SECOND EDITION

ATLAS OF PRIMARY EYECARE PROCEDURES

Linda Casser, OD
Associate Dean for Academic Programs
Clinical Professor of Optometry
College of Optometry
Pacific University
Forest Grove, Oregon

Murray Fingeret, OD
Chief, Optometry Section
Department of Veterans Affairs Medical Center
Brooklyn, New York
Associate Clinical Professor
College of Optometry
State University of New York
New York, New York

H. Ted Woodcome, OD
Private Practice
Penfield, New York
Adjunct Associate Professor of Optometry
New England College of Optometry
Boston, Massachusetts

Illustrations by
Stephanie P. Schilling
Susan C. Tilberry

With Forewords by
Lesley L. Walls, OD, MD
Louis J. Catania, OD

APPLETON & LANGE
Stamford, Connecticut

97 98 99 00 01 / 10 9 8 7 6 5 4 3 2 1

Prentice Hall International (UK) Limited, *London*
Prentice Hall of Australia Pty. Limited, *Sydney*
Prentice Hall Canada, Inc., *Toronto*
Prentice Hall Hispanoamericana, S.A., *Mexico*
Prentice Hall of India Private Limited, *New Delhi*
Prentice Hall of Japan, Inc., *Tokyo*
Simon & Schuster Asia Pte. Ltd., *Singapore*
Editora Prentice Hall do Brasil Ltda., *Rio de Janeiro*
Prentice Hall, *Upper Saddle River, New Jersey*

ISBN 0-8385-0257-1

9 780838 502570   90000

Acquisitions Editor: Linda Marshall
Production Editor: Maria T. Vlasak
Designer: Mary Skudlarek

PRINTED IN THE UNITED STATES OF AMERICA

Contributors

Michael D. DePaolis, OD
DePaolis & Ryan, OD, PC
Rochester, New York
Clinical Associate
Department of Ophthalmology
University of Rochester School of Medicine
Rochester, New York
Adjunct Assistant Professor
Pennsylvania College of Optometry
Philadelphia, Pennsylvania
Corneal Topography

Gwen R. Gnadt, OD, MPH
Eye/Vision Associates
Lake Ronkonkoma, New York
Coordinator, Optometry Prime Residency Program
Northport Veterans Administration Medical Center
Northport, New York
Adjunct Clinical Professor of Optometry
College of Optometry
State University of New York
New York, New York
*Section VII: Ocular Microbiology
and Cytology Procedures*

Joseph P. Shovlin, OD
Northeastern Eye Institute
Scranton, Pennsylvania
Adjunct Assistant Professor
Pennsylvania College of Optometry
Philadelphia, Pennsylvania
Corneal Topography

Kelly H. Thomann, OD
Supervisor of Optometric Residency Program
Optometry Service
Franklin Delano Roosevelt Veterans Affairs Hospital
Montrose, New York
Adjunct Assistant Clinical Professor
State College of Optometry
State University of New York
New York, New York
Adjunct Assistant Clinical Professor
School of Optometry
Indiana University
Bloomington, Indiana
Section X: Cranial Nerve Examination

Dedicated to Our Families

Keith E. Locke, Carolyn L. Casser, D. Jeffrey Casser
Janet and Stuart Fingeret
AnnMarie, Jonathan, Jessica, and Marissa Woodcome

Without your understanding, support, and encouragement, these and
other achievements would be unattainable.

In special memory of those who have inspired and helped us,
whom we have lost in the intervening years, and
whom we greatly miss

Donald G. Casser
Alexander Pepe, OD
Sidney Fingeret

With special appreciation to those individuals
whose personal example of hard work and dedicated effort
bring abiding joy and inspiration

Anthony and Angeline Casciaro
Drs. Harold A. Sr., Harold A. Jr., Betty Ann Woodcome, and Mom

Contents

Foreword

Optometry is an ever-changing health care profession. In fact, no profession in history has experienced such a rapid expansion of clinical practice as optometry has enjoyed over the past twenty-five years.

Optometric practice changed very little prior to 1971, an era during which, for the most part, optometrists were refractionists who also fit contact lenses. In 1971, one of the first states to statutarily expand the scope of optometric practice implementated legislation to include diagnostic pharmaceutical agents in the optometrist's patient care armamentarium. In 1976, only five short years later, the successful movement toward universal utilization of therapeutic pharmaceutical agents by doctors of optometry began. Now, some twenty years later, most optometrists are able to incorporate a wide array of both diagnostic and pharmaceutical agents in the care of their patients.

In this late twentieth century, the doctor of optometry is truly educated and trained as a primary health care practitioner. The federal government classifies the doctor of optometry as a physician, in recognition of the nature and scope of services provided. Indeed, many states allow the optometrist to use the title Optometric Physician for all purposes related to the practice of optometry.

Consonant with the pharmaceutical expansion of optometric scope of practice has been the extent and nature of the clinical procedures routinely used by the primary care optometrist. It is to the procedural aspects of clinical optometric care that this unique text is dedicated. Because of its dynamic development, optometry, as the primary eyecare profession, is in need of texts that serve as a ready reference source, enabling the optometrist to effectively provide the services needed by today's patients.

It is in this spirit, then, that I proudly and enthusiastically present this text to the optometric student, resident, and practitioner. This second edition of the *Atlas of Primary Eyecare Procedures* is completely updated not only to reflect but also to help shape the rapid changes within the profession of optometry. The inclusion of additional anterior segment procedures, the Cranial Nerve Examination, Glaucoma Evaluation and Treatment Procedures, Periocular Injection Procedures, and Ophthalmic Laser Procedures, are eminent examples of how this text will assist practicing primary care optometrists to meet the eyecare needs of their patients—not only at the close of this century, but well into the next.

It gives me great pride to introduce the second edition of this landmark text as a resource to review established procedures, to investigate new techniques and treatments, and to incorporate as an essential practice reference. I truly believe that the proper use of this text will enhance the eyecare services that you provide for your patients.

Lesley L. Walls, OD, MD

Foreword to the First Edition

Good primary eyecare requires three things of a practitioner: caring, commitment, and competency. The absence or weakness of any one of these elements effectively reduces primary care to a support service or technical skill; no doubt valuable, but not primary care.

The elements of caring and commitment are often written about, talked about, and taught in numerous innovative and provocative methods. Notwithstanding all such efforts, there are fundamental character traits and desires required in practitioners and students to be able to successfully acquire and communicate the qualities of caring and commitment. When these traits and desires are present, the results are usually self-evident and rewarding to teacher, student, and patient.

Meanwhile, the third element of primary care, competency, which encompasses examination, diagnosis, and management, is the element most textbooks address. Most optometric texts concentrate on the area of ocular diagnosis because of its critical importance in disease, and on management because of the emphasis on effective outcomes in all primary health care. However, neither effective management nor proper diagnosis would be possible without a knowledge and understanding of the procedures and techniques used. Indeed, such techniques are the means by which practitioners administer their examination, arrive at their diagnosis, and often the method by which they provide their treatment and management.

Not since Arthur H. Keeney's book, *Ocular Examination: Basis and Technique,* written in the early 1970s, has a comprehensive textbook on ocular procedures and techniques been attempted. Never, in fact, has there been an illustrated "atlas" with straightforward, step-by-step descriptions of common eye procedures used regularly in primary eyecare practice. Thus, *Atlas of Primary Eyecare Procedures* is truly a valuable and unique contribution for eyecare practitioners and optometric students who must master appropriate technique before they can hope to arrive at proper diagnoses and management plans.

Now, what if a valuable, needed, and unique textbook the nature of *Atlas of Primary Eyecare Procedures* were able to capture in its technical descriptions, the qualities of caring and commitment mentioned above as the other two fundamental elements in true primary eyecare? That accomplishment would certainly make this textbook the ideal book for every optometric practitioner and student. It would also require some very special authors with the knowledge and skills to complete such a task and the character traits and desires to turn such technical expertise into primary care. Please allow me to share with you the fact that the authors of this textbook, Murray Fingeret, Linda Casser, and Ted Woodcome are exactly the people in optometry to have achieved this extraordinary task.

I have had the honor and pleasure over a fourteen-year period of working with each of these individuals as students, residents (all at the J. C. Wilson Health Center in Rochester, New York), and now as clinical practitioners and educators in the optometric profession. From my perspective, when it comes to the qualities and skills of caring, commitment, and competency attendant to primary eyecare, these three people have added new dimensions to each of those elements. Although at one point I may have been the teacher, their depth of human qualities, caring, and commitment has turned me into their devoted student. Their contributions and dedication to the optometric profession, patient care, and education continue to help us all grow, improve, and better serve our patients.

It is with a mixture of personal and professional pride and joy that I humbly present to the optometric profession and, indeed, to the health care literature at large, this unique and valuable textbook for eyecare practitioners and students. And it is with even greater pride and joy, on behalf of my profession and the patients who shall benefit from our efforts and the knowledge gained from this book, that I thank the authors and congratulate their achievement.

Louis J. Catania, OD

Introduction

In the Introduction to the first edition of *Atlas of Primary Eyecare Procedures*, we referenced the evolution of the scope and practice of optometry over the preceding ten to fifteen years. It has now been another ten years since the writing of the first edition began, during which time the dynamic evolution of optometry has been no less impressive. This second edition of the *Atlas of Primary Eyecare Procedures* is intended not only to reflect the recent changes in optometry, but also to help set forth future directions.

The unique text-facing-illustrations format of the *Atlas* has been retained with the goal of providing a generously illustrated, yet succinctly organized, text that enables the clinician to become familiar with many of these important primary eyecare procedures. As before, each procedure section is composed of several components: Description/Indications, Instrumentation, Technique, Interpretation, and Contraindications/Complications. Our goal is for optometric students, residents, and practitioners to refer to this book in the clinical setting as these procedures are anticipated and performed. The *Atlas* is not intended as an all-inclusive textbook covering comprehensive information on the diagnosis, treatment, and management of the clinical conditions for which these techniques are performed. A Suggested Readings list is included in each section to which the reader is referred for supplementary information.

All of the material from the first edition has been extensively reviewed and updated for this volume. In addition, the contents of the second edition of the *Atlas* have been substantially expanded to include procedures that optometrists have more recently incorporated into clinical practice. The original ten sections in the first edition have been expanded to fifteen; the original eighty procedures have been increased to 103. Some specific additions to the second edition are:

- Section II: the expansion of the gonioscopy procedures
- Section III: the addition of excisional removal of verruca and papilloma, and chalazion removal
- Section IV: the addition of punctal cautery
- Section VI: the addition of anterior stromal puncture and corneal topography
- Section X: cranial nerve examination

- Section XII: glaucoma evaluation and treatment procedures
- Section XIII: periocular injection procedures
- Section XIV: ophthalmic laser procedures
- Section XV: infection control procedures

As all clinicians realize, there are often several generally accepted methods of performing any of these procedures. We have attempted to present the most widely accepted versions, citing alternative approaches whenever possible. As a result, the procedures contained in this text should not be interpreted as the only accepted clinical methods, but rather consensus versions upon which the clinician may incorporate appropriate individual variations.

More specifically, it is not expected that the reader use this text exclusively to initially perform some of the more sophisticated techniques added to the second edition. Rather, it is intended that this text supplement appropriate training and education in the clinical setting pertaining to these more advanced techniques. Without question, the well-being of the patient combined with your personal level of clinical comfort must dictate whether or not a procedure included in this text is performed.

Finally, throughout the *Atlas* certain assumptions are made that are not specified in each section:

- Appropriate clinical assessment has been made to ensure that the procedure is indicated
- Patient hypersensitivity to any listed medication has been ruled out
- Appropriate infection control measures are implemented, such as hand-washing and the use of appropriate personal protective equipment
- Instruments are appropriately cleaned and asepticized/sterilized before and after each procedure

We are grateful and appreciative of the response and feedback provided by our students and colleagues to the first edition. Our goal is to foster excellence in optometric clinical education and patient care. To this end, our hope is that the readers of this text will find that, in some small measure, it contributes to their ability to do so for the betterment of their patients.

Linda Casser, OD
Murray Fingeret, OD
H. Ted Woodcome, OD

Acknowledgments

There are countless individuals who have directly or indirectly contributed to this book, as is true for any undertaking of this nature. We will always be grateful for these many unnamed, special individuals. It is an honor and privilege to specifically acknowledge those whose contributions and efforts were invaluable to the successful outcome of this project:

- Louis J. Catania, OD, for his original vision of this work, his confidence in our abilities, his commitment to primary care optometry, his energy and enthusiasm, and his ongoing guidance and inspiration
- R. Craig Percy, for his expert guidance as editor of the first edition and his many contributions to the optometric literature
- Stanley Teplick, MD, for his supportive effort and commitment in reviewing manuscripts new to the second edition
- Lesley L. Walls, OD, MD, for his enthusiasm and energy, his many contributions to primary care optometry, and his appreciated efforts in providing the Foreword to the second edition
- Kevin L. Waltz, MD, OD, for his efforts in reviewing the first edition and for his personal commitment to optometric education
- Harvey Bonner, OD, for his insightful comments and suggestions regarding new material for the second edition
- W. David Sullins, Jr, OD, for his vision of the profession of optometry and his commitment to excellence
- Our contributing authors, Kelly H. Thomann, OD, Gwen R. Gnadt, OD, MPH, Michael D. DePaolis, OD, and Joseph P. Shovlin, OD, for their enthusiastic participation in this project
- Stephanie Schilling, for her expert artistic contributions as illustrator for the second edition, and for her patience, understanding, and support
- Cheryl Mehalik, for her guidance in the initial stages of the second edition
- Linda Marshall, for her enthusiastic support and leadership as editor

Finally, we acknowledge with great appreciation and admiration the ongoing commitment to primary eyecare exemplified by our students, residents, and colleagues everywhere.

For one of us (LC), thirteen years as a faculty member at the Indiana University School of Optometry were instrumental in formulating my approach to primary eyecare procedures. It is with heartfelt appreciation that I recognize and thank the staff, faculty, and students of the Indianapolis Eye Care Center for their many years of personal and professional support. I also extend sincere appreciation and gratitude to the optometrists of Indiana for their many years of friendship and for their long-standing commitment to primary eyecare.

Essential to the successful completion of this project was a semester of sabbatical leave completed during the 1995–96 academic year, part of which was spent at the Northeastern State University College of Optometry in Tahlequah, Oklahoma. Sincere appreciation is extended to Indiana University and the School of Optometry for this invaluable opportunity for personal and professional development. It is with deep appreciation and gratitude that I acknowledge the support and consideration of so many individuals during that time: Carl Spear, Jr, OD; Tammy Than, OD; the entire faculty and staff at NSU; the 1995–1996 NSU residents; the NSU Class of 1996; and William Monaco, OD, PhD, Paul Williams, OD, and David Tally, OD, for enabling my activity at the college. Special appreciation is also extended to George Foster, OD, and Roy Hiskett, OD, along with all colleagures in the Oklahoma Optometric Association, for their dedication to optometry and their commitment to its future.

For illustrations on the color plates, the first number is that of the procedures and the second is the figure number in the procedure. Illustrations on the color plates are also reproduced in black and white with their relevant procedures.

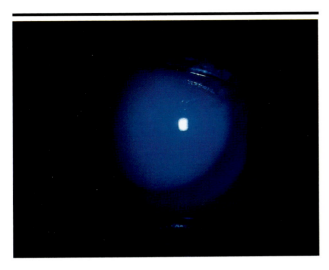

12–1. B. When illuminated with the cobalt filter, the Fleischer ring of keratoconus appears black.

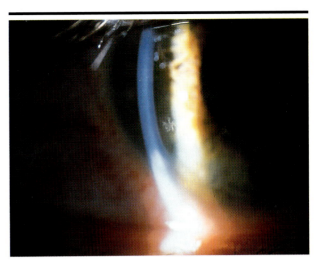

12–3. B. Two small herpes simplex dendritic ulcers are visible in indirect illumination.

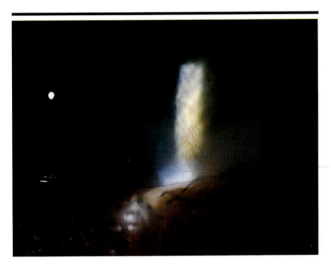

12–4. A. A limbal neovascular tuft is seen in retroillumination.

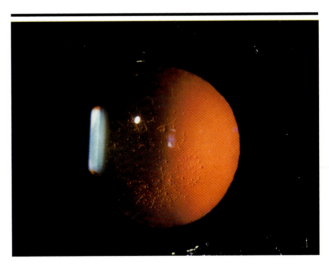

12–5. B. A pre-Descemet's corneal dystrophy is seen in fundus retroillumination.

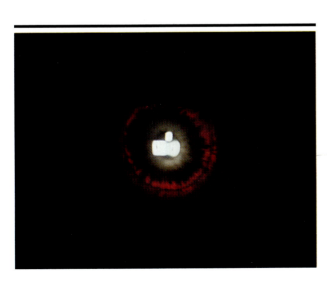

14–2. B. Extensive peripheral iris transillumination defects are present in this patient with pigment dispersion syndrome. (Courtesy of David W. Sloan, OD)

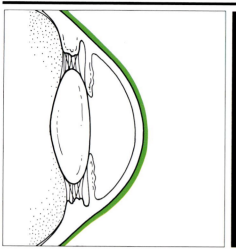
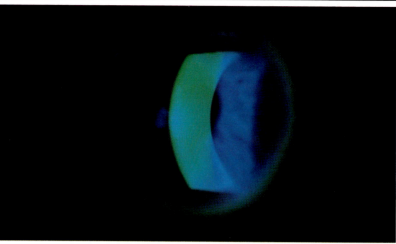

15–3. The intact precorneal tear film (schematic, left) appears uniformly green when stained with fluorescein sodium and illuminated with cobalt filter of the slit lamp (right). (Photo courtesy of Keith E. Locke, PHD)

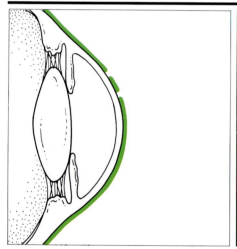
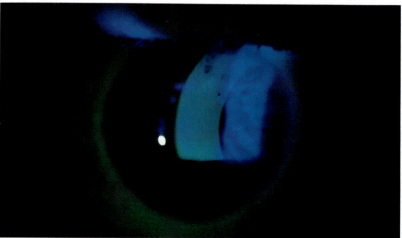

15–4. Dry areas appear as black spots or streaks in the fluorescein-stained precorneal tear film.

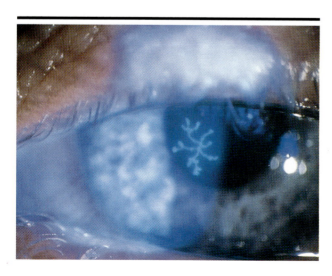

16–4. The cornea exhibits positive fluorescein sodium staining secondary to a herpes simplex dendritic ulcer.

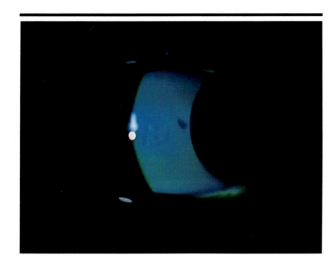

16–5. B. The cornea exhibits negative fluorescein sodium staining centrally secondary to epithelial bullae resulting from Fuchs' endothelial dystrophy.

16–6. (right) The bulbar conjunctiva and cornea exhibit rose bengal staining secondary to keratoconjunctivitis sicca.

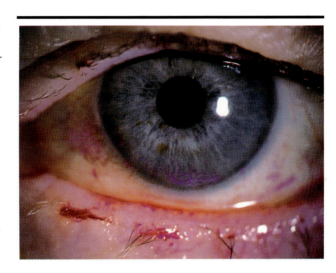

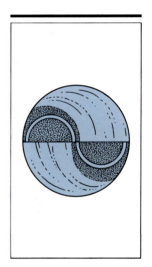

17–4. B. (far right) The corneal reflection of the applanation tonometer probe will appear as two pale blue semicircles, which are used to center the probe.

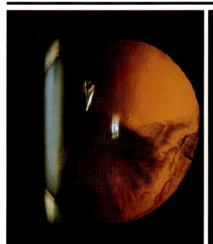

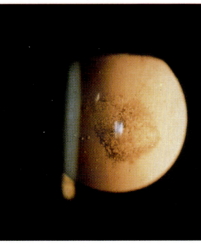

19–6. A. (far left) A cortical cataract as seen using retroillumination. B. (left) A posterior subcapsular cataract as seen using retroillumination.

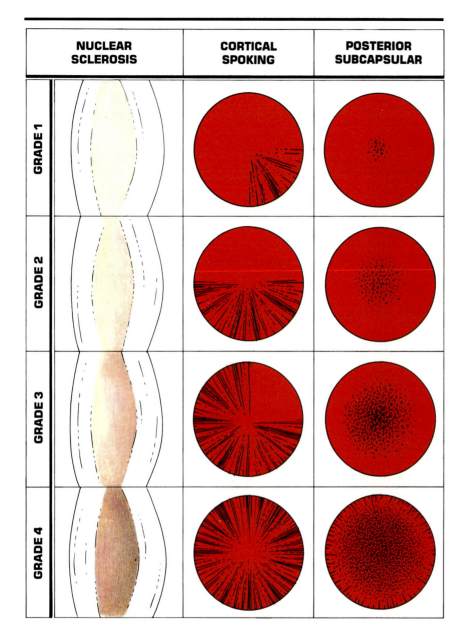

	NUCLEAR SCLEROSIS	CORTICAL SPOKING	POSTERIOR SUBCAPSULAR

19–7. A grading system for age-related cataracts. The nuclear sclerotic changes are shown in cross-section with the anterior surface to the left. The cortical spoking and posterior subcapsular changes are seen in retroillumination.

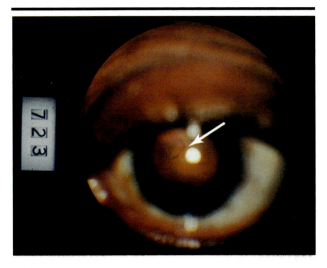

20-5. A posterior vitreous detachment may be detected by the large vitreous floater visible with distal direct ophthalmoscopy.

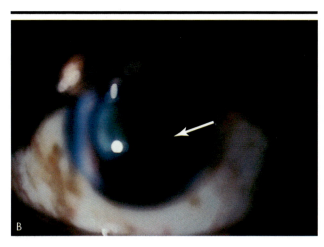

20-6. B. Following PVD, the collapsed posterior vitreous limiting layer may be visible with the slit lamp. It appears as an undulating, white wrinkled-looking veil (arrow) with optically empty fluid behind it.

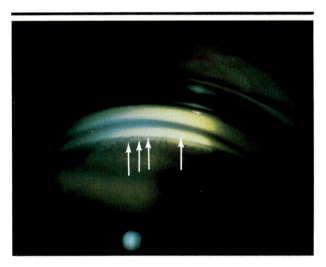

21-5. A wide-open angle as visualized with gonioscopy. The arrows going from left to right indicate the ciliary body band, scleral spur, trabecular meshwork, and Schwalbe's line.

21-12. A wide open angle is seen with all structures visible. Note the fine iris processes covering the ciliary body band.

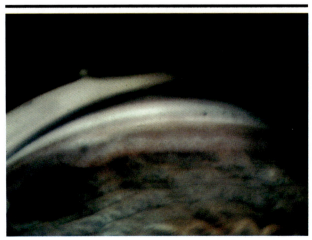

21-13. (left) An angle recession is pictured with an excessively wide open angle as evidenced by the amount of ciliary body band exposed.

21-14. A closed angle is pictured with a convex iris obscuring all angle structures.

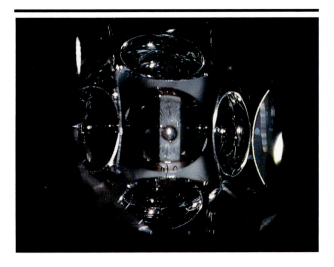

22–4. A. The minified view of the iris and pupil as seen through the center of the 4-mirror goniolens prior to corneal contact.

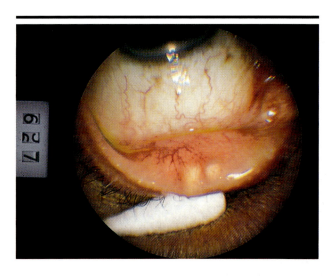

27–2. Occlusive sebaceous distention of the meibomian gland is visible as yellow "streaking" through the overlying palpebral conjunctiva.

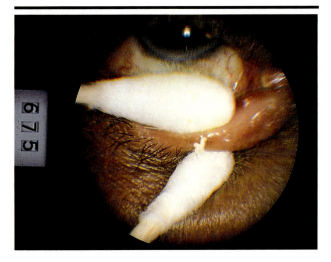

27–4. B. Cheesy sebaceous material is expressed from a meibomian gland in the right lower lid.

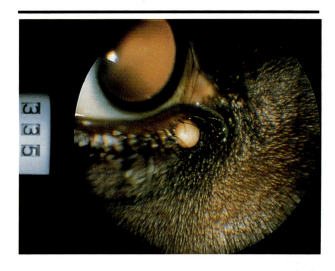

28–1. The superficial sebaceous cyst appears as a well-demarcated, creamy white, smooth, round nodule.

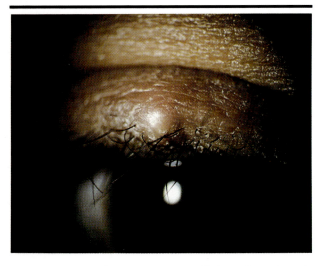

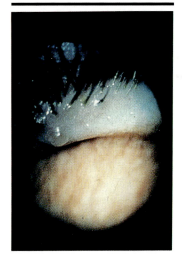

29–1. Sudoriferous cysts appear as one or more small, noninflamed, avascular, clear fluid-filled cysts on the anterior lid margin.

28–2. The deeper sebaceous cyst is more flesh-toned in color and less well demarcated.

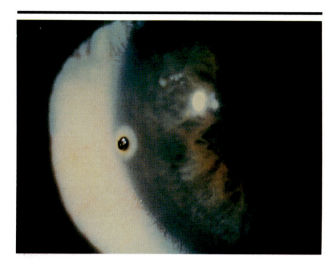

44-1. A metallic foreign body on the cornea, surrounded by a ring of rust and edema.

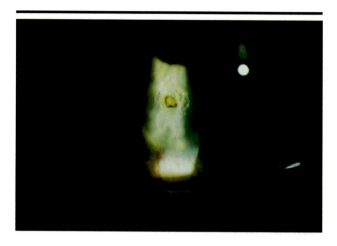

45-1. A corneal rust ring is noted following removal of an embedded metallic foreign body. The surrounding epithelial defect is also visible.

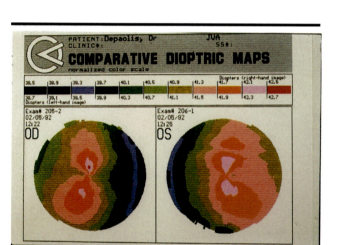

50-4. Enantiomorphism of the normal cornea: The maps of the right and left eyes are nonsuperimposable mirror images of one another.

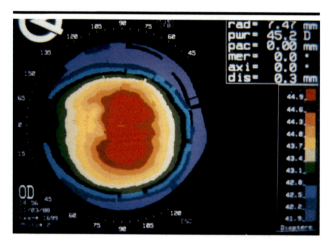

50-5. Variable asphericity of the normal cornea. Asphericity is meridional specific and the cornea flattens to a greater extent nasally than temporally.

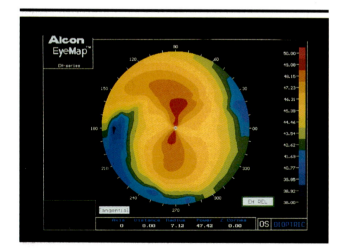

50-6. Corneal toricity. Most normal corneas have some detectable degree of corneally toricity, as represented in this symmetric with-the-rule bow tie configuration.

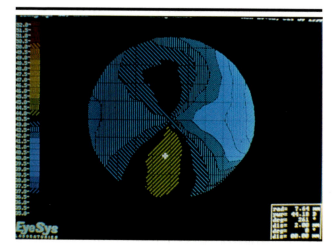

50-7. This topographic map illustrates an asymmetric bow tie configuration to the with-the-rule astigmatism.

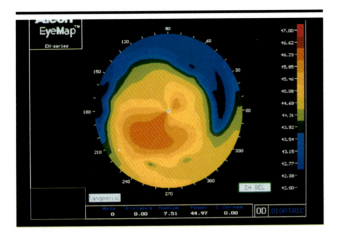

50–8. Occasionally, the steepest corneal curvature is found to be slightly displaced relative to the visual axis.

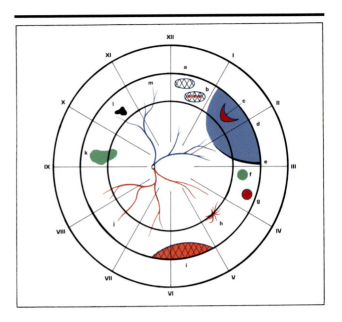

55–11. Ocular fundus with anatomical landmarks. (a) Long posterior ciliary artery and nerve. (b) Short posterior ciliary artery. (c) Vortex vein. (d) Vitreous base (nasal). (e) Vitreous base (temporal). (f) 20 D lens view. (Courtesy of Anthony Cavallerano, OD

60–6. (left) The fundus drawing color coding system. (a) Lattice. (b) Lattice with holes. (c) Flap tear. (d) Detached retina. (e) Demarcation line. (f) Operculum. (g) Retinal hole. (h) Vortex vein. (i) Retinal dialysis. (j) Retinal arterioles. (k) Vitreous opacity. (l) Retinal or choroidal nevus. (m) Retinal veins. The universal color code for fundus drawing is given below.

RED

Solid

- Retinal arterioles
- Vortex veins
- Attached retina
- Preretinal and intraretinal hemorrhages
- Normal fovea/red cross
- Retinal neovascularization
- Open areas of retinal breaks (tears/holes)
- Open area of outer layer retinoschisis holes
- Vascular anomalies (collaterals, shunts, etc.)

Crosslined

- Open area of giant tears and retinal dialysis
- Inner area of thinned retina
- Open area of inner layer retinoschisis holes
- Inner area of chorioretinal atrophy

BLACK

- Pigment within detached retina
- Borders of chorioretinal atrophy
- Choroidal nevus
- RPE hypertrophy or choroidal pigment
- Demarcation lines at attached edge of detached retina or within detached retina
- Edge of buckle beneath attached retina
- Sheathed vessels, outlined or solid, depending upon degree
- Pigmented outline of short and long posterior ciliary arteries and nerves
- Posttreatment pigmentation following diathermy, cryotherapy, or photocoagulation

GREEN

Solid

- Cotton wool patches
- Vitreous hemorrhage
- Vitreous membranes
- Intraocular foreign body
- Media opacities (label)
- Ora serrata pearls
- Prepapillary (hyaloid) annular opacity
- Outline of elevated neovascularization
- Retinal operculum

Dotted

- Asteroid hyalosis
- Snowflake deposits on lattice degeneration and retinioschisis

BLUE

Solid

- Retinal veins
- Detached retina
- Detached fovea (blue cross)
- Intraretinal cysts
- Outline of ora serrata
- Outline of lattice degeneration
- Outline of flat neovascularization
- Outline of retinal breaks (holes, tears)
- Outline of thinned retinal areas
- Vitreoretinal traction tufts
- Cystic retinal tufts
- Circumferential, fixed, meridional, or radial folds

Crosslined

- Rolled edges of retinal tear
- White with or without pressure (label)
- Inner layer of retinoschisis
- Detached pars plana epithelium anterior to detached ora serrata
- Outline of change in area or folds of detached retina because of shifting fluid

Stippled

- Peripheral cystoid degeneration

BROWN

- Pigment beneath detached retina
- Choroidal melanoma
- Ciliary processes
- Pars plana cysts
- Uveal tissue
- Striae ciliaris
- Edge of buckle beneath detached retina
- Outline of posterior staphyloma
- Outline of chorioretinal atrophy beneath detached retina
- Choroidal detachment
- Fibrous demarcation lines

YELLOW

Solid

- RPE level deposits
- Serous or hemorrhagic detached fovea drawn as yellow cross
- Long and short ciliary nerves
- Postphotocoagulation retinal edema
- Severe intraretinal and subretinal exudation

Dotted

- Drusen
- Intraretinal and subretinal exudates

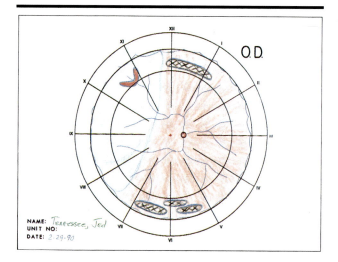

60–7. An example of fundus drawing; retinal tear with detachment.

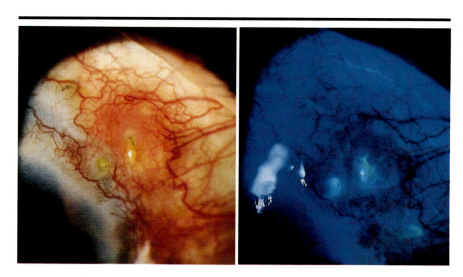

90–2. Suture barbs protruding through the bulbar conjunctiva (arrows) are visible with the slit lamp biomicroscope using white light (left) and with the cobalt filter following instillation of fluorescein sodium (right). Note the area of surrounding conjunctival edema and injection. (Courtesy of David E. Magnus, OD)

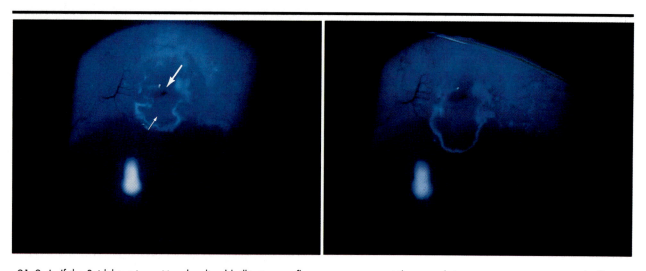

91–2 A. If the Seidel test is positive, localized brilliant green fluorescence occurs at the wound site as aqueous streams into the fluorescein. B. The bright fluorescein is displaced as the aqueous continues to leak. (Courtesy of David E. Magnus, OD)

Topographic Examination
Initial Report

Heidelberg
Retina
Tomograph

Patient: John, 04.11.1955, right eye, #

Diagnosis/Class.:

This Examination: Database entry: 15   Examination Date: 11.03.1994

Scan: Angle: 10 °, Depth: 2.50 mm, Focus: 0.00 dpt

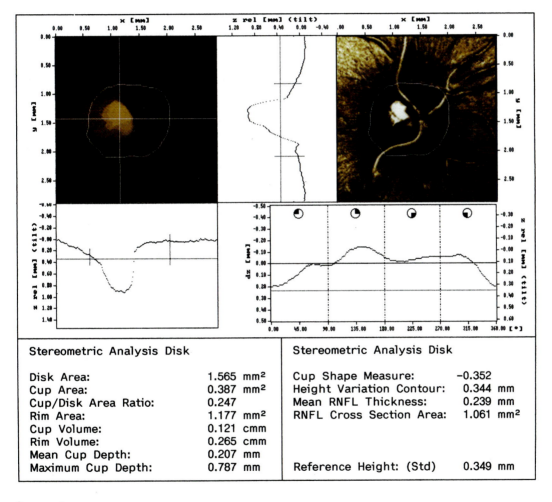

Stereometric Analysis Disk		Stereometric Analysis Disk	
Disk Area:	1.565 mm²	Cup Shape Measure:	−0.352
Cup Area:	0.387 mm²	Height Variation Contour:	0.344 mm
Cup/Disk Area Ratio:	0.247	Mean RNFL Thickness:	0.239 mm
Rim Area:	1.177 mm²	RNFL Cross Section Area:	1.061 mm²
Cup Volume:	0.121 cmm		
Rim Volume:	0.265 cmm		
Mean Cup Depth:	0.207 mm		
Maximum Cup Depth:	0.787 mm	Reference Height: (Std)	0.349 mm

Comments: _____

Software: IR1–V1.11   Date:_____   _____ M.D.

92–3. A Heidelberg Retina Tomograph (HRT) of a normal patient indicates measurements of the disc size and volume. (Courtesy of Heidelberg Engineering.)

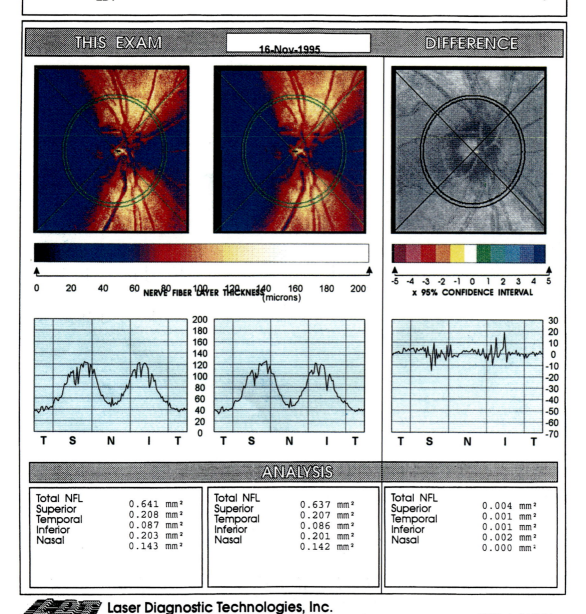

92–5. A Laser Diagnostic Technologies (LDT) nerve fiber analyzer (NFA) printout of a normal patient illustrates the results of two different examinations. (Courtesy of Laser Diagnostic Technologies.)

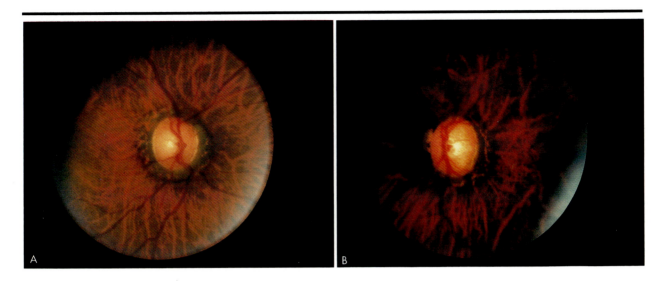

92–8. This patient has open-angle glaucoma in the right (A) and left (B) eyes.

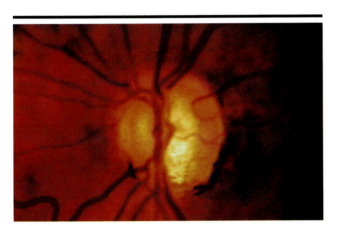

92–9. Notching of the optic disc neuroretinal rim is noted at the inferior temporal location in this patient's left eye.

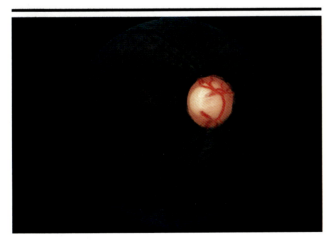

92–10. Temporal unfolding of the neuroretinal rim is noted in this patient's right optic nerve so that a very thin rim is now present temporally.

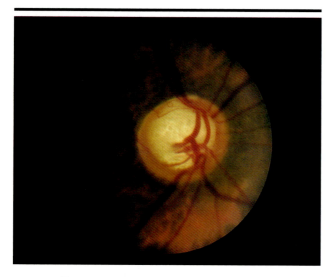

92–11. Diffuse enlargement of the cup is noted in the right eye of this patient with open-angle glaucoma. A notch is also developing at the superior temporal pole of the optic nerve. (Courtesy of Rodney Gutner, OD)

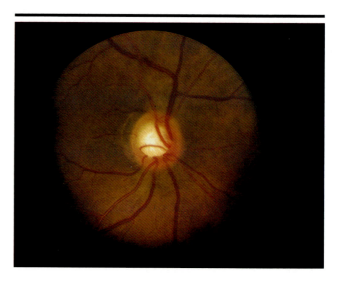

92–12. In vessel overpass, the vessels appear to be suspended over the cup as they pass over the surface due to loss of supportive disc tissue from glaucomatous damage.

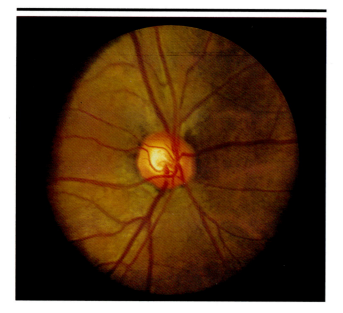

92–13. A "soft" sign associated with glaucomatous vessel change is baring of the circumlinear vessel in which a space forms between the vessel and the cup margin.

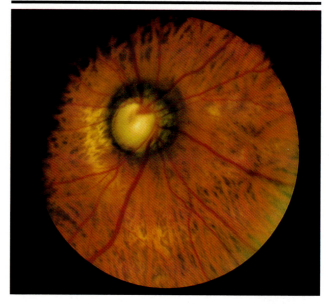

92–14. In advanced glaucoma, the optic cup may take on a "bean pot" appearance. The neuroretinal rim is undermined so that the vessels bend and are lost from view as they cross the disc margin.

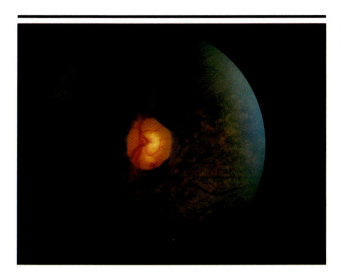

92–15. A splinter-shaped hemorrhage is noted at the 6-o'clock disc margin. It is a sign associated with open-angle glaucoma that often precedes focal rim notching and visual field loss.

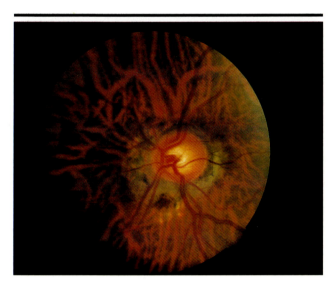

92–16. Peripapillary atrophy is another "soft" sign of glaucoma. It may be indicative of a disc that is more susceptible to damage from elevated IOP or a sign of active damage to this region.

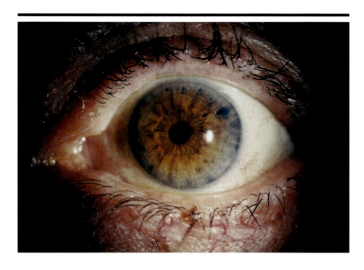

100–4. B. A photograph of a patient following laser iridoplasty.

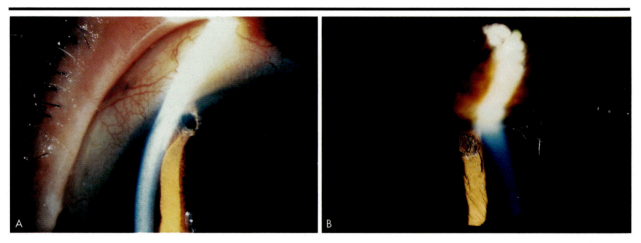

101–9. A. A patent argon laser iridotomy is visible with the slit lamp biomicroscope. B. This laser iridotomy is not patent. Note the pigment that occludes the opening.

101–11. A patent Nd:YAG laser iridotomy is noted using retroillumination with the slit lamp biomicroscope.

Ophthalmic Pharmaceutical
Procedures

1

Drop Instillation and Punctal Occlusion: Adults

■ **Description/Indications.** The use of topical ophthalmic pharmaceutical solutions or suspensions is integral to ocular examination, diagnosis, and treatment. The categories of topical ophthalmic drops used diagnostically in-office include anesthetics, mydriatics, miotics, and cycloplegics.

Systemic absorption of topical ophthalmic drops occurs through the nasopharyngeal mucosa via the puncta. Resultant adverse systemic side effects are potentially serious following the use of agents such as topical beta-adrenergic blockers. Systemic absorption of topical ophthalmic drops may be significantly reduced by punctal occlusion to minimize the amount of medication entering the nasolacrimal system. Indications for punctal occlusion following the instillation of ophthalmic drops include the use of 10% phenylephrine, to avoid a hypertensive crisis; beta-adrenergic blocking agents, to avoid breathing difficulties; and bradycardia, and other adrenergic agents, to avoid tachycardia and hypertensive crisis.

■ **Instrumentation.** Desired ophthalmic solution or suspension, facial tissues.

■ **Technique.** Recheck the label of the bottle to ensure that the correct solution or suspension was chosen, and remove the cap. When appropriate, advise the patient that a mild, transient burning sensation may be expected.

Ask the patient to tilt the head back so that the chin is slightly elevated, and to look up and back (Fig. 1). Using the forefinger of one hand, evert the lower lid slightly so that a "trough" is formed by the inferior cul-de-sac. Holding the opened bottle in the opposite hand and stabilizing it by resting the little and/or ring fingers on the patient's cheek or nose as appropriate, squeeze a drop or two as desired into the exposed cul-de-sac (Fig. 2A). Release the lower lid and ask the patient to gently blot away the excess fluid with a tissue, or blot away the excess fluid from the lid area yourself using a tissue. If desired, advise the patient to keep the lids closed for a few seconds, waiting for any associated burning to subside. Alternatively, a one-handed technique may be performed using the little and/or ring fingers to evert the lower lid while the drop is instilled (Fig. 2B).

When indicated, occlude the puncta following drop instillation. Ask the patient to close the eyes and hold your index finger firmly over the nasolacrimal sac, upper and lower canaliculi, and the medial palpebral ligament in the nasal canthus. Use relatively firm pressure to collapse the sac against the nasolacrimal bone for approximately 1 minute (Fig. 3A). Do this for each eye in which drops are instilled. The patient may be advised to bilaterally occlude the puncta himself or herself by straddling the bridge of the nose with thumb and forefinger after closing the eyes (Fig. 3B). Alternatively, instruct the patient to close the eyes for 3 minutes following drop instillation. This will significantly reduce the amount of fluid pumped into the nasolacrimal system through action of the lids and orbicularis oculi muscles.

A patient may exhibit mild to moderate anxiety upon having the eyedrops instilled, so that blepharospasm makes access to the cul-de-sac difficult. Added firmness is then required to open both the upper and lower lids. To instill drops in the right eye using this technique, use your left thumb to hold the lashes of the upper lid against the superior orbital rim. Use the little and/or ring finger of the right hand, which is holding the opened bottle, to simultaneously evert the lower lid (Fig. 4). As the patient looks up and back, squeeze the bottle to instill the drop into the palpebral fissure.

■ **Contraindications/Complications.** The examiner must be familiar with any contraindications that may preclude using a particular drug for a given patient. These contraindications may include drug allergies, drug–drug interactions, certain systemic conditions, and ocular anatomical considerations. Care must be taken to avoid contacting the tip of the dropper to the patient's cilia, lids, conjunctival surface, or tears, as contamination of the bottle's contents may occur.

A patient may rarely experience vasovagal syncope following instillation of the drop. Should this occur, basic first-aid measures are taken. These include elevating the feet above the level of the head, passing a broken ammonia inhalant ampule beneath the nostrils, and monitoring the basic vital signs.

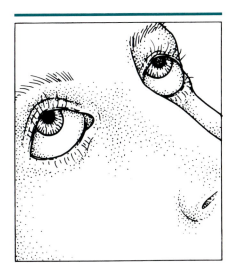

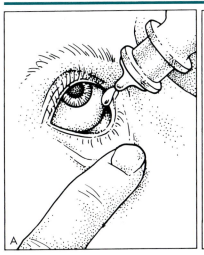

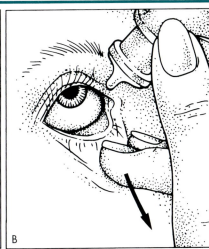

1. Instruct the patient to tilt the head back slightly and to look up and back.

2. A. Evert the lower lid slightly so that a "trough" is formed by the inferior cul-de-sac. Squeeze a drop or two, as desired, into the exposed cul-de-sac.

2. B. Alternatively, use the same hand to evert the lower lid and hold the bottle.

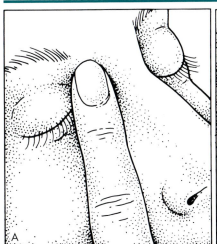

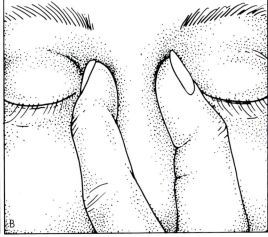

3. A. (far left) For punctal occlusion, hold your index finger firmly over the medial canthal area to occlude the canaliculi and collapse the lacrimal sac. B. (left) Patients themselves may be instructed to occlude the puncta bilaterally following drop instillation by straddling the bridge of the nose with thumb and forefinger after closing the eyes.

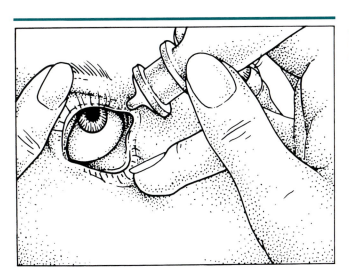

4. If blepharospasm occurs, use the left thumb to hold the upper lid lashes against the superior orbital rim. Use the little finger of the hand holding the dropper bottle to simultaneously evert the lower lid.

2 Drop Instillation and Punctal Occlusion: Young Children

■ **Description/Indications.** The use of topical ophthalmic pharmaceutical solutions or suspensions is integral to ocular examination, diagnosis, and treatment even for very young children. The categories of topical ophthalmic drops used diagnostically in-office most frequently include anesthetics, mydriatics, and cycloplegics.

Very young children may be resistant to or apprehensive about drop instillation. When gentle reassurance and persuasion with swift instillation have failed, or if the child becomes slightly combative after successful instillation of one drop in one eye, techniques of mild restraint may be instituted with the help of family members.

■ **Instrumentation.** Desired ophthalmic solution or suspension, facial tissues.

■ **Technique.** Reassure family members that the child's resistance is usually the result of apprehension rather than discomfort. Recheck the label of the bottle to ensure that the correct solution or suspension was chosen and remove the cap. Recline the young patient halfway in the examination chair. Ask an adult family member of the patient to cross the child's hands in his or her lap and to hold them firmly. Depending upon the size of the child, the family member may be able to use his or her forearms or a free arm to firmly hold the child's legs (Fig. 1).

To overcome the child's blepharospasm, firmly open the upper and lower lids. Use your left hand to hold the child's forehead steady and your left thumb to hold the upper lid against the superior orbital rim. Use the little and/or ring finger of your right hand, which is holding the opened bottle, to simultaneously evert the lower lid (Fig. 2). Squeeze the bottle and instill the drop into the palpebral fissure. Instill the drop into both eyes as quickly as possible. Blot excess fluid and tears with tissue.

With extreme resistance of the very young child, it is helpful to have an assistant gently but firmly hold the side of the child's head. Alternatively, the child's arms may be held over his or her head to help hold the sides of the head in place as the drops are instilled (Fig. 3). Further holding of the feet and legs will reduce the child's tendency to kick. The child may also be seated and gently restrained in an accompanying adult's lap.

Punctal occlusion may be desirable to reduce systemic absorption in the small child but may not be feasible if the child is restless. To occlude the punctum following drop instillation, hold your index finger or another appropriately sized finger firmly over the nasolacrimal sac, the upper and lower canaliculi, and the medial palpebral ligament in the nasal canthus, while the child's eyes are closed. Use relatively firm pressure to collapse the sac against the nasolacrimal bone for 1 minute (Fig. 4). Do this for each eye in which drops were instilled. Alternatively, instruct a family member, whose hands have been washed, to occlude the puncta.

■ **Contraindications/Complications.** The examiner must be familiar with any contraindications of using a particular type of drug for a given patient, including allergies to the drug contents, drug–drug interactions, certain systemic conditions, and ocular anatomical considerations. This is especially important for young children with their smaller body weights. Care must be taken to avoid contacting the tip of the dropper to the patient's cilia, lids, conjunctival surface, or tears, as contamination of the bottle's contents may occur. Discuss with the family member symptoms of central nervous system toxicity of any long-acting anticholinergic agents used such as cyclopentolate or atropine.

Care must be taken to ensure that the child is held firmly but gently. Due to extreme blepharospasm the held upper lid may evert, but this will not affect instillation of the drop. It may be very difficult to spread the lids apart to instill the drops. In this instance a small pool of drops may be placed in the medial canthal area. Through capillarity some of the fluid will enter the conjunctival sac (reservoir effect). If the child is kicking or moving wildly, the child may injure himself or herself or others, or may damage equipment. Once the drops are instilled, the young child will usually calm down quickly when able to move around freely.

In attempting to instill the drops, the examiner may decide in extreme instances that the risk of physical or emotional trauma outweighs the need for the diagnostic agent. Use of these agents may then be deferred to a time when the child is better able to cooperate. When use of the agent(s) is absolutely necessary, referral may be made or consultation obtained to perform the procedure under mild sedation or even general anesthesia.

It is very unusual for a young child to experience vasovagal syncope following drop instillation. Should this occur, basic first-aid measures are taken.

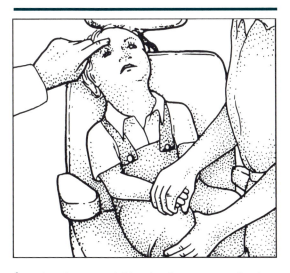

1. Recline the young child in the chair. Instruct a family member to gently restrain the child's hands and legs.

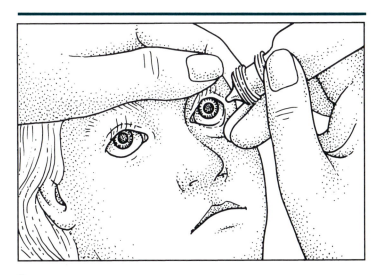

2. Use your left hand to hold the child's forehead and your left thumb to hold the upper lid. Use the little finger of your right hand to evert the lower lid.

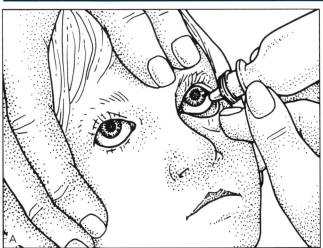

3. A. It is helpful for an assistant to gently but firmly hold the sides of the child's head.

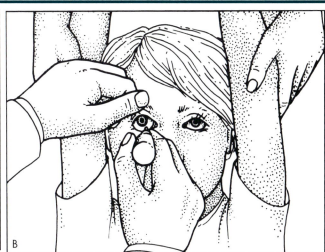

3. B. Alternatively, holding the child's arms over the head will help to hold the head in place.

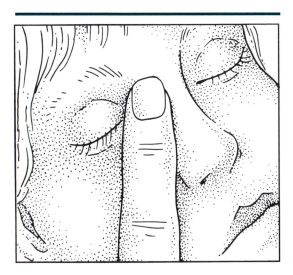

4. If indicated, hold a finger over the medial canthal area to minimize systemic absorption of the drops.

3

Pledget Use for Drops

■ **Description/Indications.** A pledget placed in the conjunctival sac may be used as a vehicle to deliver diagnostic pharmaceutical agents. Pledgets are used to maximize pupillary dilation and the effect of topical ophthalmic anesthetic solutions by enhancing ocular contact time.

Maximum pupillary dilation does not always occur despite the use of several potent mydriatic or mydriatic/cycloplegic agents. Optimal dilation can be hampered by conditions such as excessive iris pigmentation, diabetes mellitus, and posterior iris synechiae. The use of a pledget that has been saturated with the mydriatic/cycloplegic agent(s) and placed in the conjunctival sac will increase ocular contact and enhance the efficacy of these agents. This technique is especially helpful in attempting to break posterior iris synechiae.

The trend in contemporary surgical procedures such as cataract extraction is to use topical anesthesia rather than regional blocks. The use of a pledget will enhance the effect of topical ophthalmic anesthetic solutions so that the less invasive topical approach can be effectively utilized.

■ **Instrumentation.** Desired ophthalmic mydriatic or mydriatic/cycloplegic solutions, desired topical ophthalmic anesthetic solutions, sterile cotton-tipped applicators, sterile Polypore nonlinting instrument wipes, sterile jeweler's forceps, sterile ophthalmic scissors, facial tissues.

■ **Technique.**

Mydriasis/Cycloplegia: Instill 1 to 2 drops of topical ophthalmic anesthetic solution such as 0.5% proparacaine in each eye (see p. 2). Pull off the soft tip of a sterile cotton-tipped applicator, and roll it between your thumb and forefinger to form a small elongated wad approximately ¼ inch long (Fig. 1). Moisten this pledget with a routinely used combination of diagnostic agents such as 1% tropicamide and 2.5% phenylephrine. Ask the patient to look up. Holding the pledget in one hand, gently retract the patient's lower lid with the opposite hand. Place the pledget in the inferior cul-

de-sac (Fig. 2A). Use a second sterile cotton-tipped applicator to gently push the pledget into the fornix as the patient continues to look upward (Fig. 2B). Alternatively, use a sterile jeweler's forceps to place the pledget in the fornix (Fig. 3).

To enhance diagnostic pupillary dilation for effective examination of the ocular fundus, it is generally adequate to leave the pledget in place for approximately 15 to 20 minutes. For therapeutic use such as breaking posterior iris synechiae, it may be necessary to leave the pledget in place for 30 to 60 minutes to achieve the desired result. When necessary and appropriate, use greater concentrations of drugs, different mydriatic/cycloplegic agents from those routinely used, or more potent solutions to achieve adequate dilation. If maximum pupillary dilation is not achieved, instill additional agents onto the pledget while it is positioned in the conjunctival sac (Fig. 4).

Once in position, the pledget will be apparent externally as a small bulge in the lower lid, which the patient may feel as a slight fullness (Fig. 5). Instruct the patient to look up while the pledget is in place or to close the eyes. If the pledget slips or moves, reposition it with a sterile cotton-tipped applicator or jeweler's forceps.

To remove the pledget, ask the patient to look up. While retracting the lower lid with one hand, use the jeweler's forceps to carefully remove the pledget.

Topical Anesthesia: After forming the pledget as described above, saturate it with several drops of 0.5% tetracaine ophthalmic solution and place it in the inferior fornix. For additional topical anesthesia, a pledget may be similarly placed in the superior fornix. Leave the pledget(s) in place for approximately 5 to 10 minutes, and then remove.

Alternative anesthetic solutions for the pledget technique when more invasive procedures are anticipated include 4% lidocaine topical solution and lidocaine/bupivacaine combinations. The use of preservative-free versions of these solutions is helpful to avoid corneal toxicity, especially during preoperative preparation for cataract extraction.

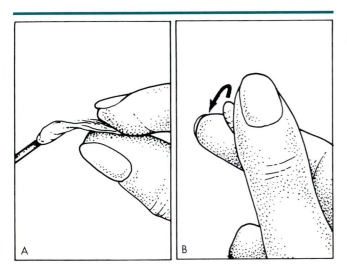

1. A. Pull off the extreme tip of a sterile cotton-tipped applicator.
B. Roll it between your fingers to form a small elongated wad.

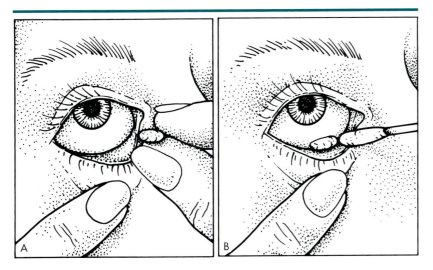

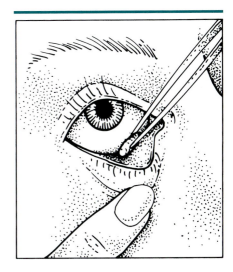

2. A. Place the moistened pledget in the inferior cul-de-sac. B. Use a sterile cotton-tipped applicator to position the pledget.

3. A jeweler's forceps may be used to place the pledget into the eye.

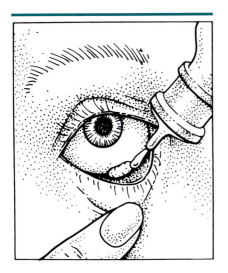

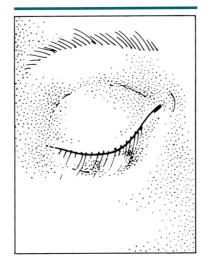

4. (far left) When necessary, resaturate the pledget with the desired pharmaceutical agent(s).

5. (left) The pledget is apparent as a small bulge in the lower lid.

Technique Variations: Alternative materials are available from which a pledget can be formed. For example, sterile non-linting instrument wipes such as Polypore (Mentor) come individually packaged and can be cut to any pledget size (Fig. 6). Although somewhat rigid when dry and initially removed from its package, the wipe readily absorbs fluid to swell slightly and form a spongy, comfortable pledget. Remove a nonlinting instrument wipe from its sterile package. Use a sterile ophthalmic scissors to cut a small rectangular pledget approximately ½ inch long and ⅛ inch wide. Saturate it with the desired ophthalmic solution(s). Once moistened and soft, place it in the conjunctival cul-de-sac as described.

As a modification of the pledget technique, an intact sterile cotton-tipped applicator can be used to focally deliver an enhanced effect of topical ophthalmic anesthetic solution. This technique tends to be less effective than an actual pledget but more effective than drops alone.

As an example, this technique can be used to provide increased local anesthetic effect at the punctum prior to dilation and irrigation of the lacrimal system (see p. 130). After instilling topical ophthalmic anesthetic solution such as 0.5% proparacaine into the conjunctival sac, saturate a sterile cotton-tipped applicator with the same solution. Ask the patient to look up and hold the saturated applicator on the lower punctum for approximately 30 seconds (Fig. 7). For procedures such as chalazion removal (see p. 118) or subconjunctival injection (see p. 432), a cotton-tipped applicator pledget soaked with 4% lidocaine topical solution may be applied to the palpebral or bulbar conjunctiva prior to administering the injection for local infiltrative anesthesia (see p. 417).

■ Contraindications/Complications.

The examiner must be familiar with any contraindications of using a particular type of drug for a given patient, including allergies to the drug contents, drug–drug interactions, certain systemic conditions, and ocular anatomical considerations (such as narrow anterior chamber angles for mydriasis/cycloplegia). Enhanced ocular contact time through the use of a pledget may result in greater ocular and systemic side effects. For this reason, some clinicians advise against using 10% phenylephrine on a pledget. Systemic absorption can be minimized if the patient is instructed to keep the eyes closed while the pledget is in place. When adding solution directly onto the pledget, care must be taken to avoid contacting the tip of the dropper to the patient's cilia, lids, conjunctival surface, or tears, as contamination of the bottle's contents may occur.

If the pledget is inadequately placed in the inferior fornix or if the patient moves the eye excessively following pledget insertion, it may slip out of position and cause corneal irritation, or it may fall out completely. Any resultant corneal irritation is generally minor and transient, usually requiring treatment only with artificial tears. Care should be taken when manipulating the jeweler's forceps and the cotton-tipped applicator near the globe.

A patient may rarely experience vasovagal syncope following placement of the pledget. Should this occur, basic first-aid measures are taken. These include elevating the feet above the level of the head, passing a broken ammonia inhalant ampule beneath the nostrils, and monitoring basic vital signs.

6. The Polypore (Mentor) sterile nonlinting instrument wipe comes individually packaged and can be cut to any pledget size. The wipe readily absorbs fluid to swell slightly and form a spongy, comfortable pledget. A sterile ophthalmic scissors has been used to cut a small rectangular pledget approximately ½ inch long and ⅛ inch wide from the sterile nonlinting instrument wipe.

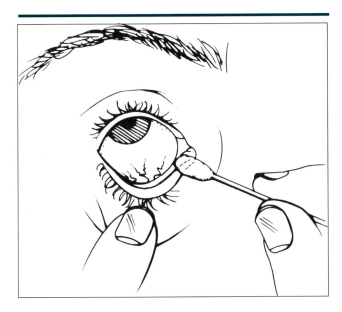

7. An intact sterile cotton-tipped applicator saturated with ophthalmic anesthetic solution can be used to focally deliver an enhanced effect. Here the punctum is specifically anesthetized by asking the patient to look up and holding the applicator in place for approximately 30 seconds.

4

Sector Pupil Dilation

■ **Description/Indications.** Patients with very narrow anterior chamber angles may require a more detailed evaluation of the media and retina than can be achieved through an undilated pupil, but because of the narrow angles full pupillary dilation is contraindicated. These patients are generally candidates for a prophylactic laser iridotomy procedure (see p. 454). As an interim or in some cases alternative measure, a vertically oval pupil may be produced by focal adrenergic stimulation of the radially oriented iris dilator muscles. This sector pupillary dilation will allow for a more thorough posterior chamber evaluation while minimizing the risk of acute angle closure glaucoma. The use of a sterile cotton-tipped applicator moistened with phenylephrine ophthalmic solution will allow for localized and controlled delivery of the diagnostic agent.

■ **Instrumentation.** Phenylephrine in a 2.5% ophthalmic solution, topical ophthalmic anesthetic drop, sterile cotton-tipped applicators, facial tissues.

■ **Technique.** Instill 1 to 2 drops of topical ophthalmic anesthetic solution in each eye (see p. 2). Moisten the tip of a sterile cotton-tipped applicator with 2 to 3 drops of 2.5% phenylephrine (Fig. 1). Ask the patient to look up. While steadying your hand on the patient's cheek, hold the moistened cotton-tipped applicator at the 6-o'clock position of the limbus for 15 to 20 seconds (Fig. 2). Repeat the procedure for the opposite eye if indicated using a fresh cotton-

tipped applicator. Monitor for sector dilation after approximately 20 to 30 minutes (Fig. 3). If the dilation is inadequate, repeat the technique for another 10 to 15-second interval.

Alternatively, moisten the 5-mm-long tip of a lengthwise portion of a Schirmer tear strip (see p. 000) with either 2.5% phenylephrine or 1% epinephrine. Position the strip centrally in the lower lid near the 6-o'clock position of the corneal limbus. When phenylephrine is used for sector dilation, keep the strip in place for approximately 30 seconds; when epinephrine is used keep the strip in place for approximately 1 minute.

■ **Contraindications/Complications.** The examiner must be familiar with any contraindications of using a particular type of drug for a given patient, including allergies to the drug contents, drug–drug interactions, certain systemic conditions, and ocular anatomical considerations. Excessive contact time of the moistened cotton-tipped applicator may result in unintentional full pupillary dilation. If the applicator is saturated with too much phenylephrine, contact of the applicator with the globe may "squeeze" excess solution into the sac and will also cause excessive dilation.

If the cotton-tipped applicator slips out of position or if the patient moves the eyes excessively, corneal irritation may result. Any resultant irritation is generally minor and transient, usually requiring treatment only with artificial tears.

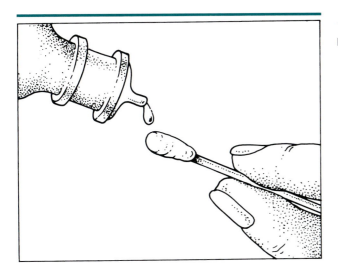

1. Moisten the cotton-tipped applicator with 2 or 3 drops of 2.5% phenylephrine.

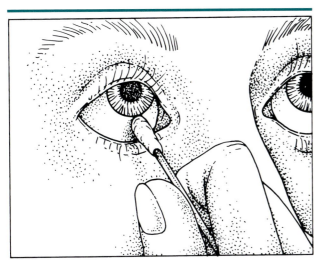

2. With the patient looking up, hold the applicator at the 6-o'clock position on the limbus for 15 seconds.

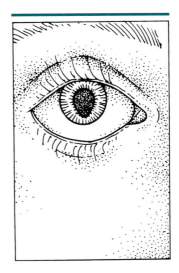

3. Resultant sector dilation of the pupil.

Ointment Application: Conjunctival Sac

■ **Description/Indications.** An indication for in-office ointment application into the conjunctival sac is the use of ophthalmic topical antibiotic ointment in therapeutic patching for a corneal wound or injury (see p. 174).

■ **Instrumentation.** Desired ophthalmic ointment, topical ophthalmic anesthetic solution, facial tissues.

■ **Technique.** Recline the patient slightly in the examination chair. As needed following the ocular evaluation, instill another drop of topical ophthalmic anesthetic solution (see p. 2).

Ask the patient to look up over his or her head. Recheck the label of the ointment to ensure that the correct preparation was chosen, and remove the cap of the tube. With the thumb and forefinger of one hand, gently pinch the lower lid away from the globe so that the inferior cul-de-sac forms a small pouch. Simultaneously squeeze a small bolus of ointment into the cul-de-sac while reminding the patient to keep looking upwards (Fig. 1). Twist the tube slightly to interrupt the ointment flow. Release the lower lid.

Release of the lower lid will often cause a small amount of the ointment to exude. To retain this exuded ointment within the conjunctival sac, gently grasp the lashes of the upper lid between the thumb and forefinger of one hand while the patient is looking up (Fig. 2A). Instruct the patient to slowly close the eyes, and while he or she does so, gently lift the upper lid up and over the exuded ointment until the lid margins are apposed (Fig. 2B). Instruct the patient to keep both eyes closed while the therapeutic patch is applied. (see p. 174)

■ **Contraindications/Complications.** The examiner must be familiar with any contraindications of using a particular type of ointment for a given patient, including allergies to the drug contents, drug–drug interactions, and so on. Care must be taken to avoid contacting the tip of the tube to the patient's cilia, lids, conjunctival surface, or tears, as contamination of the tube's contents may occur.

If excessive amounts of ointment exude when the patient closes the lids, the examiner may elect to repeat the application of ointment before pressure patching. To do so, gently wipe away excess ointment from the surface of the lids as the patient's eyes are closed. Ointment residue on the lids will make grasping of the slippery lower lid difficult for reapplication of the medication.

If grasping of the upper lid is used to reduce the amount of ointment exudation when the patient closes the lids, care must be taken not to "overshoot" the lower lid margin with the upper lid. Doing so may result in entrapment of the lower lashes so that they come in contact with the globe under the patch.

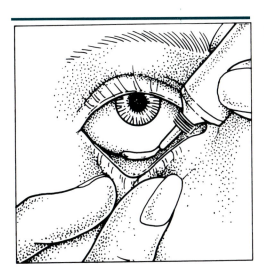

1. Gently pinch the lower lid to form a small pouch as the patient looks up. Apply the ointment into the cul-de-sac.

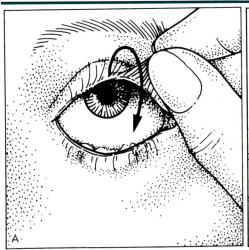

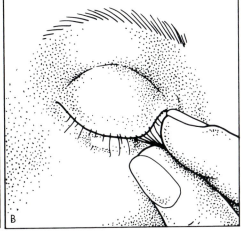

2. A. To minimize ointment exudation, grasp the lashes of the upper lid as the patient looks up. Gently lift the upper lid up and over the palpebral aperture as the patient slowly closes the lids.

2. B. Continue to gently lift the lid over the exuded ointment until the lid margins are opposed, taking care not to entrap any lower lid lashes.

6 Patient Instructions: Drop Instillation

■ **Description/Indications.** For a variety of diagnostic or therapeutic reasons a patient may be instructed to instill drops into his or her own eyes out of the office. In addition to ensuring compliance with medication dosage, it is important that the patient use an effective technique to instill the drops. Specific verbal instructions, written instructions, and in-office demonstration and practice are effective ways of maximizing patient compliance and, therefore, therapeutic effectiveness.

■ **Instrumentation.** Desired ophthalmic solution or suspension, facial tissues, wall or stand-mounted mirror.

■ **Technique.** Advise the patient to wash the hands, verify that the bottle chosen is correct, and remove the cap of the bottle. Ask the patient to look directly into a mirror. To instill drops into the right eye, have the patient tilt the head slightly to the left and gently pull down the lower lid with the index finger of his or her left hand to form a trough. As the patient holds the dropper bottle in the area of the lateral canthus with the right hand, advise him or her to squeeze 1 to 2 drops into the trough formed by the cul-de-sac and then straighten the head (Fig. 1).

The procedure is repeated for the left eye by tilting the head to the right, gently retracting the lower lid with the index finger of the right hand, and holding the dropper bottle in the left hand (Fig. 2). Alternatively, if the patient has a strongly dominant hand, the hand holding the bottle may reach across to the lateral canthal area when instilling drops into the contralateral eye.

If desired, the eyes may be closed for a few moments after instilling the drops in each eye to help retain the drops in the cul-de-sac. When indicated, to minimize systemic absorption of the solution or suspension, advise the patient to occlude the puncta bilaterally for 1 minute or to close the eyes for 3 minutes (see p. 2). A tissue may be used to blot away the excess fluid. Advise the patient to wash the hands and recap the bottle.

■ **Contraindications/Complications.** The examiner must be familiar with any contraindications of a particular type of drug for a given patient, including allergies to the drug contents, drug–drug interactions, certain systemic conditions, and ocular anatomical considerations. The patient must be advised to avoid contacting the tip of the dropper to the cilia, lids, conjunctival surface, or tears, as contamination of the bottle's contents may occur. If the patient seems to be using an excessive amount of drop refills or if the treated condition is poorly controlled, reassessing the patient's drop installation technique may be beneficial.

When appropriate, it is helpful to advise a patient that certain eyedrops may produce a mild, transient burning sensation. This patient education may prevent poor compliance due to discomfort and can be used as an indicator that the drop was properly instilled. Some preparations may be refrigerated to reduce burning, and the sensation of cold may be used to verify proper instillation. Instruct the patient using steroid suspensions to vigorously shake the bottle 15 to 30 times before instilling the drop.

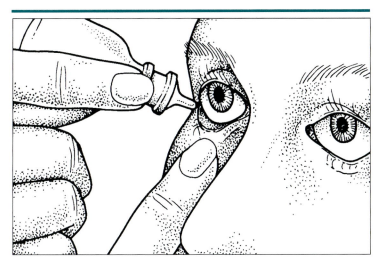

1. The patient looks into a mirror, tilts the head to the left, and retracts the right lower lid. The drop is instilled at the right lateral canthus into the trough formed by the cul-de-sac and the head is straightened.

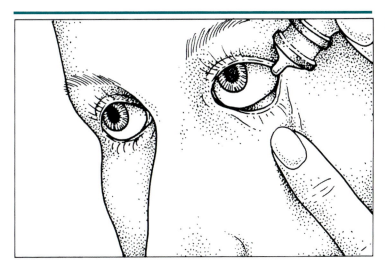

2. The technique is reversed to instill drops into the left eye.

7 Patient Instructions: Ointment Application to Lid Margins

■ **Description/Indications.** Topical ophthalmic ointment is usually the preferred drug vehicle for treating the majority of eyelid conditions. Ointments applied to the lid margins also act as drug reservoirs, providing therapeutic levels of medication to the globe by melting into the conjunctival sac. As a result, ointment applied to the lid may be chosen for the treatment of conjunctival disorders. This technique is especially useful in treating patients for whom manual dexterity is problematic or for treating very young children.

In addition to ensuring compliance with medication dosage, it is important that the patient use an effective technique to apply the ointment to the lids. Verbal instructions, written instructions, and in-office demonstration are effective ways of maximizing patient compliance.

■ **Instrumentation.** Desired ophthalmic ointment, cotton-tipped applicators, facial tissues, wall or stand-mounted mirror.

■ **Technique.** Advise the patient to wash the hands, to verify the label on the ointment to be applied, and to remove the cap of the tube. Instruct the patient to apply a ½ to ¾-inch ribbon of ointment onto one index finger (Fig. 1A). Closing the eyes, the ointment is applied along the lid margins, moving from the medial canthus to the lateral canthus (Fig. 1B). Additional reservoir effect is achieved when a small dab of the ointment is placed at the lateral canthus. This technique is repeated for both eyes. If an area of the lid other than the margin is being treated, the ointment is similarly applied in the appropriate area, using a mirror as needed. Instruct the patient to wash the hands and recap the tube.

Alternatively, ointment may be applied to the lid margins using a cotton-tipped applicator. Instruct the patient to apply a ½-inch ribbon of ointment to the applicator tip (Fig. 2A). Advise the patient to look into the mirror and carefully apply the ointment to the upper and lower lid margins (Fig. 2B and C).

When ointment applied to the lid margins is used for its reservoir effect to the conjunctiva, excess lid ointment may be gently wiped away with a tissue after 3 to 5 minutes without reducing the therapeutic effect.

■ **Contraindications/Complications.** The examiner must be familiar with any contraindications of using a particular type of drug for a given patient, including allergies to the drug contents and drug–drug interactions. The patient should be advised that transient blurred vision is common following application of ointment to the lid margins. If a cotton-tipped applicator is used to apply ointment to the lid margin, the patient must be instructed to use careful technique while looking in the mirror so that superficial injury to the globe does not occur.

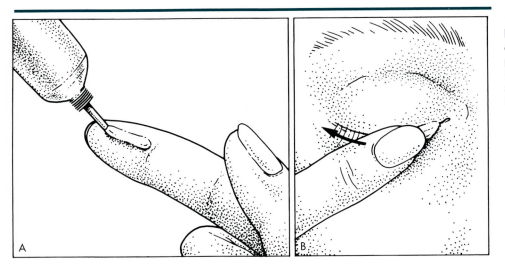

1. A. (far left) A ½ to ¾-inch ribbon of ointment is applied onto one index finger. B. (left) The patient closes the eyes and, starting at the medial canthus, spreads the ointment along the length of the lid margins.

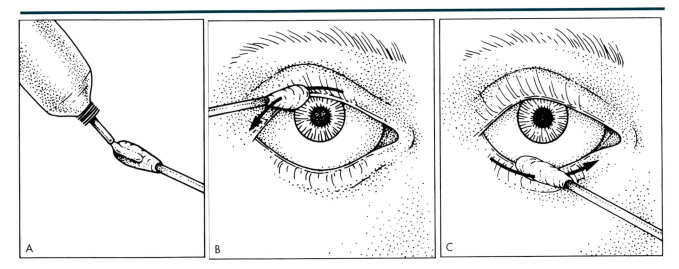

2. A. A ½-inch ribbon of ointment is applied to the cotton-tipped applicator. B. While looking in the mirror, ointment is applied with the applicator to the upper lid margin and C. to the lower lid margin.

8 Patient Instructions: Ointment Application to Conjunctival Sac

■ **Description/Indications.** Topical ophthalmic ointments applied into the conjunctival sac are prescribed for a number of anterior segment disorders. In addition to ensuring compliance with medication dosage, it is important that the patient use an effective technique to apply the ointment into the conjunctival sac. Verbal instructions, written instructions, and in-office demonstration are effective ways of maximizing patient compliance.

■ **Instrumentation.** Desired ophthalmic ointment, wall or stand-mounted mirror, facial tissues.

■ **Technique.** Advise the patient to wash the hands, verify the label on the ointment to be applied, and remove the cap of the tube. Instruct the patient to look into the mirror and tilt the chin down slightly so that the eyes roll upward. He or she then gently pinches the lower lid away from the globe between the thumb and forefinger of one hand so that the inferior cul-de-sac forms a small pouch (Fig. 1). A ½-inch ribbon of ointment is squeezed into the cul-de-sac and the tube is twisted slightly to interrupt ointment flow. The lower lid is then released (Fig. 1B). The eye may be gently massaged through the closed lid to facilitate spread of the ointment within the sac (Fig. 1C). Excess ointment is gently wiped away with a facial tissue. This procedure is repeated for the opposite eye as indicated. Instruct the patient to wash the hands and recap the tube.

Alternatively, the patient may first apply the ointment to a fingertip and transfer it into the conjunctival sac. Instruct the patient to wash the hands and to apply a ½-inch ribbon of ointment onto the fingertip of one hand (Fig. 2A). While looking into a mirror, the patient pulls down the lower lid with the index or middle finger of the opposite hand to expose the palpebral conjunctival surface (Fig. 2B). He or she then rolls or wipes the ointment onto the palpebral conjunctiva (Fig. 2C). Gently pinching the lower lid away from the globe will help to "pocket" the ointment (Fig. 1B). This technique is especially useful for ointments or gels that are more viscous in nature.

■ **Contraindications/Complications.** The examiner must be familiar with any contraindications of using a particular type of ointment for a given patient, including allergies to the drug contents and drug–drug interactions. Some types of ophthalmic ointments or gels have very specific dosage guidelines to determine the amount of medication applied into the conjunctival sac. The patient must be advised to avoid contacting the tip of the tube to the cilia, lids, conjunctival surface, or tears, as contamination of the tube's contents may occur. Proper technique must be utilized to prevent inadvertent superficial injury to the globe.

It is important to warn the patient that significant transient blurring of vision will occur following instillation of ointment into the conjunctival sac. Adverse visual effects can be minimized by controlling the amount of ointment applied as well as the timing of dosages.

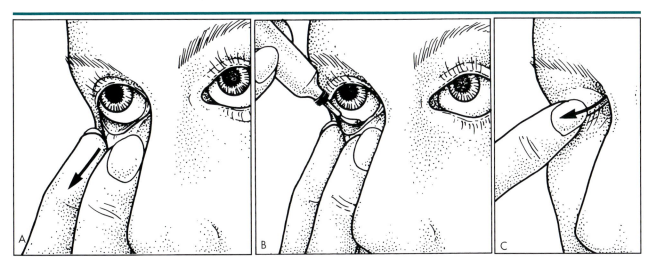

1. A. The patient looks into the mirror and tilts the chin down slightly. The lower lid is gently pinched between the thumb and forefinger of the left hand.

1. B. The ointment is applied into the conjunctival sac and the lid is released.

1. C. The eye may be gently massaged through the closed lid.

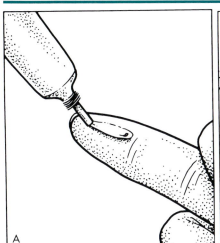
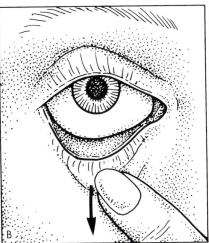
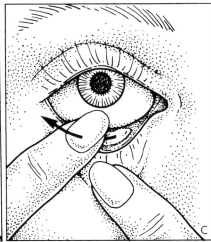

2. A. The patient applies a ½-inch ribbon of ointment onto the fingertip of one hand.

2. B. The patient pulls down the lower lid using the index or middle finger of the opposite hand.

2. C. The patient wipes the ointment onto the exposed palpebral conjunctiva.

Suggested Readings

Bartlett JD: Dilation of the pupil, in Bartlett JD, Jaanus SD (eds): *Clinical Ocular Pharmacology,* ed 3. Boston, Butterworth-Heinemann, 1995, pp 479–502.

Bartlett JD: Ophthalmic drug delivery, in Bartlett JD, Jaanus SD (eds): *Clinical Ocular Pharmacology,* ed 3. Boston, Butterworth-Heinemann, 1995, pp 21–45.

Catania LJ: Management of common eyelid problems. *Practical Hints* series, vol 1, no 1. Dresher, PA, Primary Eyecare, 1982.

Catania LJ: General therapeutic considerations in clinical practice, in *Primary Care of the Anterior Segment.* Norwalk, CT, Appleton & Lange, 1988, pp 1–14.

Locke LC, Meetz R: Sector dilation: An alternative technique. *Optom Vis Sci* 1990; **67:**291–296.

Samples JR: The use of topical beta adrenergic antagonists for the contemporary therapy of glaucoma. *Contemp Ophthalmic Forum* 1987;**5:**139–147.

Shaffer RN: Problems in the use of autonomic drugs in ophthalmology, in Leopold IH (ed): *Ocular Therapy.* St. Louis, Mosby, 1967, vol 2: *Complications and Management,* pp 18–23.

Silverman MB: Routine pupillary dilation (letter). *J Am Optom Assoc.* 1990; **61**: 356.

Terry JE: Diagnostic pharmaceutical agents, clinical uses, in Terry JE (ed): *Ocular Disease: Detection, Diagnosis and Treatment.* Springfield, IL, CC Thomas, 1984, pp 39–41.

Slit Lamp Biomicroscopy
and Adjunct Procedures

9   Overview Biomicroscopic Evaluation

■ **Description/Indications.** The slit lamp biomicroscopic examination is an integral part of most evaluations performed by the ophthalmic practitioner. Use of the slit lamp biomicroscope ("slit lamp") is indicated to perform routine comprehensive ocular health evaluations; to evaluate for ocular trauma, irritation, infection, and inflammation; and to fit and manage contact lens patients. Two of the commonly available attachments for the slit lamp allow the practitioner to perform applanation tonometry (see p. 52) and Hruby lens examination (see p. 242). Many slit lamps are adaptable for anterior segment photography. The slit lamp is integral to the use of auxiliary evaluative techniques and procedures described throughout this text.

The scattering of light due to the Tyndall effect will make most of the ocular media visible through biomicroscopy. A variety of slit lamps, including hand-held models, are commercially available, with each having two important components in common: the viewing system and the illumination system. The viewing system consists of a stereoscopic compound microscope with parallel or converging optics that is adapted to examine the human eye in vivo and mounted on a movable platform. Multiple magnification powers are available. Use of a focusing joystick along with a vertical control knob provides for movement of the microscope in the x, y, and z meridians

relative to the patient positioned in the head and chin rest (Fig. 1).

The illumination system is a light source mounted on the microscope that is variable in intensity and orientation and is projected by an optical system upon the eye. Various aperture stops and filters may be introduced to change the configuration and color of the illumination beam. The relative angle between the illumination system and the microscopic viewing system may be varied to achieve the most effective evaluative technique.

It is most clinically effective and efficient to develop a slit lamp examination routine that is identically performed on each patient. In addition, it is efficacious to establish a smooth yet dynamic sequencing of examination components using fluid hand movements to control the joystick and illumination beam settings. If an ocular lesion is detected or if more detailed evaluation of a specific ocular component is desired, additional techniques and illuminations are incorporated as indicated.

This procedure will review a suggested baseline technique for the overview slit lamp evaluation as may be performed during comprehensive patient examination. The two most commonly used illumination techniques for the general slit lamp evaluation are diffuse illumination and direct focal illumination. More structure and purpose-specific techniques are discussed in subsequent procedures.

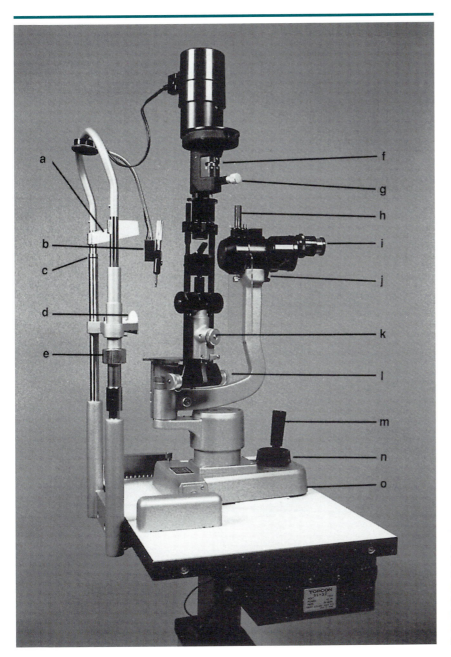

1. The major components of the slit lamp biomicroscope. (a) Forehead rest. (b) Fixation light. (c) Canthus alignment mark. (d) Chin rest. (e) Chin rest height adjustment knob. (f) Beam filters control. (g) Beam height control. (h) Tonometer mount stem. (i) Eyepieces. (j) Magnification lever. (k) Click stop knob. (l) Beam width control. (m) Joystick. (n) Vertical control knob. (o) Slit lamp base.

Diffuse illumination refers to a wide beam that is directed obliquely for general scanning of the anterior segment (Fig. 2). The field of view is maximized by using a low magnification setting. *Direct focal illumination* refers to the focusing of the light beam and the microscope in the same specific area. It does not refer to coaxial placement of the light source with the microscope. Usually medium to high magnification is used depending upon the structure being evaluated. The parallelepiped and optic section are two commonly used types of direct focal illumination, especially important for evaluating the cornea and crystalline lens. The parallelepiped illuminates a three-dimensional tissue area and is effective for detecting tissue lesions (Fig. 3). An optic section illuminates a two-dimensional area of tissue that is viewed obliquely, similar to examining a histological section, and is used to localize the depth of lesions (Fig. 4).

■ **Instrumentation.** Slit lamp biomicroscope.

■ **Technique.**

Basic Slit Lamp Setup: Set the oculars of the microscope to your pupillary distance. Set the power of the ocular eyepieces to zero or to your spherical equivalent refractive error as appropriate. Position the patient comfortably in the slit lamp. Adjust the height of the chin rest so the patient's lateral canthus is aligned with the black line on the upright bar (Fig. 1). Raise or lower the examination chair so the patient can easily rest the forehead against the head strap without straining excessively to reach it (chair too low) or hunching over (chair too high). Advise the patient to grasp the handholds if available. Turn the illumination rheostat to its lowest setting before turning on the slit lamp. Advise the patient that you will be touching the eyelids periodically during the slit lamp examination.

Diffuse Illumination: Position the microscope directly in front of the eye. Adjust the magnification knob to 6X or 10X. Position the light source at approximately 60 degrees from the microscope. Place the microscope and beam in coincident focus with the beam "in click." Adjust the apertures so that the beam is approximately 3 to 4 mm wide and of maximum height. Use the joystick and vertical control knob to focus the microscope on the desired structure illuminated by the diffuse beam (Fig. 2).

Direct Focal Illumination: Position the microscope directly in front of the eye and the light source at approximately 60 degrees from the microscope. Place the microscope and beam in coincident focus with the beam "in click." Adjust the beam to its maximum height and narrow the beam to 1 to 2 mm in width to illuminate a parallelepiped-shaped section of the cornea. Use the joystick to sharply focus the microscope and parallelepiped simultaneously (Fig. 3). To form an optic section, narrow the beam width until it is almost extinguished (Fig. 4).

VAN HERICK ANGLE ESTIMATION

Click stop:	In
Beam angle:	60 degrees
Beam width:	Optic section
Beam height:	Maximum
Filter:	None
Illumination:	Medium
Magnification:	10–16X

1. The slit lamp setup for Van Herick angle estimation.

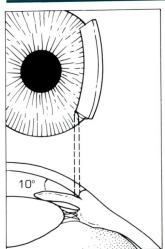

2. Photograph of Van Herick estimation of the temporal angle OS. The anterior chamber appears as a black space between the cornea and iris (arrow). (Courtesy of Keith E. Locke, PhD)

3. (below) Van Herick angle Grades 1 through 4.

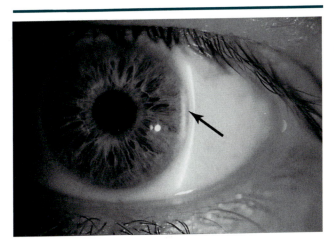
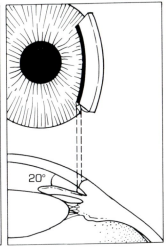
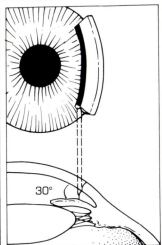
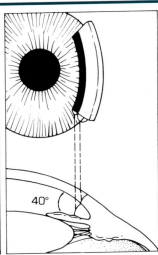

Grade 1: The width of the chamber interval is less than ¼ the width of the corneal optic section. The angle is extremely narrow and will probably close with full pupillary dilation.

Grade 2: The width of the chamber interval is approximately ¼ the width of the corneal optic section. The angle is narrow and is capable of closure.

Grade 3: The width of the chamber interval is ¼ to ½ the width of the corneal optic section. The angle is unlikely to close.

Grade 4: The width of the chamber interval is equal to or greater than the width of the corneal optic section. This is a wide-open angle.

11

Tear Meniscus Evaluation

■ **Description/Indications.** The tear layer is comprised of the outermost oily layer, the middle aqueous layer, and the innermost mucin layer. In addition to the lacrimal lake in the medial canthal area, strips of tear fluid are located at the posterior margins of both the upper and lower eyelids. The inferior marginal strip is more easily visualized and gives off a mirror-like reflection. This tear strip is actually wedge or meniscus-shaped as it simultaneously contacts the lid margin and the bulbar conjunctiva with the lid in the normal position.

In addition to diagnostic tests such as tear breakup time (p. 44) and Schirmer testing (p. 35), the quality of the tear layer may be assessed by inspection with the slit lamp biomicroscope. This technique may be added to the overview slit lamp examination (p. 26) and is indicated for patients with symptoms suggestive of keratitis sicca and for contact lens patients. If keratitis sicca is suspected following the patient history, tear meniscus evaluation should be the initial component of the slit lamp evaluation so that the effect of the lights on tearing is minimized.

■ **Instrumentation.** Slit lamp biomicroscope.

■ **Technique.** Position the patient comfortably at the slit lamp (see p. 22). Adjust the eyepieces to accommodate your pupillary distance and refractive error. Adjust the magnification to 10X to 16X. Make certain that the beam is in the "click" position. Use your right hand to control the joystick and vertical positioning knob; use your left hand to control the beam height and width levers. To evaluate the right eye, position the beam 60 degrees to the left (temporally) of the microscope. Turn the rheostat to its lowest setting and adjust the slit beam width to a 1 to 2-mm parallelepiped (Fig. 1; also see p. 24). Alternatively, keep the slit beam turned off and use ambient room lighting to focus on the tear strip.

Focus the parallelepiped on the inferior tear strip near the lateral canthus. Use the joystick to scan across the tear strip, moving nasally and keeping the strip in focus (Fig. 2). At any point the beam may be narrowed to an optic section to assess the depth of the tear meniscus.

■ **Interpretation.** The tear strip will frequently exhibit superficial colored moire reflections off the outermost oily layer. Excessive tear lipids commonly occur in patients with meibomian gland oversecretion or seborrheic blepharitis. A patient who is wearing excessive eye makeup or makeup applied close to the lid margin will often exhibit colored makeup debris in the tear strip as well as in the tears covering the entire globe. A patient with bacterial conjunctivitis will exhibit exudative debris and mucus in the tear strip. A patient who has been instilling ophthalmic ointment into the conjunctival sac will exhibit oil droplets in the tear strip once the ointment has melted somewhat.

Normally the tear meniscus should be approximately 1 mm wide. In patients with keratitis sicca, the meniscus may be significantly reduced in size due to reduced quantities of the aqueous tear component. The resultant concentration of the oily and mucin tear layers may produce significant levels of mucous strands and debris in the tear strip, especially if accompanying epithelial sloughing is present, and the tear strip will appear very viscous.

■ **Complications/Contraindications.** If the patient is a suitable candidate for slit lamp examination, no risks are associated with this technique. Turning the illumination rheostat too high may induce reflex tearing and obscure the viscosity and thinning of the tear meniscus. The tear meniscus should be evaluated prior to any planned eversion of the upper lid (p. 94). Lid eversion will result in expression of the meibomian gland secretions into the tear strip and will artifactually contribute to the appearance of debris. Lid eversion may also induce reflex tearing to interfere with evaluation of the tear meniscus.

TEAR MENISCUS EVALUATION

Click stop:	In
Beam angle:	60 degrees
Beam width:	1–2 mm Parallelepiped
Beam height:	Maximum
Filter:	None
Illumination:	Low, or use ambient lighting only
Magnification:	10–16X

1. Slit lamp set-up for tear meniscus evaluation.

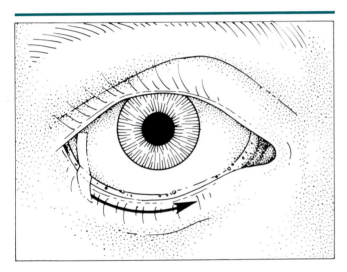

2. A parallelepiped is focused on a viscous tear strip. The arrow indicates the direction of slit lamp scanning.

12 Corneal Evaluation

■ **Description/Indications.** While using the slit lamp biomicroscope to perform an overview evaluation of the eye and adnexa (see p. 22), corneal lesions may be detected that require more thorough evaluation with additional slit lamp illumination techniques. These techniques are typically not included in routine comprehensive slit lamp examination but may be easily incorporated as indicated, either singly or in combination.

Cobalt Filter Illumination: Introduction of the cobalt filter using diffuse illumination but without the instillation of fluorescein sodium will cause corneal iron lines to appear black. This technique is especially useful in detecting subtle Fleischer rings in the diagnosis of early keratoconus.

Specular Reflection: When the microscope and illumination system are set at equal angles of incidence and reflection, the anterior and posterior surfaces of the cornea will serve as reflecting surfaces. This technique is especially useful in evaluating the corneal endothelium. It may also be used for assessing the anterior and posterior surfaces of the crystalline lens.

Indirect Illumination: The microscope is focused on an area immediately adjacent to the illuminated tissue. This technique is especially useful for evaluating refractile, nonopaque corneal lesions such as microcysts and fingerprint lines.

Retroillumination (Iris): Light is reflected off the anterior surface of the iris as the cornea is focused. Lesions will be backlighted and appear black due to absorption of the reflected light.

Retroillumination (Fundus): When the slit lamp beam is directed straight ahead through the dilated pupil, the light will reflect off the fundus through the pupil to form the "red reflex." Lesions will be backlighted and will appear black if sufficiently dense or as areas of corneal irregularity.

Sclerotic Scatter: Internal reflection characteristics of the cornea are used to evaluate its transparency. This technique was invaluable for assessing central corneal clouding (CCC) that developed secondary to polymethymethacrylate (PMMA) hard contact lens wear, but may be used whenever corneal clarity is questioned.

■ **Instrumentation.** Slit lamp biomicroscope.

■ **Technique.** Position the patient comfortably at the slit lamp (see p. 24). Adjust the eyepieces to accommodate your pupillary distance and refractive error. Make certain that the patient's eyes are in primary gaze. To assess the right eye, ask the patient to fixate toward your right ear or over your right shoulder.

Cobalt Filter Illumination: To evaluate the right eye, position the beam 60 degrees to the left (temporally) of the microscope. Make certain that the beam is in the "click" position. Use your right hand to control the joystick and vertical positioning knob; use your left hand to control the beam height and width levers. Introduce the cobalt filter. Set the magnification to 10X to 16X and open the beam width to approximately 3 mm. Turn the illumination rheostat to its highest setting. Scan the cornea looking for subtle black linear, arcuate, or circular lines (Fig. 1).

Specular Reflection: To illuminate the central cornea of the right eye, position the microscope approximately 45 degrees to the right and the illumination system 45 degrees to the left of the visual axis. Make certain that the beam is in the "click" position. Adjust the illumination rheostat to a medium setting. Use your right hand to control the joystick and vertical positioning knob; use your left hand to control the beam height and width levers. Set the magnification to 16X to 40X and open the beam to a parallelepiped approximately 1 mm wide.

Move the joystick with your right hand to position the beam at the corneal apex. A bright reflection of the slit beam filament will be visible in one ocular of the microscope and the reflection of the endothelium will be visible through the other. With the microscope in the straight-ahead position, specular reflection will naturally occur off the curved temporal and nasal sides of the cornea when the beam is placed to the temporal and nasal sides, respectively (Fig. 2).

COBALT FILTER EVALUATION

Click stop:	In
Beam angle:	60 degrees
Beam width:	3 mm
Beam height:	Maximum
Filter:	Cobalt
Illumination:	Maximum
Magnification:	10–16X

A

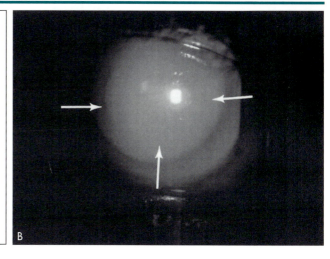

B

1. A. The slit lamp setup for cobalt filter illumination of the cornea.

1. B. When illuminated with the cobalt filter, the Fleischer ring of keratoconus appears black (arrows). (*See also* Color Plate 12–1.B.)

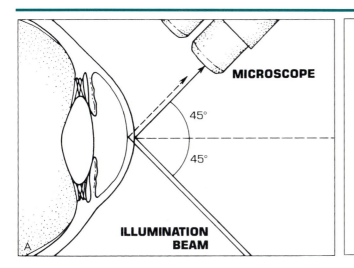

A

SPECULAR REFLECTION

Click stop:	In
Beam; microscope angles:	45 degrees to left; 45 degrees to right of visual axis, respectively
Beam width:	1 mm
Beam height:	Maximum
Filter:	None
Illumination:	Medium
Magnification:	16–40X

2. A. (above) The slit lamp setup for specular reflection of the cornea.

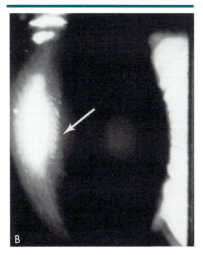

B

2. B. (left) Guttata are visible as an orange-peel-like disruption of the corneal endothelium (arrow).

Indirect Illumination: To evaluate the right eye, position the beam 60 degrees to the left (temporally) of the microscope. Adjust the illumination rheostat to a medium setting. Use your right hand to control the joystick and vertical positioning knob; use your left hand to control the beam height and width levers. Use your left hand to turn the beam to the left of the "click" position. Set the magnification to 10X to 16X and open the beam to a parallelepiped approximately 1 mm wide. Adjust the microscope so that the beam is focused to the left of the lesion and change your point of regard to the lesion (Fig. 3).

Retroillumination (Iris): To evaluate the right eye, posi-tion the beam 60 degrees to the left (temporally) of the microscope. Adjust the illumination rheostat to a medium setting. Use your right hand to control the joystick and vertical positioning knob; use your left hand to control the beam height and width levers. Make certain that the beam is in the "click" position. Set the magnification to 10X to 16X and open the beam to a parallelepiped approximately 1 mm wide. Adjust the microscope so that the corneal lesion is in focus and positioned in front of light reflected off the anterior surface of the iris (Fig. 4). Alternatively, the beam may be moved out of "click" stop so that the cornea is viewed in light reflected off the iris.

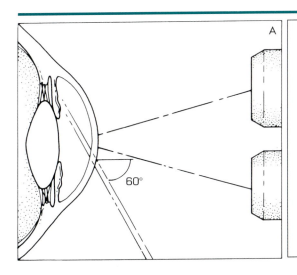

3. A. The slit lamp setup for indirect illumination of the cornea.

INDIRECT ILLUMINATION

Click stop: Out
Beam angle: 60 degrees
Beam width: 1 mm
Beam height: Maximum
Filter: None
Illumination: Medium
Magnification: 10–16X

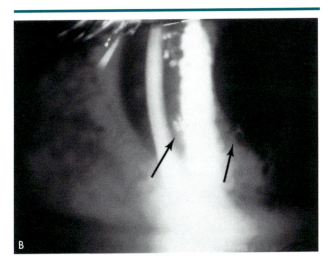

3. B. In the photograph, two small herpes simplex dendritic ulcers are visible in indirect illumination (arrows). (*See also* Color Plate 12–3.B.)

4. A. In the photograph, a limbal neovascular tuft is seen in iris retroillumination. (*See also* Color Plate 12–4.A.)

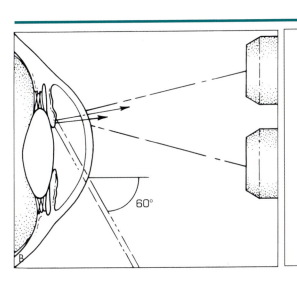

4. B. The slit lamp setup for iris retroillumination of the cornea.

RETROILLUMINATION: IRIS

Click stop: In (or out)
Beam angle: 60 degrees
Beam width: 1 mm
Beam height: Maximum
Filter: None
Illumination: Medium
Magnification: 10–16X

Retroillumination (Fundus): After pupillary dilation (see p. 2), position the light source directly in front of the microscope so that neither eyepiece is occluded. Adjust the microscope magnification to 10X to 16X. Use your right or left hand to control the joystick and vertical positioning knob; place your opposite hand on the illumination beam housing to control the slit height and width. Adjust the beam illumination to form a parallelepiped approximately 1 mm wide and 6 mm high that will fit within the pupillary area. Position the beam just inside the edge of the pupil, focus the microscope in the plane of the central cornea, and look for areas of black opacity or irregularity within the red reflex (Fig. 5).

Sclerotic Scatter: Make certain that the beam is in the "click" position. Use your right hand to control the joystick and vertical positioning knob; use your left hand to control the beam height and width levers. To evaluate the right eye, position the beam 60 degrees to the left (temporally) of the microscope. Adjust the rheostat illumination knob to medium.

Move the joystick to position a 1 mm parallelepiped at the temporal limbus of the right eye. When positioned correctly the nasal limbus will exhibit a halo or glow. Looking outside the slit lamp to the nasal side, observe for areas of milky white haze in the cornea. Using the pupil as a dark background will facilitate this assessment (Fig. 6). If necessary, rotate the viewing microscope to your left so as to not obscure your view of the cornea.

■ Interpretation.

Cobalt Filter Illumination: Iron deposits in the corneal epithelium (iron lines) will appear black with the cobalt filter. When the diagnosis of early keratoconus is suspected due to keratometer mire distortion, refractive error changes of cylinder axis and power, and slightly reduced visual acuity, a subtle partial or complete Fleischer ring may be an early corneal sign observable with the slit lamp and will aid in appropriate diagnosis. With the cobalt filter a black arc or ring will be apparent in the mid-corneal area and may be slightly decentered.

This subtle finding will be easily overlooked if the angle between the illumination system and the microscope is insufficiently large so that light reflected off the iris obscures the appearance, or if the illumination is set too low. Steroscopic appreciation that the black line is located in the cornea assists in making this assessment. The black lines are more prominent following pupillary dilation, when light reflected off the iris is less likely to interfere.

Specular Reflection: With specular reflection the normal corneal endothelium will exhibit a regular, mosaic-like appearance of polygonal cells. The higher magnification settings will be needed to fully appreciate this. When corneal guttata are present in the central cornea, areas of dimpling will appear within the corneal mosaic, similar to an orange peel (see Fig. 2B). Irregularity and/or dropout of corneal endothelial cells has also been reported following intraocular lens implant surgery and prolonged soft contact lens wear.

Indirect Illumination: Corneal microcysts will appear as refractile spherical bodies in the epithelium, giving it a ground glass appearance. Fingerprint lines, a potential component of epithelial basement membrance dystrophy, will appear as sinuous, concentric refractile lines.

Retroillumination (Iris and Fundus): Any frank corneal opacity will appear darkened or black with reillumination. The degree of light absorption will vary with the density of the lesion. Less dense, more refractile corneal lesions will produce lightened or darkened areas of irregularity in the red reflex.

Sclerotic Scatter: A normal clear cornea will not exhibit areas of light scatter with this technique and will appear black (Fig. 5B). If central corneal clouding (CCC) is present due to hard contact lens wear, a circular gray-white haze approximately 4 to 6 mm in diameter will be apparent in the central corneal area. Areas of significant corneal edema or white blood cell infiltration will also appear as milky areas with this technique.

■ Complications/Contraindications. If the patient is a suitable candidate for slit lamp examination, no risks are associated with these techniques.

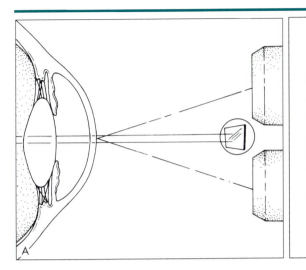

RETROILLUMINATION:	FUNDUS
Click stop:	In (or out)
Beam angle:	0 degrees (coaxial with microscope)
Beam width:	1 mm
Beam height:	6 mm
Filter:	None
Illumination:	Medium
Magnification:	10–16X

5. A. The slit lamp setup for fundus retroillumination of the cornea.

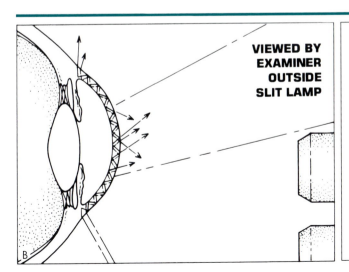

5. B. In the photograph, a pre-Descemet's corneal dystrophy is seen in fundus retroillumination. (*See also* Color Plate 12–5. B. Courtesy of Kevin L. Waltz, MD, OD).

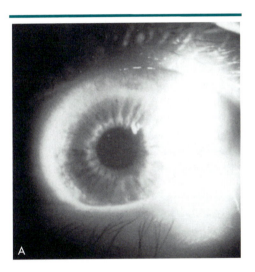

6. A. When evaluated with sclerotic scatter, the central cornea appears clear (black) against the pupillary background.

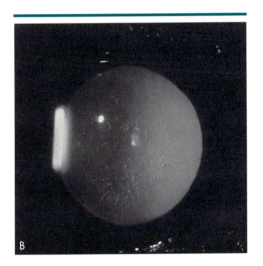

VIEWED BY EXAMINER OUTSIDE SLIT LAMP

SCLEROTIC SCATTER	
Click stop:	In
Beam angle:	60 degrees
Beam width:	1 mm
Beam height:	Maximum
Filter:	None
Illumination:	Medium

6. B. The slit lamp setup for sclerotic scatter of the cornea. Scattering of light is shown from central corneal haze.

13 Anterior Chamber Evaluation

■ **Description/Indications.** The normal aqueous humor is virtually optically empty so that the anterior chamber appears black when the slit beam passes through it. In the presence of anterior uveitis, protein and white blood cells (leukocytes) leak into the anterior chamber from inflamed blood vessels of the iris and ciliary body. The Tyndall effect will allow the visualization of this debris as it circulates in the anterior chamber via the aqueous convection currents. Also, pigment particles from the iris pigment epithelium may be released into the anterior chamber following blunt trauma, routine pupillary dilation, and in patients with pigment dispersion syndrome. Red blood cells (erythrocytes) may be observed circulating in the anterior chamber following the development of a hyphema or microhyphema. Due to the minute size of this debris, appropriate illumination and magnification obtainable with the biomicroscope are required to evaluate the anterior chamber. Debris in the anterior chamber is most easily visualized when the black pupillary area is maintained as the background against which to judge the Tyndall effect.

Assessing the status of the anterior chamber is essential to the accurate differential diagnosis of ocular infections and inflammations, especially following traumatic insult. In a noninflamed eye, chronic uveitis may be suggested by keratic precipitates (KPs) on the corneal endothelium.

This technique of anterior chamber evaluation is incorporated into the biomicroscopic evaluation whenever indicated.

■ **Instrumentation.** Slit lamp biomicroscope.

■ **Technique.** Position the patient comfortably at the slit lamp and adjust the eyepieces of the microscope properly (see p. 24). Make certain that the beam is in the "click" position and that the patient's eyes are in primary gaze. To assess the right eye, ask the patient to fixate toward your right ear or over your right shoulder.

Position the light source 60 degrees to the left (temporally) of the microscope. Adjust the microscope magnification to 16X to 25X. Use your right hand to control the joystick and vertical positioning knob; place your left hand on the illumination beam housing to control slit height and width. Adjust the slit beam height and width using your left hand to form a small round spot of light (conic section) or a short parallelepiped approximately 1 mm wide and 2 mm high. Turn the slit lamp illumination rheostat to its maximum setting (Fig. 1). Turn off all ambient room lights.

Let yourself dark-adapt for a few seconds. Focus the conic section or parallelepiped on the cornea temporal to center at the level of the temporal pupillary border. Move the joystick slightly forward to focus the beam on the anterior surface of the crystalline lens at the nasal pupil margin. As you make the forward focusing motion, carefully observe the black interval of the anterior chamber for minute particles floating vertically within the beam. Perform several of these subtle forward and back oscillatory motions between the cornea and anterior lens surface for a few seconds while observing the small particles reflected in the slit lamp beam (Fig. 2). Vertical and horizontal positional changes of the beam can also be made to assess the anterior chamber, especially when inflammatory cells are suspected but not initially seen. If reddish-brown particles are noted in the anterior chamber, introduce the red-free (green) filter to distinguish red blood cells from pigment particles since erythrocytes absorb green light and will no longer be visible.

1. (left) Slit lamp setup for anterior chamber evaluation.

ANTERIOR CHAMBER EVALUATION

Click stop:	In
Beam angle:	60 degrees
Beam width, height:	Conic section or parallelepiped 1 mm wide and 2 mm high
Filter:	None
Illumination:	Maximum, ambient room lights off
Magnification:	16–25X

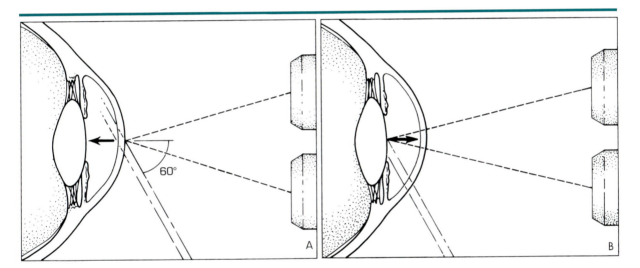

2. A. The short parallelepiped is first focused on the cornea, and then onto the front surface of the lens (B).

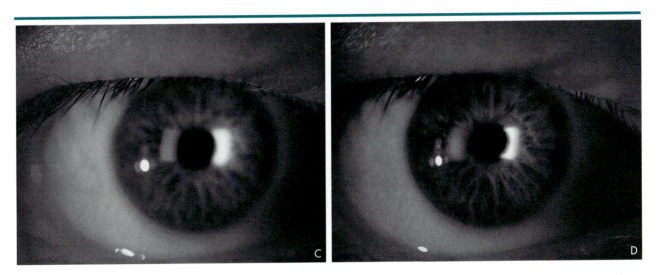

(C) To maximize the black pupillary background, focus the corneal beam temporal of center at the level of the temporal pupillary border, and then focus onto the lens at the nasal pupil border (D). (C, D courtesy of Keith E. Locke, PhD)

■ **Interpretation.** Evaluating the anterior chamber for "cells and flare" due to anterior uveitis refers to assessing for the presence of inflammatory white blood cells (leukocytes) and protein, respectively, that have leaked from inflamed iris and ciliary body vessels. White blood cells appear as whitish specks floating in the anterior chamber (Fig. 3A). Protein in the anterior chamber will not be visible as descrete floating particles but gives an overall milky appearance to the aqueous (Fig. 3B). Cells and flare in the anterior chamber are graded 0 to 4. The grading of cells and flare is determined by the quantity of each visible at any one time in the slit lamp beam (Fig. 4).

Using white light, red blood cells and pigment particles appear as reddish-brown specks floating in the anterior chamber. When the red-free (green) filter is introduced, the red blood cells appear black and will no longer be visible within the anterior chamber. Pigment particles will not absorb the red-free light and will still be visible.

■ **Complications/Contraindications.** The novice biomicroscopist will usually overlook mild to moderate anterior uveitis because of the subtleness of the findings. It is very important to use appropriate illumination and magnification settings of the slit lamp, to let yourself dark-adapt for a few seconds, and to take your time in scrutinizing the anterior chamber. Following the initial evaluation, pupillary dilation will increase the amount of black pupillary background area facilitate visualization of the cells and flare.

Significant loss of corneal clarity due to conditions such as scarring, edema and white blood cell infiltration secondary to corneal healing, and large keratic precipitate (KP) formation, may make visualization of the anterior chamber difficult. In these instances, direct the conic section or short parallelepiped beam through as clear an area of the cornea as possible. Occasionally, a difference in intraocular pressure between the two eyes, the degree of ciliary flush, and observation for fine KPs on the inferior portion of the corneal endothelium may be the only clinical signs that can be elicited to evaluate the degree of anterior chamber involvement.

When the corneal epithelium is disrupted such as following a traumatic abrasion, the anterior chamber should be evaluated prior to the instillation of fluorescein sodium (see p. 48). In this instance the fluorescein will penetrate through the cornea into the anterior chamber and will produce a green-tinged flare that may be misinterpreted as protein in the anterior chamber.

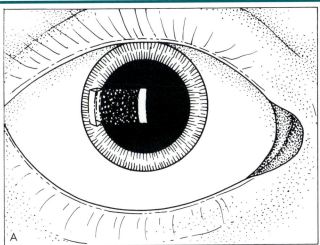

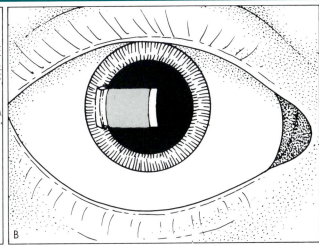

3. **A.** Cells in the anterior chamber appear as whitish specks.

3. **B.** Flare in the anterior chamber appears as a milky haze.

4. The grading of anterior chamber cells and flare.

GRADE	CELLS	FLARE
0	No cells	Complete absence
Trace (½)	Any noticed	Barely noticed
1	4–8	Mild
2	9–15	Moderate
3	Too many to count	Marked
4	Most ever seen	Severe

14 Iris Transillumination

■ **Description/Indications.** Slit lamp evaluation of the iris with diffuse or direct focal illumination (see p. 24) will not reveal defects of the iris pigment epithelium (IPE). For certain clinical entities, the identification of IPE defects through iris transillumination is important for accurate diagnosis.

Iris transillumination is based on the principle of retroillumination. When the slit lamp beam is directed straight ahead through the pupil, the light will reflect off the fundus back through the pupil to form the "red reflex." When the iris is intact and the pupil undilated, the IPE will absorb all of the retroilluminated light and the iris will appear black. If localized or diffuse IPE defects are present, the red reflex will be visible through the iris in the affected areas. Areas of frank iris loss will also transilluminate.

If a Krukenberg's spindle is present on the corneal endothelium, iris transillumination will contribute to the diagnosis of pigment dispersion syndrome. Iris transillumination may help to assess the patency of surgical iridectomy or laser iridotomy (see p. 454) performed for narrow-angle or acute angle closure glaucoma. Diffuse iris transillumination will accompany ocular or generalized albinism and may aid in determining the etiology of nystagmus. IPE defects may follow cataract surgery or ocular trauma.

This technique of iris transillumination is incorporated into the biomicroscopic evaluation when indicated.

■ **Instrumentation.** Slit lamp biomicroscope.

■ **Technique.** Perform iris transillumination before pupillary dilation. Position the patient comfortably at the slit lamp and adjust the eyepieces of the microscope properly (see p. 24). Make certain that the beam is in the "click" position and that the patient's eyes are in primary gaze. To assess the right eye, ask the patient to fixate toward your right ear or over your right shoulder.

Position the light source directly in front of the microscope (coaxial) so that neither eyepiece is occluded. Adjust the microscope magnification to 6X to 10X. Use your right or left hand to control the joystick and vertical positioning knob. Place your opposite hand on the illumination beam housing to control slit height and width. Adjust the beam illumination to form a short, wide parallelepiped approximately 2 mm wide and 2 mm high that will fit within the pupillary area. Turn the illumination rheostat to maximum levels and turn the ambient room lighting off. Position the beam within the pupil area, focus the microscope at the plane of the iris, and observe for areas of red retroillumination (Fig. 1). Make small lateral movements with the joystick if necessary to get the brightest red reflex. If the upper and lower lids are obscuring the superior and inferior peripheral iris, respectively, instruct the patient to open the eyes more widely, or gently retract the lids to expose the entire iris.

■ **Interpretation.** Overall iris transillumination will be present in ocular or generalized albinism and will appear as a diffuse pink glow. Multiple slit or wedged-shaped red areas of peripheral iris transillumination occur secondary to pigment dispersion syndrome (Fig. 2). Transillumination of the pupillary ruff develops due to exfoliation (pseudoexfoliation) syndrome or as a result of pupillary ruff atrophy in the aging process. Isolated focal peripheral iris transillumination defects result from peripheral iridectomy or laser iridotomy.

Pronounced loss of the iris pigment epithelium will produce relatively large areas of iris transillumination postsurgically or posttraumatically. Full thickness absence of the iris secondary to conditions such as essential iris atrophy and iridodialysis will also produce transillumination defects.

■ **Complications/Contraindications.** If the patient is a suitable candidate for slit lamp examination, there are no risks associated with this technique. Subtle peripheral transillumination defects due to pigment dispersion syndrome will be overlooked if the slit lamp illumination is set too low or if the lids are blocking a substantial portion of the peripheral iris.

IRIS TRANSILLUMINATION

Click stop:	In
Beam angle:	0 degrees (coaxial with microscope)
Beam width:	2 mm
Beam height:	2 mm
Filter:	None
Illumination:	Maximum, ambient room lights off
Magnification:	6–10X

1. Slit lamp setup for iris transillumination. A coaxial beam is positioned in the pupillary area and the microscope is focused in the plane of the iris.

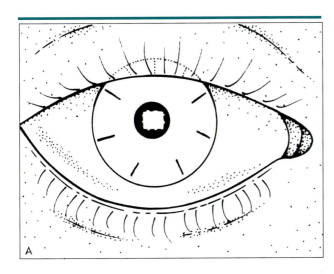

2. A. In this example of mild pigment dispersion syndrome, iris transillumination defects appear as multiple red, slit-shaped areas in the periphery of the iris. The lids should be retracted to fully reveal the extent of the transillumination defects.

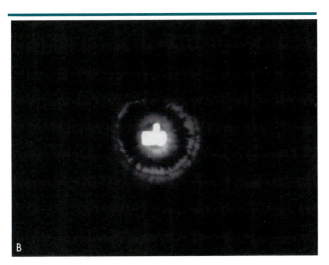

2. B. Extensive peripheral iris transillumination defects are present in this patient with advanced pigment dispersion syndrome. (*See also* Color Plate 14–2. B.) (Courtesy of David W. Sloan, OD)

15 Tear Breakup Time Determination

■ **Description/Indications.** Fluorescein sodium is an orange dye that fluoresces green when illuminated with a cobalt blue filter. The tear film is stained with fluorescein sodium dye and observed with a slit lamp biomicroscope as a means of assessing the integrity of the tears.

The tear layer is comprised of the outer lipid layer, middle aqueous layer, and inner mucin layer. Dissipation of the oily or mucin layer to cause tear evaporation will result in the formation of a dry area in the precorneal tear film. This dry area will appear as a black spot or streak that forms in the once uniformly fluorescent green tear film. Decreased tear secretion will also produce dry spots.

The amount of time it takes for dry areas to form in the fluorescein sodium-stained tear layer following a blink is known as the tear breakup time (BUT). For most patients with normal tear film integrity, the BUT is sufficiently long so that blinking approximately every 15 to 30 seconds will result in the redistribution of an intact tear layer over the globe. Although BUT testing may be of questionable reliability or repeatability, a greatly reduced BUT is probably indicative of dry eye problems (keratitis sicca).

BUT testing is usually performed following a comprehensive slit lamp examination (see p. 22) and is added when the patient has signs or symptoms suggestive of keratitis sicca, or as part of the ocular health evaluation prior to contact lens fitting.

■ **Instrumentation.** Slit lamp biomicroscope, sterile fluorescein sodium strips, sterile ophthalmic saline solution, facial tissues.

■ **Technique.** Hand the patient a fresh facial tissue. Remove a sterile fluorescein sodium strip from the package, taking care not to contaminate the fluorescein sodium-impregnated end. Holding the strip in one hand over a wastebasket or sink, use the other hand to squeeze a drop of sterile ophthalmic saline solution onto the fluorescein end of the strip (Fig. 1A). Ask the patient to look up. Gently retract the right lower lid with the index finger or thumb of the left hand. Holding the strip in your right hand, dab the moistened fluorescein dye from the end of the strip onto the inferior bulbar conjunctiva (Fig. 1B). Alternatively, ask the patient to look down, gently retract the upper lid, and dab the fluorescein onto the superior bulbar conjunctiva. Using the same fluorescein strip, repeat this procedure for the left eye. If an anterior segment infection is present, however, instill fluorescein sodium into the uninvolved eye first or use a separate strip for each eye. Discard the fluorescein strip(s). Advise the patient that the saline solution may momentarily sting slightly. The patient may use the tissue to dab away excess fluid but should not forcefully wipe the eyes.

Position the patient comfortably at the slit lamp and adjust the eyepieces of the microscope properly (see p. 24). Make certain that the beam is in the "click" position and that the patient's eyes are in primary gaze. To assess the right eye, ask the patient to fixate toward your right ear or over your right shoulder.

Position the light source 60 degrees to the left (temporally) of the microscope. Introduce the cobalt filter into the illumination beam. Adjust the microscope magnification to 6X to 10X. Use your right hand to control the joystick and vertical positioning knob; use your left hand to widen the slit to approximately 3 mm. Increase the slit lamp illumination rheostat to its highest setting (Fig. 2).

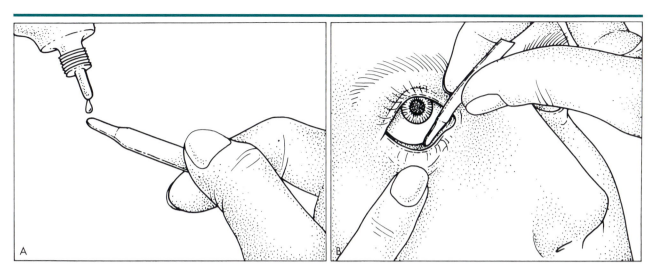

1. A. Squeeze a drop of sterile ophthalmic saline solution onto the fluorescein sodium impregnated end of the strip.

1. B. Retract the right lower lid with the index finger or thumb of your left hand and dab the strip onto the inferior bulbar conjunctiva.

TEAR BREAKUP TIME DETERMINATION

Click stop:	In
Beam angle:	60 degrees
Beam width:	3–4 mm
Beam height:	Maximum
Filter:	Cobalt
Illumination:	Maximum
Magnification:	6–10X

3–4mm   60°

2. Slit lamp setup for tear BUT determination. Diffuse illumination of maximum intensity is used along with the cobalt filter.

Ask the patient to blink fully and then to refrain from blinking until instructed to do so. Begin counting mentally to yourself in 1-second intervals. While counting, manipulate the joystick with your right hand to continually scan all portions of the fluorescein-stained precorneal tear film (Fig. 3). The appearance of one or more black dry spots in the precorneal tear film marks the end of the test (Fig. 4). Record the number of seconds that elapsed as the tear breakup time (for example, BUT = 8 sec). Repeat the procedure for the left eye.

■ **Interpretation.** A normal breakup time is considered to be 10 to 15 seconds or greater. A low breakup time may be indicative of keratitis sicca. Other tests that may be performed to assess for keratitis sicca include Schirmer tear testing (p. 124), and collagen punctal plug insertion (p. 140). Focal areas initially appearing as black spots in the tear film that persist even with repeated blinks probably represent areas of "negative" fluorescein staining due to epithelial elevation rather than tear breakup (see p. 48).

■ **Complications/Contraindications.** Tear BUT testing should be performed prior to the instillation of topical ophthalmic anesthetic solution because the BUT may be artificially lowered and corneal staining may be induced. If the patient has difficulty in refraining from blinking, gently retract the lids with your fingers with the hand not controlling the slit lamp joystick.

Fluorescein sodium can penetrate into soft contact lenses and discolor them. When indicated, a large-molecular-weight fluorescein solution (fluorexon) can be used because it is less readily absorbed by soft lens materials. Because this solution tends to fluoresce less intensely, set the slit lamp illumination at the highest level.

That portion of the bulbar conjunctiva that is touched with the fluorescein strip will stain densely and should not be interpreted as an abnormality. If the patient exhibits a Bell's reflex while the fluorescein strip is touched to the superior bulbar conjunctiva, linear staining of the cornea may be induced. Care should be taken to avoid applying too much saline solution to the fluorescein strip and inadvertently dripping fluorescein dye onto the patient's clothing. Reassure the patient that the orange discoloration of the tear film covering the cornea and conjunctiva will dissipate.

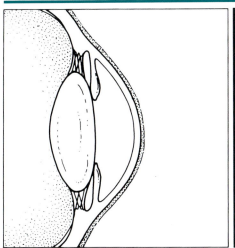 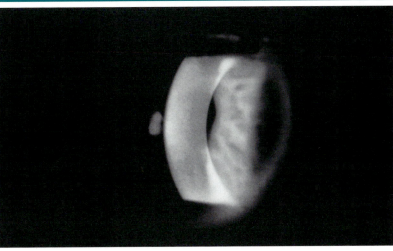

3. The intact precorneal tear film (schematic, left) appears uniformly green when stained with fluorescein sodium and illuminated with cobalt filter of the slit lamp (right). (*See also* Color Plate 15–3.)

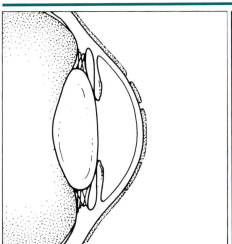 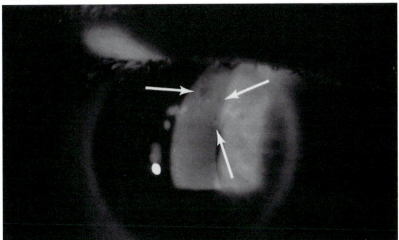

4. Dry areas appear as black spots or streaks in the fluorescein-stained precorneal tear film (arrows). (*See also* Color Plate 15–4.)

16 Vital Dye Staining

■ **Description/Indications.** Fluorescein sodium or rose bengal vital dyes are routinely used in the diagnosis of corneal and conjunctival conditions. Fluorescein sodium is an orange dye that fluoresces green when illuminated with a cobalt filter. Areas of corneal or conjunctival epithelial loss will exhibit fluorescein dye uptake and will appear bright green. This positive fluorescein staining will help to identify the extent and distribution of epithelial loss. Fluorescein staining is assessed whenever epithelial loss is suspected, such as following corneal or conjunctival trauma, contact lens removal, or foreign body removal (see pp. 164 and 156), and to assess corneal involvement secondary to conjunctival, lid, lash, and lacrimal disorders.

The conjunctival epithelium will exhibit fluorescein staining as a result of trauma. Focal inflammatory involvements, such as nodules in nodular episcleritis or phlyctenules in phlyctenular keratoconjunctivitis, will also show positive fluorescein staining. Fluorescein dye will tend to pool in the normal topographical undulations of the bulbar and palpebral conjunctiva.

Fluorescein staining will also help to assess areas of corneal epithelial elevation as occurs in a healing corneal abrasion or recurrent corneal erosion, in epithelial microcysts, and in the geographic mapping areas of epithelial basement membrane dystrophy. The elevated epithelium causes a thinning of the precorneal tear film to produce black areas within the tear layer fluorescence.

In contrast, rose bengal staining will highlight corneal and epithelial cells that are devitalized but have not desquamated and are still intact. Rose bengal staining of the inferior cornea and bulbar conjunctiva is especially indicative of keratitis sicca.

■ **Instrumentation.** Slit lamp biomicroscope, sterile fluorescein sodium strips, sterile rose bengal strips, sterile ophthalmic saline solution, facial tissues.

■ **Technique.** Hand the patient a fresh facial tissue. Remove a sterile strip of the desired vital dye from the package, taking care not to contaminate the dye-impregnated end. Holding the strip in one hand over a wastebasket or sink, use the other hand to squeeze a drop of sterile ophthalmic saline solution onto the dye end of the strip (Fig. 1A). Ask the patient to look up. Gently retract the right lower lid with the index finger or thumb of the left hand. Holding the strip in your right hand, dab the moistened dye from the end of the strip onto the inferior bulbar conjunctiva (Fig. 1B). Alternatively, ask the patient to look down, gently retract the upper lid, and dab the dye onto the superior bulbar conjunctiva. Using the same strip, repeat this procedure for the left eye. If anterior segment infection is present, however, instill vital dye into the uninvolved eye first or use a separate strip for each eye. Discard the strip(s). Advise the patient that the saline solution may momentarily sting slightly. The patient may use the tissue to dab away excess fluid but should not forcefully wipe the eyes.

Position the patient comfortably at the slit lamp and adjust the eyepieces of the microscope properly (see p. 24). Make certain that the beam is in the "click" position and that the patient's eyes are in primary gaze. To assess the right eye, ask the patient to fixate toward your right ear or over your right shoulder.

Position the light source 60 degrees to the left (temporally) of the microscope. Adjust the microscope magnification to 6X to 10X. Use your right hand to control the joystick and vertical positioning knob; place your left hand on the illumination beam housing to set the slit width at 3 to 4 mm and slit height to maximum for diffuse illumination.

Fluorescein Sodium Staining: Introduce the cobalt filter into the illumination beam and increase the slit lamp illumination rheostat to its highest setting (Fig 2). Allow the fluorescein dye to diffuse for approximately 30 seconds. Scan the cornea and bulbar conjunctiva for areas of dye uptake that appear bright green. To assess the topography of the palpebral conjunctiva, gently retract the lower lid as the patient looks up, or evert the upper lid (see p. 94).

Rose Bengal Staining: Use diffuse white light illumination of medium intensity (Fig. 3). Scan the cornea and bulbar conjunctiva for areas of dye uptake that appear as rosy red areas.

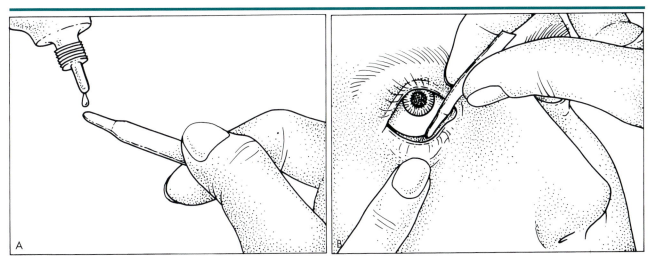

1. A. Squeeze a drop of sterile ophthalmic saline solution onto the vital dye-impregnated end of the strip.

1. B. Retract the right lower lid with the index finger or thumb of your left hand and dab the strip onto the inferior bulbar conjunctiva.

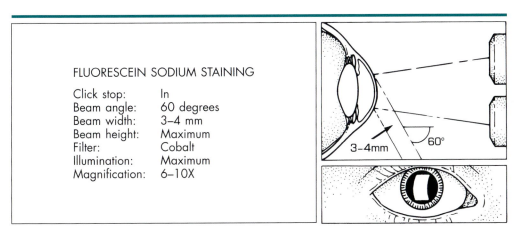

FLUORESCEIN SODIUM STAINING

Click stop:	In
Beam angle:	60 degrees
Beam width:	3–4 mm
Beam height:	Maximum
Filter:	Cobalt
Illumination:	Maximum
Magnification:	6–10X

2. Slit lamp setup for fluorescein sodium staining. Diffuse illumination of maximum intensity is used along with the cobalt filter.

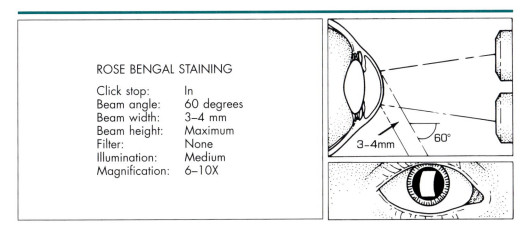

ROSE BENGAL STAINING

Click stop:	In
Beam angle:	60 degrees
Beam width:	3–4 mm
Beam height:	Maximum
Filter:	None
Illumination:	Medium
Magnification:	6–10X

3. Slit lamp setup for rose bengal staining. Diffuse white light illumination of medium intensity is used.

■ Interpretation.

Fluorescein Sodium Staining: Areas of missing corneal epithelium will take up fluorescein stain and appear bright green (Fig. 4). These areas are said to exhibit positive corneal staining. The extent and distribution of this staining will be dependent upon the etiology of the epithelial disruption. Mucus or epithelial debris in the tear film will also stain brightly with fluorescein.

In contrast, areas of epithelial elevation cause thinning of the fluorescein-stained tear layer. These areas will appear as black spots within the tear film and are said to exhibit negative fluorescein staining (Fig. 5). These areas present as persistent black spots in contrast to the dry spots of tear breakup, which transiently appear within the tear layer as the blink reflex is suppressed (see p. 44).

Fluorescein dye will pool in the normal topographical undulations of the bulbar and palpebral conjunctiva. On the bulbar conjunctiva this pooling of dye will appear as a subtle cross-hatching effect. On the palpebral conjunctiva, the fluorescein will pool around focal elevations of this tissue, and will accentuate the appearance of palpebral conjunctival follicles and papillae. In addition to this normally observed pooling effect, the conjunctiva will also exhibit frank fluorescein staining when the epithelium is disrupted.

Rose Bengal Staining: Rose bengal staining will appear as rosy red areas of dye uptake, indicative that epithelial cells are intact but devitalized (Fig. 6). Rose bengal will also stain mucus and keratin.

■ Complications/Contraindications.

Vital dye staining should be performed prior to the instillation of topical ophthalmic anesthetic solution because corneal staining may be induced. That portion of the bulbar conjunctiva that is touched with the vital dye strip will stain densely and should not be misinterpreted as an abnormality. If the patient exhibits a Bell's reflex while the vital dye strip is touched to the superior bulbar conjunctiva, linear staining of the cornea may be induced.

If the fluorescein in the tear film is not allowed to diffuse slightly, the excess fluorescein may obscure areas of positive corneal staining. Conversely, excessive diffusion of the fluorescein will prevent visualization of areas of negative staining. With significant corneal epithelial disruption, the anterior chamber should be evaluated prior to the instillation of fluorescein (see p. 38). In this instance the fluorescein will penetrate through the cornea into the anterior chamber and will produce a green-tinged flare that may be misinterpreted as protein in the anterior chamber.

Care should be taken to avoid applying too much saline solution to the fluorescein or rose bengal strip and inadvertently dripping dye onto the patient's clothing. Reassure the patient that the orange or red discoloration of the tear film covering the cornea and conjunctiva will dissipate. Fluorescein sodium will discolor soft contact lenses if instilled while the lens is in the eye. Fluorexon is less likely to penetrate most soft lenses due to a higher molecular weight and may be used for vital dye staining when reinsertion of soft lenses is necessary.

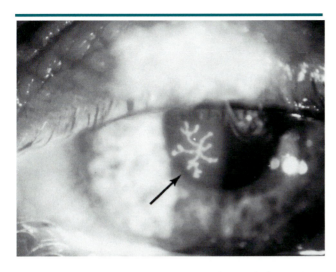

4. The cornea exhibits positive fluorescein sodium staining secondary to a herpes simplex dendritic ulcer (arrow). (*See also* Color Plate 16–4.)

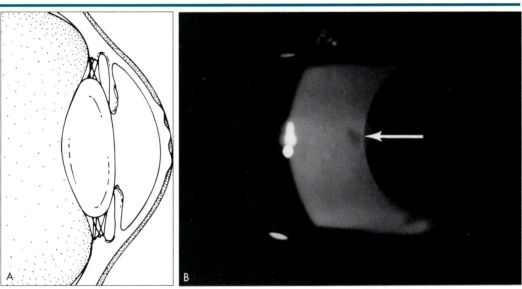

5. A. Areas of corneal epithelial elevation cause thinning of the fluorescein-stained tear film to form black spots called negative staining. B. The cornea exhibits negative fluorescein sodium staining centrally secondary to epithelial bullae resulting from Fuchs' endothelial dystrophy (arrow). (*See also* Color Plate 16–5. B.)

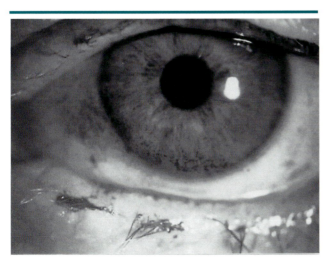

6. The bulbar conjunctiva and cornea exhibit rose bengal staining secondary to keratitis sicca. (*See also* Color Plate 16–6.)

17 Applanation Tonometry: Goldmann

■ **Description/Indications.** Measurement of the intraocular pressure (IOP) is an essential component of routine comprehensive eye examinations, is integral to assessing the efficacy of therapeutic agents for glaucoma, and is important to differentially diagnose acute anterior segment involvements.

Goldmann applanation tonometry is the technique for IOP measurement against which all other techniques are judged. The IOP is determined by measuring the amount of force necessary to flatten a constant corneal surface area. Compared with other techniques, the effects of intraocular volume change, surface tension, and corneal rigidity are negligible so that the applanation pressure corresponds well to the true IOP. Most Goldmann applanation tonometers are mounted on a slit lamp biomicroscope. The corneal area flattened by applanation will be visible through either the right or left eyepiece. A hand-held applanation tonometer (Perkins tonometer) is also available for patients who cannot be positioned in the slit lamp (see p. 58).

The three basic components of the Goldmann tonometer are the applanating probe, the probe arm mounted into a spring-loaded control box, and the measuring drum (Fig. 1). The probe is a prism that optically doubles the applanation image, displacing it into two halves. The flat tip of the probe contacts the cornea and enables the examiner to determine when a standard corneal area 3.06 mm in diameter has been flattened. The tear layer, which appears yellow-green with fluorescein sodium viewed with a cobalt filter, is used to demarcate the flattened corneal area. Where the probe contacts the cornea, the fluorescein-stained tears are pushed to the periphery of the applanation area to form a well-defined yellow-green ring. The inside border of the ring represents the line of transition between the area of the cornea flattened by applanation and that which is not. The knob on the measuring drum reads in grams of applanation force; one gram of force corresponds to 10 mm Hg of IOP.

■ **Instrumentation.** Slit lamp biomicroscope with Goldmann tonometer, asepticized applanation probe, fluorescein sodium-benoxinate ophthalmic solution or sterile fluorescein sodium ophthalmic strips with topical ophthalmic anesthetic solution, facial tissues.

■ **Technique.** Following slit lamp examination of the anterior segment (see p. 38), ask the patient to sit back from the slit lamp. Hand the patient a clean facial tissue. Instill a drop of fluorescein sodium–benoxinate ophthalmic solution into each eye, or instill a drop of topical ophthalmic anesthetic and fluorescein sodium vital dye (Fig. 2, see also p. 48). Advise the patient that a mild, transient burning may occur and that he or she may blot the excess fluid from the eyes with the tissue.

Swing the entire Goldmann tonometer to the forward position into which the clean and dry, asepticized (see p. 475) probe has been inserted. If the patient has less than three diopters of corneal cylinder as measured by keratometry, align the probe so that the white mark on the probe holder is continuous with the 180-degree line on the probe. Align the red mark on the probe holder with the line on the probe corresponding to the minus cylinder axis if more than three diopters of corneal cylinder are present. The probe arm should rock back freely when the measurement drum is on "zero." Make sure the probe "clicks" laterally into the straight-ahead position when the tonometer is positioned for measurement.

Position the slit lamp illumination source approximately 60 degrees from the eyepieces. Open the slit beam to its widest setting and introduce the cobalt filter. Set the slit lamp magnification to 6X to 10X, and turn the rheostat to its maximum setting so that the probe tip is brightly illuminated (Fig. 3). Turn the knob on the measuring drum to "1," corresponding to 10 mm Hg, causing it to rock forward slightly.

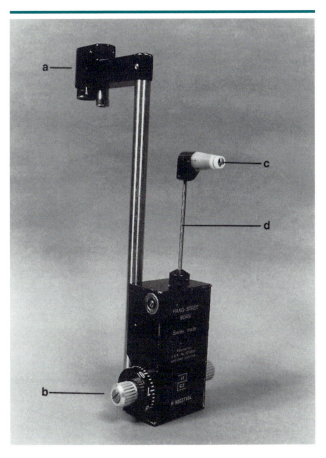

1. The components of the slit-lamp-mounted Goldmann applanation tonometer. (a) Slit lamp mounting arm. (b) Measuring drum. (c) Applanation probe. (d) Probe arm.

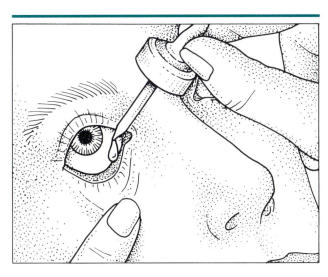

2. Instill a drop of fluorescein sodium–benoxinate solution into each eye.

GOLDMANN APPLANATION TONOMETRY

Click stop: In
Beam angle: 60 degrees
Beam width: Maximum
Beam height: Maximum
Filter: Cobalt
Illumination: Maximum
Magnification: 6–10X

3. Slit lamp setup for Goldmann applanation tonometry.

Ask the patient to position the head on the chin and forehead rests of the slit lamp. Correct positioning of the patient's head against the forehead rest is important. Occasionally an assistant or family member may need to gently hold the patient's head in place. Instruct the patient to fixate straight ahead or adjust the fixation light so that the right eye is in primary gaze. Looking outside the slit lamp, grossly center the probe approximately ¾ inch from the right corneal apex (Fig. 4A). If large slit lamp movement is necessary, move the base toward the patient while keeping the joystick vertical, making subsequent finer movements with the joystick. Looking through the slit lamp, use the joystick to move the probe slightly forward. Approximately ½ inch before corneal contact is made, the reflection of the probe off the cornea will appear as two pale blue semicircles (Fig. 4B). Use the joystick and vertical positioning knob to adjust the lateral and vertical position of the slit-lamp-mounted probe so that the pale blue semicircles are centered in the field of view and equally divided, making movements in the direction of the larger semicircle.

Ask the patient to blink fully and to keep the lids wide open, looking straight ahead. Use the joystick to move the probe toward the corneal apex while maintaining centration of the pale blue semicircles as visualized through the slit lamp. After contacting the cornea you will see two steadily pulsating fluorescent green semicircles.

The width of the fluorescein semicircles should be approximately one-tenth of the diameter of the flattened area. Make small adjustments with the joystick in the direction of the larger semicircle to exactly center and equally divide the fluorescein semicircles (Fig. 5). An alternative approach for achieving corneal contact is to sight outside of the slit lamp as the probe is positioned on the corneal apex. The limbus will exhibit a blue glow when contact is made. While using the joystick to carefully maintain corneal contact, resume sighting through the slit lamp and proceed with the technique.

While maintaining applanation with one hand on the joystick, quickly use the opposite hand to turn the measuring drum until the inner borders of the two fluorescein semicircles just touch each other. If significant pulsation is present, adjust the measuring drum so that the semicircles pulsate equally to either side of the correct endpoint (Fig. 6). Pull back on the joystick to remove the probe from the cornea. Note the IOP measurement in mm Hg by multiplying the figure on the drum by 10. Repeated measurements should be within a range of ± 0.5 mm Hg. Repeat the technique for the left eye, swinging the slit lamp illumination beam to the temporal side if desired. Swing the tonometer out from the forward position and check both corneas with the slit lamp for induced epithelial staining (see p. 48) if desired.

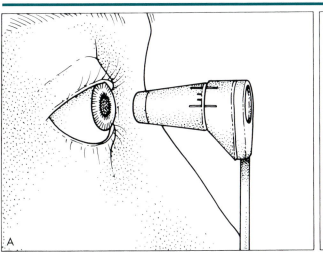 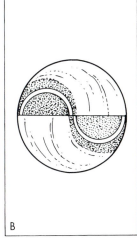

4. A. Looking outside the slit lamp, grossly center the probe approximately ¾ inch from the corneal apex.
B. Approximately ½ inch before corneal contact is made, the reflection of the probe will appear as two pale blue semicircles, which are used to center the probe. (*See also* Color Plate 17–4.B.)

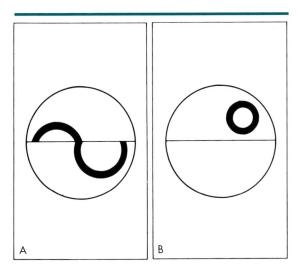

5. A. Following corneal contact, the larger inferior semicircle indicates that the probe is too high. Make small adjustments with the joystick in the direction of the larger semicircle to correctly center the probe. B. The instrument is too far to the left and too low.

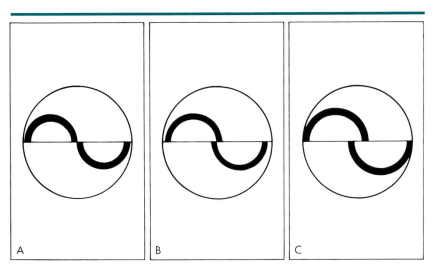

6. While maintaining centered corneal contact with the joystick, use the opposite hand to quickly turn the measuring drum until the inner borders of the semicircles just touch. A. More probe pressure is needed. B. Correct endpoint. C. Too much probe pressure.

Occasionally a patient may have difficulty keeping the lids open or may have a narrow palpebral fissure so that lid retraction is needed. Just before aligning the probe, ask the patient to look down. Use the forefinger of your left hand to gently retract the upper lid. Ask the patient to look straight ahead and use the thumb of your left hand to gently retract the lower lid. Be certain to hold the lids against the orbital rims so that pressure is not applied to the globe (Fig. 7). Proceed with the technique as described using your right hand to control the joystick. Release your right hand from the joystick to adjust the knob on the measurement drum when corneal contact is made. Because neither hand is maintaining applanation with the joystick, corneal contact is frequently lost. After adjusting the measurement drum, use your right hand on the joystick to reapplanate the cornea. Repeat this process to bracket to the applanation endpoint.

If the fluorescein semicircles are too wide, too much fluorescein is in the conjunctival sac or the lids contacted the probe during measurement (Fig. 8A). Draw back the probe, dry the probe tip with a clean tissue, ask the patient to gently blot the eyes with a tissue, and repeat the measurement. Conversely, rapid dissipation of the tears will produce semicircles that are too narrow (Fig. 8B). Draw back the probe, instill more fluorescein, and repeat the measurement.

■ **Interpretation.** If the fluorescein semicircles are too wide, the IOP measurement will be artificially high. Semicircles that are too narrow yield IOP measurements that are artificially low. Most practitioners consider normal intraocular pressures as measured by applanation to be 21 mm Hg or less, with the difference in readings between the two eyes expected to be no greater than 3 to 4 mm Hg. However, because of diurnal IOP fluctuation, along with many other factors, it is extremely important that the practitioner not rely solely on the IOP reading to rule out a diagnosis of glaucoma. Careful optic nerve head assessment, nerve fiber layer and retina evaluation, visual field analysis, and anterior segment evaluation including gonioscopy are needed to determine whether the IOP is normal for that individual (see Section XII).

■ **Complications/Contraindications.** The examiner must be familiar with any contraindications that may preclude using any of the diagnostic agents needed for applanation tonometry. Applanation tonometry is avoided in the presence of conjunctival infection to prevent probe contamination, large central corneal abrasions to prevent further epithelial disruption, and significant epithelial basement membrane dystrophy to avoid inducing a corneal abrasion. Care should be taken to avoid over-manipulating eyes that have sustained severe ocular trauma. Corneas that are extremely distorted or scarred will produce irregular mires that may prevent an accurate reading.

To minimize anxiety, it is best to avoid detailing to the patient that actual corneal contact will occur. Patient anxiety tends to artificially elevate the IOP. Continual coaxing of the patient to open both eyes widely will help to minimize interference by the lids. Touching of the lids or lashes by the probe will induce a blink reflex and should be avoided. If the examiner puts pressure on the globe while retracting the lids the IOP will be artificially elevated.

It is common to induce some superficial corneal epithelial disruption following applanation tonometry. This will occur following topical anesthetic use, due to movements of the probe on the cornea, desiccation of the cornea surrounding the contact area, and unanticipated patient eye movements. Usually no treatment is required for these minor tissue disruptions other than perhaps the use of artificial tears. The examiner should avoid, however, large repositioning movements of the probe when it is in contact with the cornea. If the appearance of the fluorescein semicircles indicates that major repositioning is needed, use the joystick to pull the probe back from the cornea and reposition before applanating again. Rarely, poor examiner technique or sudden head or eye movements by the patient while the probe is in contact with the cornea may induce a corneal abrasion.

A patient may rarely experience vasovagal syncope during this technique. Should this occur, basic first-aid measures are taken. These include elevating the feet above the level of the head, passing a broken ammonia inhalant ampule beneath the nostrils, and monitoring basic vital signs.

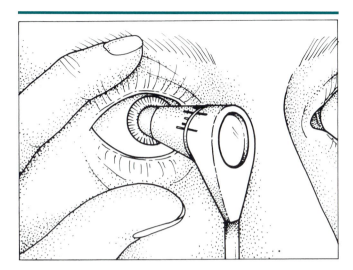

7. Gently retract the upper and lower lids against the orbital rims if necessary.

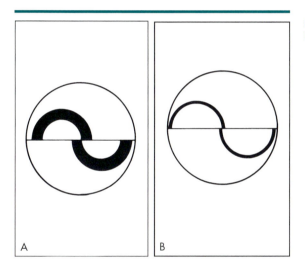

8. A. Wide semicircles indicate that too much fluorescein is present.
B. Narrow semicircles indicate insufficient fluorescein is present.

18 Applanation Tonometry: Perkins

■ **Description/Indications.** Measurement of the intraocular pressure (IOP) is an essential component of routine comprehensive eye examinations, is integral to assessing the effect of therapeutic agents for glaucoma, and is important to differentially diagnose acute anterior segment involvements.

Goldmann applanation tonometry is the technique for IOP measurement against which all other techniques are judged. The IOP is determined by measuring the amount of force necessary to flatten a constant corneal surface area. Compared with other techniques, the effects of intraocular volume change, surface tension, and corneal rigidity are negligible, so that the applanation pressure corresponds well to the true IOP. Most Goldmann applanation tonometers are mounted on a slit lamp (see p. 52). For some patients with physical constraints who cannot be positioned in the slit lamp, when a slit lamp is not available, or for wheelchair users or bedridden patients, a hand-held applanation tonometer (Perkins tonometer) may be used to obtain accurate IOP measurements. The prism arm is counterbalanced so that the instrument may be used in the horizontal or vertical position.

The applanating probe is mounted into a spring-loaded holder controlled by a measurement knob. The cobalt illumination source is self-contained in the handle of the unit and turns on when the measurement knob is turned past the zero mark. An adjustable forehead rest helps to support the instrument in place (Fig. 1). The probe is a prism that optically doubles the applanation image, displacing it into two halves. The flat tip of the probe contacts the cornea and enables the examiner to determine when a standard corneal area 3.06 mm in diameter has been flattened. The tear layer, which appears yellow-green with fluorescein viewed with a cobalt filter, is used to demarcate the flattened corneal area. Where the probe contacts the cornea, the fluorescein-stained tears are pushed to the periphery of the applanation area to form a well-defined yellow-green ring. The inside border of the ring represents the line of transition between the area of the cornea flattened by applanation and that which is not. The knob on the measuring drum reads in grams of applanation force; one gram of force corresponds to 10 mm Hg of IOP.

■ **Instrumentation.** Perkins tonometer with asepticized applanation probe, fluorescein sodium–benoxinate ophthalmic solution or sterile fluorescein sodium ophthalmic strips with topical ophthalmic anesthetic solution, facial tissues.

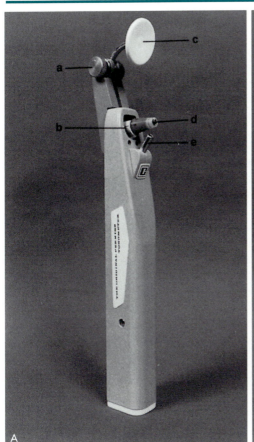

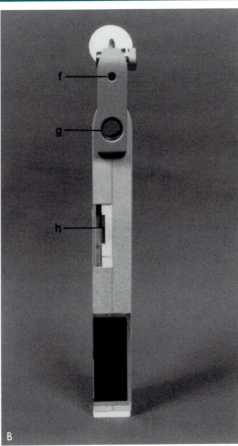

1. A. (far left) The components of the Perkins applanation tonometer. (a) Forehead rest set screw. (b) Applanating probe holder. (c) Patient forehead rest. (d) Applanating probe. (e) Illumination source.
B. (left) (f) Examiner forehead rest mount (optional). (g) Eyepiece. (h) Measurement knob.

■ **Technique.** Insert the clean and dry, asepticized probe into the tonometer holder. If the patient has less than three diopters of corneal cylinder as measured by keratometry or as interpolated from the spectacle prescription, align the probe so that the white mark on the probe holder is continuous with the 180-degree line on the probe. Align the red mark on the probe holder with the line on the probe corresponding to the minus cylinder axis if more than three diopters of corneal cylinder are present. Adjust the length of the forehead rest by loosening the locking screw and sliding the arm in or out. Tighten the locking screw at the estimated length of the arm so that when the rest is placed on the forehead the tonometer can be angled and pivoted into a position that is parallel with the front of the face (Fig. 2).

Hand the patient a clean facial tissue. Instill a drop of fluorescein sodium-benoxinate ophthalmic solution into each eye, or instill a drop of topical ophthalmic anesthetic and fluorescein sodium vital dye (Fig. 3). Advise the patient that a mild, transient burning may occur and that he or she may blot the excess fluid from the eyes with the tissue. Position the patient's line of sight so that the eyes are in primary gaze.

To measure the patient's right eye, position yourself standing or sitting in front of and slightly temporally to the right eye. Turn the measuring knob so that the cobalt illumination turns on and the dial is set at 1 (10 mm Hg). Place the forehead rest approximately in the middle of the patient's forehead and gently hold it in position with your left hand. Looking outside the instrument, pivot the handle toward the patient so that the tip of the probe is approximately ¾ inch from the corneal apex (Fig. 4).

Sighting through the viewing lens with your right eye, the reflection of the probe off the cornea before contact is made will appear as two pale blue semicircles (Fig. 5). Move the instrument handle toward the patient while maintaining centration of the pale blue semicircles. After contacting the cornea you will see two steadily pulsating fluorescent green semicircles. The width of the fluorescein semicircles should be approximately one-tenth of the diameter of the flattened area. Make small adjustments with the handle to exactly center and equally divide the fluorescein semicircles, moving toward the larger semicircle (Fig. 6).

An alternative approach for achieving corneal contact is to sight outside of the tonometer as the probe is positioned on the corneal apex. The limbus will exhibit a blue glow when contact is made. While using good hand control to carefully maintain corneal contact, resume sighting through the tonometer and proceed with the technique.

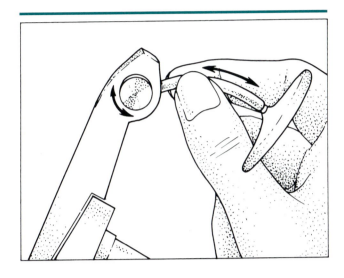

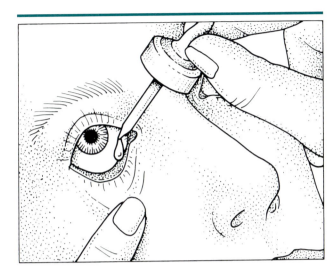

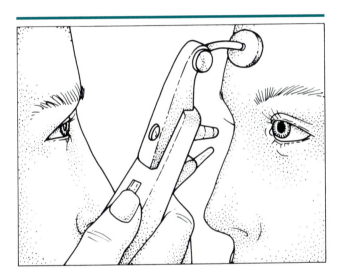

2. (above left) Loosen the locking screw, slide the forehead rest arm in or out as needed, then tighten the locking screw.

3. (above right) Instill a drop of fluorescein sodium–benoxinate solution into each eye.

4. (left) Place the forehead rest in the middle of the patient's forehead, holding it gently with your left hand. Position the probe approximately ¾ inch from the cornea.

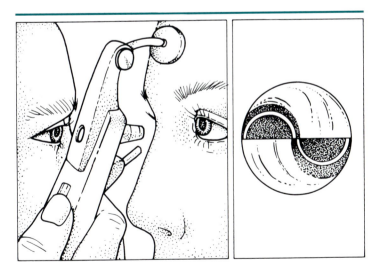

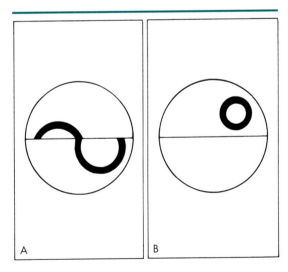

5. Looking through the instrument, the reflection of the probe off the cornea will appear as two pale blue semicircles. Move the instrument forward until two green semicircles appear. (*See also* Color Plate 17–4.B.)

6. A. Following corneal contact, the larger inferior circle indicates that the probe is too high. B. The instrument is too far to the left and too low.

Use the thumb of your right hand to turn the knurled knob controlling the measuring drum until the inner borders of the two fluorescein rings just touch each other (Fig. 7). If significant pulsation is present, adjust the measuring drum so that the rings pulsate equally to either side of the correct endpoint. Lift the instrument off the cornea. Note the IOP measurement in mm Hg by multiplying the figure on the drum by 10. Repeated measurements should be within a range of ± 0.5 mm Hg. Repeat the technique for the left eye, using opposite hands and positioning yourself to the patient's left.

Occasionally a patient may have difficulty holding the lids open, or may have a narrow palpebral fissure requiring lid retraction. Once the forehead rest is in place, the thumb and forefinger of your left hand may be used to gently retract the lids (see p. 56). Be certain to hold the lids against the orbital rims so that pressure is not applied to the globe. Proceed with the technique as described.

If the fluorescein semicircles are too wide, too much fluorescein is in the conjunctival sac or the lids contacted the probe during measurement (Fig. 8A). Draw back the probe, dry the probe tip with a clean tissue, ask the patient to gently blot the eyes with a tissue, and repeat the measurement. Conversely, rapid dissipation of the tears will produce semicircles that are too narrow (Fig. 8B). Draw back the probe, instill more fluorescein, and repeat the measurement.

■ Interpretation.

If the fluorescein semicircles are too wide, the IOP measurement will be artificially high. Semicircles that are too narrow yield IOP measurements that are artificially low. Most practitioners consider normal intraocular pressures as measured by applanation to be 21 mm Hg or less, with the difference in readings between the two eyes expected to be no greater than 3 to 4 mm Hg. However, because of diurnal IOP fluctuation, along with many other factors, it is extremely important that the practitioner not rely solely on the IOP reading to rule out a diagnosis of glaucoma. Careful optic nerve head assessment, nerve fiber layer and retina evaluation, anterior segment evaluation including gonioscopy, and visual field analysis, are needed to determine whether the IOP is normal for that individual (see Section XII).

■ Complications/Contraindications.

Good, steady technique on the part of the examiner is important to produce corneal applanation with appropriate pressure. The examiner must be familiar with any contraindications that may preclude using any of the diagnostic agents needed for applanation tonometry. Reassure the patient that the orange discoloration of the tear film will dissipate. Applanation tonometry is avoided in the presence of conjunctival infection to prevent probe contamination, large central corneal abrasions to prevent further epithelial disruption, and significant epithelial basement membrane dystrophy to avoid inducing a corneal abrasion. Care should be taken to avoid overmanipulating eyes that have sustained severe ocular trauma. Corneas that are extremely distorted or scarred will produce irregular mires that may prevent an accurate reading.

To minimize anxiety, it is best to avoid detailing to the patient that actual corneal contact will occur. Patient anxiety tends to artificially elevate the IOP. Continual coaxing of the patient to widely open the eyes will help to minimize interference by the lids. Touching of the lids or lashes by the probe will induce a blink reflex and should be avoided. If the examiner puts pressure on the globe while retracting the lids the IOP will be artificially elevated.

It is common to induce some superficial corneal epithelial disruption following applanation tonometry. This will occur following topical anesthetic use, due to movements of the probe on the cornea, desiccation of the cornea surrounding the contact area, and unanticipated patient eye movements. Usually no treatment is required for these minor tissue disruptions other than perhaps the use of artificial tears. The examiner should avoid, however, large repositioning movements of the probe when it is in contact with the cornea. Rarely, poor examiner technique or sudden head or eye movements by the patient while the probe is in contact with the cornea may induce a corneal abrasion.

A patient may rarely experience vasovagal syncope during this technique. Should this occur, basic first-aid measures are taken. These include elevating the feet above the level of the head, passing a broken ammonia inhalant ampule beneath the nostrils, and monitoring the basic vital signs.

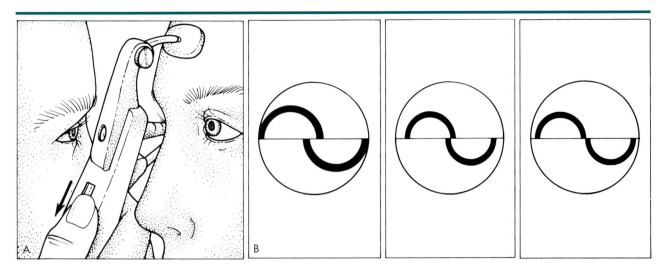

A. While maintaining corneal contact, use your thumb to turn the knurled knob until the inner borders of the semicircles just touch.

7. B. (left) Too much probe pressure; (middle) correct endpoint; (right) more probe pressure needed.

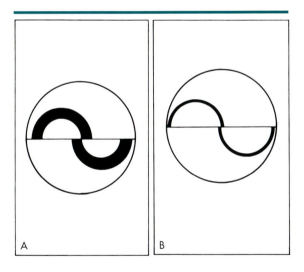

8. A. Wide semicircles indicate that too much fluorescein is present. B. Narrow semicircles indicate insufficient fluorescein is present.

19 Crystalline Lens Evaluation

■ **Description/Indication.** The crystalline lens consists of the nucleus, cortex, and capsule. The nucleus may be further subdivided into the most clinically distinguishable components: the embryonic nucleus, seen as a dark vertical band in the center of the lens; the fetal nucleus, bounded by the anterior and posterior "Y" sutures; and the adult nucleus, most visible after the age of 30. The zones of optical discontinuity visible with the slit lamp demarcate the various layers of the crystalline lens. Any zone of the crystalline lens may exhibit a loss of transparency due to age-related changes, trauma, ocular infections or inflammation, medications, or congenital opacities. Examination with the slit lamp biomicroscope allows for detailed assessment of these congenital or acquired cataracts. Because many of these changes are acquired and progressive, periodic crystalline lens evaluation is needed.

Slit lamp examination of the crystalline lens is most accurately and easily done following pupillary dilation. During comprehensive examination, crystalline lens evaluation with the slit lamp generally follows refractive analysis, undilated slit lamp examination, tonometry, and dilated fundus evaluation. Two types of slit lamp illumination are most frequently used to assess the crystalline lens, direct focal illumination and retroillumination.

Direct focal illumination refers to coincident focusing of the light beam and the microscope. It does not refer to coaxial placement of the light source with the microscope. The parallelepiped and optic section are two commonly used types of direct focal illumination. The parallelepiped produces a three-dimensional section of the lens and is useful for initial lens evaluation. An optic section illuminates a two-dimensional lens area that is viewed obliquely, similar to examining a histological section. The procedure is the same as parallelepiped illumination except that the beam width is narrowed until it is almost extinguished. When evaluating the lens, the optic section is sharply focused to localize lens opacities. Because the entire depth of the lens cannot be in focus at one time with direct focal illumination, systematic scanning of the lens is performed.

When the slit lamp beam is directed straight ahead through the dilated pupil, the light will reflect off the fundus back through the pupil to form the "red reflex" of *retroillumination.* Any frank lens opacities will absorb the reflected light and will appear as black or darkened areas in the red reflex, depending upon their density. Areas of fluid within the lens will appear as vacuolated or cleft-shaped areas of irregularity in the red reflex. This technique is especially useful to determine where the lens opacity lies relative to the visual axis and to assess what portion of the pupillary area is obscured by the opacity. Retroillumination used alone, however, will not definitively localize the lens opacity.

■ **Instrumentation.** Slit lamp biomicroscope, diagnostic pharmaceutical agents for pupillary dilation.

■ **Technique.**
Direct Focal Illumination: Position the patient comfortably at the slit lamp (see p. 24). Adjust the eyepieces to accommodate your pupillary distance and refractive error. Adjust the slit lamp rheostat to a medium setting and the magnification to 10X to 16X. Position the microscope directly in front of the eye and the light source at approximately 60 degrees temporally from the microscope. Make certain that the beam is in the "click" position and that the patient's eyes are in primary gaze. To assess the right eye, ask the patient to fixate toward your right ear or over your right shoulder. With your left hand adjust the beam to its maximum height and narrow the beam to 1 to 2 mm in width to illuminate a parallelepiped-shaped section of the lens (Fig. 1). Use your right hand on the joystick to sharply focus the microscope and parallelepiped simultaneously.

Starting at the temporal border of the dilated right pupil, use the joystick to focus the parallelepiped on the anterior half of the lens. Keep this portion of the lens in focus while scanning across the lens to the nasal border of the pupil. Move the joystick forward to focus on the posterior half of the lens, scanning across it to the temporal pupil border (Fig. 2).

DIRECT FOCAL: OPTIC SECTION

Click stop: In
Beam angle: 60 degrees
Beam width: Nearly
extinguished
Beam height: Maximum
Filter: None
Illumination: Medium
Magnification: 10–16X

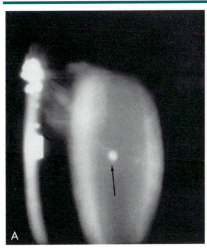

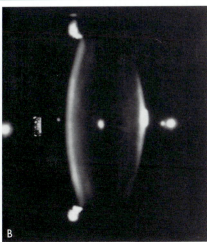

RETROILLUMINATION: LENS

Click stop: In
Beam angle: 0 degrees
Beam width: 1 mm
Beam height: 6 mm
Filter: None
Illumination: Medium
Magnification: 6–10X

3. (above left) Slit lamp setup for optic section examination of the crystalline lens.

4. A. (above center) An anterior axial embryonal cataract is detected using a parallelepiped (arrow). B. (above right) Using an optic section the opacity is localized to just anterior of the embryonic nucleus.

5. (left) Slit lamp setup for retroillumination of the crystalline lens.

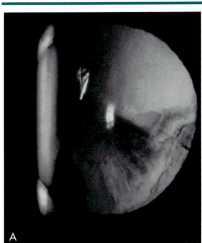

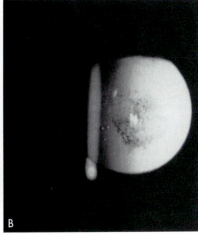

6. A. A cortical cataract as seen using retroillumination. (*See also* Color Plate 19–6.A.)

6. B. A posterior subcapsular cataract as seen using retroillumination. (*See also* Color Plate 19–6.B.)

■ **Interpretation.** The shape and location of the lens opacity will help diagnose its etiology. With direct focal illumination, most cataracts will appear white; in retroillumination they will appear black. Many vacuoles or pockets of fluid within the lens will not be visible with direct focal illumination but will be detected as round or oblong irregularities with retroillumination.

The three most common age-related cataracts are nuclear sclerosis, cortical spoking, and posterior subcapsular cataracts (Fig. 7). Grading systems are used to describe these crystalline lens changes. Depending upon its degree, nuclear sclerosis will appear as a yellow, orange, or brownish haze toward the posterior half of the lens in direct focal illumination. When pronounced, the edge of the sclerosed nucleus will create an "oil droplet" effect in the red reflex of retroillumination. Cortical spoking (cuneiform cataract) will appear as wedged-shaped opacities in the anterior or posterior cortex. Posterior subcapsular changes (cupuliform cataract) will appear as vacuolated, ground glass opacities just beneath the posterior capsule. These age-related lens changes may occur singly or in combination.

It is very important that the examiner learn to estimate the effect of cataract formation on best corrected visual acuity (VA) based on the appearance of the lens. If the VA is monocularly reduced and the crystalline lens changes are judged to be symmetric, then other causes must be sought to account for the VA difference.

■ **Complications/Contraindications.** If the patient is a suitable candidate for slit lamp biomicroscopy, there are no contraindications to performing this specific examination of the crystalline lens. The routine precautions for pupillary dilation should be followed (see p. 2). The novice biomicroscopist may have a tendency to set the slit lamp illumination rheostat too high, which may produce some discomfort for the patient due to the pupillary dilation.

	NUCLEAR SCLEROSIS	CORTICAL SPOKING	POSTERIOR SUBCAPSULAR
GRADE 1			
GRADE 2			
GRADE 3			
GRADE 4			

7. A grading system for age-related cataracts. The nuclear sclerotic changes are shown in cross-section with the anterior surface to the left. The cortical spoking and posterior subcapsular changes are seen in retroillumination. (*See also* Color Plate 19–7.)

20 Vitreous Evaluation

■ **Description/Indications.** Although the vitreous is comprised of approximately 99% water, the solid components that compose the remaining 1% reflect light sufficiently well to allow for evaluation of the vitreous using the slit lamp biomicroscope. The focal length of the slit lamp allows for observation of approximately the anterior one-third of the vitreous body. Use of auxilliary instrumentation such as the Hruby lens (see p. 242), retinal three-mirror lens (see p. 238), and the fundus biomicroscopic lens (see p. 244) will extend the focal range of the slit lamp further into the globe for more extensive examination of the vitreous.

Routine observation of the vitreous performed in conjunction with evaluation of the crystalline lens following pupillary dilation (see p. 64) will allow the practitioner to distinguish normal vitreous appearance from abnormal. Other indications for slit lamp examination of the vitreous include symptoms of floaters and light flashes (photopsia), to diagnose posterior vitreous detachment (PVD) with or without retinal complication, and to assess vitreous involvement in intraocular inflammation.

Examination of the vitreous with the slit lamp is best performed following pupillary dilation. The most useful illumination technique to evaluate the vitreous is direct focal illumination. Direct focal illumination refers to the focusing of the light beam and the microscope in the same specific area. It does not refer to coaxial placement of the light source with the microscope. The parallelepiped and optic section are two commonly used types of direct focal illumination. The parallelepiped produces a three-dimensional section of the vitreous and is most useful for its evaluation.

■ **Instrumentation.** Slit lamp biomicroscope, diagnostic pharmaceutical agents for pupillary dilation.

■ **Technique.** Position the patient comfortably at the slit lamp (see p. 24) following pupillary dilation (see p. 2). Adjust the eyepieces to accommodate your pupillary distance and refractive error. Adjust the slit lamp rheostat to a medium to medium-high setting and the magnification to 10X to 16X. Position the microscope directly in front of the eye and the light source at approximately 45 to 60 degrees temporally from the microscope. Make certain that the beam is in the "click" position and that the patient's eyes are in primary gaze. To assess the right eye, ask the patient to fixate toward your right ear or over your right shoulder. With your left hand adjust the beam to its maximum height and narrow the beam to 1 to 2 mm in width to illuminate a parallelepiped-shaped section of the vitreous. Use your right hand on the joystick to sharply focus the microscope and parallelepiped simultaneously (Fig. 1).

Starting at the temporal border of the dilated right pupil, move the joystick forward to focus the parallelepiped into the anterior vitreous. Keep this portion of the vitreous in focus while scanning across the vitreous to the nasal border of the pupil. Move the joystick further forward so as to focus into the vitreous as far as possible and scan across it to the temporal pupil border (Fig. 2). Repeating this technique with the beam positioned nasally will ensure that the vitreous is thoroughly examined. If necessary, increase the slit lamp magnification setting to evaluate the vitreous in greater detail.

■ **Interpretation.**

Normal Vitreous: The vitreous is adherent to the lens in a 9-mm diameter arcuate or circular area known as the ligament of Wieger. Within this 9-mm diameter area is the optically empty retrolental space. Frequently a small corkscrew like fibril may be seen dangling from the central portion of the posterior lens surface. This is a remnant of the hyaloid artery and may be accompanied by a Mittendorf dot.

The anterior portion of the vitreous appears as milky folds of gossamer-like texture separated by optically empty spaces. These folds appear wavy and oscillate with eye movements. In the very young patient the individual collagen fibrils may be difficult to distinguish. In the older patient, however, the folds are seen to be composed of individual crisscrossing fibrils. Small white dots or nodosities may be seen at the intersection of two fibrils. The spaces between the fibrils are otherwise optically empty in the normal vitreous.

1. Slit lamp setup for slit lamp examination of the vitreous.

PARALLELEPIPED: VITREOUS

Click stop:	In
Beam angle:	45–60 degrees
Beam width:	1–2 mm
Beam height:	Maximum
Filter:	None
Illumination:	Medium to medium-high
Magnification:	10–16X

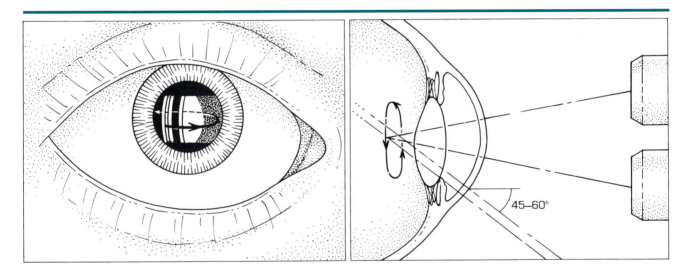

2. Focus the parallelepiped into the anterior vitreous. Beginning at the temporal pupil border, scan toward the nasal pupil border. Focus as far into the vitreous as possible and reverse the direction of scan. Repeat the scan with the beam positioned nasally.

Vitreous Cells: Multiple conditions involving the posterior segment may result in a spewing of inflammatory cells, red blood cells, or pigment cells into the vitreous. These cells will appear as small punctate opacities (Fig. 3) suspended or slowly floating within the optically empty spaces between the fibrils and in the retrolental space (space of Berger). These cells are not to be confused with nodosities that may be present at the intersection of two fibrils.

If the cells are white in color, they are probably inflammatory white blood cells (leukocytes) that are the result of intraocular inflammation such as pars planitis, toxocara canis, or active ocular toxoplasmosis. Inflammatory white blood cells may also appear in the anterior vitreous as spillover from a significant anterior uveitis. If the vitreous cells are red-brown in color they are usually red blood cells (erythrocytes) and/or retinal pigment epithelial cells (RPE cells). Known as tobacco dusting or Shaffer's sign, these red-brown cells are usually an indication that a retinal tear or detachment is present so that RPE cells have become dislodged or associated retinal vessel damage has occurred. When the red-free (green) filter is introduced, the red blood cells appear black and will no longer be visible within the vitreous. Pigment particles will not absorb the red-free light and will still be visible.

Space-occupying lesions of the posterior segment such as retinoblastoma and malignant melanoma may also produce vitreous cells.

Vitreous Fiber Clumping: With increasing age, the vitreous fibers lose some of their normal binding (gel) capacity so that the fibers and fluid become separated (syneresis). In doing so, the fibers will tend to clump together and will produce the symptom of floaters. These clumped fibers will appear as very prominent vitreous stranding when observed with the slit lamp.

Prominent vitreous stranding may also be observed following the resolution of significant posterior segment inflammation or hemorrhage in which the vitreous was involved.

Posterior Vitreous Detachment (PVD): With time, pockets of fluid (lacunae) will form within the body of the vitreous. Percolation posteriorly of the liquified vitreous through the vitreous cortex will result in a pulling away of the vitreous from its peripapillary attachment to produce a PVD (Fig. 4). The posterior vitreous cortex collapses forward so that a prepapillary annulus may be visible with retroillumination during distal direct ophthalmoscopy, and the posterior vitreous cortex may be within focusing range of the slit lamp (Fig. 5). Following PVD, the posterior limiting layer of the vitreous may be apparent as an undulating, white wrinkled-looking veil that separates the collapsed and condensed fibril-laden vitreous anteriorly from the fluid-filled, optically empty space posteriorly (Fig. 6).

Asteroid Hyalosis: Spherical calcium-containing opacities may form most commonly unilaterally, or, bilaterally, in the vitreous in a middle-aged or older patient. When present in the anterior vitreous within focusing range of the slit lamp, they will appear as very bright, yellow, reflective bodies suspended in the vitreous.

■ **Complications/Contraindications.** There are no contraindications to performing this specific slit lamp examination of the vitreous. The routine precautions for pupillary dilation should be followed (see p. 2). The novice biomicroscopist may have a tendency to set the slit lamp illumination rheostat too high, which may produce some discomfort for the patient due to the pupillary dilation.

Significant cataract formation can obscure the various vitreous landmarks. A good deal of observational skill development is needed to accurately assess the presence of vitreous cells. Likewise, the collapse of the posterior limiting layer of the vitreous in PVD can be easily overlooked if the slit lamp is not focused well into the vitreous cavity.

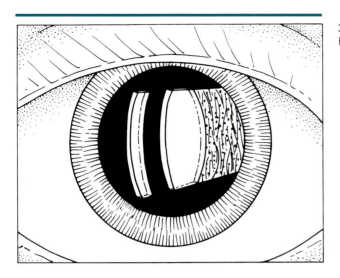

3. Cells in the anterior vitreous appear as small punctate opacities floating between the fibrils.

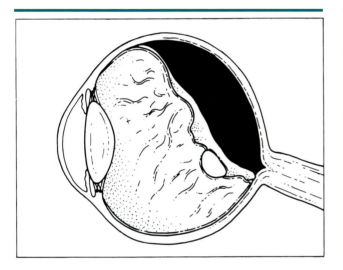

4. Percolation posteriorly of liquefied vitreous results in a posterior vitreous detachment (PVD).

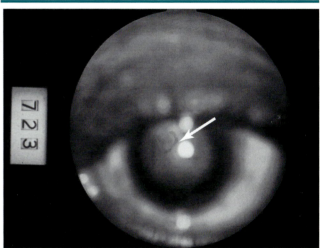

5. Clinically, a PVD may be detected by the large prepapillary annulus vitreous floater (arrow.) (*See also* Color Plate 20–5.)

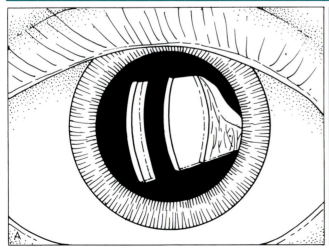

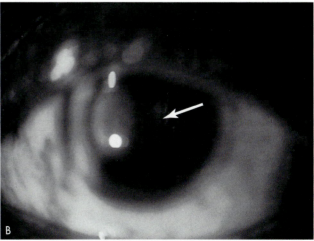

6. A. Following PVD, the collapsed posterior vitreous limiting layer may be visible with the slit lamp. B. It appears as an undulating, white wrinkled-looking veil (arrow) with optically empty fluid behind it. (*See also* Color Plate 20–6. B.)

21 Gonioscopy: Three-mirror Lens

■ **Description/Indications.** Gonioscopy is a technique used to visualize and assess the anterior chamber angle. A gonioscopic lens is a plastic cone-shaped contact lens containing reflecting mirrors that is used in conjunction with the slit lamp biomicroscope to evaluate the anterior chamber angle. Gonioscopic lenses come in various sizes and designs, containing one, two, or three mirrors (Fig. 1). The most commonly used lens is the three-mirror universal (Goldmann) design, which allows for evaluation of the angle, as well as the posterior pole and the mid and far peripheral retina (see p. 238). A coupling solution is required for use with a three-mirror lens, because the concavity of the gonioprism is greater than the radius of curvature of the cornea. The gonioscopy solution forms an interface between the lens and cornea. Solutions that may be used for this purpose include saline solution, goniogel (2.5% methylcellulose), and 1.0% carboxymethyl cellulose. Less viscous solutions, while more apt to form air bubbles, are not as irritating to the cornea and allow clear views of the fundus following gonioscopy.

Indications for gonioscopy include evaluating glaucoma suspects or ocular hypertensives; accurately diagnosing open or narrow-angle glaucoma; assessing angle pigmentation; assessing the angle as suitable for pupillary dilation in suspiciously narrow cases previously evaluated with Van Herick angle estimation (see p. 28); diagnosing suspected angle recession in cases of ocular trauma; evaluating for angle neovascularization, tumors, congenital anomalies, or foreign bodies; and assessing peripheral anterior synechiae. For situations in which the intraocular pressure (IOP) is elevated or glaucoma is suspected, the anterior chamber angle is evaluated to rule out specific causes for the rise in IOP. In particular, signs of pigment dispersion syndrome (see p. 38), pseudoexfoliation, or other material within the trabecular meshwork or angle proper must be evaluated to understand potential etiologies for the elevated IOP. Also the width of the angle and the access of aqueous to the trabecular meshwork are evaluated in these cases. Gonioscopy, using specially coated lenses to minimize reflections, is used in conjunction with a laser to deliver applications into the anterior segment for laser trabeculoplasty (see p. 444), iridoplasty (see p. 450), or peripheral iridotomy (see p. 454).

■ **Instrumentation.** Three-mirror gonioscopic contact lens (goniolens), slit lamp biomicroscope, gonioscopic solution, topical ophthalmic anesthetic solution, sterile ophthalmic irrigating solution, facial tissues.

A

1. A. A three-mirror Goldmann-style universal gonioscopy lens. Three mirrors, angled at 59, 67, and 73 degrees, are placed at 120-degree intervals. This multipurpose lens also allows for evaluation of the anterior chamber and fundus. The small semicircular 59-degree mirror is used to view the angle structures. (Courtesy of Ocular Instruments, Inc.)

B

1. B. Single-mirror Goldmann-style gonioscopy lens. This lens has a 62-degree mirror, which must be rotated into all quadrants to view the entire circumference of the angle. Its small size facilitates insertion when examining children and individuals with narrow palpebral apertures. (Courtesy of Ocular Instruments, Inc.)

■ **Technique.** Store the bottle of gonioscopic fluid in its container upside down and use proper lens filling technique to reduce the amount of bubbles that may form. Instill gonioscopic fluid into the concave surface of the goniolens by initially squeezing the fluid onto a clean facial tissue. While continuing to squeeze, move the tip of the gonioscopic fluid bottle over the concave surface of the goniolens and fill it no more than halfway (Fig. 2).

Hand the patient a clean facial tissue. Instill two drops of a topical ophthalmic anesthetic solution in each eye (see p. 2). Advise the patient that a mild, transient burning sensation may occur and that he or she may blot excess fluid from the eyes with a tissue. Adjust the room illumination so it is dark with little ambient light. This is important in the assessment of narrow angles and the differential diagnosis of sub-acute angle closure glaucoma. Minimal amounts of light will constrict the pupil, leading to a wider angle appearance than would occur in dark conditions. Adjust the eyepieces to accommodate your pupillary distance and refractive error. Adjust the slit lamp rheostat to a medium setting and the magnification to 10X. Position the microscope straight ahead and the light source directly in front of the microscope so that neither ocular is occluded. Adjust the beam width to approximately 4 mm, making certain that the beam is in "click" (Fig. 3). Position the patient comfortably at the slit lamp (see p. 24) and advise him or her that once in place, the goniolens will feel awkward but not

uncomfortable. Instruct the patient to make every effort to keep the chin and forehead completely in the slit lamp and to try not to squeeze the eyelids shut.

To insert the goniolens in the right eye, position yourself slightly to the patient's right and move the slit lamp all the way to the patient's left. Ask the patient to look up and use the forefinger or thumb of your left hand to gently retract the patient's lower lid. With your right hand place one edge of the slightly tilted goniolens into the inferior fornix and release the lower lid (Fig. 4A). Use the thumb of your left hand to gently but firmly grasp the right upper lid as the patient continues to look up (Fig. 4B). Ask the patient to look straight ahead (Fig. 4C). Quickly pivot the goniolens onto the cornea and release the upper lid. Exchange hands so that the thumb and forefinger of your left hand are holding the edge of the goniolens (Fig. 4D).

Support your left hand firmly by suspending your remaining fingers from the forehead strap, by resting the heel of your hand on a support rod attached to the upright bar of the slit lamp when available, or by resting your elbow on the slit lamp table. If the length of your forearm is too short to reach the slit lamp table, an inverted facial tissue box or arm rest may be placed under your elbow. With your right hand, use the joystick to move the slit lamp in front of the patient. Instruct the patient to look straight ahead or at the fixation light, which has been positioned in front of the left eye.

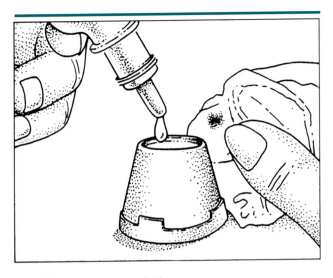

2. Instilling the gonioscopic fluid.

GONIOSCOPY: THREE-MIRROR

Click stop:	In
Beam angle:	0 degrees or 45 degrees
Beam width:	Optic section to 4 mm parallelepiped
Beam height:	Maximum
Filter:	None
Illumination:	Medium
Magnification:	10–25X

3. Slit lamp setup for three-mirror gonioscopy.

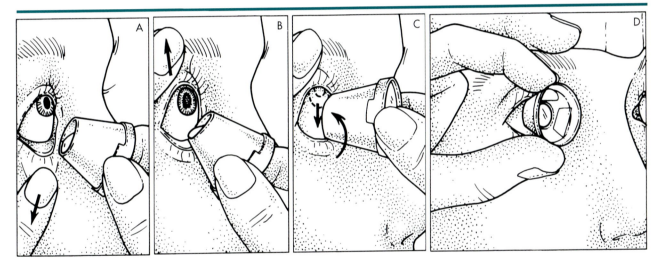

4. A. The fluid-filled lens is tilted backward slightly as the eye is approached. As the patient looks up, the lower lid is retracted. B. One edge of the lens is placed in the inferior fornix, and the thumb is used to retract the upper lid. C. The lens is pivoted onto the eye as the patient is asked to look straight ahead. D. The thumb and index finger are used to hold the lens securely against the eye, and the remaining fingers are supported on the forehead strap.

Use the joystick to position the slit lamp beam onto the center of the small semicircular shaped mirror which has been rotated to the 12-o'clock position. With the joystick move the slit lamp forward to focus on the reflected mirror image of the angle (Fig. 5). Increase the magnification to 16X to assess the angle structures. The inferior angle will be viewed which in most eyes is the widest, giving the clinician a baseline with which to evaluate the other quadrants. The slit beam may be narrowed to an optic section and moved to create an angle of approximately 45 degrees from the microscope. Assess the pupil frill of the iris initially and then follow the slit beam as it rolls along the iris surface and structures of the anterior chamber angle. The angle between the reflection of the beam off the anterior iris surface and the corneal endothelium is estimated in degrees to assess the angle size (Fig. 6A). Also follow the path of the optic section as it contours along the corneal surface. The slit beam may be inclined with certain biomicroscopes so that the beam splits into two, indicating the anterior and posterior surfaces of the cornea. The two beams come together to form a corneal wedge which identifies Schwalbe's line (Fig. 6B). Following assessment of angle size, reposition the light source in front of the microscope, reopen the beam width to 4 mm, and assess the angle structures.

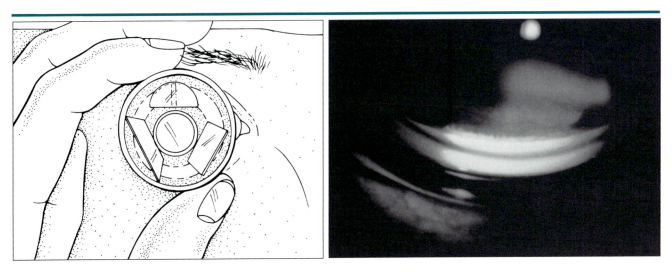

5. (above left) Position the slit beam onto the center of the semicircular mirror in the 12 o'clock position and focus forward onto the reflected image (above right). (*See also* Color Plate 21–5).

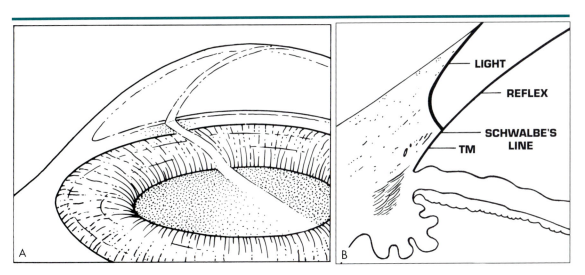

6. A. An optic section placed at 45 degrees from the microscope may be used to estimate the size of the angle using reflections off the corneal endothelium and anterior iris. B. With the slit beam inclined, a corneal wedge is created with two beams seen in the cornea, one reflected off the anterior surface and the other the posterior. The beams join at Schwalbe's line. The wedge is often a useful demarcation tool, especially in lightly pigmented eyes.

To view the entire angle, rotate the three-mirror goniolens so that all four quadrants are visualized. To do so, gently rotate the goniolens between your thumb and forefinger while maintaining good corneal contact (Fig. 7). The semicircular mirror of the goniolens is typically placed superiorly initially to analyze the inferior angle. Because this portion of the angle is the largest, it allows for comparison with remaining views of the angle. With each repositioning of the goniolens, relocate the slit lamp beam onto the angle mirror. It is usually helpful to use the right hand to hold the goniolens in place so that the thumb and forefinger of the left hand may be repositioned to allow for further lens rotation.

To remove the goniolens, ask the patient to squeeze the lids shut and the lens should pop off the eye. If not, while the patient is squeezing the lids shut, hold the lens in your right hand and use the forefinger of your left hand to gently push on the globe through the lower lid just temporal to the lens to break the suction between the goniolens and the cornea (Fig. 8). Use sterile ophthalmic saline solution to irrigate the gonioscopic solution from the conjunctival sac as the patient holds multiple paper towels around the eye (see p. 152). Repeat the procedure for the opposite eye, reversing the hands used.

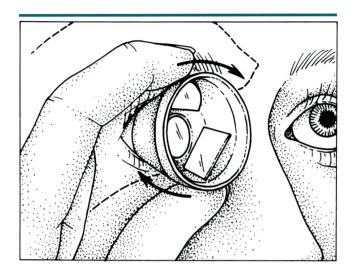

7. Rotate the goniolens between your thumb and forefinger to visualize all areas of the angle.

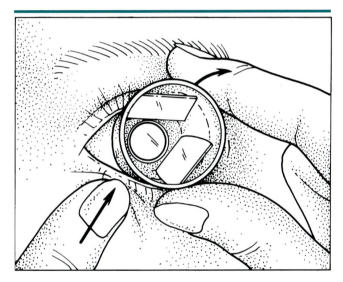

8. To remove the goniolens, use the forefinger of your left hand to gently push on the globe through the lower lid as the patient squeezes the eyes closed.

■ **Interpretation.** Because the three-mirror goniolens uses a mirror to indirectly visualize the angle, the gonioscopic image will be 180 degrees away from the mirror position. Multiple methods of interpreting and recording the gonioscopic findings have been proposed. All techniques involve determining the extent of angle structures visible. The assessment also includes evaluation of the angle made between the anterior surface of the iris and the posterior surface of the cornea (angle width), the configuration of the iris, and the insertion point of the iris root. The most commonly used angle grading system incorporates grades of 0 to 4 (Fig. 9). The Van Herick technique of angle assessment using a slit lamp optic section corresponds well with this technique (see p. 28).

The iris is evaluated at the onset of the procedure. As the slit beam rolls along the surface of the iris into the angle, a determination is made regarding iris shape and contour. The iris may be mildly convex (common); significantly convex, which is associated with hyperopia and has an increased risk of developing angle closure glaucoma; or concave, which is associated with myopia and pigment dispersion syndrome. The angle formed between the posterior corneal surface and iris is estimated in degrees. When visible, the ciliary body will appear as a light gray to brown band just anterior to the root of the iris. The ciliary body band may be wide in myopes and narrow or absent in hyperopes. It is typically the same width between eyes except in anisometropes or with angle recession following trauma. The scleral spur is just anterior to the ciliary body and appears as a thin white band. The trabecular meshwork is the next tissue observed, varying in color from tan to dark brown. Aqueous humor flows through the posterior portion of the trabecular meshwork, leading to pigment and debris deposition in this region. This band of tissue is usually relatively wide but may not be readily visible in lightly pigmented individuals. Schlemm's canal, located within the posterior portion of the trabecular meshwork, is usually not apparent except when blood or pigment is present. The most anterior structure of the angle is Schwalbe's line, which marks the end of the cornea and is seen as a thin, refractile white line.

Certain signs may be apparent within the angle that require further documentation and description. For example, iris pigment epithelial cells may dislodge and collect in the anterior chamber angle. The location, density, and quality of pigmentation is described, usually with a system of grades 0 to 4, although much subjective interpretation is involved (Fig. 10). The angle pigmentation will be densest

GRADE	ANGLE WIDTH (DEGREES)	POSTERIOR STRUCTURE VISIBLE	DESCRIPTION	RISK OF CLOSURE
4	35–45	Ciliary body band	Wide open	Impossible
3	20–35	Ciliary body may be visible/scleral spur	Open	Improbable
2	10–20	Scleral spur/ trabecular meshwork	Narrow	Possible
1	10	Anterior portion of trabecular meshwork	Extremely narrow	Probable
0	0	No structures visible	Closed	Closed

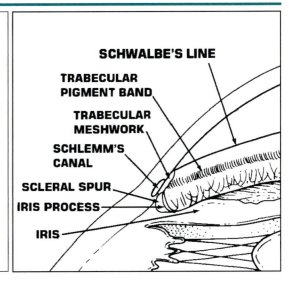

9. Grading system for angle evaluation.

GRADE	AMOUNT OF PIGMENTATION
4	Dense
3	Moderate
2	Mild
1	Trace
0	None

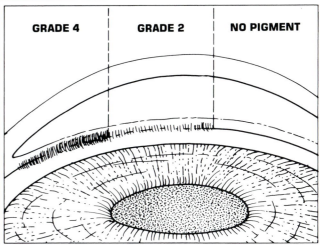

10. Grading system for angle pigmentation.

in the posterior trabecular meshwork, the area overlying Schlemm's canal, and may also be prominent anterior to Schwalbe's line (Fig. 11). The novice gonioscopist should avoid confusing the granular, dark brown pigment overlying Schlemm's canal with the smooth, gray-brown ciliary body. Other normal variations include blood in Schlemm's canal, which appears as a pale pink, indistinct band, often due to excessive lens pressure. Dense iris processes may obscure the view of the ciliary body (Fig. 12). Angle recession due to trauma appears as an abnormally wide open angle (Fig. 13). Comparison of different angle views of the same eye as well as comparable areas of the opposite eye will help in the diagnosis of subtle angle recession. Peripheral anterior synechiae (PAS) will produce a "tenting" of the iris, sometimes as high as Schwalbe's line. Neovascularization, either in the angle or on the iris, may be noted, as well as abnormal lens and anterior chamber deposits such as exfoliative material. In a closed angle, the angle structures are not visible (Fig. 14).

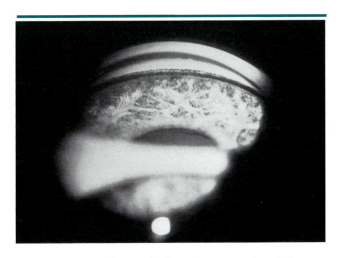

11. A gonioscopic photograph of a wide open angle with dense pigmentation of the trabecular meshwork. Note the pigment on the back of the crystalline lens, visible through the pupil.

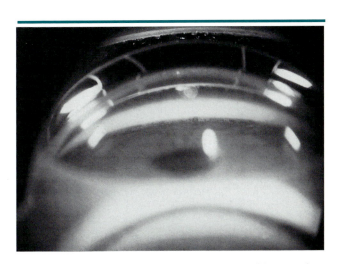

12. A wide open angle is seen with all structures visible. Note the fine iris processes covering the ciliary body band. (*See also* Color Plate 21–12.)

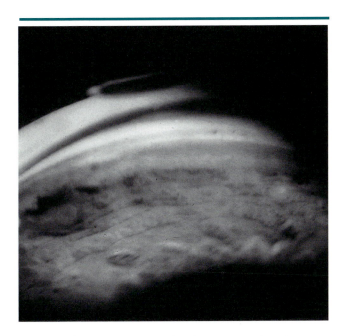

13. An angle recession is pictured with an excessively wide open angle as evidenced by the amount of ciliary body band exposed. (*See also* Color Plate 21–13.)

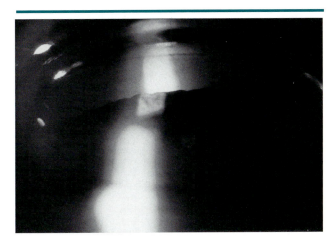

14. A closed angle is pictured with a convex iris obscuring all angle structures. (*See also* Color Plate 21–14.)

Several techniques for recording the information obtained using gonioscopy have been described. The two most straightforward methods involve using two crossed lines representing the four quadrants into which the appropriate grade is entered (Fig. 15). The angle is largest inferiorly and narrowest superiorly. This same technique can be used to record angle pigmentation in each quadrant, which is usually densest inferiorly. Another technique uses a circle to diagrammatically represent the 360 degrees of the anterior chamber angle (Fig. 16). Labeled arrows are used to illustrate the extent of each angle finding as they correspond to the hour markings on a clock. With this technique, it is relatively easy to indicate areas of angle recession, iridodialysis, peripheral anterior synechiae, and so on.

■ Contraindications/Complications.

For the novice gonioscopist, several errors of technique are commonly made. If too much gonioscopic solution is instilled, the excess will drip down the patient's cheek. Good support of the hand holding the gonioscopic lens is imperative to maintain steady control of the lens and to minimize patient discomfort. Putting too much pressure of the supporting hand against the patient's cheek will result in a tendency for the patient to back away from the slit lamp. Conversely, bubbles in the gonioscopic fluid layer may indicate that inadequate pressure is being used to hold the lens in place. Gently increasing the corneal contact pressure may rectify this. If not, gentle pressure and tilting of the goniolens may eliminate trapped air bubbles. If the bubbles cannot be eliminated and the angle image is obscured, remove the goniolens and reapply. Wiping any gonioscopic fluid from the patient's lids will facilitate lens reinsertion. Inadvertent entrapment of the patient's lower lid or lashes can usually be remedied by gently lifting the goniolens slightly and retracting the lower lid. Tilting the lens or applying too much pressure to the globe may distort the angle appearance and result in inaccurate assessments. Failure to keep the thumb and forefinger of the hand holding the goniolens on the side of the lens rim may block the slit lamp illumination onto the mirror. If the slit lamp illumination system is not in the straight-ahead (coaxial) position, one eyepiece of the microscope may be blocked and stereopsis lost.

It is common to induce transient superficial punctate keratitis (SPK) following gonioscopy and subsequent irrigation. When significant, this corneal disruption may interfere with visualization and photography of the fundus. Usually reassurance to the patient that a transient foreign body sensation may develop is all that is necessary, although artificial tears may be dispensed and used for 12 to 24 hours. Due to the suction that is created between the lens and the cornea, it is possible that significant corneal disruption could result when underlying abnormalities are present such as epithelial basement membrane dystrophy.

Uncommonly, patient anxiety may produce significant blepharospasm so that three-mirror gonioscopy cannot be performed. In these instances, the four-mirror technique may be a successful alternative (see p. 88). Also, a patient may rarely experience vasovagal syncope during gonioscopy. Should this occur, basic first-aid measures are taken. These include elevating the feet above the level of the head, passing a broken ammonia inhalant beneath the nostrils, and monitoring basic vital signs.

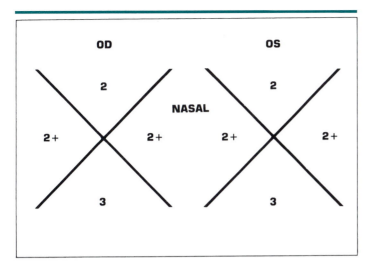

15. For recording angle size or pigmentation, two crossed lines create spaces for entering numerical gradings for the superior, inferior, nasal, and temporal angles.

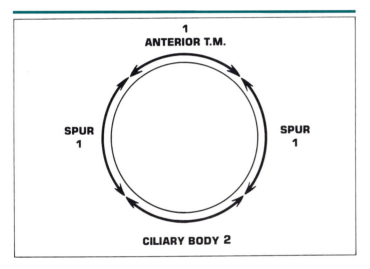

16. The circle represents the 360 degrees of the angle, with the arrows indicating the visible extent of each structure. The numbers indicate pigment grading.

22 Gonioscopy: Four-mirror Lens

■ **Description/Indications.** Gonioscopy, a technique used to visualize and assess the anterior chamber angle, may be performed with a four-mirror lens such as the Zeiss or Posner goniolens (Fig. 1). A four-mirror lens has four mirrored sides inclined equally that are used to view the anterior chamber angle. The Zeiss lens is mounted in a removable Unger holder. Other four-mirror lenses (Fig. 1) have a permanently mounted handle (Posner lens) or are hand-held (Sussman lens).

Indications for gonioscopy include evaluating glaucoma suspects or ocular hypertensives; accurately diagnosing open or narrow angle glaucoma; assessing angle pigmentation; assessing the angle as suitable for pupillary dilation in suspiciously narrow cases previously evaluated with Van Herick angle estimation (see p. 28); diagnosing suspected angle recession in cases of ocular trauma; evaluating for angle neovascularization, tumors, congenital anomalies, or foreign bodies; and assessing peripheral anterior synechiae. For situations in which the intraocular pressure (IOP) is elevated or glaucoma is suspected, the anterior chamber angle is evaluated to rule out specific causes for the rise in IOP. In particular, signs of pigment dispersion syndrome (see p. 38), pseudoexfoliation, or other material within the trabecular meshwork or angle proper must be evaluated to understand potential etiologies for the elevated IOP. Also the width of the angle and the access of aqueous to the trabecular meshwork are evaluated in these cases.

There are several advantages to four-mirror compared to three-mirror gonioscopy (see p. 74). It is performed quickly, requires no rotation of the lens, allows for rapid comparison between the two eyes, requires no gonioscopic fluid, is smaller in size and may be better suited for patients with small palpebral apertures, and may be easier for patients to tolerate. This technique tends to be less traumatic to the globe and may be performed in certain cases of ocular trauma where gonioscopy is indicated or to assess suspected acute angle closure glaucoma. Indentation gonioscopy may be performed with the four-mirror lens in individuals with narrow angles to differentiate between appositional and synechial closure. Four-mirror gonioscopy can be readily performed on a routine basis following applanation tonometry to allow the practitioner to become familiarized with anterior chamber angle evaluation.

The major disadvantages to this technique are that maintaining proper positioning of the lens can be difficult to master, because no suction is created between the lens and the cornea; and that errors in technique are more likely to result in inaccurate distortions of the angle.

■ **Instrumentation.** Four-mirror gonioscopic lens (goniolens), slit lamp biomicroscope, topical ophthalmic anesthetic solution, contact lens wetting solution or artificial tears, facial tissues.

■ **Technique.** Hand the patient a clean facial tissue. Instill two drops of a topical ophthalmic anesthetic solution in each eye (see p. 2). Advise the patient that a mild, transient burning sensation may occur and that he or she may blot excess fluid from the eyes with a tissue. If desired, instill a single drop of contact lens wetting or artificial tear solution into the concave surface of the goniolens.

Position the patient comfortably at the slit lamp (see p. 24) and adjust the eyepieces to accommodate your pupillary distance and refractive error. Adjust the room illumination so it is dark with little ambient light. This is important in the assessment of narrow angles and the differential diagnosis of sub-acute angle closure glaucoma. Minimal amounts of light will constrict the pupil, leading to a wider angle appearance than would occur in dark conditions. Adjust the slit lamp rheostat to a medium setting and the magnification to 6X to 10X. Position the microscope straight ahead and the light source directly in front so that neither ocular is occluded. Adjust the beam width to a parallelepiped approximately 2 mm wide. Make certain that the beam is in "click" (Fig. 2). Advise the patient that he or she will feel the goniolens in place but that it should not be uncomfortable. Instruct the patient to make every effort to keep the chin and forehead completely in the slit lamp and to not squeeze the eyelids shut.

To evaluate the patient's right eye, hold the handle of the goniolens with the thumb and forefinger of your left hand. Position your fingers as far up the handle as necessary to feel comfortable and to allow for hand support. Using the remaining fingers of your left hand to gently support your left hand on the patient's cheek, hold the lens approximately 1 inch from the corneal apex (Fig. 3). With your right hand, use the joystick to focus the slit lamp on the front of the goniolens. Looking through the center portion of the goniolens you will see a minified image of the iris and pupil. Using this image as a guide, approach the cornea with the goniolens while moving the joystick forward to maintain focus on the lens (Fig. 4). Once the cornea

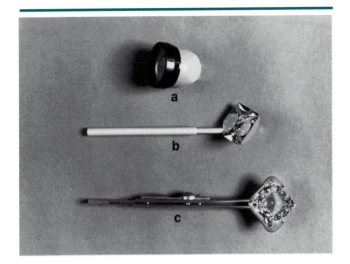

GONIOSCOPY: FOUR-MIRROR

Click stop:	In
Beam angle:	0 degrees or 45 degrees
Beam width:	Optic section to 4 mm parallelepiped
Beam height:	Maximum
Filter:	None
Illumination:	Medium
Magnification:	10–25X

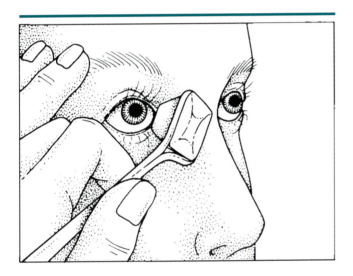

1. (above left) (a) The Sussman hand-held four-mirror lens. (b) The Posner-type four-mirror lens with a permanently mounted handle. (c) The Zeiss four-mirror lens with the Unger holding fork.

2. (above right) The slit lamp setup for four-mirror gonioscopy.

3. (left) Hold the goniolens handle between the thumb and forefinger of your left hand. Hold the lens approximately 1 inch from the corneal apex and use the remaining fingers to support your hand firmly.

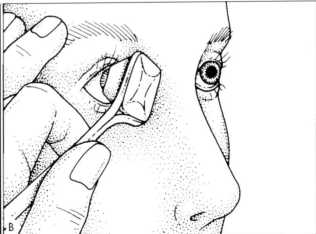

4. A. Use the minified view of the iris and pupil seen through the center of the goniolens to maintain proper lens position as the cornea is approached. (*See also* Color Plate 22–4.A.)

4. B. Once the goniolens is in position, support your left hand firmly on the patient's cheek or the upright bar of the slit lamp.

is contacted with the goniolens, support the heel of your left hand on the patient's cheek or use the remaining fingers of your left hand to brace against the upright bar of the slit lamp. Alternatively, apply the lens to the cornea while looking outside the slit lamp. Hold the lens as steady as possible and return to sighting through the slit lamp. The Sussman or other hand-held four-mirror goniolens is used in a similar fashion except that the rim of the lens is held between your thumb and forefinger.

As the patient's eye is approached with the goniolens avoid touching the lashes and inducing a blink reflex. With a narrow palpebral aperture, or if the patient has difficulty keeping the lids wide open, tilt the top of the lens slightly forward to lift up and under the upper lid as the cornea is approached (Fig. 5). Once the goniolens is properly positioned, instruct the patient to look straight ahead or at the fixation light, which has been positioned in front of the left eye. Use your right hand to control the joystick and vertical positioning knob to move the slit lamp beam onto the center of the superior mirror. Increase the magnification to 16X to assess the angle structures. Move the slit lamp forward with the joystick to focus on the reflected mirror image of the angle. Move the slit lamp beam to each of the four mirrors to assess the major quadrants of the angle. To perform indentation gonioscopy, exert gentle pressure with the lens onto the central cornea while looking at the angle through the biomicroscope (Fig. 6).

Maintain just enough pressure so that gaps do not occur in the tear film as visualized in the center of the goniolens, and corneal wrinkling is not induced. Corneal wrinkling, if seen, is an indication that too much pressure is being applied. This may occur if the goniolens is inadvertently tilted, so attempt to keep the goniolens as straight as possible.

To remove the goniolens simply lift it off the corneal apex. Irrigation of the patient's eye is not required. Repeat the procedure for the opposite eye, reversing the hands used.

■ **Interpretation.** Because the four-mirror goniolens uses a mirror to indirectly visualize the angle, the gonioscopic image will be of the angle 180 degrees away from the mirror position. The angle(s) are evaluated in a manner similar to three-mirror gonioscopy (see p. 74).

One unique feature of the four-mirror goniolens is the ability to perform indentation gonioscopy. Because the four-mirror lens has such a small-diameter contact surface, increasing pressure on the lens will indent the central cornea. The resultant increase in aqueous pressure will cause the iris root to fall away from the angle. If the angle is assessed to be very narrow or closed without indentation, this technique will allow the practitioner to distinguish between appositional and synechial closure in narrow angle glaucoma (Figs. 6 and 7). If corneal edema develops secondary to an acute intraocular pressure elevation, the instillation of topical ophthalmic anesthetic solution, followed by 1 to 2 drops of topical ophthalmic glycerin solution, will temporarily clear the cornea to allow for angle evaluation.

Other aspects of angle interpretation and recording of results are identical to those of three-mirror gonioscopy (see p. 74).

■ **Complications/Contraindications.** Maintaining adequate corneal contact without excess pressure is the most difficult aspect of four-mirror gonioscopy for the novice. Tilting the lens or applying too much pressure to the globe will distort the angle appearance and result in an overestimation of its size. If the slit lamp illumination is not in the straight-ahead (coaxial) position, one eyepiece of the microscope may be blocked and stereopsis lost.

Transient superficial punctate keratitis (SPK) may occur following four-mirror gonioscopy, especially if the lens is tilted or moved excessively on the cornea. When significant, this corneal disruption may interfere with visualization and photography of the fundus. Usually reassurance to the patient that a transient foreign body sensation may develop is all that is necessary, although artificial tears may be dispensed and used for 12 to 24 hours. It is possible that significant corneal disruption could result when underlying abnormalities are present such as epithelial basement membrane dystrophy, although this is less likely to occur than with three-mirror gonioscopy because no suction is created between the goniolens and the cornea.

Uncommonly, patient anxiety may produce significant blepharospasm so that four-mirror gonioscopy cannot be performed. A patient may rarely experience vasovagal syncope during this technique. Should this occur, basic first-aid measures are taken. These include elevating the feet above the level of the head, passing a broken ammonia inhalant beneath the nostrils, and monitoring basic vital signs.

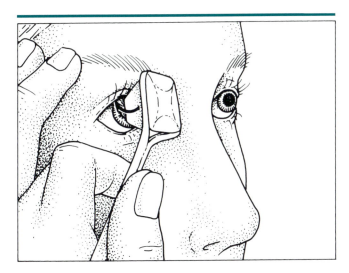

5. If necessary, tilt the top of the goniolens slightly forward and lift up and under the upper lid as the cornea is approached.

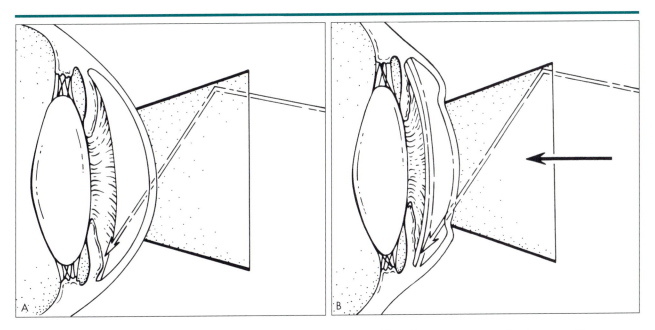

6. With the four-mirror goniolens in its normal position (A), no structures are visible in this narrow anterior chamber angle (B).

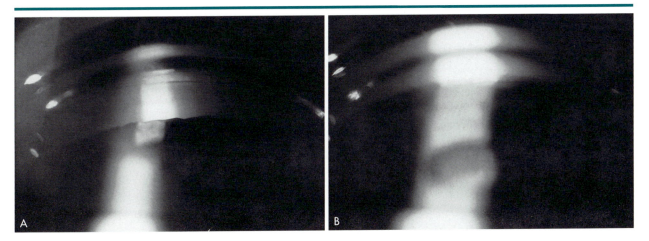

7. Indentation of the corneal apex with the goniolens (A) allows for visualization of all structures (B), indicating that peripheral anterior synechiae are not the cause of the narrow angle.

II Suggested Readings

Alward WLM: *Color Atlas of Gonioscopy.* London, Mosby-Year-book Europe, 1994.

Amos JF: Age-related cataract, in Amos JF (ed): *Diagnosis and Management in Vision Care.* Boston, Butterworths, 1987, pp 601–637.

Bartlett JD: Slit lamp, in Eskridge JB, Amos JF, Bartlett JD (eds): *Clinical Procedures in Optometry.* Philadelphia, Lippincott, 1991, pp 206–220.

Brandreth R: *Clinical Slit Lamp Biomicroscopy.* Berkeley, University of California Multimedia Communications Center, School of Optometry, 1978.

Carlson NB, Kurtz D, Heath DA, Hines C: Ocular health assessment, in *Clinical Procedures for Ocular Examination,* ed 2. Norwalk, CT, Appleton & Lange, 1996, pp 221–319.

Casser L, Lingel NJ: Diseases of the cornea, in Bartlett JD, Jaanus SD (eds): *Clinical Ocular Pharmacology,* ed 3. Boston, Butterworth-Heinemann, 1995, pp 679–746.

Cockburn DM: Tonometry (Chapter 23) and Gonioscopy (Chapter 32), in Eskridge JB, Amos JF, Bartlett JD (eds): *Clinical Procedures in Optometry.* Philadelphia, Lippincott, 1991.

Farris RL: Abnormalities of the tears and treatment of dry eyes, in Kaufman HE, Barron BA, McDonald MB, Waltman SR (eds): *The Cornea.* New York, Churchill Livingstone, 1988.

Fingeret MF, Fodera FA: Uveitis, in Bartlett JD, Jaanus SD (eds): *Clinical Ocular Pharmacology,* ed 3. Boston, Butterworth-Heinemann, 1995, pp 775–792.

Garston MJ: Light flashes and floaters . . . Making a differential diagnosis. *Contemp Optom* 1988; **7:**19–30.

Litwak AB: Gonioscopy, in Lewis TL, Fingeret M (eds): *Primary Care of the Glaucomas.* Norwalk, CT, Appleton & Lange, 1992, pp 121–136.

Locke LC: Conjunctival abrasions and lacerations. *J Am Optom Assoc* 1987;**58:**488–493.

Schnider CM: Dyes, in Bartlett JD, Jaanus SD (eds): *Clinical Ocular Pharmacology,* ed 3. Boston, Butterworth-Heinemann, 1995, pp 389–407.

Van Herick W, Shaffer RN, Schwartz A: Estimation of width of angle of anterior chamber. *Am J Ophthalmol* 1969;**68:** 626–629.

Yolton DP: Topical ophthalmic dyes, in Eskridge JB, Bartlett JD, Amos JF (eds): *Clinical Procedures in Optometry.* Philadelphia, Lippincott, 1991, pp 358–363.

Eyelid Procedures

23 Eyelid Eversion: Single

■ **Description/Indications.** Single eversion of the upper eyelid is performed whenever evaluation of the superior palpebral conjunctiva is needed. Indications for this procedure include, but are not limited to, a history of ocular foreign body or symptoms of foreign body sensation, the evaluation of contact lens patients during the prefitting assessment as well as during follow-up care, and the diagnosis of palpebral vernal conjunctivitis or superior limbic keratoconjunctivitis.

The goal is to evert or "fold" the upper lid upon itself at the uppermost aspect of the superior tarsal plate (Fig. 1). Because the tarsal plate is fibrous and relatively rigid, attempts to evert the lid within the body of the plate itself will generally be unsuccessful. This technique may be performed with or without a slit lamp biomicroscope depending upon the degree of magnification needed. Lids can be everted using your fingers alone (digital technique) or in conjunction with a cotton-tipped applicator. For patients with tight lids, the applicator technique will be easier to perform than the digital technique.

■ **Instrumentation.** Slit lamp biomicroscope (optional), sterile cotton-tipped applicators (optional).

■ **Technique.** Position the patient behind the slit lamp biomicroscope if desired (see p. 24). Use your left hand to evert the patient's right lid; your right hand to evert the patient's left lid.

Digital Method: Instruct the patient to look downward. Actual closure of the eyes should be avoided as the technique then becomes more difficult. Grasp a central section of lashes of the upper lid or the lid margin itself between your thumb and forefinger. Gently pull the lid down and out, away from the globe (Fig. 2A). Simultaneously, place your middle finger at the superior margin of the tarsal plate. Using slight downward pressure at this point along with upward rotation of the margin, "flip" or evert the lid (Fig 2B).

Applicator Method: Follow the same technique outlined above except position a cotton-tipped applicator at the superior edge of the tarsal plate with your unused hand. After the lid has been gently pulled away from the globe, use slight downward pressure with the applicator along with slight upward motion of the lid margin to evert the lid (Fig. 3). Once the lid is everted, gently slide the swab out from the lid so as to free your opposite hand. When everting smaller, tighter lids this same technique may be facilitated by using the "stick" end of the applicator placed tangentially against the lid.

While evaluating the everted lid, use your thumb to hold the lashes against the superior orbital rim with moderately firm pressure. Instruct the patient to continue to look downward (Fig. 4). Once the examination is complete, release the lashes, instruct the patient to look upward, and the lid should "snap" back into position. Reversal of the eversion may be facilitated if you provide a gentle "unfolding" movement with your thumb or forefinger as the patient looks upward.

■ **Interpretation.** The normal superior palpebral conjunctiva will appear as a glossy, smooth, well-vascularized mucous membrane. Moderately sized papillae are usually present at the superior border of the tarsal plate, medially and laterally. Lid eversion may reveal deviations from normal such as foreign bodies, follicles, small papillae, or giant cobblestone papillae.

■ **Contraindications/Complications.** Some patients may exhibit minor anxiety about this procedure. Usually reassurance that the procedure feels awkward but is not painful is all that is required. Should the patient back away while the technique is performed, the resultant pulling on the lashes and lid may cause some mild discomfort.

Loss of a few lashes following this technique is not uncommon. Should the patient have very short lashes or scanty lashes, gentle grasping of the lid margin itself may be necessary. Eversion of the upper lid will naturally cause expression of the meibomian glands so that a transiently oily tear layer may result.

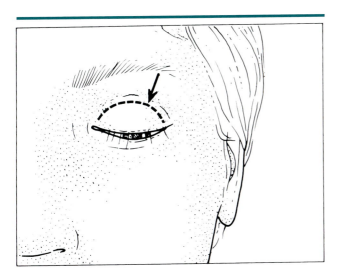

1. The superior aspect of the tarsal plate (arrow) is the pivot point for single eversion of the upper eyelid.

2. (below) Digital method. A. As the patient looks downward, grasp the lashes between your thumb and forefinger, and gently pull the lid down and out. B. Place your middle finger at the superior edge of the tarsal plate (dashed line). Use pressure as shown and evert the lid.

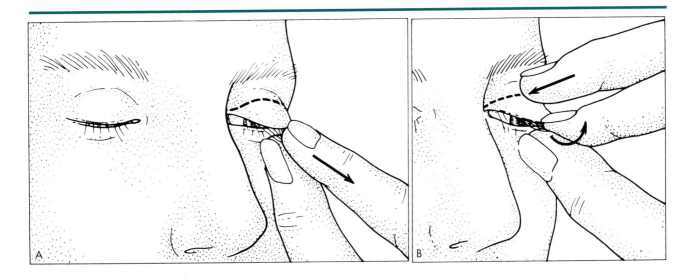

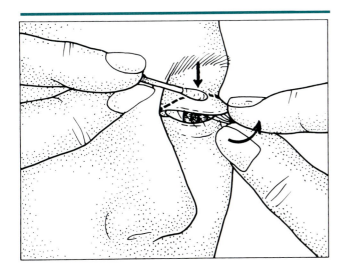

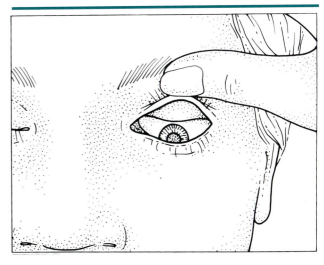

3. Applicator method. Place the cotton-tipped applicator at the superior edge of the tarsal plate (dashed line) with your unused hand. Use pressure as shown and evert the lid.

4. Using relatively firm pressure, hold the lashes against the superior orbital rim during examination of the everted lid. Instruct the patient to continue looking down.

24

Eyelid Eversion: Double

■ **Description/Indications.** Double eversion of the upper lid is performed when access to the superior fornix area is required. Two common indications for this procedure include examining for one or more hard-to-find foreign bodies, such as a displaced contact lens, and performing conjunctival irrigation (see p. 156). The term *double eversion* is somewhat of a misnomer, as the technique does not actually result in two folds of the upper lid. This technique is usually performed using a lid retractor (Fig. 1) with the patient positioned outside of the slit lamp biomicroscope.

■ **Instrumentation.** Lid retractor, sterile cotton-tipped applicators (optional).

■ **Technique.** Instill topical ophthalmic anesthetic solution (see p. 2) and perform single lid eversion (Fig. 2A; see also p. 94). Grasping the handle of the retractor between the thumb and forefinger of the unused hand and supporting the heel of this hand and/or wrist on the patient's forehead, position the retractor to "hook" the superior edge of the tarsal plate of the everted lid (Fig. 2B). As the patient continues to look downward, use the retractor to lift the upper lid gently but firmly in an upward and outward direction away from the globe to expose the superior fornix, which now may be visualized and evaluated (Fig. 3).

Once the retractor is in position, the hand that originally grasped the lashes may be removed to perform other techniques, or the hand holding the retractor may be exchanged.

■ **Interpretation.** The most common abnormality of the superior fornix region is locating a foreign body. Frequently, however, the foreign body or suspected debris cannot be visualized and irrigation will help to dislodge it.

■ **Contraindications/Complications.** Instructing the patient to continue looking downward will avoid the possibility of inducing a corneal abrasion from use of the retractor. The patient may experience symptoms of mild foreign body sensation for several hours following this procedure, which may be relieved by artificial tears.

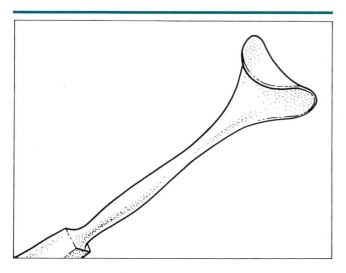

1. The lid retractor used in double eversion of the upper eyelid.

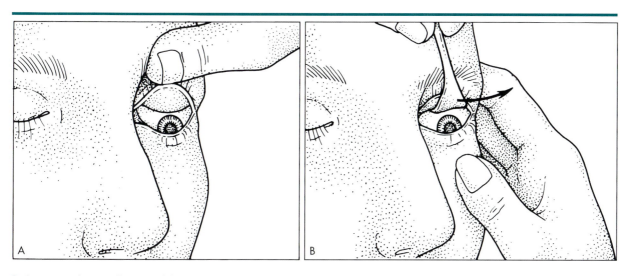

2. A. First singly evert the upper lid, instructing the patient to look downward.

2. B. Use the retractor to "hook" the superior edge of the everted tarsal plate. Lift the lid gently but firmly upward and slightly outward to expose the superior fornix.

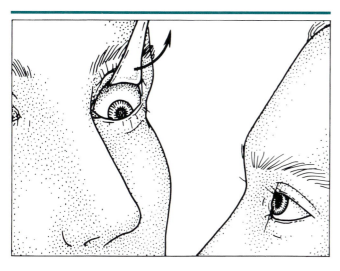

3. Through double eversion the superior fornix may be directly visualized and evaluated or irrigated.

25

Speculum Insertion

■ Description/Indications. An ophthalmic speculum is used to retract the eyelids during surgical procedures such as cataract extraction. A speculum may be used in-office for certain ophthalmic techniques when definitive lid retraction is required, such as during suture cutting (see p. 360), or when the patient is unable to voluntarily control lid movements or exhibits a tendency toward blepharospasm, such as during corneal foreign body removal (see p. 162). The spring-type (Barraquer) speculum is one of the easiest types available for lid retraction (Fig. 1).

■ Instrumentation. Barraquer speculum, topical ophthalmic anesthetic solution.

■ Technique. Instill 2 drops of topical ophthalmic anesthetic solution in each eye (see p. 2). To insert the speculum into the right eye, hold the speculum between your right thumb and forefinger so that the handle is oriented temporally. Position yourself to the side of the patient and ask him or her to look up. Use the forefinger of your left hand to gently retract the lower lid, then "hook" the medial portion of the lower lid with the inferior arm of the speculum (Fig. 2). Ask the patient to look down and use your left forefinger to gently retract the upper lid. Squeeze the speculum slightly, and "hook" the upper lid (Fig. 3). Ask the patient to look straight ahead keeping both eyes open and proceed with the necessary procedure (Fig. 4).

To remove the speculum, gently grasp the handle of the speculum between your right thumb and forefinger. Position your left thumb gently on the right upper lid. Simultaneously spread the lids apart slightly by retracting the upper lid with your left thumb and the lower lid with the remaining fingers of your right hand. Ask the patient to look down, squeeze the speculum and "unhook" the upper lid; ask the patient to look up and "unhook" the lower lid.

To insert the speculum into the left eye, repeat the procedure, using opposite hands if desired.

■ Complications/Contraindications. Some patients may be quite bothered by the awkward feeling of a speculum in place. A speculum should not be inserted when manipulation of the globe is contraindicated, such as when penetrating ocular injury is suspected. Poor insertion technique or a strong Bell's reflex on the part of the patient may induce a corneal abrasion, which should be treated appropriately. One or more small subconjunctival hemorrhages may be induced by speculum insertion.

Once the speculum is in place, it is important to keep the cornea appropriately moistened because the blink reflex is inhibited. To prevent excessive corneal desiccation it is helpful to leave the speculum in place for as short a time as possible.

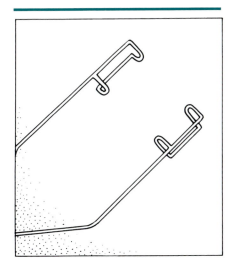

1. The spring-type (Barraquer) speculum used to retract the eyelids.

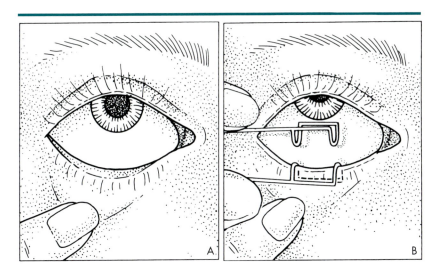

2. A. Position yourself to the side and use your left forefinger to gently retract the lower lid as the patient looks up. B. "Hook" the medial portion of the lower lid with the inferior arm of the speculum.

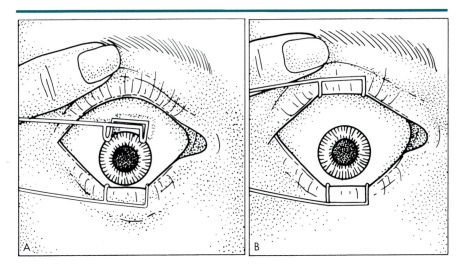

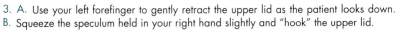

3. A. Use your left forefinger to gently retract the upper lid as the patient looks down.
B. Squeeze the speculum held in your right hand slightly and "hook" the upper lid.

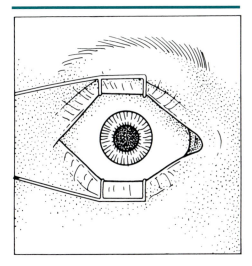

4. The patient is looking straight ahead with the speculum in place.

26 Epilation

■ **Description/Indications.** Epilation is performed when a lash (cilium) or lashes (cilia) require mechanical removal, usually because of induced ocular irritation from contact with the globe. Indications for this procedure include, but are not limited to, trichiasis and entropion. In the latter condition epilation of multiple lashes may serve as a temporary presurgical treatment measure. Less commonly, the epilation technique may be used to remove a lash that has become lodged in the inferior punctum or in a meibomian gland orifice.

Epilation may be performed with the patient positioned outside of or in the slit lamp biomicroscope. If the lash to be removed is relatively long and dark in color, epilation is easily performed without use of the slit lamp. Conversely, if the lash is short and/or light in color, epilation is difficult unless the slit lamp is utilized.

Several types of surgical-quality forceps are available for epilation (Fig. 1). The jewelers-type forceps has tapered, rather pointed tips or jaws. The cilia forceps has wider jaws, similar to a familiar tweezers, and may be squared-off, angled, tapered, or rounded. The jewelers-type forceps is useful for grasping the lash to be epilated when it is located in an area of numerous or closely spaced lashes. In this instance the wider cilia forceps may result in the inadvertent epilation of adjacent normal cilia. Use of the jewelers-type forceps is also helpful when the targeted lash is short or broken off.

■ **Instrumentation.** Desired forceps type, slit lamp biomicroscope (optional).

■ **Technique.**
Slit Lamp Technique: Position the patient comfortably in the slit lamp (see p. 24). No topical anesthetic is required. If the lash to be removed is on the lower lid, instruct the patient to look upward so that the cornea may not be inadvertently abraded during the procedure. Firmly support the heel of your hand holding the forceps on the patient's cheek, the bridge of the nose, or the upright bar of the slit lamp. Looking first outside of the slit lamp, position the tips of the forceps approximately 1 inch away from the lower lid (Fig. 2A). Using low slit lamp magnification (6X to 10X) and a wide illumination beam, observe the illuminated tips of the forceps through the slit lamp as the lid is approached. Grasp the base of the lash with the forceps and use a gentle "plucking" motion to epilate (Fig. 2B).

For epilation of the upper lid, instruct the patient to look downward. It may be helpful to slightly retract the lid to more accessibly position the upper lid lash for epilation (Fig. 3). So that you can use your free hand to control the slit lamp joystick, retraction of the upper lid may be facilitated with the help of an assistant.

External Method: Position the patient's head comfortably on the headrest of the examining chair and illuminate his or her face with the stand lamp. The techniques of patient fixation are the same as those for the slit lamp technique. You may find it helpful to rest the heel of your hand holding the forceps on the patient's cheek (Fig. 4). If difficulties are encountered localizing the cilium or cilia to be epilated, the slit lamp technique may then be used.

■ **Interpretation.** During epilation slight resistance will be felt as the lash is plucked from the follicle. If the lash is actually lodged in the orifice of the meibomian gland or punctum, the lash will glide out smoothly.

■ **Contraindications/Complications.** Successful epilation for the cooperative patient will generally have no contraindications or complications. The examiner should take reasonable care when performing epilation with the pointed jewelers forceps. If repeat epilation is necessary it is performed in approximately 2 to 4 months to coincide with the cilia growth rate. Permanent follicle destruction such as electrolysis, argon laser treatment (see p. 438), or radiosurgery may be considered when repeat epilation is performed on multiple occasions.

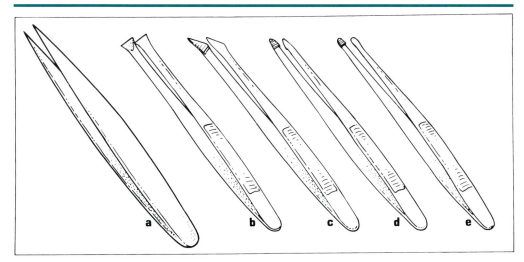

1. The surgical-quality jewelers forceps (a) has pointed tips; cilia forceps may be squared off (b, Littauer), angled (c, Bergh), tapered (d, Zeigler), or rounded (e, Beer).

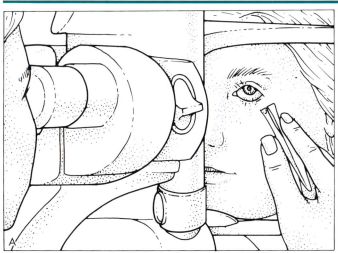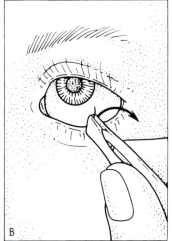

2. A. To epilate a lash on the lower lid, position the patient in the slit lamp and instruct him or her to look up. Place the tips of the forceps approximately 1 inch away from the lower lid.
B. Having approached the lower lid, support the heel of your hand on the patient's cheek. Grasp the lash near its base and use a gentle "plucking" motion.

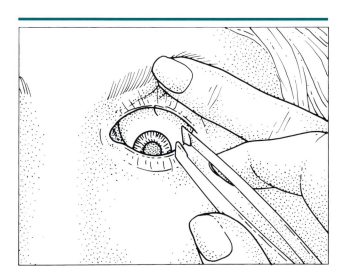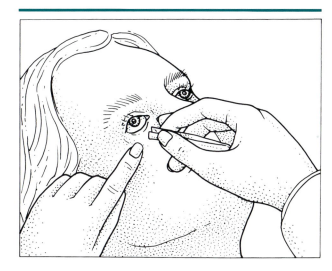

3. To epilate the upper lid, an assistant is retracting the upper lid slightly to more accessibly position the lash and the patient is looking downward.

4. Epilation without the use of a slit lamp. The patient's head is positioned on the headrest, the stand lamp illuminates his or her face, and your hand is supported on the patient's cheek.

Meibomian Gland Expression

■ **Description/Indications.** The meibomian glands, the sinuous sebaceous glands located within the tarsus of the upper and lower lids, may become clogged by an over-production of sebum and other noninflammatory debris (Fig. 1). This nonacute mechanical blockage may involve a single gland or multiple glands; the latter condition is known as chronic meibomianitis. Occlusion of the gland(s) by the cheesy sebaceous material may cause gland distention that is visible as a yellow "streaking" of the palpebral conjunctiva in the area of the affected gland(s) (Fig. 2). Opaque occlusive plugs may also be visible in the gland orifices. Mild hyperemia and edema of the corresponding lid margin may be present, apparent especially when only a single gland is involved. Mild irritation of the lid margin may be reported and an irritative conjunctivitis or kerato-conjunctivitis may result.

Meibomian gland expression is indicated to relieve chronic meibomianitis or to open a single clogged meibo-mian gland that is causing irritation. The small, translucent, waxy, nonirritative meibomian gland orifice plugs that are often noted during routine examination generally do not require expression. Another potential etiology of an isolated clogged meibomian gland that may be alleviated by expression is the residual inflammatory debris that may persist in the gland orifice following resolution of an internal horde-olum. However, gland expression is not indicated for acute internal hordeolum, nor is it included in the therapeutic regimen for chalazion.

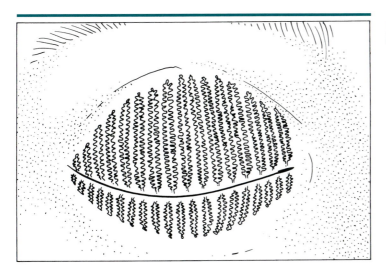

1. The meibomian glands are the sinuous sebaceous glands located within the tarsus of the upper and lower lids.

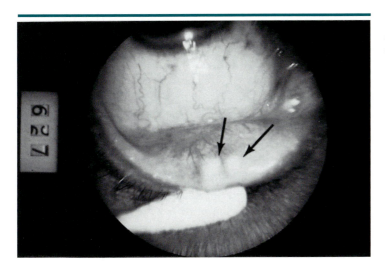

2. Occlusive sebaceous distention of the gland is visible as yellow "streaking" through the overlying palpebral conjunctiva (arrows). (See also Color Plate 27–2.)

■ **Instrumentation.** Topical ophthalmic anesthetic solution, sterile cotton-tipped applicators, sterile ophthalmic saline solution.

■ **Technique.** Instill topical anesthetic drops (see p. 2). Position the patient's head comfortably on the headrest of the examining chair, and illuminate his or her face with the stand lamp. For meibomian gland expression of the lower lid, instruct the patient to look up. Horizontally place one sterile cotton-tipped applicator that has been moistened with sterile saline in the inferior cul-de-sac in the region of the gland to be expressed (Fig. 3). Moistening the applicator will allow for smoother contact with the mucous surface of the palpebral conjunctiva. Using the other hand, place a second dry cotton-tipped applicator on the outside of the lid, just opposed to the applicator in the cul-de-sac, and with the handle oriented in the opposite direction. Lightly support the heels of the your hands on the patient's face. Gently but firmly squeeze the applicators against each other as you roll the applicators upward along the length of the gland toward the lid margin (Fig. 4). Wipe away any expressed sebaceous material with a third cotton-tipped applicator. Continue the procedure until the material can no longer be expressed.

Meibomian gland expression of the upper lid is probably easiest to perform if the lid is first singly everted using a dry cotton-tipped applicator (see p. 94). Hold the applicator in place behind the everted lid and instruct the patient to continue looking down. Place a second moistened cotton-tipped applicator on the palpebral conjunctiva of the everted lid just opposite to the applicator on the skin side of the lid and with the handle of the applicator oriented in the opposite direction. Gently but firmly squeeze the applicators against each other, as you express upward along the length of the gland and approach the lid margin (Fig. 5). Wipe away any expressed sebaceous material with a third cotton-tipped applicator.

■ **Interpretation.** Expression of normal meibomian glands will produce a clear, fluid material. In meibomianitis expression will produce a semisolid, yellow-white material that exudes like toothpaste squeezed from a tube, which may be voluminous (Fig. 4B). For a clogged gland orifice, expression will produce a single waxy solid plug.

Once expression is completed, a treatment regimen of hot compresses, lid hygiene measures (see p. 116), lid massage, artificial tears, and/or prophylactic ophthalmic antibiotic drops may be recommended. Repeated in-office meibomian gland expression may be needed for chronic meibomianitis.

■ **Contraindications/Complications.** Because the lids and lid margins are richly innervated, meibomian gland expression may produce a mild to moderate amount of discomfort for the patient. The examiner should judge the degree of pressure he or she is able to use during the procedure by the comfort level of the patient. Some clinicians elect to use a pledget of anesthetic solution before performing this technique (see p. 6). Rarely, meibomian gland expression may precipitate an acute internal hordeolum.

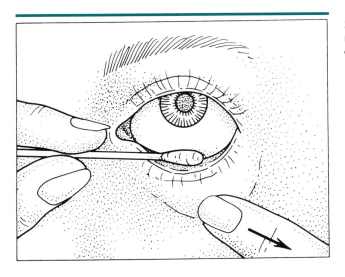

3. To express the lower lid, ask the patient to look upward. Place a moistened sterile cotton-tipped applicator horizontally in the inferior cul-de-sac in the region of the gland(s) to be expressed.

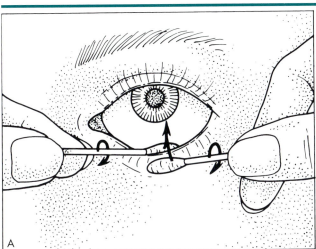

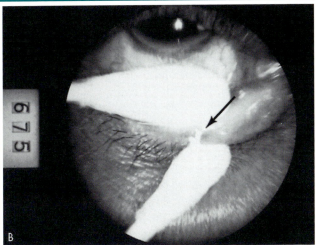

4. A. Using the other hand, place a second dry cotton-tipped applicator on the outside of the lid just opposite to the applicator in the cul-de-sac. Gently but firmly squeeze the applicators against each other, rolling them upward toward the lid margin (arrow).

4. B. Cheesy sebaceous material (arrow) is being expressed from a meibomian gland in the right lower lid. The position of the swab on the outside of the lid is slightly different than described due to examiner positioning at the camera. (*See also* Color Plate 27–4.B.)

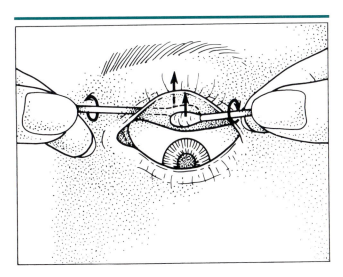

5. To express the superior glands, singly evert the upper lid, keeping the dry applicator in place. Place a second moistened applicator on the opposing palpebral conjunctiva. Gently but firmly squeeze the applicators against each other, rolling them upward.

28

Sebaceous Cyst Evacuation

■ **Description/Indications.** Sebaceous retention cysts due to duct blockages may occur on the skin of the eyelids just as they occur on other skin areas. They appear as well-demarcated smooth, round, noninflamed, nontender nodules, and one or more capillaries may surround or overlie the lesions. Sebaceous cysts occur singly or in multiples. When the lesions are superficial they are creamy white in color; cysts located deeper within the skin appear pinker or more flesh-toned in color (Figs. 1 and 2).

A superficial sebaceous cyst may be evacuated when it is sufficiently large so that a patient expresses concern about the cosmetic appearance of the lesion. Cyst evacuation is generally not indicated for lesions noted during routine examination of the asymptomatic patient.

■ **Instrumentation.** Sterile disposable 25G needle, sterile cotton-tipped applicators, topical ophthalmic anesthetic solution (optional), alcohol pads.

■ **Technique.** Position the patient's head comfortably on the headrest of the examining chair, and illuminate his or her face with the stand lamp. If the cyst to be removed is on the lower lid, instruct the patient to look up; when the cyst is on the upper lid, instruct the patient to look down. Squeeze excess fluid from an alcohol pad and use it to clean the skin overlying and surrounding the cyst; allow the skin to air dry. Topical anesthesia is generally not necessary, but if desired, hold a cotton-tipped applicator pledget saturated with topical ophthalmic anesthetic drops in contact with the cyst for approximately 30 seconds (see p. 6). Pull the skin adjacent to the cyst taut. With the heel of your hand supported on the patient's face, use a sterile 25G needle to score or puncture the top of the cyst, in a nonvascularized area if possible (Fig. 3). The wall of the cyst may be fairly tough so that repeated scoring may be necessary, or the original scoring may need to be enlarged to facilitate expression.

Using two sterile cotton-tipped applicators positioned at opposite sides of the base of the lesion, gently but firmly evacuate the cyst by rolling the applicators toward each other until the sebaceous material is completely expressed (Fig. 4). Use additional sterile applicators to wipe away sebaceous material (Fig. 5).

Instruct the patient to apply antibiotic ointment as prophylaxis against infection three or four times daily for several days until a small scab forms and the area heals. If the sebaceous cyst is located away from the lid margin, a nonophthalmic antibiotic ointment may be used for prophylaxis.

■ **Interpretation.** During sebaceous cyst evacuation, cheesy, yellow-white sebaceous material will be expressed. It is usual for a minute amount of bleeding to occur during and following expression.

■ **Contraindications/Complications.** This technique is not appropriate for the removal of deep sebaceous cysts that required incision through skin tissue. The examiner should warn the patient to monitor for the unlikely onset of secondary bacterial infection following removal of the cyst.

When the cyst is located on the lid margin, care should be taken when swabbing the skin with alcohol so as not to contaminate the eye. This might best be accomplished by using a cotton tipped applicator moistened with isopropyl alcohol. Care should be taken when scoring the lid margin cyst with the needle, and manipulation with the applicators in this area can be awkward. The patient should be informed that the sebaceous cyst may occasionally recur.

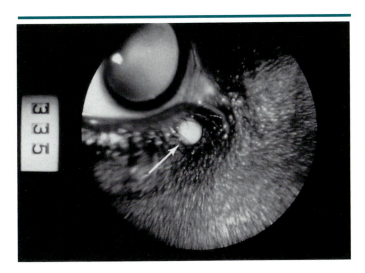

1. The superficial sebaceous cyst appears as a well-demarcated, creamy white, smooth, nontender, round nodule (arrow). One or more capillaries may surround or overlie the lesion. (*See also* Color Plate 28–1.)

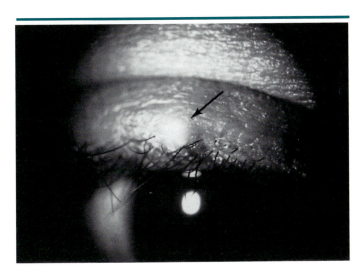

2. The deeper sebaceous cyst is more flesh-toned in color and less well demarcated (arrow). It is not a candidate for evacuation using this technique. (*See also* Color Plate 28–2.)

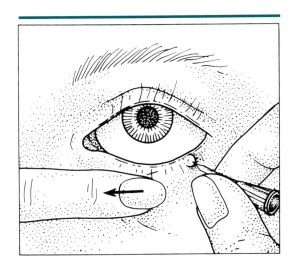

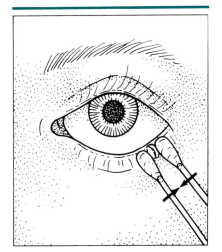

3. Pull the skin adjacent to the cyst taut and, with the heel of your hand supported on the patient's face, use a sterile 25G needle to score or puncture the top of the cyst in a nonvascularized area if possible.

4. Place two sterile applicators at opposite sides of the base of the lesion, and gently but firmly express the cyst until the cheesy sebaceous material is completely evacuated.

5. The evacuated sebaceous cyst. Antibiotic ointment is applied as prophylaxis for several days until it heals.

29 Sudoriferous Cyst Evacuation

■ **Description/Indications.** Retention cysts of the sweat glands of Moll, known as sudoriferous cysts, appear as one or more small, noninflamed, avascular, clear, fluid-filled cysts on the anterior portion of the lid margin (Fig. 1). When sufficiently large, a sudoriferous cyst may be evacuated for cosmetic reasons. Cyst evacuation is generally not indicated for lesions noted during routine examination of the asymptomatic patient.

■ **Instrumentation.** Slit lamp biomicroscope, sterile disposable 25G needle, sterile cotton-tipped applicators.

■ **Technique.** Position the patient comfortably in the slit lamp (see p. 24), and instruct him or her to keep the head firmly against the chin and forehead rests. No topical anesthetic is needed. If the cyst is located on the lower lid margin, instruct the patient to look upward. Support the heel of your hand holding the needle firmly on the patient's cheek or on the upright bar of the slit lamp. Looking first outside of the slit lamp, position the needle approximately 1 inch away from the lower lid (Fig. 2A). Using low slit lamp magnification (6X to 10X) and a wide illumination beam, observe the illuminated tip of the needle through the slit lamp as the lid

is approached. Use the tip of the needle to "puncture" the sudoriferous cyst (Fig. 2B). If needed, use a tissue or cotton-tipped applicator to wipe away the clear exudate.

When the cyst is located on the upper lid margin, instruct the patient to look down. To more accessibly expose the cyst it may be helpful to slightly retract the upper lid. In order for you to continue using your free hand to control the slit lamp joystick, retraction of the upper lid may be facilitated with the help of an assistant (Fig. 3).

Generally no topical antibiotic prophylactic treatment is required following evacuation of a sudoriferous cyst, but a one-time application of ophthalmic antibiotic ointment may be used. Advising the patient that the cyst may reform or that other cysts may appear is helpful.

■ **Interpretation.** As the sudoriferous cyst is evacuated, a minute amount of clear, watery fluid will appear.

■ **Contraindications/Complications.** Successful evacuation of a sudoriferous cyst for the cooperative patient will generally have no contraindications or complications. If the patient is poorly cooperative, inadvertent abrasion of the cornea with the 25G needle may result.

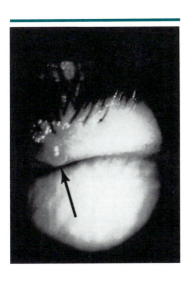

1. Sudoriferous cysts appear as one or more small, noninflamed, avascular, clear fluid-filled cysts on the lid margin (arrow). (*See also* Color Plate 29–1.) (Courtesy of Primary Eyecare Educational Services, Inc.)

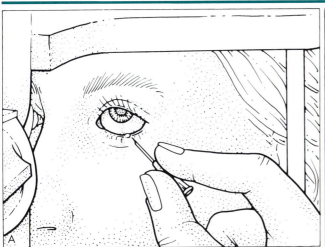

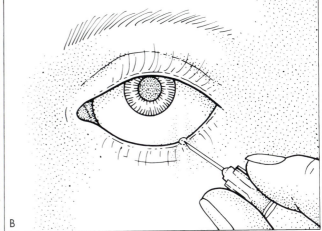

2. A. Position the patient in the slit lamp and ask him or her to look up. Place the tip of the needle approximately 1 inch away from the lower lid.

2. B. Use the tip of the needle to "puncture" the sudoriferous cyst. A minute amount of clear, watery fluid will appear, which can be wiped away if needed.

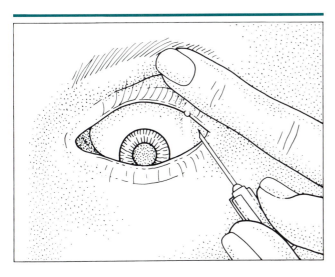

3. To evacuate a sudoriferous cyst of the upper lid, an assistant is retracting the upper lid slightly and the patient is looking downward.

30 Verruca, Papilloma Removal: Chemical

■ Description/Indications. Verrucae and papillomas (Fig. 1) may involve the skin of the lids and adnexa. Although these lesions are commonly removed for cosmetic reasons using simple excision (see p. 112), electrocautery, or radiosurgery, a chemical removal technique, is also available. Because verrucae and papillomas are viral in origin, their removal also helps to prevent dissemination.

Bichloracetic acid (dichloroacetic acid), an effective chemical keratolytic and cauterizing agent, may be used to remove verrucae and papillomas. It is available in a treatment kit that includes a bottle of acid, a micro-dropper, acid receptacles, petrolatum, and pointed wooden applicator sticks. This technique is usually performed with the patient positioned outside of the slit lamp biomicroscope, although magnification provided by a head loupe is helpful.

■ Instrumentation. Bichloracetic acid treatment kit, sterile cotton-tipped applicators, head loupe (optional).

■ Technique. Position the patient's head comfortably on the headrest of the examining chair, and illuminate his or her face with the stand lamp. Using a cotton-tipped applicator, apply a thin layer of petrolatum to the normal tissue surrounding the lesion to protect it from treatment (Fig. 2A). Transfer a small amount of bichloracetic acid to one of the acid receptacles with the micro-dropper to prevent contamination of the solution. Dip the applicator stick a few millimeters into the acid in the receptacle to moisten it, and remove excess acid by drawing the applicator over the lip of the receptacle. Apply a small amount of bichloroacetic acid to each lid lesion by touching it with the acid-moistened applicator stick (Fig. 2B). Usually only one application is necessary; however, retreatment may be performed as needed.

■ Interpretation. With application of bichloracetic acid to a verruca or papilloma, the area will immediately turn white (Fig. 2C), followed by a gray-white appearance and dark eschar (Fig. 2D). The lesion will typically desquamate in 7 to 10 days (Fig. 3).

■ Complications/Contraindications. Bichloracetic acid treatment should be avoided for lesions on the lid margin as chemical keratoconjunctivitis may result. Care should be taken that excess bichloracetic acid does not drip from the applicator stick onto areas of the skin not intended for treatment. Acid that is accidentally spilled onto normal tissue should immediately be removed by wiping with a cotton-tipped applicator or cotton pledget and rinsing with water. Some clinicians apply the bichloracetic acid with the patient in a supine position to reduce unintended dripping of the acid following application.

Because of the delicate nature of the eyelid skin, slight erythema and mild stinging may result from application of the acid. Focal hypopigmentation may occur in patients with darkly pigmented skin.

Bichloracetic acid should not be used to treat malignant or premalignant lesions. If the lid lesions are not adequately treated by bichloracetic acid, removal by an alternative technique may be necessary.

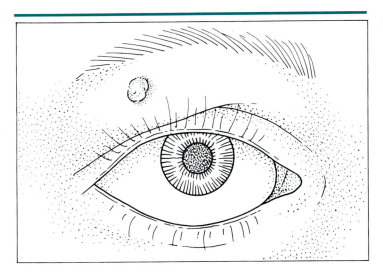

1. A papilloma is present on the upper lid.

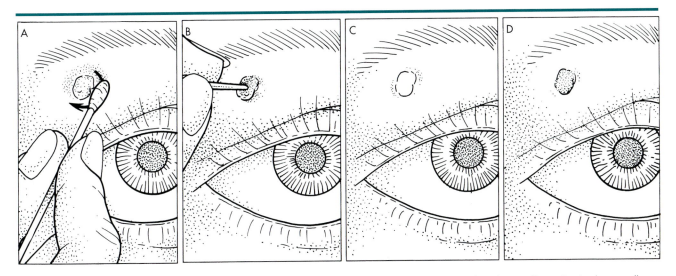

2. A. Using a cotton-tipped applicator, apply a thin layer of petrolatum to the normal tissue surrounding the papilloma. B. Apply a small amount of bichloracetic acid to the papilloma with a wooden applicator stick. The papilloma immediately turns white due to schemical cauterization by the acid (C), followed by a gray-white appearance and dark eschar (D).

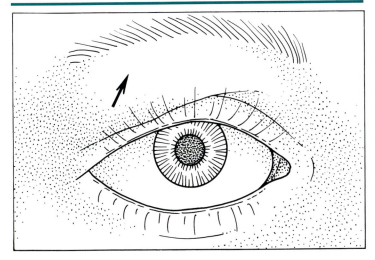

3. The papilloma has desquamated in 7 to 10 days (arrow). When necessary, retreatment may be performed.

31

Verruca, Papilloma Removal: Excisional

■ **Description/Indications.** Papilloma is a general category of frequently benign epithelial tumors that are not of viral origin. Squamous papillomae, also known as skin tags or soft fibromas, are the most common benign eyelid tumor. They usually present as pedunculated, multilobular, cauliflower-like, flesh-colored lesions made up of clusters of finger-like projections of epithelial and fibrovascular tissue. These noninfectious polyps have a roughened, granulated, non-eroded surface and are attached to the skin by variably sized stalks (Fig. 1). They often present at the mucocutaneous border of the eyelid as well as in the periorbital skin area, and are mostly of cosmetic concern to the patient. Pigmentation of these lesions can vary from amelanotic to dark. Chemical treatment (see p. 110) and surgical removal are the treatments of choice when indicated.

Viral papillomas or verrucae are benign, painless, self-limiting warts that frequently outgrow their blood supply and disappear spontaneously. Therefore, a conservative approach to treatment is advised. These human papillomavirus lesions usually appear in multiples and are readily spread by physical contact and autoinnoculation, with infection affecting the epidermal keratinocytes. They can slough off viral toxins and epithelium into the conjunctival sac, producing chronic conjunctivitis. Pinpoint black spots on their surfaces, characteristic of common warts, are believed to be thrombosed blood vessels and embedded dirt, as opposed to simple pigmentation.

Several types of verrucae (viral papillomas) are recognized clinically. The common wart or verruca vulgaris is usually elevated and multilobulated, with a keratinized surface resembling a mosaic or cauliflower-like design due to its fused cylindrical projections connected to the skin by variably sized stalks (Fig. 2A). Verruca planar is a round, slightly raised, flat-based (sessile) wart varying in size from a few millimeters to several centimeters (Fig. 2B). Another type is the verruca digitata or filiform lesion, a cutaneous horn-like lesion composed of multiple finger-like projections less fused than in the common wart and with a somewhat wider base.

The nature of the attachment between the lesion and the skin will determine the type of excisional technique used. Pedunculated lesions with small diameter stalks, usually 1 to 2 mm or slightly larger, can be removed by simple excision or snipping. Larger flat-based lesions are removed by epidermal curetting or surgical blade shaving techniques, depending upon personal preference. All of these

techniques are used when a full-thickness tissue excision for biopsy is not indicated. For any of these techniques, thermal cautery is used to control bleeding when necessary.

■ **Instrumentation.** 0.5% proparacaine ophthalmic solution; 1 to 2% lidocaine with epinephrine 1:100,000 for injection; sterile: 18G 1 ½-inch needle, 3 or 5-mL syringe, 27 or 30G ½-inch needle, mouse-toothed forceps, curved iris or probe-tipped scissors, dermal #1 curette, #15 disposable surgical blade, alcohol pads, cotton-tipped applicators, gauze pads, latex gloves; head loupe (optional), high-temperature disposable thermal cautery, specimen jar with formaldehyde, broad-spectrum ophthalmic antibiotic, eye protection (optional), appropriate infectious waste disposal container, puncture resistant biohazard sharps container.

■ **Technique.** Review the risks and benefits of the procedure with the patient and ask him or her to sign the appropriate consent form. Prepare the syringe for injection with lidocaine with epinephrine 1:100,000 (see p. 402). For appropriate infection control, wear sterile latex gloves (see p. 475) and eye protection as indicated. Recline the patient to a flat, comfortable, secure supine position that allows for easy access to the lesion. Position proper illumination for the procedure. Consider using a head loupe if desired. Inform the patient of a brief pinching sensation, followed by mild burning associated with the anesthetic injection. Instill two drops of topical anesthetic solution into the eye if reducing the blink reflex would be helpful during the procedure.

Simple Excision/Snipping: Examine the lesion for anatomical structure, noting the presence of a pedunculated stalk. If the stalk is 1 to 2 mm in width at its base, prepare the lesion by swabbing the area with a sterile alcohol pad, then allow it to air dry. Inject a small amount of anesthetic subcutaneously at the base of the lesion with a 27 or 30G ½-inch needle to achieve infiltrative anesthesia (see p. 417).

Grasp the lesion with a toothed forceps and pull upward, placing tension on its base while elevating it and the underlying skin; use the curved-tipped scissors to snip the lesion at the junction of the base and skin surface (Fig. 3). If any minor bleeding occurs, apply direct pressure with a sterile cotton-tipped applicator or sterile gauze pad. If significant bleeding continues after a few minutes, dry the area with a sterile gauze pad and briefly pinpoint cauterize the base (described later).

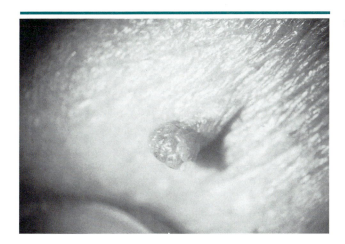

1. A pedunculated papilloma. (Courtesy of Rodney Gutner, OD)

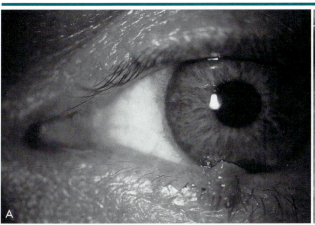

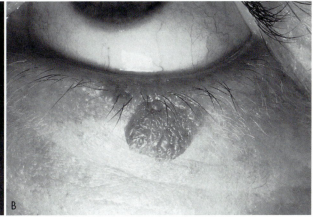

2. A. A common wart or verruca vulgaris on the lower lid margin. Note the chronic, low-grade conjunctivitis.

2. B. A flat-based (sessile) verruca planar. (Courtesy of Rodney Gutner, OD)

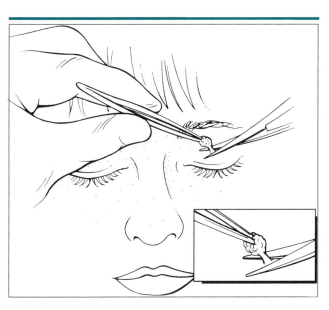

3. For simple excision or snipping, grasp the lesion with a toothed forceps and elevate upward, placing tension on the lesion and the underlying skin. The curve-tipped scissors are positioned parallel to the skin surface, straddling the base of the stalk (inset), and the lesion is snipped at the junction of the base and the skin.

Epidermal Curettage: Examine the lesion for anatomic structure. If the base is broader than 2 mm, consider epidermal curettage. Swab the area with a sterile alcohol pad, then allow to air dry. Using the 27 or 30G ½-inch needle, inject a small amount of anesthetic around the base of the lesion to achieve infiltrative anesthesia (see p. 00). This should elevate the lesion somewhat away from the skin surface. Create two-way tension on either side of the lesion with the thumb and forefinger of your nondominant hand (Fig 4A). Grasp the curette like a pencil with your dominant hand and place it firmly against the skin, enclosing the lesion in the round or oval curette opening angled at approximately 15 to 30 degrees from the surface of the skin. Support your hand on the closest facial bone, apply continuous pressure, and slide the curette back toward you with a firm, horizontal shearing motion (Fig. 4B). Place the excised lesion in specimen jar if biopsy is indicated.

After lesion removal, inspect the epidermal area for punctate bleeding and apply direct pressure with a sterile cotton-tipped applicator or gauze pad. If significant bleeding continues, dry the area with a sterile cotton-tipped applicator or gauze pad and apply brief pinpoint cautery (described later).

Shave Excision: Examine the lesion for anatomical structure. If the base is broader than 2 mm, consider shave excision. Swab the area with a sterile alcohol pad, then allow to air dry. Using the 27 or 30G ½-inch needle, inject a small amount of anesthetic around the base of the lesion to achieve infiltrative anesthesia (see p. 417). This should elevate the lesion somewhat away from the skin surface. Gently grasp the lesion with sterile forceps using the nondominant hand and place the flat surface of a #15 surgical blade against the skin and next to the lesion (Fig. 5). With a smooth stroke, draw the blade through the base of the lesion parallel to the surface of the skin. Snip the last piece of skin attachment with sterile scissors.

After removal of the lesion, inspect the epidermal area for punctate superficial bleeding and apply direct pressure with a sterile cotton-tipped applicator or gauze pad. If significant bleeding continues, swab the area dry with a sterile cotton-tipped applicator or gauze pad and apply brief pinpoint cautery (described in the next section).

Thermal Cautery: Most battery-operated high-temperature disposable cautery units come in a sterile packaged, loop tip design with a safety cap (Fig. 6). Operate it by simply depressing the side power button with the thumb as it is held with a pencil grip. The tip glows brightly and quickly after the button is depressed. Contact time and the amount of tip surface contact determines the amount of thermal energy applied to the treated area. For pinpoint cautery, momentarily touch the glowing tip to the desired area one or more times until bleeding stops.

For all techniques, place the excised lesion in the specimen jar if biopsy is indicated. Apply a broad-spectrum antibiotic ophthalmic ointment to the small epithelial defect area and instruct the patient to do so for a few days postprocedure. Recommend non-aspirin analgesics for patients with any residual discomfort.

■ **Interpretation.** After several days a small scab will form over the excised base of these lesions, which will fall off with minimal destruction to normal tissue and scarring. Lesions with very narrow stalks can often be removed without anesthetic if the patient is willing to tolerate a very brief sharp pinching sensation. Lesions needing full-thickness biopsy involve a more extensive surgical technique.

If pinpoint cautery is used, a small plume of smoke followed by small focal areas of eschar will appear as cauterization is performed.

■ **Contraindications/Complications.** Medical contraindications to epinephrine should be noted in the preprocedure work-up and avoided by using plain lidocaine for infiltrative anesthesia, especially in patients with heart disease, hypertension, and thyrotoxicosis. Any history of sensitivity to anesthetics, antibiotics, or analgesics should also be determined in the initial patient history. Patients with bleeding disorders should be cautiously considered for this procedure. The topical anesthetic agents may produce local hypersensitivity reactions, including toxic keratitis.

The major systemic side effects caused by local anesthetics are excitation of the central nervous system (CNS) and depression of the cardiovascular system. Initial CNS symptoms of anesthetic toxicity commonly include drowsiness, light-headedness, dizziness, and a metallic taste followed by nausea, garrulousness, perioral numbness, tingling, diplopia, and tinnitus. The first sign of cardiovascular toxicity is typically a reduction in blood pressure. Tremors, muscle twitching, seizures, loss of consciousness, respiratory depression, and circulatory collapse have been reported. As a result, when performing injections, it is important to ensure the prompt availability of proper equipment and personnel trained to address medical emergencies, ranging from vasovagal syncope to cardiac arrest.

Lesions that directly involve the lid margin should be treated conservatively or referred to prevent permanent eyelid dysfunction. Cautery should be limited to pinpoint treatment to minimize scarring and depigmentation. All injections should be performed cautiously, as unintentional injection of deeper tissue can have serious complications.

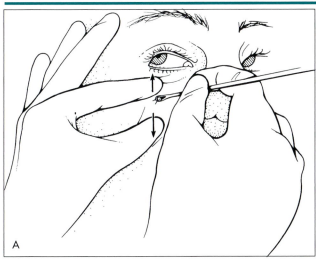

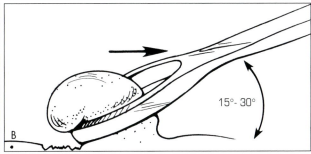

4. A. For epidermal curettage, place two-way tension on both sides of the lesion, and enclose the lesion inside of the horizontally positioned oval curette opening.

4. B. Keeping the curette angled at approximately 15 to 30 degrees from the surface of the skin, move the curette back toward you with a firm, horizontal shearing action.

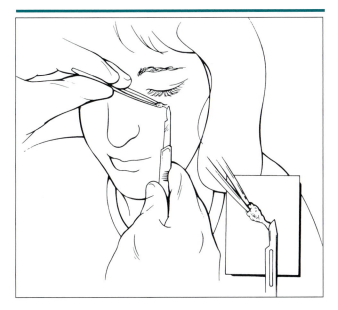

5. For shave excision, gently elevate the lesion with sterile forceps and place the flat surface of the blade against the skin. Make a smooth stroke, drawing the blade through the base of the lesion while remaining parallel to the skin surface (inset).

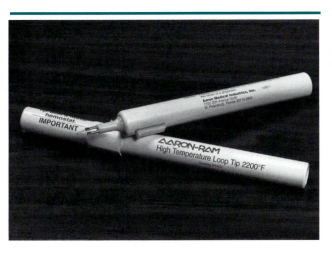

6. The disposable cautery unit is operated by depressing the side power button with the thumb. After the tip glows brightly, lightly pinpoint cauterize the base of the excised lesion to control bleeding if desired or necessary.

32 Eyelid Scrubs

■ **Description/Indications.** Eyelid cleansing measures ("lid scrubs") may be used to treat and/or control a number of disease processes that involve the lid margin. The conditions for which lid scrubs may be indicated include, but are not limited to, marginal blepharitis, *Demodex* blepharitis, and control of recurrent hordeola or chalazia. The examiner usually recommends to the patient that this procedure be done at home once or twice daily.

This technique may be performed in a variety of ways. The two common components to this procedure, however, include a solution for cleansing the lids and a mechanical technique for doing so. Although baby shampoo is frequently used for eyelid hygiene, commercially prepared lid scrub solutions are available complete with patient instructions and cleansing pads, often premoistened. Lid scrubs have also been performed using antibiotic ointments.

■ **Instrumentation.** Lid cleansing solution, clean gauze or cotton pads, or cotton-tipped applicators.

■ **Technique.**
Gauze or Cotton Pad Technique: Instruct the patient to apply a small amount of the recommended lid scrub solution to a clean gauze or cotton pad. Alternatively, instruct the patient to use a premoistened lid cleansing pad. Rubbing together two portions of the pad that are moistened with the solution will create a mild lather. Instruct the patient to close the eyes and, using firm but gentle pressure in a horizontal motion, rub the pad along the lid margins (Fig. 1). A separate pad is used for each eye.

Cotton-tipped Applicator Method: Instruct the patient to moisten a clean cotton-tipped applicator with the recommended lid scrub solution. The procedure should be done while looking into a mirror so as to carefully monitor the placement of the applicator. To clean the lower lid margin, instruct the patient to tilt the chin down slightly, causing the globe to roll upward, and retract the lower lid slightly with the index finger of one hand to expose the lid margin. Holding the cotton-tipped applicator in the opposite hand, the patient should gently but firmly rub the applicator in a hor-

izontal motion along the base of the lashes for the length of the lower lid (Fig. 2). To clean the upper lid margin, instruct the patient to elevate the chin slightly so that the globe rolls downward. While the upper lid is retracted slightly with the index finger of one hand, and holding the cotton-tipped applicator in the opposite hand, the patient gently but firmly rubs the applicator in a horizontal motion along the base of the lashes for the length of the upper lid (Fig. 3). A clean applicator is used for each eye.

A gentle rinsing of the lid area with warm water followed by drying with a clean face towel completes both procedures.

To help ensure compliance it is useful to give definitive guidelines as to the duration of the procedure, such as 10 seconds per eye or 10 scrubs per eye. Dispensing prepared written instructions outlining the recommended lid scrub technique is also helpful.

■ **Interpretation.** If the patient is compliant and performing the technique correctly, a diminution or complete resolution of lid margin debris should be noted following lid hygiene measures.

■ **Contraindications/Complications.** When compliance is problematic, it is helpful to simplify the procedure as much as possible so that it may be easily incorporated into the daily hygiene regimen.

Should lid irritation develop in the course of this therapy, the patient may be performing the technique too vigorously or too frequently. Patients who may be susceptible to this complication include those with very delicate lid tissues, such as accompanies acne rosacea. If the patient is inappropriately performing lid scrubs with a nonrecommended product, ocular and/or lid irritation may result.

Patients who are performing lid scrubs using cotton-tipped applicators should be advised to carefully position the applicator on the lid margin while looking in a mirror. Mechanical irritation of the globe may result if inadvertent slipping of the applicator occurs. Patients susceptible to this complication may include presbyopes and patients with manual dexterity difficulties.

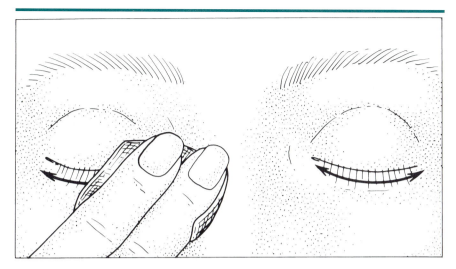

1. The patient is performing lid scrubs using a clean gauze pad that has been moistened with the recommended lid hygiene solution. Using firm but gentle pressure in a horizontal motion, the pad is rubbed along the lid margins.

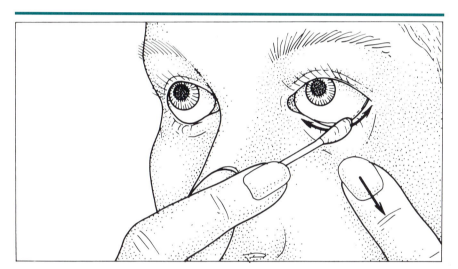

2. While looking into a mirror, the patient has tilted the chin down, and the lower lid is retracted slightly with the index finger of one hand. Holding the applicator in the opposite hand, the patient is gently but firmly rubbing in a horizontal motion along the base of the lashes for the length of the lower lid.

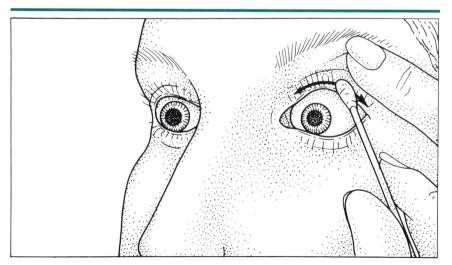

3. While looking into a mirror, the patient has tilted the chin up, and the upper lid is retracted slightly with the index finger of one hand. Holding the applicator in the opposite hand, the patient is gently but firmly rubbing in a horizontal motion along the base of the lashes for the length of the upper lid.

33 Chalazion Removal: Incision and Curettage

■ **Description/Indications.** A chalazion is a lipo-granuloma of the eyelid that usually forms after a meibomian (tarsal) gland obstruction ruptures, releasing sebum into the surrounding tarsal tissue to incite a granulomatous reaction, or following an acute internal hordeolum that evolves into a chronic sterile granuloma. Chalazia are often associated with seborrhea, chronic blepharitis, and acne rosacea, as well as *Demodex* infestation of the sebaceous glands. Most chalazia are nontender, firm, slowly enlarging masses having variable sequellae. This inflammatory tissue reaction yields single or multiple lesions which can cause pressure necrosis, tissue swelling, discomfort, cosmetic distress, and/or blurred vision.

If standard treatment with hot compresses and topical and/or systemic antibiotics is unsuccessful, lesional removal may be indicated. Patients frequently request removal, especially for cosmetic reasons. Intralesional injection of steroid (see p. 426) has been advocated by some practitioners, considered by many to be most successful if done during the early stage of granuloma formation. Chalazia located close to the nasolacrimal system appear to be a prime indication for steroid injection to avoid more invasive intervention near the canaliculi. Incision and curettage or subconjunctival total excision are the surgical methods of choice, initiated after any acute inflammation has subsided. Both methods approach the lesion from the palpebral conjunctival side, because the posterior tarsal plate containing the meibomian glands is closest to this surface of the eyelid, and also to avoid external skin scarring. Occasionally, granuloma formation can extend through the skin surface or rupture and drain through the anterior lid surface, requiring excision and minimal suturing.

■ **Instrumentation.** 0.5% proparacaine ophthalmic solution; 1 to 2% lidocaine with epinephrine 1:100,000 for injection; sterile: 18G 1 ½-inch needle, 3 or 5-mL syringe, 27 or 30G ½-inch needle, chalazion clamp, chalazion curette, scalpel (e.g., #11), toothed forceps, scissors (e.g., Westcott or Stevens), gauze pads, eye pads, cotton-tipped applicators, latex gloves; broad-spectrum antibiotic ophthalmic ointment; 1-inch micropore tape; specimen jar with formaldehyde; eye protection (optional); appropriate infectious waste disposal container; puncture resistant biohazard sharps container.

■ **Technique.** Review the risks and benefits of the procedure with the patient, and ask him or her to sign an appropriate consent form. Prepare the syringe for injection with lidocaine with epinephrine 1:100,000 for injection (see p. 402). For appropriate infection control, wear sterile latex gloves (see p. 475) and protective eye wear as indicated. Recline the patient to a flat, comfortable, secure supine position. Position proper illumination for the procedure. Inform the patient of a brief pinching sensation, followed by mild burning associated with the anesthetic injection.

Instill two drops of topical anesthetic into the eye. Swab the area of the lesion using a sterile alcohol pad, being careful not to allow any alcohol to drip into the eye, and allow it to air dry. Using the 27 or 30G ½-inch needle, inject 0.5 to 1.0 mL of lidocaine with epinephrine subcutaneously (see p. 417) under the anterior lid skin surrounding the elevated mass for initial infiltrative anesthesia (Fig. 1). One or multiple injections may be necessary depending upon the size and location of the lesion, or simply angling the needle may amply extend the range of infiltration. Do not initially inject the lesion itself. Wait a few minutes for the anesthetic to work. Evert the involved lid (see p. 94), and apply a chalazion clamp by straddling both sides of the eyelid and centering the lesion in the opened-ring side of the clamp (Fig. 2). Tighten the circular knob to secure the clamp and to achieve hemostasis. Allow the clamp to hang gently from the lid and rest on the forehead or cheek away from the cornea. If the brow is too prominent to rest the clamp on, position it so the handle is oriented horizontally toward the outer canthus. At this point, some practitioners inject the lesion itself subconjunctivally with anesthetic using the same syringe and keeping the needle anterior to the tarsal plate (Fig. 3).

Working from this exposed conjunctival side, make approximately a 3-mm vertical conjunctival incision through the length of the lesion with the #11 blade, remaining parallel to the meibomian glands (Fig. 4). Be careful not to cut any closer than 2 to 3 mm from the eyelid margin to prevent possible postprocedure lid notching. Some practitioners reverse the blade, positioning the dull edge toward the lid margin, to help prevent unintentional margin damage. Granulomatous chalazion material will often extrude through the edges of the incision.

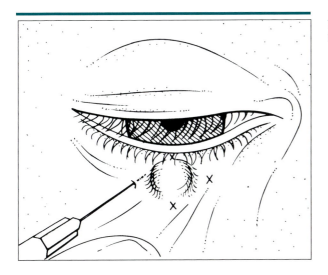

1. Inject the local anesthetic subcutaneously at one or more sites surrounding the chalazion for infiltrative anesthesia.

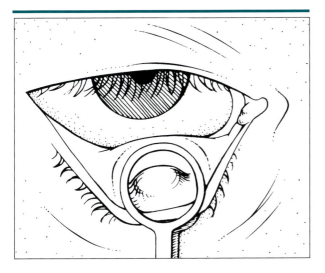

2. Apply the chalazion clamp on either side of the everted eyelid, centering the lesion in the opened ring. Tighten the circular knob, and then allow the clamp to hang or rest away from the cornea.

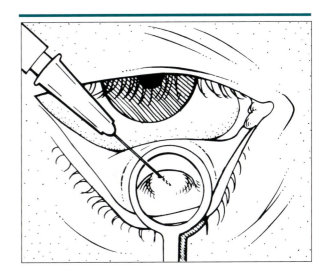

3. After applying the clamp and everting the lid, some practitioners inject the chalazion itself with anesthetic solution. Keep the injection within the lesion, avoiding penetration into the retrotarsal plate area.

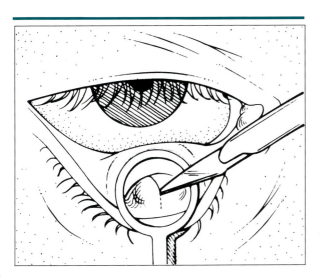

4. Make a 2 to 3-mm vertical conjunctival incision through the length of the lesion with the #11 blade, remaining parallel to the meibomian glands and staying 2 to 3 mm away from the lid margin.

Insert the curette into the newly created pocket opening and, using multidirectional movements, attempt to vigorously sweep all material out through the lesion incision (Fig. 5). Wipe material onto a sterile gauze pad between curettages. Use sterile cotton-tipped applicators to absorb any blood blocking your visibility of the incision area. If additional drainage is needed, grasp the edge of the incision flap with sterile forceps and cut away a small elliptical piece of the flap with sterile scissors (Fig. 6). Any residual fibrous sac found, especially with long-standing chalazia, should be carefully removed if possible by grasping it with the forceps and cutting it away with the scissors, avoiding disruption of normal tissue. Place any material for biopsy into a properly labeled specimen jar. With superior lid granulomas, it is easier to apply the clamp to the lid area first (Fig. 7A), and then evert the lid (Fig. 7B), recentering the lesion if necessary.

Remove the clamp and apply direct pressure with sterile gauze to control any residual bleeding. Some practitioners lightly pinpoint cauterize the base of the operated area to control bleeding. Most battery operated high temperature disposable cautery units come in sterile packaged, loop tip design with a safety cap (Fig. 8). Operate it by simply depressing the side power button with the thumb as it is held with a pencil grip. The tip glows brightly and quickly after the button is depressed. Contact time and the amount of tip surface contact determines the amount of thermal energy applied to the treated area. For pinpoint cautery, momentarily touch the glowing tip to the desired area one or more times until the bleeding stops.

Instill a broad-spectrum ophthalmic antibiotic ointment into the eye (see p. 12), and patch overnight or at least for a few hours (see p. 174). Prescribe warm compresses and ophthalmic antibiotic ointment at bedtime or more often if desired for 1 week, informing the patient that some drainage may occur for a few days. Recommend nonaspirin analgesics for patients with any residual discomfort and schedule the patient for follow-up in 5 to 7 days.

Dispose of soiled materials in an appropriate infectious waste disposal container; dispose of the needle and syringe in a puncture-resistant biohazard sharps container.

■ **Interpretation.** Postprocedure lid edema, tenderness, and redness are expected. Following incision and curettage of chalazion and with subsequent healing, the lid will resume its normal appearance and the preprocedure signs and symptoms will resolve. Occasionally, a small granuloma detectable with lid palpation may remain. A white, fibrous scar will develop on the palpebral conjunctival side, noted on lid eversion.

If pinpoint cautery is used, a small plume of smoke followed by small focal areas of eschar will appear as cauterization is performed.

The diagnosis and treatment of recurrent chalazion in the same lid location, especially in the elderly, should be made cautiously as sebaceous cell carcinoma can mimic chalazion. More extensive surgery may be required for recurrent chalazion, multiple lesions, or a poorly visualized chalazion sac. Subconjunctival total excision with biopsy is recommended for any suspicious lesion.

With experience and confidence, consider a postprocedure follow-up only if residual or new symptoms occur, or if the lesion recurs. In the event of the latter, total subconjunctival excision of the chalazion may be required.

■ **Contraindications/Complications.** Medical contraindications to epinephrine should be noted in the preprocedure workup and avoided by using plain lidocaine for infiltrative anesthesia, especially in patients with heart disease, hypertension and thyrotoxicosis. Any history of sensitivity to anesthetics, antibiotics, or analgesics should also be determined in the initial patient history. The topical anesthetic agents may produce local hypersensitivity reactions, including toxic keratitis.

The major systemic side effects caused by local anesthetics are excitation of the central nervous system (CNS) and depression of the cardiovascular system. Initial CNS symptoms of anesthetic toxicity commonly include drowsiness, light-headedness, dizziness, and a metallic taste followed by nausea, garrulousness, perioral numbness, tingling, diplopia, and tinnitus. The first sign of cardiovascular toxicity is typically a reduction in blood pressure. Tremors, muscle twitching, seizures, loss of consciousness, respiratory depression, and circulatory collapse have been reported. As a result, when performing injections, it is important to ensure the prompt availability of proper equipment and personnel trained to address medical emergencies, ranging from vasovagal syncope to cardiac arrest.

Horizontal conjunctival-tarsal incisions should be avoided, as these frequently lead to scar tissue formation in multiple meibomian ducts with subsequent gland blockage, rupture, and recurrent chalazia. Preprocedure evaluation for any accompanying cellulitis should always be performed, especially if erythema or pain is present. Systemic antibiotic treatment may be required to resolve the cellulitis before the lid procedure is scheduled. Excessive local anesthetic infiltration should be avoided, as it can distort the tissue and make the incision more difficult. Caution should be used with all injections, especially in difficult-to-reach areas, to avoid perforation of the desired tissue and unintentional injection of another, as serious side effects can result.

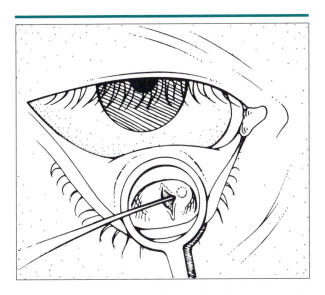

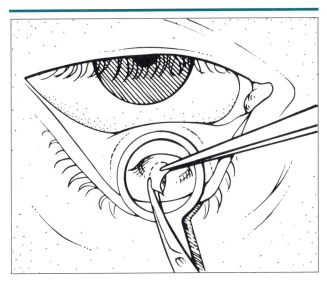

5. Insert the curette into the newly created pocket opening and, using multidirectional movements, attempt to vigorously sweep all granulomatous material out through the incision.

6. If better drainage is needed, grasp the edge of the incision with sterile forceps and cut away a small elliptical piece of the flap.

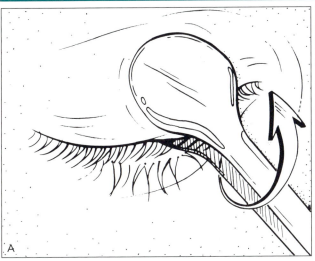

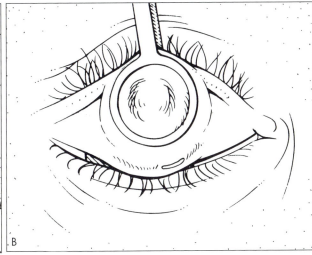

7. A. For chalazia of the upper lid, pull the lid away from the globe and straddle both sides of the lid with the clamp, attempting to center the lesion.

7. B. Push gently inward and rotate the clamp upward, everting the lid. Recenter the lesion if indicated.

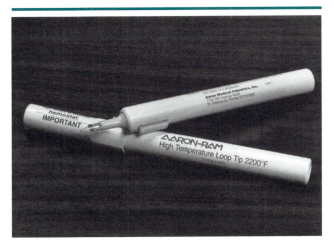

8. The disposable cautery unit is operated by depressing the side power button with the thumb. After the tip glows brightly, lightly pinpoint cauterize the area of chalazion removal to control bleeding if desired or necessary.

III Suggested Readings

Bartlett JD: Eyelid procedures, in Eskridge JB, Amos JF, Bartlett JD (eds): *Clinical Procedures in Optometry.* Philadelphia, Lippincott, 1991, pp 397–400.

Bartlett JD: Ophthalmic drug delivery, in Bartlett JD, Jaanus SD (eds): *Clinical Ocular Pharmacology,* ed 3. Boston, Butterworth-Heinemann, 1995, pp 47–74.

Bartlett JD, Melore GG: Diseases of the eyelids, in Bartlett JD, Jaanus SD (eds): *Clinical Ocular Pharmacology,* ed 3. Boston, Butterworth-Heinemann, 1995, pp 561–600.

Beyer-Machuk CK, von Norden GK: *Atlas of Ophthalmic Surgery.* Vol 1, *Lid, Orbit an Extraocular Muscles.* New York, Thiene-Stratton, 1985, pp 1.119–1.120.

Bright DC: Dermatologic conditions of the eyelids and face. *Optom Clin* 1991;**1**:89–102.

Cahill KV, Burns JA: Benign eyelid lesions. *J Dermatol Surg Oncol* 1992;**18**:1051–1055.

Carlson NB, Kurtz D, Heath DA, Hines C: Ocular Health assessment, in *Clinical Procedures for Ocular Examination,* ed 2. Norwalk, CT, Appleton & Lange, 1996, pp 221–322.

Catania LJ: Diagnoses of the eyelids, lacrimal system, and orbit, in *Primary Care of the Anterior Segment,* ed 2. Norwalk, CT, Appleton & Lange, 1995, pp 101–123.

English FP, Cohn D, Groeneveld ER: Demodectic mites and chalazion. *Am J Ophthalmol* 1985;**100**:482–483. Letter.

Habif TP: Dermatologic surgical procedures, in *Clinical Dermatology.* St. Louis, Mosby, 1996, pp 808–819.

Hersh PS: *Ophthalmic Surgical Procedures.* Boston, Little, Brown, 1988, pp 33–36.

Hurwitz JJ, Johnson D, Howarth D, Molgat YM: Experimental treatment of eyelashes with high-frequency radio wave electrosurgery. *Can J Ophthalmol* 1993;**28**:62–64.

Leone CR, Hollsten DA: Management of conjunctival diseases and chalazion, in Stewart WB (ed): *Surgery of the Eyelid, Orbit, and Lacrimal System. Ophthalmology Monographs,* vol 1. American Academy of Ophthalmology, 1993, pp 136–157.

Marines HM, Patrinely JR: Benign eyelid tumors. *Ophthalmol Clin North Am* 1992;**5**:183–185, 243–260.

McCulley JP: Meibomitis, in Kaufman HE, Barron BA, McDonald MB, Waltman SR (eds): *The Cornea.* New York, Churchill Livingstone, 1988, pp 125–138.

Melore GG: Treating eyelid and conjunctival conditions. *Optom Today,* September 1995, pp 33–38.

Melore GG: Verruca and their treatment. *South J Optom* 1985;**3**:20–22.

Soll DB, Winslow R: Surgery of the eyelids, in Duane T (ed): *Clinical Ophthalmology.* Hagerstown, MD, Harper & Row, Vol V, 1982, vol 5, pp 6–9.

White GE, Rinehart CA: How to handle eyelid problems. *Rev Optom,* May 1986, pp 75–82.

Lacrimal System Procedures

34 Schirmer Tear Test

■ **Description/Indications.** The Schirmer Tear Test is a gross measure of the aqueous volume (quantity) of the tears. It is an indicator of tear production. Although not extremely sensitive, it is easy to perform, and when used in conjunction with other tear tests (see p. 44), tear meniscus evaluation (see p. 30), corneal vital dye staining (see p. 48), and a detailed patient history, valuable information concerning tear deficiency (keratoconjuncitivis sicca, or KCS) is obtained. The test may be used for patients complaining of dry eye symptoms such as stinging, burning, foreign body sensation, tearing, and itching. The test is also helpful in documenting pseudo-epiphora, excess tearing due to ocular irritation induced by dry eye.

The Schirmer Tear Test is conducted using a pair of commercially available 5 × 40-mm strips of sterile Whatman no. 41 filter paper. When positioned in the inferior cul-de-sac, capillary action is responsible for wetting of the strips by the tears. Measurement of the length of the strips moistened by the tears is viewed as an indirect indicator of tear production.

Two types of Schirmer Tear Test strips are available. The plain white strips are unmarked, and one corner of the square end of one strip in the pair is cut off to identify the strip for the right eye (Fig. 1A). Another style of strips is marked with a line of blue dye that travels with the tear front to more easily visualize the length of tear wetting (Fig. 1B). These strips are also premarked in mm for measurement. An "R" and "L" denote the strips for the right and left eyes, respectively.

There are three variations of the Schirmer Tear Test. The Schirmer I Tear Test measures the combined reflex and basic secretory tear levels because topical anesthetic is not used. The Basic Tear Secretion Test is performed after the instillation of topical ophthalmic anesthetic solution and measures the basic secretory tear level by eliminating reflex tearing produced by ocular stimulation. This test is especially useful in individuals who find Test I irritating or uncomfortable. It is also useful in individuals who wet the strip fully in Test I, yet complain of dry eye symptoms. The Schirmer II Tear Test measures reflex tear secretion, and is done by instilling topical ophthalmic anesthetic solution and irritating the unanesthetized nasal mucosa with a cotton-tipped applicator to stimulate the lacrimal gland to produce tears. This test is performed infrequently because a lack of reflex tearing is an unusual cause of clinical problems.

■ **Instrumentation.** Schirmer Tear Test strips, topical ophthalmic anesthetic solution, cotton-tipped applicators, millimeter rule (optional).

■ **Technique.**

Schirmer I Tear Test: Prepare the strips while they are still in the package by folding the rounded end at the indentation, approximately 5 mm from the tip. Open the plastic package and remove the strip for the right eye, holding the strip by the square-cornered end. Ask the patient to look up, gently retract the right lower lid, and insert the strip into the inferior cul-de-sac, placing the fold at the lid margin (Fig. 2A). Position the strip so that it is at the lateral third of the eyelid with the longer end hanging downward over the lower eyelid. As the strip is inserted, avoid touching any part of the eye. After inserting the remaining strip into the left eye, the patient may gently close the eyes (Fig. 2B). Alternatively, the patient may blink as desired but should avoid forceful lid closure. Dim the lights in the room to enhance patient comfort.

Leave the strips in place for 5 minutes or until the strips are completely wet, whichever occurs first. Ask the patient to look up, remove the strips from the inferior cul-de-sac, and measure the length of each strip that has been wetted by the tears, beginning the measurement at the notch. A measuring guide is found on the Schirmer strip package. A template of the strip next to the guide allows for accurate measurement of the amount of strip wetting (Fig. 3). Alternatively, a millimeter rule may be used to measure the length of the strip wetted by the tears.

Basic Tear Secretion Test: Instill topical ophthalmic anesthetic solution into both eyes, wait for a few minutes for the drops to dissipate, and then proceed with this test the same as with the Schirmer I Tear Test. Leave the strips in place for 5 minutes or until they are completely wet, whichever occurs first.

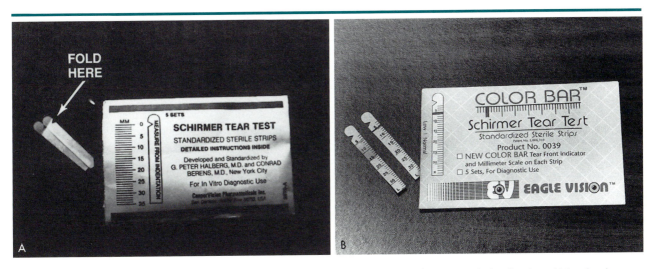

1. **A.** A package of plain Schirmer Tear Test strips. **B.** Another style of Schirmer Tear Test strips is marked with a line of blue dye that travels with the tear front to more easily visualize the length of tear wetting (note left strip).

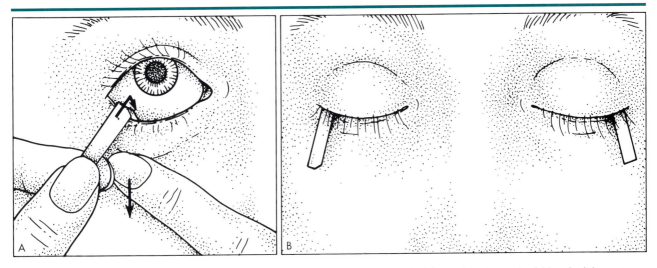

2. **A.** The Schirmer Tear Test strip is inserted into the inferior cul-de-sac at the outer third of the eyelid, placing the fold at the lid margin.
B. The Schirmer Tear Test strips are in position during the procedure with the patient gently closing both eyes.

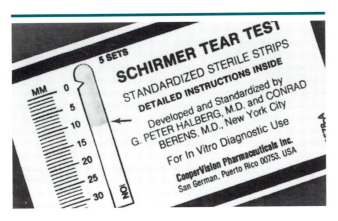

3. The length of each strip that has been wetted by the tears is measured using the ruler and template on the Schirmer Tear Test strip package.

Schirmer II Tear Test: Instill topical ophthalmic anesthetic solution into both eyes, wait for a few minutes for the drops to dissipate, and then insert the strips the same as with the Schirmer I Tear Test. Begin timing the test. Insert a cotton-tipped applicator into one nostril and gently irritate the ipsilateral nasal mucosa for 10 to 15 seconds; repeat for the other nostril (Fig. 4). Leave the strips in place for 2 minutes, then measure the length of the strip that is wetted by the tears.

■ **Interpretation.** A normal eye will wet between 10 and 30 mm of the strip when the Schirmer I Tear Test or the Basic Secretion Test is performed. The Basic Secretion Test will usually produce slightly lower readings because the reflex component is eliminated, but a normal eye will still produce more than 10 mm of wetting. Values between 5 and 10 mm are considered borderline and need to be rechecked. A result of less than 5 mm is considered to be suggestive of KCS.

If the Schirmer I Tear Test is abnormal, with results less than 5 mm, there is no need to perform the Basic Secretion Test. If the Schirmer I Tear Test is normal (the strip is wet more than 10 mm), a Basic Secretion Test may be performed to determine to what degree the strip is wet due to reflex corneal stimulation or to basic tear secretion.

A normal finding on the Schirmer I Tear Test with an abnormal finding on the Basic Secretion Test may also be indicative of a patient with KCS and pseudo-epiphora.

The Schirmer II Tear Test is evaluated differently. A reading of less than 15 mm in 2 minutes is considered to be diagnostic of a problem with reflex secretion. There should be an increase in wetting of the strip in the Schirmer II Tear Test compared to the Basic Secretion Test if reflex secretion is intact.

The results of Schirmer tear testing tend to be variable and difficult to reproduce. The Schirmer Tear Tests are not sensitive, and are best used in conjunction with other tests to obtain a diagnostic picture of KCS. When repeated over a period of time, a pattern often occurs that is diagnostic of KCS.

■ **Contraindications/Complications.** The Schirmer Tear Tests are performed before applanation tonometry or any other procedure that may irritate the cornea. If the topical ophthalmic anesthetic solution is not allowed to dissipate before inserting the strips when performing the Basic Tear Secretion Test or the Schirmer II Tear Test, the amount of tears in the eye may be overestimated. If the patient experiences minor ocular irritation following the Schirmer Tear Tests, artificial tears may be used.

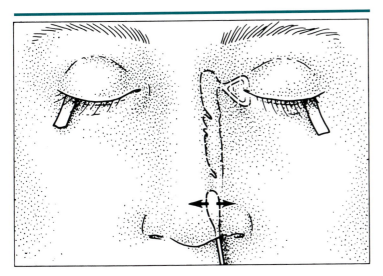

4. After instilling topical ophthalmic anesthetic solution and inserting the strips, a cotton-tipped applicator is inserted into the nostril to irritate the nasal mucosa for the Schirmer II Tear Test. The strips are left in place for 2 minutes.

35 Punctal Regurgitation/Lacrimal Sac Palpation

■ **Description/Indications.** An obstruction along the course of the nasolacrimal drainage system will affect the excretion of tears from the eye. Epiphora, an abnormal overflow of tears down the cheek, is the primary symptom associated with malfunction of the tear drainage system. Causes of nasolacrimal obstruction include anatomic malformations, debris such as mucus or dacryoliths, infection of adjacent tissues (cellulitis), or infection of the lacrimal sac (dacryocystitis).

Two important types of dacryocystitis are recognized clinically. Acute dacryocystitis describes that condition in which bacterial infection of the lacrimal sac is present and accompanied by the cardinal signs of acute inflammation. Chronic dacryocystitis refers to that condition in which mechanical blockage of the proximal end of the nasolacrimal system produces unilateral epiphora in the absence of acute bacterial inflammation or infection.

Palpation of the lacrimal sac is a useful procedure for evaluating patients with suspected dacryocystitis. When gentle pressure is applied to the sac area, regurgitation of discharge or debris from the punctum may occur. In addition, palpation of the sac within the lacrimal fossa allows the examiner to assess for masses or lumps.

■ **Instrumentation.** Slit lamp biomicroscope, sterile cotton-tipped applicators.

■ **Technique.** With the patient seated comfortably behind the slit lamp biomicroscope, place your index finger on the medial canthal ligament so it overlies the body of the lacrimal sac (Fig. 1). Exert gentle pressure over the sac while observing the punctum for discharge (Fig. 2). A cotton-tipped applicator may be used instead of your finger to apply gentle pressure on the sac (Fig. 3). Use of the cotton-tipped applicator may be preferable so that the pressure can be more locally applied.

■ **Interpretation.** The regurgitation of mucus or pus from the punctum when pressure is applied during palpation is indicative of obstruction, infection, and/or inflammation of the lacrimal sac. The accompanying signs and symptoms differentiate acute from chronic dacryocystitis as the cause of epiphora. In acute dacryocystitis, the lacrimal sac is distended due to infection, and the overlying skin is erythematous and warm to the touch. The pain is more intense with palpation of the sac, and a mucopurulent or purulent discharge will regurgitate from the punctum. If epiphora continues after treatment and resolution of acute dacryocystitis, a blockage may be present that predisposed the patient to acute dacryocystitis or a blockage may have occurred as a result of the infection. Dilation and irrigation of the nasolacrimal system (see p. 130) will confirm the blockage and dislodge it if possible.

When unilateral epiphora has been a problem for weeks to months, chronic dacryocystitis is suspected. The sac will not appear inflamed or infected, but mucoid regurgitation upon palpation is common. Lacrimal dilation and irrigation of the lacrimal system is then performed to confirm the blockage and dislodge it if possible (see p. 130). If blood regurgitates through the punctum, especially with a palpable mass, a lacrimal sac tumor should be ruled out.

■ **Contraindications/Complications.** Patient discomfort is common with acute dacryocystitis, so the indications for lacrimal sac palpation should be considered when evaluating this condition.

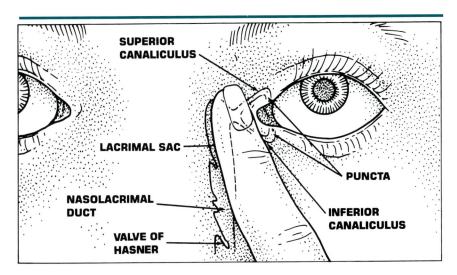

1. The index finger is placed over the lacrimal sac, pressing gently to palpate the lacrimal sac.

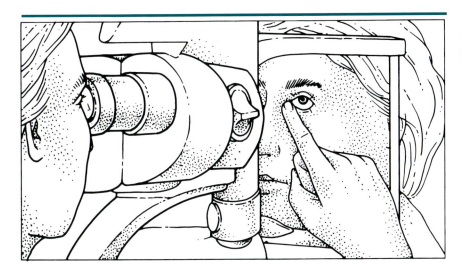

2. The lacrimal sac is palpated while viewing through the biomicroscope for the regurgitation of pus or mucus.

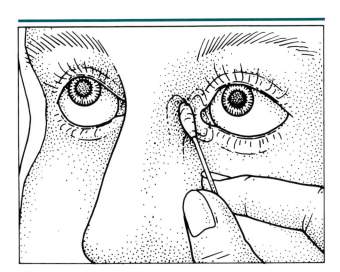

3. The lacrimal sac is palpated with a cotton-tipped applicator while the punctum is viewed with a biomicroscope.

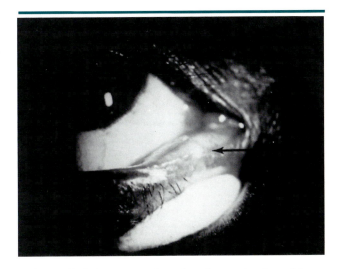

4. A mucoid discharge regurgitates from the punctum (arrow) in a case of chronic dacryocystitis.

36 Lacrimal Dilation and Irrigation

■ **Description/Indications.** Epiphora, an abnormal overflow of tears down the cheek, is a common complaint that requires careful investigation. It is often the result of actual or functional blockage within the lacrimal excretory system leading to improper tear drainage. Epiphora may be constant or intermittent, and the extent of the blockage determines the frequency of tearing. A lacrimal dilation and irrigation (D&I) procedure will help determine the patency of the lacrimal excretory system. In addition, a D&I may open a functionally blocked system by causing the release of a mucous plug or concretion. Thus, the procedure has both diagnostic and therapeutic implications. An important clinical indication for lacrimal D&I is suspected chronic dacryocystitis (see p. 128).

Lacrimal D&I is a two-stage procedure involving initial dilation ("D") of the punctum followed by irrigation ("I") of the nasolacrimal system with saline injected through a lacrimal cannula. The punctum is usually small, and needs to be temporarily enlarged with a lacrimal dilator to accommodate the lacrimal cannula. The epithelium lining the puncta and canaliculi overlies a base of elastic tissue that allows these structures to expand to approximately three times their normal diameter.

Dilators are thin, cylindrical probes that taper to a narrow tip (Fig. 1). Dilators are available in different sizes; thin and medium tapered dilators are used for most individuals. The lacrimal cannula is a short, blunted needle that is attached to a sterile disposable syringe and used to irrigate saline into the canaliculus (Fig. 1). Although they are available in different sizes and shapes, a commonly used cannula is straight with a diameter equivalent to a 23G needle.

■ **Instrumentation.** Lacrimal dilator(s), lacrimal cannula, 3 or 5-cc sterile disposable syringe, topical ophthalmic anesthetic solution, cotton pledget, sterile cotton-tipped applicators, sterile saline solution.

■ **Technique.** Prepare the syringe and cannula before beginning the procedure. Open the sterile package of a 3 or 5-cc plastic disposable syringe and remove the preattached needle or plastic cap using a slight unscrewing motion. Attach the lacrimal cannula to the tip of the syringe using a slight screwing motion. Remove the plunger and fill the syringe with sterile saline (Fig. 2A). Insert the plunger back into the barrel of the syringe and eject any remaining air from the syringe along with some of the saline. Leave the plunger in a position midway down the barrel so that the fingers may easily access the plunger to depress it while the remaining fingers hold the syringe in place (Fig. 2B).

Instill two drops of topical ophthalmic anesthetic solution into the conjunctival sac. Place an anesthetic-soaked pledget such as a sterile gauze pad or cotton-tipped applicator over the punctum for a few minutes (see p. 8) to achieve effective anesthesia (Fig. 3).

Use the index finger of your nondominant hand to gently pull the lower lid temporally and expose the inferior punctum. Use your dominant hand to hold the lacrimal dilator between your thumb, index, and middle fingers; use your remaining fingers to firmly support it on the cheek or bridge of the nose. Insert the tip of the thin tapered dilator 2 mm into the inferior punctum and vertical canaliculus, keeping it perpendicular to the lid margin (Fig. 4A). Roll the dilator between your fingers to gently expand the punctal orifice (Fig. 4B). A circular stretching motion can also be used. Once the punctum widens, switch to the medium taper dilator if necessary, rolling it back and forth to sufficiently enlarge the punctum to accommodate the cannula (Fig. 4C). Some clinicians further insert the dilator into the horizontal canaliculus to widen the punctal opening more fully.

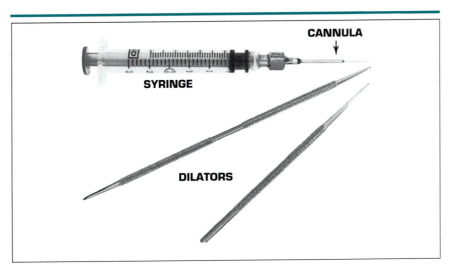

1. Instruments used for lacrimal dilation and irrigation: sterile disposable syringe, lacrimal dilators, lacrimal cannula.

2. A. (below left) The plunger is removed and the syringe is filled with sterile saline. B. (below center) The plunger is inserted back into the barrel of the syringe and any air present is ejected along with some of the saline. The plunger is left in a position midway down the barrel so that the fingers may easily access the plunger.

3. (below right) After instilling topical anesthetic drops, an anesthetic-soaked pledget such as a gauze pad is placed over the punctum for a few minutes to achieve more effective anesthesia.

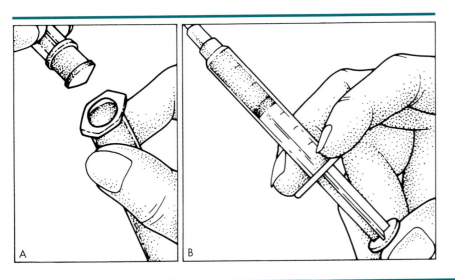

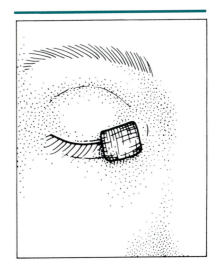

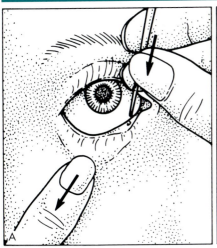

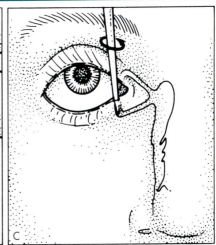

4. A. The index finger of the nondominant hand is used to gently pull the lid temporally and expose the punctum. The tip of the thin tapered dilator is inserted 2 mm into the inferior punctum and vertical canaliculus, keeping it perpendicular to the lid margin.

4. B. The dilator is rolled between the fingers to gently expand the punctal orifice. A circular stretching motion can also be used.

4. C. Once the punctum widens, a switch is made to the medium taper dilator if necessary, rolling it back and forth to sufficiently enlarge the punctum to accommodate the cannula. Note how the punctal opening has enlarged.

Remove the dilator and insert the lacrimal cannula perpendicular to the lid margin (Fig. 5A). The hand holding the syringe needs good support, provided by resting the free fingers on the cheek or bridge of the nose. Let the cannula slide downward 2 mm into the vertical canaliculus, and then gently turn the syringe horizontally so that the cannula is directed nasally. Insert it into the horizontal canaliculus another 3 to 4 mm, keeping the lid slightly taut to allow easy access (Fig. 5B). Insert the cannula far enough into the canaliculus so it will stay in place as irrigation is performed.

In some individuals the punctum does not stay stretched once the dilator is removed. If this occurs and the punctum is too small to allow insertion of the cannula, dilate the punctum again and attempt to insert the cannula more quickly after removing the dilator. An assistant may facilitate this part of the procedure by providing efficient transfer of the instrumentation.

Once the cannula is inserted, eject saline from the syringe by exerting slow, gentle pressure on the plunger (Fig. 6). Have the patient signal when saline is tasted in the back of the throat or felt in the nose. Once this occurs, withdraw the cannula. It is helpful to ask the patient to swallow after irrigating approximately 0.5 cc of saline into the nasolacrimal system to avoid a coughing reflex when saline contacts the nasopharynx.

If saline regurgitates through the superior punctum during irrigation (Fig. 7A), have an assistant occlude the superior punctum with a medium taper dilator, and then irrigate again to attempt to release the blockage (Fig. 7B). Alternatively, occlude the superior punctum by using a cotton-tipped applicator to press the superior punctum against the orbital rim, and then irrigate again. Because most blockages in the lacrimal excretory system are located in the lower canaliculus or inferior to this, performing D&I through the superior punctum is generally not necessary.

Some minor irritation of the tissues lining the nasolacrimal system is possible following D&I. In difficult cases or where irritation is suspected, prescribe a topical ophthalmic antibiotic/steroid drop, instilled two to four times a day for up to 3 days.

■ **Interpretation.** The normal outcome of lacrimal D&I is for the saline to flow unimpeded through the nasolacrimal system, and the patient tastes or feels the saline in the back of the throat or nose (Fig. 6). This result indicates that blockage is not present and another cause of the epiphora should be evaluated, that the blockage was released during the D&I, or that a functional blockage is present that may cause epiphora under the low-pressure situation of normal tear drainage. The high-pressure situation of D&I forces saline down a narrow channel that may be too constricted to allow enough drainage under some conditions. The Jones Dye Tests (see p. 134) are used to help differentiate functional blockages from patent systems.

If saline regurgitates through the superior punctum as the inferior punctum is irrigated, a blockage likely exists in the common canaliculus or lacrimal sac (Fig. 7A). The saline may be clear, or debris may be noted in the regurgitated fluid. If saline regurgitates from the inferior punctum as it is irrigated, a blockage is likely present in the inferior canaliculus (Fig. 8).

It may be difficult to move the plunger during irrigation if a blockage is present in the excretory system. Continued gentle pressure to the plunger for 10 to 15 seconds may then cause the release of a mucous plug or dacryolith. The release of the pressure will be felt by the ease with which the plunger can now be depressed. Alternatively, the plunger may be difficult to depress if the cannula has been inserted too far into the system so that it touches the lacrimal bone. In this event, withdrawing the cannula slightly will allow for irrigation of saline as the plunger is depressed.

■ **Contraindications/Complications.** Lacrimal D&I should not be performed during active acute dacryocystitis. Good support of the hand manipulating the dilator and syringe/cannula avoids extraneous tugging on the lid tissue, which can add to patient sensation. Patients may report a "fullness" or discomfort if a blockage is present that will not release during irrigation. Greatly excessive force used during irrigation could result in tissue damage. If the blockage is not relieved by lacrimal D&I or the blockage recurs after repeated procedures, more specialized evaluation is indicated.

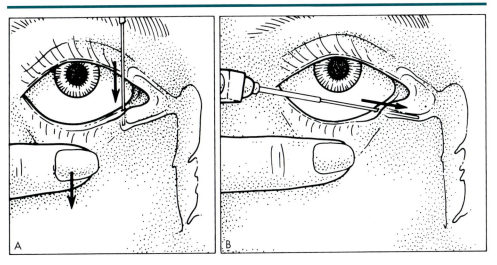

5. **A.** After removing the dilator, the lacrimal cannula is inserted perpendicular to the lid margin, letting it slide downward 2 mm into the vertical canaliculus.
B. The syringe is gently turned horizontally so that the cannula is directed nasally. The cannula is inserted into the horizontal canaliculus another 3 to 4 mm, keeping the lid slightly taut to allow easy access.

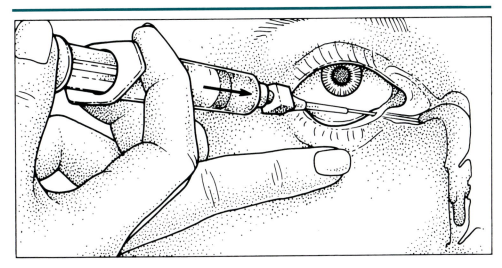

6. Gentle pressure is applied to the plunger to eject saline into the lacrimal excretory system. In the normal result, the saline flows through the system unimpeded, and the patient tastes or feels it in the back of the throat or nose.

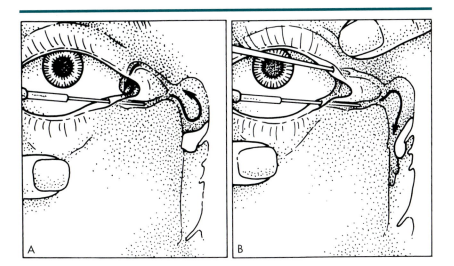

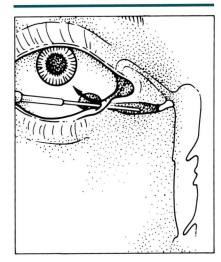

7. **A.** If saline regurgitates through the superior punctum as the inferior punctum is irrigated, a blockage likely exists in the common canaliculus or lacrimal sac. **B.** In that event, an assistant occludes the superior punctum with a medium taper dilator, and the irrigation is repeated in an attempt to dislodge the blockage.

8. If saline regurgitates from the inferior punctum as it is being irrigated, a blockage is likely present in the inferior canaliculus.

37

Jones Dye Tests 1 and 2

Description/Indications. The Jones Dye Tests 1 (primary) and 2 (secondary) are performed to determine the patency of the lacrimal drainage system. The tests are indicated when epiphora is present and the outcome of the lacrimal dilation and irrigation test is normal (see p. 130). In this situation the Jones Dye Tests will ascertain if there is a relative functional blockage of the nasolacrimal system. With a functional blockage the nasolacrimal system is open but one or more channels are too narrow to allow for effective excretion of tears under normal conditions, producing epiphora.

The Jones Dye Tests are performed by instilling fluorescein sodium vital dye into the eye and determining if it travels the length of the lacrimal drainage system.

Instrumentation. Sterile fluorescein sodium strips, sterile cotton-tipped applicators, Burton ultraviolet lamp, lacrimal dilator, lacrimal cannula, 3 or 5-cc sterile disposable syringe, sterile saline solution, white facial tissue.

Technique

Jones Dye Test 1 (Primary Dye Test): Wet four fluorescein sodium strips with sterile saline solution and instill the fluorescein by touching the inferior palpebral conjunctiva near the punctum (Fig. 1A). Do not use topical ophthalmic anesthetic solution. Blot any excess fluorescein dripping down the lower eyelid but do not reduce the volume of the lacrimal lake. Instruct the patient to sit quietly, keep the eyes open, blink normally, and not rub the eyes. After 5 minutes ask the patient to occlude the nostril on the opposite side to the eye with the fluorescein sodium and use the other nostril to blow into a white facial tissue. Inspect the tissue for evidence of fluorescein. A Burton ultraviolet lamp may aid in the inspection for fluorescein. If fluorescein is evident, the test is deemed to be positive and the lacrimal system is patent and functioning.

If fluorescein is not present in the facial tissue, wait 5 more minutes and repeat the procedure. If fluorescein is still not evident, insert a cotton-tipped applicator approximately 1 cm into the nose and hold it in place against the inferior turbinate for 10 seconds (Fig. 1B). Remove the cotton-tipped applicator and view it under the Burton lamp to detect fluorescein dye (Fig. 1C).

If fluorescein dye is not visible on the cotton-tipped applicator, gently massage the lacrimal sac and again ask the patient, with the opposite nostril occluded, to blow into a white facial tissue. If fluorescein sodium dye is evident, it indicates a narrowing or partial obstruction of the nasolacrimal duct. If no fluorescein dye is evident, a functional blockage is still possible and the Jones Dye Test 2 (Secondary Dye Test) is performed.

Jones Dye Test 2 (Secondary Dye Test): Jones Dye Test 2 is performed immediately after the primary dye test by irrigating the nasolacrimal system (see p. 130) with saline solution through the inferior punctum using a lacrimal cannula (Fig. 2). Recover some of the saline solution by having the patient lean forward and expectorate into a basin or blow the nose into a white facial tissue. Examine the solution or tissue with the Burton lamp to inspect for fluorescein sodium.

Interpretation. The Jones Dye Tests will have a positive or negative outcome. In a positive Jones Dye Test 1, fluorescein dye travels through the nasolacrimal system and is retrieved, indicating that the system is patent (Fig. 3A). In a negative Jones Dye Test 1 or 2, fluorescein dye is not retrieved (Figs. 3B, 3C). In a positive Jones Dye Test 2, fluorescein dye is retrieved after the lacrimal system is irrigated, indicating that the system has a functional blockage (Fig. 3D). Because fluorescein successfully entered the lacrimal sac, the functional blockage is likely present distal to that point. If clear saline is recovered during the Jones Dye Test 2, a functional blockage exists that is nearer to the punctum and canaliculus because fluorescein dye never entered the nasolacrimal system.

False positives in Jones Dye Testing are rare, but false negatives are possible because of the technical problems in retrieving the fluorescein dye. As a result, although a positive test indicates a patent and functioning lacrimal excretory system, a negative test is inconclusive and does not always indicate that the system is obstructed.

Contraindications/Complications. Jones Dye Testing with irrigation should not be performed during active acute dacryocystitis. Greatly excessive force used during lacrimal dilation and irrigation could result in tissue damage.

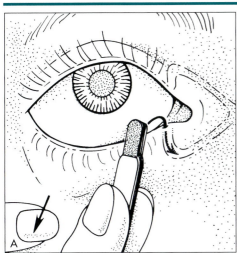
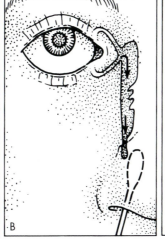

1. **A.** Jones Dye Test 1: four fluorescein sodium strips are stacked together, moistened with sterile saline, and touched to the inferior palpebral conjunctiva near the punctum to fill the lacrimal lake with fluorescein. **B.** A secondary method of retrieving the fluorescein dye is to insert a cotton-tipped applicator 1 cm into the nose and hold it against the inferior turbinate for 10 seconds. **C.** The cotton-tipped applicator is inspected under ultraviolet light to detect fluorescein dye.

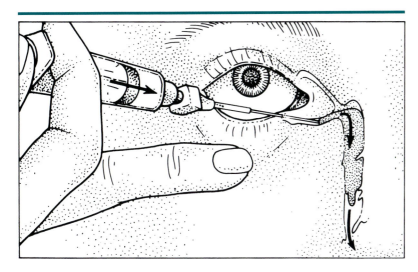

2. Jones Dye Test 2: the nasolacrimal system is irrigated with a lacrimal cannula after the instillation of fluorescein dye. The irrigated fluid is inspected for fluorescein.

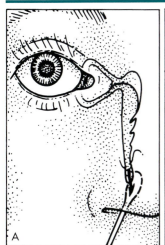
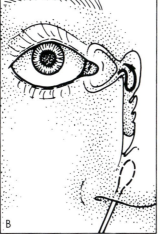

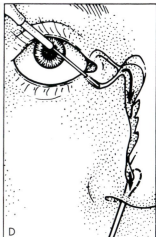

3. **A.** During the Jones Dye Test 1, fluorescein dye is draining through a patent lacrimal excretory system. The test is positive because fluorescein dye is retrieved on the cotton-tipped applicator. **B.** An example of a negative Jones Dye Test 1. A blockage in the nasolacrimal duct impedes the flow of dye. **C.** Another example of a negative Jones Dye Test 1. A stenotic nasolacrimal duct impedes the flow of fluorescein dye. **D.** An example of a positive Jones Dye Test 2. Lacrimal irrigation forces the fluorescein dye through a narrow but patent nasolacrimal duct.

38 Intracanalicular Collagen Implant

■ **Description/Indications.** Dry eye, or keratoconjunctivitis sicca (KCS), is a common ocular condition in elderly patients, contact lens wearers, patients with autoimmune and allergy-related disease, and others with tear film compromise caused by medication or the environment. When ocular signs and symptoms are not acceptably relieved with lubricating drops and ointments, alternative therapies are considered.

Punctal occlusion techniques are frequently the next line of treatment for patients with moderate to severe KCS. Prior to selecting permanent or reversible punctal occlusion, one or multiple trials of dissolvable intracanalicular collagen implants is a reasonable diagnostic approach to demonstrate to the patient the possibility of success, as well as to ascertain whether complete occlusion might result in chronic epiphora or other sequellae. Collagen implants can be easily inserted into the upper or lower puncta of one or both eyes. Once in the canaliculus, the implant expands and temporarily blocks up to 80% of the punctal drainage, thus retaining more of the natural tears in the cul-de-sac. Patient symptoms and any adverse reactions are evaluated prior to the implants dissolving in a few days. If signs and/or symptoms do improve, reversible silicone punctal plugs (see p. 140) or permanent punctal occlusion (see p. 144) can be considered.

At present, collagen implants are available in 1.6 and 2.0-mm lengths, and in diameters ranging from 0.2 to 0.6 mm, in 0.1-mm steps. Implants 0.3 and 0.4 mm in diameter are most commonly employed. One brand of collagen implants incorporates a more smoothly polished rounded surface on both ends to facilitate insertion.

■ **Instrumentation.** Sterile intracanalicular collagen implants, sterile jeweler's forceps, slit lamp biomicroscope, head loupe (optional), topical ophthalmic anesthetic solution, sterile cotton-tipped applicators.

■ **Technique.** Prepare the patient by explaining the technique and anesthetizing the punctum with topical ophthalmic anesthetic solution. Place two drops of anesthetic solution in the eye at the punctal area. For greater anesthetic effect, hold a sterile, anesthetic-saturated cotton-tipped applicator directly against the punctum for 10 to 15 seconds (see p. 8). Allow a minute to pass to ensure good anesthesia.

Remove an appropriately sized implant from its sterile foam holder with the jeweler's forceps while viewing through the slit lamp biomicroscope prior to positioning the patient, or by using a head loupe for magnification if needed (Fig. 1A). Grasp the implant firmly by the exposed end with the jeweler's forceps and pull it straight outward from the foam holder (Fig. 1B).

Position the patient comfortably at the slit lamp, ensuring that the forehead is pressed forward at all times. To insert an implant in the inferior punctum, ask the patient to look up. Place the index finger of your nondominant hand below the lid margin and retract the lid slightly to expose the punctum. Holding the implant with the jeweler's forceps, slowly approach the punctum, aligning the implant with the punctal orifice, perpendicular to the lid margin (Fig. 2). Steady your hand if needed on the patient's nose or cheek.

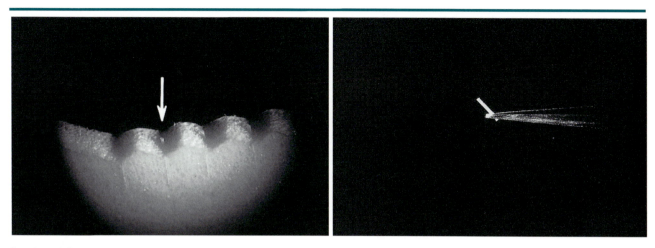

1. (above left) The intracanalicular collagen implants come in a foam insert inside sterile packaging (arrows). A jeweler's forceps (above right) is used to grasp the end of the implant and pull it straight out from the foam holder.

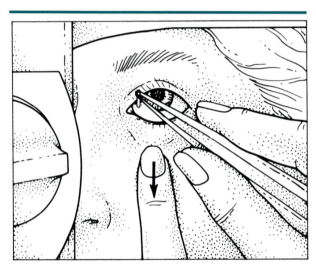

2. With the patient seated at the slit lamp and looking upward, the lower lid is retracted slightly to expose the punctum. The implant is held by the forceps and brought toward the inferior punctum for insertion.

For positioning in the vertical canaliculus, insert the end of the implant into the punctum as far as possible (Fig. 3). Release the implant, close the tips of the forceps, and gently tap the implant downward (Fig. 4A). Continue to push downward until the implant is just barely visible below the punctum (Fig. 4B). If difficulty is experienced after a few tries, consider using a smaller diameter or shorter implant.

For positioning in the horizontal canaliculus, place lateral traction on the lid to gently straighten the angle between the vertical and horizontal canaliculi. Use the tips of the closed forceps to push the implant into the horizontal canaliculus (Fig. 4C). Place an implant superiorly in the vertical or horizontal canaliculus using a similar technique, after instructing the patient to look downward. Before dismissing the patient, it may be helpful to perform a repeat slit lamp examination after a few minutes to ensure that the implants have not extruded.

This insertion procedure is performed by some practitioners outside of the slit lamp for initial placement, with or without use of a head loupe, and then the slit lamp is used for placement inspection. Insertion of the implants may be facilitated by an assistant gently retracting the lids using a cotton-tipped applicator to expose the puncta.

■ **Interpretation.** Instruct the patient to reduce the use of tear supplements as much as possible and return in 5 to 7 days to evaluate the success of the collagen implant trial. Patients frequently report improvement in their symptoms within a few days of insertion, which indicates that more permanent punctal occlusion may be considered. A monocular trial of collagen implants is frequently used for comparison of symptoms. Improvement of objective signs such as dry eye-induced keratitis may not be noted before the collagen implants dissolve.

If constant epiphora occurs after insertion of the implants in the upper and lower puncta, remind the patient that it is only temporary until the implants dissolve in a few days. Consider another trial of an implant in a single punctum in one eye to potentially eliminate the epiphora. If this is unsuccessful in reducing the epiphora, permanent occlusion is best avoided. Because collagen implants do not always produce total occlusion, their use may not accurately predict whether permanent occlusion of both the upper and lower puncta will result in epiphora.

If no improvement in dry eye signs and symptoms is noted, premature migration of the plugs might have occurred, and the practitioner should consider inserting larger implants on retrial. Some practitioners advocate the insertion of multiple collagen implants in each punctum to ensure effective tear retention.

■ **Contraindications/Complications.** Intracanalicular collagen implants should not be used in cases of acute or chronic dacryocystitis. Because the tips of the jeweler's forceps are rather sharp, care should be taken while using them, especially in the vicinity of the globe. Conjunctival and corneal irritation may result if the implants partially extrude before dissolving. In that event, they can be easily removed or repositioned with the jeweler's forceps, and appropriate therapy for the mild irritation is then instituted.

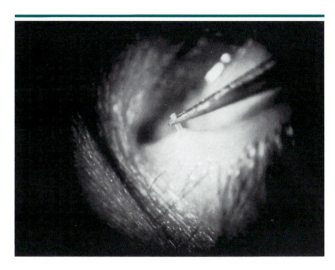

3. The end of the collagen implant is inserted into the vertical canaliculus, perpendicular to the lid margin.

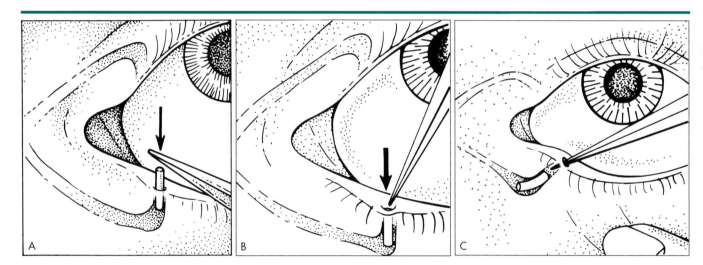

4. A. The closed tips of the forceps are used to tap the implant into the punctum. B. The closed tips of the forceps are used to gently push the implant into the vertical canaliculus until it is just visible. C. Lateral traction on the lower lid allows for positioning of the implant into the horizontal canaliculus using the closed tips of the forceps.

39

Punctal Plug Insertion

■ **Description/Indications.** Dry eye, or keratoconjunctivitis sicca (KCS), is a common ocular condition in elderly patients, contact lens wearers, patients with autoimmune and allergy-related disease, and others with tear film compromise caused by medication or the environment. When ocular signs and symptoms are not acceptably relieved with lubricating drops and ointments, alternative treatments are considered.

Punctal occlusion techniques are frequently the next line of treatment for patients with moderate to severe KCS. Successful temporary or diagnostic punctal occlusion with intracanalicular collagen implants (see p. 136) encourages consideration of more permanent occlusion with silicone punctal plugs or thermal punctal cautery (see p. 144). Silicone punctal plugs are advantageous as they can be inserted using topical anesthetic and are relatively easy to remove.

There are two styles of silicone punctal plugs. One, designed to totally occlude tear flow, is positioned at the proximal end of the canaliculus with the dome head resting just above the punctal orifice. The other, designed in theory to titrate outward tear flow, is positioned intracanalicularly. The former can be removed with jeweler's forceps, while the latter requires irrigation through the canaliculus into the lacrimal system, and the plug is not recovered. The insertion procedure for both plugs is similar to lacrimal dilation and irrigation (D&I, see p. 130), including initial punctal dilation to allow for easier insertion of the silicone plug. Punctal dilation is not always required when using the intracanalicular design.

Tapered-shaft silicone punctal plugs are available in 0.5, 0.6, 0.7, and 0.8-mm diameter sizes; 0.6 and 0.7 mm are the most popular. Several styles of preloaded insertion tools are available. One brand of silicone plugs includes a slanted collarette design to the external portion, with the reported advantage of enhancing comfort and minimizing the chance of expulsion. Intracanalicular plugs are currently available in 0.3, 0.5, and 0.7-mm diameter sizes. The 0.5-mm diameter is the size most commonly used. A set of punctal gauging instruments is available to assist in determining the appropriate size of the punctal plug.

■ **Instrumentation.** Silicone punctal plug kit including dilator/insertion tool, sterile jeweler's forceps, sterile lid fixation forceps (optional), slit lamp biomicroscope, head loupe (optional), punctal gauging set (optional), topical ophthalmic anesthetic solution, sterile cotton-tipped applicators, viscous artificial tear lubricant.

■ **Technique.** Prepare the patient by explaining the technique and anesthetizing the punctum. Instill two drops of topical ophthalmic anesthetic solution into the eye at the punctal area, and then hold a sterile, anesthetic-saturated cotton-tipped applicator directly against the punctum for 10 to 15 seconds (see p. 8). Allow a minute to pass to ensure good anesthesia. Recline the patient slightly in the examination chair if desired and illuminate the punctum using the stand lamp. Consider using a head loupe for magnification if needed.

Select a midsized punctal or intracanalicular silicone plug from the sterile packaging, unless you have assessed the punctum to be very small or large (Fig. 1). Alternatively, use the punctal gauging system. If you are not using a preloaded plug inserter or if the plug has fallen off the stylette inserter, load the plug following the manufacturer's instructions.

Punctal Occlusion Design: Lubricate the plug with a viscous tear solution. Hold the preloaded plug inserter similar to a pencil with your thumb and middle finger, and place the tip of your index finger gently above the release button (Fig. 2). Gently pull the lower lid down and temporally to expose the inferior punctum and instruct the patient to look upward (Fig. 3A). Steady your hand if needed on the patient's nose or cheek. Use the dilator end of the inserter or a 1.2-mm lacrimal dilator to enlarge the punctum, not inserting it more than 2 to 3 mm into the vertical canaliculus (see p. 128). Quickly position the inserter following dilation. Insert the plug into the punctum perpendicular to the lid margin, using a slight rotational motion (Fig. 3B). Stop insertion after the base of the dome head rests against the punctal opening. Do not force the plug into the punctum. After positioning the plug, depress the trigger, which withdraws the inserter pin, then remove the inserter. Inspect the plug position with the slit lamp (Fig. 4). Occlude the superior punctum in a similar manner if necessary, instructing the patient to look downward.

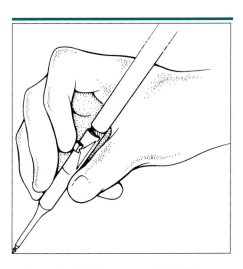

1. A. The punctal occlusion design (Freeman) silicone plug preloaded on the dilator/inserter tool. Note the tapered shaft and the domed top. (Courtesy of Eagle Vision.) B. The intracanalicular design (Herrick) silicone plug preloaded on the insertion stylette. The bell-shaped end of the plug is collapsible (Courtesy of Lacrimedics, Inc.)

2. The preloaded plug inserter is held like a pencil, with the index finger resting gently on the release button.

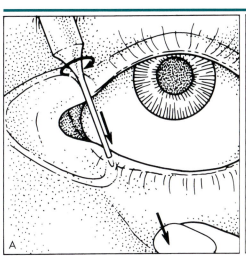

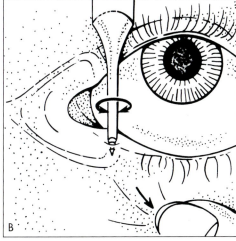

3. A. Dilation of the punctum. The punctum is anesthetized before dilation is begun, and the patient is instructed to look upward. B. The plug is inserted perpendicular to the lid margin, using a slight rotational motion.

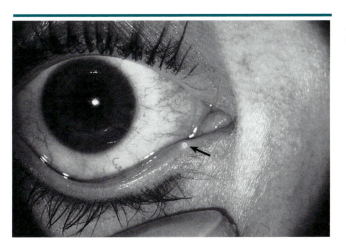

4. Proper positioning of the punctal occlusion design plug is inspected with the slit lamp. (Courtesy of EagleVision.)

Redilate the punctum if insertion is difficult, or select a different size plug if it appears too large or small. If necessary, stabilize a flaccid lower lid with a lid fixation forceps, allowing for easier insertion (Fig. 5). Hold the forceps parallel to the lid margin with the lid gently grasped just below its margin to enhance the stability of the lid. An assistant may help facilitate this procedure.

Remove the plug if desired by first anesthetizing the eye and then grasping the neck of the plug underneath the dome with jeweler's forceps, being careful not to snip off the dome. Work it gently outward along the punctal axis (Fig 6).

Intracanalicular Design: Gently pull the lower lid down and temporally to expose the lower punctum. Hold the loaded insertion stylette like a pencil perpendicular to the lid margin above the punctum. Partially insert the tip until the collapsible bell rests on the punctum (Fig. 7A). Slowly angle the top of the inserter laterally with the plug-end pointing nasally (Fig. 7B). With the assembly approximately parallel to the lid margin, the angle between the vertical and horizontal canalicular segments is straightened similar to a dilation and irrigation (D&I) procedure (see p. 130). Advance the plug down into the punctum until it is out of sight, positioning it in the horizontal canaliculus (Fig. 8A). Withdraw the inserter with a twisting motion, leaving the plug in place (Fig. 8B). Inspect the stylette to insure plug release. Using the slit lamp, inspect the punctum for adequate insertion and secondary plug extrusion.

Removal can only be accomplished with irrigation of the lacrimal system using a D&I procedure (see p. 130). This should dislodge the intracanalicular plug into the nasolacrimal sac, but the plug is usually not recovered.

■ **Interpretation.** The number of puncta occluded at the initial visit varies among practitioners. If definite improvement in signs and symptoms of dry eye occurred with the dissolvable collagen implants, one may choose to occlude both inferior puncta with silicone plugs and both superior puncta with collagen implants.

Monitor symptoms over the next two weeks to see if the patient is initially more comfortable and then becomes less so, or vice versa. If initial comfort is experienced and then decreases after the first week or so, consider silicone plugs in the superior puncta also; however, if epiphora is experienced initially but the symptoms improve after a week or so, consider occluding only the inferior puncta. Because at least 60% of tear drainage occurs through the lower puncta, frequently only these require occlusion.

■ **Contraindications/Complications.** Individuals with a history of hypersensitivity to silicone or those with an acute or chronic eye infection or dacryocystitis are not candidates for this procedure. Care must be exercised when a punctal plug is inserted, remembering that the jeweler's forceps can be rather sharp. The plug should slip into place with a minimum amount of pressure. If difficulty occurs, consider redilating the punctum or using a different size plug. Plug migration has been reported with the use of too small of a plug. Initial irritation is not uncommon after insertion; however, if it continues, removal should be considered. Entropion may be a contraindication if ocular irritation develops. A plug may be inadvertently dislodged if the eye is vigorously rubbed.

One challenge of the intracanalicular punctal plug design is that there is no definitive way of determining whether or not the plug is in place. If symptoms of dry eye recur weeks or months after insertion of the intracanalicular-style plug, consider the possibility of plug migration.

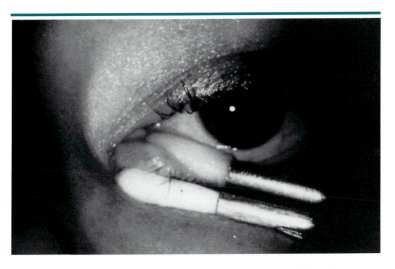

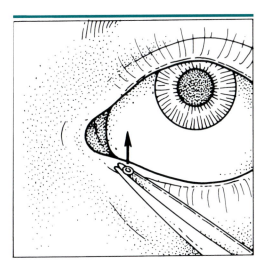

5. Lid fixation forceps are used if needed to stabilize the lower lid and punctum to facilitate plug insertion. Two moistened cotton-tipped applicators are incorporated into the forceps.

6. To remove the punctal plug, forceps are used to grasp the plug beneath the dome, and it is "worked out" along the punctal axis.

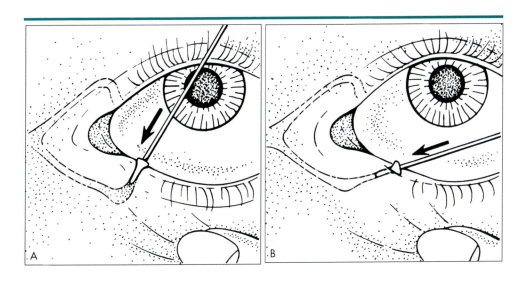

7. A. The tip of the intracanalicular plug is inserted until the collapsible bell rests on the punctum. B. The top of the inserter is then gently angled laterally with the plug end pointing nasally.

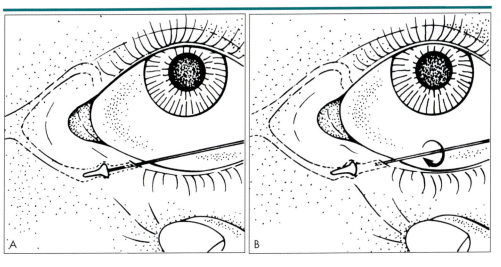

8. A. The plug is advanced 2 to 3 mm into the horizontal canaliculus. B. The inserter is withdrawn with a twisting motion, leaving the intracanalicular plug in place.

40

Punctal Cautery

■ Description/Indications.
Dry eye, or keratoconjunctivitis sicca (KCS), is a common ocular condition in elderly patients, contact lens wearers, patients with autoimmune and allergy-related disease, and those with tear film compromise caused by medication or the environment. When ocular signs and symptoms are not acceptably relieved with lubricating drops and ointments, alternative treatments are considered. Punctal occlusion techniques are frequently the next line of treatment for patients with moderate to severe KCS. A successful diagnostic trial of temporary collagen implants (see p. 136) encourages consideration of more permanent forms of punctal/canalicular occlusion such as silicone plugs (see p. 140) or punctal cautery.

Because aqueous deficiency is the tear disorder best treated by punctal occlusion, any form of permanent punctal occlusion is approached cautiously to ensure that other tear-altering entities such as blepharitis, meibomianitis, contact lens-related sequelae, eyelid closure problems, or corneal dystrophic/erosive surface anomalies are not the actual cause of the tear problem and related symptoms. When indicated, punctal cautery is performed initially on the inferior puncta. Some clinicians perform punctal cautery on the inferior punctum of only one eye to assess the response to the treatment. In severe cases of KCS, both the lower and upper puncta may be cauterized.

Punctal cautery may be performed using a battery-operated, high-temperature disposable thermal cautery or an electrocautery instrument such as the Hyfecator. Most battery-operated disposable ophthalmic cautery units come in a sterile packaged, loop-tip design with a safety cap (Fig. 1). It is operated by depressing the side power button with the thumb as it is held in a pencil grip. The tip glows brightly and quickly after the button is depressed. Contact time and the amount of tip surface contact determines the amount of thermal area delivered.

In the technique for punctal cautery described in this section, local infiltration anesthesia of the lid (see p. 417) is used before performing the technique. Some clinicians administer a very brief treatment of punctal cautery into the horizontal canaliculus with topical anesthesia alone. These clinicians have found the patient discomfort experienced by performing punctal cautery in this fashion to be no greater than the discomfort caused by the injection of anesthetic solution.

■ Instrumentation.
Sterile battery-operated disposable loop tip ophthalmic cautery or electrocautery instrument (e.g., Hyfecator), sterile punctal dilator, sterile cilia forceps, sterile 27 or 30-gauge disposable needle, sterile 3-cc disposable syringe, topical ophthalmic anesthetic solution, 2% lidocaine solution for injection, head loupe or slit lamp biomicroscope (optional), sterile cotton-tipped applicators, alcohol pads, facial tissue, sterile gauze pads, broad-spectrum ophthalmic antibiotic ointment, sterile latex gloves, puncture-resistant biohazard sharps containers.

■ Technique.
Review the risks and benefits of the procedure with the patient, and ask him or her to sign an appropriate consent form. Prepare the syringe with 2% lidocaine solution for injection (see p. 402). For appropriate infection control, wear sterile latex gloves (see p. 475). Position an adequate illumination source for punctal visualization. Pinch the loop tip of the disposable cautery together with sterile cilia forceps or an equivalent instrument to create a needle-tipped probe (Fig. 2). To resterilize the cautery, briefly turn it on until it glows, and then release the button, and recap the cautery. Instill two drops of topical ophthalmic anesthetic solution. Saturate a sterile cotton-tipped applicator with topical ophthalmic anesthetic solution, ask the patient to look up, and hold the saturated applicator on the inferior punctum for approximately 30 seconds as a pledget to deliver more effective topical anesthesia, especially if infiltration anesthesia is not used.

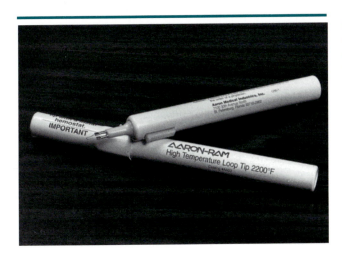

1. Punctal cautery may be performed using a battery-operated, high-temperature disposable thermal cautery. It is operated by depressing the side power button with the thumb as the cautery is held in a pencil grip.

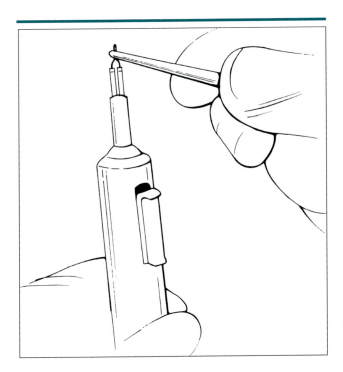

2. The loop tip of the disposable cautery is pinched with a sterile cilia forceps or an equivalent instrument to create a needle-tipped probe. The cautery is resterilized by briefly turning it on with the power button.

Inform the patient of the brief pinching and burning sensation associated with the anesthetic injection. With good neck support and the patient sitting comfortably in the examination chair, ask him or her to fixate upward. Prepare the external lid injection area with an alcohol swab. Inject 2% lidocaine solution both subcutaneously and subconjunctivally (palpebral), infiltrating the tissue around the inferior punctum and extending slightly nasally (see p. 417). Be careful not to inject the lacrimal system. Hand the patient a tissue or gauze pad, ask the patient to close the eyes, and apply firm pressure for a few minutes. This will enhance the effectiveness of the anesthetic as well as its diffusion within the lid tissue.

Assess the diameter of the punctum relative to the size of the cautery tip by attempting to insert the cool tip into the vertical canaliculus. If you are unable to insert the cautery fully, first dilate the punctum using a sterile dilator, employing the same technique used for dilation and irrigation of the lacrimal system (see p. 130). In order to dilate the punctum and canaliculus fully, it is helpful to gently turn the dilator into the horizontal canaliculus following dilation of the punctum and vertical canaliculus. Use a head loupe for magnification or the slit lamp biomicroscope if desired.

Battery-operated Cautery: Ask patient to fixate upward and use the forefinger of your nondominant hand to gently retract the lower lid and expose the inferior punctum. Hold the cautery vertically with a pencil grip (Fig. 3), resting your thumb lightly on the lateral power button and supporting your hand with the ring finger on the most accessible facial bony structure.

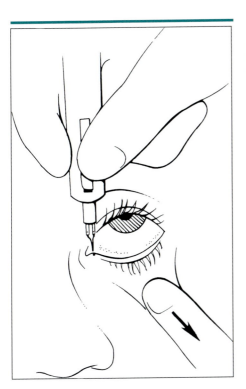

3. With the patient fixating upward, the cautery is held vertically with a pencil grip, resting the thumb lightly on the lateral power switch and stabilizing the hand on a facial bony structure. With the opposite hand, the lower lid is gently retracted to expose the inferior punctum.

Perform the deep method of cauterization by inserting the tip of the cautery into the full depth of the vertical canaliculus and turning nasally into the horizontal canaliculus to the length of the pinched loop tip (Fig. 4). Depress the power button briefly until the punctum blanches. Release the power switch. Maintain the same angle or position the cautery tip vertically, and then depress the power switch and slowly withdraw the cautery, hesitating at the punctal opening to ensure complete closure (Fig. 5). Remove the cautery after the punctum blanches again and then release the power button. Apply topical ophthalmic antibiotic ointment and schedule a follow-up examination in approximately 1 week.

Hyfecator Unit: Place the foot pedal control for convenient access on the floor. Insert the cautery cord into the low-voltage connector of the Hyfecator and initially set the dial reading between 15 and 20. Place a fine, needle-type epilation tip into the cautery handle. Position the patient comfortably in the examination chair or at the slit lamp biomicroscope. Hold the handle as you would a pencil, supporting your hand on any convenient facial bone.

Insert the probe tip into the inferior punctum to a depth of approximately 10 mm, first entering vertically and then gently angling the probe into the horizontal canaliculus. Depress the foot pedal. Watch the adjacent punctal conjunctiva until blanching begins and immediately release the pedal, which indicates probable adequate cauterization. After the first blanching, reduce the power dial by 3 or 4, withdraw the tip 2 to 3 mm, and depress the pedal again, watching for blanching. Repeat this procedure of withdrawing the probe tip/blanching until the tip reaches the punctal surface. Make sure the dial reads less than 5 as you approach the punctal surface. Very briefly and cautiously treat the punctal opening with the dial set at 3 or less.

When indicated for severe cases of KCS, the cautery procedure may also be performed on the superior puncta.

■ **Interpretation.** Punctal/canalicular cautery should provide symptomatic relief for ocular discomfort caused by insufficient tears for many patients. The endpoint of treatment should be a smooth, occluded punctal surface with no fluorescein sodium pooling at the opening. Lacrimal patency testing (see p. 130) or simple mechanical regurgitation of fluorescein sodium using digital compression will also help in determining the success of punctal closure at the follow-up visit.

Artificial tear substitutes are often continued at some level to assist with symptomatology after treatment. Deep cauterization is reported to have better long-term results than surface punctal closure alone. Repeat cauterization may be necessary for larger puncta, which appear to have a greater reopening rate.

■ **Contraindications/Complications.** Although complications of lid infiltration with anesthetic are less common than with regional blocks or general anesthesia, they have the potential to be extremely serious. Prior to performing the injection, a careful history is taken to rule out known hypersensitivity to any of the topical or injectable solutions. The topical anesthetic agents may produce local hypersensitivity reactions, including toxic keratitis.

The major systemic side effects caused by local anesthetics are excitation of the central nervous system (CNS) and depression of the cardiovascular system. Initial CNS symptoms of anesthetic toxicity commonly include drowsiness, light-headedness, dizziness, and a metallic taste followed by nausea, garrulousness, perioral numbness, tingling, diplopia, and tinnitus. The first sign of cardiovascular toxicity is typically a reduction in blood pressure. Tremors, muscle twitching, seizures, loss of consciousness, respiratory depression, and circulatory collapse have been reported. As a result, when performing injections, it is important to ensure the prompt availability of proper equipment and personnel trained to address medical emergencies, ranging from vasovagal syncope to cardiac arrest.

Despite a successful trial of punctal occlusion using collagen implants, it is possible that epiphora may result following punctal cautery, because it is believed that collagen implants occlude only 80% of the canaliculus. It is suggested that the response of the patient to cautery of the inferior puncta be assessed before the superior puncta are also cauterized.

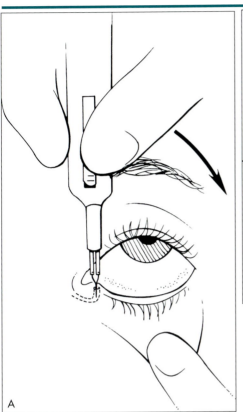

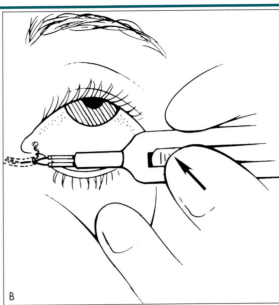

4. A. The deep method of cauterization is performed by inserting the tip of the cautery to the full depth of the vertical canaliculus and angling nasally *(arrow)* into the horizontal canaliculus. B. The power button is depressed briefly *(arrow)* until the punctum blanches. The power switch is then released.

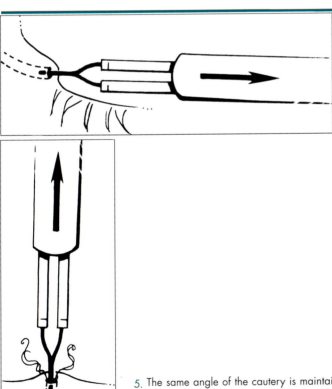

5. The same angle of the cautery is maintained *(top)* or the tip is positioned vertically *(bottom)*, the power switch is depressed, and the cautery is slowly withdrawn *(arrows)*, hesitating at the punctal opening to ensure complete closure. The cautery is removed after the punctum blanches and the power button is released.

IV Suggested Readings

Glatt HJ: Failure of collagen plugs to predict epiphora after permanent punctal occlusion. *Ophthal Surg* 1992;23:292–293.

Hecht SD: Evaluation of the lacrimal drainage system. *Am Acad Ophthalmol Otolaryngol* 1978;**85:**1250–1258.

Holly FJ, Lemp MA: Tear physiology and dry eyes. *Surv Ophthalmol* 1977;**22:**69–87.

Hornblass A, Ingis TM: Lacrimal function tests. *Arch Ophthalmol* 1979;**97:**1654–1655.

Knapp ME, Fruch BR, Nelson CC, Mush DC: A comparison of two methods of punctal occlusion. *Am J Ophthalmol* 1989;108:315–318.

Lamberts DW: Dry eye. *Int Ophthalmol Clin* 1994;34:145–150.

Lamberts DW: Punctal occlusion. *Int Ophthalmol Clin* 1994;34:145–146.

Lamberts DW: Punctal occlusion in dry eye patients, in Holly FJ (ed): *The Preocular Tear Film in Health, Disease and Contact Lens Wear.* Lubbock, TX, Dry Eye Institute, 1986.

Lemp ML: Recent developments in dry eye management. *Ophthalmology* 1987;**94:**1299–1304.

Lusthandler JM, Lemp MA: Lacrimal hyposecretion. In Roy FH (ed): *Master Techniques in Ophthalmic Surgery.* Baltimore, Williams & Wilkins, 1995, pp 736–740.

Semes LP, Clompus RJ: Diseases of the lacrimal system. In Bartlett JD, Jaanus SD (eds): *Clinical Ocular Pharmacology,* 3rd ed. Boston, Butterworth-Heinemann, 1995, pp 601–630.

Tuberville AW, Frederick WR, Wood TO: Punctal occlusion in tear deficiency syndromes. *Ophthalmology* 1982;**89:**1170.

Vrabec MP, Elsing SH, Aitken PA: A prospective, randomized comparison of thermal and argon laser for permanent punctal occlusion. *Am J Ophthalmol* 1993;116:469–471.

Willis RM, Folberg R, Krachmer J, Holland EJ: The treatment of aqueous-deficient dry eye with removable punctal plugs. *Ophthalmology* 1987;**94:**514–518.

Wright MM, Bersani TA, Freuth BR, Musch DC: Efficacy of the primary dye test. *Ophthalmology* 1989;**96:**481–483.

Conjunctival Procedures

41

Conjunctival/Ocular Irrigation

■ **Description/Indications.** Ocular tissue insult, whether from inert irritating foreign matter or from caustic chemicals in solid, liquid, or gas form, is best initially addressed by using proper conjunctival/ocular irrigation procedures. In addition to treatment for chemical injury, irrigation is used to wash small foreign bodies from the eye (see p. 156), to wash away discharge in patients with conjunctival infections, to periodically rinse the orbital socket in patients with prosthetic eyes, and to flush the viscous cushioning solution from the eye following gonioscopy or retinal three-mirror examination (see pp. 74 and 238).

Alkaline and acidic chemical burns represent true ocular emergencies requiring immediate on-site copious flushing with any water source for approximately 30 minutes, followed quickly by in-office irrigation with saline or lactated Ringer's solution to continue chemical debulking. This flushing is then followed by pH level assessment and possible continued lavage if pH imbalance is still noted, or the ocular tissue is assessed to determine the degree of damage and the indicated treatment. Concurrent with emergency treatment, information must be gathered regarding the exact components and concentrations of the offending substances, and the method and duration of exposure, along with documentation of the immediate emergency treatment performed before the patient arrived at the office. If no information is available, the patient or friend should bring the chemical container or label from the container to the office so that the components can be reviewed in an ocular toxicology reference. Contrary to most urgent office visits, immediate irrigation should be initiated for a serious chemical ocular injury before history-taking and other entrance tests are performed.

■ **Instrumentation.** Eyelid speculum, eyelid retractor, emesis basin or absorbent towels, litmus paper, topical ophthalmic anesthetic solution, sterile ophthalmic saline solution, 1000-cc IV bag(s) of sterile saline 0.9% or lactated Ringer's solution, macro-drip IV set, extension tubing, sterile cotton-tipped applicators.

■ **Technique.** Recline the patient in the examination chair. Instill two drops of topical ophthalmic anesthetic solution into each eye. Angle the patient's head so that the eye being irrigated is lower than the other to prevent accidental flushing of debris or chemicals into the opposite eye.

Position an emesis basin or large absorbent towel firmly to the temporal side of the eye to be irrigated to avoid soaking the patient's skin or clothing, or causing a floor spill. Alternatively, use multiple paper towels or facial tissue. Hold the towels below and to the side of the eye, maintaining a tight bond with the skin so fluid will not run underneath.

Ask the patient to fixate at various points depending upon which areas of the conjunctival sac and fornices will be irrigated. Remember to retract the eyelids to gain complete access to more recessed tissue under the lids. Using a new bottle of sterile ophthalmic saline solution, ask the patient to fixate superiorly while you retract the lower lid. Begin a slow steady flow of saline into the major tear reservoir of the inferior cul-de-sac and onto the bulbar conjunctiva (Fig. 1). In a systematic fashion, ask the patient to look in the opposite direction as you move nasally to flush the inner canthal area, superiorly for the bulbar conjunctiva and fornix while retracting the upper lid, and laterally for the outer canthal area and bulbar conjunctiva. Evert or double evert (see p. 94 and 96) the upper lid to enhance irrigation of the fornices and to help visualize foreign particulate matter. If necessary, use a moistened cotton-tipped applicator or dull forceps to remove sizable particulate debris (see p. 156).

For ocular foreign body debris or discharge, continue the irrigation until the offending agent is eliminated, which may be after a relatively short period (Fig. 2). For significant chemical injury, irrigate for at least 30 minutes using several bottles of sterile saline. Use an eyelid speculum (see p. 98) if the patient is unable to keep the eye open during irrigation. Use additional ophthalmic anesthetic solution during treatment if prolonged irrigation is indicated.

Depending upon your estimation of the severity of the chemical insult, use litmus paper as a guide to determine when to discontinue irrigation. Touch the end of the litmus paper to the bulbar conjunctiva close to the most involved area, or in the inferior cul-de-sac (Fig. 3A). Remove the strip after the tip appears to be saturated, and compare its new color to the color scale on the side of the litmus paper dispenser to estimate the current pH (Fig. 3B). Various shades of blue indicate levels of alkalinity, and yellow indicates acidity. Any change in color from the original green suggests that further irrigation is needed. Different litmus tests have different paper color and charts, so be sure to match the resultant color change to the appropriate package scale.

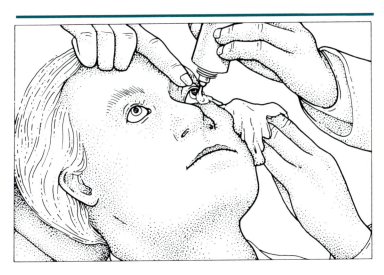

1. The eyelids are gently retracted as the eye is irrigated, and paper towels or an emesis basis are used to collect the draining fluid. When indicated, the patient's head is turned so that the eye being irrigated is lower than the other to prevent accidental flushing of chemicals into the opposite eye.

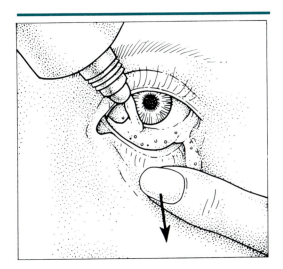

2. For nonchemical particulate debris, the eye is irrigated until the offending material is eliminated.

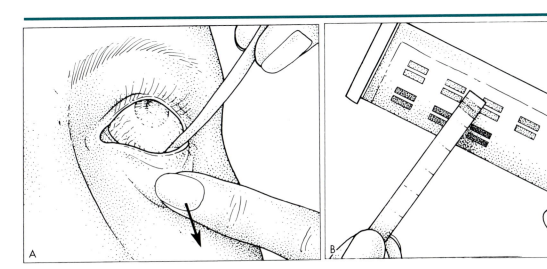

3. A. The litmus paper strip is touched to the bulbar conjunctiva close to the most involved area, or in the inferior cul-de-sac.

3. B. The saturated litmus paper strip is removed and its new color is compared to the color scale on the side of the litmus paper dispenser to estimate the current pH.

If prolonged lavage appears indicated, consider using a 1000-cc IV bag of normal saline 0.9% or lactated Ringer's solution with accompanying infusion tubing. Check the expiration date of the solution, and verify that the bag container is intact and the solution is clear. Remove the 18 gauge, macro-drip infusion set from its packaging and close the tube flow by sliding the screw clamp to pinch the tubing (Fig. 4A). After removing the bag from its protective packaging, invert the bag and pull out the protective plug at the base. Insert the large-bore piercing needle of the infusion set using a twisting motion and hang the bag on the examination stand above the patient (Fig. 4B). Attach an extension piece of tubing to the usual IV end of the tubing if extra length is needed. Turn the patient's head laterally to prevent drainage into the other eye or onto the skin. Hold the rounded end of the tubing close to the eye and slowly release the screw clamp until adequate fluid flow begins (Fig. 5). Initiate complete ocular irrigation of the globe, cul-de-sac, and adnexa. Consider using a Mediflow contact lens or Morgan lens system for continuous irrigation.

As soon as is reasonable following thorough irrigation, perform a thorough slit lamp biomicroscopic examination.

■ **Interpretation.** Management of ocular chemical injuries can be most challenging. After immediate and appropriate irrigation, comprehensive examination of all involved anterior segment tissue must be performed to assess for hyperemia, ischemia, chemosis, fluorescein staining, epithelial compromise. and corneal edema. The intraocular pressure is also assessed. Treat or triage the condition as indicated. A white quiet eye in an almost asymptomatic patient may be the most precarious of all presentations, as chemically induced ischemia and cauterization may mask severe, occult injury. Caution and a thorough knowledge of chemical insult sequellae are necessary for appropriate management.

Punctate keratitis invariably follows ocular irrigation, and this may lend confusion as to whether chemical or mechanical forces were responsible for the epithelial compromise.

■ **Contraindications/Complications.** Care should be taken not to irrigate powdered chemicals until they have been brushed away first. When irrigating one eye, avoid directing the overflow into the opposite eye or onto the skin, inducing additional damage. Superficial punctate keratitis or hyperemia are common findings following conjunctival/ocular irrigation, especially if the globe was relatively uninvolved prior to irrigation. Irrigation is contraindicated in situations where a penetrating ocular injury is suspected.

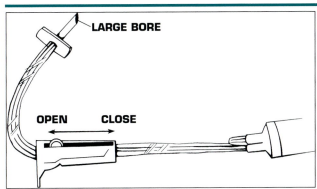

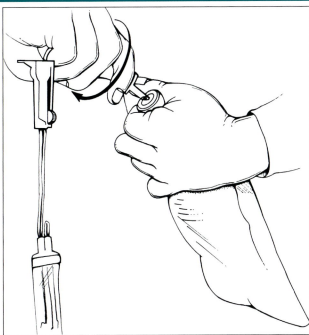

4. A. For prolonged irrigation, an IV bag of normal saline or lactated Ringer's solution may be used attached to an infusion set. The 18-gauge macro-drip infusion set is removed from its packaging and the tube flow is closed by sliding the screw clamp that pinches the tubing.

4. B. The large-bore piercing needle of the infusion set is inserted into the base opening by using a twisting motion *(arrow)*.

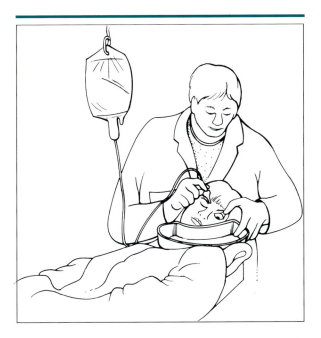

5. The rounded end of the tubing is held close to the eye and the screw clamp is slowly released until adequate flow of the irrigating solution begins. The patient's head is turned laterally and the excess liquid is collected in an emesis basin on an absorbent towel.

42 Conjunctival Foreign Body Removal

■ **Description/Indications.** A conjunctival foreign body (FB) is a frequent source of patient complaints. When visible, the FB commonly appears as a dark speck on the pink (palpebral) or white (bulbar) conjunctival surface. The superior palpebral conjunctiva is a common location for conjunctival foreign bodies. Patient symptoms may suggest a foreign body, but the object may be difficult to visualize. In that event, lid eversion (see p. 94) is used to locate the FB. Double lid eversion (see p. 96) with slit lamp magnification may be needed to localize small particulate matter such as fiberglass strands, glass, or steel, especially if it is lodged in the sulcus behind the lid margins. A hard-to-find embedded FB may be localized by an anchored mucus tag on the superior palpebral conjunctiva or by an area of focal hyperemia or edema. Fine linear foreign body tracks on the cornea that stain with fluorescein sodium (Fig. 1) are indicative of a foreign body on the lid margin or superior palpebral conjunctival surface. Foreign bodies embedded on the bulbar conjunctival surface within the palpebral aperture are easier to locate.

The assessment of conjunctival FBs includes determining the number (single or multiple); location (superior palpebral conjunctiva, bulbar conjunctiva, or inferior palpebral conjunctiva); and degree of embeddedness. Using this information, the FB is removed with the appropriate procedure such as irrigation or use of a sterile cotton-tipped applicator, spud, sterile disposable needle, or jeweler's forceps.

The use of topical ophthalmic anesthetic solution is avoided unless the patient is very uncomfortable and exhibits significant blepharospasm, or if the FB is substantially embedded. Topical anesthesia is avoided so that when the particle is located and removed, the patient will feel immediate relief, indicative that no FBs remain in the eye. On occasion the FB may irritate the cornea sufficiently so that, even following removal, the eye is still sensitive and uncomfortable. A thorough slit lamp examination with lid eversion will confirm that no other FBs remain in the eye. If necessary, topical ophthalmic anesthetic solution is used to maximize patient comfort during the procedure.

■ **Instrumentation.** Slit lamp biomicroscope; sterile: spud, 25G ⅝-inch disposable needle, jeweler's forceps, Kimura-type platinum spatula, saline solution, cotton-tipped applicators, topical ophthalmic anesthetic solution.

■ **Technique.** The simplest method for removing a superficial conjunctival FB is by irrigation with sterile saline solution (Fig. 2). Locate the FB, using lid eversion if necessary, and forcefully irrigate, aiming the saline spray at the edge of the particle so that it dislodges and washes away (see p. 152). Use sufficient irrigation so that the FB does not remain in the cul-de-sac. The use of topical ophthalmic anesthetic solution may be helpful prior to irrigation.

If irrigation has not dislodged the superficial conjunctival FB, use a sterile cotton-tipped applicator that has been moistened with sterile saline to remove it. Use the slit lamp biomicroscope and evert the lid if necessary to make the FB accessible. Gently dislodge the particle, using small strokes tangential to the plane of the eyelid (Fig 3). As with the irrigation technique, this method works best for superficial FBs, especially those in the cul-de-sac and on the superior tarsus.

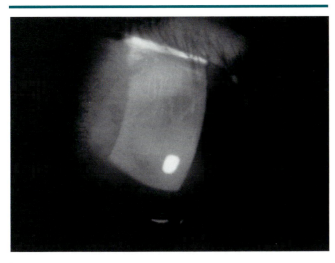

1. Fine linear foreign body tracks on the cornea that stain with fluorescein sodium are suggestive of an FB under the upper lid. (Courtesy of Ann Michael.)

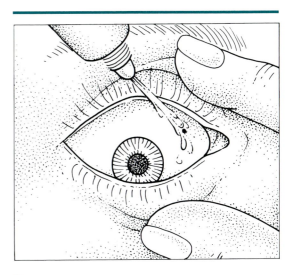

2. A superficial FB may be removed by irrigation with sterile saline. The irrigating spray is aimed at the edge of the FB on the bulbar conjunctiva in an attempt to dislodge it.

3. Following lid eversion, a moistened sterile cotton-tipped applicator may be used to wipe the surface of the palpebral conjunctiva to dislodge the FB.

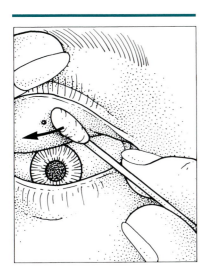

Foreign matter embedded in the conjunctiva that is not dislodged by irrigation or swabbing will require the use of a sterile spud or disposable needle for removal. The technique is similar to that used to remove a corneal FB (see p. 164). Using the slit lamp biomicroscope and following instillation of topical anesthetic solution, ask the patient to fixate appropriately to expose the FB. Set the slit lamp magnification on 10X to 16X and use diffuse illumination of medium intensity (see p. 22). Align the spud close to the eye while viewing outside the slit lamp and, once aligned, use the slit lamp for greater magnification. Use a handrest if desired or rest the elbow on the slit lamp table to achieve greater stability. Hold the spud or needle so it is tangential to the conjunctival surface and use it to slowly loosen the edges of the FB (Fig. 4A). Once the periphery is loosened, use a subtle flicking motion to lift off the FB (Fig. 4B, 4C). Irrigate the eye following dislodging of the FB to remove any remaining particles. Use a Kimura-type blunt spatula or jeweler's forceps to remove residual particulate matter (Fig. 5). Use the spatula to "scoop up" loose pieces of material; use the forceps to grasp individual pieces.

The jeweler's forceps may be used to locate suspected conjunctival foreign bodies covered by a mucus tag. Pull the tag away with the forceps. A visible embedded barb may now be exposed. Remove the barb with the spud, needle, or forceps.

If after thorough examination an FB cannot be found, saline irrigation of the superior and inferior cul-de-sacs, followed by swabbing of the anesthetized palpebral conjunctival surfaces with a moistened cotton-tipped applicator, may be successful in relieving the symptoms.

Instill ophthalmic antibiotic solution or ointment after the procedure for prophylaxis. If there is considerable tissue disruption, antibiotics may be required for a longer period. Cycloplegia and pressure patching are rarely needed because the conjunctiva heals quickly, usually within 12 to 24 hours for most epithelial disruptions. Schedule a follow-up examination as needed or ask the patient to return if FB symptoms persist.

▧ Contraindications/Complications.

Secondary infection is possible, especially if the FB was embedded. An FB on the bulbar conjunctiva may be a sign of perforating injury. This is especially true if a history of hammering metal-on-metal or working around high-speed machinery such as a grinder's wheel is elicited. A perforating injury is easily masked by a subconjunctival hemorrhage, and the Seidel test (see p. 370) aids in the differential diagnosis. Radiologic studies of the eye and orbit may be indicated under these circumstances. If signs of globe perforation are present, appropriate referral for consultation is indicated.

Reassure the patient that a small subconjunctival hemorrhage may occur following removal of a conjunctival FB. Superficial punctate keratitis may result following irrigation due to mechanical disruption of the cornea.

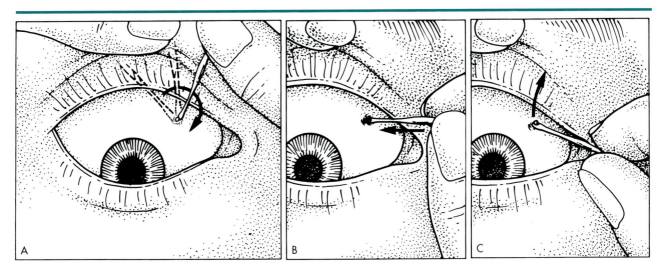

4. A. A spud is used to loosen the edges of an FB embedded in the bulbar conjunctiva. B. The spud is positioned underneath the FB. C. A subtle, upward flicking motion is used to lift off the FB.

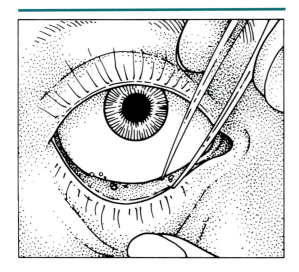

5. A jeweler's forceps may be used to grasp and remove residual particulate matter from the conjunctival sac.

43 Lymphatic Cyst Drainage

■ Description/Indications. Lymphatic cysts of the bulbar conjunctiva are somewhat common, often reported by the concerned patient as an acute "blister" (Fig. 1) or the cause of a foreign body sensation. The cysts, which may be several millimeters in length, appear singly or in multiples. They may be round in appearance or irregular and lobulated. Lymphatic cysts move with the bulbar conjunctiva freely over the sclera.

Aside from the occasional cosmetic concern, patients with lymphatic cysts of the bulbar conjunctiva are usually asymptomatic and no treatment is generally recommended. If the cyst becomes cosmetically obvious or irritated, it can be lanced and drained.

Lymphatic cysts may also occur on the inferior palpebral conjunctiva but are rarely noticed by the patient and generally cause no symptoms. Concretions of the palpebral conjunctiva may be present in association with lymphatic cysts, appearing as small areas of yellow debris within the clear cyst.

■ Instrumentation. Slit lamp biomicroscope, 25G ⅝-inch sterile disposable needle, sterile cotton-tipped applicators, topical ophthalmic anesthetic solution, 2.5% phenylephrine ophthalmic solution, sterile saline solution.

■ Technique. Instill several drops of topical ophthalmic anesthetic solution into the eye, waiting about a minute for the drops to take effect. If desired, instill two drops of 2.5% phenylephrine ophthalmic solution to produce conjunctival vasoconstriction and minimize the chance of secondary bleeding. Advise the patient that good cooperation and fixation facilitate the procedure.

Seat the patient comfortably behind the slit lamp biomicroscope with the head firmly against the forehead strap. Set the slit lamp magnification at 10X to 16X and use diffuse illumination of medium intensity. Provide the patient with a suitable target to ensure optimal fixation and to expose the lymphatic cyst. With the sterile disposable needle positioned tangentially to the globe, puncture the cyst, making a subtle stabbing-like motion to create a hole (Fig. 2A). Try to angle the needle slightly so that it points away from the ocular surface as the cyst is lanced. The cyst will often collapse spontaneously after penetration of the needle (Fig. 2B). If the cyst does not spontaneously collapse, make a second puncture.

Gentle massage through the closed lids (Fig. 3) may help evacuate the cyst. Using two fingers, make a gentle back-and-forth motion on the lids near the site of the cyst. If the cyst does not drain after massage and a patent puncture is visible, use a sterile cotton-tipped applicator moistened with sterile saline solution to evacuate it (Fig. 4). Apply pressure to the end of the cyst opposite the puncture site. Gently roll the cotton-tipped applicator over the cyst, forcing fluid through the puncture site.

Advise the patient to instill a broad-spectrum ophthalmic antibiotic solution as prophylaxis for approximately 2 days. Also instruct the patient to gently massage the collapsed cyst through the closed eyelids twice a day for a few days to help prevent recurrence.

■ Interpretation. Immediately following drainage of the lymphatic cyst, a small amount of clear fluid will appear and the elevated wall of the cyst will flatten. When considering this procedure, it is important to remind the patient that the cyst may recur following drainage. If the cyst recurs, a second procedure may be performed. Inflamed lymphatic cysts or recurrent cysts may require surgical excision and biopsy to rule out a lymphangioma or other conjunctival tumor.

■ Contraindications/Complications. A small subconjunctival hemorrhage may develop if a vessel is inadvertently ruptured during drainage of the cyst. Secondary infection is an uncommon possibility after a procedure of this nature. Do not drain a lymphatic cyst in the presence of bacterial conjunctivitis.

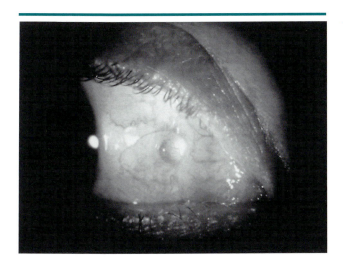

1. A bulbar conjunctival lymphatic cyst.

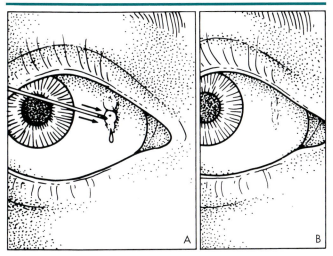

2. A. The wall of the lymphatic cyst is punctured with a sterile disposable needle to create a hole for drainage of the clear fluid. B. The collapsed cyst, seen following drainage.

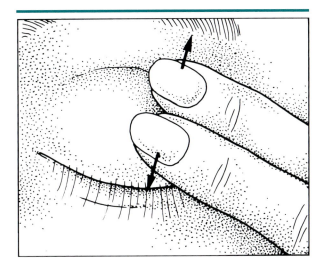

3. Massage through the eyelids is used to collapse a punctured lymphatic cyst if it does not spontaneously evacuate.

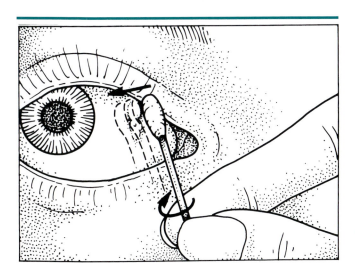

4. Following puncture with a sterile disposable needle, a moistened cotton-tipped applicator is used to collapse cysts that do not spontaneously evacuate.

Suggested Readings

Bartlett JD, Jaanus SD: *Clinical Ocular Pharmacology,* ed 3. Boston, Butterworth-Heinemann, 1995.

Casser L: Conjunctival abrasions and lacerations. *J Am Optom Assoc* 1987;**58:**488–93.

Catania LJ: *Primary Care of the Anterior Segment,* ed 2. Norwalk, CT, Appleton & Lange, 1995.

Cullom RD, Chang B: *The Wills Eye Manual,* ed 2. Philadelphia, Lippincott, 1994.

Eskridge JB, Amos JF, Bartlett JD (eds): *Clinical Procedures in Optometry.* Philadelphia, Lippincott, 1991.

Onofrey BE: Management of corneal burns. *Optom Clin* 1995;**4:**3–37.

VI

Corneal Procedures

44

Corneal Foreign Body Removal

■ **Description/Indications.** Foreign bodies may become embedded in the cornea, leading to symptoms of varying intensity. Symptoms may include redness, pain, foreign body sensation, tearing, blurred vision, and photophobia. Occasionally a patient is encountered with an asymptomatic corneal foreign body. Corneal foreign body (FB) removal is generally indicated when exogenous debris is noted.

A detailed patient history is important to determine the origin and nature of the corneal foreign body. A careful examination with the slit lamp biomicroscope (see p. 24) is needed to determine the depth and extent of the FB (Fig. 1). It is especially important to use an optic section at the site of the FB. Additional examination techniques are used to assess the involvement of other ocular structures.

Most corneal FBs become embedded in the epithelium and rarely penetrate Bowman's membrane because of its tough consistency (Fig. 2). When the patient history suggests that the FB is of high-speed origin such as from drilling, a grinder's wheel, or hammering metal-on-metal, a corneal perforating wound must be ruled out with procedures such as a careful slit lamp examination, Seidel test (see p. 370), and dilated fundus examination (see p. 244).

There are several techniques available for removal of a corneal FB. The technique chosen is determined by factors such as the location and degree of embeddedness of the FB

as well as the cooperation level of the patient. The goal of the procedure is to remove the corneal FB with as little tissue disruption as possible. Superficial particles may be removed by irrigation with sterile ophthalmic saline solution, whereas embedded particles require removal with a spud, needle, or loop (Fig. 3). An FB may appear to be superficial, but if irrigation does not dislodge it, it is considered to be embedded and an alternative removal technique is used.

A foreign body spud or sterile disposable needle is commonly used to remove embedded corneal FBs. The shape of the spud allows for excavation and "flicking off" of an FB. The spud is the instrument of choice for removing most embedded corneal FBs. Sterile disposable needles are available in different diameters and lengths (see p. 402). The higher the gauge (G) number of the needle, the smaller the diameter. A commonly used needle size for corneal foreign body removal is 25G ⅝ inch. Because of the sharpness of the needle, it must be used with great care during this technique. A foreign body loop made from nylon or other semirigid material may be used to remove loosely embedded corneal FBs. It flexes during removal of corneal FBs, which makes it useful for children with poor fixation and uncooperative patients. A disposable plastic instrument for foreign body removal is available in sterile multipacks, and the head of the unit contains multiple components that may be used (Fig. 4).

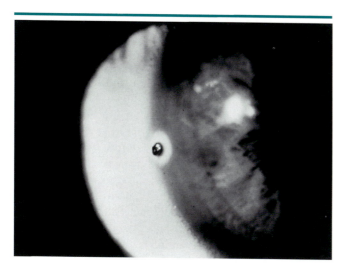

1. A metallic foreign body is noted on the cornea near the limbus. It is surrounded by a ring of rust and edema, which suggests that it has been present for a period of time. (*See also* Color Plate 44–1).

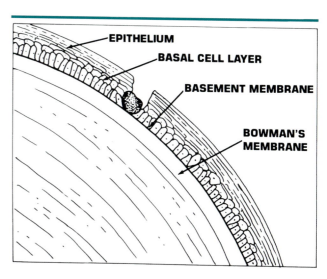

2. Most corneal foreign bodies, as shown here, become embedded in the epithelium and rarely penetrate Bowman's membrane because of its tough consistency.

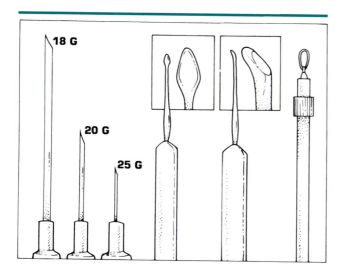

3. Embedded corneal foreign bodies are removed with a needle (left), a spud (shown centrally in frontal and side views), or a loop (right).

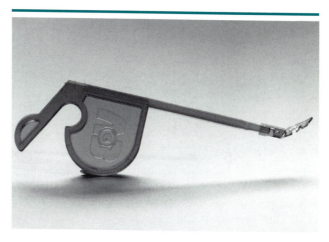

4. The Polytome is a disposable plastic instrument available for ocular foreign body removal. The head of the unit contains multiple components that may be used. (Courtesy of Eaglevision.)

A sterile cotton-tipped applicator is not widely used for corneal FB removal. When viewed under the slit lamp biomicroscope, the large head of the swab makes it difficult to remove the FB without disrupting substantial areas of the surrounding corneal epithelium (Fig. 5). In addition, the applicator tends to fragment the FB, removing the superficial particles and leaving the embedded component behind. A sterile cotton-tipped applicator moistened with sterile saline is useful for sweeping dislodged corneal FBs from the palpebral conjunctival surface.

■ **Instrumentation.** Slit lamp biomicroscope; sterile: corneal foreign body spud, 25G ⅝-inch disposable needle, corneal foreign body loop, eyelid speculum, ophthalmic saline solution, cotton-tipped applicators; topical ophthalmic anesthetic solution.

■ **Technique.** Advise the patient that good cooperation and fixation will facilitate the procedure. Instill two drops of topical ophthalmic anesthetic solution into each eye.

Irrigation: Recline the patient slightly in the examination chair, raise the upper lid with the thumb of one hand, and use the other hand to direct a stream of sterile saline irrigating solution at the edge of the corneal FB (see p. 152). If irrigation dislodges the FB into the cul-de-sac, use a moistened sterile cotton-tipped applicator to remove the FB from the eye. If irrigation is not successful, use an alternative technique to remove the FB.

Spud or Needle: Position the patient comfortably at the slit lamp biomicroscope with the head firmly against the forehead strap. Set the slit lamp magnification at 10X to 16X and use diffuse illumination or a wide parallelepiped of medium intensity. Position a fixation target for the oppo-site eye so that the orientation of the globe allows for easy access to the corneal FB. Stabilize your arm on the slit lamp table, use an arm rest if desired, or rest the fourth and fifth fingers of the dominant hand on the patient's cheek, bridge of the nose, or upright bar of the slit lamp.

Hold the spud or needle like a pencil between the thumb and forefinger, and initially align it by sighting outside of the slit lamp, positioning it in front of the FB at an angle tangential to the corneal surface (Fig. 6). Once aligned, use the slit lamp for the remainder of the procedure (Fig. 7). Ask the patient to blink, and then secure the upper eyelid with the nondominant hand if necessary. An assistant may secure the upper lid, or use an eyelid speculum (see p. 98) if patient cooperation is poor. With small strokes, use the tip of the spud or the tip of the needle with the bevel facing toward you to loosen the edges of the FB (Fig. 8A). Maintaining a tangential angle to the globe, insert the spud or the tip of the needle just beneath the FB and use a subtle flicking motion to release it from the corneal surface (Fig. 8B and 8C).

Nylon Loop: Position the patient comfortably at the slit lamp biomicroscope with the head firmly against the forehead strap. Set the slit lamp magnification at 10X to 16X and use diffuse illumination or a wide parallelepiped of medium intensity. Position a fixation target for the opposite eye so that the orientation of the globe allows for easy access to the corneal FB. Ask the patient to blink, and then secure the upper eyelid with the nondominant hand if necessary. An assistant may secure the upper lid, or use an eyelid speculum (see p. 98) if patient cooperation is poor. Stabilize your arm on the slit lamp table, use an armrest if desired, or rest the fourth and fifth fingers of the dominant hand on the patient's cheek, bridge of the nose, or upright bar of the slit lamp.

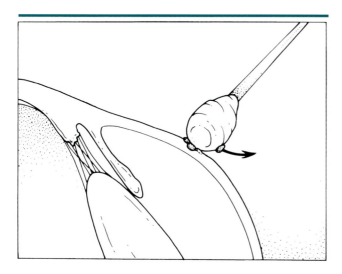

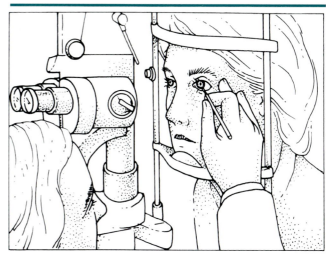

5. A sterile cotton-tipped applicator is not widely used for corneal foreign body removal. The large head tends to disrupt substantial areas of the surrounding epithelium, and fragmented, embedded particles tend to be left behind.

6. The spud, needle, or loop is held like a pencil and initially aligned by sighting outside of the slit lamp. It is positioned in front of the FB at an angle tangential to the corneal surface.

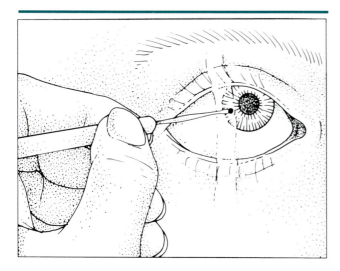

7. Once the spud is initially aligned, the slit lamp biomicroscope is used for the remainder of the procedure, and a tangential angle between the spud and cornea is maintained.

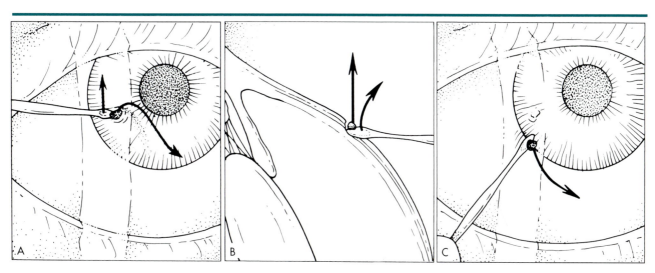

8. A. Maintaining a tangential approach, the tip of the spud is used to loosen the edge of the corneal FB. B. Once the tip of the spud is positioned underneath the FB, a subtle flicking motion is used to release it from the corneal surface. C. The edge of the spud may be used to "scoop" away a corneal FB.

Initially align the loop by sighting outside the slit lamp, positioning it in front of the FB at an angle tangential to the corneal surface. Once aligned, use the slit lamp for the remainder of the procedure. Hold the loop tangential to the corneal surface, and use it to tease the edge of the FB, loosening it from the epithelium (Fig. 9A). Insert the loop just beneath the FB and use a subtle flicking motion to release it from the corneal surface (Fig. 9B and 9C).

■ **Interpretation.** It is very common to note wrinkling of the cornea as mild pressure is applied with the spud, needle, or loop during removal of the corneal FB. An epithelial defect will remain after corneal FB removal for which appropriate treatment is instituted. Following removal of a metallic FB, a ring of rust may remain that may also require removal (see p. 170). A ring of edema may remain that will resolve as the cornea heals. If the embedded foreign body had been present for a substantial period of time, a secondary anterior uveitis may be present, which also resolves with appropriate treatment and as the cornea heals.

■ **Contraindications/Complications.** Secondary bacterial infection of the resulting corneal defect is possible after FB removal, so prophylactic antibiotic treatment is typically initiated until the cornea heals. A vegetative foreign body may result in secondary fungal keratitis. Increasing intraocular inflammation following FB removal suggests the possibility of a retained intraocular foreign body. Use caution when removing a corneal foreign body with a needle so that inadvertent corneal perforation does not occur.

If Bowman's membrane or the anterior stroma is disrupted by the foreign body or during its removal, a small corneal scar may result that tends not to affect visual acuity. For foreign bodies that are assessed to be deep within the corneal stroma or if corneal perforation is suspected, a referral for consultation is recommended.

The patient will experience discomfort to a varying degree following corneal FB removal, depending upon the initial degree of involvement as well as the ease with which the FB was successfully removed. Appropriate topical or systemic therapy for pain control may be initiated. It is also helpful to educate the patient about appropriate safety eyewear issues to help prevent future corneal FBs.

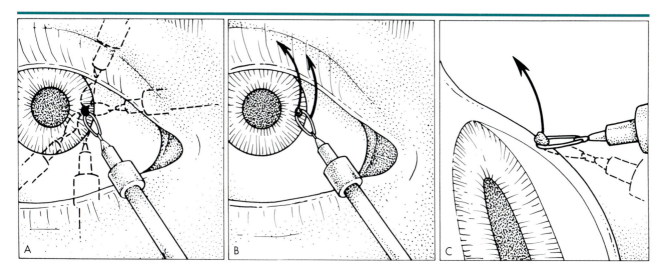

9. A. Maintaining a tangential approach, the loop is used to tease the edge of the corneal FB, loosening it from the epithelium.
B. The loop is positioned underneath the corneal FB. C. A subtle flicking motion is used to release the FB from the corneal surface.

45 Corneal Rust Ring Removal

■ **Description/Indications.** A metallic foreign body (FB) begins to oxidize (rust) within 12 to 24 hours of becoming embedded in the cornea. The resulting siderosis stains the corneal epithelial cells, basement membrane, and Bowman's membrane an orange-brown color. The rust usually forms in a ring around the metallic FB (Fig. 1). An accompanying white ring of edema may be noted around the FB or the rust ring. To avoid the development of a rust ring, metallic corneal FBs are best removed as soon as possible (see p. 170). If a substantial rust ring develops, the stained epithelial cells are removed after dislodging the metallic corneal FB.

Most metallic corneal FBs become embedded in the epithelium and rarely penetrate Bowman's membrane because of its tough consistency. When the patient history suggests that the FB is of high-speed origin such as from drilling, a grinder's wheel, or hammering metal-on-metal, a corneal perforating wound must be ruled out with procedures such as a careful slit lamp examination (see p. 22), Seidel test (see p. 370), and dilated fundus examination (see p. 244).

The Algerbrush is commonly utilized to remove a superficial corneal rust ring. It is a small, low-speed, battery-operated drill that is fitted with a tiny dental burr (Fig. 2). The Algerbrush is available with several different size burrs. The smallest size (0.5 mm) is used most often because it effectively removes the rust and tends to cause the least tissue disruption. The burrs can be removed from the drill for storage and sterilization after use. Disposable burrs are also available.

The Algerbrush has a built-in clutch mechanism that will stop the instrument when a certain degree of resistance is encountered. Bowman's membrane is of a tough consistency and requires a stronger force to penetrate than the Algerbrush can produce. As a result, when the Algerbrush contacts Bowman's membrane, it will automatically shut off.

A hand-held ophthalmic burr may also be used to remove a corneal rust ring (Fig. 3). This method is useful when the soft whirring sounds made by the Algerbrush are unsettling to the patient. The disadvantage of using the ophthalmic burr compared to the Algerbrush is that it takes longer to achieve the desired result. Alternatively, a corneal foreign body spud or sterile 25G ⅝-inch needle may be used to remove a rust ring.

■ **Instrumentation.** Slit lamp biomicroscope; Algerbrush with sterile burrs; sterile: ophthalmic burr, disposable 25G ⅝-inch needle, corneal foreign body spud, ophthalmic saline solution; topical ophthalmic anesthetic solution.

■ **Technique.** Advise the patient that good cooperation and fixation will facilitate the procedure. Instill two drops of topical ophthalmic anesthetic solution into each eye. Position the patient comfortably at the slit lamp biomicroscope with the head firmly against the forehead strap. Set the slit lamp magnification at 10X to 16X and use diffuse illumination or a wide parallelepiped of medium intensity. Position a fixation target for the opposite eye so that the orientation of the globe allows for easy access to the rust ring. Stabilize your arm on the slit lamp table, use an armrest if desired, or rest the fourth and fifth fingers of the dominant hand on the patient's cheek, bridge of the nose, or upright bar of the slit lamp.

Initially align the rust ring removal instrument by sighting outside of the slit lamp, positioning it in front of the rust ring at an angle tangential to the corneal surface. Once aligned, use the slit lamp for the remainder of the procedure. Ask the patient to blink, and then secure the upper lid with the nondominant hand if necessary. An assistant may secure the upper lid, or use an eyelid speculum (see p. 98) if patient cooperation is poor.

Hand-held Ophthalmic Burr: Hold the burr like a pencil between the thumb and forefinger at an angle tangential to the plane of the cornea. Contact the burr with the rust ring and apply gentle pressure. Twirl the burr between your fingers so that the burr head rotates on the cornea and removes the rust ring. Irrigate the eye with sterile saline solution (see p. 152) following removal of the rust ring.

Spud or Needle: Hold the corneal FB spud or sterile disposable 25G ⅝-inch needle between the thumb and forefinger like a pencil. Keeping the instrument tangential to the cornea, use small motions to scrape away the epithelium that contains the rust. Irrigate the eye with sterile saline solution (see p. 152) following removal of the rust ring.

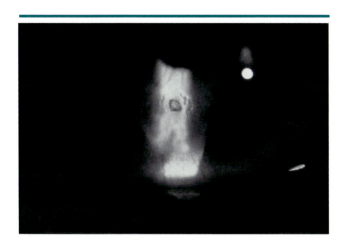

1. A corneal rust ring is noted following removal of an embedded metallic foreign body. The surrounding epithelial defect is also visible. (*See also* Color Plate 45–1.) (Used with permission from Casser L, Lingel NJ: Diseases of the cornea, in Bartlett JD, Jaanus SD (eds): *Clinical Ocular Pharmacology,* ed 2. Boston, Butterworth-Heinemann, 1995: 689.)

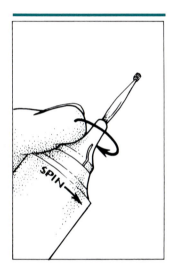

2. The Algerbrush is a small, low-speed, battery-operated drill fitted with a tiny dental burr that is used to remove a corneal rust ring. It is turned on by rotating the base of the burr in the direction indicated by the arrow on the handle.

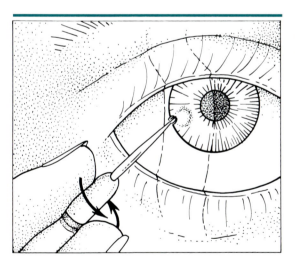

3. A hand-held ophthalmic burr may be used to remove a corneal rust ring. The burr is held tangentially in contact with the tissue and is manually twirled to rotate the burr and remove the rust ring.

Algerbrush: To alleviate patient apprehension during this technique, mention that the Algerbrush makes a soft whirring noise, and encourage the patient to ignore it if possible. Turn on the Algerbrush by rotating the base of the burr with your finger in the direction indicated by the arrow on the handle. (Fig. 2.) The burr will begin to rotate and a whirring noise will be heard.

Keeping the instrument tangential to the cornea, lightly contact the rotating burr with all areas of the rust ring (Fig. 4). Avoid applying too much pressure to the cornea. If the Algerbrush continually stops during the procedure, restart the rotation of the burr, and reduce the amount of pressure applied during the technique. Stop the rotation of the burr by putting pressure on the housing of the burr with your finger. Irrigate the eye with sterile saline solution (see p. 152) following removal of the corneal rust ring.

■ **Interpretation.** It is very common to note wrinkling of the cornea as mild pressure is applied tangentially during removal of the rust ring. While using the Algerbrush, a noticeable amount of epithelial debris will be generated. A small crater-like corneal epithelial defect will remain after removal of a superficial corneal rust ring, for which appropriate treatment is instituted (Fig. 5). A ring of edema may remain that will resolve as the cornea heals. If the embedded metallic foreign body and resultant rust ring have been present for a substantial period of time, a secondary anterior uveitis may be present, which also resolves with appropriate treatment and as the cornea heals.

In many instances the rust ring will vary in its consistency. For example, a larger, more solid component may overlie a softer, more diffuse component. In this event, it is not unusual to combine removal techniques. The spud might be most useful to remove the solid component, followed by use of the Algerbrush for the softer component.

If the amount of rust associated with the metallic corneal FB is mild or if rust ring removal proves to be difficult, it is possible to allow the rust to leach out spontaneously as the patient is followed over the next few days. A rust ring removal technique can still be used if the spontaneous leaching is insufficient.

■ **Contraindications/Complications.** Secondary bacterial infection of the resulting corneal defect is possible after rust ring removal, so prophylactic antibiotic treatment is typically initiated until the cornea heals. Increasing inflammation following rust ring removal suggests the possibility of a retained intraocular foreign body. Use caution when removing a rust ring with a needle so that corneal perforation does not occur inadvertently.

If Bowman's membrane or the anterior stroma is disrupted by the metallic foreign body or during removal of the accompanying rust ring, a small corneal scar may result that tends not to affect visual acuity. If a small amount of rust is retained, the scar will have a faint orange-brown color. For metallic foreign bodies that are determined to be deep within the corneal stroma or if corneal perforation is suspected, a referral for consultation is recommended.

The patient will experience discomfort to a varying degree following corneal rust ring removal depending upon the initial degree of involvement as well as the ease with which the FB and rust ring were successfully removed. Appropriate topical or systemic therapy for pain control may be initiated. It is also helpful to educate the patient about appropriate safety eyewear issues to help prevent future corneal FBs.

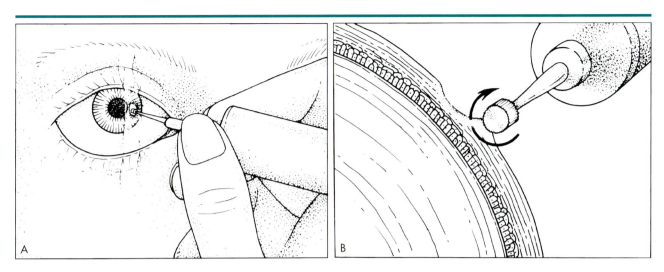

4. A. The Algerbrush is held tangentially to the cornea. B. The rotating burr is lightly touched to the corneal tissue to remove the rust ring in the area from which the metallic FB was removed.

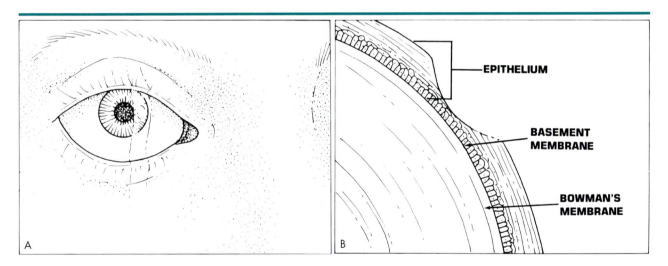

5. A small crater-like epithelial defect will remain immediately after removal of a superficial corneal rust ring, as seen using the slit lamp biomicroscope (A) and in cross-section (B).

46 Therapeutic Patching

■ **Description/Indications.** There are many indications for and methods of patching the eye. The most common indications include treatment for corneal injuries and other types of corneal epithelial compromise, temporary protection after minor surgical procedures, protection using a metal shield following more invasive ocular surgery or in the presence of a penetrating wound, as well as occlusion therapy for amblyopia.

A mainstay of treatment for corneal epithelial compromise has long been the "pressure patch," a technique intended to immobilize the eyelid to reduce discomfort and to promote the corneal healing process. Following instillation of a long-acting mydriatic/cycloplegic agent as well as topical ophthalmic antibiotic ointment, one or more eyepads are placed over the closed lid and secured with strips of hypoallergenic tape to apply pressure against the eyelid and globe. The patient is generally reexamined in 24 hours, at which time the pressure patch is removed. Pressure-free direct eyelid taping is an alternative method of therapeutic patching in which constant lid closure is desired. The eyelid is taped shut with hypoallergenic tape and then covered with a noncompressive eyepad, which is also taped in place. Patients with tender globes are often more comfortable with this technique than the traditional pressure patch. It also allows for drug reinstillation by the patient if aggressive medical therapy is needed in the first 24-hour period.

This section describes the procedures for therapeutic patching of the eye by pressure patching and direct lid taping.

■ **Instrumentation.** Sterile gauze eyepads, 1-inch hypoallergenic tape, alcohol swabs, topical ophthalmic anesthetic solution, topical ophthalmic mydriatic/cycloplegic solution(s), topical ophthalmic antibiotic ointment.

■ **Technique.** If the patient is photophobic, dim the examination room lights to enhance patient comfort. Instill a topical ophthalmic anesthetic solution to improve patient comfort and cooperation.

If indicated, instill a long-acting mydriatic/cycloplegic solution. It is optimal to ensure that the pupil is fully dilated before applying the patch. This is especially important for patients with darkly pigmented irises whose pupils may dilate poorly. Maximum pupillary dilation will increase patient comfort and will reduce the likelihood of a secondary traumatic anterior uveitis.

Recline the patient slightly in the examination chair. Inspect the patient's face from the perspective of applying the patch, especially with regard to the depth of the globe in the orbit relative to the orbital rim, which will determine the positioning and number of eyepads used. Ask the patient to look up and instill a small ribbon of topical ophthalmic antibiotic ointment into the inferior cul-de-sac (see p. 12). Ask the patient to close both eyes for the remainder of the procedure. Squeeze excess fluid from an alcohol pad and swab the skin of the cheek and forehead where the tape will be applied to remove oil from the skin and enhance adherence of the tape.

Pressure Patching: Push any hair away from the face. Fold one patch in half and place it over the closed eyelid (Fig. 1A). Place a second and third patch over the initial patch, angling them slightly along an imaginary line connecting the bridge of the nose and the ipsilateral ear (Fig. 1B). For shallow orbits two patches may suffice, while deep orbits may require a fourth patch to create pressure on the cornea. Keep the patches in place by asking the patient to gently hold a finger on the patch. Tip the patient's head slightly backward to balance the patches on the eye, or apply a short piece of tape over the eyepads.

Cut a 6 to 7-inch piece of tape, place one end at the midpoint of the forehead, and use the thumb of one hand to securely hold it in place. With the free hand lay the tape diagonally across the patches, pulling it taut as it runs toward the cheek and top of the mandible (Fig. 2A). Keep the tape away from the nasolabial fold and side of the mouth so that the patient may chew or talk comfortably without loosening the tape. Pinch the skin of the cheek upward where the end of the tape will be positioned. Release the pinched skin as the tape is placed on the skin (Fig. 2B). This increases the pressure of the patch. Ask the patient to attempt to open the eye; if he or she cannot, the patch has been properly applied and the remaining pieces of tape can be secured.

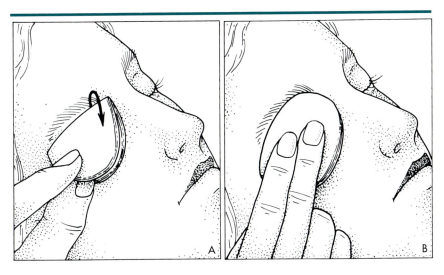

1. A. For pressure patching, a folded eyepad is placed over the closed eye. B. Two or three additional eyepads are used as indicated to patch the eye. The patient holds the patches gently in place until a strip of tape is applied.

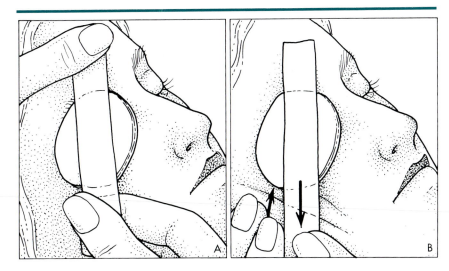

2. A. The first strip of tape is placed down the center of the patch, and is anchored on the forehead and on the cheek. B. The cheek is pinched upwards as the first strip of tape is placed. This tends to tighten the tape once the skin is released.

Cut a second piece of tape about 6 inches in length, starting it closer to the bridge of the nose and overlapping the first piece (Fig. 3A). Curve or contour this piece so it follows and covers the superior and lateral edges of the patch. Apply a third piece of tape, about 6 inches in length, starting temporally to the original piece of tape (Fig. 3B). Overlap the original strip of tape at the superior and inferior temporal edges. Apply a fourth piece of tape, 7 inches in length, in a downward direction along the route of the first strip. Pull this trip taut, making sure it overlaps the inner edges of strips two and three and covers all ends of the tape on the cheek (Fig. 3C). Use a fifth piece of tape, about 4 inches in length, to close off the lateral aspect of the patch, if still exposed.

Prescribe an analgesic if the patient is in considerable discomfort. Instruct the patient to leave the patch in place until reexamined in 24 hours, and to avoid taking a shower or getting the patch wet. Also explain that the eye may feel worse once the topical anesthetic has worn off.

Remove the pressure patch by pulling down on the skin of the cheek and at the same time, with the other hand grasping the end of the first strip of tape, lift the end of the tape, starting from the bottom and advancing toward the forehead (Fig. 4). The eyepads will lift off as the tape is removed.

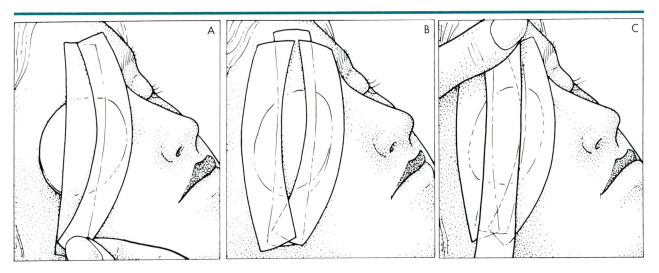

3. A. The second strip of tape is placed inside the original strip. It follows the contour of the patch before ending on the cheek. B. The third strip of tape is placed to the outside of the original strip. C. The fourth strip of tape is centered over the patches. It overlaps the sides of the other strips of tape.

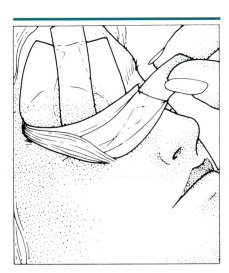

4. The pressure patch is removed by grasping the bottom piece of tape and pulling upward to remove the tape and eyepads.

Direct Lid Taping: Place a strip of tape horizontally along the closed upper eyelid of the affected eye while applying lateral pressure (Fig. 5A). Fold one corner of the strip of tape to provide an easily accessible tab for anticipated removal. Apply a second strip of tape vertically, starting superiorly so that it is perpendicular to and superimposed upon the first strip. After adherence of the two strips, pull gently downward on the closed eyelid and apply the strip across the eyelashes onto the cheekbone area (Fig. 5B). Ask the patient to attempt to open the eye to ensure proper closure technique. For general protection and to avoid patient access to the tape, gently secure one or two eyepads in a noncompressive manner using three or four strips of adhesive tape, as shown in Figure 3.

When removing the direct lid tape after removing the eyepads, pull the superior end of the vertically oriented strip downward to help prevent discomfort by pulling on the eyelashes. Grasp the tab of the horizontal strip to remove it.

Although the 24-hour pressure patch using eyepads and tape has been widely used for a long period of time, recent studies and clinical experience suggest that very successful alternative techniques are available. These alternative techniques have been viewed to increase patient comfort, to reduce corneal healing time, and to enhance visual function by eliminating the source of monocular occlusion and by retaining stereopsis. These alternative methods of treating corneal epithelial lesions include the use of topical ophthalmic antibiotic drops or ointment along with mydriatic/cycloplegia without the use of a patch, or using a disposable soft contact lens with topical ophthalmic antibiotic drops. The use of topical ophthalmic nonsteroidal anti-inflammatory drugs to control pain and secondary inflammation has also been described.

■ Interpretation/Management.

After the patch is removed, wipe away any lid debris. Wait a few minutes before taking a visual acuity to allow the patient to become reacclimated. Use a penlight and slit lamp to assess the size and shape of the remaining corneal abrasion, corneal edema, discharge, hyperemia, and cells and flare (see p. 22).

Mild to moderate abrasions usually heal in 24 to 36 hours, while larger abrasions may take 48 to 72 hours or longer to resolve. If after 24 hours the abrasion has not totally healed, repatch with appropriate pharmaceutical agents, and ask the patient to return again in 24 hours. Infants and children heal extremely quickly while diabetics often heal slowly. Recurrent corneal erosions may require several days to resolve, especially in cases of anterior basement membrane dystrophy. Patching can be discontinued when re-epithelialization is complete.

■ Contraindications/Complications.

Beards may interfere with adhesion of the tape during patching. Placement of the tape may need to be modified or an alternative technique chosen. A pressure patch should never be applied whenever a penetrating injury is suspected. A protective shield should be applied and the patient referred promptly. Epithelial defects associated with contact lens wear may predispose the patient to bacterial keratitis, so pressure patching is best avoided for these patients.

Anterior uveitis may be part of the spectrum of sequelae due to the corneal injury. Treatment with a steroid suspension is generally delayed until a patch is no longer required, since in most cases the inflammation is secondary to the epithelial loss and will resolve once re-epithelialization occurs. Discharge, especially if increasing in severity, is a sign of ocular infection and must be dealt with promptly.

After removing the patch, several corneal changes may be noted due to the mechanical effects of patching. Punctate staining secondary to the irritative effects of the ointment may be seen. This will resolve as the ointment is discontinued. Corneal edema or folds in the stroma and Descemet's membrane may be due to the pressure effects of the patch on the cornea. The folds and edema will disappear with discontinuation of the patch. Five percent sodium chloride solution may hasten the recovery.

Some individuals' skin may be sensitive to either the mechanical or allergic effects of the tape. A mild red erythematous area occurs on the skin where the tape was placed. This will disappear in several days after the patch is removed. A low-dose topical dermatologic steroid may hasten the recovery.

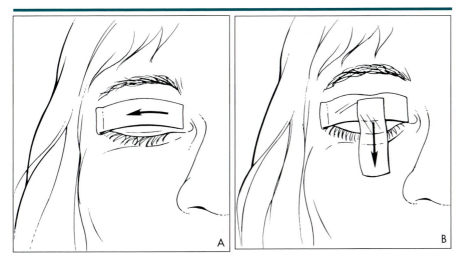

5. A. For direct lid taping, a strip of tape is placed horizontally along the closed upper eyelid while lateral pressure is applied. B. A second strip of tape is placed vertically, starting superiorly so that it is perpendicular to and superimposed upon the first strip. Gentle downward pressure is applied to the closed eyelid, and the strip is adhered across the eyelashes onto the cheekbone area.

47 Corneal Debridement

■ **Description/Indications.** Loose or damaged corneal epithelium is frequently removed as a therapeutic measure to enhance corneal healing. This corneal debridement procedure provides for a "clean" edge of epithelium from which the centripetal movement of epithelial resurfacing may be facilitated. For example, corneal debridement is used to remove loose tissue or "flaps" surrounding a corneal abrasion or recurrent corneal erosion, corneal filaments in filamentary keratitis, and the milky coagulation of epithelium (eschar) in mild corneal thermal burns.

Two methods of corneal debridement are described here. A "minimal wipe" form removes only the loose, damaged epithelium and is performed with a sterile cotton-tipped applicator. A more extensive form of corneal debridement is performed with an Algerbrush, which is used, for example, to remove epithelial flaps surrounding a corneal abrasion or recurrent corneal erosion that cannot be "wiped" away with a cotton-tipped applicator. Debridement of normal corneal epithelium is performed using a blunt spatula (e.g., Paton) prior to photorefractive keratectomy (PRK).

The Algerbrush is a low-speed, battery-operated drill that is fitted with a tiny dental burr. The Algerbrush is available with several different-size burrs. The smallest size burr (0.5 mm) is used most frequently. The burrs can be removed from the drill for storage and sterilization after use. Disposable burrs are also available.

The Algerbrush has a built-in clutch mechanism that will stop the instrument when a certain degree of resistance is encountered. Bowman's membrane is of a tough consistency and requires a stronger force to penetrate than the Algerbrush can produce. As a result, when the Algerbrush contacts Bowman's membrane, it will automatically shut off. It may also stop when more normal areas of epithelium are encountered during corneal debridement.

■ **Instrumentation.** Slit lamp biomicroscope, Algerbrush with sterile burrs, sterile cotton-tipped applicators, topical ophthalmic anesthetic solution, sterile ophthalmic saline solution.

■ **Technique.** Advise the patient that good cooperation and fixation will facilitate the procedure. Instill two drops of topical ophthalmic anesthetic solution in each eye. Position the patient comfortably at the slit lamp biomicroscope with the head firmly against the forehead strap. Set the slit lamp magnification at 10X to 16X and use diffuse illumination or a wide parallelepiped of medium intensity. Position a fixation target for the opposite eye so that the orientation of the globe allows for easy access to the area to be debrided. Stabilize your arm on the slit lamp table, use an arm rest if desired, or rest the fourth and fifth fingers of the dominant hand on the patient's cheek, bridge of the nose, or upright bar of the slit lamp.

Initially align the debridement instrument by sighting outside of the slit lamp, positioning it in front of the globe at an angle tangential to the corneal surface. Once aligned, use the slit lamp for the remainder of the procedure. Ask the patient to blink, and then secure the upper lid with the nondominant hand if necessary. An assistant may secure the upper lid, or use an eyelid speculum (see p. 98) if patient cooperation is poor.

Cotton-tipped Applicator: Moisten the sterile cotton-tipped applicator with sterile ophthalmic saline solution and hold it between the fingers like a pencil at an angle tangential to the plane of the cornea (Fig. 1A). Use gentle small strokes to "wipe" away the damaged epithelium, working the applicator in one direction (Fig. 1B). Irrigate the eye with sterile saline solution (see p. 152) following debridement with the cotton-tipped applicator.

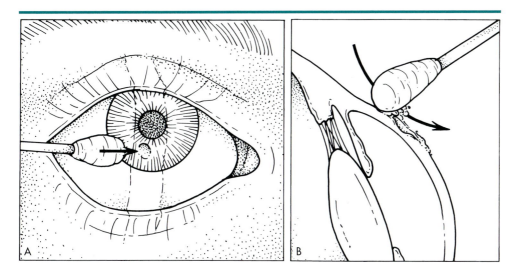

1. A. A moistened sterile cotton-tipped applicator held tangentially to the plane of the cornea may be used for corneal debridement. B. Gentle, small, unidirectional strokes are used to "wipe" away the damaged epithelium.

Algerbrush. To alleviate patient apprehension during this technique, mention that the Algerbrush makes a soft whirring noise, and encourage the patient to ignore it if possible. Turn on the Algerbrush by rotating the base of the burr with your finger in the direction indicated by the arrow on the handle (Fig. 2A). The burr will begin to rotate and a whirring noise will be heard.

Keeping the instrument tangential to the cornea, lightly contact the rotating burr with all portions of the epithelium to be debrided (Fig. 2B). Avoid applying too much pressure to the cornea and avoid removing areas of normal epithelium. If the Algerbrush continually stops during the procedure, restart the rotation of the burr, and reduce the amount of pressure applied during the technique. Stop the rotation of the burr by putting pressure on the housing of the burr with your finger. Irrigate the eye with sterile ophthalmic saline solution (see p. 152) following corneal debridement with the Algerbrush.

■ **Interpretation.** It is very common to note wrinkling of the cornea as mild pressure is applied tangentially during corneal debridement. While using the Algerbrush, a notice-able amount of epithelial debris will be generated. The endpoint for the procedure is removal of the damaged or abnormal epithelium. An epithelial defect of varying size with "clean" edges will remain after corneal debridement, for which appropriate treatment is instituted. If debridement was performed as part of the treatment for a large corneal abrasion, a secondary anterior uveitis may be present, which resolves with appropriate treatment and as the cornea heals.

■ **Contraindications/Complications.** Secondary bacterial infection of the resulting corneal defect is possible following corneal debridement, so prophylactic antibiotic treatment is typically initiated until the cornea heals. Debridement is contraindicated in cases of suspected globe penetration or obvious ocular infection.

Excessive corneal debridement will result in the removal of healthy corneal epithelium. The patient will experience discomfort to a varying degree following corneal debridement, depending upon the size of the epithelial defect following the procedure. Appropriate topical or systemic therapy for pain control may be initiated.

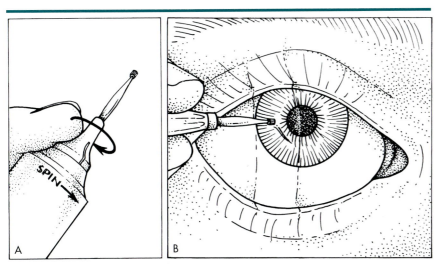

2. A. The Algerbrush is a small, low-speed, battery-operated drill fitted with a tiny dental burr that may be used for corneal debridement. It is turned on by rotating the base of the burr in the direction indicated by the arrow on the handle. B. The Algerbrush is held tangentially to the cornea, and the rotating burr is lightly touched to all portions of the epithelium to be debrided.

48

Corneal Sensitivity Testing

■ **Description/Indications.** The loss of corneal sensitivity to touch may result from specific ocular conditions as well as neurological disorders that affect the corneal nerves. As a result, corneal sensitivity testing can aid in the differential diagnosis of various corneal conditions by ruling out those not associated with diminished corneal sensation. In addition, corneal sensitivity testing is included in the cranial nerve examination (see p. 328) to assess the somatic sensory function of the ophthalmic branch (V1) of the trigeminal nerve (CN5). Loss of corneal sensitivity is often the first sign of damage to the trigeminal nerve.

Some specific ocular conditions in which corneal sensitivity may be reduced include herpes simple keratitis, herpes zoster keratitis, long-term contact lens wear, certain corneal dystrophies and degenerations, dense corneal scars, neurotrophic keratitis, trachoma, and certain types of glaucoma. Corneal sensitivity may be reduced for several months to years after ocular surgery in which corneal nerves were disrupted. Central nervous system disorders and systemic diseases such as diabetes mellitus may reduce corneal sensation. Some conditions may permanently affect corneal sensation; in others, corneal sensitivity will return to normal levels once the underlying process is resolved.

A cotton wisp is frequently used clinically to assess corneal sensitivity. Gross qualification of the sense of touch is made by the patient, comparing one eye to the other. A commercially available device, the Cochet-Bonnet anesthesiometer, specifically quantifies corneal sensation. The instrument is a pen-shaped device with a nylon filament protruding from one end. The pressure exerted on the cornea by the nylon filament is dependent upon its length, which is adjustable. For example, the longer the nylon filament, the smaller the pressure needed to elicit minimum perceptible sensation, and therefore the more sensitive the cornea.

■ **Instrumentation.** Sterile cotton-tipped applicators, sterile fluorescein sodium strips.

■ **Technique.** Provide a brief explanation to the patient as to how the procedure is performed. Explain that he or she may feel a sensation as the eye is touched, but that it will not be painful. Ask the patient to signal as soon as the sensation is felt.

Examine both corneas with the slit lamp biomicroscope (see p. 24). Wash your hands and prepare a cotton wisp by drawing out a small tuft of cotton from a sterile cotton-tipped applicator (Fig. 1A). Twirl the end of the cotton tuft to form a fine wisp (Fig. 1B).

Ask the patient to fixate slightly upward. Hold the cotton-tipped applicator between the thumb and forefinger, and rest the remaining fingers on the patient's cheek. Move the cotton wisp carefully toward the center of the cornea, initially avoiding the patient's line of sight. Gently touch the central cornea, keeping the wisp perpendicular to the corneal plane (Fig. 2). Continue to touch the

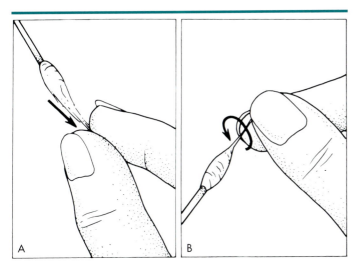

1. A. (far left) To prepare the cotton-tipped applicator for corneal sensitivity testing, a small tuft of cotton is drawn out from the tip.
B. (left) The end of the cotton tuft is twirled to form a fine wisp.

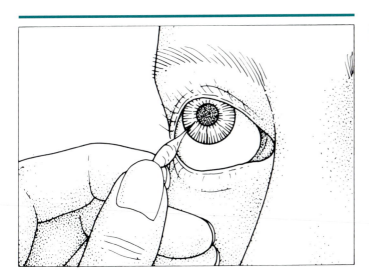

2. The patient is asked to fixate slightly upward, the wisp is held between the thumb and forefinger, and the remaining fingers are supported on the patient's cheek. The wisp is moved toward the center of the cornea while avoiding the patient's line of sight, and the central cornea is gently touched.

wisp to the central cornea until the patient signals that it is felt or until the wisp, while in contact with the cornea, bends slightly (Fig. 3). Alternatively, observe the patient to see if he or she blinks or begins tearing when the wisp contacts the cornea.

Test the other eye in the same fashion, asking the patient to subjectively compare the sensation of one eye to the other. Perform one corneal stroke with the wisp at a time. If necessary, repeat the test a few seconds later to confirm the results. If the test is repeated, it may be helpful to intermittently withhold the wisp from the cornea but continue to ask the patient to respond as if the cornea were being touched. This allows for assessment of the reliability of patient responses.

If necessary, fluorescein sodium dye can be instilled into the eyes after corneal sensitivity testing to assess for any irritation induced by the procedure (see p. 48).

■ **Interpretation.** The patient is asked two questions: Do you feel the wisp touching the eye, and, if so, can you quantify the sensation felt in one eye compared to the other? Corneal sensitivity will be reduced on the side with the related corneal or trigeminal compromise. This will manifest as the absence of sensation on one side compared to the other, a reduction of sensation on one side compared to the other as subjectively described by the patient, or by the absence of a spontaneous blink reflex when one side is tested.

Most individuals will demonstrate a blink reflex when the normal cornea is touched with the wisp. Unfortunately, the blink reflex is not always a reliable sign of intact corneal sensitivity, because the patient may blink as a protective reflex when the wisp approaches the cornea.

■ **Contraindications/Complications.** Topical ophthalmic anesthetic solution cannot be instilled prior to testing corneal sensitivity. In addition, any other procedure that may irritate the cornea should be performed after corneal sensitivity testing.

Care should be taken whenever corneal sensitivity testing is performed on a diseased cornea. In this instance, a separate cotton-tipped applicator should be used for each eye, or the applicator should be used on the healthy cornea first.

Uncommonly, corneal sensitivity testing may result in minor corneal irritation. In that event, explain to the patient that a mild foreign body sensation may be felt for a few hours. Appropriate treatment is instituted if needed, such as antibiotic prophylaxis or artificial tear therapy.

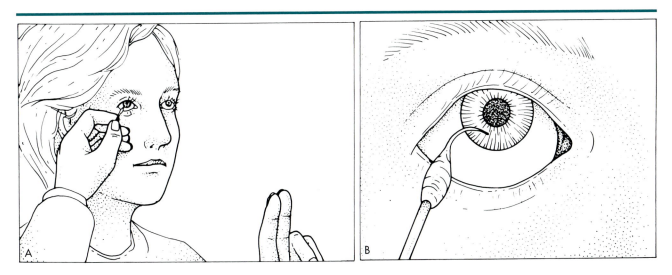

3. Potential end-points of corneal sensitivity testing. The wisp is touched to the central cornea until the patient signals that it is felt (A), or until the examiner is able to touch the wisp to the cornea with sufficient force so that it bends, even if the patient does not signal that it is felt (B).

49

Anterior Stromal Puncture

Description/Indications. Recurrent corneal erosion (RCE) is a common clinical condition that occurs weeks, months, or even longer following previous corneal injury. It occurs most frequently following a linear corneal abrasion such as a fingernail scratch or paper cut. RCE may also occur in association with corneal dystrophic or degenerative conditions such as anterior basement membrane dystrophy (ABMD).

RCE is the result of compromise to the normally firm adhesion between the epithelial basement membrane and Bowman's layer. This loss of tight adhesion leads to recurrent, spontaneous breakdown or sloughing of the epithelial layer of the cornea. Additional corneal compromise from further injury, inflammation, dry eye, or loss of corneal sensation can all contribute to exacerbation of this condition.

Symptoms of pain, foreign body sensation, tearing, photophobia, and blurred vision, ranging from mild to debilitating, which occur upon awakening, comprise the classic clinical presentation of RCE. Reduced overnight tear secretion, coupled with edema from reduced oxygen levels under the closed eyelids, predisposes the poorly wetting surface epithelial cells to adhere to the palpebral conjunctiva with subsequent cell disruption, denudement, and sloughing when the lids are opened. Slit lamp biomicroscopic findings typically reveal an epithelial defect surrounded by loose, gray, edematous epithelium that stains both positively and negatively with fluorescein sodium dye (Fig. 1). These areas frequently exhibit negative staining in the absence of a frank epithelial defect associated with an acute RCE.

When a patient presents with an RCE but without a previous history of corneal injury, the condition is likely the result of a corneal dystrophy or degeneration that causes poor epithelial adhesion. In order to assess this potential cause of the RCE, close examination using the slit lamp biomicroscope is indicated to assess for corneal changes characteristic of ABMD such as maps, dots, fingerprints, and intraepithelial microcysts, which are best visualized using indirect and retroillumination slit lamp techniques (see p. 24). Because ABMD and other corneal dystrophies and degenerations tend to be bilateral, careful examination of the fellow, asymptomatic eye for characteristic changes may assist in determining the etiology of the RCE.

Standard and very successful treatments for RCE consist of different combinations of corneal debridement (see p. 180), ocular lubricants, hypertonic solutions and ointments, pressure patching (see p. 174), bandage soft contact lenses, and collagen shields. Alternative treatment considerations include anterior stromal puncture (ASP), also referred to as epithelial reinforcement, superficial keratectomy, Nd:YAG laser treatment, and diathermy/surface cautery. Anterior stromal puncture is an in-office procedure performed at the slit lamp biomicroscope that involves needle penetration and disruption of the epithelium and Bowman's layer to allow for normal healing, which secures the epithelium and basement membrane to the anterior stroma. These shallow corneal penetrations theoretically stimulate production of laminin, fibronectin, collagen, and other agents needed to produce epithelial adhesion and progressive reorganization over a period of months.

The broad tip of a sterile 20G needle is felt by many to be the best size for anterior stromal puncture, despite other suggestions supporting the use of a 25, 27, or 30G needle. The tip of the needle is bent at the bevel so that the corneal penetrations can be made without a straight-on approach of the needle. A specially designed sterile, disposable 25G anterior stromal puncture needle is available for this technique (Fig. 2). Its design is intended to eliminate the risk of corneal perforation during ASP and to reduce subsequent corneal scarring. The preset 90-degree angle of the distal tip of the ASP needle limits the depth of the corneal punctures. The preset angle at the proximal end of the ASP needle shaft is intended to keep the practitioner's fingers below the patient's line of sight to reduce patient anxiety and to enhance comfort and cooperation.

1. A recurrent corneal erosion (RCE) is noted in the inferior cornea. The epithelial defect is surrounded by loose, edematous epithelium that stains both positively and negatively with fluorescein sodium dye. Used with permission from Casser L, Lingel NJ: Diseases of the cornea, in Bartlett JD, Jaanus SD (eds): *Clinical Ocular Pharmacology*, ed 2. Boston, Butterworth-Heinemann, 1995, p 694.)

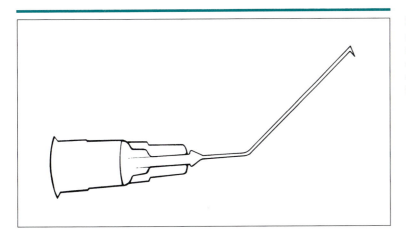

2. The specifically designed sterile, disposable 25G anterior stromal puncture needle is shown. The preset 90-degree angle of the distal tip limits the depth of the corneal punctures, and the preset angle at the proximal end is intended to keep the practitioner's fingers below the patient's line of sight.

■ **Instrumentation.** Slit lamp biomicroscope, sterile disposable 25G anterior stromal puncture needle, topical tetracaine ophthalmic solution, topical ophthalmic non-steroidal anti-inflammatory solution, topical ophthalmic broad-spectrum antibiotic solution and ointment, topical ophthalmic mydriatic/cycloplegic solution(s), sterile fluorescein sodium strips, sterile saline.

■ **Technique.** Instill topical ophthalmic nonsteroidal anti-inflammatory drops into the eye every 15 minutes for 1 hour before the procedure to alleviate postprocedure pain. Instill several drops of antibiotic solution over the same period to reduce the external bacteria count. Instill a few drops of topical ophthalmic anesthetic solution into the treatment eye for comfort and one drop in the fellow eye to reduce the blink reflex. Instill fluorescein sodium dye (see p. 48) to better visualize the extent of the involved epithelium as well as the puncture marks as they are made.

Advise the patient that good cooperation and fixation will facilitate the procedure. Position the patient comfortably at the slit lamp biomicroscope with a reminder that the head must be kept firmly against the forehead strap. Set the slit lamp magnification at 10X to 16X and use diffuse illumination or a wide parallelepiped of medium intensity. Position a fixation target for the opposite eye so that the orientation of the globe allows for easy access to the area for ASP. Do not debride the cornea before treatment unless a loose flap of epithelium is present and moves with each blink.

Initially align the ASP needle by sighting outside of the slit lamp and positioning it in front of the corneal area to be treated. Hold the specially designed disposable anterior stromal puncture needle perpendicular to the cornea, resting your remaining fingers on the patient's cheek for stability (Fig. 3). Inspect the fluorescein pattern and begin making nonconfluent, closely placed puncture marks throughout the entire erosion area, approximately 0.5 to 1.0 mm apart (Fig. 4). The stroma is penetrated to the depth allowed by the preset 90-degree angle of the distal ASP needle tip. Extend the punctures approximately 1 to 2 mm beyond the lesion onto normal corneal tissue, using retroillumination (see p. 42) to better define the edges of the erosion area.

■ **Interpretation.** During the procedure, corneal wrinkling and indentation will be noted as the ASP penetrations are made. After the procedure, multiple focal corneal epithelial defects will remain at the site of the ASP penetrations. Instill drops of topical ophthalmic antibiotic, nonsteroidal anti-inflammatory, and mydriatic/cycloplegic solutions. Instill a topical ophthalmic antibiotic ointment and apply a pressure patch (see p. 174). Prescribe systemic pain medication if needed and schedule a follow-up examination for the next day.

Continue patching with antibiotic ointment and nonsteroidal anti-inflammatory drops, with cycloplegia if necessary, until positive fluorescein sodium staining is no longer present following healing of the corneal epithelium. This usually takes 2 to 3 days, at which time this treatment can be discontinued. At this time, prescribe 5% sodium chloride hypertonic ointment four times a day for 1 week, and then at bedtime only or more frequently as needed for at least 6 months because mild symptoms may persist. As the cornea heals, small corneal scars may persist at the site of the ASP treatments.

■ **Contraindications/Complications.** The patient should be informed that at least one repeat procedure is possible in approximately 20% of patients. Although loss of acuity or glare do not appear to be significantly reported problems, limit or avoid ASP treatments in the visual axis unless necessary for a successful outcome. Poor technique during ASP may result in corneal perforation.

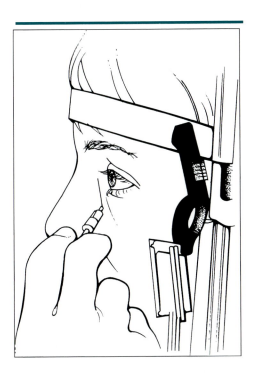

3. While viewing through the slit lamp biomicroscope, the hand holding the ASP needle is stabilized on the patient's cheek in preparation for making the puncture marks.

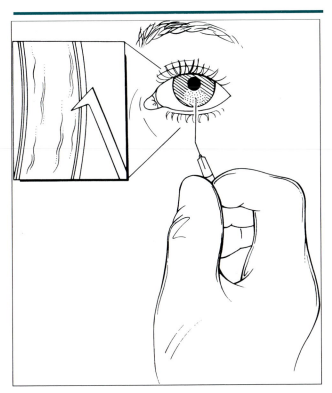

4. Nonconfluent, closely placed corneal puncture marks are made approximately 0.5 to 1.0 mm apart throughout the entire erosion area, extending 1 to 2 mm beyond the lesion onto normal corneal tissue. The stroma is penetrated to the depth allowed by the preset 90-degree angle of the distal tip of the ASP needle (inset).

50
Corneal Topography

■ **Description/Indications.** Clinicians have long recognized the importance of assessing corneal structure but have lacked the means by which to accurately assess its surface characteristics. The keratometer measures an annulus of approximately 2.5 to 3.5 mm, but it does not assess the central and peripheral cornea. The theory behind keratometry also assumes that corneal curvature is constant across any meridian and that the major power meridians are orthogonal. Although these assumptions are acceptable for the healthy cornea, they are not valid for many patients who wear contact lenses, have undergone refractive surgery, have experienced ocular trauma, or manifest corneal disease. It is for these reasons that computerized corneal topography, or videokeratography, has become a more integral part of clinical practice.

The indications for computerized corneal topography can be classified into three categories: baseline applications, differential diagnosis, and therapeutic decision-making. Corneal topography is indicated for those patients contemplating refractive surgery, or who have a history of corneal trauma or suspected pathology. Many clinicians incorporate this procedure as part of the contact lens fitting, especially for rigid contact lens wearers. Corneal topography serves as an adjunct in fitting standard contact lenses or may be reserved for those requiring specialty fits such as toric, multifocal, and orthokeratology contact lens designs.

Corneal topography is valuable in evaluating patients with a questionable diagnosis. For example, subtle differences in corneal topography assist in the differential diagnosis between contact lens warpage and keratoconus. In addition, corneal topography often identifies irregular astigmatism undetected by other instruments, thereby accounting for decreased vision of unknown etiology. This is particularly important in evaluating the patient with a tentative diagnosis of amblyopia.

Numerous studies demonstrate the value of corneal topography in planning astigmatic keratotomy, radial keratotomy, and excimer laser photorefractive keratectomy, as well as in selective suture removal following ocular surgery. Perhaps one of the most valuable applications of corneal topography in differential diagnosis relates to the post-refractive surgery patient. Corneal topography performed following radial keratotomy assists in identifying individuals in need of enhancement, those with irregular astigmatism, and those at risk of diurnal fluctuations in vision. For the patient who has undergone photorefractive keratectomy, corneal topography aids in detecting atypical wound healing, central islands or divots, and decentered ablation zones.

With few exceptions, corneal topography units operate on the principle of reflective photokeratoscopy. Each unit is comprised of five key components (Fig. 1). The first is a self-illuminated, multiple-ring placido disc. The placido disc is projected onto the anterior corneal surface, where the reflected rings form a virtual image in the anterior chamber. Depending upon the corneal curvature and the type of topography unit, the reflected rings can represent a corneal diameter of over 10 mm. One or more video cameras housed within the placido cone photograph the image. Next, the photograph is scanned and digitized, resulting in up to 10,000 raw data points. The data points are analyzed by a central processing unit to generate the topography map. Most topography units operate in a DOS or Windows system and use a Pentium chip processor.

Once a captured corneal image has been deemed accurate, it is processed to generate a topography map. The computer analyzes the placido photokeratoscope photography, digitizes the data points, and converts the raw data into a topography map. Each instrument employs its own proprietary algorithm to generate the map. Although there is considerable debate as to which manufacturer offers the most accurate and reproducible algorithm, all are spherically biased and have certain inherent limitations. In addition, each performs a certain amount of extrapolation to fill in data point voids. In this sense, a map is not a true point-by-point replication of the entire corneal surface. One of the many benefits of corneal topography, however, is the ability to evaluate these data in a number of different formats.

■ **Instrumentation.** Corneal topography unit, including placido photokeratoscope, central processing unit, color video monitor, and printer; artificial tears.

■ **Technique.** Instill a drop of artificial tears in each eye to maximize the integrity of the corneal refractive surface, particularly for those patients with dry eye or epithelial compromise.

Turn on the corneal topography unit. This is usually accomplished by one switch, but inspect the computer, placido photokeratoscope, video monitor, and printer to confirm that each component is operating. The instrument quickly performs a number of internal system checks, and then it is ready for use.

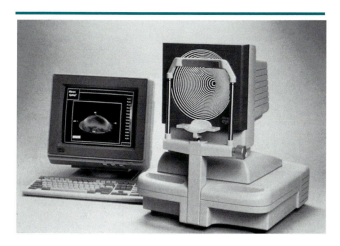

1. An example of a corneal topography unit, which includes a self-illuminated multiple ring placido disc and a computerized processing unit. (Courtesy of Alcon.)

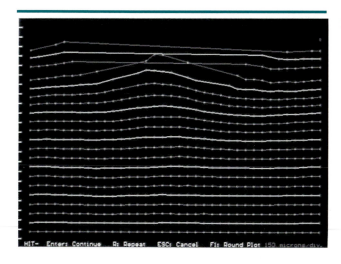

2. The analysis verification screen demonstrates the number of rings imaged and the number of data points acquired per ring. This example demonstrates a number of smooth and complete rings, exemplifying a good image. (Courtesy of EyeSys.)

Enter pertinent patient data into the computer. Many topography instruments provide for the entering of diagnosis, refractive findings, and freelance text regarding the patient's history. Seat the patient comfortably at the topography unit, ensuring that his or her head is properly positioned, with the chin in the rest and the forehead against the strap.

Position the placido photokeratoscope in front of the eye to be imaged, and ask the patient to view the central fixation light. Perform final alignment of the patient and refine the focus of the placido disc rings. Certain topography units require that this step be performed manually, while others offer an integrated auto focus and alignment.

Instruct the patient to maintain fixation, blink once, and then open the eye widely. The topography image is captured by pushing the appropriate button.

Image acquisition is followed by computerized analysis. Many corneal topography units have validation checks to assure image accuracy prior to processing. One such feature is the analysis verification screen (Fig. 2). This screen demonstrates the number of rings imaged and the number of data points acquired per ring. In this particular example, the requested density is a data point every 10 degrees per ring, with up to 23 rings being processed. This particular example demonstrates a number of smooth and complete rings, exemplifying a good image. A screen in which the lines intersect or in which there are few data points per line suggests a poor image. In this event, capture another image prior to processing.

Proceed with the desired analysis options, described in the following subsections.

Normalized Display: The color scale is created around the median dioptric point for that particular map. The result is a customized scale according to the patient's individual corneal topography, and smaller dioptric variations are more dramatically displayed. The disadvantage of this display is that different maps are not easily compared. For instance, the color red can represent a different dioptric value for one eye compared to the other.

Absolute Display: In this format, the color scale represents a large, fixed dioptric range. A specific color represents a certain dioptric value regardless of the patient's corneal dioptric range. The benefit of this display is that map-to-map comparisons are easily made. The limitations are that a color represents a larger dioptric range, so that subtle topography variations are not readily discernible.

Keratometer Display: This format generates a simulated keratometry. Instead of using two data points in each of two orthogonal meridians as in traditional keratometry, the instrument samples multiple points along the steepest and flattest meridians. The benefits of this display include obtaining a more accurate reading than with keratometry alone, and the major meridians are not assumed to be orthogonal.

Comparative Display: In this format the instrument is used to compare two maps. The benefits of this display include the ability to compare right and left maps for asymmetry and to compare sequential maps for the same eye.

Difference Display: This option allows for a digital subtraction of two maps. It is particularly valuable in assessing the impact of contact lens wear or surgical keratoreformation.

Meridional or Profile Display: This option dissects the topography across a specified meridian and is an excellent means for demonstrating irregular astigmatism.

Three-dimensional Display: This option displays the corneal topography in an elevation map format and is excellent for patient education purposes.

Numeric Display: This format is actually the framework upon which the color maps are constructed. It is an excellent option for assigning a dioptric value to a specific point, but it is not particularly valuable as a qualitative overview.

Sagittal Versus Tangential Display: These maps represent different ways in which to interpret raw data. It is generally accepted that the tangential map is more representative of actual corneal curvature and is the standard in many of the instruments.

Read the desired topographical data as displayed on the color monitor, or print a hard copy. Once an image is captured, reposition the placido photokeratoscope in front of the fellow eye and repeat the procedure.

■ **Interpretation.** In interpreting corneal topography, the clinician first evaluates the color scale. As previously indicated, color scales are expressed in a normalized or absolute mode. The universal standard dictates that flatter dioptric values correlate with cooler (blue) colors, while steeper dioptric values are represented by hotter (red) colors. Once the color scale is established, the dioptric sensitivity is evaluated. A generally accepted protocol correlates an incremental color shade change for every 0.50 diopter of topographic variation. In this fashion, a reasonable degree of sensitivity is evident, yet extraneous information is avoided from excessively small dioptric increments (Fig. 3).

Several tenets of normal corneal topography have been observed, one of which is enantiomorphism. This implies that the topographical maps of the right and left eyes are nonsuperimposable mirror images of one another (Fig. 4). The clinical significance of this characteristic is evident in primary idiopathic keratoconus, in which the lack of enantiomorphism is an early diagnostic finding.

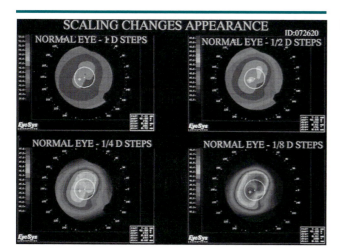

3. The resultant difference in the appearance of a corneal map is shown as the incremental dioptric color shade change is varied.

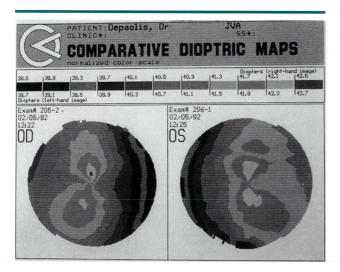

4. Enantiomorphism of the normal cornea: The maps of the right and left eyes are nonsuperimposable mirror images of one another. (*See also* Color Plate 50–4.)

A second consideration of normal corneal topography is that of variable asphericity (Fig. 5). Topography has helped to provide a better understanding of the nonconoidal nature of the cornea. It is generally accepted that corneal asphericity is meridional specific, and that the average cornea flattens to a greater extent nasally than temporally. The clinical significance of this feature as evaluated by corneal topography is that more patient-specific contact lens designs can be created.

Yet another feature of normal corneal topography is that most patients have some detectable degree of corneal toricity. The orientation of the astigmatism is with-the-rule (Fig. 6) in approximately two thirds of all cases, against the rule in approximately one sixth, and oblique in the remaining one sixth. Relatively few normal corneas are entirely free of astigmatism. Qualifying and quantifying the astigmatism allows those individuals performing the contact lens fitting and the refractive surgery to plan an appropriate course.

The astigmatic configuration of the cornea is a hallmark of normal topography as well. Approximately 50% of normal eyes have a bow tie astigmatic configuration, 21% are oval, 21% are round, and fewer than 8% are irregular in profile. Within the bow tie category, controversy exists regarding the significance of symmetric versus asymmetric configurations (Fig. 7). Occasionally, a simple shift in patient fixation changes the irregular bow tie to a more normal-appearing topography. The importance of this feature lies in the fact that many corneal diseases, poorly fit contact lenses, and less than optimal surgical outcomes manifest an irregular profile.

One final aspect of normal topography is that the corneal apex is in close proximity to and often encompasses the patient's line of sight. Occasionally, the steepest corneal curvature is slightly displaced relative to the visual axis, but not substantially so (Fig. 8). This aspect is clinically significant as there are a number of apical shift disorders that do not conform to this standard.

■ Complications/Contraindications.

If the patient has a dry, irregular corneal surface, additional drops of artificial tears may be instilled to enhance the image acquisition. If the photokeratoscopic rings are obstructed due to a prominent supraorbital rim or nose, the patient's head may be rotated slightly while he or she maintains fixation. In this fashion, greater ring exposure is assured prior to capturing an image.

There are no known risks to a patient when performing corneal topography. Anatomic or postural difficulties may preclude the patient from being successfully positioned at the topography unit.

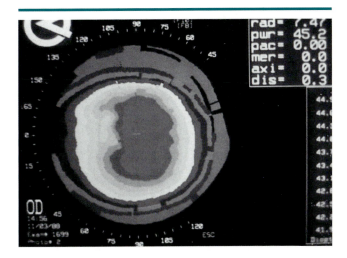

5. Variable asphericity of the normal cornea: Asphericity is meridional specific and the cornea flattens to a greater extent nasally than temporally. (*See also* Color Plate 50–5.)

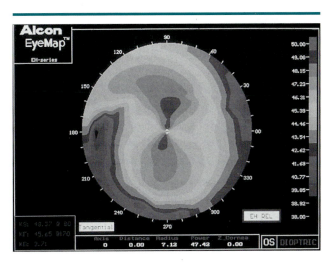

6. Corneal toricity: Most normal corneas have some detectable degree of corneal toricity, as represented in this symmetric with-the-rule bow tie configuration. (*See also* Color Plate 50–6.)

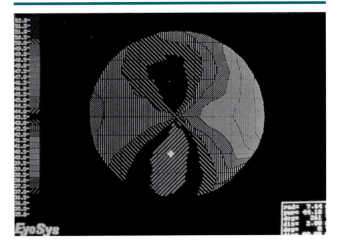

7. This topographic map illustrates an asymmetric bow tie configuration to the with-the-rule astigmatism. (*See also* Color Plate 50–7.) (Courtesy of EyeSys.)

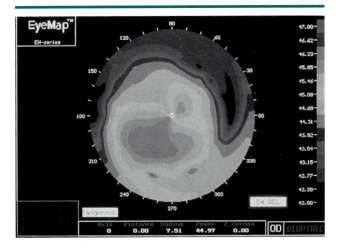

8. Occasionally, the steepest corneal curvature is found to be slightly displaced relative to the visual axis. (*See also* Color Plate 50–8.)

VI Suggested Readings

Bartlett JD: Ophthalmic drug delivery, in Bartlett JD, Jaanus SD (eds): *Clinical Ocular Pharmacology,* ed 2. Boston, Butterworth-Heinemann, 1995, 47–74.

Bogan SJ, et. al: Classification of normal corneal topography based on computer-assisted videokeratography. *Arch Ophthalmol* 1990;**108:**945.

Buratto L (ed): *Corneal Topography: The Clinical Atlas.* Thorofare, NJ, Slack, 1996.

Casser L, Lingel NJ: Diseases of the cornea, in Bartlett JD, Jaanus SD (eds): *Clinical Ocular Pharmacology,* ed 2. Boston, Butterworth-Heinemann, 1995, pp 679–745.

Catania LJ: *Primary Care of the Anterior Segment,* ed 2. Norwalk, CT, Appleton Lange, 1995.

Eskridge JB, Amos JF, Bartlett JD (eds): *Clinical Procedures in Optometry,* Philadelphia, Lippincott, 1991.

Frucht-Pery J, Stiebel H, Hemo I, et al: Effect of eye patching on ocular surface. *Am J Ophthalmol* 1993;**115:**629–633.

Hulbert MFG: Efficacy of eyepad in corneal healing after foreign body removal. *Lancet* 1991;**337:**643.

Kirkpatrick JNP, Hoh HB, Cook SD: No eye pad for corneal abrasion. *Eye* 1993;**7:**468–471.

McLean EN, MacRae SM, Rich LF: Recurrent erosion: treatment by anterior stromal puncture. *Ophthalmology* 1986;**93:**784–788.

Rubinfeld RS: Recurrent corneal erosion. In *Master Techniques in Ophthalmic Surgery.* Baltimore, Williams & Wilkins, 1995, pp 184–191.

Rubinfeld RS, Laibson PR, Cohen EJ, et al: Anterior stromal puncture for recurrent erosion: Further experience and new instrumentation. *Ophthalmic Surg* 1990;**21:**318–326.

Sanders DR, Koch DD (eds): *An Atlas of Corneal Topography.* Thorofare, NJ, Slack, 1993.

VII

Ocular Microbiology and Cytology Procedures

51 Cultures

■ **Description/Indications.** Certain external infections that threaten the integrity of the eye require microbiological laboratory analysis to identify the microorganism(s) involved. Ocular laboratory studies center on two areas, cytology and cultures. Whereas cytological studies (see p. 210) help identify bacteria, viruses, fungi, and allergens, the latter by the eye's cellular response to these stimuli, microbiological culture techniques are mainly used for bacterial identification. Viral cultures are also available and becoming more commonly used.

Culture studies involve the growth of colonies of microorganisms on compatible media. A small amount of material from the eye containing the microorganisms is spread onto solid media plates. The plates are incubated and evaluated for the growth of distinct colonies. The characteristics of growth are specific for each microorganism and aid in identification. After each microorganism is grown and isolated, the characteristics of each pathogen are described.

Culture results are also used to study the sensitivity of microorganisms to specific antibiotics. The resistance pattern of each organism to specific antibiotics is studied, leading to more effective antibiotic usage. Sensitivity studies are generally requested whenever cultures are taken. With bacteria, it takes 24 to 48 hours before culture results are available, so treatment is usually initiated with broad-spectrum agents just after the culture is taken. The treatment is modified if the culture and sensitivity results indicate that other antibiotics might be more effective.

Cultures are indicated when clinical findings are insufficient to arrive at a diagnosis, when the tissue reaction is severe, or when the infection has not responded in a suitable time frame to appropriate treatment. Specific indications for culture include hyperacute conjunctivitis, neonatal conjunctivitis, postoperative infections, chronic conjunctivitis, and central corneal ulcers not of viral antigenic origin.

Agar plates are the solid medium used to grow microorganisms for isolation and identification. Blood agar is the most commonly used plate. It is a general-purpose medium that will grow most bacterial organisms. *Neisseria* and *Haemophilus* do not grow well on blood agar; therefore, chocolate agar (a polypeptone agar enriched with hemoglobin) is also used. These plates are typically incubated in 10% CO_2 to enhance the growth of these organisms. Blood and chocolate agar plates are requested for all eye cultures. Other media such as Sabouraud's agar (fungi isolation) and Thayer-Martin agar (gonococcal identification) might be required, depending on the case presentation. The media plates are refrigerated until use and are brought to room temperature prior to inoculation. Thioglycolate broth (liquid medium) is useful as a transportation medium and will grow facultative anaerobic organisms as well as aerobes and fungi.

A Culturette is a commercially prepared transport container used for cultures. It is readily available and consists of a rayon-tipped applicator packaged in a cylindrical container containing modified Stuart's medium. Because the eye may have very few organisms and fastidious organisms cause several of the more serious eye infections, a Culturette may not recover the pathogens. The use of direct plating onto solid media or a more hearty transport medium like thioglycolate broth is recommended.

The noninvolved eye is generally cultured for comparison. Because there are common pathogens in all eyes, misinterpretation can be avoided by comparing the normal flora to pathogenic flora. When possible, specimens are directly inoculated onto the solid media plates and promptly delivered to a laboratory. When not feasible, transport media are available. Amies, Stuart, Cary-Blair, Transgrow, and liquid thioglycolate broth are examples of transport media used to keep bacteria viable until the sample is plated by the laboratory. The laboratory will often supply preferred choices of transport and growth media with specific instructions.

Because ophthalmic anesthetic solutions have a bacteriostatic effect, lid and conjunctival cultures need to be taken before anesthetic instillation. Proparacaine 0.5% is the anesthetic solution of choice when needed because it inhibits bacterial growth the least of all topical anesthetics. Cultures are therefore taken before scrapings and smears, for which an anesthetic is required. Antibiotics also limit the number of organisms available for culture. It is necessary to take the culture before the initiation of any antibiotics or to discontinue the antibiotic at least 1 and preferably 2 days before culturing.

Applicators used to collect material from the lids and conjunctiva may be made from cotton, calcium alginate, or Dacron polyester. Calcium alginate swabs are preferred because they are soft, inert, and soluble.

■ **Instrumentation.** Sterile cotton-tipped applicators, calcium alginate swabs, Kimura platinum spatula, alcohol lamp, 0.5% proparacaine ophthalmic anesthetic solution, sterile nonpreserved saline, blood agar plates, chocolate agar plates, Sabouraud's agar plate, specialty agar plates, trypticase soy broth, thioglycolate broth (transport medium), slit lamp biomicroscope, eyelid speculum.

■ **Technique.**

Sterile conditions are recommended for any microbiological test so that extraneous microorganisms do not contaminate the findings. Wear gloves, be meticulous and clean with each step of the procedure, and obey all rules for universal precautions (see p. 475).

Eyelids: Before culturing the eyelid margins, clean away any crusts or debris. Moisten a sterile cotton-tipped applicator with nonpreserved saline solution to scrub the lid margins. Moisten a separate applicator with trypticase soy broth (if available) or nonpreserved sterile saline solution. The moisture increases the adherence of organisms to the swab and increases the comfort to the patient. Pull the lid away from the eye and wipe the applicator along the margin of the eyelid (Fig. 1). Roll the applicator along the lid margin three or four times so that it absorbs some material. Do not rub the lid margins. Immediately inoculate the solid media plates.

To streak an agar plate with a sample from the right eyelid, place the applicator in the lower part of the plate and slowly streak a capital "R" on the surface of the medium (Fig. 2). This is the designated symbol for a culture specimen taken from the right eyelid. A capital "L" is the symbol for material from the left lid margin. Place material from the eyelids toward the bottom of a plate and material from the conjunctiva toward the top as the agar plate is facing you.

Roll the applicator on the surface of the plated medium (Fig. 3A, 3B), avoiding the edges. Do not let the applicator dig into the medium and break the surface. (Fig. 3C). Use a separate plate for each eye to prevent crowding of the growth, to avoid interpretation difficulties. Routinely inoculate both blood and chocolate agar plates as well as any other media indicated.

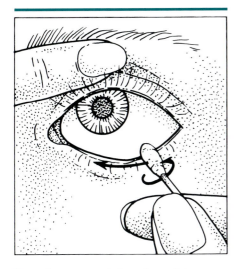

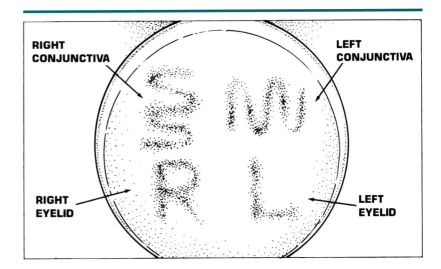

RIGHT
CONJUNCTIVA

LEFT
CONJUNCTIVA

RIGHT
EYELID

LEFT
EYELID

1. To obtain a sample for culture of the eyelids, a sterile cotton-tipped applicator is moistened and wiped along the margin of the eyelid.

2. The symbols shown are made when streaking culture material from the eyelids or conjunctiva onto the agar plate. By convention, material from the eyelids is placed toward the bottom of the agar plate, and material from the conjunctiva is placed toward the top of the plate.

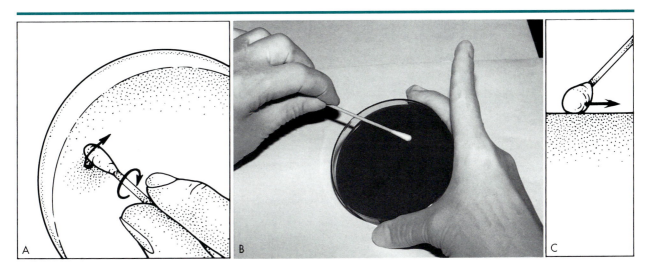

A

B

C

3. To transfer the sample to the agar plate, the applicator is rolled on the surface of the plated medium (A), avoiding the edges (B). The applicator should not break the surface of the medium as the sample is plated (C).

It is preferable to inoculate the solid medium plates immediately after obtaining the sample. When solid medium plates are unavailable, use a transport medium, preferably thioglycolate broth in a glass tube. For sterilization purposes, remove the cap and flame the rim of the tube, allowing the tube to heat for a few seconds (Fig. 4A). Place the applicator tip first into the tube of thioglycolate broth, breaking off any part of the wooden stick that has been touched (Fig. 4B). Reflame the top of the tube and cap tightly. It is important that the wooden stick remaining in the tube be untouched. Therefore, when using the applicator try to touch only the very end of the wooden stick.

Label the sample with the patient's name, doctor's name, time and date of sample, eye, and medications used and if they have been discontinued (Fig. 5). Fill out the laboratory forms and request which antibiotics are to be tested in the sensitivity studies.

If a Culturette is chosen, use the applicator to obtain the culture sample and slide it back into the container so the top of the applicator fits flush at the end of the tube. Squeeze the ampule at the bottom of the tube, breaking the seal and allowing the liquid medium to surround the applicator tip (Fig. 6). Recap, place the container back in its original envelope, label, and ship to the laboratory.

Lacrimal Sac/Meibomian Glands: Samples from the lacrimal sac or meibomian glands can also be plated and are placed in the eyelid position on the media plates. To obtain meibomian secretions, express the meibomian glands (see p. 102). Using a moistened applicator, collect the secretions by rolling an applicator along the lid margins. Plate the collected material or place it in a suitable transport medium. To obtain a sample from the lacrimal sac, gently palpate the sac (see p. 128), watching for discharge to regurgitate from the punctum. Collect the discharge with a moistened applicator, plate it immediately or place the material in a suitable transport medium. Label each sample, indicating the source of the material.

Conjunctiva: The inferior palpebral conjunctiva is the usual site for obtaining conjunctival specimens. Evert the lower lid, pulling it down and away from the eye. Gently roll a moistened applicator along the entire inferior palpebral conjunctiva (Fig. 7). Allow the applicator to absorb as much material as possible. Roll the applicator several times to collect as much material as possible. Do not rub the conjunctiva and avoid touching the applicator to the lashes, lid margins, or your hand. Plate it immediately or place the material in a transport medium. A vertical zigzag or helical pattern, placed on the top part of the media plate, is the symbol for material from the right conjunctiva, and a horizontal zigzag pattern is the symbol for material from the left conjunctiva (Fig. 2).

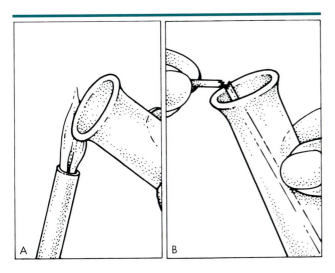

4. When necessary, a transport medium is used for the sample, preferably thioglycolate broth in a glass tube. After removing the cap, the rim of the tube is flamed for sterilization (A). The end of the wooden stick of the applicator that has been touched is broken off after insertion of the sample into the tube (B).

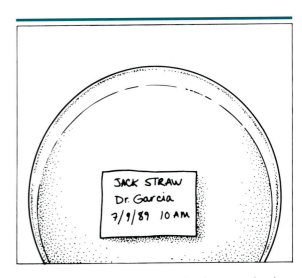

5. After covering the agar plate that has been inoculated with the sample, an identification label is affixed.

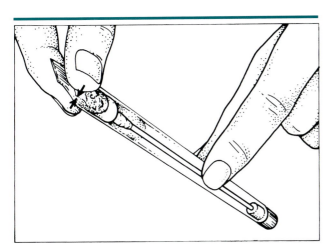

6. The ampule of a Culturette is squeezed, breaking the seal and providing transport medium for the specimen on the applicator.

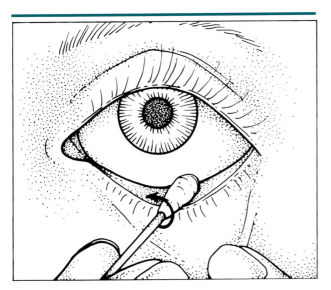

7. To obtain a sample for culture of the conjunctiva, a moistened sterile cotton-tipped applicator is rolled along the entire inferior palpebral conjunctiva.

Cornea: Use a Kimura platinum spatula to obtain specimens for cultures from a corneal ulcer. Instill a drop of 0.5% proparacaine ophthalmic anesthetic solution in each eye. Using an alcohol lamp, flame a Kimura spatula for sterilization, heating it for several seconds and allowing it to air cool. Platinum heats and cools very rapidly. Focus on the ulcer using a slit lamp biomicroscope and place the spatula temporally and tangentially to the corneal lesion. Use the edge of the spatula and gently scrape and discard any necrotic tissue and debris surrounding the ulcer. Gently scrape the advancing edge and then the central ulcer bed (Fig. 8–A), removing only the surface cells. The advancing edge and the ulcer bed each comprise a separate sample, and are plated separately. Always move the spatula in a downward motion away from the eye, taking care not to use excessive force to avoid corneal perforation if the patient moves. The spatula must not contact anything but the ulcer, to avoid contamination of the sample. When blepharospasm or fixation are problems, an eyelid speculum may be of help. Eyelid and conjunctival cultures are obtained before scraping a corneal ulcer, and if a lid speculum is required, it is inserted after obtaining lid and conjunctival specimens.

Take multiple samples of both areas of the ulcer, flaming the spatula after each sampling. Place the first samples retrieved on blood, chocolate, and Sabouraud's agar plates by lightly streaking the spatula over the surface. Make a minimum of two rows of "C's" (Fig. 9), each "C" representing a separate sample. Streak the Sabouraud plate last because it contains antibiotics that may inhibit the growth of bacteria if transferred to the blood or chocolate agar plates. Label the plates. Because of reduced growth, transport media are not used for cultures from corneal ulcers; however, a broth may be inoculated in addition to the solid media for increased chances of recovery. The specimen for Giemsa and Gram staining (see p. 210) should be plated on the slide last to avoid potential contamination of the media.

■ **Interpretation.** When growth on the culture medium is seen, the density, shape, and description of the colonies is important. Colonies are described looking at the size, pigmentation, shape, surfaces, odor, transparency, and consistency (Fig. 10). Any of these characteristics can be quantified from 1+ to 4+. The growth can also be quantified from 1+ to 4+ or in colony-forming units (CFUs). If changes to the medium such as hemolysis occur, these need to be noted. From the description of the culture growth, a microorganism may be identified. Any growth away from a streak is viewed as contamination and not due to microorganisms. Preliminary results are usually available in 24 hours, with the final results in 48 to 72 hours. In a conjunctival infection, if streaks from both the lids and the conjunctiva are plated, the greatest growth should be observed in the conjunctival streak. In evaluating the rows of streaks from a corneal ulcer, if a microorganism is present in two streaks on two rows, this is evidence that the pathogen has been isolated. Further growth in thioglycolate, if used, is evidence that a microorganism has been isolated and identified.

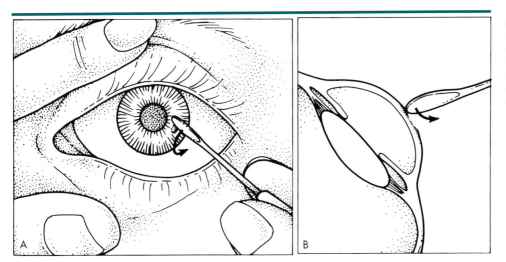

8. To obtain a sample for culture of the cornea, a sterile Kimura spatula is used to scrape the ulcer, using a downward motion away from the eye (A). Both the advancing edge (B) and the bed of the ulcer are scraped and plated as separate samples.

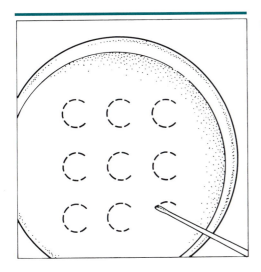

9. The spatula is used to directly inoculate the cornea culture samples onto the agar plate, forming rows of "C's."

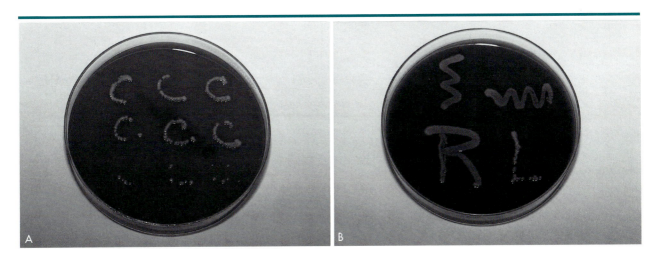

10. A. A plated culture sample taken from the cornea shows 48 hours of organism growth. B. A plated culture sample on chocolate agar taken from the eyelids and conjunctiva exhibits excellent growth from the conjunctiva of both eyes. Minimal growth is noted on the sample from the left eyelid.

In the laboratory, discs containing specified antibiotics are placed on special agar plates once growth of the microorganisms has been identified. The zones of the inhibition of growth around each disc are analyzed (Fig. 11). These zones are indicators if specific antibiotics will be effective. Drugs requested for testing may include ampicillin, bacitracin, cefazolin, erythromycin, gentamicin, sulfonamides, and the antibiotic with which treatment was initiated.

■ Contraindications/Complications. Care must be taken whenever any part of the lids, conjunctiva, or cornea is cultured. Create as little trauma as possible, especially when corneal scrapings are done, because an infected cornea is weakened and prone to perforate with excessive pressure. The number of samples may need to be limited for corneas extensively thinned by inflammation and in danger of perforation.

The collected ocular material may be infectious and even dangerous. Obey all rules for universal precautions, using gloves, washing hands, and cleaning and sterilizing all equipment (see p. 475). Adhere to regulations regarding in-office microbiological laboratories.

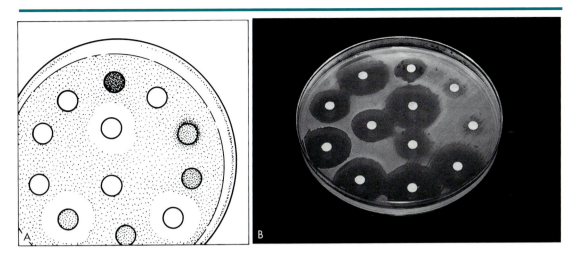

11. A. Discs impregnated with antibiotics to inhibit microorganism growth are used for sensitivity studies and to quantify the level of resistance. B. Zones of inhibition of organism growth around multiple discs on this plate indicate that most of the antibiotics chosen are efficacious against the organism in question.

52 Cytology (Smears and Scrapings)

■ **Description/Indications.** Ocular cytological studies (smears and scrapings) are indicated when an ocular infection or inflammation presents whose appearance and questionable assessment suggest the need to identify or exclude certain organisms to arrive at a diagnosis. Smears and scrapings provide information regarding the morphology of the microorganism(s), inflammatory cellular response, and epithelial cell composition. This information is used to better understand possible etiologies and to formulate a treatment regimen.

Specific indications for obtaining cytological studies include any central corneal ulcer not of viral origin, hyperacute purulent conjunctivitis, neonatal conjunctivitis, postoperative infections, and chronic or recurrent conjunctivitis. In addition, noninfectious inflammations, allergies, toxic reactions, degenerative diseases, and neoplasms are other indications for obtaining cytological studies.

Scrapings are taken after culturing (see p. 201) since a topical ophthalmic anesthetic solution is usually required to obtain samples and, due to its bacteriostatic effect, can decrease the number of viable organisms available for culture. Samples are also preferably obtained before antibiotics are used.

A cotton-tipped or calcium alginate applicator and Kimura spatula are used to lightly scrape epithelial cells from the surface of the eyelids and conjunctiva. A spatula can collect more material than an applicator; if upon microscopic examination insufficient cells are present after using an applicator to obtain the conjunctival sample, retake the sample using a spatula. Only a Kimura or Lindner platinum spatula is used to scrape corneal ulcers. Once obtained, the sample is placed on a glass slide, fixed, stained, and examined under a microscope. The practitioner may read the slide or use a community laboratory for this purpose. Smear results are usually available the same day, which is an advantage as compared to cultures.

The stain(s) used for the reading of slides depend(s) upon the presentation and clinical suspicions. The two most commonly utilized are the Gram and Giemsa stains. The Gram stain is used to differentiate bacterial microorganisms into two groups, Gram positive and Gram negative, and to provide information regarding morphology of the organism. This division of organisms into smaller, more specific groups helps in their identification and diagnosis. The Giemsa stain

or a modified variation (Wright's stain) is used when the etiology of the condition is unknown and information is needed regarding the cytological response. The Giemsa stain does not provide a great deal of information regarding bacterial pathogens because, whether Gram positive or negative, all will stain alike. The Giemsa stain is useful to differentiate a viral from allergic from bacterial response, especially for conjunctivitis, by determining the type of inflammatory cells, condition of epithelial cells, and presence of cytoplasmic inclusion bodies. The Giemsa stain also identifies fungi (hyphae), yeast forms, and the bacterial morphology, though the Gram stain may better accomplish the latter. In general, both the Gram and Giemsa stains are used for each case, since they tend to complement each other.

The monoclonal antibody test is used to diagnose chlamydial infections. A smear is stained with the monoclonal antibody and read using a fluorescent microscope. Other special stains are available to evaluate fungal, atypical bacterial responses, and Acanthamoeba.

■ **Instrumentation.** Sterile cotton-tipped applicator, calcium alginate applicator, Kimura-type platinum spatula, 0.5% proparacaine ophthalmic anesthetic solution, alcohol lamp, glass slides, 95% methyl alcohol, slit lamp biomicroscope, grease pencil.

■ **Technique.**
Eyelids: If scales or crusts cover the lid margin, use a moistened applicator to gently scrub the margins prior to obtaining a scraping. Pull the lid taut and, using a dry sterile cotton-tipped or calcium alginate applicator, rub the margin of the eyelid in one direction at or near the base of the lashes alongside the lid margin (Fig. 1). Do not roll the applicator. Transfer the material to a clean glass slide by gently rocking the applicator on the center (Fig. 2). Spread the material firmly and evenly in a thin layer over a small area in the center of the glass slide. If the material is dry, add several drops of unpreserved saline solution to allow the specimen to be spread evenly. Circle the area with the grease pencil to note to the laboratory where the material may be found. Fix the slide promptly. The preferred method, especially for Giemsa stain, is to place the slide in a 95% methyl alcohol solution for at least 5 minutes (Fig. 3). After 5 minutes, remove the slide, allow it to air dry,

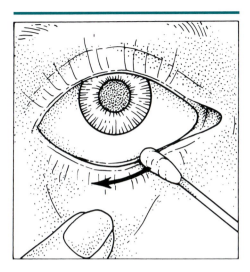

1. A dry applicator is used to obtain a smear sample from the lid margin. Note that the applicator is rubbed in one direction only.

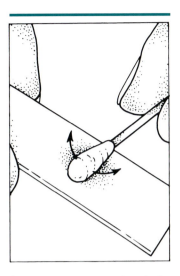

2. The applicator is gently rocked on the center of the glass slide to transfer the smear sample.

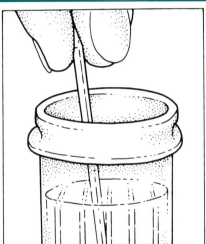

3. After transferring the smear sample, the slide is fixed promptly by placing it in a bath of 95% methyl alcohol for 5 minutes.

label, and prepare for transport to a local laboratory. Alternate methods for fixing the slide include air-drying or placing the slide over a flame for a few seconds. When a flame is used, hold the slide above it so the bottom is gently heated without being touched (Fig. 4). The method of fixation depends on the stain desired and it is best to contact the laboratory to determine the proper method.

Lacrimal Sac/Meibomian Glands: Samples from the lacrimal sac or meibomian glands can also be obtained for cytological staining. Obtain meibomian secretions by expressing the meibomian glands (see p. 102) and collecting the material with a dry applicator, smearing the material onto the center of a glass slide, and fixing. Collect secretions from the lacrimal canaliculus and lacrimal sac by palpating the lacrimal sac (see p. 128) until material regurgitates from the punctum. Collect the material with a sterile dry applicator, smear it onto a clean glass slide, and promptly fix it.

Conjunctiva: Obtain conjunctival specimens using a dry applicator or spatula. Usually the sample is taken from the inferior palpebral conjunctiva, but the superior palpebral conjunctiva is scraped when it is the predominant tissue affected. To obtain a sample from the inferior cul-de-sac,

have the patient look up, and evert the lower eyelid. Move the applicator over the inflamed area or gently scrape the conjunctiva if a specific pathology is not seen. Start at one point and advance the applicator several times, moving approximately one-quarter inch in one direction only (Fig. 5). Do not roll the applicator. Place the material on a clean glass slide and promptly fix.

A platinum spatula may also be used to obtain samples from the palpebral conjunctiva. Sterilize the spatula, placing the blade into the flame of an alcohol lamp for several seconds. Remove and allow it to cool to room temperature, not letting it touch anything that may affect its sterility. Remove any excess secretions with a moistened cotton-tipped applicator. Instill topical ophthalmic anesthetic solution, ask the patient to look up, and evert the lower eyelid. Use the spatula to gently scrape the conjunctiva, holding the spatula blade perpendicular to the conjunctival surface to collect the cells (Fig. 6). Move in one direction only for several passes. The conjunctiva will blanche mildly as it is scraped, but if bleeding occurs, reduce the force applied. Gently tap the side of the spatula blade on the edge of the glass slide to remove excess fluid (Fig. 7A). Turn the spatula over and, while holding it flat, gently tap it in the center of the glass slide, transferring the material in a smooth, even fashion (Fig. 7B). Fix the slides.

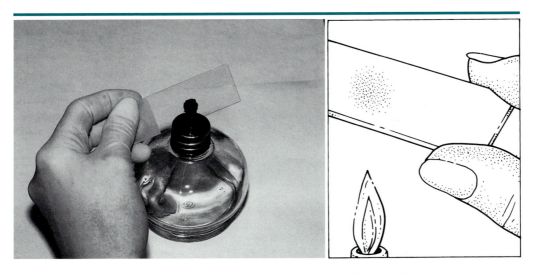

4. An alternative method for fixing the slide with the smear sample is to hold it over a flame for a few seconds.

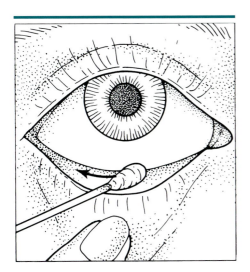

5. A dry applicator is used to obtain a smear sample from the inferior palpebral conjunctiva. Note that the applicator is rubbed in one direction only.

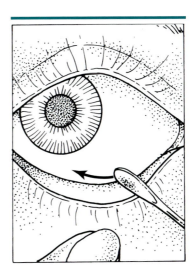

6. An alternative method of obtaining a sample from the inferior palpebral conjunctiva is to use a platinum spatula to gently scrape the tissue after instilling topical ophthalmic anesthetic solution.

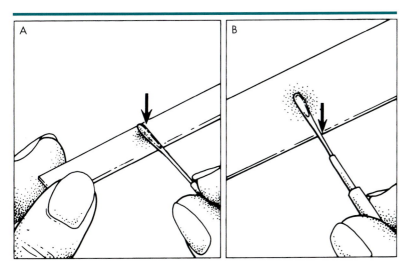

7. A. The spatula is lightly tapped on the edge of the slide to release excess fluid. B. The spatula is then tapped over the center of the glass slide to release its contents.

Cornea: Scrape corneal ulcers using a Kimura or Lindner platinum spatula. Instill several drops of topical ophthalmic anesthetic solution. Pass a Kimura spatula through a flame for sterilization and allow it to cool. Use a slit lamp biomicroscope to better visualize the ulcer and, with a moist applicator, gently remove any excess necrotic tissue or discharge from the ulcerated area. This material may be used for culture (see p. 201). Using the side of the spatula blade, gently scrape the bed and advancing edge of the ulcer (Fig. 8), avoiding excessive force to the cornea. Spread the material onto glass slides and fix it. Gram and Giemsa stains are indicated on any specimen collected from a corneal ulcer.

Label any slide being prepared for transport to a laboratory. Include the name of the patient and doctor, date and time of the sample, and the eye from which the specimen was taken. Note if any antibiotics have been used. Complete a form for each test required and place the slide(s) in the container or envelope provided by the laboratory for transport.

■ **Interpretation.** The Gram stain is used to divide bacteria into two groups: those retaining (Gram positive) or losing (Gram negative) the primary crystal violet stain when treated with 95% methanol (Fig. 9). Gram-negative organisms do not retain the primary stain and are subsequently counterstained with safranin, appearing red under the microscope. The makeup of the cell wall determines if the stain is preserved. The Gram stain is also useful in describing the morphologic appearance of the microorganisms. Three shapes (cocci, rods, bacilli) and four organizational patterns (single, pairs, clusters, chains) can be identified (Fig. 10). Not all shapes occur for all organized patterns. Gram-positive cocci may be observed as single units, in pairs, in clusters (staphylococci), or in chains (streptococci). Gram-positive rods or diplococci (pneumococci) may be seen, and Gram-negative organisms may appear as diplococci *(Neisseria),* diplobacilli *(Moraxella),* and rods *(Pseudomonas aeruginosa, Haemophilus).* Organisms having a similar morphologic appearance with Gram's stain may be definitively diagnosed with a culture (see p. 201). The Gram stain will also identify hyphae from fungal infections, seen as large filaments through the microscope. Although hyphae usually pick up the Gram stain, this is not absolute, and on occasion filaments may be noted on a smear not picking up the stain. The Gram stain is especially useful to evaluate bacterial corneal ulcers, providing guidance on the microorganism involved and the choice of therapeutic agents.

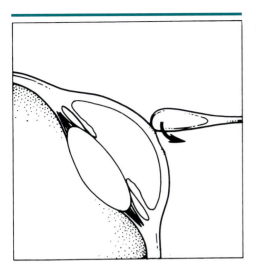

8. To obtain a sample from the cornea, the spatula is used to scrape the bed of the ulcer as well as the advancing edge.

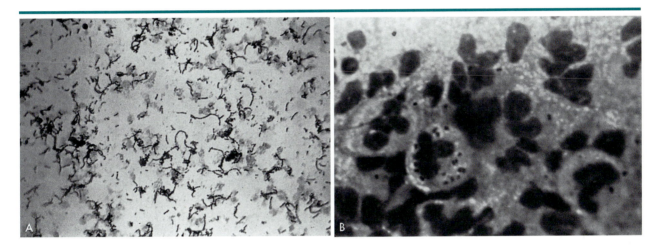

9. A. These streptococci organisms are Gram positive because they retain the primary crystal violet stain after being treated with methanol. Note that the organisms are arranged in chains. B. These *Neisseria* diplococci are Gram negative because they do not retain the primary crystal violet stain and appear red.

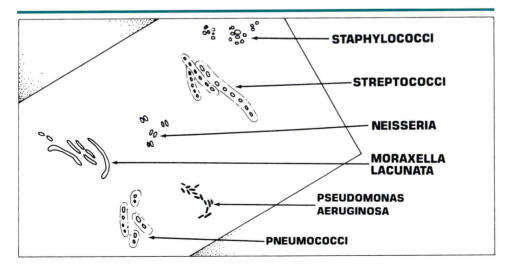

STAPHYLOCOCCI

STREPTOCOCCI

NEISSERIA

MORAXELLA LACUNATA

PSEUDOMONAS AERUGINOSA

PNEUMOCOCCI

10. The morphologic appearance of the various organisms can also be identified using the Gram stain on the smear or scraping sample.

The Giemsa stain provides information regarding the inflammatory cell response, condition of the epithelial cells, and presence of cytoplasmic inclusion bodies within the epithelial cells (Fig. 11). When polymorphonuclear leukocytes (PMNs) are the predominant cell, a bacterial infection is suspected. Fungal infections and conjunctivitis associated with membrane formation may also give a predominant PMN response. Mononuclear cells (lymphocytes) are associated with adenoviral infections, viral infections, and toxic reactions. A predominant response of eosinophils is found in allergic and hypersensitivity conditions. Epithelial cell changes include intracytoplasmic inclusion bodies, seen in neonatal Chlamydial infections, and keratinization associated with keratitis sicca. Intracytoplasmic inclusion bodies are less commonly seen in adult forms of Chlamydia. Like the Gram stain, the Giemsa stain can also provide information on cell morphology.

On occasion the number of cells available for interpretation may be small, leading to a negative report. This is more common when a dry applicator is used to obtain the sample. The specimen may be retaken, using a spatula to generate a larger representation.

■ **Contraindications/Complications.** Care must be taken when using a spatula or applicator to obtain samples from the eye. Bleeding, while not uncommon since cells are being removed from the superficial layers of the eyelids and conjunctiva, is an indication that excessive force is being applied. Corneal ulcers can be particularly problematic to test because the cornea may already be thinned and any additional force may lead to perforation. When taking a cytological specimen, avoid touching a structure other than the one being scraped to avoid contamination.

The collected ocular material may be infectious and even dangerous. Obey all rules for universal precautions, using gloves, washing hands, and cleaning and sterilizing all equipment (see p. 475). Adhere to regulations regarding in-office microbiological laboratories.

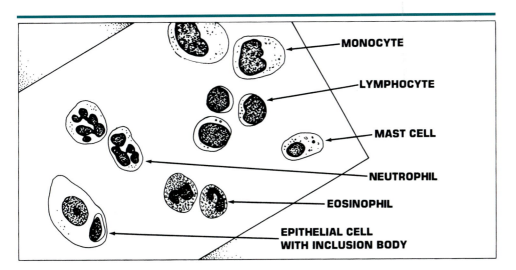

MONOCYTE

LYMPHOCYTE

MAST CELL

NEUTROPHIL

EOSINOPHIL

EPITHELIAL CELL
WITH INCLUSION BODY

11. The Giemsa stain is used to identify the various inflammatory cells, the condition of the epithelial cells, and the presence of cytoplasmic inclusion bodies within the epithelial cells on the smear or scraping sample.

VII Suggested Readings

Casser L, Lingel NJ: Diseases of the cornea, in Bartlett JD, Jaanus SD (eds): *Clinical Ocular Pharmacology,* ed 3. Boston, Butterworth-Heinemann, 1995, pp 679–745.

Fedukowicz HB, Stenson S: *External Infections of the Eye.* Norwalk, CT, Appleton & Lange, 1985.

Finegold SM, Baron EJ: *Bailey and Scott's Diagnostic Microbiology.* St. Louis, Mosby, 1986.

Fuller DG: Cytology in anterior segment disease. *Optom Clin* 1992;**2:**27–40.

Leibowitz HM: *Corneal Disorders: Clinical Diagnosis and Management.* Philadelphia, Saunders, 1984.

VIII

Posterior Segment Procedures

53

Direct Ophthalmoscopy

■ **Description/Indications.** Direct ophthalmoscopy allows for the visual examination of the retina and ocular media. The hand-held direct ophthalmoscope uses the patient's eye as a simple magnifier by aligning its viewing and illuminating beams (Fig. 1). This produces an erect, magnified, well-detailed real image of the retina. Compared to other fundus-viewing instruments, it is the easiest to master, provides for greatest patient comfort, can be used through smaller pupils, and provides the most accurate estimate of the patient's visual compromise due to media opacification. Disadvantages of the direct ophthalmoscope include its limited illumination, lack of stereopsis, close working distance, dependence on refractive errors for clarity and magnification, and small field of view (approximately two disc diameters). Although acceptable screening views are obtained through an undilated pupil, routine pupillary dilation enhances the field of view. The examined eye's pupillary margin and crystalline lens peripheral optical distortions limit the extent and quality of off-axis and peripheral fundus views.

Direct ophthalmoscopy is indicated for ocular fundus examination, evaluation of an eye's media, and evaluation of a patient's fixation pattern.

The ophthalmoscope head (Fig. 2) connects to a handle that serves as the power source. The head contains a variable range of plus and minus lenses used to compensate for refractive errors. The light is projected through a variably sized aperture and correcting lens to illuminate the fundus. Adjusting the aperture changes the beam size, which helps control reflections. A red-free filter is available to more easily identify hemorrhages and the nerve fiber layer. A fixation target is included in many ophthalmoscopes to assess the fixation pattern (visuoscopy).

Magnification is determined by the patient's and examiner's refractive powers, axial lengths of their globes, and compensating lenses used. A myopic person's inherent uncorrected plus power, along with the correcting minus ophthalmoscope lens, yield a magnified image (Galilean telescope design) for the emmetropic examiner. The hyperopic eye minifies (reversed telescopic design) the usual 15X magnified image created when both the examiner and the patient are emmetropic. High astigmatic or spherical refractive errors require that spectacle correction be worn by the examiner and/or patient to improve the clarity of the image, avoid distortion, and/or avoid unacceptable image size.

■ **Instrumentation.** Direct ophthalmoscope, topical ophthalmic mydriatic/cycloplegic solution(s).

■ **Technique.** Dilate the pupils with topical mydriatic/cycloplegic solution(s). Position the patient's eyes at a similar level to yours. Ask the patient to fixate a nonaccommodative distance target. Dim the room lights to maximize pupil dilation and reduce glare. Holding the ophthalmoscope in your right hand, align your right eye with the ophthalmoscope's aperture and brace it against your cheekbone. Attempt to keep your opposite eye open to minimize accommodative spasm and eyelid discomfort. Place the right index finger along the right side of the lens dial wheel. Dial in a +10 lens. Push down and rotate the rheostat illumination dial, usually located toward the top of the handle. Set the illumination in the midrange of beam intensity, varying it as needed to improve the clarity of the image. To examine for media opacities, direct the ophthalmoscope's light beam into the patient's right pupil at a distance of 10 to 12 inches, angled from a slight temporal position (Fig. 3). Move forward until the red retinal reflex is in focus and examine for opacities. If an opacity is present, ask the patient to look in a certain position while you keep the ophthalmoscope stable, or move the ophthalmoscope beam keeping the patient's eye stable. Determine if the opacity moves in the same or opposite direction as your movement. Same-direction movement indicates that an opacity is in front of the posterior crystalline lens area (optical center of eye), while against movement indicates an opacity posterior to the lens. Use the slit lamp to confirm any findings.

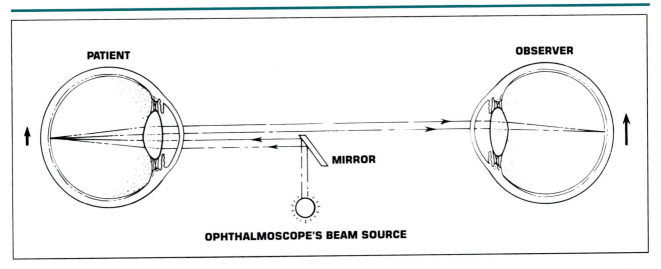

1. Basic optical principle of direct ophthalmoscopy. The viewing and illumination systems are aligned, using the patient's eye as a simple magnifier.

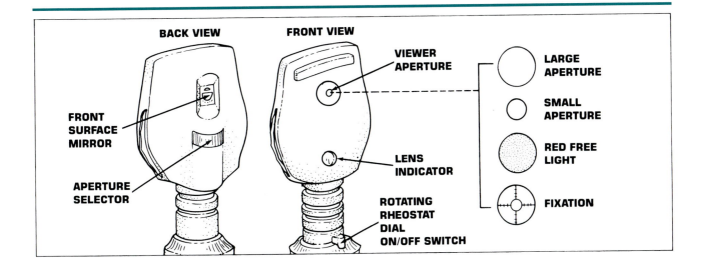

2. (above) Direct ophthalmoscope head components and aperture selections.

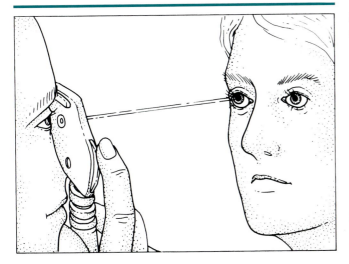

3. (left) Positioned at 10 to 12 inches in front of the patient, the examiner moves forward and observes the red reflex for opacities, judging their location.

Reduce the plus power as the patient's eye is approached. Attempt to keep your head position vertical so as to not block the patient's fixation with his or her opposite eye. Stop when your knuckles lightly touch the patient's cheek (Fig. 4A). This area of contact can act as a rotational point for examination movements, insuring a close working distance and resultant optimal field of view (Fig. 4B). Slowly continue with plus reduction until the retina is in focus, noting any anomalies along the way. A circular area approximately two disc diameters in size is visualized when emmetropia (Fig. 5) is present. Direct your fixation slightly nasally and inferiorly to locate the optic disc. Note its color, margins, shape, peripapillary retinal changes, presence or absence of spontaneous venous pulsation, and the horizontal and vertical cup/disc ratios. Observe disc tissue for sloping margins of the cup and/or pallor. Estimate the depth of the cup by focusing at the anterior-most cup edge and then reducing plus power until the bottom of the cup is clear (1 diopter = ⅓ mm).

Follow the retinal blood vessels outward from the disc into the posterior pole in a systematic quadrantal fashion (Fig. 6). Go as far as possible, noting the A/V ratio, crossing appearances, vessel caliber, arterial light reflex, and the surrounding retinal tissue for blood, fluid, exudate, elevation, or pigment alteration. Make small dioptric power adjustments if needed to compensate for ocular movements, unsteadiness, and changes in tissue area observed. Increase the range of the retinal area visualized by asking the patient to look in the same direction as the quadrant being examined. To examine the retinal periphery, view from 180 degrees away and angle your head to go out as far as possible (nasally for temporal retinal exam, inferiorly for superior retinal exam).

Examine the macula area. Ask the patient to look directly into the ophthalmoscope beam for the exact localization of the foveal area. Note the presence or absence of the foveal light reflex. To determine the patient's fixation pattern, change the ophthalmoscope's aperture to the fixation target, instruct the patient to occlude the opposite eye with his or her hand and to fixate on the center of the target.

Gently hold the patient's upper lid against the superior orbital rim with your opposite thumb for viewing the inferior fundus, for photophobic patients, or for patients with small palpebral apertures. It may also be necessary to secure the sensitive patient's lower lid downward against the inferior orbital rim with the ring finger of the hand holding the ophthalmoscope to keep the eyelids open. Record all pertinent data in the patient's record.

Repeat the entire procedure on the opposite eye by moving to the patient's opposite side and using your left hand and eye.

■ **Interpretation.** The optic disc is evaluated for its color, margins, shape, peripapillary retinal changes, presence or absence of spontaneous venous pulsation, and the horizontal and vertical cup/disc ratio, noting any accompanying disc tissue sloping and/or pallor. Fundus vasculature, pigment changes, and clarity of ocular media should all be noted. Although with a dilated pupil the examiner is capable of visualizing the far peripheral retina, the ophthalmoscope's magnification and limited field of view do not lend themselves to an efficient examination of the retinal periphery.

■ **Contraindications/Complications.** Aside from some discomfort due to glare, this noncontact procedure should present no risk to the patient. Patient and examiner health may be better protected by the examiner wearing a surgical mask.

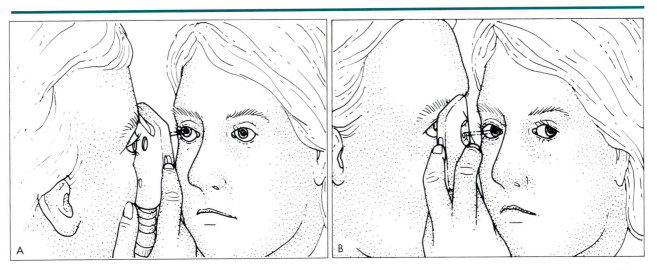

4. A. Proper examiner–patient alignment during direct ophthalmoscopy, using the knuckles as a point of rotation during examination. B. The examiner should rotate in the opposite direction of the fundus area being examined.

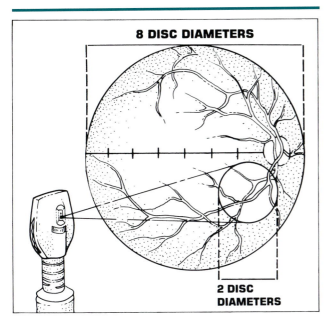

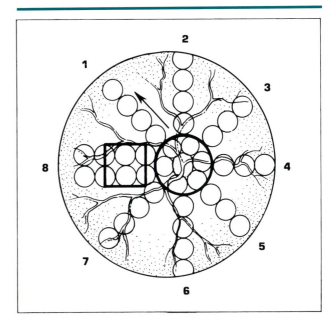

5. In an emmetropic eye, direct ophthalmoscopy yields a field of view that is two disc diameters in size, while binocular indirect ophthalmoscopy using a 20-diopter condensing lens yields a field of view that is eight disc diameters in size.

6. In the systematic evaluation of the fundus, after viewing the optic disc (large dark circle), the retinal blood vessels are followed in an organized pattern outward from the disc (as shown in steps 1 through 8), finishing with an examination of the macula (large square).

54 Monocular Indirect Ophthalmoscopy

■ **Description/Indications.** Monocular indirect ophthalmoscopy combines the advantages of increased field of view (indirect ophthalmoscopy) with erect real imaging (direct ophthalmoscopy) to produce a viewing system for ocular fundoscopy. By collecting and redirecting peripheral fundus-reflected illumination rays, which cannot be accomplished with the direct ophthalmoscope (see p. 220), the indirect ophthalmoscope extends the observer's field of view approximately four to five times. An internal relay lens system reinverts the initially inverted image to a real erect one, which is then magnified. This image is focusable using the focusing lever/eyepiece system (Fig. 1). The end result is an ophthalmoscope with a 40 to 45-degree (eight disc diameters) field of view and approximately 5X magnification.

The instrument itself has an illumination rheostat at its base, a focusing lever for image refinement, a filter dial with red-free and yellow filters, a forehead rest for steady proper observer head positioning, and an iris diaphragm lever to adjust the illumination beam diameter (Fig. 2). Its disadvantages include lack of stereopsis, limited illumination, fixed magnification, and fair to good resolution.

Indications for use of monocular indirect ophthalmoscopy include the need for an increased field of view of the retina, small pupils, uncooperative children, patient's intolerance of the brighter light from the binocular indirect ophthalmoscope, basic fundus screening, one-handed examination technique, and a monocular examiner unable to appreciate the advantages of a binocular instrument. Binocular indirect ophthalmoscopy (see p. 226), however, with its superior stereoscopic viewing system, still remains the technique of choice whenever possible.

■ **Instrumentation.** Monocular indirect ophthalmoscope, topical ophthalmic mydriatic/cycloplegic solution(s).

■ **Technique.** Dilate the patient's pupils with topical ophthalmic mydriatic/cycloplegic solution(s). To examine the right eye, stand to the patient's right side, remove any spectacle correction the patient is wearing, and have him or her fixate straight ahead. Keep your habitual refractive correction in place, turn on the instrument rheostat, dim the room lighting, push the iris diaphragm lever fully to the left to maximally increase the aperture size, and center the red dot on the filter dial to position the open aperture for normal viewing. Slide the front dust shield button fully downward to prevent illumination and viewing obstruction.

Place the forehead rest against your forehead and align your right eye through the instrument eyepiece with the patient's right eye, holding the handle with your right hand. Position yourself several inches in front of the patient and focus through the patient's pupil onto the fundus using your thumb on the focusing lever (Fig. 3). As you approach, stop approximately 4 to 5 inches from the patient's eye. Adjust the focusing and iris diaphragm levers to produce a clear, maximally illuminated fundus view. Continue to approach the patient until your knuckle lightly touches the patient's cheek. As your working distances decreases, fundus magnification will increase. Angle the light slightly nasally to illuminate the optic disc.

After scanning the tissue surrounding the optic disc, ask the patient to look upward and scan the superior posterior pole, pivoting around the pupil as a rotational center. Direct the patient to look superior temporally, then superiorly, and finally, superior nasally. With each position of gaze, direct the ophthalmoscope light beam from the opposite direction (Fig. 4), focus on the central posterior pole, and track anteriorly as far as possible to examine as much retinal tissue as can be visualized. Repeat the same procedure nasally, temporally, and then inferiorly in a similar fashion. Use the opposite hand to control obstructive eyelids. Make fine adjustments with the focusing lever as your vertex distance varies.

Repeat the same procedure on the left eye, using your left eye, left hand, and positioning yourself at the patient's left side.

■ **Interpretation.** As with direct ophthalmoscopy, observe any media opacities as you focus through the eye onto the fundus. The optic nerve, retinal vasculature, and retinal tissue should be examined for anomalies. Use of the red-free filter will enhance the contrast of the retinal vasculature and any hemorrhages.

Although vitreous base views are possible with monocular indirect ophthalmoscopy, its greatest effectiveness extends anteriorly to the peripheral equatorial region. The 40+ degree field of view of the monocular indirect is approximately the same as that of the binocular indirect ophthalmoscope.

■ **Contraindications/Complications.** This non-contact, moderate illumination procedure, when performed properly, presents no potential risk to the patient.

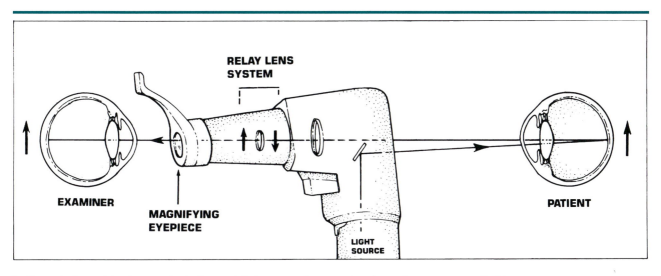

RELAY LENS
SYSTEM

EXAMINER

MAGNIFYING
EYEPIECE

LIGHT
SOURCE

PATIENT

1. The optical principle of monocular indirect ophthalmoscopy, demonstrating the resultant erect, magnified image.

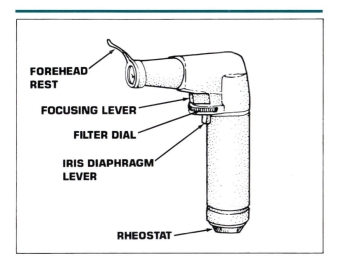

FOREHEAD
REST

FOCUSING LEVER

FILTER DIAL

IRIS DIAPHRAGM
LEVER

RHEOSTAT

2. The components of the monocular indirect ophthalmoscope.

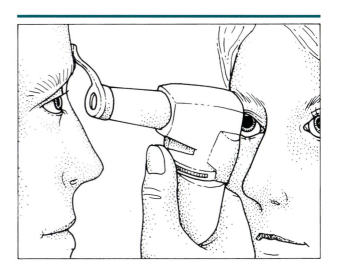

3. The examiner is properly positioned with thumb on the focusing lever.

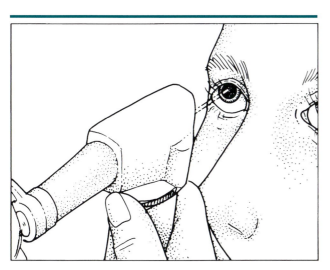

4. The patient is asked to look in the same direction as the fundus area being examined, while the light beam is directed from the opposite direction.

55 Binocular Indirect Ophthalmoscopy

■ **Description/Indications.** Binocular indirect ophthalmoscopy (BIO) is a technique used to evaluate the entire ocular fundus. It provides for stereoscopic, wide-angled, high-resolution views of the entire retina and overlying vitreous. Its optical principles and illumination options allow for visualization of the fundus regardless of high ametropia, hazy ocular media, or central opacities. The examiner's use of different-powered condensing lenses, variable illumination intensity, scleral indentation (see p. 234), and multiple viewing angles, allows for total fundus inspection. A more detailed inspection of certain retinal areas may require the complementary use of fundus biomicroscopy (see p. 244), fundus contact lens (see p. 238), or Hruby lens (see p. 242) techniques.

The optics of BIO (Fig. 1) consist of light beams directed into the patient's eye that produce reflected observation beams from the retina. These beams are focused to a viewable, aerial image following placement of a high plus-powered condensing lens at its focal distance in front of the patient's eye. The resultant image is real, magnified 1.5X to 3.5X, reversed left to right, inverted top to bottom, and located between the examiner and the condensing lens (Fig. 2). The examiner views this image through the oculars of the head-borne indirect ophthalmoscope.

The BIO (Fig. 3) consists of a headband apparatus, optical viewing system, and rheostatically controlled illumination source. The headbands provide proper and comfortable instrument placement with adjustment controls located at the crown of the head and occipital notch area. Some styles of BIO are spectacle-mounted.

The variable-intensity illumination beams of the light source are directed downward and reflected laterally by an adjustable mirrored surface located in the instrument's main housing. These optics allow the fundus-directed illumination beams to pass off-axis to the returning reflected observation beams, minimizing corneal light reflexes. The ocular lens system has knobs or sliding track adjustments to horizontally align the low plus-powered eyepieces (+2.00 to +2.50 D) with the examiner's interpupillary distance (IPD). Prisms incorporated into the instrument optically reduce the examiner's IPD, allowing it to be imaged along with the illumination beam within the patient's pupil. Stereoscopic viewing is thus produced. Therefore, the two images of the examiner's pupils and that of the light source are located inside the patient's dilated pupil for binocular viewing. The small-pupil BIO has the ability to further condense these three points to allow passage through undilated pupils.

Condensing lenses are double aspheric with a multilayered antireflective coating and are available in various powers, diameters, tints, and designs. During examination the more convex lens surface faces toward the examiner, while the less convex surface faces the patient's eye (noted by a white or silver line encircling the lens). The standard +20 D lens produces approximately 2.5X magnification and a 35-degree or eight-disc diameter field of view. This is in contrast to a direct ophthalmoscope, which produces approximately 15X magnification and a two-disc diameter fundus view (Fig. 4). As the condensing lens power is decreased, the resultant visual field decreases and magnification increases; therefore, compared to the standard +20 D lens, a +14 D lens yields 3.5X magnification and smaller field, while a +28 D yields 1.5X magnification and larger field. Clear and amber lenses are available. Amber or yellow lenses appear to increase patient comfort by reducing scattered light, thereby reducing irritating glare. They produce an image as sharp as a clear lens. Examiners have their own preferences relative to fundus color perception with a clear versus a yellow condensing lens.

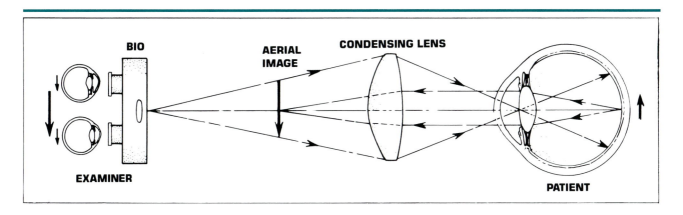

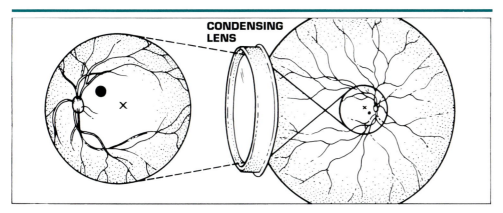

1. (above) BIO optical principles: light beams are directed into the patient's eye that produce reflected observation beams from the retina. These beams are focused to an aerial image with a condensing lens.

2. (left) BIO with a condensing lens produces a real, magnified, reversed, inverted aerial fundus image for examiner inspection.

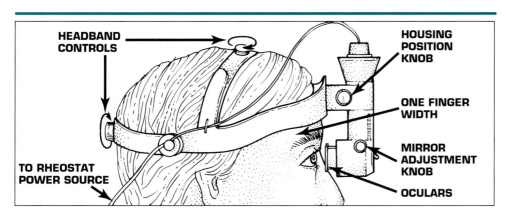

3. (left) BIO is balanced and secured on your head. The crown headband is initially adjusted to absorb most of instrument's weight, and then the occipital headband is tightened. The front headband is positioned approximately one index finger width above the eyebrows. The oculars are placed close to your eyes or lightly abutting any spectacles.

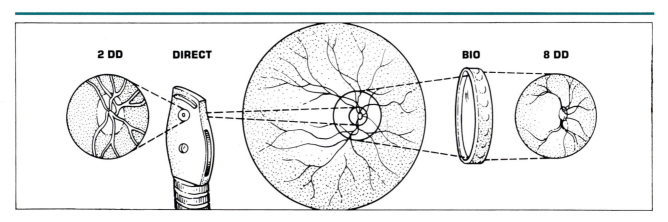

4. The field of view comparison between the direct ophthalmoscope (2 DD) and BIO (8 DD).

Advantages of BIO include stereopsis, large field of view, bright illumination, minimal peripheral view distortion, and complete peripheral tissue access when used with scleral indentation. Other advantages include a comfortable working distance and relative independence from patient refractive error or moderate media opacification. Disadvantages include the need for pupil dilation, patient's moderate glare discomfort, initial examiner adjustment to the inverted/reversed image, low magnification with loss of fine detail, and the initial learning time needed to become comfortable and proficient with its use.

Indications for BIO examination include thoroughness of routine comprehensive ocular health assessment; patient symptoms of flashes, floaters, spots, or other symptoms consistent with vitreous detachment, syneresis, inflammation or hemorrhage, or retinal tear or detachment; and patient history of peripheral vision loss, blunt ocular trauma, previous retinal detachment or peripheral retinal disease, diabetes, significant vascular disease, metastatic carcinoma, posterior vitreous detachment, or parasympathomimetic therapeutic drug treatment (pilocarpine therapy). Airborne communicable disease that might be passed with a closer working distance unless a mask is worn, or uncooperative patient behavior most commonly found in children, are also indications for this technique.

■ **Instrumentation.** Binocular indirect ophthalmoscope, condensing lens(es), topical ophthalmic mydriatic/cycloplegic solution(s), reclinable examination chair or table.

■ **Technique.**
BIO Adjustment: Loosen both the crown and occipital headstraps. Place the loosened BIO onto your head and position the bottom of the front headband approximately one index finger width above your eyebrows (*see* Fig. 3). Tighten the crown strap until this headband position begins to stabilize as most of the instrument's weight begins to rest on the top of your head. Position the back headstrap on or below the occipital notch and tighten until the instrument is securely positioned. Make fine adjustments as needed. Loosen the knob(s) that control the instrument's main housing (oculars and light tower). Fixating straight ahead and level, vertically position the oculars to within eyelash distance from your uncorrected eyes aligned tangential to or slightly angled downward from the ocular surface. This should maximize your visual field and minimize horizontal diplopia. If you wear spectacles, lightly abut the oculars up against their front surface.

Horizontally align each ocular by closing one eye and fixating your centrally positioned thumb held at 16 to 20 inches. Adjust the ocular alignment knob or slide the oculars to place an identical centrally positioned thumb in each ocular's field of view (Fig. 5). After individual alignment, view the thumb binocularly as a single clear object, thus creating an optimal setting for stereoscopic viewing. Make fine vertical and horizontal adjustments as needed to maximize the optics. Turn on the BIO power source and fixate straight ahead on a wall or your hand at 16 to 20 inches, looking at the projected light source. Use the mirror knob to vertically place the light source at the upper one-half to one-third of the field. The illumination beam will then pass superior to the reflected observation beam. In a darkened room, this step would precede centration of the oculars. Observe the location of the light filament in each ocular's field of view to ensure that it is horizontally centered or displaced slightly nasally. Refer to the manufacturer's guide if it is not. These light filaments should be defocused at the 18 to 20-inch working distance.

The only required major adjustment to a BIO personally used by one practitioner is the occipital headstrap adjustment. A brief review of all adjustments and alignments should be made with each BIO use, however.

BIO Technique: Dilate both of the patient's pupils with topical ophthalmic mydriatic/cycloplegic solution(s), preferably using both a parasympatholytic and sympathomimetic agent to maximize dilation and patient comfort. Seat the patient in a reclinable examination chair which, when reclined, will give 270 degrees access at the patient's head. Carefully recline the patient using good head support until his or her facial plane is parallel to the floor and approximately at the level of your hips to allow for extension of your arms with a slight bend (Fig. 6). Direct the patient to fixate straight upward at the ceiling. Dim the room lighting to eliminate any overhead glare sources. With the BIO headset in place and with the voltage set to midrange, stand to the right shoulder side of the reclined patient at his or her 8-o'clock position. Gently secure the patient's right upper lid against the superior orbital rim with your left thumb and rest your remaining fingers on the patient's forehead for self-support and for future condensing lens support (Fig. 7). Hold a clean +20 D condensing lens with the thumb, index, and middle fingers of your right hand, positioning the more convex surface toward you or the lens' white-ringed edge toward the patient. Place your thumb between the knurled rings of the lens and place your index and middle fingers on the upper and lower knurled rings, respectively, for maximum lens control. Lightly secure the right lower lid against the inferior orbital rim with the ring and/or smallest finger of the same hand, completing palpebral aperture separation and establishing a pivot position for adjustments of the condensing lens.

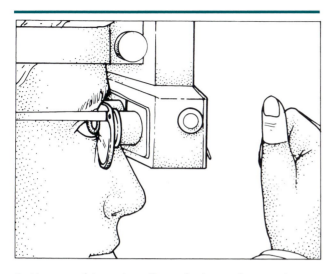

5. Alignment of the oculars: Alternately close each eye and view the centrally placed thumb at 16 to 20 inches. Slide the oculars until each eye is seeing identical, centered images with resultant stereopsis.

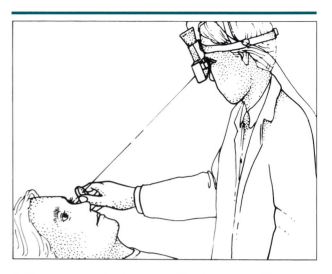

6. The patient is reclined using good head support until his or her face is parallel to the floor and approximately at the level of your hips to allow for extension of your arm with a slight bend.

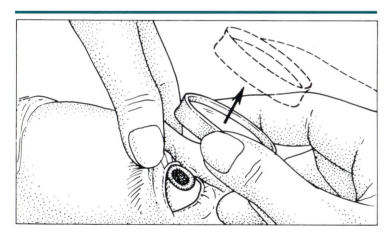

7. The patient's upper and lower lids are gently retracted while centering the condensing lens over the red reflex; lens movement upward in a "tromboning" motion (arrow) will yield a full-lens fundus view.

From a working distance of 18 to 20 inches (arm's length) and positioned almost above the patient, direct the light beam into the pupil, producing a complete red pupillary reflex. Place the condensing lens close to the ocular surface between you and the patient, noting an erect image of the patient's eye through the lens. Pull upward on the lens, maintaining the central position of the pupil reflex, until the entire lens fills with a fundus image. Use this "tromboning" movement of the lens continuously during BIO. Make fine adjustments in the lens tilt and vertex distance to produce a distortion-free, full-lens view. Increase the illumination when poor visualization occurs secondary to media opacification. At this point an "optical viewing system" has been created consisting of your fixation line through the BIO oculars to the focused aerial image, through the condensing lens' optical center, through the center of the pupil, to the fundus area of regard (Fig 8). An imaginary rod through these points reminds the examiner to bend the torso in unison with the lens in order to maintain this identical alignment as the condensing lens is tilted to view other fundus areas.

If a single, stereoscopic, clear image is seen, initiate systematic examination of the fundus, beginning with the less photosensitive peripheral retina. Direct the patient to look back toward the 12-o'clock position at his or her forehead. Tap the forehead with your fingertips if fixation assistance is needed. From a position 180 degrees opposite to the patient's direction of gaze, in this instance inferiorly, direct the illumination beam into the right eye, using the just discussed "optical system" design. Begin posteriorly near the equator and track superiorly toward the ora serrata, attempting to maintain a full condensing lens view and an intact "optical system." This will require you to lean slightly over the patient and then tip your torso at the hip backward and to the right, as fixation is directed more and more superiorly. With the pupil as the rotation point, illuminate and view any specific retinal area by rotating yourself and the light source opposite in direction to the area of regard, thus directing the beam onto the retina from 180 degrees away.

Note that the far peripheral retina is viewed through an optically oval or elliptical pupil opening, reducing the lens image quantity or lens filling and your stereopsis (Fig. 9A, B). Frequently tilt your head to reposition the illumination beam and ocular alignments in the pupil (Fig. 9C). After reaching the peripheral limit of the superior retina, direct the light source out of the patient's pupil, ask him or her to blink and then to look superior nasally. Reposition the light back into the "optical system," begin equatorially and again smoothly track the retina anteriorly. Repeat this procedure in a clockwise direction for all eight cardinal meridians. View and review overlapping areas. Ask the patient to look in the direction of the quadrant to be examined. Circle the patient's head as you examine downward toward the inferior retina. To prevent patient distress and light intolerance, remove the light source by lifting your head and allow the patient to blink briefly following changes in fixation.

Having completed the peripheral retina inspection, reposition yourself at the patient's 8-o'clock position and ask him or her to fixate the ceiling. With minimal torso and "optical system" movements, scan the superior and lateral posterior pole meridians beginning near the disc and moving anteriorly to the vortex areas. Ask the patient to look toward each of your shoulders as you examine the inferior posterior pole meridians with similar movements. View and review overlapping areas.

Repeat the same examination on the left eye either by carefully leaning over the patient or by positioning yourself on the opposite side of the patient at his or her 4-o'clock position. Rotate the head of the chair away from the instrument stand to create the needed 270 degrees of access area. Ambidextrous examination is encouraged, as it will be needed for scleral indentation (see p. 234). After examining the periphery and posterior pole of the left eye, ask the patient to look directly at the light source with each eye for better macular examination. Use a lower-powered condensing lens than the standard +20 D if greater magnification is needed.

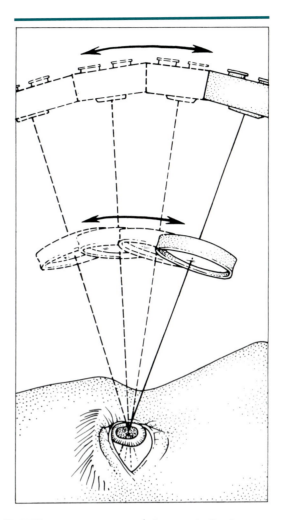

8. All examiner movement during examination is performed maintaining the patient's pupil as the center of rotation as the examiner's visual axis and condensing lens are moved in unison.

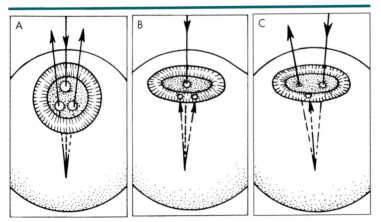

9. A. A normal round pupil area contains the illumination beam and the examiner's visual axes. B. While viewing the far retinal periphery, an oval pupil can obstruct the examiner's visual axis. C. Examiner's head tilting can reposition the three beams for better viewing.

BIO teaching mirrors are available that allow another observer to simultaneously view the same fundus with the examiner (Fig. 10).

■ Interpretation.

Recognition of fundus anatomical landmarks (Fig. 11) assists the novice BIO practitioner as he or she develops proficiency and confidence with the instrument. These same landmarks are helpful to the more experienced practitioner for specific localization and recording of significant fundus findings (see p. 248). Approximately 60 to 70% of the entire fundus is considered posterior pole. Posterior pole reference points include the optic disc; central retinal artery and vein; fovea; and the anatomical macula, which includes the area between the major superior and inferior temporal vascular arcades. The actual posterior pole anterior limit is identified by connecting the vortex vein ampullae with an imaginary line. These prominent, thicker ampullae, numbering 4 to 15 per eye, represent the merging of multiple swirling choroidal venous tributaries as they exit posteriorly from the choroid through the scleral canal. The equatorial region is immediately anterior to these large collecting vessels, which are most commonly found in each oblique quadrant and best seen in patients with lightly pigmented fundi.

The peripheral retina comprises the remaining 30 to 40% of the fundus and is divided into superior and inferior regions by the long posterior ciliary arteries and nerves. This artery and nerve emerge at the retinal equator and traverse anteriorly to the ora serrata in a characteristic "ribbonlike" hyper- and hypopigmented pattern at 3:00 and 9:00. The short ciliary arteries of the choriocapillaris and their accompanying nerves, numbering 10 to 20, run perpendicular to the ora serrata. These pigment-mottled lines are most commonly seen in the vertical meridians (6 and 12-o'clock).

The ora serrata represents the end of the choroid and the retina. The choroid continues on as the pigmented pars plana while the retina becomes the nonpigmented single epithelial layer on the pars plana surface. The temporal ora serrata border is characteristically smooth while the nasal border has a scalloped surface. Just posterior to the ora serrata is an age-related, circumferentially oriented, wide band of mottled pigment that represents the vitreous base or posterior firm attachment of the posterior vitreous to the retina.

The initial work with the smaller, inverted, reversed, condensing lens image can be quite trying. It is important to remember that it is only the lens view that is different. If you are directing light into the superior aspect of the fundus, you are indeed looking at superior retina. As you scan more anteriorly, the newly illuminated retinal tissue image appears in the condensing lens at its opposite edge closest to you. Much of the initial concern with image reversal and inversion can be reduced by performing most of the BIO examination standing at the head of the reclined chair, facing the patient's feet. When looking straight down at the patient from this position you have changed your viewing relationship, such that your face is now inverted and reversed relative to the patient's. This nullifies the image change and the orientation of what you see is now a "normal" fundus view. Fundus drawing (see p. 248) will also help to overcome this hurdle.

If only a red reflex is seen or if the lens is only partially filled with fundus details, trombone the condensing lens off the pivot finger. If no details are seen, place the condensing lens at 2 inches and move your headset light source closer or further away. If no fundus details are still seen, suspect media obstruction. Poor fundus visualization due to patient blepharospasm may be decreased by reducing the light intensity, holding the eyelids more gently, or providing a specific fixation target.

■ Contraindications/Complications.

Maximal pupillary dilation may be contraindicated in certain patients. Physical or vascular conditions may prevent reclining of the patient. In this case, examination can be done in the sitting position, which requires additional repositioning of both the patient and examiner during examination.

The examiner's inability to hold the condensing lens stable can reduce viewing quality. Consider bracing the edge of the condensing lens against the thumb of the hand holding the upper lid and also against the patient's nose in certain positions.

Significant corneal disruption or opacification hinders fundus visualization with indirect ophthalmoscopy. Therefore, performing fundus contact lens examination prior to BIO is avoided.

Vertical diplopia is frequently the result of a tilted BIO housing, which can be corrected by gross tilting of the headset. Horizontal diplopia is commonly caused by incorrect IPD settings or a working distance too close to the patient. Too close a working distance with a smaller pupil will not allow fundus visualization. A tight headband adjustment will induce unnecessary examiner discomfort.

American National Standards Institute (ANSI) modified findings recommend that with voltage set at half power, continuous viewing of a single fundus area should not exceed 40 seconds in duration.

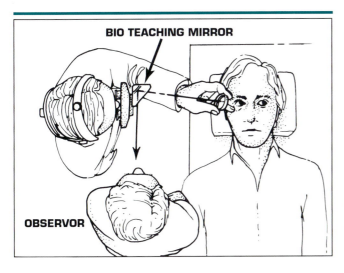

10. (left) A teaching mirror is attached to the BIO for simultaneous fundus viewing by two people. The observer should be positioned at twelve inches or less from the mirror.

11. (below) Ocular fundus with anatomical landmarks. (a) Long posterior ciliary artery and nerve. (b) Short posterior ciliary artery. (c) Vortex vein. (d) Vitreous base (nasal). (e) Vitreous base (temporal). The circled areas represent successive views observed with the BIO. (See also Color Plate 55–11.) (Courtesy of Anthony Cavallerano, OD)

56 Scleral Indentation

■ Description/Indications. Views of the anterior ocular fundus are limited by the iris, edge of the crystalline lens, and the patient's globe–orbit configuration. Even with maximum pupillary dilation, these factors make viewing the pars plana, ora serrata, and some areas of the peripheral retina difficult when solely using the binocular indirect ophthalmoscope (BIO) (Fig. 1A). Scleral indentation is a technique used to inwardly displace optically inaccessible or poorly defined areas of the peripheral fundus, aligning them with the examiner's axis of observation (Fig. 1B). Scleral indentation not only allows for the simple inward displacement of tissue, but also allows it to be viewed stereoscopically from multiple angles by elevating and rolling the tissue with a scleral depressor. Lesions that might otherwise go undetected or misdiagnosed can be identified by employing this technique. It is optimal to master the BIO technique (see p. 226) before learning scleral indentation.

Indications for scleral indentation include symptoms of flashes, floaters, spots, or hazy or decreased vision; history of blunt trauma; high axial myopia; aphakia; or any previously diagnosed peripheral retinal anomaly.

One purpose of peripheral fundus examination is to identify retinal breaks or areas with rhegmatogenous potential. Proper indentation technique attempts not only to place the area of concern on the examiner's observation axis, but also to produce a change in viewing perspective to assist in diagnosis. Placement of the area along the sloping edge of the indentation (Fig. 1C) produces a darkened subretinal appearance with resultant enhanced contrast between the intact retina and any retinal break. Indentation also produces oblique viewing, which increases apparent tissue layer density, thus reducing retinal translucency and increasing the contrast between a retinal break and the retina. Indentation allows for greater ease in viewing tissue layer separation and surface irregularities by creating multiple viewing angles along and between tissue layers.

There are several types of scleral depressors available, with the choice depending mostly upon personal preference. The thimble type (open or closed tip), double-ended flat, and cotton-tipped applicators are commonly employed (Fig. 2). Ambidexterity with both the condensing lens and the depressor greatly facilitates the technique. The anatomic configuration of the patient's face usually determines whether the right or left hand is used. A gentle touch during indentation yields the best results.

■ Instrumentation. Binocular indirect ophthalmoscope, condensing lens (20 D and 30 D), scleral depressor (indentor), topical ophthalmic mydriatic/cycloplegic solution(s), cotton-tipped applicators.

■ Technique. Maximally dilate each eye with topical ophthalmic mydriatic/cycloplegic solutions. Recline the well-dilated patient, allowing for enough room at the patient's head for unrestricted movement around it. Perform BIO before scleral indentation to identify fundus areas warranting further study.

In preparation for superior retinal examination, stand at the patient's right side. Hold the depressor between the left thumb and index finger, with the middle finger placed along its shaft, and ask the patient to look downward. Locate the superior lid fold, which corresponds to the top of the tarsal plate, and place the depressor tip at this point with its curve directed toward the globe (Fig. 3A). Ask the patient to slowly look backward just beyond the straight up position, allowing the depressor to maintain its lid position as it follows the eye back into the orbit (Fig. 3B). The depressor is now positioned perpendicular to, and with its tip tangential to, the globe. Place the depressor between 7 (ora) and 14 mm (equator) from the limbus, along the side of the globe corresponding to the area of regard, and apply gentle pressure (Fig. 3C). If the patient is uncomfortable, too much pressure is probably being applied, the depressor is not tangential, or you are indenting too far anteriorly.

With the depressor in position, tilt your torso to the right. Shine the indirect beam into the pupil, directing it superiorly, attempting to place the depressor tip and the light on the same observation axis. Standing 180 degrees away, observe the overall red reflex and note the presence of a darkened alteration to the reflex corresponding to the depressor position. Practice finding this reflex change using only the BIO and the depressor. Place the condensing lens in front of the eye's darkened reflex area, follow the depressor shaft into the eye, and look for an elevation of the retina at the opposite side of the lens. If not present, do not add any additional pressure. First, scan the adjacent fundus, adding a little movement to the depressor for easier recognition. If still unsuccessful, reposition the light or the depressor, making sure that gentle pressure is being applied tangentially, not perpendicularly, to the globe.

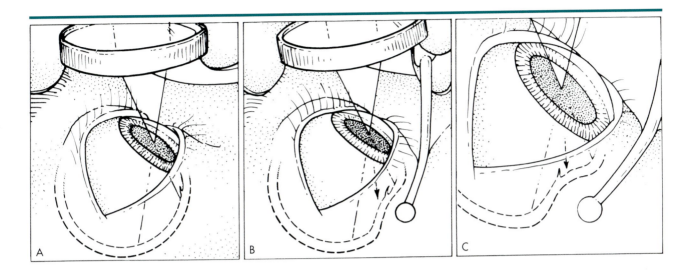

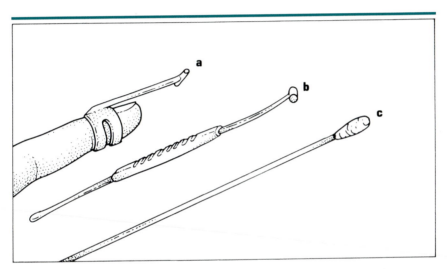

1. (above) A. Even with extreme gaze and maximum pupillary dilation, some anterior ocular fundus tissue cannot be seen with the BIO alone. B. Scleral indentation displaces tissue inwardly to place it into the examiner's axis of observation. C. The area of regard is placed along the sloping edge of the indented tissue for different viewing perspectives.

2. (left) Three common designs for scleral depressors are the (a) thimble design, (b) double-ended flat, and (c) cotton-tipped applicator.

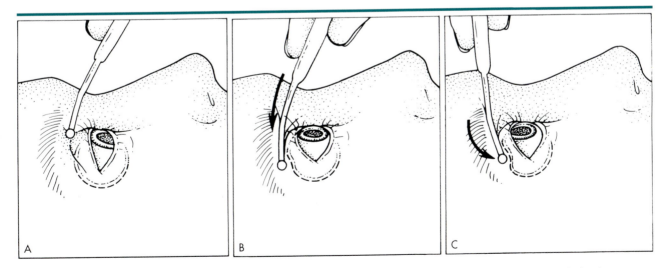

3. With the patient looking downward, the depressor is placed at the superior lid fold (A). As the patient looks backward, the depressor is allowed to follow the eye into the orbit (B) tangential to the globe. Apply gentle pressure to the globe with the tip of the depressor (C).

Attempt to maintain a common axis between the BIO, condensing lens, pupillary center of rotation, and the depressor (Fig. 4). If the retinal elevation is seen but is not in the proper position, move the depressor opposite to the direction you want the visualized area to move, or ask the patient to look into that position of gaze. To visualize the ora serrata, have the patient look further backward toward his or her forehead and your depressor. To view more posteriorly, instruct the patient to partially lower the eyes. During the learning process, make correcting movements with the depressor horizontally and vertically to visualize the elevated area, eventually progressing to oblique corrective movements. Reposition the plane of the patient's face to assist in bypassing anatomical obstructions. For example, a patient with a prominent frontal bone will require the chin elevated to tip the frontal bone out of the way for inferior fundus viewing (Fig. 5).

Each circumferential placement of the depressor usually allows for visualization of 1 ½ clock hours of the fundus. The need for repositioning of the depressor at each clock hour to be examined depends upon the age of the patient and his or her accompanying tissue flaccidness. For an older patient with flaccid lids, attempt to move the depressor one additional clock hour by sliding the depressor without the patient's refixation. For additional circumferential examination, reposition the depressor at the desired position(s). For younger patients with firmer orbital texture, reposition the depressor for each clock position.

To perform inferior scleral indentation, ask the patient to initially look upward toward his or her forehead. Place the depressor at the inferior-most edge of the lower tarsal plate, then ask the patient to look straight ahead or downward while keeping the chin level or tilted slightly upwards (Fig. 6A). As the eye returns downward to the straight ahead or inferior gaze position, allow the depressor to follow the globe back into the orbit (Fig. 6B). Examine the inferior fundus by clock hours in the same manner as the superior fundus.

Difficulty may arise when the 3 and 9-o'clock areas are indented. Begin as if you were going to examine the 10 or 2-o'clock position. After placement of the depressor at the edge of the superior tarsal plate, "drag" the lid around to the 9 or 3-o'clock position, exerting gentle pressure (Fig. 7). If poor results occur, anesthetize the globe with a topical solution and depress directly on the scleral tissue.

■ **Interpretation.** Contrast enhancement of a retinal defect is produced because part of the incident light beam from the indirect ophthalmoscope is reflected obliquely away from the examiner's view, yielding a darker choroidal/retinal pigment epithelial background against the inner translucent retina. In addition, angular displacement may place another structure optically behind a defect, also enhancing tissue contrast. Whenever a translucent tissue is viewed obliquely, its apparent tissue density is increased, resulting in increased contrast. Retinal surface irregularities leading to retinal holes, tears, or other peripheral anomalies are more easily detected when viewed from different angles produced with indentation.

■ **Contraindications/Complications.** Incomplete pupillary dilation will frequently result in unsuccessful scleral indentation. Placement of the condensing lens prior to visualization of the darkened reflex will often lead to poor depressor localization. The gentle depression of the globe must be tangential rather than perpendicular to attain the desired results. Slight discomfort may be reported by some patients during testing. Depression on the tarsal plate or too close to the limbus and ciliary body will also produce patient discomfort. Extreme gaze toward the quadrant of regard is not always needed for good anterior retina visualization. Inadequate examiner torso tilting can limit fundus views.

Proper scleral indentation is not believed to enlarge retinal holes or cause retinal detachment. Do not perform indentation on eyes that have undergone recent intraocular surgery. Use caution when depressing patients with glaucoma, as IOP does increase during this technique. Do not perform scleral depression on eyes that may have a penetrating injury, hyphema, or ruptured globe.

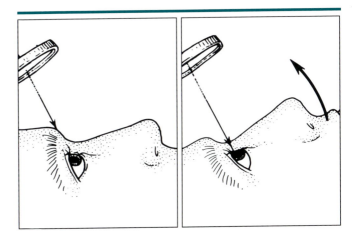

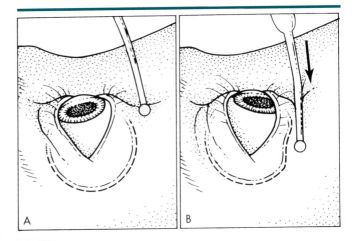

5. To avoid anatomical restrictions during examination, tilt the patients face away from the obstructive structure.

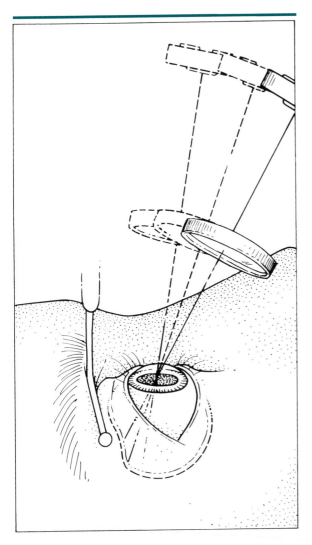

4. A common axis between the examiner, condensing lens, pupillary center, and area of indentation should be maintained during examination.

A

B

6. A, B. The depressor is placed at the inferior tarsal plate margin of the lower lid and this position is maintained as it follows the globe downward.

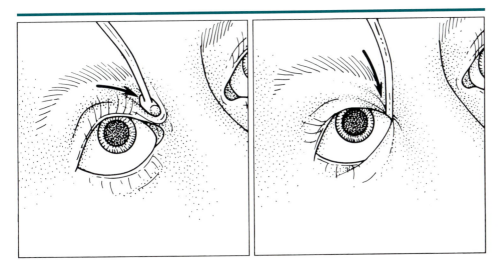

7. The horizontal meridians are examined by "dragging" the edge of the superior lid downward and then indenting.

57 Retinal Evaluation: Three-Mirror Lens

■ **Description/Indications.** The three-mirror fundus contact lens, used with the slit lamp biomicroscope, allows for stereoscopic examination of the retina extending from the optic disc to the ora serrata, including the vitreoretinal interface. The entire vitreous cavity can also be visualized and studied. It is helpful to perform binocular indirect ophthalmoscopy (see p. 226) prior to three-mirror lens examination so that specific areas requiring further scrutiny can be identified.

The inner concave surface of the fundus lens is placed centrally in contact with the anesthetized cornea, similar to the positioning of a gonioscopic lens (see p. 74). A viscous ophthalmic solution or gel is used as a cushioning and bonding agent. The direct contact bonds the lens and ocular surfaces, producing an optical continuity that yields a view with few distortions or reflections. The lens neutralizes the corneal refractive power, extending the biomicroscope's range of focus posteriorly to the retina (Fig. 1). Lateral and axial biomicroscopic views with this lens, through a maximally dilated pupil, are relatively independent of the patient's refractive error.

The name of the lens is somewhat of a misnomer because not only does it have three mirrors for fundus viewing, but also a central viewing lens. Lens design (Fig. 2A) consists of a 64-diopter central lens power with an inner surface 7.6 mm radius of curvature, capable of displaying the central fundus 30 degrees from the axis. The optic disc and macula can be examined for subtle changes with this centrally positioned lens.

The three enclosed reflecting mirrors are spaced 120 degrees apart with varying angles of inclination (73, 67, and 59 degrees) corresponding to the equatorial fundus, anterior equator to posterior ora serrata, and ora serrata/pars plana regions, respectively (Figs. 2B and C). The latter mirror is also used in gonioscopy for viewing of the anterior chamber angle (see p. 38). The 73 and 67-degree mirrors are frequently used for the differential diagnosis of peripheral retinal holes, tears, or other anomalies.

Selection of the desired mirror depends upon the fundus area to be examined. The resultant views are reversed in an antero-posterior direction (inverted) only, not laterally as in binocular indirect ophthalmoscopy. The fundus lens–biomicroscope combination allows for a variety of magnified views using different slit widths and illumination options. The additional magnification with the three-mirror lens is a

clear advantage over the binocular indirect ophthalmoscope when a detailed examination is required.

■ **Instrumentation.** Three-mirror fundus contact lens, slit lamp biomicroscope, topical ophthalmic anesthetic solution, topical ophthalmic mydriatic/cycloplegic solutions, cushioning solution or gel, sterile ophthalmic saline solution.

■ **Technique.** Maximally dilate the pupil with topical ophthalmic mydriatic/cycloplegic solution(s). Anesthetize the cornea with topical ophthalmic anesthetic solution. Place 2 or 3 bubbleless drops of cushioning solution or gel in the clean, concave surface of the lens. Position the patient in the slit lamp, encouraging him or her maintain contact with the slit lamp forehead and to not squeeze the eyes shut during testing.

Pull the slit lamp away to allow adequate room for lens placement. Instruct the patient to look upward and open the eyes widely. Hold the lens with your thumb, index and middle finger, tilting slightly backward to retain the fluid (Fig. 3A). Depending upon the palpebral aperture size, tightness of the lids, and patient cooperation, the thumb of the opposite hand may be needed to secure the upper lid against the superior orbital rim. Place the lens on the eye with either hand; however, since the outside hand (left for the right eye, and vice versa) usually holds the lens in position during the procedure, it might be easier to perform the insertion procedure with the same hand.

Steady your hand by placing your ring finger on the inferior orbital rim while pulling the lower lid down to widen the cul-de-sac. Tuck the inferior edge of the lens into the inferior cul-de-sac (Fig. 3B) placing it in contact with the bulbar conjunctiva to assist with continued control of the inferior lid margin. Bring the top of the lens forward and ask the patient to look straight ahead (Fig. 3C). Look for a central cornea image, which indicates proper alignment, and release the upper lid (Fig. 3D). Keep mild pressure on the lens during testing; however, if placement is insecure, apply additional pressure. Watch for corneal folds or striae or induced arterial pulsation, which are indicators of excessive lens pressure. Utilize an elbow rest if additional stabilization is needed and secure the lens by placing your remaining fingers on the patient's cheek or on the upright bar of the biomicroscope.

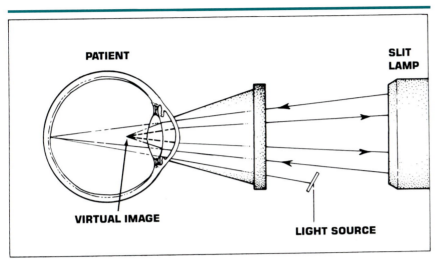

1. (left) Optical principle of the three-mirror fundus contact lens. The lens neutralizes the corneal refractive power and extends the slit lamp's range of focus.

2. (below) A. Frontal view of the lens with its four optical surfaces (1 = central posterior pole; 2 = equatorial area; 3 = anterior peripheral fundus; 4 = ora serrata, pars plana.) B. Diagrammatic projections of viewing range for each lens component. C. Panoramic diagram of specific viewing areas for each lens surface.

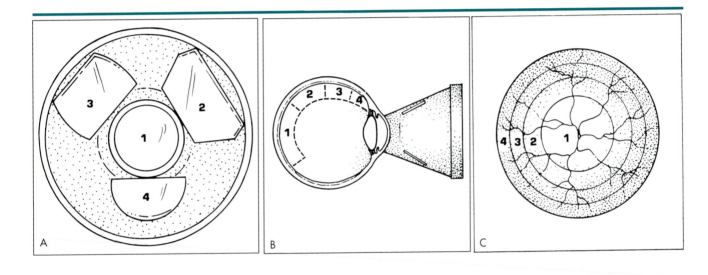

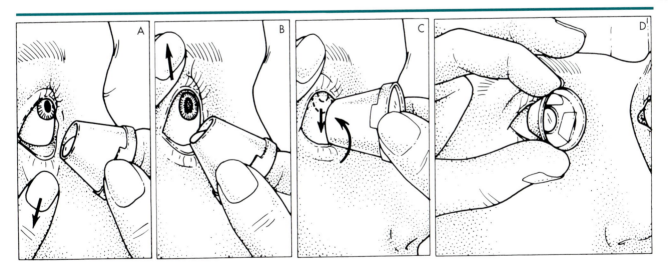

3. A. The fluid-filled lens is tilted backward slightly as the eye is approached. As the patient looks up, the lower lid is retracted. B. One edge of the lens is placed in the inferior fornix, and the thumb is used to retract the upper lid. C. The lens is pivoted onto the eye as the patient is asked to look straight ahead. D. The thumb and index finger are used to hold the lens securely against the eye, and the remaining fingers are supported on the forehead strap.

Set the slit lamp magnification initially at 10X and the beam width at 3 to 4 mm with the light beam and microscope placed coaxially (Fig. 4). Instruct the patient to look straight ahead at a fixation target placed directly in front of the opposite eye. Move the slit lamp forward, keeping the beam centered in the middle of the lens. Continue moving forward through the pupillary red reflex until the posterior pole is in focus. Stop the axial movement behind the crystalline lens if central vitreous inspection is needed. Position the joystick vertically to allow for fine fingertip focusing. Examine any desired area of the central 30 degrees of the fundus, making small horizontal and vertical beam movements. Adjust magnification, beam width, light intensity, illumination angle (0 to 20 degrees), and beam rotation as needed. Ask the patient to look directly at the beam for central macular examination.

Examine the remaining posterior pole and equatorial regions by directing the light beam into the rectangular peripheral mirror. Rotate the lens on the eye using the thumb and middle or index finger to position this mirror directly opposite (180 degrees) to the retinal area to be examined (Fig. 5A). Rotate the light beam parallel to the meridian of regard (Fig. 5B). Place the illuminating column (light beam) on the same side as the mirror being used when obliquely examining the inferior retina with a superiorly positioned mirror. Place the illuminating column to the opposite side of the mirror being used when obliquely examining the superior retina with an inferiorly positioned mirror. Maintain adequate pressure on the lens with rotation movements to prevent air bubbles from entering and disrupting the view, or to keep an eyelid from sliding under the lens and squeezing it out from the eye. Attempt to eliminate acquired bubbles with lens rotation, tilting, and gentle pressure. Remove and reinsert the lens if obstructive bubbles persist.

Use the same procedure with the trapezoid mirror when examining the peripheral retina from the equator to the vitreous base. Use the small semicircular mirror with wide dilation to visualize the vitreous base, ora serrata/pars plana, and lens zonular areas, as well as the anterior chamber angle when used for gonioscopy. Tilt the lens in the same direction as the specific examining mirror to extend its peripheral range of view (Fig. 6A), or ask the patient to look in the opposite direction as the mirror to also extend the range (Fig. 6B). Pull back on the joystick slightly to examine the overlying vitreous.

Remove the fundus lens by asking the patient to look upward and blink firmly; or alternatively, ask the patient to continue to fixate straight ahead as you grasp the lens, while with the opposite hand's thumb you press on the globe at the inferotemporal edge of the lens. Press through the patient's lower lid to ensure cleanliness (Fig. 7).

Lightly irrigate the cul-de-sac areas with sterile ophthalmic saline solution after lens removal (see p. 152) to remove residual cushioning solution. Inform the patient that he or she may experience some temporary blur and irritation during the remainder of the day. No prophylactic treatment is generally needed.

■ **Interpretation.** The three mirrors yield an image that is reversed in an anterior-posterior direction (Fig. 5B). For example, the inferior retina is seen inverted and directly in a superiorly positioned mirror. As you move peripherally on the mirrored surface or "climb the mirror," new fundus tissue will appear on the inner edge of the lens.

■ **Contraindications/Complications.** Apprehensive, young, or poorly fixating patients may make this procedure difficult to perform. Inadequate pupil dilation or significant media opacities can all hinder success. Patients with surgical wounds, pathologic epithelial keratopathies, possible perforating injuries, or recent significant blunt trauma injury should not be examined with this contact technique. The cushioning solution frequently causes punctate staining or haze, affecting corneal transparency; therefore, photography or other noncontact procedures are generally completed prior to three-mirror evaluation. Minor corneal abrasions are possible with poor technique. IOP is temporarily decreased following fundus lens use, also necessitating that IOP measurement be performed first. A vasovagal reflex is possible with compressive procedure of the globe.

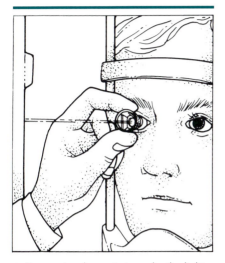

4. To examine the posterior pole, the light beam is directed centrally into the lens and focused on the retina.

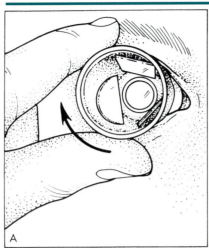

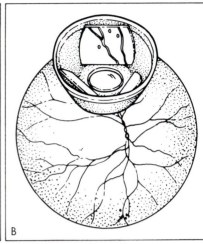

5. A. Fingertip rotation of the lens is done while maintaining adequate pressure against the eye. B. The beam of the biomicroscope is directed into the lens mirror positioned at 12-o'clock to produce an inverted image of a 6-o'clock fundus lesion.

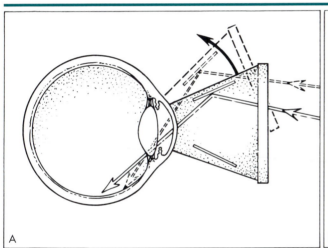

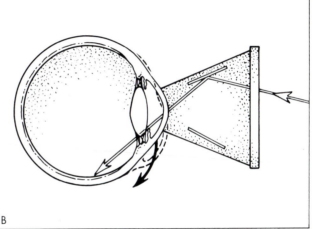

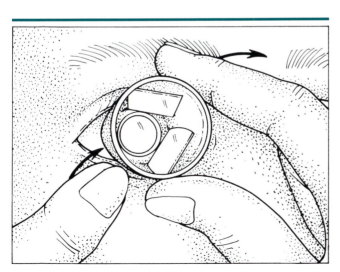

6. (above) A. The lens is tilted opposite in direction to the area being examined in order to extend the view anteriorly. B. Alternate method: The patient is asked to look slightly opposite in direction to the employed mirror to extend the anterior range of view.

7. (left) To remove the fundus lens, suction can be broken by gently indenting the globe through the patient's lower lid.

58 Hruby Lens Examination

■ **Description/Indications.** The Hruby lens is a −58.6 diopter plano/concave lens mounted on the slit lamp biomicroscope that extends the focal range of the microscope posteriorly to the retinal plane. By effectively neutralizing the eye's refractive power, this system results in an erect, stereoscopic, virtual image located in the anterior segment near the posterior lenticular surface (Fig. 1). The iris, located anterior to the lens image, acts as a diaphragm or field stop limiting or extending the stereoscopic field of view.

The major function of the Hruby lens is noncontact examination of the optic disc, macula, posterior pole, and central vitreous. Prefocused or focusable Hruby lenses are available on specific slit lamps. The easily accessible, noncontact features of this lens make it useful in many situations. Reflections off the lens and the eye's anterior surface can produce bothersome aberrations.

■ **Instrumentation.** Hruby lens, slit lamp biomicroscope, topical ophthalmic mydriatic/cycloplegic solution(s).

■ **Technique.** Dilate the patient's pupils with ophthalmic mydriatic/cycloplegic solution(s). Position the patient comfortably at the slit lamp biomicroscope with instructions to always keep the forehead in contact with the headstrap. Insert the post of the Hruby lens into the slotted sliding track with the concave lens surface facing the patient (Fig. 2). The Zeiss slit lamp has a self-adjusting Hruby lens that swings down into place and is operational after pushing a small release button on the mechanism arm (Fig. 3). Instruct the patient to fixate straight ahead with the nontested eye, while positioning the lens as close to the tested eye as possible (approximately 10 to 20 mm). Make initial adjustments with gross movements of the slit lamp, and refinements with subtle movements of the Hruby lens handle (Fig. 4). Position the slit lamp joystick in the vertical position, allowing for fine focus adjustments during the examination with your fingertips. Adjust the slit beam to a 2 to 3-mm width, in direct align-

ment with the center of the Hruby lens; set magnification at 6X or 10X; and set illumination intensity to a moderate level. Move the slit lamp forward, maintaining lens focus and centration of the pupillary red reflex. Pass through the crystalline lens, making note of any opacities seen with the induced retroillumination. Continue the movement forward through the vitreous until retinal tissue and blood vessels are clearly in focus.

Make fine adjustments by varying the beam width and height, magnification, illumination intensity, and the angle of illumination (0 to 10 degrees) to improve the image. Make fine adjustments also with the Hruby lens focusing handle. Control fixation with the slit lamp fixation light or with another fixation light or target. Position the latter target beside your ear on the side of the nontested eye. Move the fixation target to centrally position the desired area for examination, noting that the ocular tissue in view will move in the opposite direction as the target movement. Continue to make fine joystick focusing adjustments during the examination, remembering that the more centrally positioned the red reflex and the smaller the lens distance to the cornea, the better the stereoscopic view.

Pull back on the joystick to place the vitreous in focus when examination is desired.

■ **Interpretation.** The resultant Hruby lens image is erect, stereoscopic, and magnified. This provides for adequate examination of the optic disc, macula, and central retinal tissue and lesions.

■ **Contraindications/Complications.** Poor patient fixation, slit lamp positioning difficulties, poor glare tolerance, limited pupillary dilation, and significant media opacities can all yield poor results or limited success. The multiple optical interfaces of this system allow for fair to good views due to induced reflections and aberrations. Consider using a fundus contact lens (see p. 238) or fundus biomicroscopy (see p. 244) if the Hruby lens views are unacceptable.

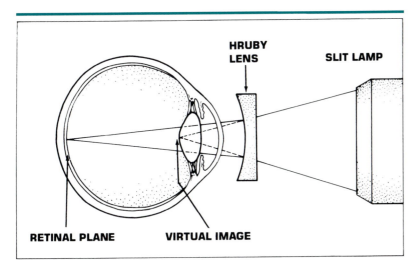

1. Optical principles of the Hruby lens. By effectively neutralizing the eye's refractive power, this −58.6 diopter plano/concave lens produces an erect, stereoscopic, virtual image near the posterior lenticular surface.

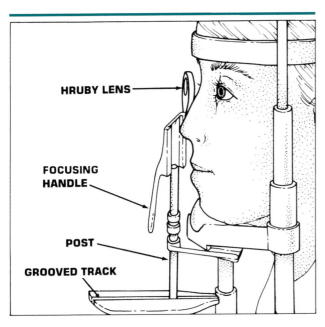

2. The post of the focusable Hruby lens is placed in the slotted slide track and then the lens is adjusted for proper positioning.

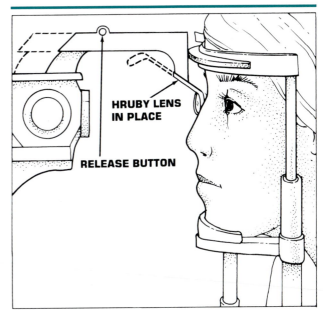

3. The self-focusing, slit lamp-mounted Hruby Lens (Zeiss model) is placed in position by pushing the release button followed by downward rotation of the lens.

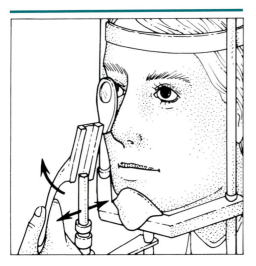

4. To decrease the lens vertex distance, pull backward on the handle; to increase vertex distance, push forward.

59
Fundus Biomicroscopy

■ **Description/Indications.** The clinical standard for posterior segment examination is fundus biomicroscopy. Noncontact fundus lens designs have continued to evolve, and due to their relative ease of use and high-quality optics, fundus biomicroscopy has developed into a procedure of choice for routine posterior segment examinations, as well as for assessing many specific clinical entities. This technique provides for a noncontact, stereoscopic, well-illuminated view of the choroid, retina, vitreous, and optic nerve. It is considered a better alternative to the Hruby lens (see p. 242) and an easier one than the retinal three-mirror lens (see p. 238).

As with binocular indirect ophthalmoscopy (BIO, see p. 226), a high plus-powered ophthalmic condensing lens is used to focus diverging illuminated posterior segment light rays to form an aerial image. The resultant optical system provides the examiner with a magnified, real, inverted, and reversed image (Fig. 1). The small size of the image requires the variable magnification capabilities of the slit lamp biomicroscope for detailed examination (Fig. 2). The condensing lens used for fundus biomicroscopy is double aspheric, optically coated, and most frequently hand-held. The asphericity produces fewer optical aberrations and more uniform illumination.

Clear and yellow lenses for fundus biomicroscopy are available in powers of +60, +78, and +90 diopters (D); in addition, there are full-field, high-resolution, and small-pupil design lenses (Fig. 3). The optional yellow tint eliminates ultraviolet and short-wave (blue and violet) visible wavelengths, and reduces patient glare sensitivity and the very small potential for retinal photochemical damage. The 78D and 90D lenses remain the most popular at present; however, the full-field designs are quickly gaining in popularity.

Image magnification and field of view are directly related to the pupil aperture diameter and the dioptric power of the lens. The average working distance for the most popular lenses is 6.5 to 7.0 mm.

Successful lens alignment requires visual axis centration, proper and stable vertex distancing and lens tilting, along with continuous minor readjustment of the lens throughout the procedure. Pupillary dilation is required for maximum viewing, and the patient experiences a moderate amount of glare during the procedure. Small-pupil lenses are now available and have been met with mixed reviews. These lenses may, for example, be helpful for assessing the optic nerve heads of glaucoma patients during follow-up examination when pupillary dilation is not indicated.

The hand-held, noncontact aspect of this technique allows for ease of performance, and the procedure can be easily interrupted or discontinued as needed. A steady lens holder is available as an alternative lens positioning technique. Some practitioners have created their own holders by using the slit lamp fixation light and a properly placed elastic band. Fundus biomicroscopy can be used for routine posterior segment examination of cooperative patients, apprehensive patients, young individuals, and patients with recent ocular trauma, as well as in other situations that may preclude the use of other more involved, contact-type examination techniques. High-quality stereoscopic views of the optic nerve head allow for comprehensive glaucoma and glaucoma-suspect evaluation (see p. 372). Visualization of the posterior pole, peripheral retina, underlying choroid, and vitreous tissues can be accomplished by choosing the appropriate lens, biomicroscopic magnification, and patient position of gaze.

■ **Instrumentation.** Slit lamp biomicroscope, fundus biomicroscopic condensing lens(es), topical ophthalmic mydriatic/cycloplegic solution(s), steady lens holder (optional).

■ **Technique.** Maximally dilate the patient's pupils with topical ophthalmic mydriatic/cycloplegic solution(s). Position the patient comfortably at the biomicroscope with instructions to keep the forehead pressed up against the forehead rest. Adjust the slit lamp beam to 2 to 3 mm in width, at moderate illumination, and set the magnification at either 6X or 10X. Reduce the beam width and height if patient discomfort is encountered. Align the biomicroscope directly in front of the eye to be examined. Direct the light source perpendicular to the corneal apex (coaxial with the biomicroscope), or up to 10 degrees off-axis, and move it forward to within a few inches of the eye. This should produce a large retroilluminated red pupillary reflex. Instruct the patient to fixate straight ahead with the opposite eye looking past your ear, or to fixate the properly positioned slit lamp fixation light.

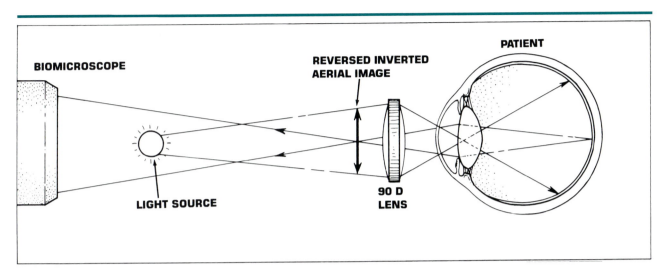

1. The optical principles of fundus biomicroscopy.

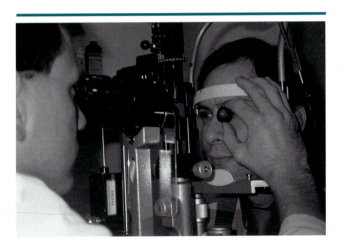

2. The small size of the image produced by fundus biomicroscopy requires the variable magnification capabilities of the slit lamp for detailed examination (Courtesy of Daniel Reiser, OD, and Steven Hill, OD).

3. Various fundus biomicroscopy lenses are illustrated, including yellow add-on filters. (Courtesy of Volk Optical.)

Grasp the perimeter of the lens with your thumb and index finger. Viewing from outside the biomicroscope, introduce and center either surface of the double aspheric lens directly in front of the patient's eye at a distance of approximately 1.0 to 1.5 cm (½ inch). Stabilize the lens by holding the remaining fingers of your hand against the patient's cheek (Fig. 4A), the slit lamp upright bar, or the forehead strap. Use your middle finger to secure the upper eyelid and the ring finger to hold the lower lid against the orbital rim if an adequate palpebral aperture width cannot be maintained by the patient (Fig. 4B).

While viewing through the oculars, pull back on the slit lamp joystick until the aerial image of the narrowed red reflex beam from the retina is in focus. As with the BIO, make minor adjustments in the centration, tilt, and vertex distance of the condensing lens to improve the image. Gradually widen the slit beam as much as the patient will tolerate without creating added problems due to reflection or discomfort. Place the joystick in the upright position to allow for fine focusing. Scan the fundus with lateral and vertical movements of the joystick. Do this in a systematic manner for all nine cardinal meridians. One suggested technique is to begin at the optic disc, move the beam inferiorly with the joystick or vertical knob, and track the superior vascular arcade and surrounding retina temporally (Fig. 5). After reaching the temporal limit of the lens without patient eye movements, move the light beam superiorly and track the inferior arcade back toward the disc. Examine the nasal retina next.

After completing the examination of the retina and choroid of the posterior pole, extend your views anteriorly in any quadrant by asking the patient to look toward each direction of the posterior segment that you desire to examine further with the lens, remembering to tilt the lens as fixation changes. Tilt the lens to the left with left gaze, and to the right with right gaze. Tilt the inferior edge inward and closer to the globe with upgaze (Fig. 6A). Tilt the superior edge inward and closer to the eyebrow with downward gaze, retracting the upper lid as needed (Fig. 6B). The full-field lens design allows for greater topographical retinal viewing.

Pull back on the joystick for examination of the overlying vitreoretinal interface. Even with optimum viewing technique and conditions, the vitreous can be difficult to visualize. Optic section examination of the vitreous with some variation in beam width seems to allow for better visualization of detail. Vitreous syneresis and detachments, coalesced and condensed lamellar sheets of fibrils (wavy off-white tissue), and liquefaction with lacunae (empty pockets), are visualized, along with inflammatory, pigment, or hemorrhagic cells.

■ **Interpretation.** As with binocular indirect ophthalmoscopy, it takes time to adapt to interpreting the resultant reversed and inverted lens image. It is only the lens view itself, however, that is different, as the quadrant that you are examining is the quadrant being seen.

True fundus color discrimination may be adversely affected by the optional yellow tint, which explains why many practitioners prefer clear fundus biomicroscopy lenses. Nerve fiber layer viewing with red free light is also adversely affected. Extremely subtle posterior segment changes may still require the high-quality views attained only with a fundus contact lens (see p. 238).

■ **Contraindications/Complications.** Photophobic patients greatly restrict the quality and length of examination time for fundus biomicroscopy. Proper placement of the condensing lens and a reasonable exposure time to the illuminating light source produces no danger to the ocular tissue using either clear or yellow-tinted lenses. Unsteadiness on the part of the examiner may be resolved by using the available steady mount lens holder.

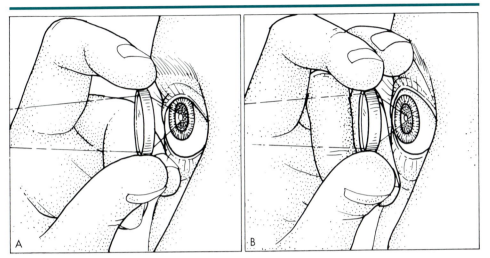

4. A. The lens is positioned approximately ½ inch in front of the patient's eye and stabilized by resting the fingers on the patient's cheek. B. The middle finger is used to secure the upper lid and the ring finger for the lower lid if the patient cannot maintain an adequate palpebral aperture.

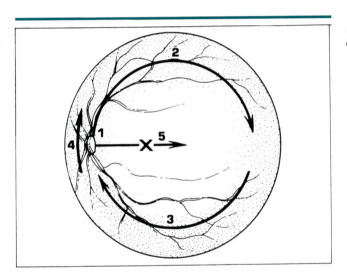

5. After examining the optic disc, the fundus is scanned in a systematic manner as illustrated.

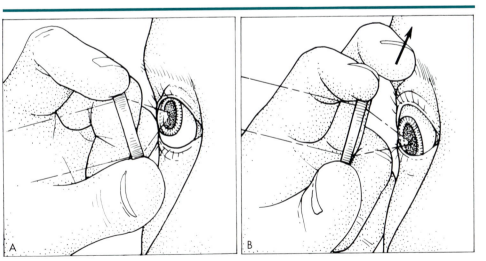

6. A. The lens is tilted backward with upgaze to view the superior retina more anteriorly. B. The lens is tilted downward and the upper lid secured against the superior orbital rim to view the inferior retina more anteriorly.

60

Fundus Diagramming

■ **Description/Indications.** A fundus diagram or drawing is used to illustrate and record retinal conditions and associated vitreous anomalies. It is especially useful in illustrating conditions such as large retinal detachments that occupy areas too large in size to be documented by a single photograph. The technique of fine detailed fundus drawing or retinal diagramming is developed with practice, patience, and being a "stickler for detail." Mapping out a complete fundus appearance requires sound binocular indirect ophthalmoscopy (see p. 226) and scleral indentation (see p. 234) skills.

Fundus drawings assist the novice practitioner in mastering the concept of the inverted, reversed, and smaller image created with binocular indirect ophthalmoscopy (BIO). An accurate drawing is the result of a systematic and thorough fundus examination using good spatial orientation skills. It requires that the examiner be precise in his or her descriptions and use the universal color code for fundus drawings that allows other practitioners to understand them. These detailed geographic recordings are excellent for publication or for future review, and may prove invaluable in situations where media opacification occurs between the office visit and scheduled surgery.

The standard fundus diagramming chart (Fig. 1A) provides a graphic, anatomical skeleton upon which normal and abnormal ocular conditions are located and recorded. Projection of the eye's spherical surface onto this flat plane recording sheet produces a disproportionate amount of area allotted for the peripheral ocular tissue (Fig. 1B), yielding lateral and circumferential distortion. Since fundus drawing is commonly performed for peripheral retinal anomalies, this works in the examiner's favor for additional drawing space, but actual dimensions must be kept in perspective when reviewing the total picture.

Three concentric circles on the standard chart circumferentially designate subdivisions of the fundus. The inner or equatorial circle, which in a three-dimensional drawing would actually have the largest diameter, encloses the posterior pole (disc, macula, and major vasculature). The middle circle represents the posterior border of the ora serrata and the termination of retinal photoreceptors. Between the inner and middle circle is the peripheral retina, which in actuality makes up 30 to 40% of the entire retina. The outer circle represents the anterior limit of the fundus (pars plana) visible to the examiner with scleral indentation (see p. 234).

The recording chart has other helpful subdivisions, increasing the accuracy of the fundus representation. Roman numerals (I to XII) or numbers (1 to 12) are positioned to designate the clock hours around the perimeter of the drawing, with accompanying radial lines directed toward the posterior pole running through the concentric circles. Lesions can thus be described by clock hour and anterior-posterior fundus position. These radial lines also allow for superior and inferior fundus delineation (above and below the 3 and 9-o'clock positions) as well as temporal and nasal (left or right of the 12 and 6-o'clock positions). The point at which the 12 to 6 and 3 to 9-o'clock lines would cross if extended designates the fovea or center of the diagram.

In the upper-right-hand corner of the chart (the XII end) is the designation of OD or OS. In a corner at the opposite end of the chart (the VI end) are the inverted and reversed words "inverted image." When the recording chart is positioned for use, these words can be read normally when standing at the patient's feet and looking toward his or her head. There is additional space designated on the chart for the patient's name and date.

Regardless of which eye is being examined on a reclined patient, the chart is always positioned with the XII (12) closest to the patient's feet and the VI (6) closest to the head (Fig. 2). To gain a better perspective as to actual in vivo fundus dimensions and orientation, the examiner designates retinal distances using the common nonlinear measurement of the disc diameter (DD). An 18 to 20 diopter condensing lens provides an 8-DD view (Fig. 3). The equator is 6 DD from the fovea and also 2 DD anterior to the vortex vein ampullae. Between the equator and the ora serrata, enclosing the peripheral retina, is a 4-DD distance. Comparing actual ocular dimensions to the chart, the distance between each clock hour at the equator is approximately 6 DD, whereas, at the ora it is approximately 3 DD.

■ **Instrumentation.** Binocular indirect ophthalmoscope (BIO), condensing lenses, scleral depressor, fundus diagramming recording charts, clipboard, common lead pencil, colored pencils or markers (red, black, blue, green, yellow, brown), topical ophthalmic mydriatic/cycloplegic solution(s).

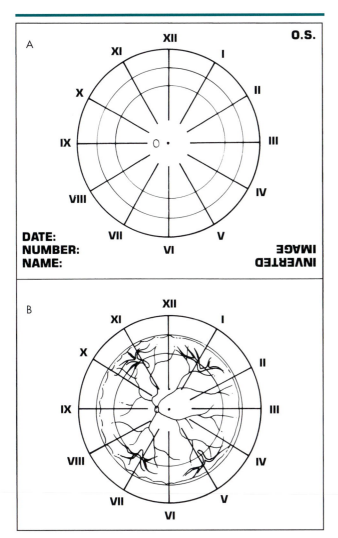

1. A. An example of standard fundus drawing chart. B. The peripheral fundus has a disproportionate amount of space allotted to it, requiring the examiner to place it in proper overall perspective.

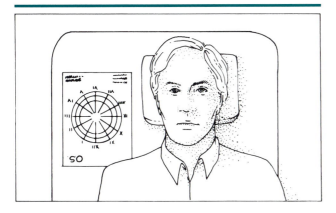

2. The fundus chart is positioned at the patient's right shoulder with the XII designated position closest to his or her feet.

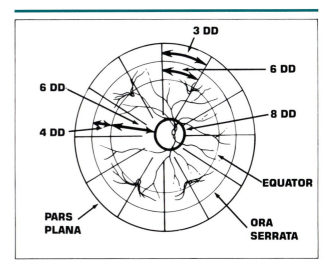

3. Disc diameter (DD) measurements provide for a more realistic overview of actual fundus distances. A 20 diopter BIO condensing lens provides a field of view of approximately 8 DD.

■ **Technique.** Following pupillary dilation, perform a complete fundus examination with the BIO and any other fundus viewing technique required for detailed assessment. Use a higher-powered condensing lens with its larger field of view when extensive retinal tissue involvement exists.

To prepare for ocular fundus diagramming, recline the well-dilated patient in the examination chair or on a retinal examination table. Secure the recording sheet to a clipboard with the Roman numeral XII facing the patient's feet and VI toward the head, which is effectively inverting and reversing the chart. Place the clipboard beside the patient's right ear on the examination table or on a separate table. Left-handed examiners may choose to place the board to the left side of the patient's head.

First, document any significant posterior pole findings. Stand at the head of the chair or table looking down at the patient (Fig. 4) placing yourself in an inverted and reversed position relative to the patient. Begin with the right eye if both eyes are to be diagrammed. Ask the patient to fixate straight up at the ceiling. Lean slightly over the patient and, using the BIO, observe the fovea seen to your left and the optic disc to your right in the condensing lens. Direct the patient's fixation to your left ear, examining the nasal disc area and beyond, and record directly on the chart as seen. Direct his or her fixation to your right ear, examining the temporal disc and macula areas, and record. Direct fixation to your chin for superomacular viewing, and to your forehead for inferomacular viewing. This technique should provide a view of the central posterior pole region. Record your findings directly onto the chart, drawing them exactly as seen in your condensing lens view. Place a red dot or cross in the foveal area, slightly inferotemporal to the disc, if this area is normal. Do not attempt to draw C/D ratios or other disc anatomy from BIO viewing as there are other more accurate techniques for this (see p. 244).

Examine the equatorial and oral areas using the following technique for each clock hour of the fundus. Stand 180 degrees away from the area to be examined and ask the patient to look toward the same area under examination.

Record your findings on the area of the chart closest to you and corresponding to 180 degrees away from the quadrant examined (Fig. 5). For example, to examine the patient's right eye at the 2-o'clock position, stand on the patient's right side at his or her 8-o'clock position, ask the patient to look up and to the left toward 2-o'clock, and examine this area. Record your findings at the Roman numeral II chart area (8-o'clock position) exactly as seen in the lens. Remember that as you scan peripherally toward the ora, new retinal tissue will appear in the condensing lens closest to you at the near side of the lens. With each view, concentrate not only on retinal tissue, but also on any overlying vitreous changes.

Continue in a systematic fashion to scan and examine each clock hour starting posteriorly and moving toward the ora serrata, viewing from 180 degrees opposite to the examined area. Complete examination will require you to circle the patient's head. Repeat the oral region examination with the scleral depressor for any areas with incomplete views.

Record all initial findings in regular lead pencil for ease of correction until the fundus diagram is completed. Draw and color all necessary findings (Fig. 6) using the universal color code (see Color Plate 60–6). Draw only the retinal vessels that are specifically helpful to the fundus diagram. It is usually easier to draw the required vasculature from the far periphery posteriorly.

Repeat the entire procedure for the left eye if indicated.

■ **Interpretation.** The composite drawing can illustrate any normal and abnormal finding seen in the fundus. An example of fundus diagramming is presented (Fig. 7).

■ **Contraindications/Complications.** Prolonged fundus viewing of a single area to study detail should be avoided. American National Standards Institute (ANSI) modified findings recommend that with voltage set at half power, continuous viewing of a single fundus area should not exceed 40 seconds in duration. Scleral indentation is avoided when contraindicated (see p. 234).

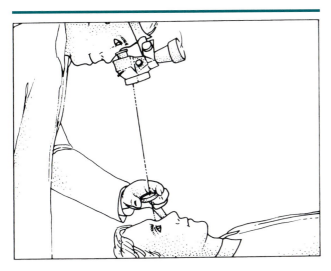

4. By standing at the patient's head and changing spatial orientation, the reversed and inverted image produced by the condensing lens can effectively be nullified for simpler viewing.

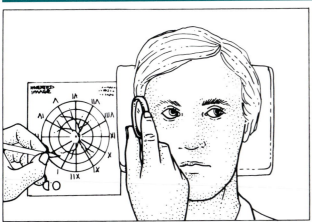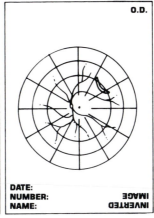

5. Direct the BIO light beam from 180 degrees away from the retinal quadrant under examination (here, the patient's right eye), and ask the patient to look toward the same examined quadrant.

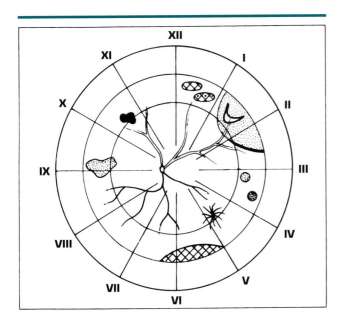

6. The fundus drawing color coding system. (*See* Color Plate 60–6 for the universal color chart.)

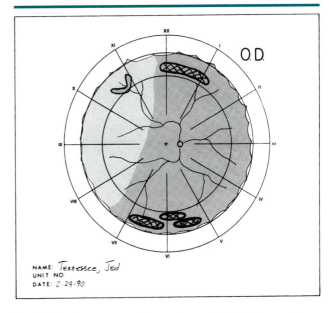

7. A fundus drawing example: retinal tear with detachment. (*See also* Color Plate 60–7.)

61

Amsler Grid Test

■ **Description/Indications.** Amsler grid testing is used to examine for and monitor functional disturbance(s) of the central visual field, 10 degrees on all sides of fixation. It is useful in detecting central and paracentral scotomas and distortion.

The standard Amsler chart consists of a perfectly squared, white-lined grid pattern with a central white fixation dot superimposed on a dull black background (Fig. 1). The squared edges, straight lines, and good contrast provide a geometric design on which the eye can best identify pattern "errors" or disturbances. When the target grid is held at 28 to 30 cm (approximately 12 inches) and viewed by a patient wearing his or her best near corrective lens, each 5-mm square subtends a visual angle of 1 degree. The overall chart is 20 by 20 degrees square, projecting itself over the macular area (Fig. 2).

The standard Amsler grid is used the majority of the time, but a set of seven different grids (Amsler grid book) is available for use in specific circumstances. For example, chart 3 (red grid on a black background) may be used to test for a small central scotoma associated with optic neuritis. A central field weakness (relative scotoma) may manifest better with this chart due to red desaturation from optic nerve disease (see p. 260).

A patient with unexplained visual acuity loss, despite a healthy macular appearance, is a candidate for detailed central field assessment with an Amsler grid. This test is performed prior to pharmacologic mydriasis/cycloplegia. The standard Amsler grid charts and instructions are often sent home with patients with macular disease for daily or frequent self-monitoring of inactive, active, or potential maculopathies.

■ **Instrumentation.** Amsler grid chart or book, patient's best near corrective lens, recording sheets.

■ **Technique.** Seat the patient comfortably and instruct him or her to wear a current near spectacle correction. If the patient's best near correction is not available, put the appropriate near Rx in a trial frame. Ask the patient to hold the uniformly illuminated chart in front of the testing eye at 28 to 30 cm (approximately 12 inches) (Fig. 3). Occlude the opposite eye, avoiding globe compression.

Ask the patient if he or she sees the central white spot on the chart and make note of the answer. If "yes," remind the patient that central fixation must continue throughout the entire test. Continually remind the patient of central fixation during testing.

Ask the patient the following standard questions and note the responses:

1. Do you see the white spot in the center of the squared chart?
2. While you are looking only at the spot, do you also see all four corners of the chart at the same time?
3. While you are still looking at the spot, do you see an uninterrupted, even network of lines and squares; or do you see spots, holes, or any blurry or missing lines?
4. While you continue to look at the spot, are all the vertical and horizontal lines straight and parallel, or are they distorted or wavy? Are all the small squares equal in size and perfectly regular?
5. Still looking at the white spot, do you see anything else, such as vibrations, shining, colors, tint, or wavering lines?
6. Still looking at the white spot, at what distance from this center point do you see the blur or distortion(s)? How many boxes away is it and how many boxes are involved?

Record all significant data. Switch the occluder to the other eye and repeat the questions. In the case of subtle grid changes, alternately cover each eye and ask the patient to compare.

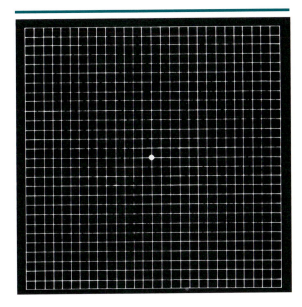

1. The standard Amsler grid testing chart (Chart 1) consists of a perfectly squared, white-lined grid pattern with a central white fixation dot superimposed on a dull black background.

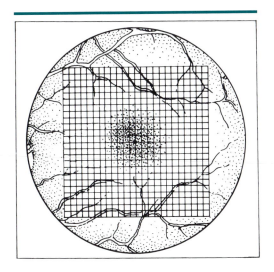

2. Amsler grid tests the majority of the macular area by assessing a 20 by 20-degree square area.

3. The patient holds a uniformly illuminated Amsler chart at 28 to 30 cm while wearing the best near corrective lens and occluding the opposite eye.

■ **Interpretation.** If the patient answers yes to question 1, then there is no central scotoma; move on to question 2. If the answer is "yes, but it's blurred," then there may be a relative central scotoma. Ask the patient to describe the extent of central grid involvement and move to question 2. If the answer is no, then there probably is a dense central scotoma. Switch to Chart 2 (Fig. 4) for the last five questions, because it has two diagonal white lines that cross in the center of the chart where the white spot would be. This should allow the patient to estimate where the center of the grid is for fixation purposes as the other questions are asked. The validity of the grid test decreases when poor central fixation is present.

If the answer to question 2 is yes, then continue on to 3. If the answer is no, then other visual field testing is indicated.

If the answer to question 3 is no, then continue on to 4. If the answer is yes, then relative or absolute juxta-central and paracentral scotoma(s) exist (Fig. 5). Have the patient point to and describe the defect(s). The patient may use the black on white recording grid sheets to better demonstrate them. Chart 4 has spots with no lines, which may be helpful in localizing scotomas.

If the answer to question 4 is yes, then continue to 5. If the answer is no, metamorphopsia is present. (Fig. 6). Ask the patient to localize the area(s) of metamorphopsia. Use the patient recording grid sheets for documentation or ease of reporting. Chart 5, which has one-directional lines capable of being oriented horizontally or vertically, may assist in identifying the involved areas. Chart 6, which has doubling of the Amsler grid lines horizontally along the reading axis, may also be helpful for metamorphopsia testing.

If the answer to question 5 is no, then continue on to 6. If the answer is yes, then entopic phenomena may be present as an early indicator of maculopathy.

Question 6 has probably been answered by this stage. The goal is to localize the retinal problem. Chart 7 may help with fine central changes as it has duplication and finer subdivision of the central Amsler grid. A table format helps to summarize the potential responses to the questions (Fig. 7).

If the patient calls the office reporting any changes on his or her take-home Amsler grid, schedule an examination within the next 24 to 48 hours.

■ **Contraindications/Complications.** This is a noninvasive test that presents no risk to the patient. Poor central fixation or reduced near-point acuity will markedly decrease the test's reliability. If the patient's bifocal addition size or type is such that the Amsler grid cannot be viewed in its entirety, then false positives in testing may occur. The patient's understanding of the test and his or her ability to relate subjective findings to the examiner also determine the success of Amsler grid testing.

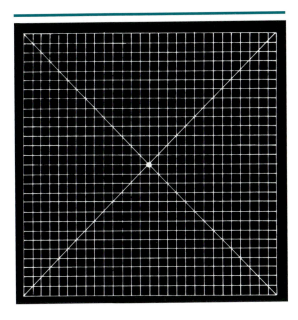

4. The Amsler grid with centrally crossing diagonal lines (Chart 2) is used to aid patient fixation when a central scotoma is present.

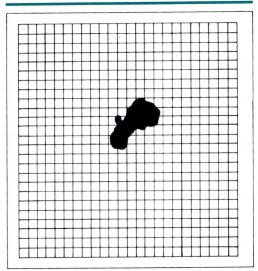

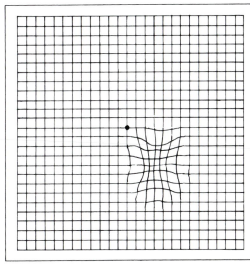

5. (far left) An example of a juxtacentral scotoma detected with Amsler grid testing.

6. (left) An example of paracentral metamorphopsia detected with Amsler grid testing.

SUMMARY TABLE OF AMSLER GRID TESTING		
QUESTION NO.	"YES" RESPONSE	"NO" RESPONSE
1	No central scotoma; proceed to question 2.	Central scotoma; switch to Chart 2 for remaining questions. Other visual field testing indicated.
2	Continue to question 3.	Continue to question 4.
3	Juxtacentral/paracentral scotoma; Chart 4 may be useful.	Metamorphopsia present.
4	Continue to question 5.	Continue to question 6.
5	Entoptic phenomenon.	

7. Potential responses to the standard Amsler grid testing questions. Question 6 asks the patient to specifically localize and quantify the size of the scotoma on the grid.

Photostress Recovery Test

■ **Description/Indications.** The photostress recovery test measures the return of visual function to the macula after a timed exposure to a bright light stimulus. A test light bleaches the visual pigments to produce a subsequent decrease in visual acuity. The time of recovery to within one line of the best corrected visual acuity is measured. The recovery of visual acuity is the result of resynthesis of the photoreceptor visual pigments. This process is dependent upon the metabolic ability of the involved photoreceptors, the juxtapositioned retinal pigment epithelium (RPE), and the photoreceptor–RPE complex interactions. Any disease process that disrupts photopigment resynthesis or separates the receptors and RPE could lead to an increased photostress recovery time.

The photostress recovery test is indicated when a patient presents with decreased vision and equivocal ocular findings, requiring differential diagnosis between early optic nerve and macular disease, or "dry" versus "wet" macular disease.

■ **Instrumentation.** Penlight or transilluminator, visual acuity chart, watch with second hand.

■ **Technique.** Do not dilate the patient's pupils prior to the test. Determine and record the patient's best corrected visual acuities. Remove any spectacle correction. Totally occlude the involved poorer-seeing eye. Place a steady bright penlight or transilluminator 3 to 5 cm (1½ to 2 inches) in front of the "normal" eye (Fig. 1). Ask the patient to stare at this light for 10 seconds. Remove the light, continue to occlude the opposite eye, replace any spectacle Rx, and ask the patient to look at the distance acuity chart (Fig. 2). Have the acuity chart already set up to display the patient's previously recorded best acuity and one line less

in resolution (for example, 20/20 BVA and 20/25). Ask the patient to begin to read the letters as soon as focus returns. Time and record how long it takes for acuity to return in order to read one line less than the original best corrected visual acuity.

Occlude the just tested eye and repeat the same test on the opposite eye. Record your results.

■ **Interpretation.** The relative difference between photostress recovery times in each eye is the best criterion for analyzing the results. Normal recovery time is 50 to 60 seconds. Abnormal recovery time can range from 90 to 180 seconds, or greater. Recovery time is age related, and therefore patients over 40 years of age will probably show some symmetric increase in "normal" recovery times.

Optic nerve disease is a conduction deficit unrelated to bleaching and regeneration of photopigments. Therefore, optic nerve disease should yield a negative photostress recovery test. Macular disease such as central serous choroidopathy will show a positive photostress recovery test. A positive test may indicate the need for more advanced testing such as intravenous fluorescein angiography (see p. 262).

Validity of this test markedly decreases with best corrected visual acuity less than 20/80. Also, significant media opacification may yield a relative asymmetry in photostress recovery time caused by decreased light stimulation rather than retinal disease.

■ **Contraindications/Complications.** There are no contraindications or complications associated with the photostress recovery test. It is important that the illumination source have fresh batteries or be well charged. Alternatively, a binocular indirect ophthalmoscope headset (moderate setting) may be used for this procedure.

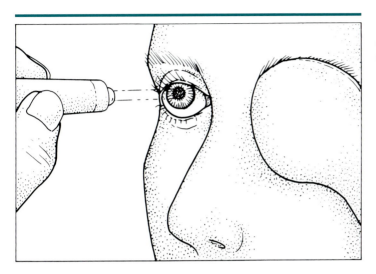

1. The eye in question is occluded and a steady bright light source placed 3 to 5 cm in front of the "normal" eye. The patient is asked to stare at the light for 10 seconds.

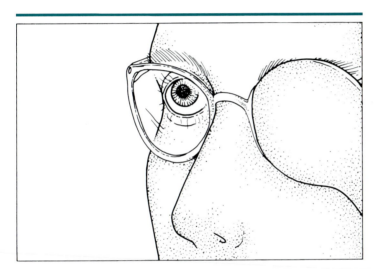

2. After replacing any spectacle correction and keeping the nontested eye occluded, the recovery time is measured for return of acuity to one line less than the best corrected visual acuity. The same procedure is repeated on the opposite eye.

63 Brightness Comparison

■ **Description/Indications.** The confirmation of optic nerve disease can be aided by a few basic in-office tests. The brightness comparison test involves the alternate presentation of a bright light stimulus to each eye followed by a series of questions on the subjective quantification of the "brightness" perceived by each eye. A steady bright penlight, transilluminator, or binocular indirect ophthalmoscope (moderate setting) is used as the light source. A clean white, evenly illuminated card may also be used as a target.

This test aids in the differential diagnosis between fundus disease and optic nerve disease when the ocular health appearance is equivocal. Optic nerve lesions usually produce a generalized depression in light sensitivity, perceived by the patient as objects appearing dimmer. However, fundus disease, even with extensive pathology, tends not to be reported as dimmer, provided the testing light diffusely illuminates the interior of the eye.

This test is considered to be the subjective parallel to the swinging flashlight test for an afferent pupillary defect.

■ **Instrumentation.** Penlight, transilluminator or binocular indirect ophthalmoscope.

■ **Technique.** Occlude the patient's left eye and direct the bright light stimulus toward the right eye (Fig. 1). Ask the patient to look directly at the light with the right eye. Quickly occlude the right eye and present the identical stimulus at the same viewing distance and angle toward the left eye (Fig. 2), again asking the patient to look directly at the light. Alternately cover each eye (Fig. 3) and ask the patient if a brightness difference exists between the light stimulus as seen with each eye. Shine the light into each eye for about 1 to 3 seconds.

If the patient notices a difference in brightness, ask him or her to place a value on the level seen as the test is repeated. Present the light stimulus again, first to the healthier, better-seeing eye. Ask that if this light were worth one dollar in brightness value, then how much is the other eye's image worth? Ninety cents? Fifty cents? Present the same light stimulus to the suspicious eye and record the patient's subjective response. Record the response as RE and LE (for example, RE 100 and LE 50).

■ **Interpretation.** A definite brightness difference between the two eyes supports the suspicion that optic nerve dysfunction may be present. In the example recording of RE 100 and LE 50, this would be interpreted that the perceived brightness in the left eye is only half that of the right, lending support to the diagnosis of optic nerve disease in the left eye.

■ **Contraindications/Complications.** A marked difference in ocular media clarity between each eye could produce a false-positive result. Incorrect results are possible if the light source is not strong enough to maintain stable, identical intensity during testing. The illumination source should have fresh batteries or be well charged. Nonidentical angles of stimulus presentation or unequal testing distances may also induce error. The patient's ability to describe any difference seen can limit the test's value.

The amount or duration of the light stimulus during testing presents no danger to the patient.

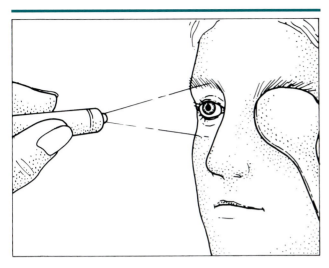

1. A bright white stimulus is presented to the patient's right eye for 1 to 3 seconds while the left is well occluded, asking the patient to note the level of perceived brightness.

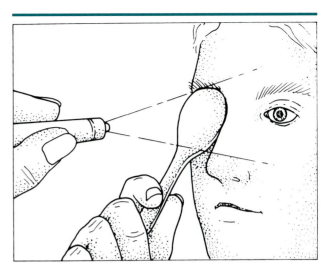

2. The patient's right eye is occluded and the identical stimulus is presented to the left eye, again asking the patient to note the level of brightness.

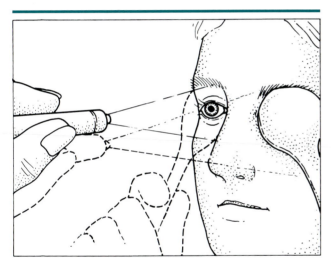

3. The light source is alternately presented to each eye and the patient is asked if a difference in brightness exists. The patient is also asked to subjectively quantify the brightness difference.

64 Red Desaturation Test

Description/Indications. The perception of certain colors frequently decreases or appears desaturated in the presence of optic nerve dysfunction. In contrast, macular disease does not usually affect gross color recognition. Red desaturation testing, along with other basic screening tests such as the brightness comparison test (see p. 258) and photostress recovery test (see p. 256), is performed when unexplained loss or dysfunction of vision occurs.

In-office screening for differences in red color perception between the patient's two eyes or in the different fields of vision of one eye may be diagnostic for optic nerve disease. The presence of optic nerve dysfunction and its accompanying diminished conduction may elevate pure cone threshold, thus acting as a filter barrier to the more sensitive cones with a resultant decrease in color perception. An afferent pupillary defect is frequently found in an eye that exhibits red desaturation. The level of color desaturation does not always correlate with the degree of visual impairment. Red desaturation in different areas of the visual field may be diagnostic for suspected chiasmal disease. Simultaneous field comparison of red stimuli may assist in the diagnosis.

Instrumentation. Red mydriatic/cycloplegic ophthalmic solution caps or comparable red targets.

Technique. Do not perform any bright light testing prior to red desaturation testing so each eye will be at an equal state of light adaption. Place the overhead light of the instrument stand behind the patient and direct it forward to evenly illuminate yourself and the patient's visual field (Fig. 1).

Alternating Red Comparison: Occlude the eye in question and ask the patient to look at a red cap with the "normal" eye (Fig. 2A). After a few seconds, switch the occluder (Fig. 2B) to the opposite eye, asking if there is any difference in the intensity of the red color. If no definite response is given, repeat the test, asking the patient if the cap is equally red, dimmer, brighter, or appears washed-out in color as it is viewed by each eye. Record the answer in relative value terms such as "slightly dimmer, much dimmer," and so on.

Simultaneous Testing (Foveal Versus Parafoveal Areas): An alternative method to test for central red desaturation is by unilateral simultaneous presentation. Ask the patient to fixate a centrally positioned red cap with the eye in question. Present another red cap simultaneously several inches to one side of center. Hold the targets at your chest level, allowing your white lab coat to act as an even background (Fig. 3). Ask the patient to look directly at the central red cap and tell you if the central or the peripheral cap color is equal to or brighter than the other. Be sure that both caps are evenly illuminated and the opposite "normal" eye is occluded.

Monocular Visual Field Color Comparison: Another method of red desaturation testing is monocular visual field color perception comparison. This is used most commonly with suspected early temporal field deficit in pituitary tumors, looking for possible quadrantic or hemispheric defects. Occlude one of the patient's eyes. Place two red caps approximately 8 to 12 inches apart at arm's length in front of the patient. Instruct him or her to fixate a target in between the two caps, such as your lab coat button or a properly positioned pin (Fig. 4A). Ask the patient to look at the central fixation target and decide if either red cap seems brighter or dimmer than the other. To more closely examine the superior quadrant, especially the superior temporal quadrant, keep the fixation point the same but elevate both targets to the superior quadrants (Fig. 4B). Record the answers, occlude the opposite eye, and repeat the testing.

Interpretation. A positive response of a dimmer or desaturated red stimulus between eyes, especially with any subjective report of visual dysfunction, may necessitate further neurologic workup such as meticulous pupillary, visual field, or visual evoked response testing, neurology consultation, CT scan, or MRI.

While looking at the central red fixation cap and comparing it to the peripheral red cap, the central cap should be as red or redder than the other. If the central cap is reported as a dimmer or duller red, a central scotoma and optic nerve disease are suspected.

In cases of pituitary tumor, the temporal fields, or more specifically the superior temporal fields, may exhibit characteristic weakness to red stimuli. If a positive response is given, visual field testing is initiated.

Contraindications/Complications. As with any subjective test, the examiner's interpretation of the responses and the patient's reliability can lead to false positive or negative results. Uneven illumination of the testing objects can also introduce error. If two red caps are used, it is important to make sure that they are equal in color.

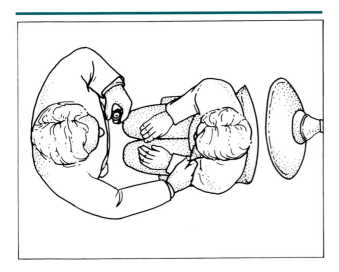

1. The examiner is centrally positioned with even illumination directed from behind the patient onto the targets.

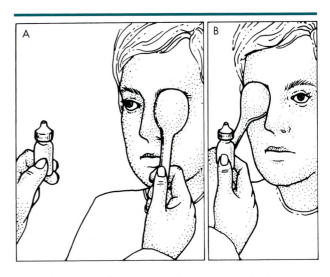

2. A. Alternating red comparison: The patient's involved eye is occluded as a red stimulus is presented to the opposite eye. B. The occluder is switched to the opposite eye and the identical red stimulus is presented to the involved eye.

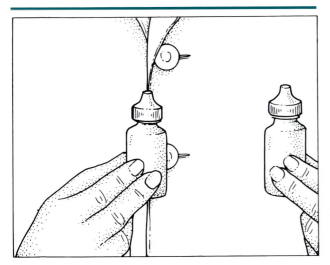

3. Simultaneous Testing (Foveal vs Parafoveal): The nontested eye is occluded while one red target is centrally positioned and another is placed off-center. Ask the patient to fixate centrally and state whether the center or off-center red target is brighter.

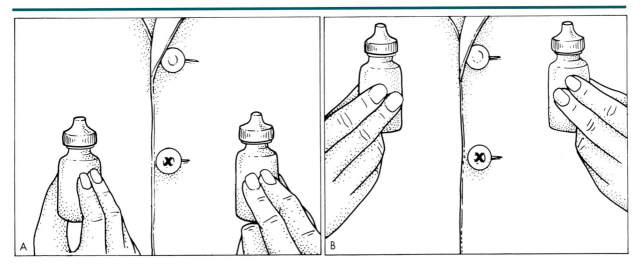

4. Monocular visual field color comparison: The patient fixates a centrally positioned fixation target ("X") between the two red caps and is asked if there is a difference in redness between the caps (A). To more closely examine the superior quadrant, keep the fixation point ("X") the same, but elevate both caps (B).

65

Fluorescein Angiography

■ **Description/Indications.** Fluorescein angiography (FA) is a diagnostic photography procedure used to detect vascular compromise of the retina, choroid, and optic nerve. It may also be used to identify areas of the fundus amenable to laser treatment, and to evaluate and monitor postlaser success. FA studies the presence and extent of intra-, extra-, and subretinal vasculature alterations that may not be observable ophthalmoscopically or detected with other examination techniques. Many vision-threatening conditions require FA for differential diagnosis and treatment.

Fluorescein sodium is a stable, pharmacologically inert vegetable dye. Following intravenous injection, 80% of it binds to plasma proteins, mostly albumin. The remaining 20% is free and unbound within the bloodstream and is responsible for actual fluorescence during testing. When light energy of 465 to 490 nanometers (blue light) is directed at these fluorescein molecules, they fluoresce yellow-green with a peak emission of 520 to 530 mm.

A fluorescein camera (Fig. 1) has a blue excitation filter (such as the Kodak Wratten 47) through which the camera flash passes. The resultant blue light continues into the patient's eye, exciting the intraocular free fluorescein to its fluorescing nanometer level. These fundus-reflected and emitted lights (blue and fluorescent yellow-green, respectively) return out of the eye through an introduced yellow-green filter barrier (such as Kodak Wratten G 15). This filter absorbs the reflected blue light and allows only the emitted fluorescent light to be transmitted and recorded on high-speed black-and-white film in the camera.

The low molecular weight of fluorescein sodium allows it to easily diffuse out of most of the body's capillaries, except for the normal vessels of the central nervous system, including the retinal vascular endothelium. This diffusion leads to the jaundiced appearance of the patient's skin for a few hours after testing and the brilliant yellow color of his or her urine for 24 to 48 hours.

Posterior to the retina, the fenestrated endothelial cells of the choriocapillaris allow intravascular fluorescein to easily leak outward into the extravascular space, creating a relatively uniform fluorescent background during testing referred to as the *choroidal flush*. Fluorescein sodium is incapable of perfusing through a healthy retinal pigment epithelium (RPE).

Depending upon the level of pigmentation, the RPE acts as a filter barrier between the retina and choroid, limiting the transmitted and visualized choroidal flush (Fig. 2). This is especially true of the macular areas, where the pigmentation is quite dense. Conversely, dropout of the RPE will lead to bright areas of visible hyperfluorescence.

In contrast to the choroidal system (Fig. 3), healthy retinal blood vessels have tightly bound endothelial cells that do not allow fluorescein to leak into the extravascular space.

There are several tenets behind fluorescein angiography. Normal blood flow transit time to and through the retina is relatively fixed, normal vascular patterns are well known, and nondiseased retinal vessels are nonpermeable. These tenets allow the patient's fluorescein angiography study to be compared to established standards and interpreted.

■ **Instrumentation.** Angiography camera and appropriate filters, ASA 400 black-and-white film (36 exposures), 35-mm color film, two camera backs (one motor driven with timer), 5 mL of 10% fluorescein sodium for injection, sterile 5-cc syringe, sterile 20-gauge (1½-inch) needle, sterile 23-gauge butterfly or scalp-vein needle, normal saline, tourniquet, alcohol swabs, armrest, small bandage, standard emergency room equipment tray, emesis basin, topical ophthalmic mydriatic/cycloplegic solution(s).

■ **Technique.** Explain the purpose and procedure of the test to the patient. Mention that this is a photographic test, not an x-ray, and that the injection method is very similar to having blood drawn. Ask the patient to read and sign the fluorescein angiography consent form. Explain that immediately following the injection and up to 30 seconds afterwards, he or she may experience a brief feeling of warmth or nausea that will quickly pass. Dilate the patient's pupils fully with topical ophthalmic mydriatic/cycloplegic solution(s).

Focus the camera eyepiece by turning it counterclockwise to add plus power, relaxing your accommodation, and blurring the crosshair fixation target. Turn the eyepiece clockwise until the fine crosshairs are in sharp focus. Position the patient comfortably at the camera with a reminder

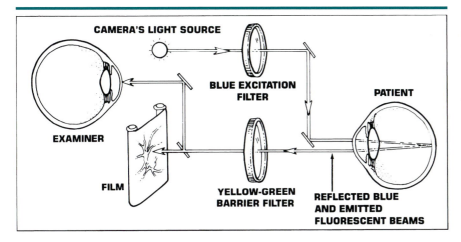

1. The excitation filter of the fluorescein camera produces blue light, which excites the unbound fluorescein sodium molecules. The reflected blue light is absorbed by the barrier filter, allowing only the emitted fluorescent yellow-green light to be recorded on the high-speed black-and-white film.

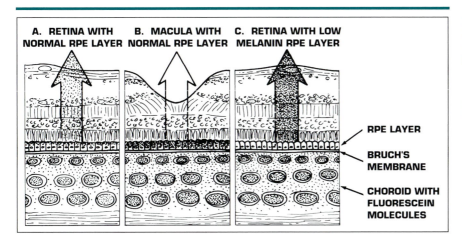

2. A. The RPE acts as a filter barrier between the retina and choroid, limiting the transmitted and visualized choroidal flush. B. Little to no choroidal flush is noted in the macular area, where the RPE melanin is quite dense. C. The choroidal flush is prominent in areas of the retina where the RPE melanin is reduced or absent.

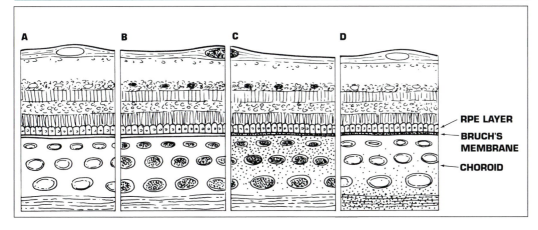

3. A. Before the fluorescein injection. B. Early arteriovenous phase with intravascular fluorescein. C. Arteriovenous phase with diffuse choroidal vessel leakage only. D. Late phase with extravascular fluorescein only.

that the forehead must remain against the forehead strap at all times. Focus onto the patient's fundus to ascertain that clear quality photos are possible, and observe the patient's response to the camera's bright light. Take any necessary color photos with the alternate camera back for documentation and comparison with the fluorescein photos. Make sure that the fundus area(s) to be photographed are clearly visible.

Change to the motor-driven, timer camera back containing 36-exposure black-and-white ASA 400 film (such as Tri-X film). Use the self-contained high plus camera lens, low strobe power, and red-free filter to photograph a small card containing the patient's name, date, and other desired information. Remove the high plus lens, adjust to the proper strobe power, and take photos (2 to 4) of the involved area(s) using a green (red-free) filter (such as Kodak Wratten 57 or 58). This will increase fundus contrast and identify any areas that appear to fluoresce without dye injection (autofluorescence). Decide which fundus areas will be photographed, which require blood transit studies, and which will need late shots.

Leave the camera focused on the retinal area to be examined, remove the red-free filter, insert the camera's blue excitation and yellow-green blocking filters, and adjust the strobe power to the camera's standard setting. After comfortably positioning the patient's arm on an armrest or table, have the trained or certified person administering the injection insert an intravenous, 23-gauge butterfly needle into the patient's antecubital vein. If this is not possible with these veins, the administrating individual should consider those veins on the back of the hand or the thumb side of the wrist. Inject a small amount of saline and observe the injection site to ensure that the fluorescein will not extravasate from the vein due to poor needle placement. Connect a prepared 5-cc syringe of 10% fluorescein to the butterfly needle using short tubing.

Following a signal from the person injecting, start the camera timer simultaneously with dye injection (Fig. 4). Take a photo upon completion of the injection, which is administered at a rate of 1 cc per second (5 to 7 seconds). Begin taking photos every 1 to 2 seconds for the first 20 to 30 seconds (10 to 12 photos); and then every 10 to 20 seconds for the next minute or two (6 to 10 photos). After the completion of the venous phase, wait 8 to 10 minutes before taking any desired late shots to reveal late fluorescein leakage, intraretinal dye accumulation, or fluorescein leakage pattern formation. During this 8 to 10-minute waiting period, take any full venous-phase photos of the opposite eye, if indicated. Take late shots of this opposite eye also if desired. If the opposite eye requires a complete fluorescein study on the same day, wait approximately 1 hour before repeating the procedure.

Remind the patient that his or her skin will appear yellow for a few hours, and that the urine will be yellow for 24 to 48 hours.

■ **Interpretation.** Red-free photos showing autofluorescence include retinal pigment granules, myelinated nerve fibers, and certain lipid materials, while pseudofluorescence from imperfect filters is most commonly seen at the optic disc and with drusen.

In the normal fluorescein transit study, following antecubital injection the dye bolus reaches the choroid in approximately 8 to 12 seconds by way of the short posterior ciliary arteries. The choroidal vessel pattern appears in the initial prearterial phase, followed rapidly by the expected fluorescein leakage in the choriocapillaris with its resultant choroidal flush (Fig. 5). Any visible cilioretinal arteries or optic disc capillaries will also fill at the same time. The intensity of the choroidal flush, dependent on RPE melanin density, will be noticeably reduced in the darkened macular area where the pigment is the most dense and the fluorescein-absorbing retinal xanthophyll pigment is also abundant.

The early arteriovenous phase begins immediately afterwards (10 to 15 seconds postinjection). During this phase, the arteries quickly fill with fluorescein and early laminar flow to the veins begins (Fig. 6). Fluorescein characteristically travels along the venous walls to create this laminar effect. In the late arteriovenous phase, complete artery and arteriole filling occurs along with marked venous lamellar flow (Fig. 7). The venous phase at 20 to 30 seconds exhibits maximum venous filling and reduced artery fluorescence (Fig. 8). The choroidal vessels continue to fluoresce but with reduced intensity.

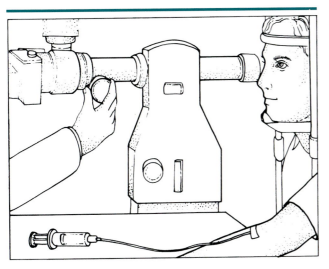

4. Set up for fluorescein angiogram. The patient is positioned at the camera and venous access is obtained.

5. (below left) In the prearterial phase, a uniform choroidal background flush appears (arrows). (Courtesy of Retina Consultants, Providence, RI.)

6. (below right) In the early arteriovenous phase, the arteries and arterioles fill with fluorescein (small arrow), while the veins exhibit very early laminar flow (large arrow). (Courtesy of Retina Consultants, Providence, RI.)

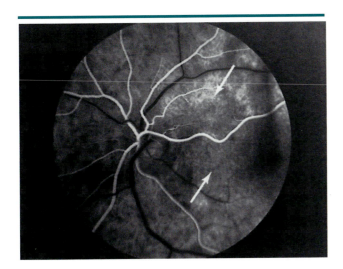

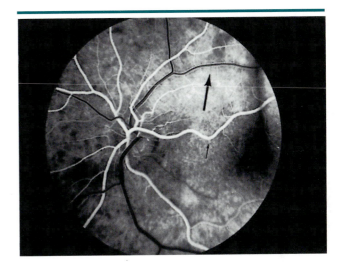

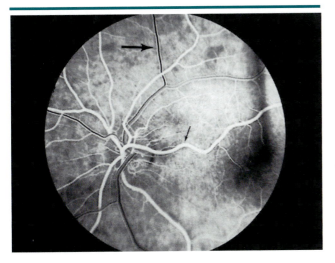

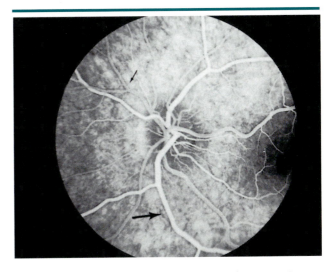

7. In the arteriovenous phase, all arterial vessels are filled (small arrow), with marked laminar flow in the veins (large arrow). (Courtesy of Retina Consultants, Providence, RI.)

8. In the venous phase, maximum venous filling (large arrow) is present with reduction in arterial fluorescence (small arrow). (Courtesy of Retina Consultants, Providence, RI.)

The normal fundus is devoid of most of the fluorescein after approximately 10 minutes. Because the entire vessel lumen is seen on angiography versus only the blood column with ophthalmoscopy, the retinal vessels will appear larger in caliber during angiography.

When studying the initial dye transit through the fundus, it is helpful to remember that healthy retinal vessels do not leak fluorescein and that, aside from the "black" macular hypofluorescence, the remainder of the choroidal flush is evenly distributed. The examiner looks for areas of hypofluorescence caused by blockage of the emitted light due to hemorrhage, exudates, glial tissue, or pigmentation (Fig. 9), or by vascular compromise from occlusion, nonperfusion, emboli, or arteriosclerosis (Fig. 10). The examiner also looks for areas of hyperfluorescence due to abnormal vasculature or RPE dropout. Abnormal vascular changes include vessel tortuosity, retinal or subretinal neovascularization (Fig. 11), or aneurysm. Vascular leakage may occur due to papilledema, capillary leakage, cystoid macular edema (Fig. 12), or subretinal neovascularization. RPE melanin variations also produce "window defects" with hyperfluorescence from increased choroidal flush transmission due to absence of "filtering" pigment cells.

■ Contraindications/Complications.

Patient photophobia from the camera flash, squinting, Bell's reflex, or illness from the injection greatly affect the quality of the photographs. The patient may have to be allowed to briefly close the eyes, blink more frequently when instructed, or sit back for a moment to gain composure in order to obtain satisfactory angiographic results.

Patients with known hypersensitivity to fluorescein sodium should only be tested when absolutely necessary, following proper medical precautions. Performing FA on pregnant patients should be avoided unless absolutely necessary.

In decreasing order of frequency, the most common side effects reported with FA are nausea, vomiting, urticaria/pruritus, extravasation, dyspnea, and syncope. In addition, there are reported cases of more serious anaphylactic shock and myocardial infarction. For those patients for whom the test is indicated, the benefits of preservation of vision usually far outweigh the risks involved. In any case, an emergency resuscitation kit should be in the testing room at all times.

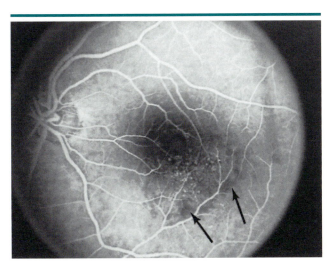

9. Hypofluorescence: Diabetic circinate exudative ring blocks normal fluorescence (arrows). (Courtesy of Retina Consultants, Providence, RI.)

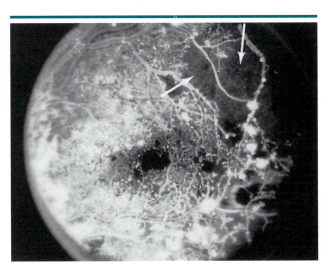

10. Hypofluorescence: Large areas of nonperfusion in a diabetic patient (arrows). (Courtesy of Retina Consultants, Providence, RI.)

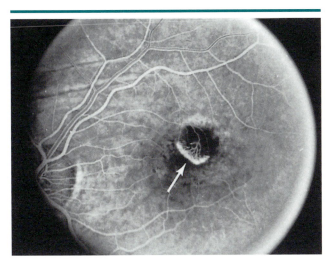

11. Hyperfluorescence: Choroidal neovascular membrane (arrow) with feeder vessel. (Courtesy of Retina Consultants, Providence, RI.)

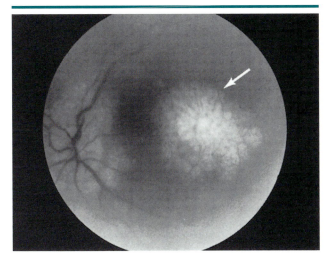

12. Hyperfluorescence: Cystoid macular edema (arrow). (Courtesy of Retina Consultants, Providence, RI.)

66 B-Scan Ultrasound

■ **Description/Indications.** B-scan ophthalmic ultrasound (echography) is a diagnostic procedure used for the detection and differentiation of ocular and orbital disorders. Its most common use is in a contact mode for the evaluation of the posterior segment in eyes with dense media opacification. B-scan ultrasound is also useful in the management of identified lesions to monitor for progression. B-scan instrumentation can be modified to an immersion technique for anterior segment study.

B-scan ophthalmic ultrasound consists of focused, short-wavelength, acoustic waves with frequencies of approximately 10 MHz. An echographic probe with an internal oval cylinder contains a laterally oscillating piezoelectric crystal near its tip, which converts electrical energy into mechanical energy. This energy is emitted as an advancing acoustic wavefront into the eye (Fig. 1A). The intraocular and orbital velocity of the wavefront differs as it passes through various ocular tissues.

Distinct tissues reflect, refract, and scatter sound waves in characteristic ways. The acoustic interface reflections at adjacent tissues create recordable echoes that are affected by the angle of sound wave incidence; different degrees of absorption, scattering, and refraction; and the size and shape of each interface.

The emitted sound waves enter the eye, and their reflected components are received by the probe's transducer. These waves are then amplified, filtered, and displayed as a two-dimensional echogram on a video screen (Fig. 1B). The focused beam's reflection or echo is represented as a dot on the screen with its strength indicated by its brightness. The stronger the echo, the brighter the projected dot.

The coalescence of these dots forms the two-dimensional B-scan screen image. The horizontal axis of the echogram represents tissue depth, and the vertical axis represents the scanned segment of the globe or orbit. Successive cross-sections are represented on the screen. As the procedure is performed, the examiner tries to summate the two-dimensional sections into a three-dimensional visualization.

The round or oval probe has a line, dot, or logo marker along the shaft near its tip, which corresponds to the lateral-oscillating direction of the crystal. This reference point designates the area represented on the upper portion of the B-scan display or echogram. The probe's surface is represented as the first line on the left side of the echogram, while the fundus is represented on the right. The best resolution is found centrally on the echographic display.

The value of B-scan is poorly represented by a single echographic Polaroid photo. Rather, the test is a dynamic kinetic study of the globe and orbit. It is referred to as "real-time" ultrasound because most of the information derived from the procedure is obtained by the examiner during testing. This explains why more practitioners are videotaping ultrasounds to appreciate the continuous flow of information during testing. Tissue mobility induced during the procedure for differential diagnosis purposes is an example of the value of dynamic studies.

B-scan ultrasound screening is most commonly indicated in cases of opaque media where information regarding the ocular status posterior to the opacity is desired to determine whether surgical intervention is indicated. For example, B-scan may be performed when a large vitreous hemorrhage (Fig. 2) is present to establish the etiology as vascular leakage, retinal tear or detachment, tumor, or vascular disease with a secondary detachment. Serial B-scans are used to follow this hemorrhage over time until it clears to insure proper diagnosis or to identify complications. B-scan screening is performed both on a high and low-sensitivity or gain setting. The former is more sensitive for gross fundus lesions and vitreal opacities, whereas the latter is capable of detecting subtle fundus elevations.

B-scan yields information about topography—the location and configuration of lesions—along with their gross reflectivity. Positive B-scan screening findings indicate the need for complete B-scan topographic examination (Fig. 3), such as in the event of opaque ocular media, vitreous hemorrhage (previtrectomy), suspected ocular tumors, intraocular foreign bodies, retinal detachment, optic disc anomalies, suspected extraocular muscle disease, and proptosis. A negative B-scan in search of an intraocular or orbital foreign body is followed by a more sensitive CAT scan. When B-scan is used in conjunction with echographic A-scan, it is referred to as *standardized echography*. A-scan provides more information regarding lesion size measurement, internal structure, and intrinsic vasculature (see p. 356).

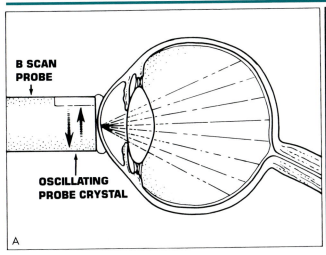

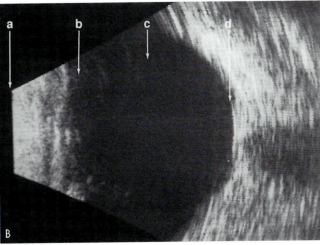

1. A. The B-scan ophthalmic ultrasound probe contains an oscillating piezzoelectric crystal near its tip, which converts electrical energy into mechanical energy. This energy is emitted as an advancing acoustic wavefront into the eye.

1. B. Normal B-scan. A two-dimensional echogram records tissue-specific reflected echoes. The horizontal axis represents tissue depth and the vertical axis the scanned segment of the globe. (a) Probe and corneal surface. (b) Posterior lens surface. (c) Vitreous. (d) Retina. (Courtesy of Retina Consultants, Providence, RI.)

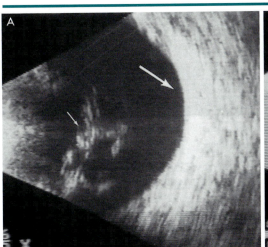 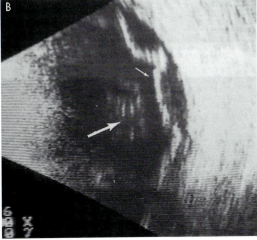

2. A. (far left) Vitreous hemorrhage (small arrow) with attached retina (large arrow).
B. (left) Vitreous hemorrhage (large arrow) with detached retina (small arrow). (Courtesy of Retina Consultants, Providence, RI.)

SECTION[a]	PROBE MARKER ORIENTATION
Transverse	
Horizontal: nasal and temporal	Superiorly
Vertical: superior and inferior	Nasally
Vertical: obliques	Superiorly
Axial	
Vertical	Superiorly
Horizontal	Nasally
Longitudinal	
Horizontal, vertical, obliques	Toward center of cornea

[a]The longer diameter of the probe is placed parallel to the limbus for transverse sections, and perpendicular to the limbus for longitudinal sections.

3. Summary of B-scan sections and probe orientation.

B-scan screening (transverse and axial sections) of eyes with opaque media requires a systematic approach. Transverse or circumferential scans are taken in the eight cardinal meridians, beginning at the posterior fundus and progressing anteriorly. These transverse scans (horizontal, vertical, and oblique) assist in determining the presence and lateral extent of a lesion (Fig. 4). The probe is oriented so its longer diameter or the tip marker is parallel to the limbus in all three orientations. Examination therefore occurs circumferentially on both sides of a particular meridian from the posterior to anterior fundus. The meridian lying in the middle of the circumferential scan is referred to as the *designated meridian.* Some practitioners screen only in the four main quadrants.

Axial scans are the next step in B-scan screening. Ultrasound waves are directed straight back through the cornea and lens to assist in documenting certain lesions and membranes relative to the optic nerve. The orientation of axial scans is both horizontal and vertical (Fig. 5).

Complete topographical B-scan includes longitudinal scans in addition to transverse and axial. Longitudinal scans examine the suspected area in an antero-posterior, radial-like direction (Fig. 6). The probe is oriented perpendicular to the limbus with the marker always positioned toward the center of the cornea.

■ Instrumentation.
B-scan ultrasound unit, ophthalmic methylcellulose solution, topical ophthalmic anesthetic solution.

■ Technique.
Instill 2 drops of topical ophthalmic anesthetic solution in each eye. Position the ultrasound unit behind the patient to allow you to simultaneously view both the probe and video screen (Fig. 7). Recline the patient and ask him or her to fixate a target on the ceiling, exposing the inferior conjunctiva and sclera. Apply a small amount of ophthalmic methylcellulose solution to the probe tip.

For initial transverse screening scans, place the probe parallel to the inferior limbus (6-o'clock) directly on the conjunctiva at the limbal border with the marker oriented nasally. Hold the probe steady on the globe and observe the screen. Take three or four overlapping scans as you slide the probe inferiorly from the limbus toward the far inferior fornix area (Fig. 8) at the 6-o'clock position. Continually monitor the echogram for abnormal echoes. Repeat a similar limbus to fornix scanning at every 1½ clock hour posi-

tion (6:00, 4:30, 3:00, 1:30, 12:00, 10:30, 9:00, 7:30). Orient the marker superiorly for both nasal and temporal scans, nasally for both superior and inferior scans, and superiorly for any required oblique scans. For example, to evaluate the nasal fundus, ask the patient to fixate nasally while the probe is placed limbally on the temporal conjunctiva with the probe marker oriented superiorly. Perform all scans at both a high and low-gain setting.

To take axial scans, first ensure that there is adequate topical anesthesia. Instruct the patient to look straight up at the ceiling target with the nontesting eye. Place a drop of methylcellulose on the probe tip, then place the probe in direct contact with the cornea. Hold the probe in place as you observe the screen. Take the first scan with the marker oriented superiorly to perform a vertical axial scan. Rotate the marker to a nasal position for a horizontal axial scan. Perform these at both high and low-gain settings.

For longitudinal scans, orient the probe perpendicular to the limbus by positioning the probe marker toward the center of the cornea for all meridians. Hold the probe on the conjunctiva as you observe the screen. The peripheral fundus will appear superiorly at the top of the echogram, while the optic disc and posterior fundus will be located on the lower portion of the screen.

Although not theoretically correct, many practitioners perform all of the procedures described (see Fig. 3) through the patient's closed lid. They monitor proper eye positioning by observing the opened, nontesting eye and the expected anatomical finding on the screen.

■ Interpretation.
An example of a vitreous hemorrhage with and without retinal detachment is seen in Figure 2. If a lesion is detected with the B-scan screening technique, complete topographical examination (transverse, axial, and longitudinal scans) is indicated in the area of the lesion. The best way to improve interpretation skills is to perform this test on eyes with clear media for which the diagnosis is known.

■ Contraindications/Complications.
B-scan is avoided on an eye that has had recent intraocular surgery, or may have a scleral laceration or a perforating injury. When performed properly, B-scan ultrasound presents no danger to the eye or orbit. A minor corneal abrasion or irritation from the probe or testing solution may occur, but usually does not require treatment.

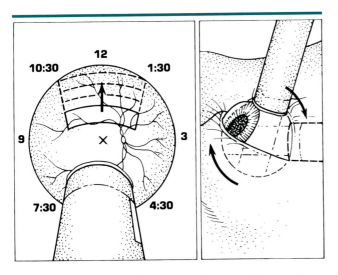

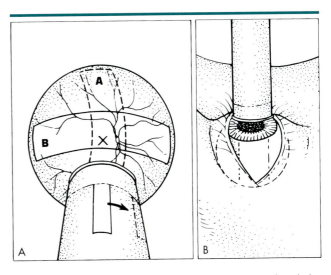

4. Transverse scanning involves moving the "band-like" circumferentially oriented acoustic waves in a posterior-to-anterior globe direction in each of the eight cardinal meridians.

5. Axial scans are performed in two directions: A. Vertical, with the probe marker superiorly. B. Horizontal, with the probe marker oriented nasally.

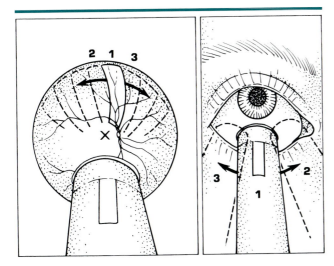

6. Longitudinal scans are performed radially in a posterior to anterior direction after a lesion has been identified (probe marker toward central cornea.)

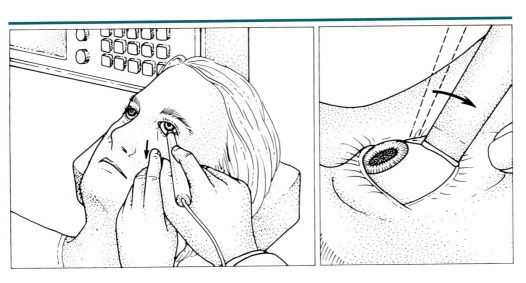

7. (far left) The B-scan screen is positioned behind and close to the patient's head for simultaneous examiner viewing during testing.

8. (left) The probe is slid along the globe in overlapping positions from the limbus toward the furthest extent of the inferior fornix.

VIII Suggested Readings

Alexander LJ: *Primary Care of the Posterior Segment,* ed 2. Norwalk, CT, Appleton & Lange, 1994.

Amsler M: *Amsler Grid Book.* London, Hamblin, 1984.

Anderson DR: *Perimetry With and Without Automation,* ed 2. St. Louis, Mosby, 1987.

Barker FM: Vitreoretinal biomicroscopy: A comparison of techniques. *J Am Optom Assoc* 1987;**58:**985–992.

Benson WE: *Retinal Detachment Diagnosis and Management.* Hagerstown, MD, Harper & Row, 1980.

Cavallerano A, Gutner R, Garston M: Indirect biomicroscopy techniques. *J Am Optom Assoc* 1986;**57:**755–758.

Cavallerano A, Semes L, Potter JW: How to perform scleral indentation. *Rev Optom,* Dec 1986, pp 51–59.

Eskridge JB, Amos JF, Bartlett JD (eds): *Clinical Procedures in Optometry.* Philadelphia, Lippincott, 1991.

Gass JDM: *Stereoscopic Atlas of Macular Diseases: Diagnosis and Treatment.* St. Louis, Mosby, 1987, pp 12–41.

Green RL, Byrne SF: Diagnostic ultrasound, in Ryan SJ, Ogden TE (eds): *Retina.* St. Louis, Mosby, 1989, vol 1, pp 191–271.

Gutner R, Cavallerano A, Wong D: Fundus biomicroscopy: A comparison of four methods. *J Am Optom Assoc* 1988; **59:**388–390.

Havener WH, Gloeckner S: *Atlas of Diagnostic Techniques and Treatment of Retinal Detachment.* St. Louis, Mosby, 1967, pp 1–51.

LaMotte JO, Holt LJ, Aguero CB: Comparison of patient attitudes about the wearing of masks during direct ophthalmoscopy (abstract). *Optom Vis Sci* 1996;12S:193.

Potter JW, Semes LP, Cavallerano AA, Garston MJ: *Binocular Indirect Ophthalmoscopy.* Boston, Butterworth, 1988.

Schatz H: Fluorescein angiography: Basic principles and interpretation, in Ryan SJ, Schachat AP, Murphy RP, Patz A (eds): *Retina.* St. Louis, Mosby, 1989, vol 2, pp 3–77.

Shammas HJ: *Atlas of Ophthalmic Ultrasonography and Biometry.* St. Louis, Mosby, 1984.

Tolentino FI, Schepens CI, Freeman HM: *Vitreoretinal Disorders: Diagnosis and Management.* Philadelphia, Saunders, 1976, pp 45–108.

Walters GB: The technique of scleral depression. *J Am Optom Assoc* 1982;**53:**569–573.

IX

Physical Examination Procedures

67 Preauricular Lymph Node Palpation

■ **Description/Indications.** Palpation of the preauricular node area for lymphadenopathy (glandular swelling) is a useful diagnostic procedure, helpful in the differential diagnosis of a "red eye." Adenopathy of these superficial nodes presents as a nodular enlargement and is most prominent in children and young adults, who are most prone to lymphatic hyperplasia.

The preauricular nodes are located immediately anterior to (1 cm), and slightly inferior to, the tragus of the external ear at the temporomandibular joint (Fig. 1). Inflammatory fluid and debris from the superior eyelid and the outer one third of the inferior eyelid commonly drain into these regional lymph glands. Lymph glands represent a component of the body's defense system. These macrophage-laden nodes act as bloodstream filters by trapping and phagocytizing foreign cells and matter. Anti-inflammatory lymphocytes and plasma cells are also produced in the center of these glands, explaining their characteristic swelling and possible tenderness.

■ **Instrumentation.** None.

■ **Technique.** Seat the patient and have him or her face toward you. Place the tips of your index and middle fingers of each hand in front of the tragus of the external ear (Fig. 2A). With mild pressure feel for the slight bony depression at the temporomandibular joint. Slide the skin with your fingers over the underlying bony structures in a back-and-forth semicircular motion (Fig. 2B) searching for the depression (normal) or an elevated nodular lesion (inflammation). Compare the two sides, noting laterality, asymmetry, size, tenderness, or absence of node enlargement.

■ **Interpretation.** An enlarged preauricular node can feel just like a small pebble under the skin just in front of the ear. Tender or nontender mobile nodes most often reflect lymphadenitis or hyperplasia in response to acute inflammation. Viral conjunctivitis is usually accompanied by preauricular lymphadenopathy, often greater on the side of the more involved eye. Accompanying ear, nose, and throat symptoms usually suggest a viral conjunctivitis or, less likely, localized bacterial infection. Bacterial lid conditions such as hordeola, preseptal cellulitis, and impetigo can also produce this lymphatic tissue response. Unilateral, large, visible, tender nodes are commonly found with severe adenovirus infection and with Parinaud's oculoglandular conjunctivitis.

These nodes can be subtle or obvious; therefore, including this technique with every red eye workup will aid the practitioner in making a differential diagnosis. Nodes may stay enlarged for weeks following resolution of ocular infection.

■ **Contraindications/Complications.** There are no contraindications or complications in performing this technique, aside from being gentle with those patients who have tenderness associated with preauricular lymphadenopathy.

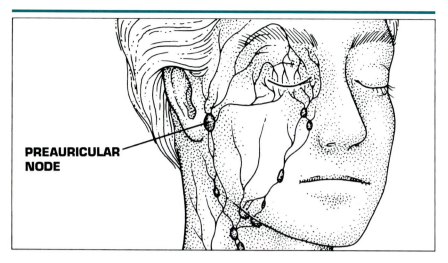

1. The lymphatic vessels of the superior eyelid and the outer one third of the inferior lid drain into the preauricular lymph nodes, which are located 1 cm anterior and slightly inferior to the tragus of the external ear.

PREAURICULAR NODE

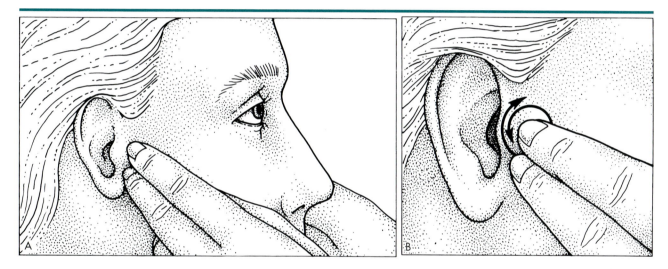

2. A. The tips of the index and middle finger of each hand are placed in front of the tragus of the external ear. B. Keeping the two fingertips close together, slide the underlying skin back and forth in a semicircular motion over the node and/or bony depressed area to palpate for an enlarged preauricular node.

68 Digital Intraocular Pressure Assessment

■ **Description/Indications.** Measurement of the intraocular pressure (IOP) is an integral component of most ocular evaluations. Goldmann applanation tonometry, either slit lamp mounted or hand-held, is the technique for IOP measurement against which all other techniques are judged (see p. 52). Occasionally, however, the examiner encounters a patient on whom it is impossible to obtain an IOP measurement with standard instrumentation. Patients typically included in this category are very young children, extremely anxious patients, or developmentally delayed individuals. Digital IOP assessment is a technique for grossly evaluating the IOP of these patient types. Digital IOP assessment may be utilized during assessment of a patient with an anterior segment infection when a noncontact tonometer is unavailable.

Using gentle pressure on the globe with the tips of the right and left index fingers, relative assessment of globe softness may be made. Incorporating this technique into the routine examination will allow the examiner to gain experience in assessing eyes in which the IOP is known and normal. When a clinical situation arises necessitating digital IOP assessment, the examiner will have already gained confidence in his or her ability to differentiate normal from abnormal globe firmness.

■ **Instrumentation.** None.

■ **Technique.** Ask the patient to look down. Gently rest the tips of both index fingers on the center of the patient's upper lid (Fig. 1). Push gently on the globe through the lid with the tip of one finger, and the tip of the other finger will rebound slightly (Fig. 2A). Alternately palpate the globe in this fashion two or three times using both fingertips (Fig. 2B). While doing so, subjectively assess the degree of firmness of the globe. Repeat the technique for the opposite eye.

■ **Interpretation.** The firmness of the globe is subjectively evaluated as soft, medium, or hard. The harder the globe the higher the IOP.

■ **Contraindications/Complications.** This technique poses no risk to the patient when the globes are intact. Avoid applying excessive pressure to the globe, however, so as not to induce any mild discomfort. Rarely, the patient may object to having the eyes touched and will be unable to cooperate even for this technique. Encourage the patient not to close the eyes, since the normal Bell's reflex will cause the cornea to roll upward beneath the portion of the lid that is palpated, which is best avoided.

Digital IOP assessment is contraindicated for eyes with a recent history of blunt trauma, penetrating ocular injury, or intraocular surgery.

Digital IOP evaluation is a gross assessment that does not substitute for quantifiable IOP measurement when it can be performed. For an acute problem or when glaucoma is suspected, consultation should be obtained for sedation of the patient so that more accurate IOP measurement with instrumentation may be performed.

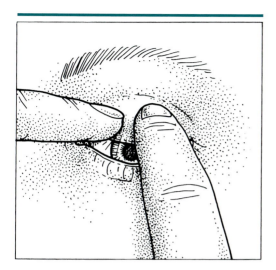

1. For digital IOP assessment, ask the patient to look down and gently rest the tips of both index fingers on the center of the upper lid.

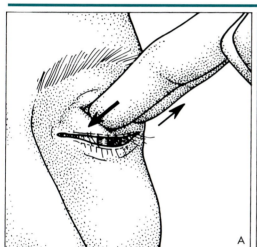

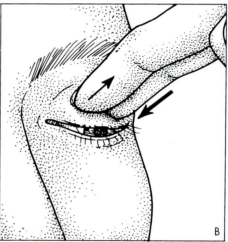

2. A. Indent the globe slightly with one fingertip; the opposite fingertip will rebound slightly. B. Alternately palpate the globe two or three times to assess the degree of firmness of the globe.

69 Globe Reposition

■ **Description/Indications.** Orbital congestion due to a space-occupying lesion, vascular anomaly, or edema may be evaluated in-office by globe reposition. Both globes are simultaneously reposited manually back into their respective orbits. Any asymmetry in the pressure needed to displace the globe into the orbit is recorded. In addition, patient discomfort during the procedure is noted. Prior to reposit, gentle palpation for pulsating exophthalmus can be performed when indicated. A positive pulsation finding is the hallmark of a vascular fistula.

Potential signs and symptoms of orbital congestion and indications for globe reposition include eyelid swelling, conjunctival injection, telangiectasia (pseudoconjunctivitis), chemosis, exophthalmos (unilateral or bilateral), extraocular muscle restriction, diplopia, decreased visual acuity, and ocular discomfort.

As with any less commonly occurring clinical finding, it is optimal that the clinician perform this technique on many normal patients to become familiar with its normal variants.

■ **Instrumentation.** None.

■ **Technique.** Seat the patient comfortably at eye level facing you. Instruct the patient to close the eyes. With your hands in the "thumbs up" position, rest the four fingers of each hand perpendicular to the patient's zygomatic arch area or over the preauricular node area (Fig. 1). Place each thumb on the patient's closed lids and attempt to gently push the globes posteriorly into their respective orbital cavities (Fig 2). Compare each side, noting any asymmetry in displacement between the eyes as well as any limitations. Some examiners prefer to reposit each globe individually at first and then simultaneously to aid in their comparison. Also note any discomfort expressed by the patient during testing.

■ **Interpretation.** Asymmetry in globe displacement is usually indicative of an orbital problem such as a space-occupying lesion, systemically induced orbital congestion, or a vascular anomaly. Aside from thyroid disease with bilateral exophthalmos, bilateral limited reposition is usually secondary to anatomically shallow orbits. Discomfort upon reposition may accompany inflammation such as retrobulbar optic neuritis.

■ **Contraindications/Complications.** Globe reposition should not be performed on anyone with a history of recent blunt ocular trauma, especially if a scleral rupture or laceration is suspected or if a hyphema is present. Other contraindications include any individual who has recently had ocular surgery, is suspected of having a corneal foreign body, or has angle-closure glaucoma.

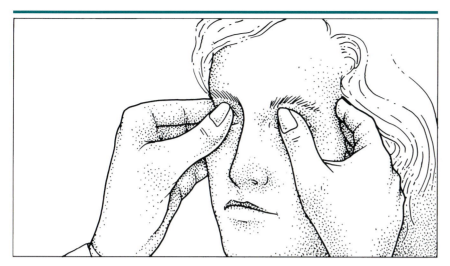

1. Hands and fingers are positioned along the zygomatic arches with upward-directed thumbs resting on the closed eyelids.

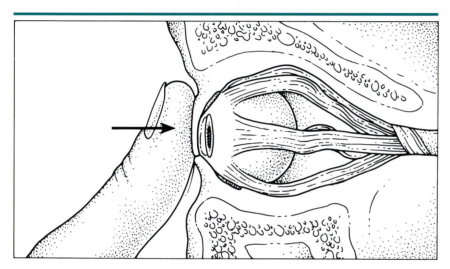

2. Gentle and even pressure is applied to each globe through the closed eyelids, attempting to displace the globe posteriorly into the orbit.

70 Exophthalmometry

■ **Description/Indications.** The forward protrusion or backward displacement of the eye(s) may be indicative of a traumatic, infectious, inflammatory, infiltrative, vascular, or neoplastic disorder affecting the orbit or globe. Exophthalmometry measures the anterior projection of the cornea relative to the lateral orbital rim. Each eye is measured in millimeters, with the value for each eye compared to the other and against an expected range of "normals." A significant difference between the two eyes or deviations from the norm may be a sign of orbital disease. The progression or resolution of an orbital condition may be monitored by successive comparison of exophthalmometry readings over time.

Indications for exophthalmometry include the appearance of proptosis (unilateral or bilateral), enophthalmos (unilateral or bilateral), orbital cellulitis, Grave's disease, or a tumor of the orbit.

The Luedde and Hertel exophthalmometers are two types frequently used. The Luedde exophthalmometer is made of transparent plastic with a millimeter rule on the side. At one end is a notch that conforms to the lateral orbital rim. The Hertel exophthalmometer is composed of two yokes separated by a crossbar with a measuring scale. Each yoke fits over the bony temporal margin of the lateral orbit rim. One yoke is fixed and the other slides to allow their variable separation and measurement of the biocular distance. The biocular distance should be set at the same scale reading each time a patient's exophthalmometer readings are taken. On each yoke is a scale with two mirrors, one above the other. The position of the apex of the cornea, seen on the scale visible in the upper mirror, determines the position of the globe within the orbit.

■ **Instrumentation.** Luedde exophthalmometer or Hertel exophthalmometer.

■ **Technique.**

Luedde Exophthalmometer: Ask the patient to be seated with the head erect, looking straight ahead. With the thumb or index finger, palpate the bony ridge indicating the lateral orbital rim (Fig. 1). Place the notch of the exophthalmometer firmly against the lateral orbit rim (Fig. 2) with the scale facing toward the side. Keep the exophthalmometer perpendicular to the plane of the face. Look from the side through the transparent exophthalmometer and sight where the corneal apex intersects the mm scale (Fig. 2). If necessary, shine a penlight on the cornea from below to accentuate the corneal apex. Take three readings and repeat the procedure for the opposite eye. Record the findings.

1. To correctly place the Luedde exophthalmometer, the index finger is used to palpate the bony ridge indicating the lateral rim of the orbit.

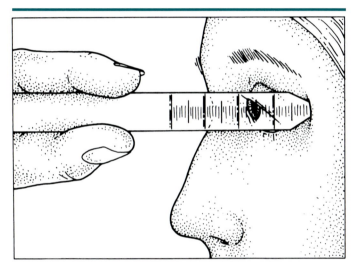

2. The notch of the Luedde exophthalmometer is placed firmly against the lateral orbital rim. The corneal apex is viewed through the exophthalmometer to sight where it intersects the scale.

Hertel Exophthalmometer: Prepare the Hertel exophthalmometer (Fig. 3) by loosening the locking screw on the crossbar and ensuring that the numeral scale on the crossbar is erect. Ask the patient to be seated with head erect, looking straight ahead. Sit or stand in front of the patient and adjust the patient's chair so that your eyes are both on the same plane. With the thumb or index finger, feel for the bony ridge indicating the lateral rim of the orbit (Fig. 1). Ask the patient to close the eyes. Slowly bring the exophthalmometer forward, keeping the exophthalmometer parallel to the floor with the scale on the crossbar visible. Place the internal arc of the yoke against the bony temporal orbital rim of the right eye (Fig. 4A). Slide the second yoke along the crossbar until the inner arc wraps around the lateral orbital rim of the left eye. Tighten the locking screw located on the crossbar and note the reading (Fig. 4B).

Ask the patient to open the eyes and to look straight ahead. Look into the two mirrors located above each other. Take the measurement where the apex of the cornea, seen in the lower mirror, is superimposed on the scale seen in the upper mirror (Fig. 5). Note this point and record. If the exophthalmometer has red vertical lines on the mirrors, superimpose them before the readings are taken. This will ensure that parallax errors do not affect the measurements. Use the same technique to measure the left eye. Repeat the readings for each eye and compare to previous results.

■ **Interpretation.** An example of an exophthalmometry reading is 17/18 @100, indicating a biocular measurement of 100 mm with the right eye measuring 17 mm and the left eye 18 mm. Normal exophthalmometry readings range from 12 to 20 mm for whites and 12 to 24 mm for blacks.

Readings greater than this are an indication of possible proptosis and merit further investigation. Measurements between the two eyes are usually within 2 mm of each other. A difference between the two eyes of 3 mm or greater is an indication for further investigation, even if all readings fall within the normal range. A comparison is also made of serial measurements over time. Any increase in a reading, after using the same biocular base value, may be an indication for further investigative testing. The deterioration or resolution of an orbital condition can be monitored by comparing successive measurements over a period of time.

The accuracy of the test hinges on careful alignment of the instrument on the patient's face along with meticulous alignment of the patient's corneal plane in the mirrors and on the scale of the exophthalmometer. Repeated readings over time require presetting of the biocular base distance. Poor fixation, convergence, parallax errors, head movement, and blepharospasm may affect the reliability of the results. The Hertel exophthalmometer, being a biocular instrument, is the instrument of choice.

The visual appearance of exophthalmos is not always confirmed with measurements. Factors such as ptosis, lid retraction, and asymmetry of the palpebral fissure may lead to a pseudoexophthalmic appearance. Patient history and old photographs may help in the differential diagnosis.

■ **Contraindications/Complications.** This test poses no risk to the patient. Following proper procedure, there are no contraindications to the test. Individuals with facial bone dysformity may not allow for the parallel placement of the instrument on the face, leading to unreliable measurements.

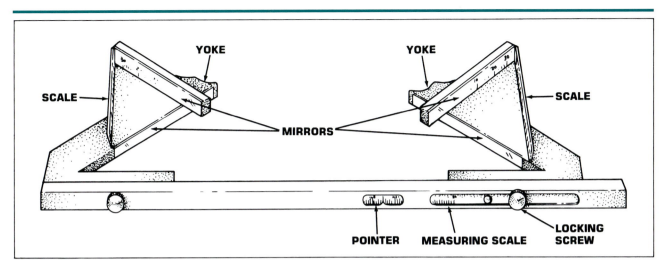

3. The Hertel exophthalmometer.

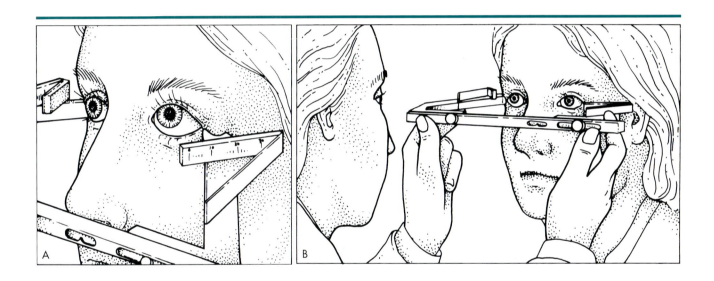

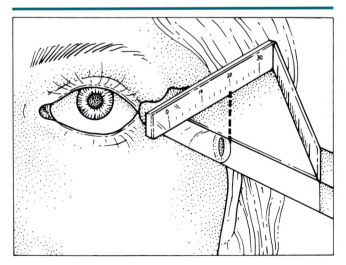

4. A. (above left) The inner arcs of the yokes of the Hertel exophthalmometer are placed on the bony ridges of the lateral walls of the orbits. B. (above right) The Hertel exophthalmometer in position on the patient's face after the locking screw on the crossbar has been tightened. If vertical red lines are present, they are aligned to eliminate parallax errors.

5. (left) A reading for the Hertel exophthalmometer is obtained by noting where the image of the corneal apex, seen in the lower mirror, is superimposed on the scale seen in the upper mirror.

71 Infraorbital Nerve Testing

■ **Description/Indications.** Direct mechanical injury or indirect edematous compression to the infraorbital branch of the trigeminal nerve (cranial nerve V) can lead to diminished sensation (hypoesthesia) of the skin and subcutaneous tissue along its distribution (see p. 284). In particular, blowout fractures of the orbit are associated with infraorbital nerve damage, producing numbness inferior and nasal to the orbit. These areas include the lower lid, the ipsilateral cheek, the lateral aspect of the nose, and the upper lip area.

The maxillary (V2) branch of the trigeminal nerve gives rise to the infraorbital nerve. This nerve travels anteriorly and centrally in the infraorbital sulcus from the lateral posterior aspect of the orbit. Approximately 15 mm posterior to the inferior orbital rim the nerve becomes enclosed in a bony canal, bends inferiorly below the rim, and exits through the infraorbital foramen of the maxillary bone, distributing sensory innervation (Fig. 1).

Direct blunt trauma to the orbital rim may cause various fractures to the bony components with subsequent damage to the surrounding tissue and nerves, leading to hypoesthesia. Blowout fractures result when the blunt trauma is sufficient to cause compression of the orbital contents. This pressure is frequently released by expulsion of orbital soft tissue through the anatomically thinner floor and medial walls of the orbit. Any maxillofacial or orbital trauma may affect the integrity of the infraorbital nerve.

■ **Instrumentation.** Cotton-tipped applicator, cotton ball or facial tissue.

■ **Technique.** Seat the patient comfortably and remove any spectacles. Twirl a clean cotton ball, cotton-tipped applicator, or facial tissue to form a wisp (Fig. 2). Instruct the patient to close the eyes and tell you when he or she feels a sensation.

Lightly touch the wisp to the lateral portion of the lower lid and move it nasally along the eyelid (Fig. 3). Pass the cotton wisp downward along the lateral aspect of the nose, temporally across the lower cheek area, and finally across the upper lip to the midline (Fig. 4). After each area is tested, ask if the patient is able to feel each stimulus. Mentally record the results.

Repeat the exact testing sequence for the opposite facial side. Ask the patient to compare the sensation on one side of the face to that of the contralateral side. It is helpful to begin testing on the normal, uninvolved side followed by testing on the involved side. Repeat any area in question, or perform the stimuli simultaneously on each side for direct comparison. Make every attempt to touch the skin with the same amount of pressure with each stroke. Assess the reliability of the patient's responses by not actually touching the patient at least once, but still asking for a response.

■ **Interpretation.** History of blunt ocular trauma accompanied by definite or even questionable infraorbital nerve hypoesthesia may indicate the need for motility testing and radiologic examination to rule out a blowout fracture. Infraorbital nerve hypoesthesia is usually temporary. The nerve commonly regenerates within 3 months, with retesting used to follow the restoration of nerve function.

■ **Contraindications/Complications.** This test presents no risk to the patient.

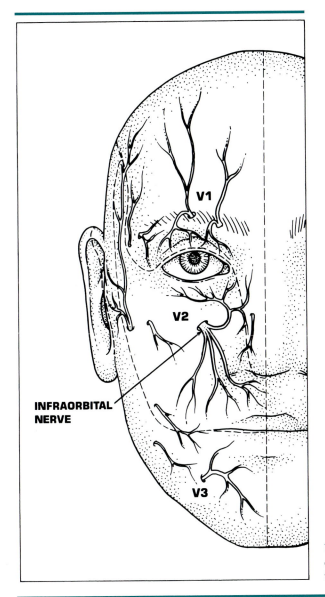

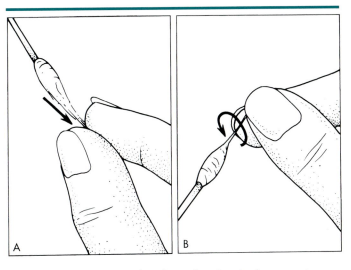

2. To prepare a cotton-tipped applicator for infraorbital nerve testing, first draw out the soft portion from the head (A), and then twirl it to form a wisp (B).

1. (left) The infraorbital nerve exits its foramen of the maxillary bone and distributes sensory fibers to the ipsilateral lower lid, cheek, lateral aspect of the nose, and upper lip to the midline.

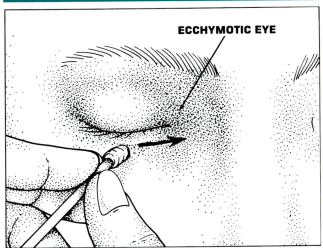

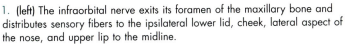

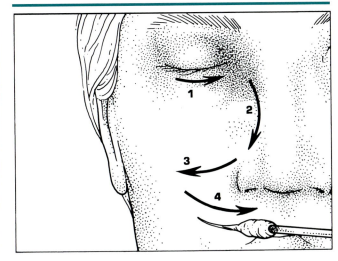

3. The wisp is initially touched to the lateral portion of the lower lid and moved nasally.

4. Following testing of the lower lid (1), the lateral aspect of the nose (2), the lower cheek (3), and the upper lip to the midline (4) are tested in a similar manner. After each area is tested, the patient is asked if the stimulus was felt.

72 Sphygmomanometry

■ **Description/Indications.** Sphygmomanometry is the method of measuring blood pressure (BP) indirectly with a sphygmomanometer (blood pressure cuff) and stethoscope. Measurements are obtained in millimeters of mercury (mm Hg) of the systolic pressure, the arterial pressure at the height of pulsation from cardiac contraction, and the diastolic pressure, the arterial pressure during ventricular relaxation between cardiac contractions (Tables 1 and 2). These measurements are obtained by auscultating (listening with a stethoscope) the Korotkoff sounds (Phases I to V) produced by completely compressing the brachial artery with the sphygmomanometer and then releasing cuff pressure until initial refilling occurs.

Indications for sphygmomanometry in the eyecare setting include screening for undiagnosed or uncontrolled hypertension, as well as reinforcing patient compliance with hypertension treatment regimens. In addition, BP measurement may be important in the use of ophthalmic diagnostic and therapeutic agents such as topical phenylephrine, hydroxyamphetamine, epinephrine and related compounds, and beta-adrenergic blocking agents; and may aid in or augment the diagnostic process of ophthalmic conditions such as chronic open-angle glaucoma, low-tension glaucoma, hypertensive retinopathy, retinal embolic phenomena, amaurosis fugax, and papilledema.

TABLE 1. FOLLOW-UP CRITERIA FOR INITIAL BP MEASUREMENT: Adults ≥ 18 Years

Initial BP Screening (mm Hg)		
Systolic	Diastolic	Recommended Follow-Up[a]
<130	<85	Recheck in 2 years
130–139	85–89	Recheck in 1 year
140–159	90–99	Confirm within 2 months
160–179	100–109	Refer within 1 month
180–209	110–119	Refer within 1 week
≥210	≥120	Refer immediately for medical care

[a]If recommendations for follow-up of recorded diastolic and systolic BP are different, the shorter recommended time for recheck and referral should take precedence.
Adapted with permission from The Fifth Report of the Joint National Committee on Detection, Evaluation, and Treatment of High Blood Pressure (JNC V). Arch Intern Med 1993;**153:**154–183.

TABLE 2. HIGH NORMAL BP READINGS: INFANTS, CHILDREN, AND ADOLESCENTS

Systolic	Diastolic	Age
141	91	16–18 years
135	85	13–15 years
125	81	10–12 years
121	77	6–9 years
115	75	3–5 years
111	73	≤ 2 years

Adapted with permission from The Fifth Report of the Joint National Committee on Detection, Evaluation, and Treatment of High Blood Pressure (JNC V). Arch Intern Med 1993;**153:**154–183.

The BP cuff is a nonstretchable fabric bag with Velcro cloth strips at the ends for closure and contains an inflatable rubber bladder. An inflating bulb with a pressure release valve and a manometer gauge for measuring pressure in the bladder are connected to the cuff by one or more rubber tubes (Fig. 1). The length of the arterial segment compressed by the inflated cuff influences the accuracy of the BP reading.

Sphygmomanometry in the average-sized adult is most accurate when performed with a cuff 12 to 14 cm wide (regular adult cuff). When necessary, choose an alternate cuff size having a rubber bladder that encircles at least two thirds of the arm circumference. The most common cuff sizes used are child, adult, and large adult. In the clinical setting the cuff pressure is usually registered by either a mercury or aneroid manometer that is hand-held (combined manometer gauge and inflation bulb), wall-mounted, table-mounted, or stand-mounted.

As pressure in the BP cuff is controlled, the Korotkoff sounds are auscultated with a stethoscope. Most stethoscopes have a chestpiece with two components, a bell and a diaphragm (Fig. 2). The diaphragm best transmits high-frequency sounds; the bell best transmits low-frequency sounds such as heart or vascular sounds. Either the bell or diaphragm side of the chestpiece is rotated ("clicked") into position to transmit sounds through the stethoscope. Usually the diaphragm side of the chestpiece, or a modification known as a corrugated diaphragm, is used for BP measurement.

■ **Instrumentation.** Adult, large adult, or child-sized sphygmomanometer; stethoscope with diaphragm.

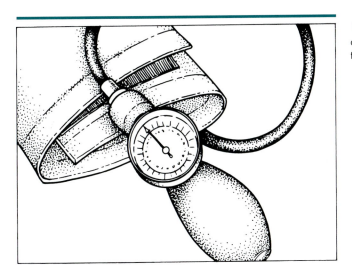

1. A hand-held aneroid sphygmomanometer. An inflating bulb with a pressure release valve and a manometer gauge are connected to the bladder in the cuff by one or more rubber tubes.

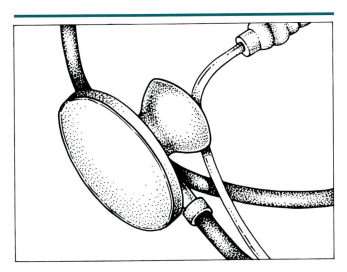

2. This stethoscope chestpiece has both a diaphragm and a bell. Either the bell or diaphragm side is "clicked" into position by rotating the chestpiece to transmit sounds through the stethoscope.

■ Technique.

It is recommended that BP measurement be taken after 5 minutes of quiet rest and that caffeine consumption, smoking, and exercise be avoided within 30 minutes of measurement. Support the seated patient's arm on the arm of a chair or table just above waist level and slightly bent with the palm turned upward so that the stethoscope head will be positioned at the level of the heart. Free the forearm of clothing and ensure that a rolled-up sleeve does not excessively constrict the upper arm. The BP may be successfully measured through a single layer of thin fabric such as the sleeve of a nylon jacket or lightweight blouse.

Palpate the brachial artery just below the antecubital crease, the bend of the elbow, so that the BP cuff can be properly positioned (Fig. 3). Center the bladder of the cuff on the upper arm overlying the brachial artery, aligning the appropriate arrow on the cuff for the arm being used. Wrap the cuff smoothly and secure it snugly so that the lower border of the cuff lies approximately 2.5 cm (1 inch) above the antecubital crease (Fig. 4). Palpate the systolic pressure to avoid an artificially low reading produced by auscultatory gap. Use the forefinger and middle finger of one hand to gently palpate the radial artery at the wrist, and inflate the cuff to approximately 30 mm Hg above the level at which the pulse disappears (Fig. 5). Deflate the cuff smoothly at a rate of approximately 2 to 3 mm Hg per second until the pulse is first palpated, and mentally note the manometer reading. Rapidly and steadily deflate the cuff completely.

Insert the earpieces of the stethoscope into your ears so that they angle forward toward your face as the stethoscope is put on. Turn the chestpiece so that the diaphragm side is transmitting. Place the diaphragm of the chestpiece gently but firmly over the brachial artery between the antecubital crease and the lower edge of the cuff, avoiding contact between the chestpiece and the cuff (Fig. 6). Inflate the cuff to approximately 20 to 30 mm Hg above the systolic pressure as determined by palpation. Turn the manometer release valve to slowly and smoothly release air from the bladder at the rate of approximately 2 to 3 mm Hg per second. Mentally note the first audible Korotkoff sound, Phase I (soft tapping sounds), which is the systolic reading.

Korotkoff sounds Phases II (swishing murmur), III (crisper sounds, increasing in intensity), and IV (abrupt sound muffling) will be audible with continued deflation of the cuff. Phase V, the disappearance of sounds, is the generally accepted diastolic reading for most patients. Mentally note the manometer reading when Phase V occurred, listen for an additional 10 to 20 mm Hg to confirm sound cessation, and then rapidly and completely deflate the cuff. If repeat measurement is necessary, wait 1 to 2 minutes to permit the release of blood trapped in the forearm venous system. If indicated, also take a measurement on the opposite arm.

By convention, record both the systolic and diastolic readings to the nearest even-number mm Hg. Indicate the position of the patient and which arm was used for measurement. For example, an entry of "160/100 R.A. Sit" indicates that BP measurement was performed on the right arm with the patient sitting down. If a cuff size other than the regular adult was used, note this information as well.

■ Interpretation.

Hypertension is not diagnosed on the basis of a single elevated in-office reading. Usually two or three readings taken in the course of several visits are necessary to diagnose essential hypertension. If two readings are taken during a visit, they are averaged, and if these first two measurements differ by more than 5 mm Hg, additional readings are taken and averaged. A 5 to 10 mm Hg difference in the readings between the right and left arms is considered normal. However, if you find the BP to be severely elevated (see Tables 1 and 2), even after a single reading, refer the patient immediately for medical care.

Tables 1 and 2 indicate normal BP readings, as well as recommended referral criteria for adults.

■ Contraindications/Complications.

This procedure poses no risk to the patient; however, patient anxiety will often produce artificially high in-office readings ("white coat" hypertension). If the BP cuff is too small for the patient's arm circumference, falsely high readings will also be obtained. Make certain that the sphygmomanometer is in good working order. It is recommended that aneroid manometers be calibrated against a perfectly working mercury manometer at least annually.

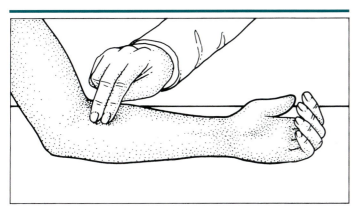

3. The brachial artery is palpated just below the antecubital crease (the bend of the elbow) so that the BP cuff can be properly positioned.

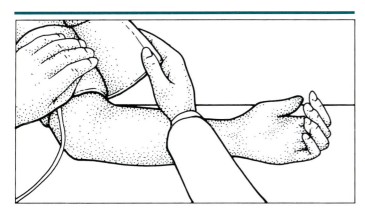

4. The cuff is wrapped smoothly and snugly so that the lower border lies approximately 1 inch above the antecubital crease and the bladder of the cuff is centered over the brachial artery.

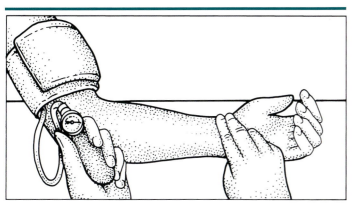

5. The systolic pressure is initially estimated by palpating the radial artery and inflating the cuff to approximately 30 mm Hg above the level at which the pulse disappears. The cuff is smoothly deflated until the pulse is first palpated, followed by rapid deflation.

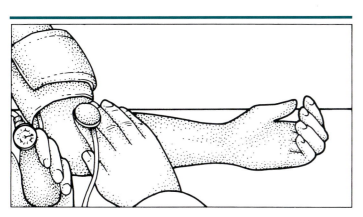

6. The diaphragm of the chestpiece is placed gently but firmly over the brachial artery between the antecubital crease and the lower edge of the cuff and the BP measurement is taken.

73 Carotid Pulse Palpation and Auscultation

■ **Description/Indications.** Bruits ("noises") are rushing sounds heard over medium and large arteries caused by vibrations of the blood vessel walls induced by turbulent blood flow. This blood flow turbulence and vessel wall vibration may be caused by partial vessel lumen occlusion from atherosclerotic plaque formation with or without accompanying thrombosis (clotting). Although generally not audible until the vessel is approximately 50% occluded, bruits are detected by auscultating ("listening to") the affected artery with a stethoscope.

The right and left common carotid arteries derive from the right brachiocephalic (innominate) artery and aortic arch, respectively, and course up through the neck between the trachea and sternocleidomastoid muscles. At the angle of the jaw the common carotids bifurcate into the external carotid arteries, which supply the scalp, and the internal carotid arteries, which supply the brain. The first branch of the internal carotid artery is the ophthalmic artery, serving the globe and adnexa (Fig. 1).

Atherosclerotic plaque formation within either common carotid artery is more likely to occur at the proximal and distal ends where bifurcation occurs. Auscultation of the carotid arteries for bruits is an in-office procedure that helps to screen for atherosclerotic plaque formation related to certain ocular signs or visual symptoms. The evaluation for common carotid artery bruits will also serve as a barometer for atherosclerotic plaque formation elsewhere within the arterial system. A gross assessment of carotid artery integrity may also be made by palpating the pulse of the right and left common carotids.

Indications for carotid auscultation include symptoms or signs of atherosclerotic plaque formation within the cerebrovascular arterial system that may occur in the middle-aged to elderly patient. These signs and symptoms include amaurosis fugax, transient ischemic attacks (TIAs), Hollenhorst plaques, retinal occlusive phenomena, asymmetric diabetic retinopathy, and anterior segment ischemic syndromes; or symptoms of vertebrobasilar artery disease such as equilibrium disorders, bilateral visual disorders, unsteadiness, and auditory symptoms.

Carotid auscultation is performed with a stethoscope. Most stethoscopes have a chestpiece (head) with two components, a bell and a diaphragm (Fig. 2). Either the bell or diaphragm side of the chestpiece is rotated ("clicked") into position to transmit sounds through the stethoscope. The diaphragm best transmits high-frequency sounds; the bell best transmits low-frequency sounds such as heart or vascular sounds. As a result, the bell setting is preferred for carotid auscultation; however, the diaphragm may be tried if difficulty in eliciting sounds is encountered.

■ **Instrumentation.** Double-head stethoscope.

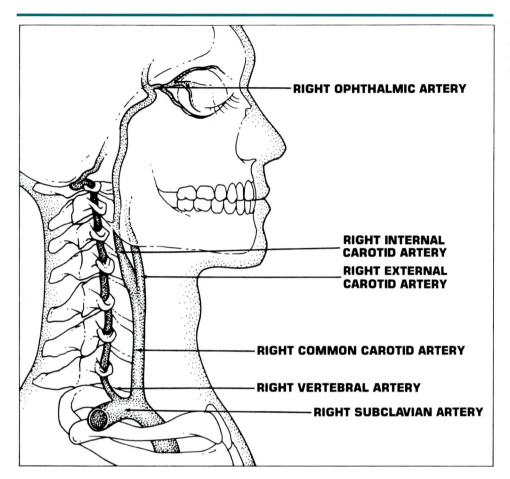

RIGHT OPHTHALMIC ARTERY

RIGHT INTERNAL
CAROTID ARTERY

RIGHT EXTERNAL
CAROTID ARTERY

RIGHT COMMON CAROTID ARTERY

RIGHT VERTEBRAL ARTERY

RIGHT SUBCLAVIAN ARTERY

1. The common carotid artery is accessible to palpation as well as auscultation for bruits due to atherosclerotic plaque formation.

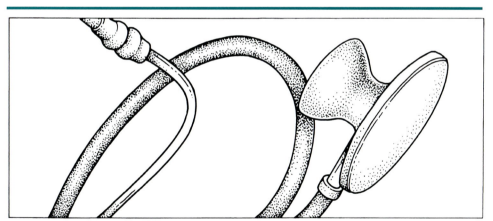

2. This stethoscope chestpiece has both a diaphragm and a bell. Either the bell or the diaphragm side is "clicked" into position by rotating the chestpiece to transmit sounds through the stethoscope.

■ **Technique.** Adjust the headrest on the examination chair so that the patient's head is resting back slightly with the chin slightly elevated. Use the tips of the first and second fingers of one hand to gently palpate the pulse of the right common carotid artery in the fleshy groove lateral to the trachea (Fig. 3).

Insert the earpieces of the stethoscope into your ears so that they angle forward toward your face as the stethoscope is put on. Turn the chestpiece so that the bell side is transmitting. Gently place the head of the stethoscope over the artery approximately 1 inch above the clavicle (Fig. 4). To minimize the distracting noise of the patient's breathing, ask him or her to stop breathing in mid-expiration. Carefully listen for bruits for a few seconds, and then ask the patient to resume breathing. Reposition the stethoscope head further up the common carotid artery and repeat the procedure two or three times along the length of the carotid. Repeat the technique on the left side.

■ **Interpretation.** Palpation of the carotid pulse may be graded as follows: Grade 0, no pulse; Grade 1+, detectable but faint pulse; Grade 2+, stronger pulse but decreased in intensity; Grade 3+, normal pulse; Grade 4+, bounding or forceful pulse. Atherosclerotic plaque formation will reduce carotid blood flow, which may be evident as a diminished pulse by palpation.

When a bruit is present, a blowing or "whooshing" type sound will be heard superimposed on the normal sound of the pulse. If an atherosclerotic plaque is present at the distal or proximal end of the common carotid artery, the bruit may become louder as that partially obstructed portion of the artery is auscultated. Bruits may be subjectively graded 1 to 4. Because of normal vessel elasticity, bruits are common but benign in children and young adults. Significant heart murmur may also be transmitted along the vessels and interpreted as a bruit.

Carotid bruits may be indicative of potentially life-threatening cerebrovascular or cardiovascular disease and referral should be made for appropriate medical assessment. The absence of bruit does not necessarily rule out carotid artery plaque formation, however, since the vessel lumen may be occluded to such an extent that blood flow turbulence is greatly diminished.

■ **Contraindications/Complications.** Care must be exercised so as not to apply excess pressure on the common carotid artery when palpating the pulse or auscultating with the stethoscope. If atherosclerotic plaque formation is present, excess pressure may mechanically occlude the vessel, interrupt blood flow, and induce a TIA. During carotid pulse assessment, the right and left common carotids should not be palpated simultaneously so that blood flow to the brain is not interrupted. As a result of anatomical variation or excessive neck tissue, it may be difficult to detect the pulse or vascular sounds of the common carotid artery.

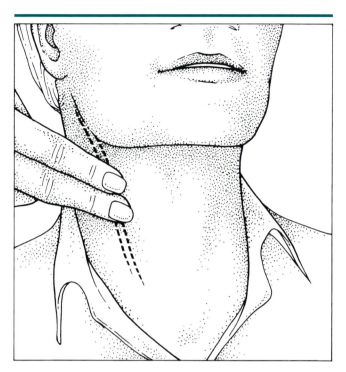

3. The common carotid artery is palpated to assess the pulse and to localize it for auscultation by gently positioning the tips of the first and second fingers in the fleshy groove between the trachea and the sternocleidomastoid muscle.

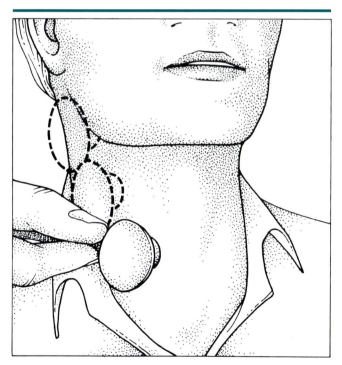

4. To auscultate the common carotid, the bell side of the stethoscope is gently placed over the artery approximately an inch above the clavicle. Auscultation is performed at three or four positions along the length of the common carotid.

74 Orbital Auscultation

■ **Description/Indications.** Orbital congestion due to a space-occupying lesion, vascular anomaly, or edema may be further investigated in-office with orbital auscultation. Similar in many ways to carotid auscultation (see p. 290), orbital auscultation is performed through the closed eyelid to detect a bruit, diagnostic of a vascular anomaly. Performing this test on normal patients will help the examiner learn the expected orbital sounds.

Orbital auscultation is performed with a stethoscope. Most stethoscopes have a chestpiece (head) with two components, a bell and a diaphragm (Fig. 1). Either the bell or the diaphragm side of the chestpiece is rotated ("clicked") into position to transmit sounds through the stethoscope. The diaphragm best transmits high-frequency sounds; the bell best transmits low-frequency sounds such as heart or vascular sounds. As a result, the bell setting is preferred for orbital auscultation.

■ **Instrumentation.** Double-head stethoscope.

■ **Technique.** Seat the patient comfortably in the examination chair and instruct him or her to close both eyes. Insert the earpieces of the stethoscope into your ears so that they angle forward toward your face as the stethoscope is put on. Turn the chestpiece so that the bell side is transmitting.

Place the bell portion of the stethoscope over the closed eyelid of one eye (Fig. 2). Ask the patient to hold his or her breath. Listen carefully for a few seconds, and then ask the patient to resume breathing. If a bruit is not heard, move the bell temporally towards the lateral canthus in an effort to enhance the orbital sounds (Fig. 3).

Repeat the procedure on the opposite eye for comparison. Multiple attempts may be necessary to detect subtle bruits.

■ **Interpretation.** When an orbital bruit is present, a blowing or "whooshing" type sound will be heard superimposed on the normal sound of the pulse. Either the patient's subjective awareness of a bruit, reported as head sounds similar to that of "swishing" or running water, or the examiner's detection of a bruit are both indicators of a positive test.

Detection of an orbital bruit suggests referral to rule out an orbital vascular anomaly, a posteriorly located carotid-cavernous fistula, or, less commonly, an orbital or intracranial tumor.

■ **Contraindications/Complications.** When performed gently, orbital auscultation poses no known risk to the patient. Caution should be used when examining an eye that has undergone recent intraocular surgery or has recently sustained blunt trauma.

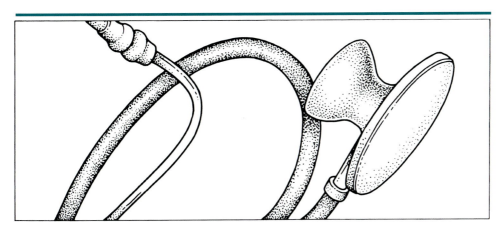

1. This stethoscope chestpiece has both a diaphragm and a bell. The bell side is "clicked" into position by rotating the chestpiece to transmit sounds through the stethoscope for orbital auscultation.

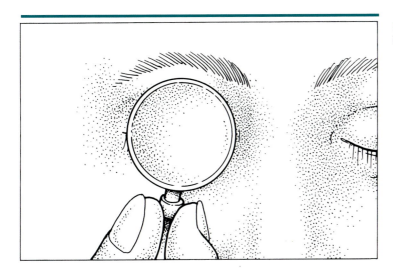

2. To auscultate the orbit, the bell portion of the stethoscope is placed over the closed eyelid.

3. The bell can be moved temporally toward the lateral canthus in an effort to enhance orbital sounds.

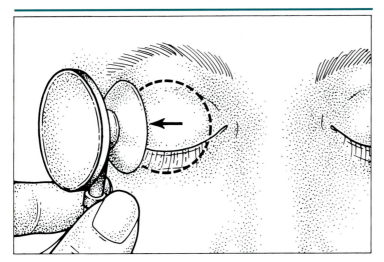

75

Ophthalmodynamometry

■ Description/Indications. Ophthalmodynamometry (ODM) is a technique that measures the relative ophthalmic artery pressure. When used in conjunction with other tests and procedures (such as ascultation, angiography, and Doppler studies), a profile of carotid artery insufficiency may be obtained.

Carotid artery insufficiency is a vascular condition with both ocular and systemic significance. In this condition the common and/or internal carotid arteries, the major vessels supplying blood to the head and neck (see p. 290), are focally narrowed due to stenosis, artheromatous build-up, or thrombosis. with subsequent decrease in blood flow to the eye and brain. The resultant ischemic condition may cause symptoms that include transient monocular blindness (amaurosis fugax), headache, aphasia and tingling, paraesthesias, or weakness of a limb. Signs of carotid artery involvement include Hollenhorst plaques, central or branch retinal artery occlusion, venous stasis retinopathy, retinal artery pulsation, asymmetric retinopathy, or unilateral reduced intraocular pressure. There are effective medical and surgical approaches for the treatment of carotid artery occlusive disease if detected; however, if undetected, a great many patients may go on to experience cerebral or ocular stroke.

During ODM, external pressure is applied to the sclera, leading to a rise in intraocular pressure, while the arterial tree at the disc is observed. When the intraocular pressure is greater than the diastolic arterial pressure but less than the systolic pressure, an arterial pulse is observed as the vessel collapses and reopens. The first arterial pulse indicates the diastolic pressure, and loss of this pulse, the systolic pressure. Under normal conditions an arterial pulse is not observed but may be seen in glaucoma, syncope, and aortic valve insufficiency. At least 50% of individuals have a normal spontaneous venous pulse because the intraocular pressure of 15 to 20 mm Hg approximates ophthalmic venous diastolic pressure.

There are two methods of ODM, compression and suction. Compression ODM is the more commonly used. The instrument itself has either a linear or dial scale (Fig. 1), both of which function by spring tension. The dial type has two needle arrow indicators, one active and the other passive. The passive indicator will remain at the highest scale reading after pressure is released or the instrument is removed from the eye. The linear type consists of a spring-loaded sliding rod with graduated markings along a cylinder. The movement of the rod, scale, and footplate are controlled by a button that must be depressed for movement to occur. The rod is locked in position when the button is released, holding the last reading on the scale. Any prior measurements must be visually read off the scale by the examiner or an assistant.

Direct ophthalmoscopy, binocular indirect ophthalmoscopy, or fundus biomicroscopy (see pp. 220, 226, 244) may be used to observe the retinal arteries during the procedure. Advantages to using the direct ophthalmoscope are that it requires only one person to perform and provides greater magnification. Its disadvantage is the limited field of view such that small ocular movements may cause the examiner to lose sight of the artery during the procedure. Steady, perpendicular globe alignment and compression with the ODM, while simultaneously viewing the retinal artery, with the direct ophthalmoscope, makes this form the most difficult of the ODM procedures to do.

The advantages of using a binocular indirect ophthalmoscope (BIO) for this procedure are the greater field of view, increased working distance allowing for easier access for an assistant to maneuver, greater illumination, and stereopsis. Sufficient magnification is obtained with a condensing lens ranging in power from +14D to +20D. With the increased field of view and reduced magnification, small eye or head movements made during the procedure by the patient may be compensated for by the examiner without losing sight of the artery. The disadvantages of using a BIO are the need for two individuals and discomfort for the patient due to the bright light.

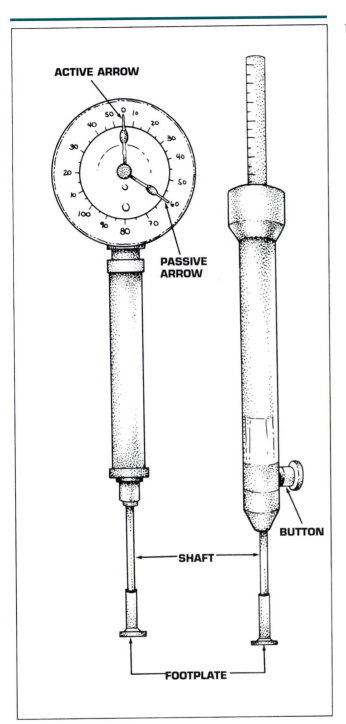

1. The dial (left) and linear ophthalmodynamometers.

■ **Instrumentation.** Ophthalmodynamometer, binocular indirect ophthalmoscope, direct ophthalmoscope, fundus biomicroscopy lens, slit lamp biomicroscope, topical ophthalmic mydriatic/cycloplegic solution(s), topical ophthalmic anesthetic solution, Goldmann tonometer, sphygmomanometer, double head stethoscope.

■ **Technique.** Explain the purpose of ODM to the patient and how it requires cooperation to obtain reliable results. Measure the intraocular pressure (see p. 276) in each eye and obtain bilateral brachial blood pressure readings (see p. 286). This information is used in the interpretation of ODM results. Dilate each eye with the desired mydriatic/cycloplegic solution(s). Begin the ODM phase of the procedure once the pupils are adequately dilated. Instill topical anesthetic solution in each eye. Use moderate room illumination so the scale on the ophthalmodynamometer is visible during the procedure.

Direct Ophthalmoscopy: Holding the direct ophthalmoscope in the hand corresponding to the eye being examined, locate a visible major artery on the optic disc near the rim. Hold the ophthalmodynamometer horizontally, like a pencil. Use the thumb, index, and middle fingers to hold the instrument and rest the remaining two or three fingers on the cheek to increase stability of the instrument (Fig. 2). With a linear-scale instrument, position the scale and button toward you and use the thumb or index finger to depress the button, allowing movement of the rod (Fig. 3).

With the patient sitting erect in the examination chair, provide a fixation target that positions the testing eye slightly up and in. Place the footplate tangentially on the globe, approximately 1 cm behind the limbus at the level of the insertion of the lateral rectus muscle (Fig. 4). Do not angle the instrument. Make sure the scale is visible to the individual noting the readings, either examiner or assistant (Fig. 5). Ask the patient to look straight ahead.

Locate the artery to be observed and apply even pressure with the ODM at a rate of approximately 20 grams per second. Have the assistant call the readings off the scale as pressure is increased. Disregard a venous pulse if present, concentrating only on the chosen artery. Stop as soon as the first initial pulse (diastole) is seen, and record the reading directly from the instrument in grams. Return the index pointer to zero or depress the button on the linear scale to reset the rod. Resume applying pressure, going past the initial pulse and watching the artery until the pulse stops and the vessel collapses (systole). Quickly remove the instrument and record this reading. Take three readings of the diastolic and systolic pressure for each eye, waiting one minute between each. Discard any disparate reading and average the results.

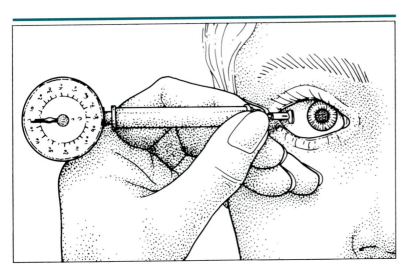

2. The ophthalmodynamometer is held between the thumb and index finger, and the remaining fingers are supported on the cheek for stability.

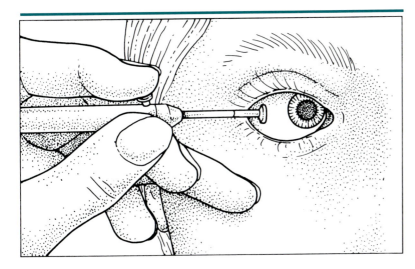

3. The index finger is used to depress the button on the linear ophthalmodynamometer to allow movement of the shaft.

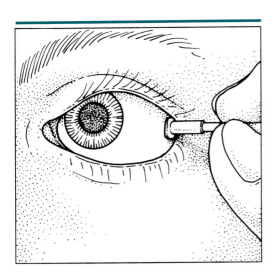

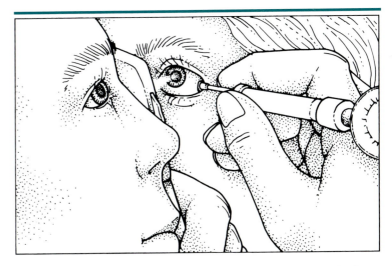

4. The footplate is placed tangentially on the globe with the shaft held horizontally as the patient looks slightly up and in.

5. The patient is asked to look straight ahead, and ODM is performed by the examiner alone using the direct ophthalmoscope.

Binocular Indirect Ophthalmoscopy: Try both the +14 D and +20 D condensing lens to see which provides the preferred view of the artery. Locate a large artery on the disc near the rim and have the assistant place the footplate on the globe, 1 cm behind the limbus. When the view of the artery is clear and stable, instruct the assistant to begin applying steady pressure (Fig. 6). Stop as soon as the first pulse (diastole) is seen and record the measurement in grams directly off the scale. Zero the instrument and repeat the procedure. Increase the pressure until the pulse occurs (diastole) then disappears (systole), remove the instrument quickly, and record. Take three separate readings for each eye, waiting 1 minute between each, discard any disparate results, and average the rest.

Fundus Biomicroscopy: Position the patient comfortably at the slit lamp biomicroscope. Obtain a clear view of the central retinal artery through the fundus biomicroscopy lens. Have an assistant position the ODM and apply pressure to the globe. Proceed with the technique to the diastolic and systolic end-points as described. Although the biomicroscope provides for a wide range of illumination and magnification settings, the headrest of the instrument may interfere with performing the procedure.

■ **Interpretation.** Readings in grams of pressure approximate but are not equal to those in mm Hg. By using a nomogram, the readings in grams are plotted against intraocular pressures to arrive at mm Hg. However, the absolute values in grams are usually used since the relative difference between the eyes is the most important factor.

The diastolic arterial reading is approximately 45 to 60% of the diastolic blood pressure measurement. This gives expected values between 30 and 50 mm Hg. The systolic arterial measure is approximately 54 to 70% of the brachial artery blood pressure, normally between 60 and 85 mm Hg. A greater than 20% decrease from the expected is considered a positive test. For borderline cases, repeat the test at a subsequent visit with the patient standing. For an individual with hypertension, a 20 to 25% reduction is needed before the diagnosis of carotid artery insufficiency can be made. A 20% increase in the diastolic measure as compared to the diastolic blood pressure is suggestive of increased intracranial pressure.

In normal individuals there should be no more than a 10% difference between the eyes. When a 15% difference is seen, the test is considered a positive indicator of carotid artery insufficiency on the side of the lower reading. Any positive test is an indicator for prompt referral to the patient's internist, neurologist, cardiologist, or vascular surgeon.

■ **Contraindications/Complications.** Care must be used whenever ODM is performed, especially since the individuals being tested probably have a compromised vascular system. The procedure should not take more than 5 to 6 seconds once pressure to the globe is initiated. If the view of the artery is lost or a pulse not seen after 6 seconds, stop the test and begin again.

Because of concern for permanently occluding a retinal artery during a systolic phase of the procedure, some authors propose that only diastolic readings be taken. However, it has been shown that without systolic readings some individuals with carotid artery insufficiency will be missed. These individuals may have equal diastolic ODM readings, and any difference between the two eyes may not manifest until systolic ODM measurements are taken. A recommended approach is to take diastolic readings first and if a 20% difference between the two eyes is seen, the test is considered positive and systolic readings are not indicated. If the test is negative or inconclusive, systolic ODM readings are warranted, especially in symptomatic individuals.

Proper technique and patient cooperation are crucial to obtaining accurate results. Misalignment of the footplate or angulation of the instrument will negatively affect the results. Any of these may also cause the eye to be displaced, losing the ophthalmoscopic view. Cataracts, media opacities, or poor fixation, which affect the examiner's view of the retinal arteries, can affect the results.

Relative contraindications to the test include a recently operated eye, ectopia lentis, recent penetrating or blunt injuries, history of retinal tears or retinal detachment, high myopia with peripheral retinal weakness, or neovascularization of the iris or retina.

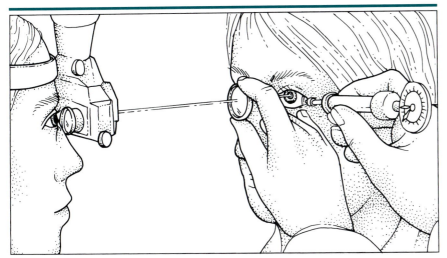

6. ODM using the binocular indirect ophthalmoscope as performed by two people, the examiner and an assistant.

76 Forced Duction Testing

■ **Description/Indications.** Forced duction testing is used to investigate the passive movements of extraocular muscles in their fields of action to determine whether an ocular motility abnormality is due to mechanical myopathic resistance or paresis, usually of neurogenic origin (see p. 302). In the instance of ocular trauma, this procedure can provide important diagnostic information.

Forced duction testing is indicated when diplopia is of acute onset, a history of trauma precedes an ocular motor disturbance, or diplopia occurs in certain positions of gaze. Following topical ophthalmic anesthesia, the technique may be performed one of two ways, using a fixation "toothed" forceps or a cotton-tipped applicator. Cotton-tipped applicators do not provide the leverage and force that forceps do, but they are easier to use, less traumatic, and work well in the majority of cases. With the forceps, the eye can be pushed and pulled to evaluate for abnormal resistance, while with the cotton-tipped applicators, the eye is only pushed.

■ **Instrumentation.** Sterile cotton-tipped applicators, fixation "toothed" forceps, eyelid speculum, topical ophthalmic anesthetic solution.

■ **Technique.** Instill topical ophthalmic anesthetic solution, and use a pledget to deliver additional topical anesthesia near the insertion of the rectus muscle(s) to be tested (Fig. 1A; see also p. 6).

Forceps: Use the toothed forceps to grasp the conjunctiva and Tenon's fascia at the insertion of the muscle to be tested, approximately 5 mm posterior to the limbus and in the opposite quadrant to where the globe will be rotated (Fig. 1B). Ask the patient to hold his or her finger in the direction the eye will be moved, and ask him or her to look at it to control innervation and help ensure cooperation. Gently rotate the eye in the indicated direction of movement (Fig. 1C). Once the eye is moved into the position of gaze or a restriction is felt, release the forceps from the conjunctiva, allowing the eye to return to its natural position. If indicated, test the contralateral eye in a similar manner to compare the resistance between the two eyes.

Cotton-tipped Applicator: Following topical anesthesia, place a sterile cotton-tipped applicator tangential to the globe and just posterior to the limbus. Gently push the globe with the cotton-tipped applicator in a similar method as with the forceps (Fig. 2). Move the involved eye into the affected positions of gaze, asking the patient to look at a target such as his or her hand to facilitate eye movement.

An alternative approach to placing the forceps or cotton-tipped applicator in the quadrant opposite to where the eye will be rotated is to place it 90 degrees away. For example, when testing the right lateral rectus muscle, grasp the conjunctiva above the superior limbus and push the globe nasally.

The use of an eyelid speculum (see p. 98) may help in keeping the eyelids separated, especially in traumatic cases with eyelid edema. The speculum is also useful for testing individuals who are having difficulty cooperating.

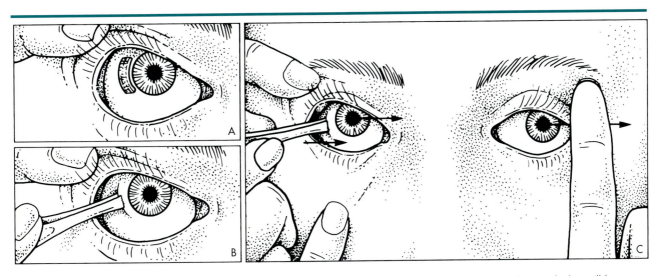

1. A. A pledget of topical ophthalmic anesthetic is placed on the conjunctiva over the insertion of the extraocular muscle that will be assessed with forced duction testing. B. A toothed forceps is used to grasp the conjunctiva and Tenon's fascia approximately 5 mm posterior to the limbus. C. The patient is asked to fixate his or her finger, and the eye is gently rotated manually in the direction indicated.

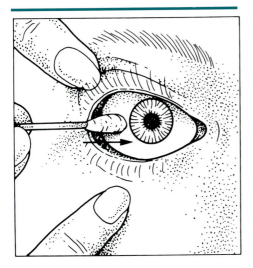

2. For this alternative method of forced duction testing, a cotton-tipped applicator is placed posterior to the limbus and used to manually rotate the globe.

■ **Interpretation.** With forced rotation, the globe should move freely in its excursions (negative test). If resistance is encountered (positive test), greater force is needed to move the eye. The opposite eye is used for comparison, especially in subtle cases of fibrosis or contracture. To obtain the feel of a normal excursion, do the test on "normals" to sense what the expected minimal resistance is.

In motility disturbances due to mechanical restrictions, the globe will move only with increased force and, at times, not at all (Fig. 3). The increased resistance occurs in grades and not in an "all or none" fashion. In most cases of fibrosis, if enough force is applied, the eye can be made to move to some extent into any position of gaze.

In motility disturbances of neurogenic origin, whether secondary to trauma or ischemia, the globe will move easily with forced duction testing, giving a negative test. With traumatic damage, the orbital or intracranial nerves supplying the extraocular muscles may be contused, leading to the paretic muscles (Fig. 4). If the traumatic damage is severe, whereby the extraocular muscles are severed, a supranormal test will result where little if any resistance is sensed upon forced duction testing.

In cases of trauma, the forced duction test is used to determine if the muscle dysfunction is due to injury to the motor nerves supplying the muscles, extraocular muscle contusion, orbital edema, or entrapment of the inferior recti or inferior oblique muscles within a blow-out fracture site. If the test is positive and increased resistance is felt, suspect a muscle or soft tissue to be entrapped. The test is negative if the eye movements are smooth and a paretic muscle, probably secondary to neurologic injury, is suspected. A neurogenic injury, edema, or muscle contusion should resolve with time, while an entrapment injury will not and may require treatment; yet all may look identical upon preliminary examination.

If the force applied pushes the eye backward, the globe may be displaced posteriorly, giving the false impression of full motilities.

In individuals with a thyroid condition who present with diplopia, suspect a myopathy. The diplopia is usually on upgaze with an accompanying inferior heterotropia. The inferior rectus is frequently involved, becoming fibrotic, leading to the eye's inability to elevate. The superior rectus muscle is not abnormal, although it appears to be on first assessment. Differential diagnosis includes a paretic muscle versus a myopathy. If resistance is felt when the eye is elevated, a probable myopathy of the inferior rectus is present.

In Brown's tendon sheath syndrome, an apparent congenital paresis of the inferior oblique is noted. Upon forced duction testing with the eye in the adducted position, resistance is felt with elevation. This positive forced duction test differentiates Brown's syndrome from an inferior oblique paresis.

■ **Contraindications/Complications.** Uncooperative patients looking in unintended positions of gaze during forced duction testing may innervate antagonistic muscles, giving the false impression of mechanical resistance. If voluntary eye movements cannot be controlled, the test cannot be done with topical anesthesia. Avoid pressing or pushing the globe into the orbit during rotation, since this may simulate ocular movement, leading to improper observations.

Forced duction testing is difficult to do on children or other individuals not capable of controlling their fixation. In these cases, false positives are possible, since resistance may be felt that does not truly exist. The test can be uncomfortable and, in cases of inadequate anesthesia, painful if a forceps is used. A mild dull ache in and around the eye may occur for several hours after the procedure. Small subconjunctival hemorrhages are not uncommon. Cotton-tipped applicators must be carefully used since they may slip, causing a secondary corneal abrasion.

Forced duction testing is contraindicated during an acute hyphema or when globe penetration is suspected. The test is often uncomfortable and difficult to accomplish in acute cases of trauma with marked lid edema and pain. In such cases, a delay of several days may be needed.

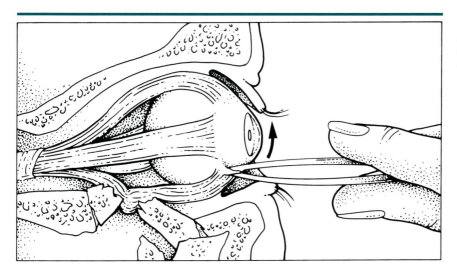

3. In a blowout fracture with extraocular muscles entrapped in the orbital floor, the eye will not elevate with forced duction testing.

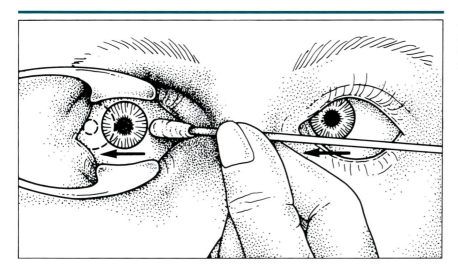

4. An ecchymotic right eye is seen with a sixth-nerve paresis following trauma. With forced duction testing, the globe can be moved freely in a temporal direction.

77 Forced Generations Testing

■ **Description/Indications.** Forced generations testing is used to diagnose and grossly quantify ocular muscle abnormalities of neurogenic origin. It is indicated in the examination of suspected nerve paresis with extraocular muscle dysfunction, especially secondary to trauma. A traumatic neurogenic etiology may be differentiated from muscle restriction. This test is often used as a companion to forced duction testing (see p. 302).

Forced generations testing is also used to follow and grossly quantify resolution of neurogenic muscle paresis, such as third or sixth-nerve palsy. In this instance the test is done periodically over time, with the degree of resistance encountered recorded.

■ **Instrumentation.** Sterile cotton-tipped applicators, topical ophthalmic anesthetic solution, eyelid speculum.

■ **Technique.** Instill several drops of topical anesthetic solution into each eye, using a pledget to deliver the topical anesthetic if necessary (see p. 6). Place a cotton-tipped applicator approximately 5 mm posterior to the limbus to correspond to the insertion of the muscle to be tested, keeping the applicator tangential to the eye (Fig. 1). Give the patient a target to look at such as his or her finger, and ask the patient to look hard into the field of action of the muscle and nerve to be tested. Apply slight pressure to the applicator, attempting to push the eye in the opposite direction of gaze. Grade and record the degree to which the eye can or cannot be moved against the action of the muscle. Test each quadrant of both eyes in a similar fashion.

An eyelid speculum (see p. 98) may assist in keeping the eyelids separated, especially in the event of trauma with eyelid edema. The lid speculum is also useful to test patients who are having difficulty cooperating for this technique.

A suspected traumatic right sixth-nerve paresis with impaired abduction may require differential diagnosis between muscle entrapment or neurogenic paresis. First place the cotton-tipped applicator nasally, and then inferiorly and superiorly at the limbus, asking the patient to look toward the applicator. Attempt to push the eye in the opposite direction. Finally, place the applicator at the temporal limbus of the right eye, asking the patient to look right (temporally) while the left eye is observed, making sure it turns directly toward the nose. Attempt to push the right eye toward the nose using the cotton-tipped applicator placed at the limbus.

■ **Interpretation.** In the case of normal extraocular muscle function, it is difficult to move the eye against the field of action of the muscle tested. A "pull" or "tug" will be felt on the cotton-tipped applicator, and the eye will remain firmly in its original position. This result indicates a negative forced generations test (Fig. 2). In cases of partial or total extraocular muscle paresis, the application of gentle pressure can move the eye against the field of action of the tested muscle. This indicates a positive forced generations test (Fig. 3).

The degree of resistance found depends upon the degree of neurogenic involvement. In the case described under "Technique," if the right eye does not move nasally when force is applied at the temporal limbus during gaze to the right, then forced generations testing is negative and sixth-nerve function is intact. As a result, another cause of the paresis must be found and additional testing is needed, such as forced duction testing (see p. 302), to rule out muscle restriction. If abduction weakness is present and the eye can be moved nasally with forced generations testing, then a right sixth-nerve paresis is confirmed.

Forced generations testing can be quantified, noting the degree of resistance (mild, moderate, severe), and may be repeated at regular time intervals (biweekly for several months) to assess for change.

To determine what normal extraocular muscle tone and resistance feel like, forced generations testing can be performed on normal patients, testing each quadrant of each eye.

■ **Contraindications/Complications.** Care should be taken to apply sufficient tangential force with the cotton-tipped applicator to prevent it from slipping and inducing a corneal abrasion. Mild conjunctival injection or subconjunctival hemorrhage may result from this technique. Forced generations testing is contraindicated in the presence of hyphema or suspected globe penetration.

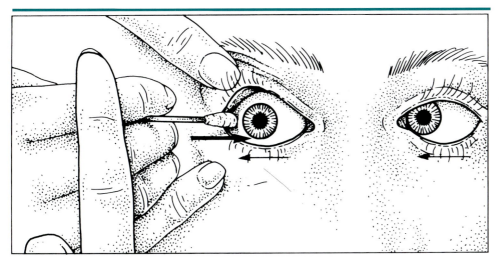

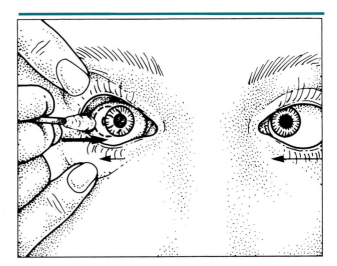

1. For forced generations testing, the cotton-tipped applicator is placed posterior to the limbus, and the patient is asked to look at his or her finger. Gentle pressure is applied to the applicator, attempting to move the globe against the field of action of the muscle tested.

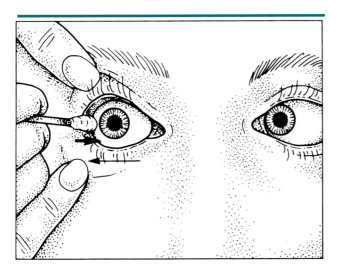

2. An example of a negative forced generations test. The eye remains in its position of gaze (narrow arrow) as pressure is applied in the opposite direction (wide arrow).

3. An example of a positive forced generations test. The application of gentle pressure (wide arrow) successfully moves the eye against the field of action of the tested muscle (narrow arrow).

IX Suggested Readings

Berguer R, Weiss H (eds): *The Carotid and the Eye.* New York, Praeger, 1985.

Fifth Report of the Joint National Committee on Detection, Evaluation, and Treatment of High Blood Pressure (JNC V). *Arch Intern Med* 1993;**153:**154–183.

Greenberg DA: Basic evaluation of exophthalmos. *J Am Optom Assoc* 1977;**48:**1431–1433.

Kaplan NM: *Clinical Hypertension,* ed 4. Baltimore, Williams & Wilkins, 1986.

Keeney AH: *Ocular Examination: Basis and Technique,* ed 2. St. Louis, Mosby, 1976.

Locke LC: Sphygmomanometry, in Eskridge JB, Amos JF, Bartlett JD (eds): *Clinical Procedures in Optometry.* Philadelphia, Lippincott, 1991, pp 267–278.

Locke LC: Induced refractive and visual changes, in Amos JF (ed): *Diagnosis and Management in Vision Care.* Boston, Butterworths, 1987, pp 313–367.

Miller NR (ed): *Walsh and Hoyt's Neuro-Ophthalmology.* Baltimore, Williams & Wilkins, 1988, pp 994–1017.

Pence NA: Ophthalmodynamometry. *J Am Optom Assoc* 1980; **51:**49–55.

Smith, JL (ed): How to really do the forced ductions/generations test, in *Neuro-ophthalmology Audio Journal,* vol 11, no. 4. Miami, Neuro-ophthalmology Tapes, 1988.

Smith JL, Zeiper IH, Cogan DG: Observations on ophthalmodynamometry. *JAMA* 1959;**170:**1403–1407.

Terry JE (ed): *Ocular Disease: Detection, Diagnosis, and Treatment.* Springfield, IL, Thomas, 1984.

Wood, FA, Toole JF: Carotid artery occlusion and its diagnosis by ophthalmodynamometry. *JAMA* 1957;**165:**1264–1270.

Cranial Nerve Examination

78 Olfactory Nerve (CN1) and Optic Nerve (CN2) Examination

■ **Description/Indications.** The cranial nerves provide motor and sensory innervation to the head and neck. Ten of the twelve cranial nerves (CN3 to CN12) have nuclei that originate within the brainstem (Fig. 1), and after they exit, travel a specific pathway to their final destinations. The olfactory (CN1) and optic (CN2) nerves differ anatomically from the other cranial nerves because neither is a true peripheral nerve or has a nucleus located in the brainstem.

The function of the cranial nerves may be impaired by supranuclear lesions (involving central connections to the cranial nerves), nuclear lesions, or infranuclear lesions (involving the peripheral nerve). The cranial nerve examination tests the status of the individual nerves and the integrity of these pathways through straightforward procedures requiring minimal time and equipment. Because each nerve has a right and left component, each side is tested separately and compared. When dysfunction is found, characteristics of the cranial nerve deficit may provide clues to localize the site of the lesion or indicate the need for further diagnostic testing. For example, a lesion between the motor cortex and the cranial nerve nucleus (upper motor neuron) will cause weakness without atrophy along with increased reflexes (spastic paralysis). A lesion to a somatic motor nerve after it exits the cranial nucleus (lower motor neuron) will produce weakness with muscle atrophy and diminished or absent reflexes (flaccid paralysis). Thus, knowledge of the anatomy and routes of the cranial nerves can be valuable in localizing diseases within the central nervous system and also in the diagnosis of systemic disease.

The sole function of the olfactory nerve (CN1) is the sense of smell. Bipolar cells for olfaction are located in the nasal mucosa. They synapse in the olfactory bulbs, and a pair of fibers (the olfactory nerves) are produced, which travel throughout the cortex, making numerous connections. Disorders of the sense of smell may be caused by a lesion involving any part of the peripheral nerve or its central connections. The result may be a total loss of smell (anosmia), decreased sense of smell (hyposmia), or other alterations in the sense of smell such as hyperosmia (increased olfactory acuity), parosmia (distorted sense of smell), or cacosmia (olfactory hallucinations).

The optic nerve (CN2) transmits visual information from the retina to the brain. The rods and cones in the retina synapse in the retinal bipolar layer, and then again with the retinal ganglion cells, providing the origin of the optic nerves. A lesion anywhere along the retinal pathway involving the optic nerve, tract, or brain may cause a corresponding deficit in visual field or visual acuity.

This section describes in-office examination of the first and second cranial nerves. The remaining ten cranial nerves are discussed in subsequent sections.

■ **Instrumentation.** An aromatic substance, visual acuity chart or equivalent, direct ophthalmoscope or slit lamp biomicroscope and a fundus biomicroscopic lens, halogen transilluminator or binocular indirect ophthalmoscope headset.

■ **Technique.**

CN1—Olfactory Nerve: A mildly aromatic substance such as vanilla, coffee, or chocolate is used to test olfaction. Noxious substances such as alcohol or ammonia are to be avoided, because they will stimulate a portion of the trigeminal nerve that innervates the nasal mucosa, thus mimicking the sensation of smell.

Instruct the patient to shut his or her eyes and occlude the left nostril (Fig. 2). Present the substance beneath the open right nare and ask the patient if he or she can smell anything and identify it. Occlude the right nostril and repeat the procedure with the same or another aromatic substance beneath the open left nare. If the nasal passages are congested, clearing them with a nasal spray such as 0.25% neosynephrine prior to testing is acceptable and will not alter the test results.

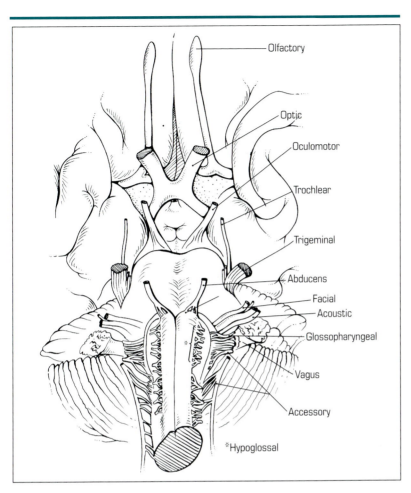

1. Basal view of the brain and the 12 cranial nerves.

Olfactory

Optic

Oculomotor

Trochlear

Trigeminal

Abducens

Facial

Acoustic

Glossopharyngeal

Vagus

Accessory

*Hypoglossal

2. To test olfaction, a pleasant-smelling substance is used. With the eyes closed and one nasal passage occluded, the patient is asked if a scent is detected and if it can be identified.

CN2—Optic Nerve: The right and left optic nerves are assessed through direct observation using techniques such as direct ophthalmoscopy (see p. 220) and fundus biomicroscopy (see p. 244), as well as indirect tests that measure their function. These indirect tests include, but are not limited to, best corrected visual acuity, visual field (see p. 386), and pupillary testing. Pupillary testing techniques that indirectly assess optic nerve function include direct and consensual pupillary testing as well as the swinging flashlight test.

Instruct the patient to look at a distant target in a room that is dimly lit yet bright enough to visualize the patient's pupils. Note pupillary size and shape under these conditions. Using either a halogen transilluminator or a binocular indirect ophthalmoscope headset with the illumination set at a medium to high level, shine the light at the right pupil (Fig. 3). Observe the promptness and completeness of constriction as well as the final pupil size in the right eye. Repeat two more times, noting any change in the pupillary response with testing fatigue. To evaluate the consensual pupillary response, shine the light into the right eye, but observe the left eye response. Repeat both direct and consensual testing, this time shining the light into the left eye.

Test the equality of the direct and consensual pupillary responses with the swinging flashlight test (Fig. 4). Shine the light source at the right pupil for approximately 3 seconds, and then rapidly swing the light across to the left eye. The rate at which the light is swung from the right to left eye varies with the rate at which the pupils respond directly to light, but the maximum swinging time should be 1 second. Note the initial reaction of the left pupil. Swing the light back to the right eye at the same speed, noting the initial reaction of the right pupil. Repeat the procedure, performing a series of multiple, studied swings. Care should be taken not to leave the light stimulus on one eye longer than the other because this can result in a false relative afferent defect.

The swinging flashlight test can be done when one pupil is fixed (e.g., due to posterior synechiae or pharmacological mydriasis). Observe only the functional pupil as the light is swung from the right to left eye and back to the right eye.

The accommodative pupillary response is used to evaluate the parasympathetic portion of the oculomotor nerve (CN3) and is discussed on page 316.

3. Right direct pupillary light response: As the patient fixates a distant target, the light beam is directed towards the patient's right pupil and the examiner observes the pupillary response in that eye. Right consensual pupillary light response: The examiner shines the light into the right eye and observes the response of the left eye.

4. Left relative afferent pupillary defect testing. The patient is asked to fixate a distant target. The light source is directed at the right pupil for 3 to 5 seconds and quickly swung to the left eye. The initial response is observed when the left pupil first receives the light.

■ Interpretation.

CN1—Olfactory Nerve: Failure to detect the scent of the substance presented indicates dysfunction of the sense of smell. However, anosmia (complete loss of the sense of smell) is not considered to be present if the patient can detect the scent but cannot identify it.

Anosmia may indicate damage to the olfactory fibers or tract, or injury at a higher level in the brain. Common causes of bilateral anosmia include upper respiratory infections, sinus conditions, rhinitis, heavy cigarette smoking, and trauma. Unilateral anosmia may indicate a lesion at the base of the frontal lobe. Olfactory hallucinations (cacosmia) may occur with lesions in the higher cortical areas.

CN2—Optic Nerve: Complete interpretation of optic nerve dysfunction is beyond the scope of this text. However, it is important to determine whether the damage is prechiasmal, chiasmal, or postchiasmal. Direct visualization of the optic nerve along with adjunct tests of optic nerve function, particularly visual field examination, can help make this determination.

The presence of a relative afferent pupillary defect provides strong evidence of prechiasmal optic nerve dysfunction. Because the pupillary motor fibers decussate twice, the direct and consensual pupil responses are equal in both eyes in the presence of normal optic nerve function (Fig. 5A). With unilateral optic nerve damage, the pupil of the involved eye reacts as if less light were entering the eye (relative to the good eye), and thus both pupils remain larger during direct pupillary testing of the involved eye (Fig. 5B). When the light is swung from the eye with the damaged optic nerve to the good eye, the initial reaction in both pupils is constriction (Fig. 5C). When it is swung back to the involved eye, both pupils dilate because the neural input is weaker relative to the better functioning optic nerve. This test may also be done in the presence of a fixed pupil (e.g., due to posterior synechiae). In these cases, only the functional pupil is observed as the light is swung between the two eyes while the direct and consensual responses are compared (Fig. 6).

Careful confrontation visual fields or perimetry may reveal a defect in one or both eyes, depending on the site of the lesion. Optic nerve damage anterior to the optic chiasm will result in a unilateral visual field defect. If a chiasmal lesion is present, the defect will usually be bitemporal, with variations possible corresponding to the portion of the chiasm damaged. If a lesion occurs posterior to the chiasm, visual field loss will involve both eyes and will respect the vertical midline.

Optic nerve evaluation through direct observation may reveal a disc that is elevated, flat, excavated, pale, hyperemic, or normal in color. These conditions can be the sequelae of conditions such as isolated optic nerve disease (e.g., anterior ischemic optic neuropathy or glaucoma), neurological disease (e.g., papilledema from a space-occupying lesion or optic neuritis in multiple sclerosis), or infectious disease (e.g., optic neuritis in Lyme disease or syphilis). Other optic nerve variations, both normal (e.g., myelinated nerve fibers) and pathologic (e.g., hemorrhages) may also be present.

■ Contraindications/Complications.
These tests present no risk to the patient. See pp. 220 and 224 for contraindications/complications of direct ophthalmoscopy and fundus biomicroscopy.

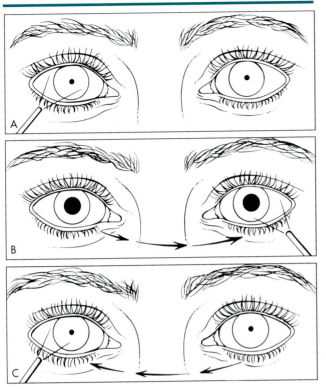

5. Left relative afferent pupillary defect. A. The right pupil constricts in response to direct stimulation. The left pupil constricts equally via consensual response. B. The light is swung over to the left eye. The right pupil dilates because the consensual response from the left eye is less than the direct response in the right eye. The left pupil dilates because the left direct response is less than the right consensual due to left optic nerve damage. C. The light is swung back to the right eye. The right pupil constricts because the right direct response is greater than the left consensual. The left pupil constricts because the right consensual response is greater than the left direct response.

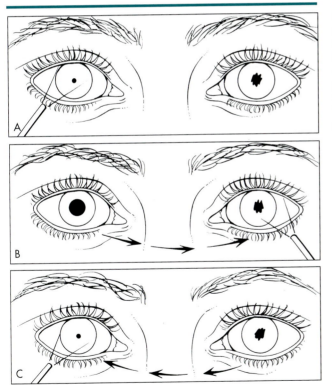

6. Reverse afferent pupillary defect testing. Testing for the presence of a relative afferent pupillary defect of the left eye when the pupil is fixed due to posterior synechiae. Only the functional pupil is observed. A. The light is shone on the right pupil, which constricts as part of the direct light response. B. The light is swung to the left eye. The right pupil dilates, because the left consensual response is reduced as a result of left optic nerve damage. C. The light is quickly swung back to the right eye, which constricts because the right direct response is greater than the left consensual response.

Oculomotor Nerve (CN3) Examination

■ **Description/Indications.** The cranial nerves provide motor and sensory innervation to the head and neck. Ten of the twelve cranial nerves (CN3 to CN12) have nuclei that originate within the brainstem (see p. 311), and after they exit, travel a specific pathway to their final destinations. The olfactory (CN1) and optic (CN2) nerves differ anatomically from the other cranial nerves because neither one is a true peripheral nerve or has a nucleus located in the brainstem.

The function of the cranial nerves may be impaired by supranuclear lesions (involving central connections to the cranial nerves), nuclear lesions, or infranuclear lesions (involving the peripheral nerve). The cranial nerve examination tests the status of the individual nerves and the integrity of these pathways through straightforward procedures requiring minimal time and equipment. Because each nerve has a right and left component, each side is tested separately and compared. When dysfunction is found, characteristics of the cranial nerve deficit may provide clues to localize the site of the lesion or indicate the need for further diagnostic testing. For example, a lesion between the motor cortex and the cranial nerve nucleus (upper motor neuron) will cause weakness without atrophy along with increased reflexes (spastic paralysis). A lesion to a somatic motor nerve after it exits the cranial nucleus (lower motor neuron) will produce weakness with muscle atrophy and diminished or absent reflexes (flaccid paralysis). Thus, knowledge of the anatomy and routes of the cranial nerves can be valuable in localizing diseases within the central nervous system and also in the diagnosis of systemic disease.

The oculomotor nerve (CN3) has both parasympathetic and somatic motor functions. The efferent portion of the pupil and the accommodative reflexes are relayed through the parasympathetic component of the oculomotor nerve, which innervates the pupillary sphincter and ciliary muscles. Direct and consensual pupillary responses, along with the accommodative response, will therefore test the integrity of this portion of the oculomotor nerve. Ocular motility testing assesses the somatic motor portion of the oculomotor nerve, which innervates the medial rectus, superior rectus, inferior rectus, and inferior oblique extraocular muscles.

This section describes the in-office evaluation of the oculomotor nerve (CN3). The remaining cranial nerves are discussed in the previous and subsequent cranial nerve sections.

■ **Instrumentation.** Fixation target, halogen transilluminator or binocular indirect ophthalmoscope headset.

■ **Technique.**

CN3—Oculomotor Nerve, Parasympathetic: Instruct the patient to look at a distant target in a room that is dimly lit yet bright enough to visualize the patient's pupils. Note pupillary size and shape under these conditions. Using either a halogen transilluminator or a binocular indirect ophthalmoscope headset with the illumination set at a medium to high level, shine the light at the right pupil (Fig. 1). Observe the promptness and completeness of constriction as well as the final pupil size in the right eye. Repeat two more times, noting any change in the pupillary response with testing fatigue. To evaluate the consensual pupillary response, shine the light into the right eye, but observe the left eye response. Repeat both direct and consensual testing, this time shining the light into the left eye.

The swinging flashlight test is used to test the equality of the direct and consensual pupillary responses as an indirect assessment of the optic nerve (CN2). This test is discussed on p. 310.

To test the accommodative reflex, instruct the patient to look at his or her finger held approximately 4 inches in front of his or her nose (Fig. 2). Gently tap the patient's finger to help elicit a strong accommodative response. Look for bilateral pupillary constriction.

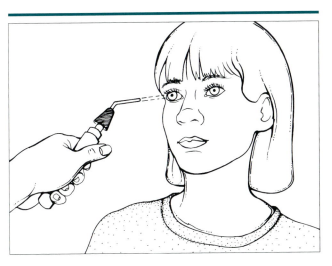

1. Right direct pupillary light response: As the patient fixates a distant target, the light beam is directed towards the patient's right pupil and the examiner observes the pupillary response in that eye. Right consensual pupillary light response: The examiner shines the light into the right eye and observes the response of the left eye. The technique is repeated for the left eye.

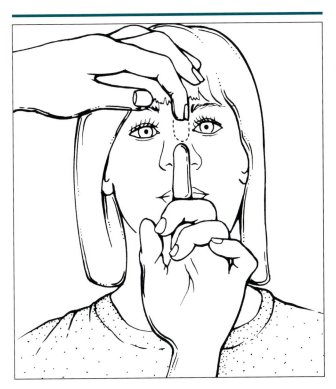

2. Accommodative response. The pupil size is observed while the patient fixates a distant target. The patient is asked to hold his or her finger about 4 inches from the eyes, just below the level of the distant target. The examiner taps the finger to elicit the response and observes the quantity and quality of pupillary constriction in both eyes.

CN3—Oculomotor Nerve, Somatic Motor: Ocular motility testing assesses the somatic motor portion of the oculomotor nerve that innervates the medial rectus, superior rectus, inferior rectus, and inferior oblique extraocular muscles. Motility testing also evaluates the function of the superior oblique muscle, innervated by the trochlear nerve (CN4), and lateral rectus muscle, innervated by the abducens nerve (CN6).

Ask the patient to follow a fixation target, held approximately 40 cm in front of the face, through the nine cardinal positions of gaze, noting if the eyes lose alignment at any time (Fig. 3). Also ask the patient to report if the target doubles. A red lens and/or maddox rod may also be used to elicit diplopia and, in conjunction with a prism bar, to measure the extent of a paretic muscle.

The doll's head (oculocephalic) maneuver may be used in infants or developmentally delayed patients who are not capable of following a fixation target. Instruct the patient to fixate straight ahead or use an engaging fixation target (e.g., a small toy or hand puppet) to maintain attention. Turn the patient's head to the left to test gaze-right horizontal eye movements (Fig. 4), and vice versa. Move the patient's head up and down to test vertical eye movements.

The somatic motor portion of the oculomotor nerve also innervates the levator palpebrae muscle so that dysfunction will result in ptosis. Measure the palpebral apertures at their widest point by resting a PD ruler against the zygomatic bone (Fig. 5). Record the palpebral aperture height in millimeters.

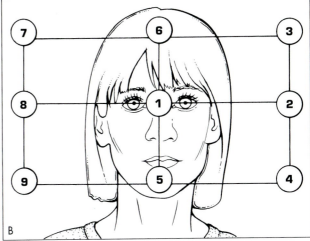

3. Ocular motility testing. A. A fixation target is placed in front of the patient in the primary position. B. The fixation target is moved in the nine cardinal positions of gaze.

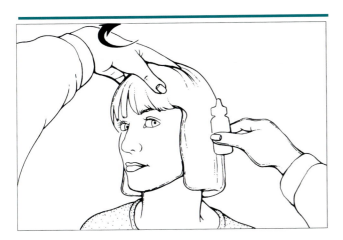

4. Doll's-head maneuver. The patient fixates an engaging target while the examiner moves the head to elicit reflex eye movements in the opposite direction.

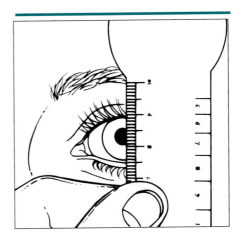

5. The palpebral apertures are measured at their widest portion by resting a PD ruler on the cheek or zygomatic bone.

■ **Interpretation.** A patient with a complete third-nerve palsy will have a unilateral ptotic lid, a fixed and dilated pupil, and an eye positioned in an outward and slightly downward position due to the unopposed action of the superior oblique and lateral rectus muscles (Fig. 6A, B). However, partial third-nerve palsies may also be encountered, depending upon the etiology and site of the lesion. For example, trauma to the superior division of the oculomotor nerve in the superior orbital fissure may impact only the superior rectus and levator palpebrae muscles.

Ocular motility testing evaluates all of the extraocular muscles; however, it is sometimes difficult to interpret which muscles are paretic when more than one is involved. The diagnosis is straightforward when all of the extraocular muscles innervated by the oculomotor nerve are paretic. There will be limited adduction, elevation, and depression of the globe (Fig. 6C to F). If only the superior rectus muscle is involved, the eye will be unable to elevate, adduct, and intort. The only function of the medial rectus is to adduct the eye; therefore, if this muscle is affected, only adduction will be limited. If the inferior rectus muscle alone is involved, the eye will have difficulty depressing, adducting, and extorting. The inferior oblique muscle is primarily involved in extorting and elevating the eye in primary gaze and plays a minor role in abducting the eye. The Parks three-step test (see p. 322) may be used to isolate a paretic inferior oblique, inferior rectus, superior rectus, or superior oblique (CN4) muscle.

Asymmetry of the palpebral apertures will be noted if the levator palpebrae muscle is partially or fully involved in a third-nerve palsy. This may range from a subtle to complete ptosis. Asymmetry of the palpebral apertures may also occur with anatomic variations of the lid (e.g., dermatochalasis, congenital ptosis) as well as other neural causes (e.g., seventh-nerve palsy, Horner syndrome), neuromuscular disorders (e.g., myasthenia gravis), and muscle dysfunction (e.g., thyroid eye disease).

If an ocular motility dysfunction is found, the site of impairment must be localized to the muscle, neuromuscular junction, or nerve. Ocular motility impairment due to muscle entrapment (e.g., trauma) or enlargement (e.g., thyroid ophthalmopathy) will often be evident as a result of the history and associated systemic signs; however, other clues may be elicited through motility testing. Ductions will be better than versions in the same direction in an eye with motility impairment due to neuropathy. Versions and ductions will be impaired equally in an eye with muscle restriction. Forced ductions and forced generations (see pp. 302 and 306) can give further useful information regarding a neural versus muscular etiology in motility dysfunction. If the neuromuscular junction is compromised, the motility dysfunction generally follows a fluctuating course and tends to worsen as the day progresses. Variable muscles may be paretic depending upon the time of day they are tested. Sleep, ice pack, Tensilon, or acetylcholine receptor antibody testing may be used to provide evidence for dysfunction at the neuromuscular junction.

Ischemia, trauma, aneurysm, and neoplasms are the most common causes of third-nerve palsies in adults. The most important distinction to make in a third-nerve palsy is whether or not the pupillary fibers are involved. The presence of a fixed, dilated pupil usually indicates a compressive lesion, most likely an aneurysm of the posterior communicating artery. The pupil will usually be spared in damage caused by ischemia (e.g., diabetes or hypertension); however, any pupil-sparing third-nerve palsy should be watched carefully for subsequent pupil involvement.

■ **Contraindications/Complications.** Pupil and ocular motility testing present no risks to the patient. The doll's-head maneuver must be performed with caution or avoided in patients with neck injury. See pp. 302 and 306 for contraindications/complications of forced ductions and forced generations testing.

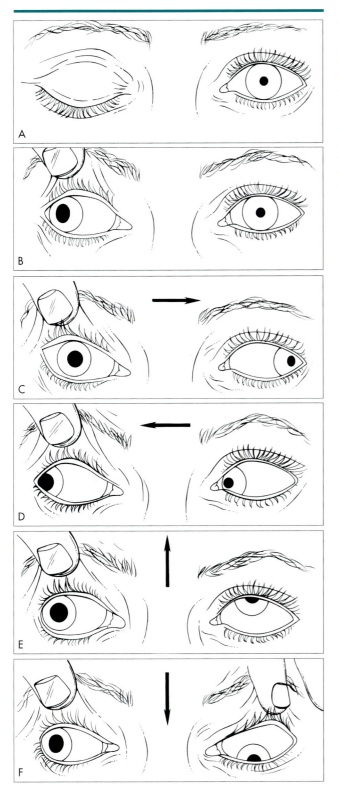

6. Complete right oculomotor nerve palsy (arrows show patient's attempted position of gaze with ocular motility testing. A. The lid is ptotic due to levator palpebrae muscle weakness. B. In primary position, the affected eye is in an out and slightly down position due to the unopposed actions of the lateral rectus and superior oblique muscles. Note the fixed and dilated pupil. C. The right eye cannot adduct due to medial rectus muscle weakness. D. The right eye is able to abduct because the lateral rectus muscle (innervated by the abducens nerve) is functional; however, it may not fully abduct because the inferior oblique muscle participates in this movement. E. The affected eye cannot elevate due to weakness of the superior rectus and inferior oblique muscles. F. The right eye cannot depress fully due to weakness of the inferior rectus. The functional superior oblique muscle allows it to depress slightly.

80 Trochlear Nerve (CN4) Examination

■ **Description/Indications.** The cranial nerves provide motor and sensory innervation to the head and neck. Ten of the twelve cranial nerves (CN3 to CN12) have nuclei that originate within the brainstem (see p. 311), and after they exit, travel a specific pathway to their final destinations. The olfactory (CN1) and optic (CN2) nerves differ anatomically from the other cranial nerves because neither one is a true peripheral nerve or has a nucleus located in the brainstem.

The function of the cranial nerves may be impaired by supranuclear lesions (involving central connections to the cranial nerves), nuclear lesions, or infranuclear lesions (involving the peripheral nerve). The cranial nerve examination tests the status of the individual nerves and the integrity of these pathways through straightforward procedures requiring minimal time and equipment. Because each nerve has a right and left component, each side is tested separately and compared. When dysfunction is found, characteristics of the cranial nerve deficit may provide clues to localize the site of the lesion or indicate the need for further diagnostic testing. For example, a lesion between the motor cortex and the cranial nerve nucleus (upper motor neuron) will cause weakness without atrophy along with increased reflexes (spastic paralysis). A lesion to a somatic motor nerve after it exits the cranial nucleus (lower motor neuron) will produce weakness with muscle atrophy and diminished or absent reflexes (flaccid paralysis). Thus, knowledge of the anatomy and routes of the cranial nerves can be valuable in localizing diseases within the central nervous system and also in the diagnosis of systemic disease.

The trochlear nerve (CN4) innervates the superior oblique muscle, which plays a role in intorting, depressing, and abducting the eye. It is the only cranial nerve that exits the brainstem dorsally. This section describes the evaluation of the trochlear (CN4) nerve. The remaining cranial nerves are discussed in the previous and subsequent cranial nerve sections.

Ocular motility testing assesses the somatic motor portion of the oculomotor nerve (CN3), which innervates the medial rectus, superior rectus, inferior rectus, and inferior oblique extraocular muscles. It also evaluates the function of the superior oblique muscle, innervated by the trochlear nerve (CN4), and lateral rectus muscle, innervated by the abducens nerve (CN6).

The Parks three-step test can be used to isolate the superior oblique muscle when motility testing is positive and a vertical deviation is present. In this test, the examiner determines the more hyper-deviated eye in three different head positions until the dysfunctional muscle is isolated.

■ **Instrumentation.** Fixation target.

■ **Technique.** To test ocular motility, ask the patient to follow a fixation target, held approximately 40 cm in front of the face, through the nine cardinal positions of gaze, noting if the eyes lose alignment at any time (Fig. 1). Also ask the patient to report if the target doubles. A red lens and/or maddox rod may also be used to elicit diplopia and, in conjunction with a prism bar, to measure the extent of a paretic muscle.

To assess the Parks three-step test, place a red lens over the patient's right eye to further dissociate the images. Ask the patient to look at a distant light source such as an isolated spot from a projector acuity chart or a halogen transilluminator held across the room. While in primary gaze, ask the patient to report which image is higher, the red image (seen by the right eye) or white image (seen by the left eye) (Fig. 2). The higher image

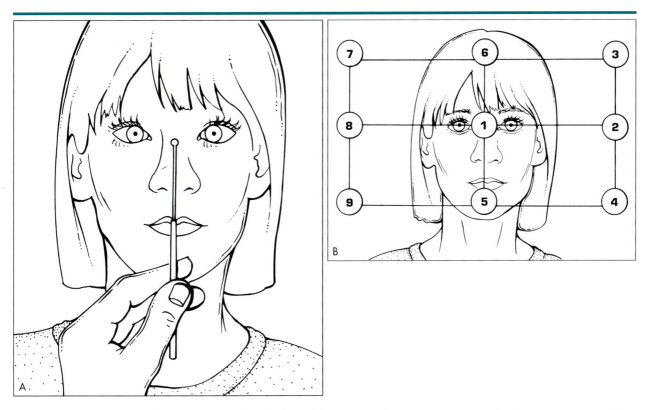

1. Ocular motility testing. A. A fixation target is placed in front of the patient in the primary position. B. The fixation target is moved in the nine cardinal positions of gaze.

2. Step one of the Parks three-step test: primary gaze position. The patient fixates a distant light source while holding a red lens over the right eye and is asked to report whether the red or white image is higher.

corresponds to the lower eye. This step narrows the possible paretic muscles from eight to four. Next ask the patient to turn his or her head to the left and look ahead, so he or she is effectively gazing to the right (Fig. 3A). Repeat this step with the patient's head turned to the right (gaze left) (Fig. 3B). Ask the patient which position caused the images to become more vertically misaligned. Record the position of gaze, not the direction of the head turn. This eliminates two more muscles. Lastly, ask the patient to tilt the head to the right while looking straight ahead (Fig. 4A). Repeat this with the head tilted to the left, again asking the patient to report which position causes the images to become more separated (Fig. 4B). If the superior oblique muscle is paretic, this step will isolate the muscle when the head is tilted to the same side as the eye with the paretic muscle. For example, with a right fourth-nerve palsy, tilting the head toward the right causes the images to be further separated.

If the patient is not able to identify or verbalize the relative locations of the red and white images, distance cover testing may be performed in the various head positions to determine the hyper-deviation. If necessary, prism bar neutralization may be used to quantify the comparisons.

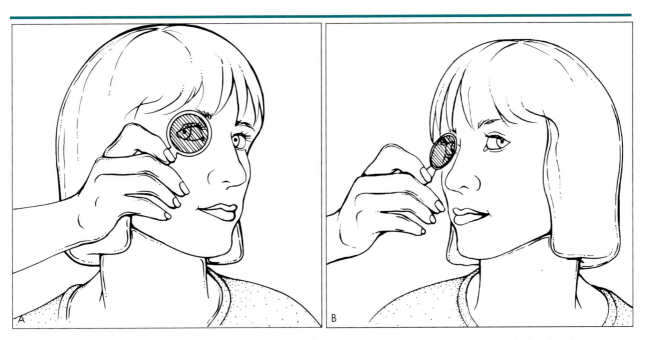

3. Step two of the Parks three-step test: Gaze right (A) and left (B) are simulated by asking the patient to turn the head to the opposite side. The patient is asked to compare the images in right and left gaze and report in which position the separation of the red and white images is greater.

4. Step three of the Parks three-step test: Head tilt right (A) and left (B). The patient is asked to compare the separation of the red and white images with the head tilted to the right and left and to report in which position the separation is greater.

■ **Interpretation.** Superior oblique muscle weakness causes the affected eye to assume an extorted position due to the unopposed action of the inferior oblique muscle. The vertical position of the eye depends on which eye is fixating. When the paretic eye fixates, it will be hypertropic, and when the nonparetic eye fixates, it will be hypotropic. Over time, the vertical deviation may decrease due to inferior oblique muscle overaction, subsequent contracture, and eventual spread of the deviation to other fields of gaze. When tested, the deviation will be the same with either eye fixating.

The patient with a fourth-nerve palsy will often assume a characteristic head tilt toward the unaffected side (Fig. 5A). This causes the normal eye to intort and align with the extorted eye to maintain single vision. Tilting the head toward the same side as the dysfunctional muscle will worsen the diplopia (Fig. 5B). Ocular motility testing will reveal weakness of downward and lateral gaze, and the results of the Park's three-step test can be used to isolate the superior oblique muscle (Fig. 6).

Similar to other oculomotor palsies, the site of damage must be localized to the muscle, neuromuscular junction, or nerve when superior oblique dysfunction is found. Testing and clinical considerations are similar to those discussed in the section on interpretation of oculomotor nerve palsy (see p. 316).

Congenital trochlear nerve palsies and trauma are the most common causes of trochlear nerve dysfunction. These may often also be bilateral. Other causes of trochlear nerve paresis include ischemia (e.g., diabetes), tumor, aneurysm, and demyelination.

■ **Contraindications/Complications.** These tests present no risks to the patient. Caution should be used when performing the Park's three-step test in patients with neck disorders.

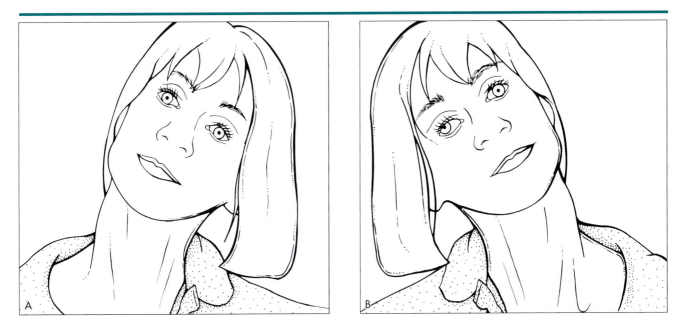

5. Right trochlear nerve palsy. A. When the head is tilted toward the opposite (left) shoulder, the patient attains single vision. B. When the head is tilted toward the same shoulder as the superior oblique palsy, the vertical deviation and diplopia are worsened.

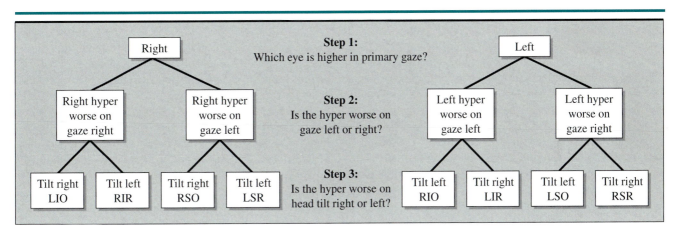

6. The Park's three-step test is used to isolate the muscle causing the hyper-deviation as listed at the bottom of the flowchart.

81 Trigeminal Nerve (CN5) Examination

■ **Description/Indications.** The cranial nerves provide motor and sensory innervation to the head and neck. Ten of the twelve cranial nerves (CN3 to CN12) have nuclei that originate within the brainstem (see p. 311), and after they exit, travel a specific pathway to their final destinations. The olfactory (CN1) and optic (CN2) nerves differ anatomically from the other cranial nerves because neither one is a true peripheral nerve or has a nucleus located in the brainstem.

The function of the cranial nerves may be impaired by supranuclear lesions (involving central connections to the cranial nerves), nuclear lesions, or infranuclear lesions (involving the peripheral nerve). The cranial nerve examination tests the status of the individual nerves and the integrity of these pathways through straightforward procedures requiring minimal time and equipment. Because each nerve has a right and left component, each side is tested separately and compared. When dysfunction is found, characteristics of the cranial nerve deficit may provide clues to localize the site of the lesion or indicate the need for further diagnostic testing. For example, a lesion between the motor cortex and the cranial nerve nucleus (upper motor neuron) will cause weakness without atrophy along with increased reflexes (spastic paralysis). A lesion to a somatic motor nerve after it exits the cranial nucleus (lower motor neuron) will produce weakness with muscle atrophy and diminished or absent reflexes (flaccid paralysis). Thus, knowledge of the anatomy and routes of the cranial nerves can be valuable in localizing diseases within the central nervous system and also in the diagnosis of systemic disease.

The trigeminal nerve (CN5 or "V") has both somatic sensory and somatic motor functions that are tested separately as part of the cranial nerve examination. The sensory portion of the trigeminal nerve has three divisions (Fig. 1): ophthalmic (V1), maxillary (V2), and mandibular (V3). The external dermatomes supplied by these sensory divisions are tested using light touch and pain sensations. The motor portion of the trigeminal nerve controls jaw movement. Jaw weakness may result from upper motor neuron (e.g., from

the motor cortex to the trigeminal nucleus) or lower motor neuron lesions. Characteristics typical of upper motor neuron lesions (e.g., increased reflexes, normal muscle mass) and lower motor neuron lesions (e.g., diminished reflexes, muscle atrophy) should be sought during the examination to help determine the site of the lesion.

This section describes the evaluation of the sensory and motor components of the trigeminal nerve. The remaining cranial nerves are discussed in the previous and subsequent cranial nerve sections. Testing of the infraorbital nerve, a branch of V2, is discussed on p. 284.

■ **Instrumentation.** Sharp and blunt objects (e.g., a safety pin and cotton-tipped applicator), reflex hammer.

■ **Technique.**

CN5—Trigeminal Nerve, Somatic Sensory: Prior to testing, advise the patient that you are going to be testing facial sensation. Demonstrate dull and sharp in the palm of the patient's hand using the dull and sharp ends of a safety pin or a wooden cotton-tipped applicator broken in half. Next, instruct the patient to shut the eyes and tell you whether a sharp or dull sensation is felt when the object is lightly touched to the facial skin. Randomly test all three divisions of the trigeminal nerve on the right and left sides, alternating sharp and dull (Fig. 1). If hypoesthesia is found in any area, thoroughly test that division with both modalities to determine the extent of dysfunction.

Sensory innervation from the cornea via V1 and motor innervation from the facial nerve to the orbicularis oculi muscles form the corneal reflex. A wisp of cotton pulled out from a cotton-tip applicator is used to test the reflex. Instruct the patient to look up and away so he or she does not see the cotton strand coming toward the eye and also to avoid a reflex blink. Touch the center of the right cornea with the cotton. Repeat the procedure on the left eye. Alternatively, ask the patient to compare relative corneal sensation on the right and left sides. Because sensitivity varies across the cornea, touch approximately the same position on each side.

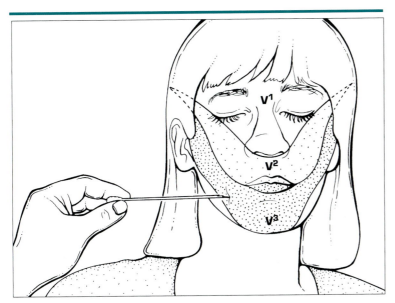

1. The sensory divisions of the trigeminal nerve: ophthalmic (V1), maxillary (V2), and mandibular (V3). With the eyes shut, the patient is asked to report whether a sharp or dull sensation is felt. Randomly test all three divisions on the right and left sides, alternately touching the dull and sharp ends of a wooden cotton-tipped applicator broken in half.

CN5—Trigeminal, Somatic Motor: Instruct the patient to clench the teeth tightly while you palpate each masseter muscle (Fig. 2A). Next ask the patient to open the mouth and look for deviation of the jaw to the right or left side (Fig. 2B). Lastly, ask the patient to forcefully move the jaw to the right side while you push against it (Fig. 2C). Repeat on the left side and compare the relative strength of each side.

The jaw jerk is a monosynaptic reflex that is tested if weakness of the jaw is noted. Ask the patient to relax the jaw and allow the mouth to hang open slightly. Place your index finger on the midline of the mandible below the lower lip. Tap your finger with the reflex hammer (Fig. 3).

■ **Interpretation.** If the sensory portion of the trigeminal nerve is damaged, symptoms may include loss or altered sensation in parts of the eye, face, and/or head. Testing each division carefully and localizing the exact area of decreased sensation is necessary. The sensory nucleus of the trigeminal nerve runs the length of the brainstem, and sensory modalities (proprioception, touch, pain, and temperature) are separated within it by function. Therefore, once abnormal pain and/or touch sensation are found, further information regarding the lesion site may be obtained by testing the other sensory modalities (e.g., proprioception).

Loss of the corneal reflex is often the first sign of damage to the trigeminal nerve, specifically to the ophthalmic division. When corneal sensitivity is reduced (see p. 184), testing the involved cornea will fail to produce prompt, complete lid closure of both eyes. When the normal cornea is tested and the motor portion of the reflex is intact, bilateral lid closure will occur. The patient may be aware of subtle changes in corneal sensitivity; therefore he or she should be asked if there is a subjective difference in corneal sensitivity.

With upper motor neuron damage to the trigeminal nerve, weakness of the jaw muscles will be present and the jaw will deviate in the direction of the weak side. The lesion will be on the side opposite the direction of jaw deviation because of the decussation of motor fibers. Muscle bulk will not be lost. If the lower motor neurons are damaged, the jaw will deviate toward the side of the lesion and atrophy of the muscles will occur.

The jaw jerk reflex also provides information regarding the type of lesion. This reflex is absent or very mild in the normal population. With supranuclear damage (from the motor cortex and pyramidal tract prior to the trigeminal nucleus), this reflex will be exaggerated. If it is a lower motor neuron lesion (between the trigeminal nucleus and the muscle), the reflex will be absent.

The motor fibers and the mandibular portion of the trigeminal separate from the rest of the nerve before it enters the cavernous sinus. Therefore lesions proximal to this location usually involve the motor and all sensory divisions. A lesion distal to this point will spare the motor fibers and sensation to the chin area (distribution of V3).

Vascular lesions, neoplasms, degenerative changes, or inflammatory disease may damage either the supranuclear pathway or trigeminal nucleus. Peripheral nerve involvement may involve the sensory or motor fibers, or both. Trauma is often the etiology in such cases. Each of the divisions is prone to trauma in different locations (e.g., ophthalmic during sinus surgery, maxillary in blowout fractures).

■ **Contraindications/Complications.** These tests present no risks to the patient. Care should be taken when performing corneal sensitivity testing in the presence of corneal disruption or external ocular infection.

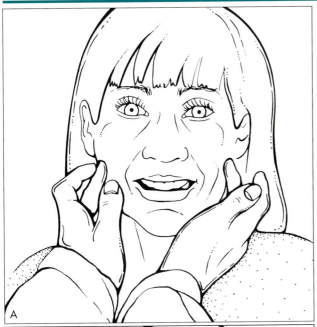

2. Evaluating the musculature of the jaw. A. The patient is asked to clench the jaw tightly while the examiner palpates the masseter muscles on each side. B. The patient is asked to open the jaw. C. The patient is asked to push the jaw against the resistance of the examiner's hand.

3. Jaw jerk reflex. The patient is asked to relax the jaw and open the mouth slightly. The examiner rests his or her index finger against the patient's chin and taps the finger gently with a reflex hammer.

82

Abducens Nerve (CN6) Examination

■ **Description/Indications.** The cranial nerves provide motor and sensory innervation to the head and neck. Ten of the twelve cranial nerves (CN3 to C12) have nuclei that originate within the brainstem (see p. 311), and after they exit, travel a specific pathway to their final destinations. The olfactory (CN1) and optic (CN2) nerves differ anatomically from the other cranial nerves because neither one is a true peripheral nerve or has a nucleus located in the brainstem.

The function of the cranial nerves may be impaired by supranuclear lesions (involving central connections to the cranial nerves), nuclear lesions, or infranuclear lesions (involving the peripheral nerve). The cranial nerve examination tests the status of the individual nerves and the integrity of these pathways through straightforward procedures requiring minimal time and equipment. Because each nerve has a right and left component, each side is tested separately and compared. When dysfunction is found, characteristics of the cranial nerve deficit may provide clues to localize the site of the lesion or indicate the need for further diagnostic testing. For example, a lesion between the motor cortex and the cranial nerve nucleus (upper motor neuron) will cause weakness without atrophy along with increased reflexes (spastic paralysis). A lesion to a somatic motor nerve after it exits the cranial nucleus (lower motor neuron) will produce weakness with muscle atrophy and diminished or absent reflexes (flaccid paralysis). Thus, knowledge of the anatomy and routes of the cranial nerves can be valuable in localizing diseases within the central nervous system and also in the diagnosis of systemic disease.

The abducens nerve (CN6) innervates the lateral rectus muscle, which abducts each eye. This section describes the evaluation of the abducens nerve. The remaining cranial nerves are discussed in the previous and subsequent cranial nerve sections.

■ **Instrumentation.** Fixation target.

■ **Technique.** Ocular motility testing assesses the somatic motor portion of the oculomotor nerve (CN3), which innervates the medial rectus, superior rectus, inferior rectus, and inferior oblique extraocular muscles. It also evaluates the function of the superior oblique muscle, innervated by the trochlear nerve (CN4), and lateral rectus muscle, innervated by the abducens nerve (CN6).

Ask the patient to follow a fixation target, held approximately 40 cm in front of the face, through the nine cardinal positions of gaze, noting if the eyes lose alignment at any time (Fig. 1). Also ask the patient to report if the target doubles. A red lens and/or maddox rod may also be used to elicit diplopia and, in conjunction with a prism bar, to measure the extent of a paretic muscle.

The doll's-head (oculocephalic) maneuver may be used in infants or developmentally delayed patients who are not capable of following a fixation target. Instruct the patient to fixate straight ahead or use an engaging fixation target (e.g., small toy or hand puppet) to maintain attention. Turn the patient's head to the left to test gaze-right horizontal eye movements, and vice versa.

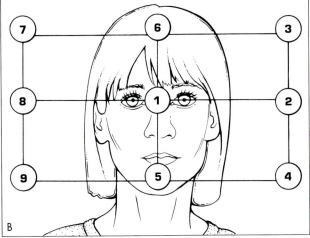

1. Ocular motility testing. A. A fixation target is placed in front of the patient in the primary position. B. The fixation target is moved in the nine cardinal positions of gaze.

■ **Interpretation.** A sixth-nerve palsy causes horizontal diplopia that is worse at distance than near. The diplopia will be reduced if the patient turns the head toward the side of the lesion. Esotropia will be more obvious in distance gaze, and ocular motility testing will reveal a partial or complete inability to abduct due to lateral rectus muscle weakness (Fig. 2).

When lateral rectus muscle dysfunction is found, the lesion site should be localized to the muscle, neuromuscular junction, or nerve. Specific tests of ocular motility may provide clues to help make the differential diagnosis. When saccades are performed and the weakness is due to a muscle problem (e.g., muscle entrapment), the eye will come to an abrupt halt when moving into the field of action of the paretic muscle. If muscle weakness is due to a nerve palsy, the paretic eye glides into the field of action of the dysfunctional muscle, called a glissade. Comparing ductions and versions may also provide useful information. When there is muscle dysfunction (e.g., muscle restriction), ductions and versions will be equal. If weakness is due to neural damage, ductions will be better than versions owing to Herring's law of equal innervation. A muscular deficit can be confirmed through forced duction testing (see p. 302).

Defects at the neuromuscular junction may also cause impaired abduction. Variability of the diplopia and worsening with fatigue are key signs of neuromuscular disorders. Sleep, ice pack, Tensilon, or acetylcholine receptor antibody testing may be used to provide evidence for dysfunction at the neuromuscular junction.

The sixth nerve is the most frequently damaged ocular motor nerve. In adults, common causes of dysfunction include ischemia (e.g., hypertension or diabetes), trauma, lumbar puncture or spinal anesthesia, increased intracranial pressure, neoplasms (metastatic or primary), and infection. In children, infection, trauma, and tumors are among the more common causes.

■ **Contraindications/Complications.** Ocular motility testing presents no risks to the patient. The doll's-head maneuver must be performed with caution or avoided in patients with neck injury.

2. This patient with right abducens nerve palsy exhibits a deficit of abduction on attempted right gaze during ocular motility testing due to lateral rectus muscle weakness.

Facial Nerve (CN7) Examination

■ **Description/Indications.** The cranial nerves provide motor and sensory innervation to the head and neck. Ten of the twelve cranial nerves (CN3 to CN12) have nuclei that originate within the brainstem (see p. 311), and after they exit, travel a specific pathway to their final destinations. The olfactory (CN1) and optic (CN2) nerves differ anatomically from the other cranial nerves because neither one is a true peripheral nerve or has a nucleus located in the brainstem.

The function of the cranial nerves may be impaired by supranuclear lesions (involving central connections to the cranial nerves), nuclear lesions, or infranuclear lesions (involving the peripheral nerve). The cranial nerve examination tests the status of the individual nerves and the integrity of these pathways through straightforward procedures requiring minimal time and equipment. Because each nerve has a right and left component, each side is tested separately and compared. When dysfunction is found, characteristics of the cranial nerve deficit may provide clues to localize the site of the lesion or indicate the need for further diagnostic testing. For example, a lesion between the motor cortex and the cranial nerve nucleus (upper motor neuron) will cause weakness without atrophy along with increased reflexes (spastic paralysis). A lesion to a somatic motor nerve after it exits the cranial nucleus (lower motor neuron) will produce weakness with muscle atrophy and diminished or absent reflexes (flaccid paralysis). Thus, knowledge of the anatomy and routes of the cranial nerves can be valuable in localizing diseases within the central nervous system and also in the diagnosis of systemic disease.

The primary function of the facial nerve (CN7) is to control the muscles of facial expression, including the frontalis, orbicularis oculi, orbicularis oris, and buccinator muscles. The facial nerve also carries taste from the anterior two thirds of the tongue, and provides parasympathetic innervation to the lacrimal and salivary glands.

This section describes the evaluation of the facial nerve. The other cranial nerves are discussed in the previous and subsequent cranial nerve sections.

■ **Instrumentation.** Salt, sugar, tongue depressors or forceps, paper towel.

■ **Technique.** To test the frontalis muscle, instruct the patient to look up or wrinkle the forehead (Fig. 1A). The orbicularis oculi muscles are tested by asking the patient to shut his or her eyes tightly and resist as you attempt to pry them open (Fig. 1B). Compare the strength on each side and determine if one or both eyes can be pried open. To test the orbicularis oris muscle, ask the patient to smile or purse the lips (Fig. 1C). Lastly, instruct the patient to frown or pull down the corners of the mouth to test the function of the buccinator muscles (Fig. 1D). In each set of muscles, note the presence or absence of symmetry.

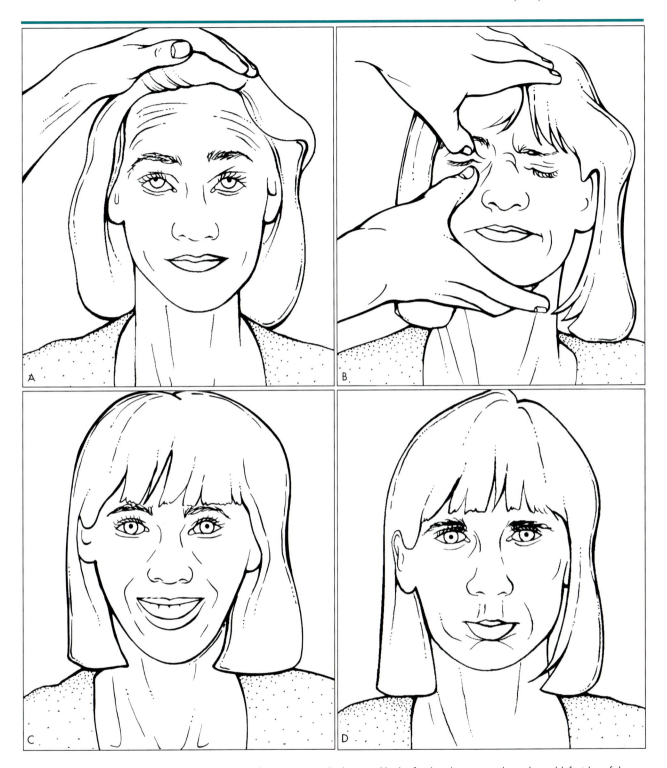

1. Evaluating the muscles of facial expression. A. The patient is asked to wrinkle the forehead to assess the right and left sides of the frontalis muscle. B. To test the orbicularis oculi muscles, the patient is asked to shut the eyes tightly and resist as the examiner attempts to open each of them. C. To assess the orbicularis oris muscle, the patient is asked to smile. D. The patient is asked to frown or pull down the corners of the mouth to evaluate the buccinator muscles.

When muscle weakness is found, taste can be tested to help localize the site of the lesion (Fig. 2). Advise the patient you will be testing his or her ability to identify a taste on the tongue. Blot the tongue dry with a paper towel and place a few crystals of salt or sugar on the anterior portion of the right side using forceps or a tongue depressor. Gently rub the crystals with a tongue depressor to dissolve them. Ask the patient to identify the taste. Repeat on the left side of the tongue using the same or different taste.

■ **Interpretation.** Marked asymmetry of the face is usually obvious on inspection when facial nerve damage is present, especially when it occurs at the level of the lower motor neuron. A patient with a lower motor neuron facial palsy will have unilateral diminished forehead furrowing, ptosis, flattened nasolabial fold, and drooping of the mouth and lips. When the patient tries to forcibly close the eyes, the eyelids will remain open on the weakened side. The patient may have epiphora if the puncta are malpositioned and unable to drain the tears. Evidence of exposure keratitis from incomplete blink due to orbicularis oculi weakness may also be present. If the patient attempts to smile, the weakened side of the mouth will not be drawn back, and he or she will be unable to frown or pucker the lips in an attempt to whistle. Eating may be problematic due to food collecting between the cheek and gums.

Bell's palsy, or idiopathic facial nerve paresis, is the most common type of facial nerve injury. This manifests clinically as complete paralysis to one half of the facial musculature (Fig. 3). Taste and salivary function may or may not be affected. Other causes of seventh-nerve damage are variable and include infection (e.g., herpes zoster, Lyme disease), ischemia (e.g., diabetes), demyelination, neoplasms, vascular lesions (e.g., stroke), and trauma (e.g., basal skull fracture or peripheral nerve injury).

When a lower motor neuron facial palsy is diagnosed, further testing can help localize the anatomical site of the lesion. Weakness of a group of facial muscles or one isolated facial muscle indicates the site of the lesion is distal to the stylomastoid foramen. Weakness of the facial muscles only (the somatic motor portion) with all other nerve functions intact localizes the lesion past the exit of the chorda tympani nerve and prior to the stylomastoid foramen. If taste and salivary gland function are decreased on the ipsilateral side, the lesion site is probably between the branch to the stapedius muscle and chorda tympani nerve. Hyperacusia (increased hearing on one side) may also be present if the nerve to the stapedius muscle (which dampens excessive movement of the ossicles) is involved. This helps to localize the lesion to a point between the geniculate ganglion and the branch to the stapedius muscle. The Schirmer tear test should be done if symptoms of decreased taste, salivary function, and increased hearing are found. If decreased tear function is found on the involved side, it provides evidence of a lesion in the internal auditory canal. An eighth cranial nerve palsy may also occur with a lesion in the internal auditory canal (see p. 340).

Facial asymmetry due to upper motor neuron damage is not as obvious as lower motor neuron damage because the upper portion of the head is innervated bilaterally from the cortex. Therefore the forehead can still be elevated on both sides in the presence of upper motor neuron damage. Fibers from the cortex that innervate the lower portion of the face decussate and, as a result, upper motor neuron (cortical) lesions (e.g., infarction) cause facial paresis to the lower facial muscles on the opposite side. There is also some bilateral innervation to the lower facial musculature and therefore there will be less weakness in upper motor neuron damage than in lower motor neuron facial nerve palsy. Facial contour will remain normal because muscles do not undergo atrophy with upper motor neuron damage. Emotional facial movements follow a somewhat different pathway than volitional movements. These movements (emotional or mimetic facial movements) may be retained with an upper motor neuron lesion, so that the face may appear to be innervated normally when the patient is conversing animatedly.

■ **Contraindications/Complications.** These tests present no risks to the patient. Care should be taken when forcibly opening the eyelids of a patient in the presence of inflammation or trauma of the surrounding adnexa.

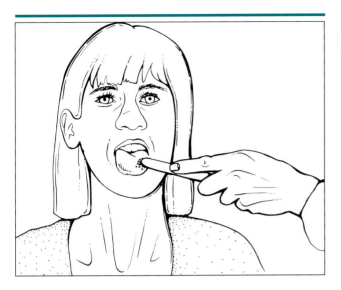

2. Taste is tested by rubbing salt or sugar crystals on each side of the tongue with a tongue depressor. Repeat on the right side of the tongue.

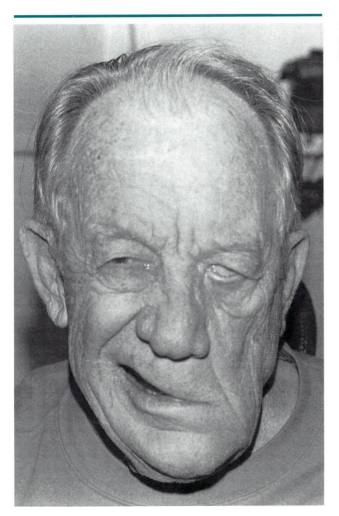

3. A patient is shown with a left Bell's palsy, or idiopathic facial paralysis, which affects all of the muscles of facial expression on one half of the face.

84 Acoustic Nerve (CN8) Examination

■ **Description/Indications.** The cranial nerves provide motor and sensory innervation to the head and neck. Ten of the twelve cranial nerves (CN3 to CN12) have nuclei that originate within the brainstem (see p. 311), and after they exit, travel a specific pathway to their final destinations. The olfactory (CN1) and optic (CN2) nerves differ anatomically from the other cranial nerves because neither one is a true peripheral nerve or has a nucleus located in the brainstem.

The function of the cranial nerves may be impaired by supranuclear lesions (involving central connections to the cranial nerves), nuclear lesions, or infranuclear lesions (involving the peripheral nerve). The cranial nerve examination tests the status of the individual nerves and the integrity of these pathways through straightforward procedures requiring minimal time and equipment. Because each nerve has a right and left component, each side is tested separately and compared. When dysfunction is found, characteristics of the cranial nerve deficit may provide clues to localize the site of the lesion or indicate the need for further diagnostic testing. For example, a lesion between the motor cortex and the cranial nerve nucleus (upper motor neuron) will cause weakness without atrophy along with increased reflexes (spastic paralysis). A lesion to a somatic motor nerve after it exits the cranial nucleus (lower motor neuron) will produce weakness with muscle atrophy and diminished or absent reflexes (flaccid paralysis). Thus, knowledge of the anatomy and routes of the cranial nerves can be valuable in localizing diseases within the central nervous system and also in the diagnosis of systemic disease.

The acoustic nerve (CN8) transmits information related to hearing and equilibrium from the special sensory organs located in the inner ear. A low-frequency sound stimulus, such as that made by a ticking watch or by rubbing the thumb and index fingers together, can be used to grossly test hearing. When a difference in hearing acuity is noted, further testing is necessary to determine if the dysfunction is due to a neural or conduction deficit. Both the Weber and Rhinne tests, which use a low-frequency (256 CPS) tuning fork, will help to localize the deficit by testing the relative efficiency of bone and air conduction to sound vibrations.

This section describes the in-office evaluation of the acoustic nerve. The other cranial nerves are discussed in the previous and subsequent cranial nerve sections.

■ **Instrumentation.** Ticking watch, tuning fork.

■ **Technique.** To assess hearing, instruct the patient to close the eyes, and hold a ticking watch approximately 40 cm from the patient's right ear. Move the watch toward the ear (Fig. 1). Ask the patient to report when he or she first hears the sound. Note the distance from the ear. Repeat the procedure on the left side, again noting at what distance the patient can detect the sound.

To perform the Rhinne test, generate vibration of the tuning fork by striking it on a firm but not rigid object (e.g., the side of the first knuckle of your index finger). Place the vibrating tuning fork on the mastoid process behind the right ear (Fig. 2A). Instruct the patient to tell you when the sound is no longer heard. Once the patient can no longer hear it, move the still-vibrating tuning fork next to the right ear (Fig. 2B). Ask if the patient can again hear it. Strike the tuning fork again and repeat on the left side.

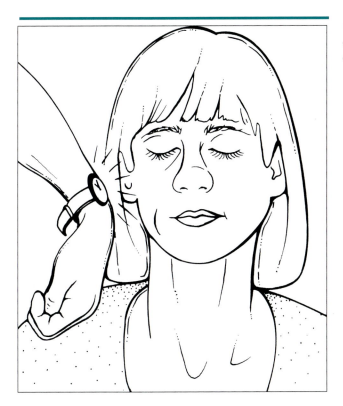

1. To test hearing, the patient is asked to shut the eyes and respond when the sound of a ticking watch is heard as it is brought toward the ear.

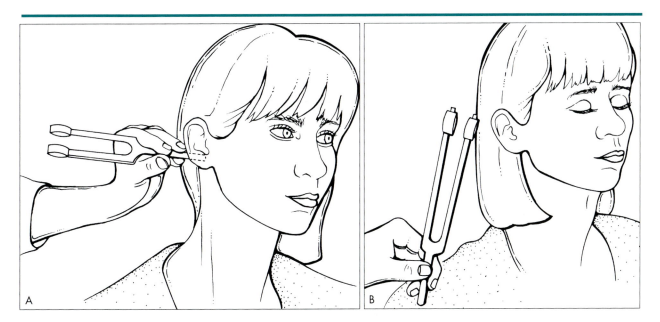

A

B

2. Rhinne test. A. vibrating tuning fork is held on the mastoid process behind the ear and the patient is asked to report when the sound is no longer heard. B. The still-vibrating fork is then moved beside the ear and the patient is asked if the sound continues to be heard.

The Weber test compares bone conduction within each side of the head. Place the vibrating tuning fork on the center of the forehead (Fig. 3). Ask the patient to report if the sound is heard more loudly on either side.

■ **Interpretation.** Decreased hearing may be due to sensorineural damage or conduction loss. Therefore, if a problem with hearing is found, further testing will help localize the site of the lesion. Sensorineural loss may be caused by disease of the cochlea, cochlear nerve, or nuclei, or the central pathways for hearing. Conduction deficits are due to interference in the transmission of sound within the internal auditory canal.

Unilateral decreased hearing may be caused by a number of mechanisms. Conduction deafness may be caused by obstruction to the auditory canal by cerumen or other substances located against the tympanic membrane, a foreign body inserted into the auditory canal, tympanic membrane perforation, or middle ear infection. The peripheral portion of the acoustic nerve can be injured, involving both the cochlear and vestibular nerves. Also, decreased hearing may be caused by a central lesion, which can damage either nerve separately, or both. A major disorder affecting both hearing and balance is Ménière's disease, a syndrome characterized by episodes of severe vertigo associated with deafness and tinnitus caused by edema of the labyrinths (composed of the semicircular canal, the saccule, and the utricle). More common causes of sensorineural loss at the peripheral nerve involving both vestibular and cochlear nerves include otitis media, meningitis, skull fracture, otosclerosis, basal tumors, and infectious or degenerative diseases. Acoustic neuroma, a tumor of the eighth cranial nerve, may additionally damage the seventh cranial nerve.

The Rhinne test is considered negative or normal if the sound is still heard after the fork is removed from the mastoid process and placed beside the ear. If hearing loss is sensorineural, the Rhinne test will remain negative. If hearing loss is the result of a conduction deficit, the Rhinne test will be positive (the sound will not be heard when the fork is next to the ear), because bone conduction has been increased and is now greater than air conduction. With sensorineural hearing loss, the Weber test will be lateralized (sound heard louder) to the side that hears better. If there is a conduction deficit, the sound from the tuning fork will be heard more loudly on the same side with decreased hearing.

The vestibular nerve (a branch of the acoustic nerve) and the structures it innervates (the semicircular canals, saccule and utricle of the inner ear) are responsible for equilibrium, coordination, and orientation in space. They provide positional information about the head and correlate head and eye movements with somatic muscle activity. This portion of the eighth cranial nerve is usually not evaluated during routine testing. However, if sensorineural hearing loss is found, it is important to ascertain if the vestibular nerve is also involved. With vestibular nerve damage the patient may experience symptoms such as dizziness, vertigo, oscillopsia, nausea, and anxiety. These are similar to the symptoms of motion sickness. Signs of vestibular nerve dysfunction include nystagmus, postural deviation, sweating, pallor, vomiting, and hypotension.

The oculocephalic reflex (doll's-head phenomenon) may be induced to evaluate vestibular function. The patient's head is moved by the examiner from side to side or up and down (pg. 318). The normal response is an involuntary conjugate deviation of the eyes in the direction opposite the head movement. Nystagmus may be noted during this maneuver in a patient with vestibular nerve damage. Caloric irrigation and tests for postural deviation or past pointing are often done in a neurological examination to elicit further information regarding the vestibular nerve.

■ **Contraindications/Complications.** These tests present no risks to the patient. Caution should be used in performing the doll's-head maneuver in patients with neck injury.

3. Weber test: The vibrating tuning fork is placed on the center of the forehead, and the patient is asked if the sound is heard equally in each ear or if it is greater on one side.

85 Glossopharyngeal Nerve (CN9) and Vagus Nerve (CN10) Examination

■ **Description/Indications.** The cranial nerves provide motor and sensory innervation to the head and neck. Ten of the twelve cranial nerves (CN3 to CN12) have nuclei that originate within the brainstem (see p. 311), and after they exit, travel a specific pathway to their final destinations. The olfactory (CN1) and optic (CN2) nerves differ anatomically from the other cranial nerves because neither one is a true peripheral nerve or has a nucleus located in the brainstem.

The function of the cranial nerves may be impaired by supranuclear lesions (involving central connections to the cranial nerves), nuclear lesions, or infranuclear lesions (involving the peripheral nerve). The cranial nerve examination tests the status of the individual nerves and the integrity of these pathways through straightforward procedures requiring minimal time and equipment. Because each nerve has a right and left component, each side is tested separately and compared. When dysfunction is found, characteristics of the cranial nerve deficit may provide clues to localize the site of the lesion or indicate the need for further diagnostic testing. For example, a lesion between the motor cortex and the cranial nerve nucleus (upper motor neuron) will cause weakness without atrophy along with increased reflexes (spastic paralysis). A lesion to a somatic motor nerve after it exits the cranial nucleus (lower motor neuron) will produce weakness with muscle atrophy and diminished or absent reflexes (flaccid paralysis). Thus, knowledge of the anatomy and routes of the cranial nerves can be valuable in localizing diseases within the central nervous system and also in the diagnosis of systemic disease.

The glossopharyngeal nerve (CN9) supplies many internal body structures. It provides motor innervation to the stylopharyngeus muscle, which elevates the pharnyx during swallowing and speech. It supplies visceral motor innervation to the otic ganglion, which sends secreto-motor fibers to the parotid gland. It carries subconscious sensation from the carotid body and sinus as well as general sensation from parts of the tongue, tympanic membrane, and a small portion of the ear. The glossopharyngeal nerve stimulates taste in the posterior two thirds of the tongue.

The vagus nerve (CN10) is the longest cranial nerve and it also innervates numerous internal body structures. It provides motor innervation to striated and smooth muscles of the pharynx, larynx, and tongue, as well as the thoracic and abdominal viscera. It carries visceral sensory information from the larynx, trachea, esophagus, thoracic and abdominal viscera, aortic arch and aortic bodies. It also carries general sensory information from small parts of the ear and pharynx.

The vagus and glossopharyngeal nerves function together in many locations and are tested in tandem with one another. Swallowing (deglutition) and speech are primarily controlled by CN9 and CN10. They may both be assessed if dysfunction to either or both nerves is suspected. The gag reflex is also tested, because the sensory component is transmitted by the glossopharyngeal nerve and the motor portion by the vagus nerve.

This section describes the in-office evaluation of the glossopharyngeal and vagus nerves. Evaluation of the other cranial nerves is discussed in previous and subsequent cranial nerve sections.

■ **Instrumentation.** Tongue depressor, cotton-tipped applicator.

■ **Technique.** Instruct the patient to open the mouth and sustain an "ah" sound. Look at the arch formed by the tonsillar pillars (not the uvula in the center) and note the presence or absence of symmetry (Fig. 1). To test the

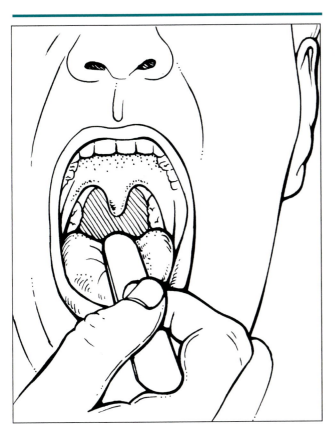

1. Evaluating the glossopharyngeal and vagus nerves. The elevated soft palate is observed as the patient phonates, noting the presence or absence of symmetry in the arch formed by the tonsillar pillars.

gag reflex, instruct the patient to open his/her mouth widely. Use a tongue depressor or cotton-tipped applicator to touch one side of the pharynx (Fig. 2A). The reflex consists of the prompt elevation of the soft palate, constriction of the pharyngeal muscles, and the sensation of gagging. Test the other side in the same manner, looking for elevation of both sides of the palatal arches. (Fig. 2B).

Appraise the patient's speech while conversing with him or her during the history and examination. If it is normal, there is no need for further testing. If dysarthria is noted or if the voice is hoarse, the "K-L-M" test may be done. Tell the patient to say, "kuh, kuh, kuh", "la, la, la", and "mi, mi, mi". The "kuh" sound tests the soft palate, innervated by CN9 and CN10. The "la" sound tests the tongue, innervated by CN12. The "mi" sound tests CN7, which innervates the lips.

Ask the patient if he or she has any difficulty swallowing. The patient can also be given a glass of water and asked to drink it. Watch for difficulty swallowing or regurgitation of fluid through the nose.

■ Interpretation

CN9—Glossopharyngeal Nerve: Dysfunction can cause loss of the gag reflex, slight dysphagia, loss of taste in the posterior one third of the tongue, loss of sensation in the pharynx, tonsils, uvula, and back of the tongue, and loss of constriction of the posterior pharyngeal wall when saying "ah." During the cranial nerve examination, glossopharyngeal dysfunction may be detected during gag reflex testing. When sensory input from the pharynx is decreased, the afferent division of this reflex is lost, and the motor response (bilateral elevation of the tonsillar pillars) does not occur.

The glossopharyngeal nerve is rarely injured in isolation; usually the vagus nerve is also involved. With a brainstem lesion involving the medulla, the hypoglossal nerve (CN12) (see p. 348) is also often affected because the nuclei of cranial nerves 9, 10 and 12 are situated nearby to one another. Possible causes of isolated glossopharyngeal nerve palsy include syphilis, tuberculosis, basal tumors, jugular vein thrombosis, trauma, and aneurysm at the circle of Willis. Compression, inflammation, and trauma may involve the glossopharyngeal as well as the vagus nerve.

CN10—Vagus Nerve: Motor signs of vagus nerve dysfunction include aphonia or dysphonia, dysphagia, and paralysis of the soft palate. Sensory signs may include pain or paresthesia of the pharynx, larynx, and external auditory meatus. The patient may sound hoarse or have a persistent cough. During the cranial nerve examination, deviation of the palatal arch may be noted so that the uvula shifts toward the unaffected side. The paretic side will fail to elevate following stimulation in gag reflex testing. When speech is tested, the patient may be unable to vocalize the "kuh" sound due to paresis of the vocal cords. Difficulty swallowing or regurgitation of fluid through the nose during drinking may also be evident.

Causes of nuclear injury are similar to those involving the glossopharyngeal nucleus. Peripheral vagus nerve damage may involve any portion of the nerve because its branches are widely distributed. Ischemia, space-occupying lesions, and trauma are possible etiologies of vagus nerve injury occurring anywhere along its long course.

■ Contraindications/Complications. These tests present no risks to the patient.

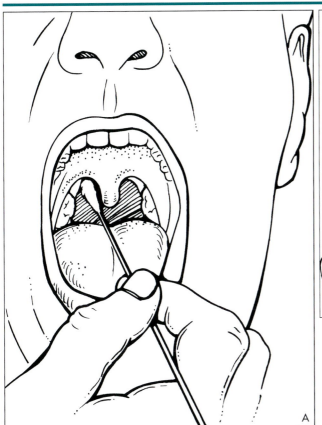

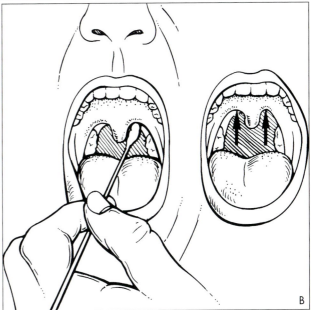

2. B. The other side of the pharyngeal wall is tested in the same manner, looking for elevation of both sides of the palatal arches (inset).

2. A. One side of the pharyngeal wall is touched to elicit the gag reflex looking for elevation of both palatal arches.

86 Accessory Nerve (CN11) and Hypoglossal Nerve (CN12) Examination

■ **Description/Indications.** The cranial nerves provide motor and sensory innervation to the head and neck. Ten of the twelve cranial nerves (CN3 to CN12) have nuclei that originate within the brainstem (see p. 311), and after they exit, travel a specific pathway to their final destinations. The olfactory (CN1) and optic (CN2) nerves differ anatomically from the other cranial nerves because neither one is a true peripheral nerve or has a nucleus located in the brainstem.

The function of the cranial nerves may be impaired by supranuclear lesions (involving central connections to the cranial nerves), nuclear lesions, or infranuclear lesions (involving the peripheral nerve). The cranial nerve examination tests the status of the individual nerves and the integrity of these pathways through straightforward procedures requiring minimal time and equipment. Because each nerve has a right and left component, each side is tested separately and compared. When dysfunction is found, characteristics of the cranial nerve deficit may provide clues to localize the site of the lesion or indicate the need for further diagnostic testing. For example, a lesion between the motor cortex and the cranial nerve nucleus (upper motor neuron) will cause weakness without atrophy along with increased reflexes (spastic paralysis). A lesion to a somatic motor nerve after it exits the cranial nucleus (lower motor neuron) will produce weakness with muscle atrophy and diminished or absent reflexes (flaccid paralysis). Thus, knowledge of the anatomy and routes of the cranial nerves can be valuable in localizing diseases within the central nervous system and also in the diagnosis of systemic disease.

The spinal accessory nerve (CN11) primarily innervates two muscles, the sternocleidomastoid muscle, coursing through the neck from the mastoid process to the medial end of the clavicle, and the trapezius muscle, coursing across the top of the shoulder. The hypoglossal nerve (CN12) innervates the muscles that control all tongue movements.

This section describes the in-office evaluation of the spinal accessory and hypoglossal nerves. Evaluation of the other cranial nerves is discussed in the previous cranial nerve sections.

■ **Instrumentation.** None.

■ **Technique.**

CN11—Accessory Nerve: To test the right sternocleidomastoid muscle, ask the patient to turn the head to the left and push against your resistance. At the same time, place your hand on the patient's left cheek and try to push the head toward the midline (Fig. 1A). Retest on the other side, comparing the relative muscular strength.

To evaluate the trapezius muscles, inspect the shoulders, noting if they are equal in appearance or if one is higher than the other. Next, instruct the patient to elevate the shoulders against your resistance. Place your hands on the shoulders and push down (Fig. 1B). Compare muscle strength on each side.

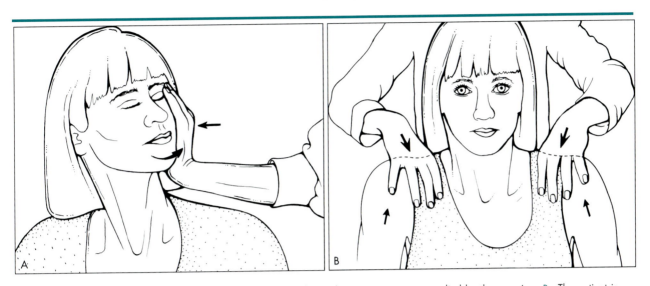

1. Testing the accessory nerve. A. The patient is asked to turn the neck against resistance applied by the examiner. B. The patient is asked to elevate the shoulders against resistance applied by the examiner.

CN12—Hypoglossal Nerve: Instruct the patient to stick his or her tongue out of the mouth (Fig. 2A). Inspect the bulk of each side of the tongue, and note if it protrudes toward one side. Also note the presence of any fasiculations (fine muscular twitching). Next, instruct the patient to stick the tongue to the right side of the mouth and try to push out the right cheek. Place your hand over the cheek and apply resistance (Fig. 2B). Repeat on the left side, noting relative tongue muscle strength on each side.

■ Interpretation.

CN11—Accessory Nerve: Paresis will manifest as weakness of the sternocleidomastoid and trapezius muscles. The most obvious evidence of sternocleidomastoid paresis is weakness of rotation when the patient is asked to turn the head against resistance. A difference in muscle strength will be evident when each side is compared. Lower motor neuron damage will also cause muscle atrophy. This may be evident when examining the tone, volume, and contour of the sternocleidomastoid muscle.

If the trapezius muscle is weak, the patient will have difficulty elevating the shoulder on the involved side and it will be weaker than the opposite side. The examiner will be able to push the weaker side down when tested. Muscle atrophy in a lower motor neuron lesion may also be noted as decreased shoulder volume and contour.

Common etiologies of accessory nerve dysfunction include trauma or neoplasms located at the base of the skull or neck. In these cases, the lower motor neurons will be affected to result in muscle atrophy and weakness. Upper motor neuron damage may be caused by conditions such as cerebral vascular accidents, degenerative disorders, neoplasms, or inflammatory conditions. In these cases, unilateral or bilateral muscle weakness will be found with retention of muscle bulk and contour.

CN12—Hypoglossal Nerve: Dysfunction manifests as weakness of the tongue. It is important to distinguish between lower motor neuron and upper motor neuron damage. If the lesion is located in the lower motor neuron, the tongue will deviate toward the side of the lesion and muscle atrophy will occur over time. Fasiculations may also be noted on the paretic side. Upper motor neuron innervation goes to the opposite hypoglossal nucleus. Therefore a lesion proximal to the hypoglossal nucleus will cause the tongue to protrude toward the opposite side. Atrophy or fasiculations will not be present in these cases.

Supranuclear and nuclear causes of hypoglossal nerve dysfunction include neoplasms and vascular lesions. Hypoglossal nerve injury may occur with trauma (e.g., neck wounds or during neck surgery), infections, or neoplasms involving the neck, tongue, or salivary glands.

■ Contraindications/Complications. These tests present no risks to the patient. Caution should be used when testing muscle strength in patients with neck or shoulder disorders.

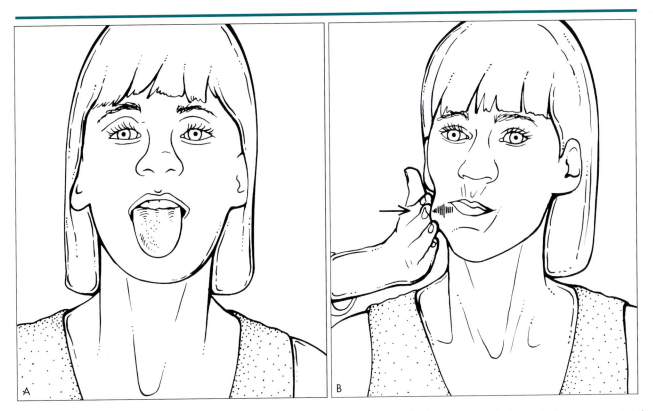

2. Testing hypoglossal nerve function. A. The patient is asked to stick out the tongue. B. The patient is asked to push the tongue against the inside of the cheek while the examiner applies resistance to the outside.

Suggested Readings

Dale R: *Fundamentals of Ocular Motility and Strabismus.* Grune and Stratton, New York, 1982.

DeJong R: *The Neurologic Examination,* ed 4. Harper & Row, Baltimore, 1979.

DeMeyer W: *Technique of the Neurologic Examination, A Programmed Text,* ed 2. McGraw-Hill, New York, 1974.

Muchnick BG: The neurologic examination, in Muchnick BG (ed): *Clinical Medicine in Optometric Practice.* St. Louis, Mosby, 1994, pp 22–36.

Newman NM: *Neuro-ophthalmology, A Practical Text.* Norwalk, CT, Appleton & Lange, 1992.

Thomann KH, Dul MW: The optometric assessment of neurologic function. *J Am Optom Assoc* 1993;**64:**421–431.

Wilson-Pauwels L, Akesson E, Stewart P: *Cranial Nerves, Anatomy and Clinical Comments.* BC Decker, Ontario, 1988.

XI

Preoperative and Postoperative Cataract Procedures

87

Potential Acuity Meter

■ **Description/Indications.** The assessment of retinal visual acuity through mild to moderate ocular media opacification may be performed with a potential acuity meter (PAM). Cataract and other surgical procedures that correct media opacification may be preceded by measurement of the potential visual acuity to prevent unnecessary procedures, surgical risks, and disappointing postoperative visual acuity.

The PAM uses a Maxwellian view optical system to project a bright miniature Snellen acuity chart onto the retina through an aperture of 0.1 mm (Fig. 1). This single beam can be directed through less dense or "window" areas of mild to moderate opacities to maximize beam transmission. The internally projected eyechart has letters ranging from 20/400 to 20/20 presented simultaneously. An additional numeric chart is also available. The patient identifies these familiar eyechart letters during testing for the examiner. Because the PAM depends entirely on the intensity of the light reaching the retina for best response, its reliability diminishes with increasing density of the cataract or other opacity.

The Guyton-Minkowski PAM (Fig. 2) is slit lamp mounted and portable, utilizing an incandescent light source. The projected Snellen chart is achromatically imaged and optically "folded" by internal condensing lenses and prisms. A spherical equivalent correction dial with −10 to +13 diopter powers is incorporated for best visual performance. This dioptric dial and an external Snellen chart for examiner viewing facilitate testing. The on–off switch and facial illumination knob are also located on this instrument panel.

■ **Instrumentation.** PAM, slit lamp, biomicroscope, topical ophthalmic mydriatic/cycloplegic solution(s).

■ **Technique.** Dilate the pupils with topical mydriatic/cycloplegic solution(s). With slit lamp retroillumination (see p. 32), scan the patient's dilated pupillary red reflex for clear "windows" or less dense opacification. Do not perform any prolonged "light" testing (such as binocular indirect ophthalmoscopy or photostress) before the procedure. Attach the PAM to the slit lamp following the manufacturer's guide. With the Haig-Streit-style slit lamp, this involves placing the mounting pin of the PAM into the focusing post hole, orienting its alignment notch with the slit lamp's alignment tab. Tighten the locking knob and plug the cord into an electrical outlet, then turn the instrument on.

Position the dilated patient in the slit lamp, with his or her refractive spherical equivalent dialed in on the PAM. Direct the patient to close the eyes as the perpendicularly directed light beam is focused on the eyelid (Fig. 3A). Upon opening the lids and with slight downward gaze (approximately 14 degrees), the patient should see the illuminated chart (Fig. 3B). Place the beam in a "window area" using mainly horizontal and vertical movements, with slight inward movement if required (Fig. 4A). Make fine patient subjective alignment adjustments to obtain uniform illumination of the silvered eye chart. Ask the patient to read the chart, starting with the largest letters. As the endpoint of acuity measurement is approached, attempt a brief subjective vision improvement using the dioptric dial. Two or more letters read correctly at the end-point identifies the final potential acuity reading.

■ **Interpretation.** False-negative results (predicted visual acuity worse than final acuity) are associated with dense opacification (Fig. 4B) and subsequent poor light penetration with the PAM. Entoptic phenomena, electrodiagnostic testing, or ophthalmic ultrasound testing (see p. 356) may be considered as alternative methods of assessing potential visual acuity.

False-positive results (predicted visual acuity better than final acuity) have been found with cystoid macular edema, serous detachments of the macula, and age-related macular degeneration. All allow for the possibility of healthy parafoveal tissue stimulation, yielding an erroneous reading. Maculopathy-related visual acuity loss produces more false positives with the interferometer than the PAM, but still the examiner's fundus impression and patient history are important in preventing false predictions and unnecessary surgery. The brightness level of the PAM chart, greater than a normal Snellen chart, may also contribute to false positive results.

The measurements obtained are intended as "estimates" of the expected acuity. No exact correlation exists.

■ **Contraindications/Complications.** This is a noninvasive procedure that presents no danger to the patient. Eyes that do not dilate well, or those in which dilation is contraindicated, can test poorly. Overaccommodation due to proximity of the instrument to the eye, especially with younger patients, may require adjustment of the dioptric dial.

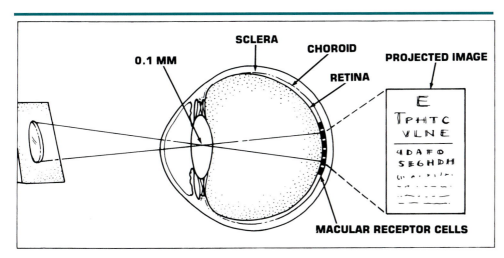

1. Optical principles of the potential acuity meter (PAM). A Maxwellian view optical system projects a bright miniature Snellen chart onto the retina through an aperture of 0.1 mm. The projected image is shown upright as seen by the patient.

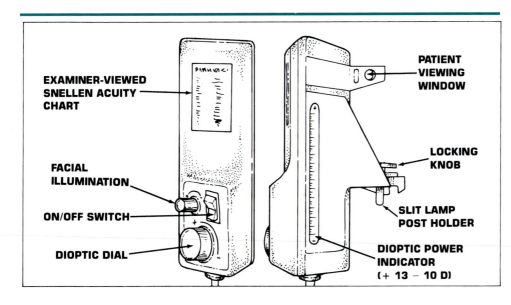

2. The components of the slit lamp-mounted PAM as seen from the examiner's side (left) and the patient's side (right).

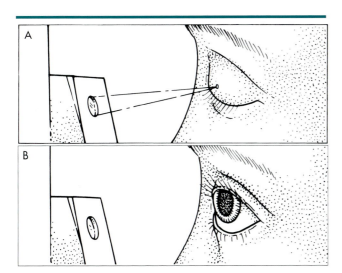

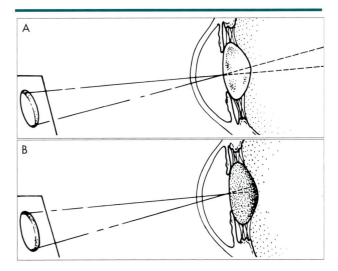

3. A. After proper patient positioning, the light beam is focused on the patient's closed eyelid. B. The patient is asked to open the eyes and look into the illuminated opening to view the projected acuity chart.

4. A. The beam is directed through the least dense area of the cataract or media opacity. B. A dense cataract will not allow light transmission to the retina. This may produce a false-negative result.

88 A-Scan Ultrasound: Biometry

■ **Description/Indications.** The axial length of the eye can be measured with quantitative A-scan ultrasound. Of the techniques available, applanation A-scan biometry is the one commonly employed. An ultrasonic transducer crystal placed in front of the eye emits and receives sound waves along the patient's optical axis. Rapid emission of sound waves by the crystal in the probe, alternating with emission suppression and subsequent retinal-rebound wave reception, yields a time-amplitude recording. This is converted into an electrical distance measurement and displaced on an oscilloscope screen along with other pertinent patient information (Fig. 1). Each spike on the graph represents an ultrasonic echo from a specific ocular tissue area (Fig. 2). Five principal echoes from the following structures are typically present: cornea, anterior crystalline lens, posterior crystalline lens, retina, and scleral/orbital fat. These deflected lines represent the measured time intervals between echoes recorded along the optical axis.

A primary use of A-scan ultrasound (biometry) is to determine the appropriate dioptric power of the intraocular lens (IOL) implanted at the time of cataract extraction surgery. To do so, the examiner combines the linear value of axial length, as determined by A-scan, with the two major corneal meridian curvature measurements (keratometry readings), an anterior or posterior IOL "constant" adjustment value (surgeon-selective), and the desired final spectacle lens power. All data are then entered into the microprocessor, which uses a surgeon-selected IOL calculation formula to arrive at the final implant power.

A hand-held or slit lamp-mounted probe/transducer is connected by a cable to the microprocessor with a display screen (Fig. 3). The transducer tip has a small light emitting diode (LED) to assist patient fixation. An attached printer for one-dimensional linear tracing is interconnected for permanent recording and interoffice communication.

■ **Instrumentation.** A-scan ultrasound unit with printer, keratometer, topical ophthalmic anesthetic solution, alcohol swabs, slit lamp biomicroscope.

■ **Technique.** Take multiple, accurate keratometry readings on both eyes with a calibrated, focused instrument prior to ultrasound measurement. Record the average of each of the major corneal meridians without noting the axis.

Turn the ultrasound unit on and enter the day's date and patient name (if desired). Calibrate the instrument daily following the manufacturer's instructions. Asepticize the probe tip with an alcohol swab, and allow sufficient time for it to air dry (2 to 3 minutes). Anesthetize both corneas by instilling topical ophthalmic anesthetic solution.

Set the instrument in the automatic mode if available, or in the manual mode. Use the manual mode if no readings are obtainable in the automatic mode or if closer analysis of the "in vivo" reading is needed. Place the pedal of the unit on the floor by your foot. Select the proper crystalline lens status entry (cataract, aphakic, or normal) for the tested eye. An improper lens status selection (phakic versus aphakic) in the automatic mode will cause the instrument to continue to search for the presence or absence of a lens structure, never selecting an "acceptable" reading. Ask the patient to fixate a target straight ahead with the nontested eye, or to look directly at the LED with the tested eye if better fixation is needed.

Two techniques for positioning the A-scan probe are described.

Hand-held Probe: Position the patient sitting upright in the examination chair with good neck support from the headrest to prevent backward movement. Secure the patient's upper lid gently against the superior orbital rim with the thumb of the nontesting hand, and secure the lower lid against the inferior rim with the ring finger of the opposite hand. Using the thumb, index finger, and side of the middle finger to hold the probe, stabilize your hand on the inferior orbital rim and place the tip of the probe perpendicular to and in light contact with the corneal apex. Attempt to align the probe tip with the optical axis, avoiding pressure that could create corneal compression (Fig. 4).

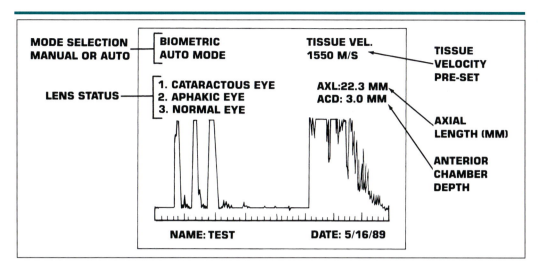

MODE SELECTION MANUAL OR AUTO

BIOMETRIC AUTO MODE

TISSUE VEL. 1550 M/S

TISSUE VELOCITY PRE-SET

LENS STATUS

1. CATARACTOUS EYE
2. APHAKIC EYE
3. NORMAL EYE

AXL:22.3 MM
ACD: 3.0 MM

AXIAL LENGTH (MM)

ANTERIOR CHAMBER DEPTH

NAME: TEST

DATE: 5/16/89

1. An acceptable A-scan reading is displayed on the oscilloscope screen of the instrument along with other pertinent information.

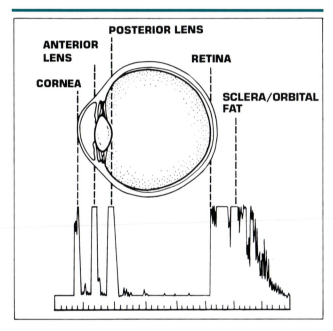

POSTERIOR LENS

ANTERIOR LENS

RETINA

CORNEA

SCLERA/ORBITAL FAT

2. Each spike on the A-scan graph represents a specific ocular area as the ultrasound waves echo off the individual structures. The time intervals are measured between the tissue echoes along the patient's optical axis.

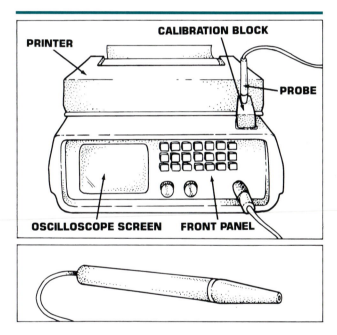

PRINTER

CALIBRATION BLOCK

PROBE

OSCILLOSCOPE SCREEN

FRONT PANEL

3. The various components of the A-scan biometry unit are shown (top). The probe (bottom) contains the ultrasonic transducer crystal that emits and receives sound waves. The transducer tip also has a small light emitting diode (LED) to assist patient fixation.

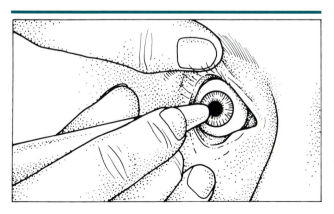

4. Hand-held probe A-scan technique. With the patient's upper lid gently retracted and the hand holding the probe securely positioned on the inferior orbital rim, the transducer probe is held perpendicular to and in light contact with the corneal apex.

Slit Lamp-mounted Probe: Place the probe in the applanation tonometer biprism holder and position the patient in the slit lamp biomicroscope with instructions to keep the forehead firmly against the head strap (see p. 24). Ask the patient to fixate straight ahead with the opposite eye or to look directly at the probe LED if poor fixation is noted. Ask the patient to blink a few times and then to open the eyes widely. Move the probe forward, similar to the technique of applanation tonometry (see p. 52), using the joystick to perpendicularly align and lightly touch the corneal apex (Fig. 5). Make every effort to avoid corneal compression.

Corneal contact by the probe using either technique will cause a continuous emission of ultrasonic waves, signified by repeated "beeping" sounds. With proper corneal alignment, the screen, which is positioned for simultaneous viewing, should display approximately equal spike heights for the cornea, anterior and posterior crystalline lens surfaces, and retina (Fig. 2). The rise of the retinal spike must be reasonably sharp at 85 to 90 degrees off the baseline. Subtle realignment of the probe may be needed at times to produce this result.

The automatic mode accessory interprets spike equality and reading acceptability, and signals this by emitting a high-pitched sound. This is followed by cessation of the beeping sounds and a freezing of the screen recording (variations exist between units). In the manual mode, view the screen simultaneously and freeze an acceptable frame by depressing the foot pedal. After a poor reading, the anterior chamber depth (ACD) reading location is replaced by a message indicating where the first problem occurred. Take at least three readings that are within 0.15 mm of each other, and average them to help ensure accuracy. After each reading, regardless of the mode used, depress the foot pedal to clear the graph before taking the next reading. Poor readings need to be repeated (Fig. 6). Use the save mode on the instrument to store one copy of a good reading to be printed out with the calculations after testing. Make sure that the anterior depth measurements (ACD) are consistent between readings to ensure against corneal compression. Scans with the longest ACD are those most likely to be unaffected by corneal compression.

Most A-scan units use a microprocessor to calculate IOL power. A printed readout of the best scan diagram is made, accompanied by the IOL calculations. Perform biometry on both eyes to allow for comparison. The average expected axial length difference is 0.2 to 0.3 mm between eyes. If inconsistencies exist, recheck for corneal compression and repeat your readings.

■ Interpretation.
Some of the modern formulas (surgeon-selected) used for IOL calculations include the Binkhorst (T) and SRK II (R). To perform the calculations, select the formula to be used (Fig. 7). The average keratometry readings from the two major meridians (K1 and K2), the average ultrasound axial length (AXL), the surgeon's anterior and posterior IOL constants (A1 and A2), and the desired final postoperative spectacle lens power (7 and 9) are entered into the microprocessor in their respective screen spaces. Multiple IOL dioptric powers are automatically calibrated for spectacle powers at the desired prescription, and for powers above and below the specified prescription value.

Both anterior and posterior chamber intraocular lens implant values are calibrated. Two IOLs (anterior and posterior) with the appropriate powers are brought to surgery, because a surgical plan calling for a posterior chamber implant may have to be changed to an anterior chamber design during surgery. When the final desired spectacle prescription is greater than 2.00D from Plano power, additional methods of calculation need to be considered and compared.

■ Contraindications/Complications.
This procedure is noninvasive and poses no risk to the patient. It requires that the examiner be accurate and precise with all readings and calculations. Repetition with consistent readings is the key to success. Caution should be exercised to prevent corneal compression with the probe, causing a reduction in the ACD and subsequent underestimation of the ocular axial length. Use of the hand-held method increases the risk of corneal compression and improper alignment. Poor patient fixation can lead to poor results. Corneal distortion and disease hinder accurate keratometry readings. Small pupils accompanied by significant lens opacification may require pupil dilation if initial testing results are poor. An induced corneal abrasion or toxic reaction to the anesthetic solution are possible but uncommon. Infrequent or incorrect calibration of any of the instruments, or incorrect data entry, can yield undesirable postsurgical acuity results.

Contact lens wearers should discontinue use of their rigid or soft lenses until a stable series of keratometry readings can be obtained. Because a keratometric error of 1.0D results in about 1.0D of IOL power calculation error, consider repeating keratometric measurements on any patient with readings less than 40D or more than 47D, when there is greater than 1.0D difference in cylinder between eyes, or when the corneal cylinder correlates poorly with the refractive cylinder.

Because a 0.3-mm error in axial length results in a 1.0D error in IOL power, consider taking more measurements when the axial length is less than 22 mm or more than 25 mm, when there is 0.3 mm difference in axial length between eyes, or with uncooperative or poorly fixating patients.

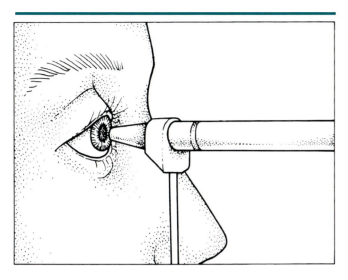

5. Slit lamp-mounted probe A-scan technique. With the probe positioned in the tonometer biprism holder, the joystick is used to perpendicularly align and lightly touch the tip to the corneal apex.

6. (below) A. This A-scan reading is unacceptable because the retinal echo is poor. B. This A-scan reading is unacceptable since the crystalline lens echoes are poor.

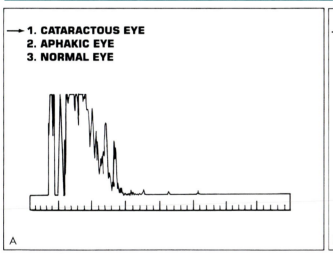

A

1. **CATARACTOUS EYE**
2. **APHAKIC EYE**
3. **NORMAL EYE**

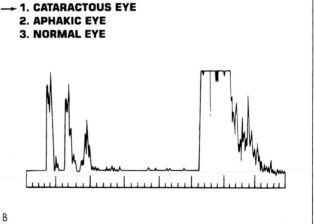

B

1. **CATARACTOUS EYE**
2. **APHAKIC EYE**
3. **NORMAL EYE**

IOL CALCULATIONS	REGRESSION PROGRAM
1. K1 = 43.50 D	(=) Clear all entries
2. K2 = 45.00 D	(←) Binkhorst
3. AXL = 22.80 mm	(→) Colenbrander
4. A1 = 115.3	**5.** A2 = 116.5

	IOL	REFR		IOL	REFR	
ANTER CHMBR LENS	+20.5	−1.62		+21.5	−1.46	POST CHMBR LENS
	+20.0	−1.22		+21.0	−1.06	
	+19.5	−0.82		+20.5	−0.66	
	+19.0	−0.42		+20.0	−0.26	
6. →	+18.5	−0.02	← **7.**	+19.5	+0.14	← **9.**
	+18.0	+0.38	**8.** →	+19.0	+0.54	
	+17.5	+0.78		+18.5	+0.94	
	+17.0	+1.18		+18.0	+1.34	
	+16.5	+1.58		+17.5	+1.74	

	EMMETROPIA (ACL)	(PCL)	CONTACT LENS PWR	APHAKIC REFR
Binkhorst	+18.13	+20.21	+14.27	+12.18
Regression	+18.47	+19.68	+13.52	+11.81
Colenbrander	+16.67	+19.65	+13.10	+11.32

1. K1: One major meridian keratometry reading
2. K2: Other major meridian keratometry reading
3. AXL: Axial length (mm)
4. A1: Anterior IOL surgical constant
5. A2: Posterior IOL surgical constant
6. Calculated anterior chamber IOL power
7. Desired post-op spectacle Rx power
8. Calculated posterior chamber IOL power
9. Desired post-op spectacle Rx power

7. The data used to calculate the appropriate dioptric power of the intraocular lens (IOL) implant include the keratometry readings of the two major corneal meridians, the axial length as measured by A-scan, an anterior or posterior IOL surgeon-specific "constant," and the desired postoperative spectacle lens power.

89

Suture Cutting

■ **Description/Indications.** Ocular suturing techniques may be performed in an interrupted or running (continuous) pattern (Fig. 1). After each suture is tied in an interrupted pattern used to close, for example, a large incision at the corneosclera junction, the knot is rotated superiorly to abut the scleral suture opening (Fig. 2A, B). The loose ends of the knot are trimmed, then covered with the surgical conjunctival flap (Fig. 2C, D). If running or continuous sutures are used to close an incision at the corneosclera junction, a single interlacing, shoestring-like pattern is used.

Suturing techniques at the corneosclera junction can affect the final shape of the cornea (Fig. 3). In an ideal suturing outcome, the sutures are equidistant, they are at the same tissue depth, they involve an equal amount of tissue on both sides of the incision, they are positioned as radially as possible, and they are tied with equal tension. Tight wound closure will steepen the central cornea in the meridian of the tight suture(s) because the circumference of the globe is decreased, resulting in a shortened radius of curvature. Indicators of tight sutures are induced postoperative corneal astigmatism, corneal wrinkling, perisutural tissue necrosis, and posterior gaping of the wound.

With the interrupted suturing technique at the cornea/sclera junction, wound compression results in a shortening (steepening) of the vertical corneal meridian, yielding with-the-rule astigmatism (Fig. 3B), in contrast to the running/continuous suturing technique, which usually results in against-the-rule astigmatism. Loose interrupted suture(s) can create wound gap with subsequent against-the-rule astigmatism (Fig. 3C). Cutting tight suture(s) in the meridian 90 degrees from the correcting minus cylinder axis reduces the astigmatic value. Therefore, a patient with 3 diopters of induced postoperative refractive cylinder at axis 180 will require cutting of the interrupted suture at the 12-o'clock (axis 90) position.

The appropriate time for cutting sutures is variable. It is dependent upon the closure technique, suture material, the amount of topical steroid used postoperatively, and the quality of healing. Good wound healing exhibits closed incision edges, the absence of an overlying conjunctival bleb, and a negative Seidel test (see p. 368). Thus, both the sutures and wound need to be examined before sutures are cut. If the wound appears healed, removal can be attempted. It is rare to cut sutures before 6 weeks postoperatively. The removal of sutures to adjust induced astigmatism is usually accomplished within 3 months.

■ **Instrumentation.** Keratometer; slit lamp biomicroscope; sterile: jeweler's forceps, scalpel or blade-breaker with razor blade, eyelid speculum, cotton-tipped applicators, fluorescein sodium strips, saline solution; topical ophthalmic anesthetic solution; broad-spectrum topical ophthalmic antibiotic solution.

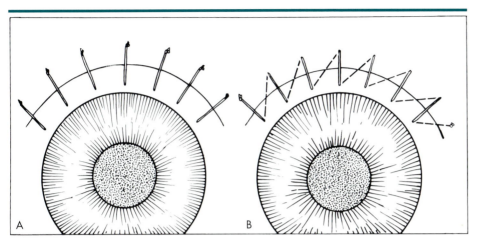

1. Potential suturing patterns used to close a large incision at the superior corneosclera junction. A. Interrupted. B. Running/continuous.

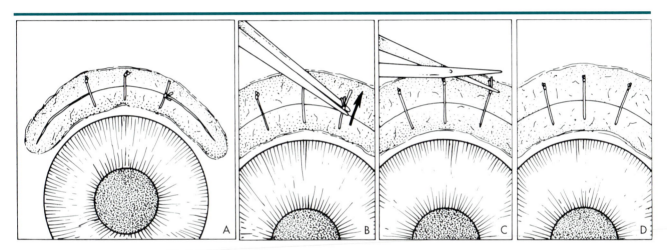

2. A. The interrupted sutures are tied to close the surgical incision. B. The suture knot is grasped and rotated superiorly to abut the scleral suture opening. C. The loose ends of the knot are trimmed. D. The sutures lie flat as the surgical conjunctival flap is positioned over the incision.

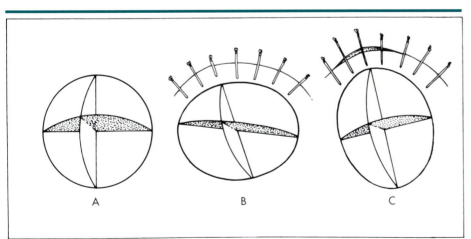

3. The suturing technique can affect the final shape of the cornea. A. The cornea is spherical since the two major meridians are the same shape. B. Tight interrupted sutures at the superior corneosclera junction will shorten and steepen the vertical meridian, inducing with-the-rule astigmatism. C. Loose interrupted sutures can create wound gap and a flattened vertical meridian, inducing against-the-rule astigmatism.

■ **Technique.** Obtain keratometry readings and the present refractive status. With this information, use the slit lamp biomicroscope to identify the surgical suturing technique and the probable tight suture(s). This suture(s) should be located approximately 90 degrees from the correcting minus cylinder. Instill 2 drops of topical ophthalmic anesthetic solution into the eye. If desired, use a pledget to deliver more effective topical anesthesia by saturating a sterile cotton-tipped applicator with topical ophthalmic anesthetic solution and holding it to the suture site for 15 to 30 seconds (see p. 6). After a few minutes, instill 2 drops of a broad-spectrum ophthalmic antibiotic solution into the eye prophylactically before cutting any suture.

Position the patient at the slit lamp biomicroscope with instructions to keep the forehead firmly against the headstrap. Have the patient look slightly downward, securing the upper lid with the thumb of your nondominant hand (Fig. 4A). Hold the cutting instrument in your opposite hand. Brace the instrument hand on the patient's bridge of the nose or inferior orbital rim.

From a perpendicular direction, move the blade forward, lightly contacting the inferior portion of the suture (corneal side) through the conjunctiva with the blade tip (Fig. 4B). The taut suture should "snap" upward when cut. The superior area will show the residual subconjunctival radial suture above the surgical incision (Fig. 4C), while the inferior suture end should disappear into the sclera. The suture usually remains subconjunctival and is removed only if it penetrates the conjunctival surface. Perform a Seidel test (see p. 368) to ensure that no wound leakage has been induced. Instill 2 additional drops of broad-spectrum ophthalmic antibiotic solution following the procedure for further prophylaxis.

Cutting running sutures can have greater tension-releasing effect and increased variability than cutting the interrupted type. Usually, a longer waiting period is used prior to cutting these sutures. Because running sutures techniques vary, more knowledge of the specific surgical technique used as well as the expected healing process is necessary prior to intervention.

■ **Interpretation.** A patient presenting 6 weeks postoperatively with induced corneal astigmatism may require one or more sutures cut. For example, if the keratometry readings are 44.50 D at 180 and 48.00 D at 90, and the refractive correction is +2.00 − 3.00 × 180, the tight suture(s) at the same axis (90) as the steepest keratometry reading (90 degrees away from the minus cylinder axis) should be cut (Fig. 5). Usually the refractive cylinder axis and the keratometry axis are approximately the same. If not, single suture cutting is done based on the keratometry reading.

Sutures are rarely cut before 6 weeks postoperatively, unless one wishes to correct a very high induced cylinder at the fourth or fifth week. Expect a 1.50 to 2.00 D cylinder change with each suture cut. A maximum of two sutures are cut at one session, and this is only done in cases of very high induced astigmatism (6 to 8 D). Cutting more than two sutures at one time reduces refractive predictability and increases the chance of wound gap. A small to moderate amount of residual with-the-rule astigmatism remaining after surgery will reduce over the years as healing continues.

■ **Contraindications/Complications.** Premature suture cutting prior to proper healing can lead to poor wound closure (wound gap), subsequent aqueous leakage, and possible endophthalmitis. Improper sterile or surgical technique may lead to secondary external and/or internal infection. Incorrect suture cutting calculations and selection can yield a less than desirable astigmatic result. A subconjunctival hemorrhage may result from this procedure and the patient should be so advised. Improper technique may result in damage to the ocular tissue.

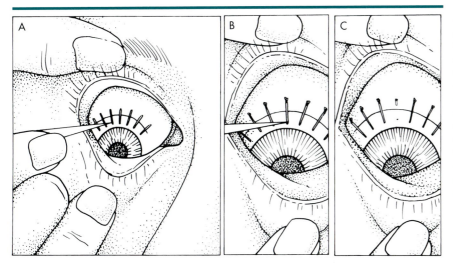

4. Suture cutting of interrupted sutures at the superior corneosclera junction: A. After positioning the patient at the slit lamp biomicroscope, he or she is asked to look slightly downward, the upper lid is secured, and the dominant hand holding the cutting instrument is stabilized. B. Approaching carefully from a position perpendicular to the globe, the tip of the blade is gently passed through the conjunctiva to nick the inferior portion of the tight suture. C. The loosened residual suture is visible above the incision line, while the inferior end retracts back into the scleral suture opening.

5. An example of corneal astigmatism induced postoperatively by a tight interrupted suture at the 12-o'clock location, as well as the change in keratometry readings and refraction following cutting of the tight suture.

Postop Keratometry (K) Reading: 44.50 @ 180/48.00 @ 90

Postop Refraction: +2.00 – 3.00 @ 180 20/20

Suture Cutting at 90-degree Position (90 degrees from correcting minus cylinder axis)

Post-suture Cutting K Reading: 44.50 @ 180/46.25 @ 90

Post-suture Cutting Refraction: +0.75 – 1.00 @ 180 20/20

Suture Barb Removal

■ **Description/Indications.** Sutures used to close ocular surgery incisions can later produce symptomatic irritation, often the result of an elevated knot of an intact suture, an elevated knot of a broken suture, or the knotless end of a broken suture (Fig. 1). The frequently used nondissolvable 10/0 nylon sutures have the potential to weaken, stretch, break, or rotate with time. The suture knot or broken suture end can rotate, elevate, and perforate the overlying tissue to form a barb that causes foreign body sensation, marked discomfort, or a secondary papillary reaction of the palpebral conjunctiva. Symptomatic elevated sutures frequently have a small area of surrounding conjunctival edema, elevation, and injection accompanied by a fine mucus tag on the barb itself (Fig. 2).

A loose protruding suture in the presence of good wound healing should be removed. Two to three months postoperatively is the desired waiting period for relatively safe, uncomplicated suture barb removal. In some instances, a bandage soft contact lens may be fit over the sutures to enhance patient comfort, allowing more time for further wound healing prior to suture removal.

■ **Instrumentation.** Slit lamp biomicroscope; sterile: jeweler's forceps, scalpel or blade-breaker with razor blade, eyelid speculum, cotton-tipped applicators, fluorescein sodium strips, saline solution, topical ophthalmic anesthetic solution, broad-spectrum topical ophthalmic antibiotic solution.

■ **Technique.** Locate the involved suture with the slit lamp biomicroscope and identify the suture pattern as interrupted or running (see p. 361). Attempt to determine whether the barb is the result of a broken suture (knot or loose end) or a rotated, protruding but intact suture. Make sure the wound is well healed and the globe is otherwise not infected or inflamed. Instill 2 drops of a broad-spectrum topical ophthalmic antibiotic solution. After a few minutes, instill 2 drops of topical ophthalmic anesthetic solution. If desired, use a pledget to deliver more effective topical anesthesia by saturating a sterile cotton-tipped applicator with topical ophthalmic anesthetic solution and holding it to the suture barb area for 15 to 30 seconds (see p. 6).

Position the patient at the slit lamp biomicroscope with instructions to keep the forehead firmly against the headstrap. Depending upon the degree of difficulty of suture barb removal as well as the level of patient cooperation, either a sterile eyelid speculum (see p. 98) or the examiner's or the assistant's fingers can be used to secure the eyelids. Without an eyelid speculum and in the event of a suture barb located at the 12-o'clock position, ask the patient to look down. Secure the upper lid against the superior orbital rim with the thumb of the nondominant hand. Stabilize the hand holding the suture barb removal instrument on the patient's bridge of the nose or the inferior orbital rim. Ask the patient to continue looking downward throughout the procedure.

In the case of a broken interrupted suture, grasp the knot with the jeweler's forceps and gently pull the entire suture out (Fig. 3). If only the knotless end is visible, gently grasp the loose suture end with the forceps and pull upward, exposing as much of the suture as possible (Fig. 4). Trim the suture by passing the sharp edge of a scalpel or blade under the forceps and as close to the surface of the globe as possible. To cut the suture, move the scalpel or blade in a direction away from the cornea. The cut end should snap back into the suture opening.

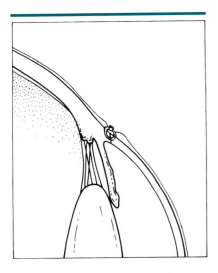

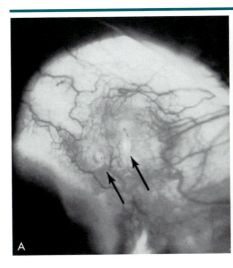

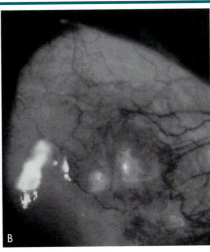

1. One source of ocular irritation from a suture may be an elevated knot of an intact suture that has broken through the overlying tissue.

2. Suture barbs protruding through the bulbar conjunctiva (arrows) are visible with the slit lamp biomicroscope using white light (left) and with the cobalt filter following instillation of fluorescein sodium (right). Note the area of surrounding conjunctival edema and injection. (*See also* Color Plate 90-2.) (Courtesy of David E. Magnus, OD)

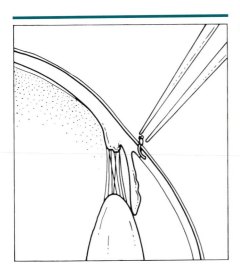

3. In the case of a broken interrupted suture, the knot is grasped with the jeweler's forceps and the suture is gently pulled out.

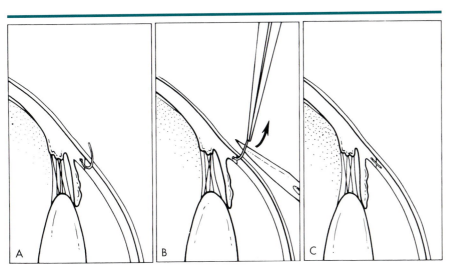

4. A. If only the knotless end of a broken interrupted suture is visible, the loose suture end is gently grasped with the forceps and pulled upward to expose as much of the suture as possible. B. The suture is trimmed at its base with the tip of a scalpel or blade in a direction away from the cornea. C. After the suture is cut, it snaps back into the suture opening.

In the case of an unbroken interrupted suture that has eroded through the overlying tissue (Fig. 5A), first gently pull on it with the jeweler's forceps to determine if it is fragile enough to break. If not, gently grasp the suture with the forceps and lift it upward away from the surface of the globe sufficiently far enough to allow the tip of the scalpel or blade to be passed under it (Fig. 5B). Using a motion directed away from the cornea, cut the suture on one side of the knot. Grasp the knotted end of the cut suture with the forceps and pull gently for removal (Fig. 5C).

Running suture barb repair is similar, except that the suture has to be cut at two points on either side of the protruding barb. Once the suture is cut twice, use the forceps to remove the free segment. Familiarize yourself with the specific running suture pattern before making any cuts.

Following suture barb removal, instill 2 additional drops of broad-spectrum topical ophthalmic antibiotic solution. A Seidel test (see p. 368) may be performed before dismissing the patient to assess for leakage at the suture opening at the site of barb removal.

■ **Contraindications/Complications.** Wound leakage caused by wound gap or dehiscence is possible if sutures are removed prior to adequate postoperative healing. Leakage is also possible from the suture opening where the knot or knotless end of the suture is pulled out. Some practitioners advocate pulling the exposed knotless end of a broken suture, when no knot is visible, back through the scleral suture canal, anterior chamber, corneoscleral junction, and out, followed by several days of topical antibiotic drops. These patients require close follow-up for aqueous leakage. Tissue "openings" or technique injury may both cause secondary bacterial infection. The Seidel test and topical broad-spectrum antibiotics are used to safeguard against these sequelae.

Since different running suture techniques exist and since cutting a running suture can have more tension-release effect on an eye than cutting an interrupted suture, extra care must be taken. Be sure that the area has had more than adequate time to heal and that the specific running suture technique and its repair are known to the examiner. When in doubt concerning suture removal, consult the surgeon whenever possible.

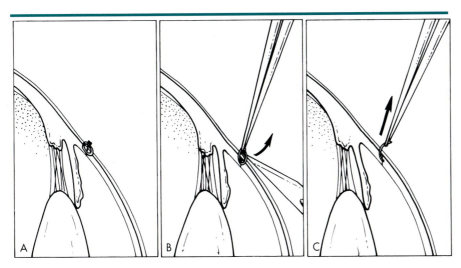

5. A. An intact interrupted suture has eroded through the overlying tissue to cause a protruding barb. B. The suture is grasped with a jeweler's forceps and lifted so that it can be cut on one side of the knot with the tip of a scalpel or blade in a motion directed away from the cornea. C. The cut interrupted suture is grasped at the knot with the jeweler's forceps and removed.

91 Seidel Test

■ **Description/Indications.** The Seidel test is used to evaluate for possible wound/aqueous leakage through an external fistula following ophthalmic surgery such as cataract extraction, suture removal, or suspected penetrating injury to the globe. A common sign of wound/aqueous leakage is a diffuse conjunctival filtering bleb-like appearance overlying the involved area, which can frequently be difficult to distinguish from postoperative conjunctival chemosis. Microcystic subepithelial changes to the overlying conjunctiva may also occur.

Other more obvious indicators of wound gap or a penetrating injury are peaking of the pupil with iris plugging at the wound opening, a large shift to against-the-rule astigmatism, a shallow anterior chamber, hypotony as measured by tonometry, decreased visual acuity, corneal laceration, and prolapsed intraocular contents. Wound leakage creates an unequal pressure gradient between the anterior and posterior chambers. The higher pressure in the posterior chamber may push the iris toward the gap in the wound. This can lead to iris prolapse and/or pupillary block secondary to a forwardly displaced vitreous.

■ **Instrumentation.** Slit lamp biomicroscope with cobalt filter, sterile fluorescein sodium strips, sterile ophthalmic saline solution.

■ **Technique.** At the appropriate point during Seidel testing, the patient is properly positioned at the slit lamp biomicroscope (see p. 22) and the cobalt filter is introduced. Three ways to perform the Seidel test are as follows:

1. Instill fluorescein sodium into the eye from a saturated sterile strip (see p. 134). Carefully search the wound or sutured area with the slit lamp biomicroscope and cobalt blue filter for indicators of wound/aqueous leakage such as clear aqueous streaming, localized brilliant hyperfluorescence,

bleb-like formation, or surface bubbles (Fig. 1A). If the IOP is extremely low and no positive Seidel test is apparent, gently press the eyelid against the globe and observe the suspicious area again very closely for leakage.

2. Ask the patient to look in the opposite direction of the area to be examined. After instilling fluorescein sodium, pool the fluorescein tear lake over the suspicious area using the lower lid. Examine for signs of wound/aqueous leakage (Fig. 1B).

3. Hold a sterile dry fluorescein strip in apposition to the area of concern while viewing through the slit lamp. Look for a trickle of aqueous moistening the strip (Fig. 1C).

■ **Interpretation.** If the Seidel test is positive, the aqueous is best observed leaking externally using a slit lamp with a fluorescein-saturated tear film. With close observation, wound leakage is identified by clear aqueous streaming into the fluorescein, a localized brilliant green fluorescein appearance at the leakage site, or dots or bubbles forming on the involved surface (Fig. 2).

A positive Seidel test necessitates immediate consultation to prevent endophthalmitis or other postsurgical complications such as hypotony or poor visual acuity. When wound leakage is suspected but Seidel testing is negative, intermittent leakage following intraocular pressure changes may be occurring. Consultation in this instance is also indicated.

■ **Contraindications/Complications.** Instillation of contaminated fluorescein or saline can lead to serious infection. Failure to instill an adequate amount of fluorescein can yield a false negative result. All manipulation of a postoperative eye or an eye with a suspected penetrating injury is performed with extreme care.

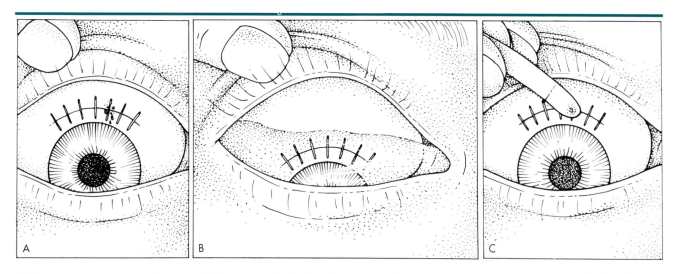

1. There are three ways to perform the Seidel test. A. After instilling fluorescein sodium, the wound area is closely examined for hyperfluorescence, bleb-like formation, or surface bubbles. B. After instilling fluorescein sodium, the fluorescein-filled tear lake is pooled over the suspected area of leakage. C. A dry sterile fluorescein sodium strip is held to the area of suspected leakage, and the area is examined closely to assess for wetting of the strip from externally leaking aqueous.

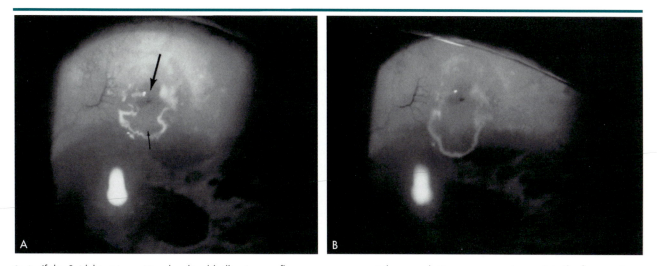

2. A. If the Seidel test is positive, localized brilliant green fluorescence occurs at the wound site as aqueous streams into the fluorescein. B. The bright fluorescein is displaced as the aqueous continues to leak. (*See also* Color Plates 91–2A and 91–2B.) (Courtesy of David E. Magnus, OD)

XI

Suggested Readings

Bass SJ, Sherman J: Ophthalmic ultrasonography, in Eskridge JB, Amos JF, Bartlett JD (eds): *Clinical Procedures in Optometry.* Philadelphia, Lippincott, 1991, pp 530–549.

Bezan DJ: Postoperative care of the cataract patient, in Bartlett JD, Jaanus SD (eds): *Clinical Ocular Pharmacology,* ed 3. Boston, Butterworth-Heinemann, 1995, pp 793–808.

Cavallerano A: Potential acuity assessment, in Eskridge JB, Amos JF, Bartlett JD (eds): *Clinical Procedures in Optometry.* Philadelphia, Lippincott, 1991, pp 470–481.

Guyton DL: Preoperative visual acuity evaluation, in Smolin G, Friedlaender M (eds): *Int Ophthalmol Clin* 1987;**27:**140–147.

Melore GG, Accettura J: Suture barb syndrome. *South J Optom* 1987;**5:**70–73.

Murrill CA, Stanfield DL, VanBrocklin MD: *Primary Care of the Cataract Patient.* Norwalk, CT, Appleton & Lange, 1994.

Sanders DR, Retzlaff JA, Kraff MC: A-scan biometry and IOL implant power calculations. Focal Points: Clinical Modules for Ophthalmologists. *Am Acad Ophthalmol* 1995;**13:**1–14.

XII

Glaucoma Evaluation
and Treatment Procedures

92 Optic Nerve, Nerve Fiber Layer, and Retina Evaluation

■ **Description/Indications.** Open-angle glaucoma describes a condition of many potential etiologies that is recognized by its characteristic optic neuropathy. This optic neuropathy and the structural integrity of the eye is most commonly evaluated using different forms of ophthalmoscopy, although more sophisticated imaging techniques such as confocal laser scanning are becoming more widespread. The structural changes associated with glaucoma include loss of the retinal nerve fiber layer, enlargement of the cup/disc ratio, asymmetry in the cup/disc ratio between eyes, baring of circumlinear vessels on the disc, flame-shaped hemorrhages at the optic disc margin, and loss of neuroretinal rim tissue. The examiner's challenge is to ascertain which signs are truly due to glaucoma and rule out conditions such as large physiologic cupping, optic nerve drusen, optic pits, or tilted discs that have similarities in appearance to glaucomatous optic neuropathy.

Several techniques and instruments are used in combination to comprehensively examine the optic nerve, retinal nerve fiber layer (RNFL), and other retinal features when evaluating for glaucomatous optic atrophy. Fundus biomicroscopy through a dilated pupil using either a noncontact fundus lens, Hruby lens, or a Goldmann-style three-mirror fundus contact lens is the preferred method for evaluating the optic nerve and posterior pole since the stereopsis and magnified view provide detailed imagery (see pp. 74). A 60 or 78D fundus lens provides ample magnification with high resolution to view the optic nerve in great detail with the slit lamp biomicroscope magnification set at 10X. Using a clear fundus lens along with a red-free (green) filter on the biomicroscope also allows for evaluation of the retinal nerve fiber layer. The three-mirror fundus contact lens provides a high-resolution image of the optic disc and posterior pole but necessitates that a lens be placed onto the eye. While the image obtained with a noncontact fundus lens is not quite of the quality as that seen with the fundus contact lens, the view is excellent nonetheless and the technique is relatively quick and easy to perform.

The stereoscopic examination, performed initially and at least on a yearly basis, usually leads to the recognition of a larger cup/disc ratio than estimated using a monocular instrument such as the direct ophthalmoscope. Direct ophthalmoscopy does have a place in the glaucomatous optic nerve evaluation because it can provide views of the optic nerve and retina through a nondilated pupil; however media opacities as well as the small pupil can limit this view. Direct ophthalmoscopy is performed at every glaucomatous follow-up evaluation through the undilated pupil. Another important use of the direct ophthalmoscope is in the gross estimation of the size of the optic disc. The small spot of light, one of the illumination options on most direct ophthalmoscopes, is designed to approximate one disc diameter in size (Fig. 1). By superimposing this spot onto the optic disc, an estimation of disc size is possible. This step in the evaluation of the glaucomatous optic disc provides greater insight into the potential for physiologic cupping, because it will be associated with a larger optic disc. If the disc margins are larger the small illumination spot, the disc is larger than average and more likely to be associated with large physiologic cupping.

Another instrument used for evaluation of the fundus in glaucoma is the binocular indirect ophthalmoscope (BIO), which provides an expanded field of view with low magnification (see p. 226). The BIO allows the diagnosis of retinal conditions that may produce visual field defects that mimic glaucoma, such as a chorioretinal scar in the nerve fiber bundle (Fig. 2). The BIO is not a useful instrument in estimating C/D size due to the low magnification of the image size, although it may be helpful in examining individuals with poor fixation or limited cooperation.

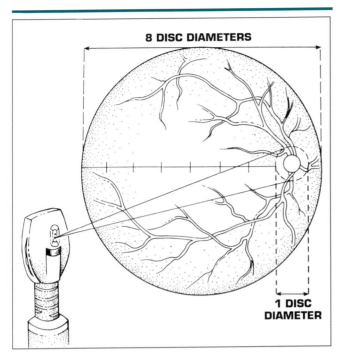

8 DISC DIAMETERS

1 DISC DIAMETER

1. The direct ophthalmoscope may be used to grossly estimate the size of the optic disc. The small aperture spot of light, designed to approximate one disc diameter in size, is superimposed onto the optic disc and its size relative to the disc is noted. Large optic discs tend to be associated with larger physiologic cupping.

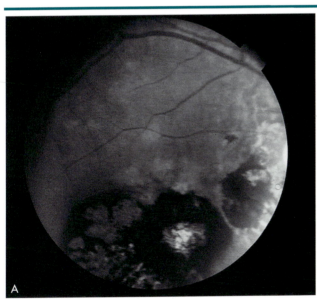

2. A. A large pigmented chorioretinal scar is noted inferior temporal to the optic disc in this patient's right eye.

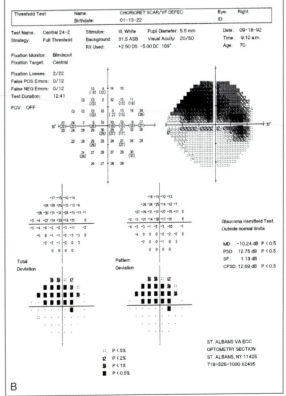

2. B. The visual field defect corresponding to the chorioretinal scar mimics that seen from glaucomatous loss.

The newest technique in imaging the optic nerve, nerve fiber layer, and retina is confocal laser scanning ophthalmoscopy (LSO). The Heidelberg Retinal Tomograph (Heidelberg Engineering) and the TopSS Topographic Scanning System (Laser Diagnostic Technologies) are two such instruments. LSO provides topographic information by imaging the retina and optic nerve in three dimensions. Light is reflected by an illuminated area at a focal plane and registered as it passes through the detector diaphragm or confocal stop. Scattered light outside the focal plane is not registered. An optical section with high resolution is created that leads to measurements of the disc size and volume, cup area, cup size, shape of the cup, peripapillary retinal height, and height variation (Figs. 3 and 4). This information is repeatable and reliable, allowing for careful follow-up to detect change in the retinal surface height or cup size. The retinal surface height measurement correlates to the thickness of the retinal nerve fiber layer. Laser Diagnostic Technologies has a separate LSO in which low-intensity polarized light is used to measure the polarization properties of the birefringent nerve fiber layer to calculate its thick-

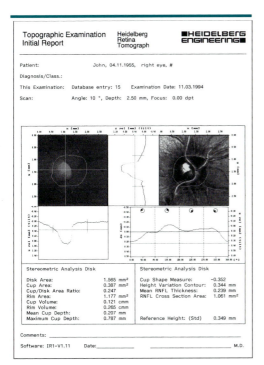

3. A Heidelberg Retina Tomograph (HRT) of a normal patient indicates measurements of the disc size and volume; cup area, size, and shape; and the peripapillary retinal height and height variation, which is correlated to the thickness of the nerve fiber layer. (*See also* Color Plate 92–3). (Courtesy of Heidelberg Engineering.)

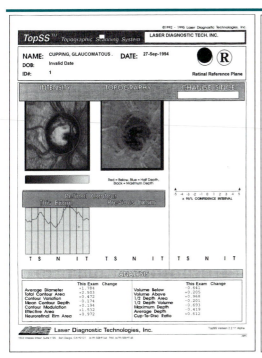

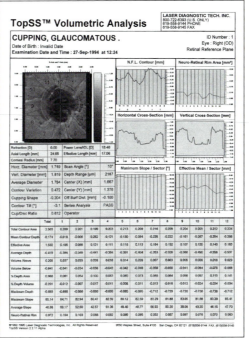

4. A. A Topographic Scanning System (TopSS) image is shown of a patient with advanced open angle glaucoma. The intensity and topographic image are presented along with the retinal contour surrounding the optic disc. B. TopSS volumetric analysis from the same patient is presented. Measurements of the optic disc, cup/disc ratio, disc and cup volume, slope, and neuroretinal rim area are shown. Contour maps of the nerve fiber layer and the neuroretinal rim area are illustrated along with horizontal and vertical cross sections of the optic disc. (Courtesy of Laser Diagnostic Technologies.)

ness (Fig. 5). Other advantages of LSO are that it allows imaging to occur through cataracts and without the need to dilate the pupil. The intensity of light used in LSO is similar to that in direct ophthalmoscopy.

■ **Instrumentation.** Direct ophthalmoscope, slit lamp biomicroscope, fundus biomicroscopic condensing lens (e.g., 60D, 78D, 90D), three-mirror fundus contact lens, Hruby lens, binocular indirect ophthalmoscope, 20D condensing lens, topical ophthalmic anesthetic solution, topical mydriatic/cycloplegic solution(s).

■ **Technique.** Dilate the pupil with mydriatic/cycloplegic solution(s). Perform fundus biomicroscopy to assess the optic nerve and nerve fiber layer integrity (see p. 244). Using a 60 or 78D fundus lens and the biomicroscope, focus a thin slit of light onto the optic disc. As the light is moved across the optic disc, observe the color, integrity, size, shape, and evenness of the entire neuroretinal rim area. View the course and location of the blood vessels, both as they emerge from the cup and as they run along the surface of the optic disc (Fig. 6). Evaluate the size, shape, contour, depth, and position of the cup as well as the area surrounding the disc (peripapillary area). Compare the size and shape of the optic disc and cup between eyes, noting any differences. Finally, note any disc abnormalities or unusual features such as a flame hemorrhage at the optic disc margin or optic nerve head drusen.

Using the fundus lens and biomicroscope, evaluate the surrounding retina, starting superior temporal to the disc and working peripherally as far as possible. Move to the superior quadrant and work in a clockwise fashion, observing the macula and posterior pole last. Next evaluate the retinal nerve fiber layer (RNFL). Utilize the red-free filter on the slit lamp to enhance the RNFL appearance and focus superior temporal to the disc so that a small portion of the disc along with the surrounding retina are observed simultaneously. Decrease the magnification to 6X if necessary so that an area several disc diameters in size is viewed simultaneously, concentrating on the area approximately two to three disc diameters from the optic nerve where the RNFL is thickest. View the superior temporal region first, moving inferiorly towards the macula, and then observe the inferior temporal RNFL last. The RNFL striations should appear bright, glistening, and evenly illuminated (Fig. 7); areas of thinning or dropout will appear as dark streaks, slits or

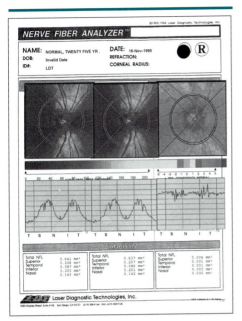

5. A Laser Diagnostic Technologies (LDT) nerve fiber analyzer (NFA) printout of a normal patient illustrates the results of two different examinations. The figures show a color-coded diagram correlating to retinal nerve fiber layer thickness. The yellow and red appearance noted in the superior temporal and inferior temporal regions is consistent with a thick, healthy nerve fiber layer. The graphical representation of a normal nerve fiber pattern is that of a double hump, indicating elevations in the areas superior temporal and inferior temporal to the optic disc. This retina is deemed to be stable because little change is noted between the two tests. (*See also* Color Plate 92–5.) (Courtesy of Laser Diagnostic Technologies.)

6. A photograph (below left) of a normal optic nerve head is shown along with an accompanying drawing (below right). The cup is small with a normal blood vessel pattern.

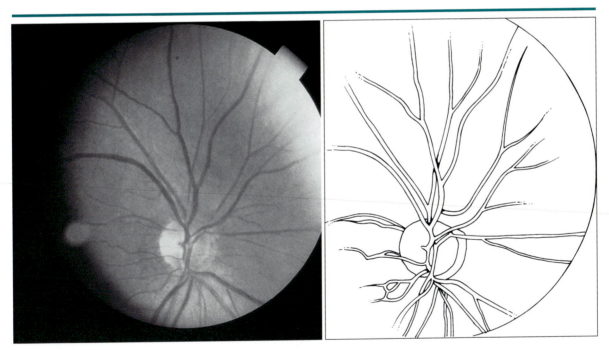

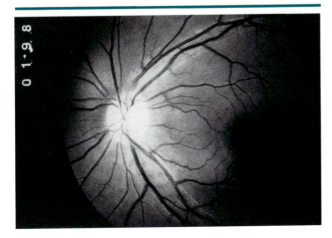

7. A retina is shown with a normal nerve fiber layer (NFL) appearance. The NFL should appear bright, glistening, and evenly illuminated.

wedges within this area. The RNFL is brighter closer to the optic nerve and dims more peripherally or towards the macula region. As the RNFL is observed, be attentive to the appearance of the underlying retinal vessels.

Use a direct ophthalmoscope and its large apurture spot of light to evaluate the optic nerve. Also, dial into the direct ophthalmoscope head, the small aperture spot of light, illuminate the optic disc, and compare the relative size of the light spot and the optic nerve (Fig. 1). Finally, perform a thorough binocular indirect ophthalmoscopic examination (BIO) with a 20D condensing lens (see p. 226). Evaluate the retina in its entirety, looking for chorioretinal scars or other abnormalities that may contribute to a glaucoma-like visual field defect.

■ **Interpretation.** When evaluating for glaucoma, one area assessed as the optic nerve is evaluated as the size and shape of the optic cup. Only 1% of normal patients have a cup/disc (C/D) ratio of 0.7 or greater. As the C/D ratio approaches 0.6, the risk for glaucoma increases and careful observation is required. Although the cup tends to have a slight vertically oval shape, any obvious vertical elongation should be noted. Only 4% of normal patients have a difference in the C/D ratio between eyes of 0.2 or greater so that an asymmetry of this magnitude or more requires careful evaluation (Fig. 8).

The neuroretinal rim must be carefully evaluated to assess its size, shape, color, and symmetry. The neuroretinal rim tends to be consistent in size and shape in a normal individual but as glaucoma develops, different patterns of neuroretinal rim tissue loss may occur. Focal abnormalities such as notching may arise due to thinning in one specific area. Notching usually occurs either at the 6 or 12-o'clock position and is often associated with RNFL dropout and a vertically elongated cup (Fig. 9). Another pattern of neuroretinal loss occurs in the temporal region (temporal unfolding) as the cup enlarges, narrowing this area of the neuroretinal rim (Fig. 10). Further change will affect the superior and temporal poles, ultimately leading to a vertically shaped cup. A final pattern of neuroretinal rim tissue loss is that of a large,

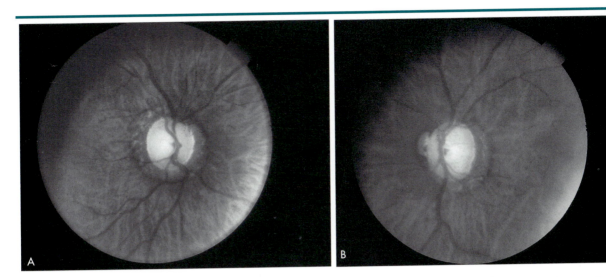

8. This patient has open-angle glaucoma in the right (A) and left (B) eyes. Note the asymmetry in the glaucomatous changes; the left eye shows a thin neuroretinal rim and enlarged cup compared to the right eye. Both eyes also exhibit peripapillary optic atrophy. (*See also* color Plate 92–8).

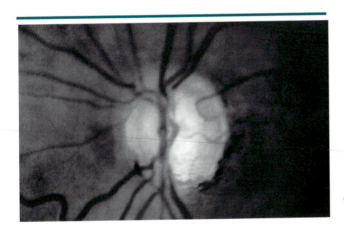

9. Notching of the optic disc neuroretinal rim is noted at the inferior temporal location of this patient's left eye. (*See also* Color Plate 92–9.)

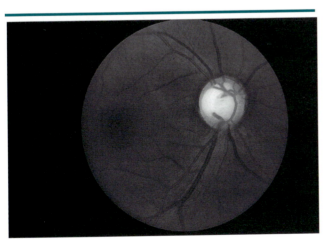

10. Temporal unfolding of the neuroretinal rim is noted in this patient's right optic nerve so that a very thin rim is now present temporally. (*See also* Color Plate 92–10.)

symmetrically thinned neuroretinal rim resulting in a large glaucomatous cup (Fig. 11).

As tissue is lost from the disc due to glaucoma, certain changes also occur to the blood vessels coursing over the optic disc. As the supportive disc tissue is lost, the vessels may appear to be suspended (vessel overpass) over the cup (Fig. 12). With further damage and as time passes, these vessels usually collapse into the bottom of the cup. A "soft" glaucomatous sign associated with vessel change is baring of the circumlinear vessel in which a space forms between the vessel and cup margin (Fig. 13). Felt to be the result of lost disc tissue, this sign has also been observed in healthy individuals. As glaucoma advances, the excavation of the optic cup enlarges over time, leading to the "bean pot" appearance (Fig. 14). In this glaucomatous change associated with advanced disease, the neuroretinal rim is undermined so that the vessels bend and are lost from view as they cross the disc margin.

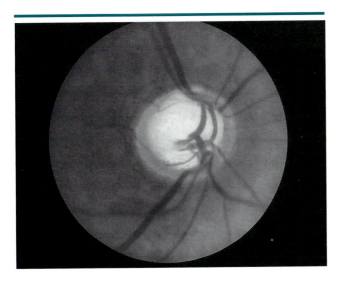

11. Diffuse enlargement of the cup is noted in the right eye of this patient with open-angle glaucoma. A notch is also developing at the superior temporal pole of the optic nerve. (*See also* Color Plate 92–11.) (Courtesy of Rodney Gutner, OD)

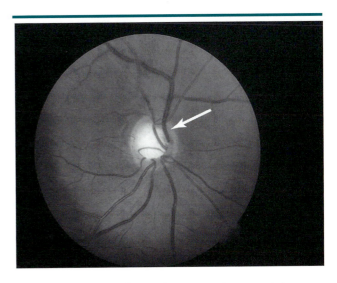

12. In vessel overpass, the vessels appear to be suspended over the cup as they pass over the surface due to loss of supportive disc tissue from glaucomatous damage (arrow). (*See also* Color Plate 92–12.)

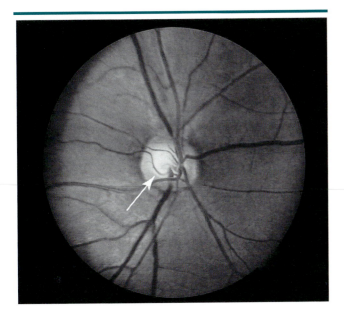

13. A "soft" sign associated with glaucomatous vessel change is baring of the circumlinear vessel in which a space forms between the vessel and the cup margin (arrow). (*See also* Color Plate 92–13.)

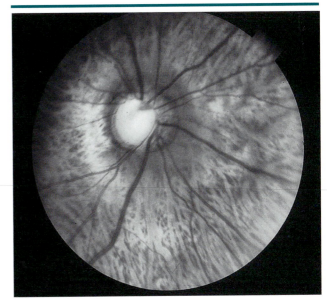

14. In advanced glaucoma, the optic cup may take on a "bean pot" appearance. The neuroretinal rim is undermined so that the vessels bend and are lost from view as they cross the disc margin. (*See also* Color Plate 92–14.)

Small splinter-shaped hemorrhages at the disc margins, typically seen at the superior or inferior poles, are a sign associated with open-angle glaucoma that often precedes focal rim notching and visual field loss (Fig. 15). They are often associated with progressive damage or an unstable glaucomatous condition. Splinter hemorrhages occur in 4 to 7% of patients with primary open-angle glaucoma, and in 6 to 25% of individuals with normal-tension glaucoma. They are transient, last between 4 and 6 weeks, and tend to recur. Splinter hemorrhages are most often seen in the inferotemporal location on the disc and their presence merits reevaluation of the patient's condition.

Peripapillary atrophic changes such as crescents or halos are created by a misalignment of the neurosensory retina, retinal pigment epithelium, choroid, and sclera and are a "soft" sign associated with glaucomatous damage (Fig. 16). Peripapillary atrophy may be indicative of a disc that is more susceptible to damage from elevated IOP or a sign of active damage to this region. Optic disc pallor is another "soft" sign of glaucoma due to ischemia of the disc, often associated with advanced disease.

RNFL defects are an early sign of glaucoma, although their appearance may also be due to diabetes. RNFL dropout occurs in different patterns such as slits, wedges, or diffuse

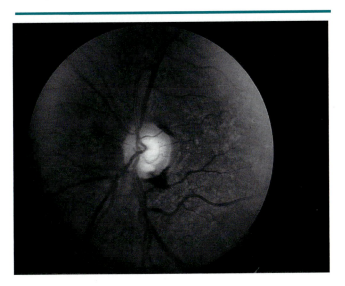

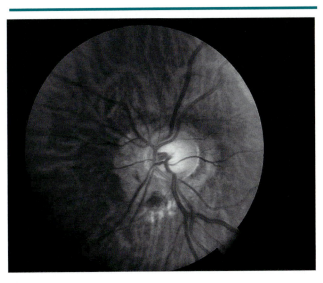

15. A splinter-shaped hemorrhage is noted at the 6-o'clock disc margin. It is a sign associated with open-angle glaucoma that often precedes focal rim notching and visual field loss. (*See also* Color Plate 92–15.)

16. Peripapillary atrophy is another "soft" sign of glaucoma. It may be indicative of a disc that is more susceptible to damage from elevated IOP or a sign of active damage to this region. (*See also* Color plate 92–16.)

atrophy. As retinal nerve fibers are lost, the underlying structures are more easily observed, giving rise to a darkened appearance in a slit or wedge configuration. Slits are multiple, thin areas of dropout, while wedges are at least 2 vein diameters in width (Figs. 17 and 18). True slit or wedge defects extend all the way back to the optic nerve. Diffuse atrophy of the RNFL is difficult to observe, as its main sign is the greater visibility of the underlying retinal vasculature.

■ Contraindications/Complications. As noncontact procedures, fundus biomicroscopy, direct ophthalmoscopy, and BIO offer little risk to the patient, although care must be taken to ensure that the patient is suitable for pupillary dilation. Apprehensive, young, or poorly fixating patients may make the procedure(s) more difficult to perform. Inadequate pupil dilation or significant media opacities can also hinder success. A small corneal abrasion or vasovagal reaction is possible with use of the three-mirror fundus contact lens if undue pressure is exerted on the eye. Individuals with recent ocular trauma, postoperative surgical wounds, infection, or inflammation are not candidates for this contact technique.

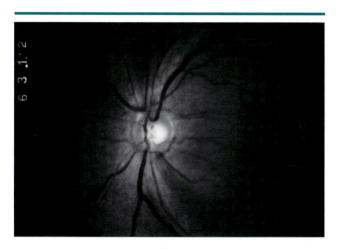

17. Retinal nerve fiber layer (RNFL) dropout in a slit pattern is visible inferior temporal to the disc. Note the beginning notch that corresponds to the RNFL dropout.

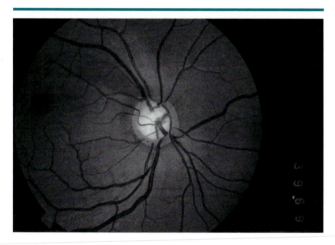

18. Wedged-shaped retinal nerve fiber layer dropout is noted superior temporal to the disc. Note the accompanying notch of the neuroretinal rim.

93

Automated Perimetry

■ **Description/Indications.** Measurement of the visual field is an important test in the diagnosis and management of a host of ocular and neurological conditions. Automated perimetry has replaced manual plotting of the visual field for most ocular conditions and is crucial to the management of individuals with glaucoma. In automated perimetry, a computerized instrument is used that performs many of the roles formally done by a technician. The automated process allows any ophthalmic practice to perform high-quality visual fields without the necessity of having a highly trained perimetrist. Still, an astute technician is required to provide instructions and position the patient properly into the instrument, as well as keeping him or her motivated and attentive throughout the test. Although bridging the gap from manual to automated perimetry has taken the "art" out of performing perimetry, the interpretation of perimetry is still an art that requires careful attention and experience.

In automated perimetry, stimuli are presented in a randomized fashion as the visual field is explored. Different test patterns are available, and selection of the one that will best test areas of the field most likely to be affected is dependent upon the patient's ocular or neurological condition. Light stimuli are presented in a static or nonmoving fashion at predetermined locations, varying in intensity until a threshold measurement is recorded. The most widely used automated perimeters, such as the Humphrey Field Analyzer, Dicon perimeter, and Octopus perimeter, have a normative patient database built into the instrument's onboard computer or accompanying software that becomes the reference of comparison for the locations tested. The database is divided by age, because the sensitivity of the visual field declines as one gets older. The measurements from the points tested are compared individually against the database, and points that fall outside the expected range of values are statistically flagged.

■ **Instrumentation.** Automated perimeter, topical ophthalmic mydriatic/cycloplegic solution(s).

■ **Technique.** If the visual acuity is different from prior examinations or if there is a question that the spectacle prescription may have changed, recheck the refraction before proceeding to perimetry. Optimal visual correction is needed for accurate perimetry results because a small error in central acuity can cause a diffuse visual field loss. Dilate the patient's pupils if they are 3 mm or less. Before dilation, inspect the anterior chamber with the biomicroscope to make sure the eye is suitable to dilate.

Before the test commences, explain to the patient the purpose of automated perimetry and what is expected of him or her. Include in this discussion that automated perimetry tests the side or peripheral vision with a small spot of light that turns on and off in the periphery as the patient looks straight ahead. The spot will vary in intensity and location within the instrument's bowl. When the patient believes the spot of light has been seen, the patient response button should be depressed. Advise the patient to always look at the bright yellow spot straight in front of him or her and not to move the eyes or try to look at the targets. In addition, this central fixation spot should be clear. Make the patient aware that it is acceptable to click the response button after the spot has gone off, as the machine will pause and answers need not be rushed. A new algorithm, SITA (Swedish Interactive Thresholding Algorithm, Humphrey Instruments), reduces testing time in part because it keeps track of patient reaction time and adjusts the stimulus presentation accordingly. Explain that if the patient gets tired, to hold the patient response button down to suspend the test, and that some of the targets may not be visible. Further, brief the patient to ignore any noises associated with the instrument, to concentrate only on the lights projected in the bowl, and to keep the forehead against the rest at all times. Patient cooperation is crucial to obtaining reliable results, and performance is improved if the patient is aware of what is occurring during visual field testing.

Determine which test pattern will be run. For the Humphrey Field Analyzer, a central field test using either the 24-2 or 30-2 test pattern is most commonly performed. The 24-2 and 30-2 patterns are similar; the 24-2 tests fewer points and extends to 24 degrees in all quadrants except nasally, where 2 points are tested at 30 degrees (Fig. 1). The 24-2 pattern is often preferred because it accomplishes many of the goals required for a central threshold test and takes less time. Individuals with severely reduced fields of vision may require a 10-degree field such as the 10-2 test pattern. The target may also need to be enlarged to a size V target for patients with reduced visual fields or acuity. In addition, decide if the test is to be run in the standard threshold configuration or if test parameters need to be modified. Modifications include using the "fastpac" or "SITA fast" strategy for the Humphrey Field Analyzer, in which testing time is reduced because the points are brack-

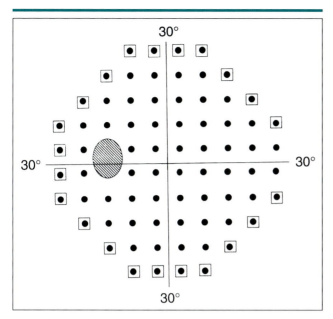

1. A template for a Humphrey Field Analyzer 30-2 and 24-2 test pattern is shown for the left eye. The 30-2 points are shown by solid dots. All edge points (marked with a box) except for the two nasally are omitted in a 24-2 test. There are 76 points tested in a 30-2 test and 55 points in a 24-2 test.

eted in one rather than two directions or the test location error measurement end-point is adjusted. Other instrument modifications may include using a smaller test target (size II) for blind spot evaluation when an excess number of fixation losses are noted, or using the "gaze tracker" for the Humphrey perimeter as an alternate method of fixation monitoring. Also decide if the foveal threshold will be tested. Once the test pattern and modifications are selected, program the patient's data into the instrument. The correct date of birth is necessary for the instrument to statistically analyze the field accurately as well as for calculating the requisite trial lens. Insert the narrow rim trial lens into the lens holder, checking to make sure the lenses are clean before placing them into the instrument.

Place an eye patch over the untested eye and position the patient into the chin and forehead rest. Proper patient positioning is crucial to obtaining accurate results. The patient should be sitting erect with a very slight bend to the back (Fig. 2A). The patient should not have to droop the shoulders or stretch the neck to position into the chin rest (Fig. 2B, 2C). Adjust the table height and the position of the stool until the patient is positioned properly. For individuals with a prominent nose, turn the head very slightly in the direction of the occluded eye to increase the patient's peripheral field of view and decrease the obstruction from the nose. The head turn is slight and the patient still must fixate directly straight ahead. Also, for individuals with prominent brows that may obstruct the superior field of vision, position the chin with a slight tilt upward to move the brow back and away from the field of vision. A lid droop is not a contraindication to performing perimetry, but taping of the eyelids may be required to ensure reliable results. Apply a single piece of tape to the lid to pull it upwards towards the brow (Fig. 3).

Ask the patient to fixate straight ahead and determine if he or she is comfortable. If so, bring the trial lens as close to the patient's eye as possible without touching the eyelashes or globe. Observe the position of the eye in the monitor and adjust the height of the trial lens so that it is centered in front of the pupil (Fig. 4). Hand the patient the response button and instruct him or her to press once a target is visible. Run the demonstration test if this is the patient's first automated perimetry experience and alert the patient to watch for targets. Have a technician in or near the testing room to monitor the patient's progress, results, and fixation. The technician needs to periodically coach the patient, providing encouragement and letting him or her know how much time is remaining. If a patient exhibits many fixation losses, stop the test and replot the blind spot. If a patient is a "happy clicker," giving many false-positive responses, also stop the test and reinstruct the patient on what is expected. Once the test is completed, save the field

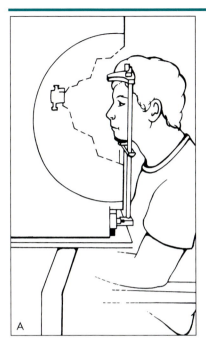

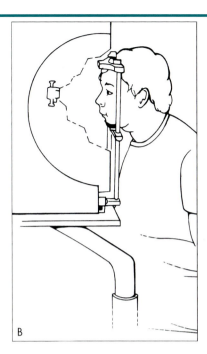

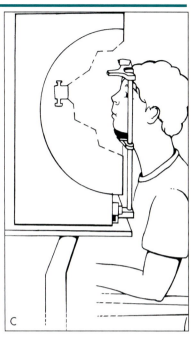

2. A. Patient positioning at the perimeter is important for a successful, reliable test. The patient needs to be comfortably positioned close to the instrument with the head centered and back straight.

2. B. Improper positioning leads to an uncomfortable patient who tires easily and moves noticeably during the test. This patient is positioned too far from instrument, causing him or her to stretch to get into the unit.

2. C. This patient is also positioned improperly at the perimeter. The instrument is too high so that the patient must stretch the neck to get into position.

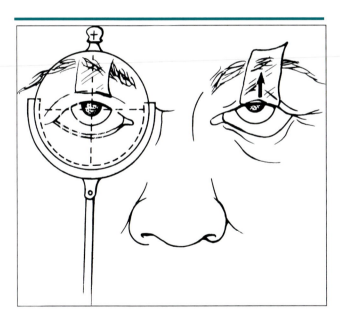

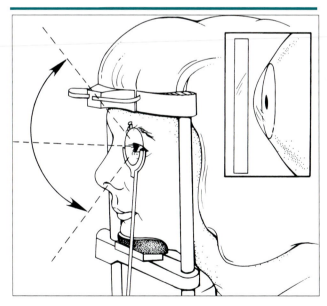

3. A piece of tape is applied to the upper lid to lift it and reduce the effects of physiologic ptosis on the results of visual field testing.

4. The trial lens must be positioned as close to the eye as possible (inset), without touching the eyelashes or globe, to ensure that the field is not obstructed by the rim of the lens.

data to the disk, test the other eye, and print the results in the desired format. Formats include the standard single field printout, an overview printout that lists chronologically all visual fields performed in a condensed fashion printed vertically on a page, and a glaucoma change probability printout that is used to monitor for change after a patient has performed several field tests (Fig. 5).

Another method to perform perimetry is with a screening strategy in which points are tested using a suprathreshold light stimulus. This test is an excellent way to perform the initial visual field as it tends to be quick and less taxing for the patient. Disadvantages of screening fields include not providing quantified information regarding the extent to which a point may be depressed, and missing subtle early defects. The screening strategy is the preferred method to test the peripheral field, because this region is relatively insensitive with great variability, and the more detailed threshold strategy provides no further benefit. There are different methods to perform screening fields with the recommended strategy one that accounts for the patient's age and test point location. The screening pattern and strategy most often used for glaucoma is the 120-point 3-zone full field pattern in which points are tested centrally and peripherally (Fig. 6). Any point missed on initial presentation, which is based upon the expected hill of vision corrected for the patient's age, is retested with a very bright stimulus.

5. A. (top left) An automated perimetry 30-2 single field printout showing a normal, full field. The gaze tracker is the horizontal line on the bottom of the page, indicating excellent eye position throughout the test. Vertical deflections upward indicate a change in gaze position, and lines deflected downward are indicative of a blink or closure of the eyes. B. (top right) An overview printout of a patient with glaucoma showing three fields performed over an 18-month period. The overview printout allows a quick analysis of several fields. In this case, the visual field defect appears to have increased both in size and density. C. (bottom left) The glaucoma change probability printout of the patient in 5B. The first two fields are averaged and each additional field is compared to this baseline. Open triangles indicate points improved from baseline and closed triangles indicate those that are worse. In this example several of the points did change from the baseline fields, indicating possible progression of the visual field defect.

6. (bottom right) A 120-point full-field three-zone screening field. This patient has glaucoma, indicated by the inferior nasal step with breakthrough into the superior field. Screening fields give a gross approximation of the field and allow an appreciation of how large a defect is. Alternatively, threshold fields give quantifiable measurements that are used to monitor for change over time.

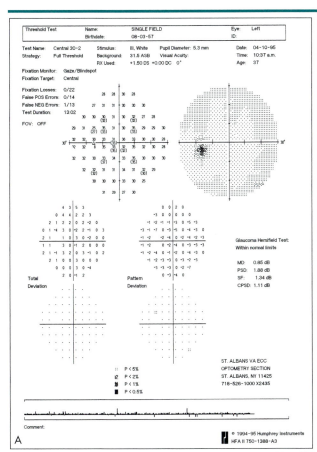

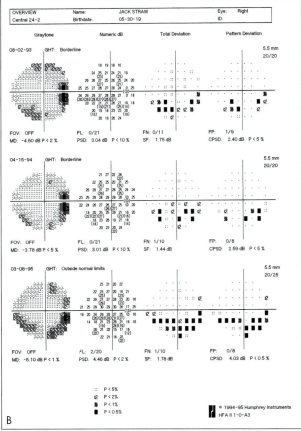

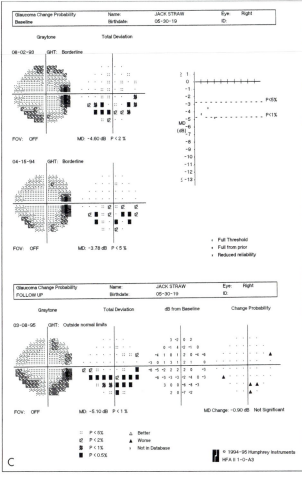

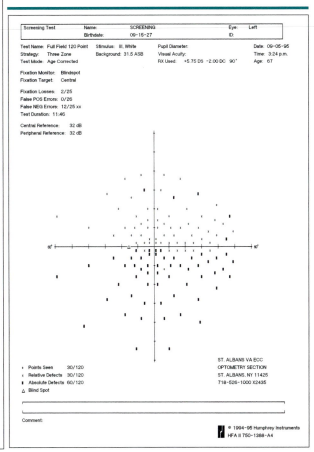

■ **Interpretation.** The threshold visual field is comprised of six different components, each having a role in the interpretation (Fig. 7). The first area requiring attention contains the reliability indices, which consist of fixation losses, false-positive responses, false-negative responses, and short-term fluctuation. The reliability indices need to be reviewed collectively rather than in isolation. A high number of fixation losses with excellent outcomes of the remaining indices is indicative of a head tilt or misaligned patient and not poor performance (Fig. 8A). The Humphrey Field Analyzer HFA II comes with an automated gaze tracking system that provides a readout of the patient's gaze position throughout the test (Fig. 7). This readout is often more descriptive of actual patient fixation performance, and its use allows the blind spot fixation monitor to be shut off, reducing test time. A high number of false-negative responses with excellent outcomes of the remaining indices is often observed in moderate to advanced glaucomatous field loss and not indicative of poor performance (Fig. 8B). Elevated short-term fluctuation with excellent reliability indices is associated with possible early glaucomatous loss or poor patient performance if the other reliability indices are also reduced. The one reliability parameter that can greatly diminish the quality of the field and needs to be carefully monitored is an excess number of false-positive responses. The instrument will alert the examiner when fixation losses are greater than 20%, or false-positive or false-negative responses are greater than 33% of the trials.

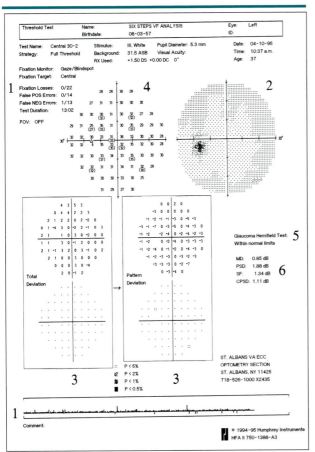

7. (left) There are six components used to evaluate visual fields. The reliability indices (1) are the first area to be evaluated, and the gray scale (2) is assessed next. The total and pattern deviation symbols (3) are reviewed in tandem and any difference must be explained. The raw data (4) are reviewed to understand the actual depth to which each point is damaged. The GHT (5) is evaluated next; the global indices (6) are evaluated last and used to confirm damage already noted.

8. A. (below left) This is an example of pseudofixation loss. Upon quick inspection, this patient appears to have been a poor test taker due to the excessive number of fixation losses. On closer inspection, the remaining reliability indices are excellent as is the short-term fluctuation. This patient either shifted gaze during the test or the blind spot was not properly set at the beginning of the test, leading to an excessive number of fixation losses. The technician performing the test noted the patient did have excellent fixation during the test. If pseudofixation loss is seen early in the test, it is wise to replot the blind spot. **B.** (below right) An example of a patient with moderate glaucoma with both hemifields damaged. All the reliability indices are excellent except for an excessive number of false-negative errors. This is often seen in moderate to advanced glaucomatous fields and is not due to a poor test taker. Rather, the damaged receptors do not recuperate in time for the visual system to respond when retested, and as a result, a very bright stimulus is not seen at a point previously evaluated.

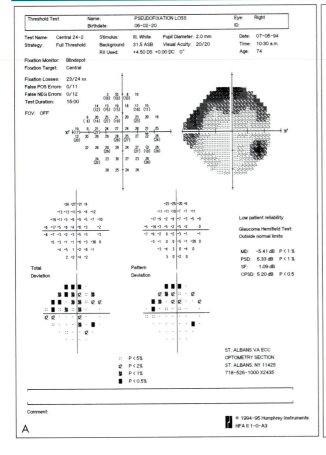

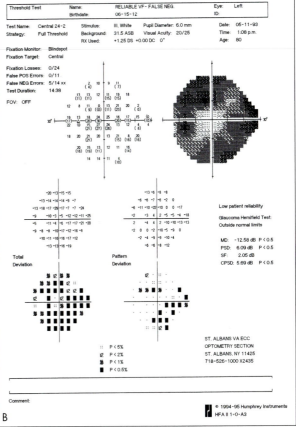

The second area to review is the gray scale, which is a shaded gross approximation of the visual field. Darker areas correspond to reduced sensitivity. The gray scale can be misleading and should be used sparingly, because other areas of the printout are more indicative of the state of the visual field.

The third area to evaluate is the total and pattern deviation areas, which are reviewed in tandem. A database of expected values for each test location is stored within the computer and categorized by age. The reading at each test location is compared against the expected value, and the difference appears in the numeric total deviation table. Just below the numeric value is a statistical probability plot, which indicates by numeric significance the potential for this score to be seen in a "normal" individual. Dark boxes indicate a probability of less than 0.5%, and four dots in a box indicate a significance of less than 5%. A 0.5% probability means that less than one-half of one percent of normal individuals will have that score. Adjacent to the total deviation table and plot are the pattern deviation table and significance plots, which are a further calculation of the total deviation table utilizing the overall field depression or elevation. The probability plots tend to be the best overall indicator of performance, and a comparison of the pattern and total deviation symbols gives indication whether a cataract or some other element may have affected the field. A pattern deviation plot that appears better than the total deviation plot could be caused by either a cataract, advanced glaucoma, inaccurate refraction, dirty trial lens, or the wrong age entered into the instrument (Fig. 9A). A clinical examination including slit lamp biomicroscopy (see p. 22) and optic nerve evaluation (see p. 310) should provide insight into this discrepancy. When the pattern deviation plot looks worse than the total deviation plot, it is usually due to a patient who is overanxious and clicking the patient response button too quickly without actually visualizing the targets (Fig. 9B). A high false-positive ratio and white scotomas on the gray scale may also be associated.

The fourth area to review is the raw threshold data, the actual numeric value in decibels of each point tested. The higher the decibel reading, the more sensitive the spot tested and the dimmer the light visualized. The raw data area is not heavily used and is referred to when further information is required regarding the sensitivity of the tested points.

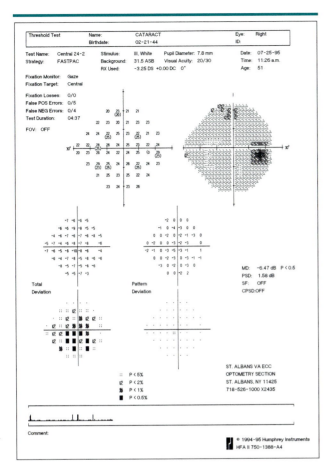

9. A. An example of a field reduced due to a cataract. The mean defect is reduced (MD) and the total deviation plot is affected but the pattern deviation plot is clear. This display can also be seen due to diffuse visual field loss from an improper refraction or advanced glaucoma. The ocular health examination confirmed that a cataract was the cause of the visual field defect.

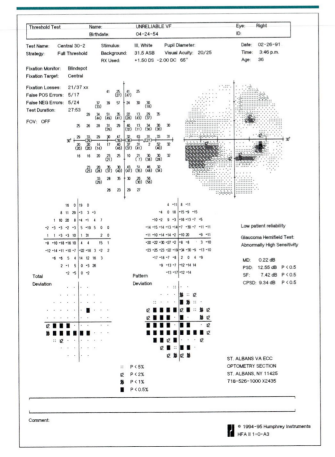

9. B. A visual field from an unreliable patient. There are several signs on the printout indicating a poor test taker, such as the excessive number of fixation losses, high number of both false-positive and false-negative errors, and high short-term fluctuation. Also the GHT message reads "abnormally high sensitivity," and white scotomas are present on the gray scale, indicating areas of abnormally high sensitivity. Upon inspection of the raw data, many points are abnormally elevated with readings in the 40s and 50s (in dB).

The fifth area to review, if available, is the glaucoma hemifield test (GHT), which compares clusters of points in one hemifield to their mirror-image counterparts in the other hemifield. Open-angle glaucoma is a condition that tends to be asymmetric in its involvement of the optic nerve between eyes and even in the same eye. Thus, one half of the eye (hemifield) tends to be affected to a greater extent, especially early in the condition. The GHT is a sensitive test that contains different evaluation messages, such as "within normal limits," "borderline," "reduced sensitivity," or "outside normal limits." A GHT message of "outside normal limits" needs to be viewed with concern.

The last area to review is the global indices, which comprise the mean deviation or overall measure of depression for the entire field, pattern standard deviation or measure of localized areas of loss, short-term fluctuation (SF) or intratest variability, and corrected pattern standard deviation, which is a refinement of pattern standard deviation that takes SF into account.

Review the six areas of the field together along with the results of a detailed eye examination to understand and interpret any defects noted (Figs. 10 to 13). Care must be taken when interpreting automated perimetry results, especially if analyzing the patient's first field. Localized defects

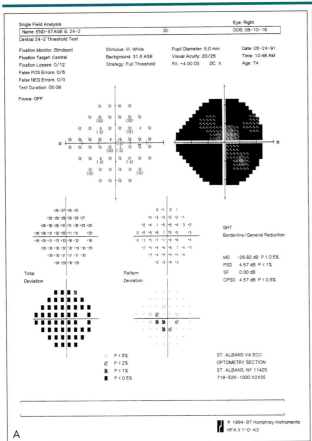

Single Field Analysis   Eye: Right
Name: END-STAGE G. 24-2   ID: DOB: 08-10-16
Central 24-2 Threshold Test

Fixation Monitor: Blindspot   Stimulus: III. White   Pupil Diameter: 5.0 mm   Date: 05-24-91
Fixation Target: Central   Background: 31.5 ASB   Visual Acuity: 20/25   Time: 10:48 AM
Fixation Losses: 0/12   Strategy: Full Threshold   RX: +4.00 DS   DC X   Age: 74
False POS Errors: 0/6
False NEG Errors: 0/0
Test Duration: 05:08
Fovea: OFF

GHT
Borderline / General Reduction

MD   -28.82 dB P < 0.5%
PSD   4.57 dB P < 1%
SF   0.00 dB
CPSD   4.57 dB P < 0.5%

Total Deviation   Pattern Deviation

:: P < 5%
∅ P < 2%
▧ P < 1%
■ P < 0.5%

ST. ALBANS VA ECC
OPTOMETRY SECTION
ST. ALBANS, NY 11425
718-526-1000 X2435

© 1994-97 Humphrey Instruments
HFA II 1-0-A3

A

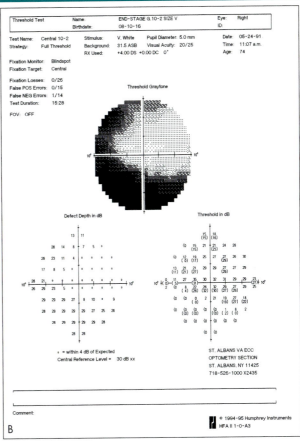

Threshold Test   Name: END-STAGE G.10-2 SIZE V   Eye: Right
Birthdate: 08-10-16   ID:

Test Name: Central 10-2   Stimulus: V. White   Pupil Diameter: 5.0 mm   Date: 05-24-91
Strategy: Full Threshold   Background: 31.5 ASB   Visual Acuity: 20/25   Time: 11:07 a.m.
RX Used: +4.00 DS +0.00 DC 0°   Age: 74

Fixation Monitor: Blindspot
Fixation Target: Central
Fixation Losses: 0/25
False POS Errors: 0/15
False NEG Errors: 1/14
Test Duration: 15:28
FOV: OFF

Threshold Graytone

Defect Depth in dB   Threshold in dB

∘ = within 4 dB of Expected
Central Reference Level = 30 dB xx

ST. ALBANS VA ECC
OPTOMETRY SECTION
ST. ALBANS, NY 11425
718-526-1000 X2435

Comment:

© 1994-95 Humphrey Instruments
HFA II 1-0-A3

B

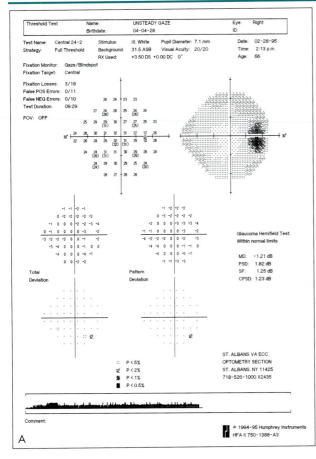

Threshold Test   Name: UNSTEADY GAZE   Eye: Right
Birthdate: 04-04-28   ID:

Test Name: Central 24-2   Stimulus: III. White   Pupil Diameter: 7.1 mm   Date: 02-28-95
Strategy: Full Threshold   Background: 31.5 ASB   Visual Acuity: 20/20   Time: 2:13 p.m.
RX Used: +3.50 DS +0.00 DC 0°   Age: 66

Fixation Monitor: Gaze/Blindspot
Fixation Target: Central
Fixation Losses: 3/18
False POS Errors: 0/11
False NEG Errors: 0/10
Test Duration: 09:29
FOV: OFF

Glaucoma Hemifield Test:
Within normal limits

MD: -1.21 dB
PSD: 1.82 dB
SF: 1.25 dB
CPSD: 1.23 dB

Total Deviation   Pattern Deviation

:: P < 5%
∅ P < 2%
▧ P < 1%
■ P < 0.5%

ST. ALBANS VA ECC
OPTOMETRY SECTION
ST. ALBANS, NY 11425
718-526-1000 X2435

Comment:

© 1994-95 Humphrey Instruments
HFA II 750-1388-A3

A

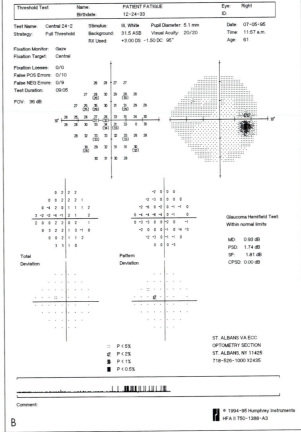

Threshold Test   Name: PATIENT FATIGUE   Eye: Right
Birthdate: 12-24-33   ID:

Test Name: Central 24-2   Stimulus: III. White   Pupil Diameter: 5.1 mm   Date: 07-05-95
Strategy: Full Threshold   Background: 31.5 ASB   Visual Acuity: 20/20   Time: 11:57 a.m.
RX Used: +3.00 DS -1.50 DC 95°   Age: 61

Fixation Monitor: Gaze
Fixation Target: Central
Fixation Losses: 0/0
False POS Errors: 0/10
False NEG Errors: 0/9
Test Duration: 09:05
FOV: 36 dB

Glaucoma Hemifield Test:
Within normal limits

MD: 0.93 dB
PSD: 1.74 dB
SF: 1.81 dB
CPSD: 0.00 dB

Total Deviation   Pattern Deviation

:: P < 5%
∅ P < 2%
▧ P < 1%
■ P < 0.5%

ST. ALBANS VA ECC
OPTOMETRY SECTION
ST. ALBANS, NY 11425
718-526-1000 X2435

Comment:

© 1994-95 Humphrey Instruments
HFA II 750-1388-A3

B

XII

Suggested Readings

Airaksinen PJ, Drance SM, Schulzer M: Neuroretinal rim area in early glaucoma. *Am J Ophthalmol* 1985;**99:**1–4.

Anderson DR: *Automated Static Perimetry*. St. Louis, Mosby, 1992.

Choplin NT, Edwards RP: *Visual Field Testing With the Humphrey Field Analyzer*. Thorofare, NJ, Slack, 1995.

Haley MJ: *The Field Analyzer Primer*. San Leandro, CA, Humphrey Instruments, 1987.

Kaiser HJ, Flammier J: *Visual Field Atlas*. Basel, University Eye Clinic, 1992.

Lachenmayer BJ, Vivell MO: *Perimetry and its Clinical Correlations*. New York, Thieme, 1993.

Lalle PA: Visual Fields, in Lewis TL, Fingeret M (eds): *Primary Care of the Glaucomas*. Norwalk, CT, Appleton & Lange, 1993, pp 159–195.

Lieberman MF, Drake MV: *Computerized Perimetry. A Simplified Guide*. Thorofare, NJ, Slack, 1992.

Litwak AB: Evaluation of the optic nerve in glaucoma, in Lewis TL, Fingeret M (eds): *Primary Care of the Glaucomas*. Norwalk, CT, Appleton & Lange, 1993, pp 137–158.

Litwak AB: Evaluation of the retinal nerve fiber layer in glaucoma. *J Am Optom Assoc* 1990;**61:**390–397.

Ritch R, Shields MB, Krupin T: *The Glaucomas*. St. Louis, Mosby, 1996.

Sommer A, Quigley HA, Robbin AL, et al: Evaluation of nerve fiber layer assessment. *Arch Ophthalmol* 1991;**109:**77–83.

Varma R, Spaeth GL, Parker KW: *The Optic Nerve in Glaucoma*. Philadelphia, Lippincott, 1993.

XIII

Periocular Injection Procedures

94

Preparing the Equipment and Medication

■ **Description/Indications.** Local injections into the periocular tissues are used for a variety of purposes, the most common of which is to achieve local anesthesia for minor lid procedures (see p. 417). Periocular injection is also used to deliver a more concentrated, localized dosage of medication than can be achieved by topical or systemic administration, and to locally administer medication that poorly penetrates the epithelium of the cornea or conjunctiva. This chapter describes the technique of preparing the equipment and medication used for injection. The following chapters describe specific techniques related to periocular injection.

Sterile, single-use disposable stainless steel needles are used for periocular injections. They come individually packaged and capped in a protective plastic sheath or cap (Fig. 1A). To prevent needle contamination and accidental needle sticks, the protective plastic cap is kept in place until the needle is used. The hub of the needle attaches to the desired sterile syringe (Fig. 1B).

Needles are available in various lengths. Those used most commonly range from 3/8 inch to 2 inches long. Needles also come in various widths or gauges, ranging from 16 to 30G. The relative width or bore of the needle is inversely proportional to the numeric designation; that is, an 18G needle is larger in diameter than a 30G (Fig. 2). Not all gauge sizes come in every length.

The length of the needle used is determined by the anticipated depth of the injection and the amount of medication to be delivered. For example, a shorter, higher-gauge needle is used to inject a small amount of medication intradermally for tuberculosis diagnostic testing, whereas a longer, lower-gauge needle is used to inject a larger amount of medication intramuscularly. An advantage of higher-gauge needles is that they produce less discomfort and a smaller break in the skin than do lower-gauge needles. However, the smaller lumen size of the higher-gauge needles means that it is necessary to apply more force on the plunger of the syringe to eject the solution as compared to the lower-gauge needles. In addition, more than one needle size may be used in the course of preparing for and administering an injection. For example, it is common to use a longer, lower-gauge needle to aspirate the injection solution into the syringe, and then change to a shorter, higher-gauge needle for periocular injection.

Sterile, single-use disposable plastic syringes are used for periocular injections. They come in various sizes in individual sterile packaging (Fig. 3A). The size of the syringe chosen will be determined by the amount of drug to be injected as well as the relative ease of manipulating the syringe in the periocular area. In general, syringes used in periocular injection tend to be smaller in size, ranging from 1 cc (tuberculin syringe) to 5 cc (Fig. 3). The tip of the syringe is threaded to accommodate the hub of the needle, with the exception of the tuberculin syringe, which has a smooth tip over which the hub of the needle is placed. The syringe may come prepackaged with a specific needle size already attached, which can be removed if necessary. Alternatively, the syringe may come with only a small protective plastic cap attached to the tip, which is removed to attach the appropriate needle.

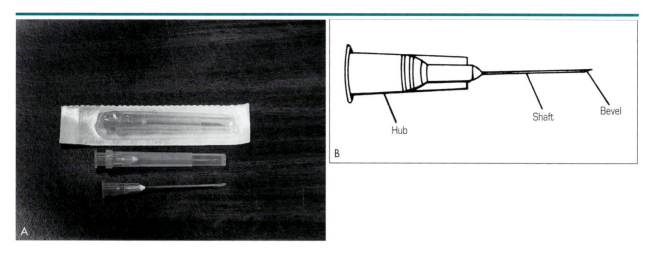

1. A. A single-use disposable stainless steel 18G 1½-inch needle is shown in its sterile package (top), with the protective plastic cap in place (middle), and without the protective plastic cap (bottom). B. The major components of the disposable needle are illustrated.

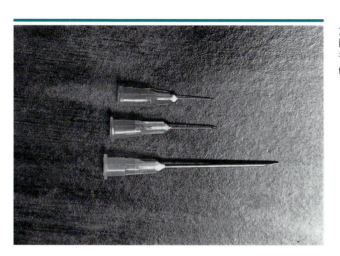

2. Sterile disposable needles come in various bore sizes (gauges) and lengths. Shown for comparison are a 30G ½-inch needle (top), a 25G ⅝-inch needle (middle), and an 18G 1½-inch needle (bottom). Note that the 18G needle is larger in diameter than the 30G.

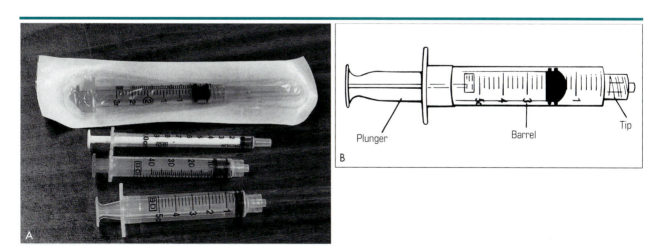

3. A. A single-use disposable 3-cc syringe is shown in its sterile package with a preattached 25G ⅝-inch needle (top). Various sizes of syringes are shown ranging from 1 cc (tuberculin syringe) to 5 cc. B. The major components of the disposable syringe are illustrated.

Commonly used medications for periocular injection are solutions or suspensions that come in multiuse glass vials (Fig. 4A). The mouth of the vial is covered with a self-sealing rubber stopper diaphragm through which medication is aspirated using a sterile needle and syringe. A small metal or plastic cap is placed over the rubber stopper of the vial when it is not in use. Because a partial vacuum can be created in the rubber-sealed vial making it difficult to aspirate solution, air is initially injected into the vial. Before solution is aspirated from the vial, an alcohol pad is used to clean the rubber stopper. More than one vial may be used if solutions are to be mixed in the syringe.

Some brands of injectable fluorescein sodium solution used for intravenous fluorescein angiography come in small, single-dose glass ampules (Fig. 4B). The ampule is opened by breaking the thin neck, which has been prescored by the manufacturer.

■ **Instrumentation.** Sterile syringe of desired size, sterile 18G 1½-inch needle(s), sterile needle of desired size for injection, sterile 20G 1½-inch needle, vial(s) or ampule(s) of medication, sterile alcohol pads, sterile gauze pads, puncture-resistant container for needle and syringe disposal (biohazard sharps container).

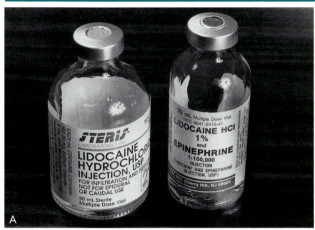

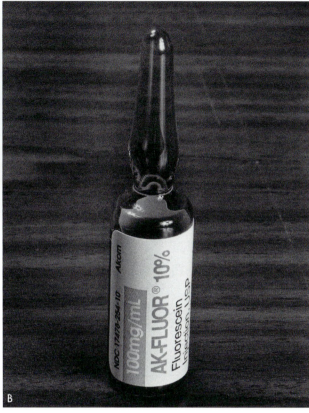

4. Commonly used medications for periocular injection come in multiuse glass vials (A) or single-dose glass ampules (B). Note that the multiuse glass vial has a self-sealing rubber stopper that is covered with a protective cap when not in use.

■ Technique

Preparing the Syringe From a Single Medication Vial:
Verify on the label of the vial that the correct medication has been chosen for injection. Remove the metal or plastic cap from the rubber seal of the medication vial, and swab the rubber seal with a sterile alcohol pad (Fig. 5). Open the sterile package of a plastic disposable syringe, and remove the preattached needle or plastic cap using a slight unscrewing motion. Attach an 18G 1½-inch needle to the tip of the syringe using a slight screwing motion (Fig. 6A). Remove the needle cap and keep it on the counter or tabletop in the nearby vicinity (Fig. 6B). Pull back on the plunger to draw

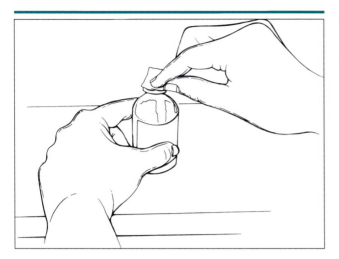

5. Before the needle is inserted to withdraw the medication, the rubber stopper of the multiuse glass vial is swabbed with a sterile alcohol pad.

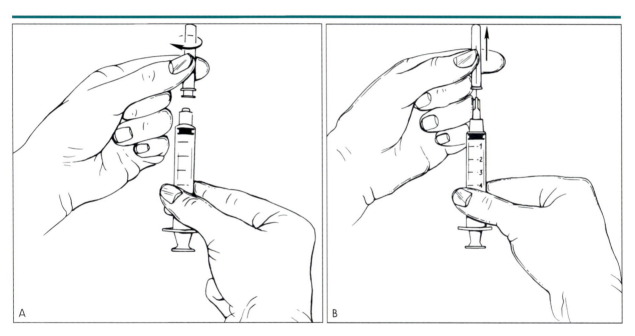

A

B

6. A. A slight screwing motion is used to attach a sterile 18G 1½-inch needle to the syringe. B. The protective cap is removed and placed on a counter or tabletop in the nearby vicinity.

air into the syringe equal in volume to the amount of solution to be aspirated (Fig. 7A). Hold the vial between the thumb and middle fingers of the nondominant hand, invert the vial, and with the vial at eye level, insert the needle through the center of the rubber seal with the bevel towards you so that its position is easily visualized (Fig. 7B). Hold the tip of the needle above the fluid level in the vial and inject the air into the vial (Fig. 7C). Withdraw the syringe slightly to position the tip of the needle below the fluid level. Grasp the end of the syringe barrel and plunger between the thumb and forefinger of the dominant hand and withdraw the plunger slightly to fill the syringe with the desired volume of solution (Fig. 8A). Be sure to hold the vial and syringe vertically so that the fluid level may be properly read on the markings on the barrel of the syringe. When the desired volume of solution has been aspirated, withdraw the needle from the vial by pulling back on the barrel of the syringe (Fig. 8B).

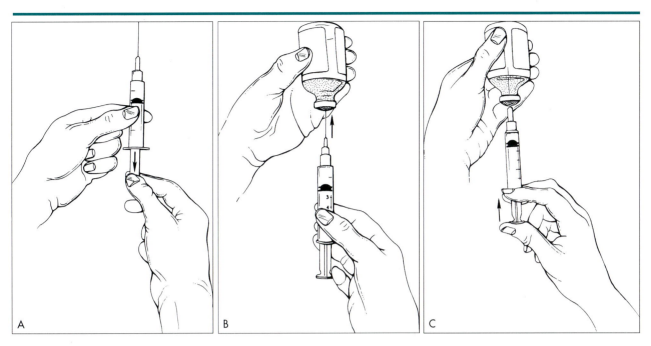

7. The plunger is withdrawn to aspirate air into the syringe (A), the vial is inverted, and the needle is inserted through the center of the rubber seal (B). The tip of the needle is positioned above the fluid level in the vial and the aspirated air is injected into the vial (C).

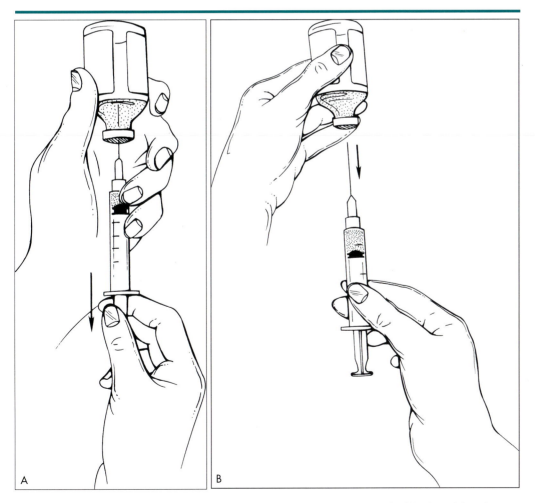

8. A. The syringe is withdrawn slightly to position the tip of the needle below the fluid level, and then the plunger is withdrawn to fill the syringe with the desired volume of solution. B. The needle is withdrawn from the vial by pulling back on the barrel of the syringe.

Hold the syringe and needle vertically at eye level with the needle upward. Gently tap the side of the syringe to remove any air bubbles, which will appear at the top of the fluid level (Fig. 9A). Pull back on the plunger slightly, and then push the plunger upward to fully eject the air (Fig. 9B).

If the syringe and needle have been prepared at a location other than chairside for the patient, recap the needle until the injection is administered. To avoid accidental needle-stick injury, use a one-handed technique to guide the needle into the cap while the cap is still lying on the counter or tabletop, being careful not to contaminate the needle (Fig. 10A). Once the needle is well inserted into the cap, use your other hand to snap the protective cap in

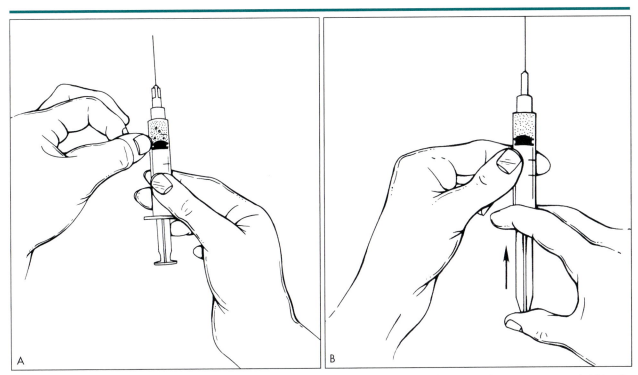

9. A. The syringe and needle are held vertically at eye level, and the side of the syringe is gently tapped to remove any air bubbles. B. The plunger is slightly withdrawn then pushed upward to fully eject residual air in the syringe.

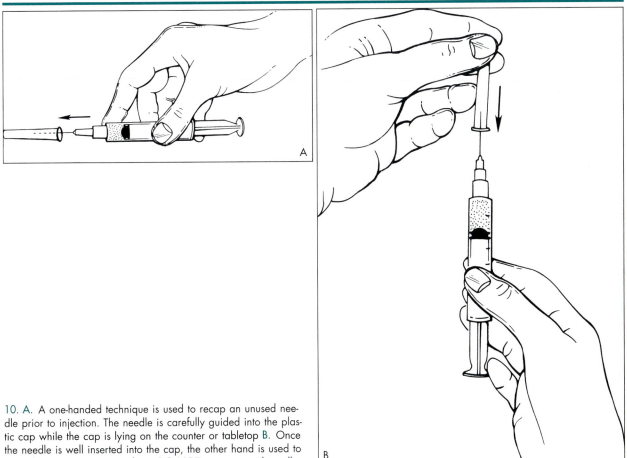

10. A. A one-handed technique is used to recap an unused needle prior to injection. The needle is carefully guided into the plastic cap while the cap is lying on the counter or tabletop B. Once the needle is well inserted into the cap, the other hand is used to snap the protective cap in place. DO NOT recap a used needle.

place (Fig. 10B). Recap the medication vial. Remove the capped 18G needle from the syringe and attach the capped sterile needle of desired length and gauge for periocular injection.

Preparing the Syringe From Two Medication Vials: Verify on the labels of the vials that the correct medications have been chosen for injection. To mix two solutions into a single syringe from two multidose vials (vials X and Y), use two 18G 1½-inch needles. Attach one of the needles to the syringe and aspirate air into the syringe equal in volume to the dose of medication from vial X. Inject the air into vial X as described (Fig. 11A). Recap the needle using the one-handed technique. Remove the 18G needle for vial X from the syringe and attach the sterile 18G needle for vial Y. Aspirate a volume of air equal to the dose of medication from vial Y. Inject the air into vial Y as described, and then aspirate the desired solution from vial Y (Fig. 11B). Withdraw the needle for vial Y and recap it using the one-handed technique. Reattach the capped needle for vial X, insert it into vial X, and aspirate the desired

solution dosage (Fig. 11C). Eliminate excess air from the syringe, recap the needle using the one-handed technique (Fig. 10), and attach the desired size needle, as described above.

Preparing the Syringe From a Glass Ampule: Attach a sterile capped 20G 1½-inch needle to a sterile 5-mL syringe, saving the original cap from the syringe. Verify on the label of the ampule that the correct medication has been chosen for injection. Gently tap the stem of the ampule to ensure that all the medication is in the body of the ampule (Fig. 12). Wrap a small gauze pad around the top of the ampule, and using a quick snapping motion, break off the top of the ampule along the prescored line at the neck (Fig. 13). Snap the top of the ampule toward you so that the break is away from your body. Place the opened ampule on a flat surface.

Uncap the needle; do not draw air into the syringe. Insert the needle into the ampule, taking care not to contaminate the needle by touching the rim of the ampule. Pull back on the plunger to draw the medication into the syringe while it is lying on a flat surface or while it is inverted after

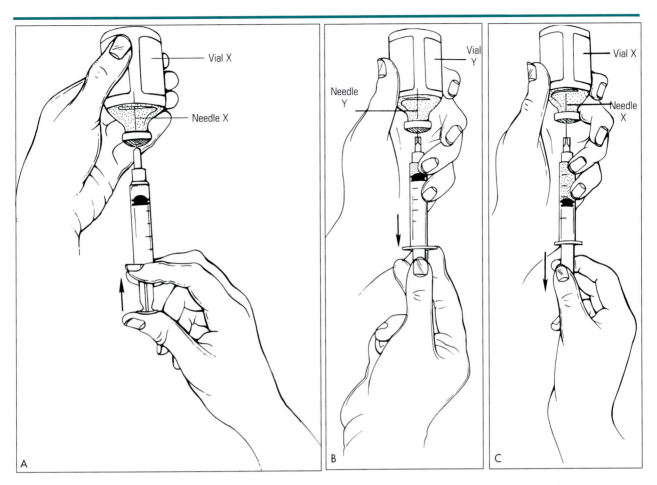

11. A. To prepare the syringe from two medication vials (vials X and Y), needle X is first attached, air is aspirated into the syringe, and the air is injected into vial X. The needle is recapped using the one-handed technique, and then needle X is removed. B. Needle Y is attached, more air is aspirated into the syringe, the air is injected into vial Y, and the desired volume of solution is aspirated from vial Y. The needle is recapped using the one-handed technique, and then needle Y is removed. C. Needle X is reattached and the desired volume of solution is aspirated from vial X. Excess air is eliminated from the syringe, and the desired size needle is attached.

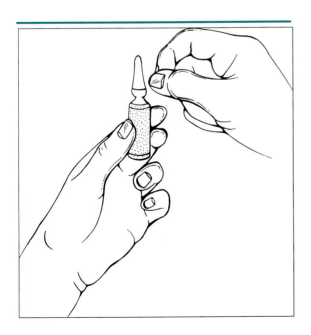

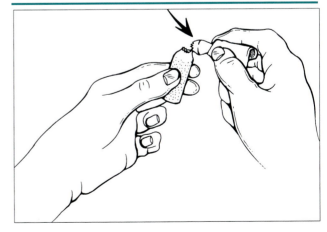

12. (left) To withdraw medication from a glass ampule, the stem of the ampule is first gently tapped to ensure that all the medication is in the body of the ampule.

13. (above) To open the ampule, a small gauze pad is wrapped around the top of the ampule and it is snapped toward you so that the break is away from your body.

the needle has been inserted (Fig. 14). Recap the needle using the one-handed technique (Fig. 10). Remove the capped needle from the syringe and replace it with the original syringe cap in preparation for attaching the filled syringe to the plastic tubing of the butterfly needle for fluorescein angiography (see p. 262).

■ Contraindications/Complications.
If air is not initially injected into the vial, the resultant negative pressure will make it difficult to withdraw the desired amount of solution. Conversely, if too much air is initially injected into the vial, the resultant positive pressure may force too much solution into the syringe or cause the plunger to eject from the syringe. If solutions are mixed in a single syringe, it is important to ensure that they are compatible. The use of improper technique for mixing solutions in a single syringe may result in contamination of a multidose vial. Some clinicians use the same needle to withdraw the medication as will be used for the actual injection (e.g., 25 or 30G) rather than the 18G needle described in this technique.

Packaged needles and syringes should be stored in a locked cabinet or drawer. During preparation of the equipment, proper care and technique must be used to avoid contamination of the injection equipment and solution as well as to prevent accidental needle sticks. Adhere fully to proper procedures for universal precautions (see p. 475). The one-handed technique described here for recapping a needle that has not yet been used for injection does not apply to used needles. Used needles should be disposed of in a biohazard sharps container without recapping.

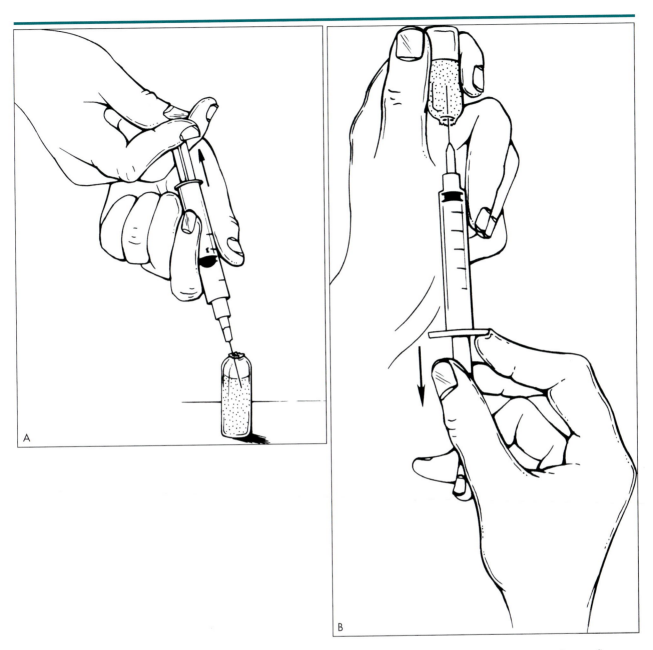

14. To fill the syringe from an open ampule, either the medication is withdrawn from the ampule while it is sitting upright on a flat surface (A), or the ampule is inverted and the medication is withdrawn after the needle has been inserted (B).

95

Local Infiltration Anesthesia of the Lid

■ **Description/Indications.** Local infiltration anesthesia of the lid is essential to performing minor invasive lid procedures. The purpose of this section is to describe focal subcutaneous infiltration of the lid with local anesthetic to block the nerves traversing the injected area. This is in contrast to regional anesthetic nerve blocks, which are used in more invasive surgery.

The skin of the lid is among the thinnest in the body. It is maximally 1 mm thick in the region of the preorbital septa and the tarsal plates. As a result, a short, high-gauge needle introduced at a shallow angle to the skin effectively penetrates into the subcutaneous area of the lid. The subcutaneous portion of the lid is relatively loose, which readily allows for infiltration of the tissue with anesthetic solution.

Topical anesthetic drops are instilled into the conjunctival sac prior to performing subcutaneous lid injection to enhance patient comfort. Both 0.5% proparacaine and 0.5% tetracaine ophthalmic solutions are readily available for topical instillation. Proparacaine is more widely used diagnostically than tetracaine because it produces less patient discomfort and is less toxic to the cornea. Although the onset, intensity, and duration of topical anesthesia obtained with proparacaine and tetracaine are pharmacologically comparable, many clinicians view tetracaine to be more effective and may instill both agents prior to more invasive techniques. Instilling the proparacaine before the tetracaine may enhance patient comfort when both agents are used. Other clinicians use just tetracaine alone when more effective topical anesthesia is required. Instilling 10% phenylephrine ophthalmic solution additionally produces a vasoconstrictive effect that may reduce the potential for hemorrhage if anesthetic is injected into the lid from the conjunctval side.

The most commonly used injectable anesthetic solutions for local infiltration of the lid are lidocaine hydrochloride (Xylocaine) and bupivacaine hydrochloride (Marcaine). Lidocaine has both a shorter onset of action and duration compared to bupivacaine. As a result, these two anesthetic solutions are commonly combined in equal amounts in a single syringe to achieve both a rapid onset and prolonged duration of anesthetic effect with local lid infiltration. The lidocaine provides rapid onset of anesthesia that lasts for about an hour; the longer-lasting effect of the bupivacaine provides postprocedure analgesia for 4 to 6 hours. In addition, the combination of the vasoconstrictor epinephrine with an injectable anesthetic prolongs the duration of anesthesia, reduces the rate of systemic absorption, and decreases local bleeding. Commercial preparations of lidocaine anesthetic for injection are commonly combined with epinephrine. A common combination of anesthetic solutions for injection is 2% lidocaine with epinephrine 1:100,000 and 0.5% bupivacaine. An alternative combination of 2% lidocaine with epinephrine 1:200,000 and 0.75% bupivacaine is preferred by others, although this is more typically used for regional nerve block injections rather than local infiltrative anesthesia. One percent lidocaine with 1:100,000 or 1:200,000 epinephrine may alternatively be used in combination with the bupivacaine. Most clinicians use 2% lidocaine with epinephrine 1:100,000 or 1:200,000 alone as a single, short-acting anesthetic agent without bupivacaine.

To reduce discomfort associated with lid infiltration, the use of a small amount of injectable sodium bicarbonate solution has been recommended by some as an additive to adjust the acidic pH (2.74 to 3.91) of infiltration anesthetic agents with epinephrine. Sodium bicarbonate injectable solution may be added to the syringe at a ratio equivalent to approximately ⅓ cc sodium bicarbonate to 10 cc of injectable anesthetic solution with epinephrine.

■ **Instrumentation.** 0.5% proparacaine ophthalmic solution; 0.5% tetracaine ophthalmic solution; 10% phenylephrine ophthalmic solution; 2% lidocaine solution with epinephrine 1:100,000 for injection; 0.5% bupivacaine solution for injection, sodium bicarbonate solution for injection; sterile: 18G 1½-inch needles, 3 or 5-cc syringe, 27 or 30G 1½-inch needle, tissue forceps, alcohol swabs, facial tissues, gauze pads; cotton-tipped applicators, puncture-resistant container for needle and syringe disposal (biohazards sharps container).

■ **Technique.** Review the risks and benefits of the procedure with the patient and ask him or her to review and sign an appropriate consent form. Prepare the syringe with the desired injection solution(s) of 1.5 cc lidocaine with epinephrine, 1.5 cc bupivacaine if appropriate, and a small amount (equivalent to a few drops) of sodium bicarbonate if desired (see p. 402). Select the appropriate type and quantity of injection solution(s) based upon the anticipated procedure as well as the size of disposable syringe chosen.

Instill one or two drops of proparacaine and/or tetracaine ophthalmic solution into the conjunctival sac (see p. 000). If local infiltration of the lid administered through the conjunctival side is anticipated, optionally instill one or two drops of 10% phenylephrine ophthalmic solution. Wait a few minutes for the topical drops to take effect. The eyelid skin at the injection site may be carefully wiped with an alcohol pad prior to injection. Squeeze out excess alcohol from the pad and ask the patient to shut the eyes before wiping the eyelid skin, taking care to avoid the lid margins. Let the lid air dry.

To inject the upper lid subcutaneously, position yourself to the side of the patient, and ask him or her to look down. Use the index finger of your left hand to pull the lid gently laterally so that the eyelid skin is slightly taut (Fig. 1). Hold the flange of the syringe barrel between your index and middle fingers, put your thumb on the plunger, and position the needle and syringe tangential to the surface of the lid so that the needle bevel is facing you (Fig. 2A). It is helpful to gently support the syringe on the finger holding the lid taut. Advise the patient that he or she will feel a slight needle stick. Use a subtle stabbing motion of the syringe directed just beneath the eyelid skin to introduce the needle into the subcutaneous portion of the lid at an angle of approximately 15 degrees to the surface of the skin (Fig. 2B). Inject approximately 0.5 cc of the anesthetic solution, which will appear as a

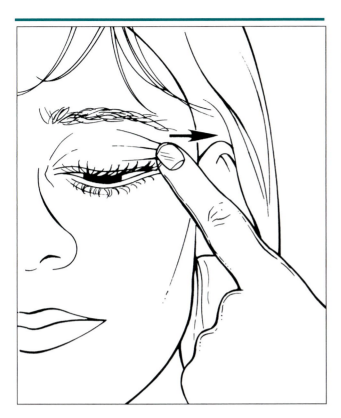

1. To inject the upper lid subcutaneously, the patient is asked to look down, and the index finger is used to pull the eye gently laterally so that the eyelid skin is slightly taut.

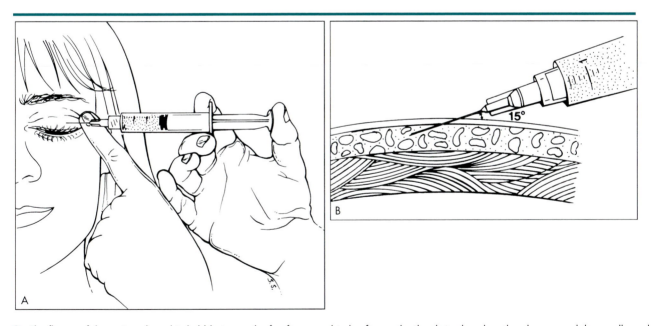

2. The flange of the syringe barrel is held between the forefinger and index finger, the thumb is placed on the plunger, and the needle and syringe are positioned tangential to the surface of the lid so that the needle bevel is facing you (A). A subtle stabbing motion directed just beneath the eyelid skin is used to introduce the needle into the subcutaneous portion of the lid at an angle of approximately 15 degrees with the surface of the lid (B).

small mounded distention of the eyelid skin surrounding the tip of the needle (Fig. 3).

Inject a sufficient amount of anesthetic to infiltrate the lid in the immediate vicinity of the desired area; however, large amounts of anesthetic solution are generally not necessary. Using a very gentle turning motion of the needle during injection will help to distribute the anesthetic. To fully infiltrate or surround the desired area with anesthetic solution, it may be necessary to reintroduce the needle at additional lid sites using the same technique (Fig. 4). It is helpful to reintroduce the needle through skin that has already been anesthetized. To infiltrate the lower lid, ask the patient to look up before performing the injection(s) (Fig. 5).

When sufficient anesthetic solution has been injected into the subcutaneous lid, withdraw the needle. Ask the patient to close the eyes. Apply firm pressure to the lid area with a tissue or gauze pad for a few minutes, or ask the patient to do so (Fig. 6). This will increase the effectiveness of the anesthetic and will help the solution to diffuse within the lid.

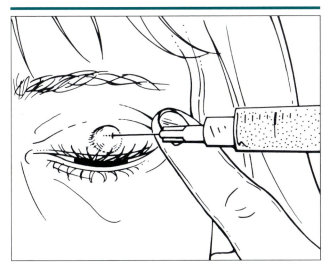

3. Approximately 0.5 cc of the anesthetic solution is injected, which will appear as a small mounded distention of the eyelid skin surrounding the tip of the needle.

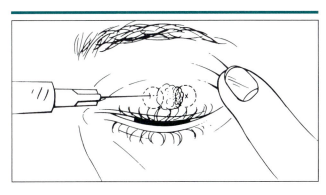

4. Here two injection sites are used to surround a lid lesion with adequate anesthetic solution. The first injection site is to the right of the lesion.

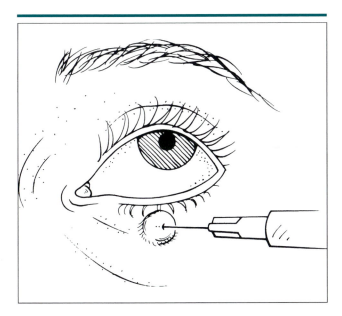

5. For infiltrative anesthesia of the lower lid, the patient is asked to look up before injecting.

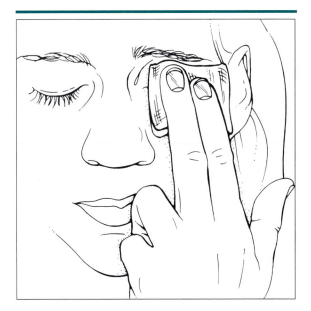

6. After injecting the anesthetic solution, the patient is asked to close the eyes and firm pressure is applied for a few minutes using a tissue or sterile gauze pad. This will enhance the effectiveness of the anesthetic as well as its diffusion within the lid.

If desired or necessary, additional anesthetic solution may be introduced through the conjunctival side of the lid. After infiltrating the upper lid subcutaneously, evert the upper lid (see p. 94). Holding the needle (bevel facing you) and syringe tangential to the lid, introduce the needle tangentially into the conjunctiva at the base of the tarsal plate and inject approximately 0.2 cc of anesthetic solution (Fig. 7A). For the lower lid, ask the patient to look up and inject the anesthetic at the base of the inferior tarsal plate (Fig. 7B).

Dispose of the used syringe and needle appropriately in a puncture-resistant container (biohazard sharps container) that has been placed in close proximity. DO NOT recap a used needle.

An alternative approach is to fully recline the patient for this procedure, positioning yourself seated to the side of the patient's head for the injection. Also, some clinicians use a metal or plastic Jaeger plate to protect the globe during local infiltration anesthesia of the lid. Before injecting the upper lid, ask the patient to look down, retract the upper lid, gently slide the Jaeger plate between the globe and the lid with the concave surface toward the globe, and then release the upper lid (Fig. 8). Have an assistant hold the plate in place during the injection. If desired, a similar technique is used to position the Jaeger plate under the lower lid after asking the patient to look up.

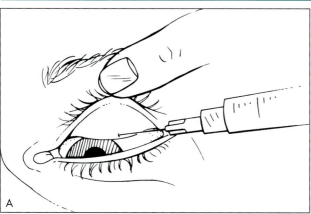

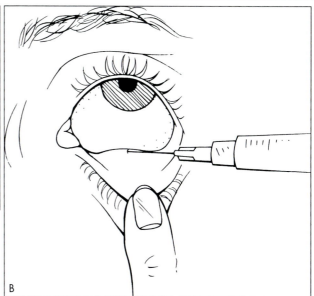

7. If desired, additional anesthetic solution may be introduced through the conjunctival side of the lid. For the upper lid, the lid is everted and the needle is introduced tangentially into the conjunctiva at the base of the superior tarsal plate (A). For the lower lid, the patient is asked to look up and the anesthetic is injected at the base of the inferior tarsal plate (B).

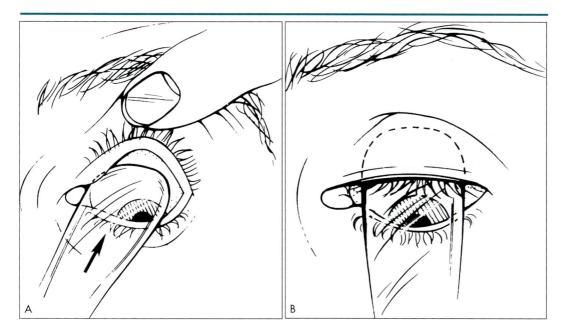

8. A metal or plastic Jaeger plate may be used to protect the globe during local infiltration anesthesia of the lid. To use the Jaeger plate when injecting the upper lid, the patient is asked to look down, the lid is retracted, and the Jaeger plate is gently positioned between the globe and the lid with the concave surface toward the globe (A). The upper lid is then released (B) and the injection is performed.

■ **Interpretation.** As the anesthetic takes effect, a slight blanching of the skin will appear from the epinephrine. Allow 5 to 10 minutes for the anesthetic to take effect. Use a tissue forceps to gently pinch the lid skin in the area of anesthetic infiltration (Fig. 9). Anesthesia is confirmed if the patient does not feel the forceps pinch, and the lid procedure can proceed.

■ **Contraindications/Complications.** Although complications of lid infiltration with anesthetic are less common than with regional blocks or general anesthesia, they have the potential to be extremely serious. Prior to performing the injection, a careful history is taken to rule out known hypersensitivity to any of the topical or injectable solutions. Patients with hypertension, diabetes, cardiovascular disease, or thyrotoxicosis are especially susceptible to the serious potential side effects of epinephrine. The topical anesthetic agents used may produce local hypersensitivity reactions, including toxic keratitis.

The major systemic side effects caused by local anesthetics are excitation of the central nervous system (CNS) and depression of the cardiovascular system. Initial CNS symptoms of anesthetic toxicity commonly include drowsiness, light-headedness, dizziness, and a metallic taste followed by nausea, garrulousness, perioral numbness, tingling, diplopia, and tinnitus. The first sign of cardiovascular toxicity is typically a reduction in blood pressure. Tremors, muscle twitching, seizures, loss of consciousness, respiratory depression, and circulatory collapse have been reported. As a result, when performing injections, it is important to ensure the prompt availability of proper equipment and personnel trained to address medical emergencies, ranging from vasovagal syncope to cardiac arrest.

Clinical anecdotal mention of focal skin hyperpigmentation related to sodium bicarbonate injection has been cited. Excessive aspiration of sodium bicarbonate into the anesthetic solution will cause a milky precipitate to appear in the syringe. If the patient reports discomfort during the course of the lid procedure, it is appropriate to inject additional anesthetic at the desired site(s). Use of the Jaeger plate may result in some minor discomfort for the patient.

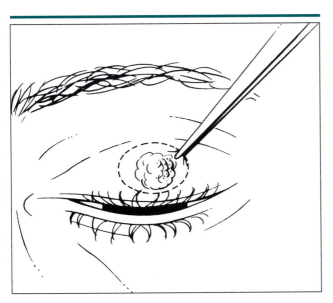

9. To confirm the effect of the anesthetic, a tissue forceps is used to gently pinch the lid a few minutes after the injection. Local infiltration anesthesia is confirmed if the patient does not feel the forceps pinch.

96

Steroid Injection of Chalazion

■ **Description/Indications.** A chalazion is a granuloma of the upper or lower eyelid that forms as a chronic, localized inflammatory response to the retention of sebum in a meibomian gland or following resolution of an acute hordeolum. Chalazia are often associated with seborrhea, chronic blepharitis, and acne rosacea, as well as *Demodex* infestation of the sebaceous glands. A chalazion manifests clinically as a nontender, firm, palpable lump in the lid, several millimeters in diameter, that may slowly enlarge to cause multiple signs and symptoms, including discomfort, cosmetic distress, and blurred vision. Single or multiple lesions may be present.

If the lesion does not spontaneously resolve or if standard treatment with hot compresses and topical and/or systemic antibiotics as indicated is unsuccessful, removal of the lesion is often pursued as an elective procedure upon patient request. Injection of chalazia with triamcinolone acetonide is a convenient and reasonably effective alternative to incision and curettage of these lesions (see p. 118).

Triamcinolone acetonide is a synthetic corticosteroid in a sterile aqueous suspension that has marked anti-inflammatory action. The 10 mg/mL concentration is used for intra-articular injections to treat the inflamed joints of rheumatoid arthritis and for intradermal injection of inflammatory lesions.

Although conflicting opinions are reported in the literature, clinical anecdotal evidence suggests that the duration and palpated density of the chalazion tend to have little effect on the response of the lesion to steroid injection. Many clinicians prefer to proceed with incision and curettage rather than attempt intralesional injection for large chalazia (approximately 8 mm and larger). Intralesional steroid injection is reported to be preferred over incision and curettage for children and for lesions located close to the lacrimal puncta or lid margin. In the instance of the latter, removal of the chalazion could result in damage to the nasolacrimal system or the integrity of the lid margin. Injection is also preferred for patients who express uneasiness about more invasive therapy or who have multiple chalazia.

Both paralesional and intralesional steroid injection of chalazia have been described. The walls of a chalazion can be rather tough in consistency, which means that resistance may be encountered as the needle is inserted intralesionally, and only a relatively small volume of the steroid (approximately 0.05 cc) may be accommodated within the lesion itself. As a result, both an intralesional approach and a paralesional modification will be discussed in this section.

Depending upon clinician preferences, this technique can be performed with or without local infiltration anesthesia of the lid, and the approach for the steroid injection can be through the palpebral conjunctiva (transconjunctival or through the lid skin (percutaneous). The technique described in this section is percutaneous and includes the use of local infiltration anesthesia. Multiple chalazia may be injected with steroid at the same visit.

■ **Instrumentation.** 0.5% proparacaine ophthalmic solution, 0.5% tetracaine ophthalmic solution, 2% lidocaine solution for injection, 0.5% bupivacaine solution for injection, 10 mg/mL triamcinoline acetonide suspension for injection, sterile 18G 1½-inch needles, sterile 27 or 30G 1½-inch needles, sterile 3 or 5-cc syringe, sterile 25G ⅝-inch needles, sterile tuberculin syringe, sterile chalazion clamp, alcohol pads, facial tissues, sterile gauze pads, sterile cotton-tipped applicators, puncture-resistant container for needle and syringe disposal (biohazard sharps container).

■ **Technique.** Review the risks and benefits of the procedure with the patient, and ask him or her to sign an informed consent. Instill topical ophthalmic anesthetic drops.

Initial Infiltration Anesthesia of the Lid (see p. 417): Attach a sterile 18G 1½-inch needle to a sterile 3 or 5-cc syringe and fill it with a mixture of injection solutions of 1.5 mL lidocaine and 1.5 mL bupivacaine (see p. 402). After preparing the syringe, attach a sterile 27 or 30G ½-inch needle.

Ask the patient to close the eyes. Squeeze out extra fluid from an alcohol pad and use it to wipe the eyelid skin at the injection site, being careful to avoid the eyelid margins. Let the lid air dry.

For a chalazion of the upper lid, position yourself to the side of the patient and ask him or her to look down. Use the index finger of your left hand to pull the lid gently laterally so that the eyelid skin is slightly taut. Hold the syringe by the flange of the barrel between your index and middle fingers, with your thumb on the plunger. Use a subtle stabbing motion of the syringe directed just beneath the eyelid skin to introduce the needle into the subcutaneous portion of the lid a few millimeters superior to the edge of the chalazion (Fig. 1). Inject sufficient anesthetic solution

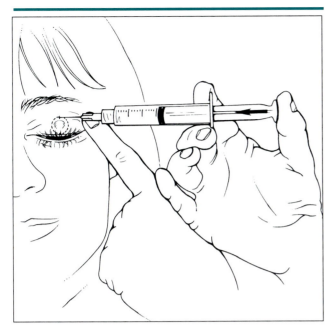

1. For initial infiltration anesthesia, the patient is asked to look down, and the index finger is used to pull the lid gently laterally. The syringe is held by the flange of the barrel between the index and middle fingers, the thumb is placed on the plunger, and a subtle stabbing motion is used to introduce the needle into the subcutaneous portion of the lid a few millimeters superior to the edge of the upper lid chalazion. Sufficient anesthetic solution is injected so that an adequately sized bleb surrounds the chalazion, changing the angle of the needle or repositioning it if necessary.

so that an adequately sized bleb surrounds the chalazion. Changing the angle of the needle during injection or repositioning the needle may be necessary in order to effect an adequately sized bleb. Withdraw the needle.

Ask the patient to close the eyes. Apply firm pressure to the lid area with a tissue or gauze pad for a few minutes or ask the patient do to so (Fig. 2). This will allow the anesthetic solution to diffuse into the lid for the desired effect. In addition, diffusion of the anesthetic will allow the borders of the chalazion to once again be visualized prior to the injection of steroid.

Intralesional Steroid Injection: Thoroughly shake the vial of 10 mg/mL triamcinolone acetonide suspension, and then prepare a sterile tuberculin syringe with approximately 0.5 cc of the suspension (see p. 402). Attach a sterile 25G ⅝-inch needle. Be sure to perform the steroid injection soon after preparing the syringe to avoid precipitation of the active ingredient out of suspension.

For intralesional injection of the upper lid, ask the patient to look down. Use the index finger of your left hand to gently pull the lid laterally to tauten the eyelid skin and to minimize movement of the chalazion nodule. Again hold the syringe by the flange of the barrel between your index and middle fingers, with your thumb on the plunger.

The approach of the needle will be dependent upon the amount of skin elevation produced by the chalazion but should be relatively shallow to avoid full-thickness perforation of the lid. Although resistance may be encountered, insert the needle directly into the center of the chalazion using the same technique described for infiltration anesthesia (Fig. 3). Inject a small volume of steroid suspension intralesionally, approximately 0.05 cc. If successful, withdraw the needle.

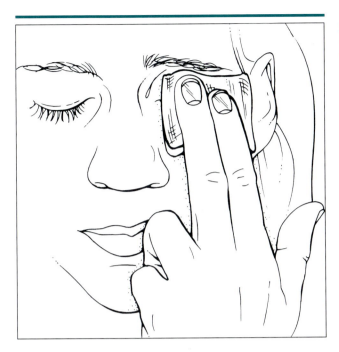

2. After injecting the anesthetic, ask the patient to close the eyes. Apply firm pressure to the lid area with a tissue or gauze pad for a few minutes, or ask the patient to do so.

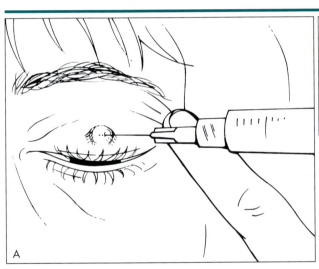

A

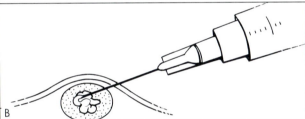

B

3. For intralesional steroid injection, the patient is asked to look down, the index finger of the nondominant hand is used to gently pull the lid laterally, (A) and a relatively shallow approach is used to insert the needle into the center of the chalazion. (B) Approximately 0.05 cc of steroid suspension is injected into the lesion.

If intralesional injection is unsuccessful, a paralesional modification may be attempted. Attempt to insert the needle through the chalazion but still within the lid (Fig. 4). This is judged by the nature of resistance felt as the needle is inserted, and also by noting changes in the lid surface as the needle is inserted. Again, a shallow approach is necessary to avoid inadvertent lid perforation. Inject approximately 0.1 cc of the steroid suspension, and then withdraw the needle. Alternatively, reinsert the needle intralesionally from another percutaneous location and inject approximately 0.1 cc of steroid suspension. The resultant second opening in the chalazion will effect paralesional injection of steroid.

Use a similar technique for chalazia of the lower lid. For infiltration anesthesia, ask the patient to look up and insert the needle a few millimeters inferior to the edge of the chalazion (Fig. 5). Proceed with intralesional or paralesional injection of steroid as described above. For a transconjunctival approach for injection of steroid, evert the lid first and maintain a relatively shallow approach with the needle for insertion into the chalazion (Fig. 6).

The use of a chalazion clamp (see p. 118) for intralesional steroid injection has been described as a method of stabilizing the lid during the injection but also for protecting the globe should lid perforation occur during the percutaneous injection. Use of a Jaeger plate for the latter purpose has also been described (see p. 417). A chalazion clamp may also be used for an injection approach from the conjunctival side.

Dispose of the used syringes and needles appropriately in a puncture-resistant container (biohazard sharps container) that has been placed in close proximity. *Do not recap a used needle.* Following steroid injection of the chalazion, schedule a follow-up appointment in 1 to 4 weeks.

■ Interpretation.

Resolution of the chalazion will be noted within approximately 1 month if the injection was successful. Many patients report resolution in approximately 1 week. If satisfactory resolution of the lesion does not occur in approximately 1 month, then a second injection or incision and curettage of the lesion may be considered. Large chalazia treated with injection therapy are more likely to require more than one injection and may carry a greater likelihood of recurrence.

Although rare, sebaceous gland carcinoma should be considered as a differential diagnosis if a lesion does not respond to treatment or if structural changes in the lid are noted, especially in older patients.

■ Contraindications/Complications.

If local infiltration anesthesia of the lid is not used for this technique, the patient may experience noticeable pain following the steroid injection. Atrophy of the skin has been reported following steroid injection of cutaneous lesions, but it has not been widely reported following steroid injection of chalazia.

Another reported side effect of intralesional triamcinolone injection of chalazia is focal hypopigmentation of the skin in the vicinity of the injection, particularly if the patient has darkly pigmented skin. An alternative transconjunctival approach of the steroid helps to minimize this potential risk.

Crystalline or insoluble preparations of corticosteroid (slowly absorbing, "depot" forms) are more likely to produce permanent atrophic changes in the eyelid skin and are not recommended for this technique. Microembolic occlusion of the retinal and choroidal vasculature has been reported after intraoperative administration of a depot steroid (methylprednisolone) at the site of chalazion excision.

Although complications of lid infiltration with anesthetic are less common than with regional blocks or general anesthesia, they have the potential to be extremely serious. Prior to performing the injection, a careful history is taken to rule out known hypersensitivity to any of the topical or injectable solutions.

The topical anesthetic agents used may produce local hypersensitivity reactions, including toxic keratitis. The major systemic side effects caused by local anesthetics are excitation of the central nervous system (CNS) and depression of the cardiovascular system. Initial CNS symptoms of anesthetic toxicity commonly include drowsiness, lightheadedness, dizziness, and a metallic taste followed by nausea, garrulousness, perioral numbness, tingling, diplopia, and tinnitus. The first sign of cardiovascular toxicity is typically a reduction in blood pressure. Tremors, muscle twitching, seizures, loss of consciousness, respiratory depression, and circulatory collapse have been reported. As a result, when performing injections, it is important to ensure the prompt availability of proper equipment and personnel trained to address medical emergencies, ranging from vasovagal syncope to cardiac arrest.

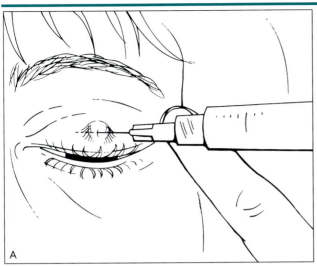

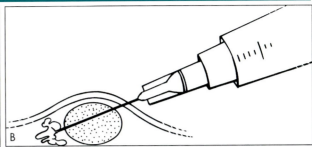

4. A. For paralesional steroid injection, a relatively shallow approach is used to attempt to insert the needle through the chalazion but still within the lid. This is judged by the resistance felt as well as by noting changes in the lid surface as the needle is inserted. B. Approximately 0.1 cc of steroid suspension is injected.

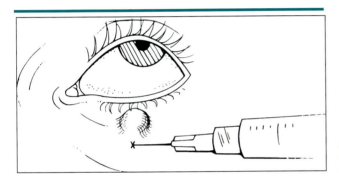

5. For initial infiltration anesthesia of the lower lid, the patient is asked to look up and the needle is inserted a few millimeters below the edge of the chalazion.

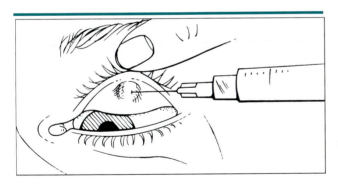

6. For a transconjunctival approach for steroid injection, the lid is everted and a relatively shallow approach is maintained for insertion of the needle into the chalazion.

97 Subconjunctival Injection

■ **Description/Indications.** Subconjunctival injection is used to treat a variety of ocular conditions and, when indicated, offers a number of advantages over other methods of drug administration. Subconjunctival injection delivers a more concentrated, localized dosage of medication than can be achieved by topical or systemic administration, and high concentrations of the drug can be delivered locally in small quantities to substantially reduce adverse effects. This technique provides an alternative method of local drug delivery for medications that poorly penetrate the epithelium of the cornea or conjunctiva. Lastly, subconjunctival injection may be a necessary and helpful alternative for patients who are not compliant with topical or systemic medication.

The conjunctiva lies loosely on the underlying tissues so that it readily "balloons" to accommodate medication injected subconjunctivally. Although the injection site can be placed anywhere on the globe, the superotemporal area is typically chosen because it is the only quadrant lying between two rectus muscles that is not traversed by an oblique extraocular muscle or tendon. The injection site is placed well beyond the equator superiorly or in the fornix inferiorly so that cosmesis and patient comfort are maximized. Steroid suspensions for the treatment of conditions such as intraocular inflammation or cystoid macular edema are examples of medications that may be injected subconjunctivally.

Both short and long-acting agents may be used for local anesthesia prior to injecting medication subconjunctivally. Short-acting anesthesia is achieved using topical ophthalmic drops; long-acting anesthesia and analgesia may be achieved, if desired, by subconjunctival injection of bupivacaine (Marcaine), which has a duration of effect of 4 to 6 hours.

Both 0.5% proparacaine and 0.5% tetracaine ophthalmic anesthetic solutions are readily available for topical instillation. Proparacaine is more widely used diagnostically than tetracaine because it produces less patient discomfort and is less toxic to the cornea. Although the onset, intensity, and duration of topical anesthesia obtained with proparacaine and tetracaine are pharmacologically comparable, some clinicians view tetracaine to be more effective and may instill both agents prior to more invasive techniques. Instilling the proparacaine before the tetracaine may enhance patient comfort when both agents are used. In addition, the instillation of 10% phenylephrine ophthalmic solution produces conjunctival vasoconstriction as a method of hemostasis.

■ **Instrumentation.** 0.5% proparacaine ophthalmic solution, 0.5% tetracaine ophthalmic solution, 10% phenylephrine ophthalmic solution, 0.5% bupivacaine solution for injection, desired therapeutic medication(s) for subconjunctival injection, sterile 18G 1½-inch needles, sterile 1, 3, or 5-cc syringes, sterile 27 or 30G ½-inch needles, facial tissues, sterile gauze pads, puncture resistant container for needle and syringe disposal (biohazard sharps container).

■ **Technique.** Review the risks and benefits of the procedure with the patient and ask him or her to review and sign an appropriate consent form. Prepare one syringe with 1 mL of bupivacaine; prepare a second syringe with the desired therapeutic medication(s) for subconjunctival injection (see p. 402). Attach a sterile 27 or 30G ½-inch needle to each syringe.

Instill one or two drops each of proparacaine and/or tetracaine ophthalmic solution (see p. 2). If desired, additionally instill 10% phenylephrine ophthalmic solution into the conjunctival sac, spacing the drops to avoid overflow from the sac. Wait a few minutes for the drops to take effect.

Position yourself in front of the patient and ask him or her to look down. Use the thumb of your left hand to gently retract the upper lid (Fig. 1A). Hold the syringe containing the bupivacaine by the flange of the barrel between your index and middle fingers, put your thumb on the plunger, and position the needle and syringe tangential to the globe so that the needle bevel is facing toward the globe. Direct the needle posteriorly, at the equator or beyond. Use a very subtle stabbing motion of the syringe directed tangential to the globe and just beneath the surface of the conjunctiva to introduce the needle into the subconjunctival space (Fig. 1B). Inject approximately 0.25 cc of the anesthetic solution, which will appear as a translucent elevation of the conjunctiva (Fig. 2). Withdraw the needle and ask the patient to close the eyes. Apply firm pressure with a tissue or gauze pad for a few minutes or ask the patient to do so (Fig. 3). Allow several minutes for the anesthetic to take effect.

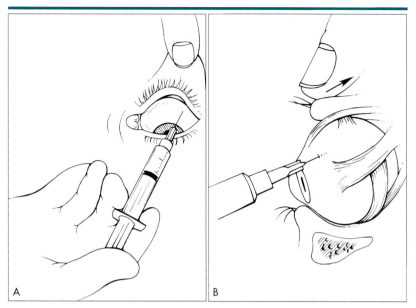

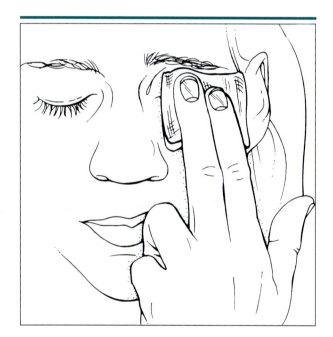

1. A. For subconjunctival injection in the super-otemporal quadrant, the patient is asked to look down and the thumb of the left hand is used to gently retract the upper lid. The syringe containing the bupivacaine is held by the flange of the barrel between the index and middle fingers, the thumb is placed on the plunger, and the needle and syringe are positioned tangential to the globe. B. The needle is directed posteriorly, at the equator or beyond, and a very subtle stabbing motion is directed tangential to the globe and just beneath the conjunctival surface to introduce the needle into the subconjunctival space.

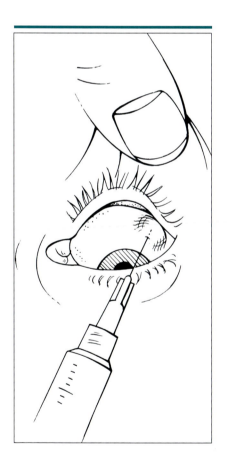

3. After injecting the anesthetic solution and withdrawing the needle, the patient is asked to close the eyes. Firm pressure is applied for a few minutes using a tissue or sterile gauze pad.

2. Approximately 0.25 cc of the anesthetic solution is injected, which will appear as a translucent elevation of the conjunctiva.

Hold the second syringe containing the medication(s) for subconjunctival injection as before, and position the needle tangential to the portion of the conjunctiva that is now elevated by the injected anesthetic (Fig. 4A). Insert the needle into the elevated conjunctiva at a site other than the initial injection (Fig. 4B). Inject the desired amount of medication, usually approximately 0.5 to 1 cc. A small amount of medication may leak from the original injection site. Reintroducing the needle at a third site and injecting the medication may reduce the amount of leakage.

When sufficient medication has been injected into the subconjunctival space, withdraw the needle. Ask the patient to close the eyes. Apply pressure to the lid area with a tissue or gauze pad for a few minutes or ask the patient to do so. This will help the medication diffuse within the subconjunctival space and control bleeding.

If desired or necessary, additional medication may be injected into the inferior subconjunctival space. Ask the patient to look up and use the forefinger of your left hand to gently retract the lower lid (Fig. 5A). Insert the needle into the inferior fornix (bevel facing toward the globe) at an angle tangential to the globe (Fig. 5B) and inject approximately 0.25 cc of anesthetic solution. A medication bleb will not appear. As described above, ask the patient to close the eyes and apply firm pressure with a tissue or gauze pad for a few minutes. Allow several minutes for the anesthetic to take effect. After injecting the desired medication into the superotemporal subconjunctival area, use the inferior fornix approach to inject the medication into the inferior subconjunctival space.

Dispose of the used syringe and needle appropriately in a puncture-resistant container (biohazard sharps container). *Do not* recap a used needle. Dismiss the patient with instructions to apply a cold pack to the eye three or four times over the next 24 hours, which will assist in pain control and will help to reduce swelling. Schedule a follow-up examination at an interval appropriate to the condition being treated.

■ **Interpretation.** After injecting into the superotemporal subconjunctival area, the medication will visibly elevate the conjunctiva. Injection of the clear anesthetic solution bupivacaine will result in a translucent conjunctival bleb. When a steroid suspension is injected subconjunctivally, the bleb will take on a milky appearance. A medication bleb will generally not appear when the transfornix approach is used for subconjunctival injection inferiorly.

■ **Contraindications/Complications.** Although complications of subconjunctival injection are not common, they have the potential to be extremely serious. Prior to performing the injection, a careful history is taken to rule out known hypersensitivity to any of the topical or injectable solutions.

The topical anesthetic agents used may produce local hypersensitivity reactions, including toxic keratitis. The major systemic side effects caused by local anesthetics are excitation of the central nervous system (CNS) and depression of the cardiovascular system. Initial CNS symptoms of anesthetic toxicity commonly include drowsiness, light-headedness, dizziness, and a metallic taste followed by nausea, garrulousness, perioral numbness, tingling, diplopia, and tinnitus. The first sign of cardiovascular toxicity is typically a reduction in blood pressure. Tremors, muscle twitching, seizures, loss of consciousness, respiratory depression, and circulatory collapse have been reported. As a result, when performing injections, it is important to ensure the prompt availability of proper equipment and personnel trained to address medical emergencies, ranging from vasovagal syncope to cardiac arrest.

In addition, the contraindications and potential complications, both local and systemic, of the therapeutic medication injected subconjunctivally should be reviewed in detail.

The appearance of a subconjunctival hemorrhage following subconjunctival injection is common. The patient should be advised of this potentiality in advance and reassured. In addition, if steroid suspension has been injected, it is not uncommon for a small amount of the medication to seep from the injection site, producing a short-lived, milky discharge. Once again, patient education is all that is necessary.

If poor technique is used and the angle at which the needle is introduced into the subconjunctival space is excessive, then scleral perforation may occur.

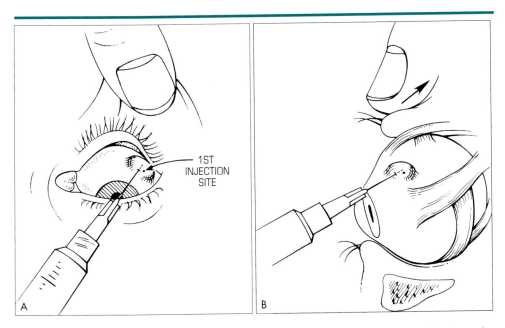

4. The needle of the second syringe containing the medication for injection is inserted into the elevated conjunctiva at a site other than the initial injection (A). The needle is positioned tangential to the portion of the conjunctiva that is elevated by the injected anesthetic (B), and the desired amount of medication is injected, usually 0.5 to 1 cc.

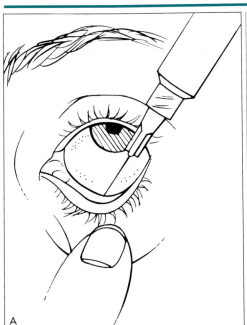

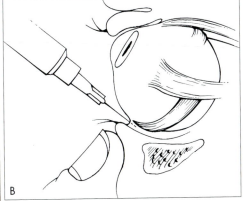

5. A. To inject into the inferior subconjunctival space the patient is asked to look up and the forefinger of the left hand is used to gently retract the lower lid. B. The needle is inserted into the inferior fornix at an angle tangential to the globe and approximately 0.25 cc of medication is injected.

XIII Suggested Readings

Bartlett JD: Ophthalmic drug delivery, in Bartlett JD, Jaanus SD (eds): *Clinical Ocular Pharmacology,* ed 3. Boston, Butterworth-Heinemann, 1995, pp 47–74.

Bartlett JD, Jaanus SD: Local anesthetics, in Bartlett JD, Jaanus SD (eds): *Clinical Ocular Pharmacology,* ed 3. Boston, Butterworth-Heinemann, 1995, pp 117–130.

Bartlett JD, Melore GG: Diseases of the eyelids, in Bartlett JD, Jaanus SD (eds): *Clinical Ocular Pharmacology,* ed 3. Boston, Butterworth-Heinemann, 1995, pp 561–600.

Castren J, Stenborg T: Cortiscosteroid injection of chalazia. *Acta Ophthalmologica* 1983;938–942.

Cohen BZ, Tripathi RC: Eyelid depigmentation after intralesional injection of a fluorinated corticosteroid for chalazion. *Am J Ophthalmol* 1979;**88:**269–270. Letter.

Dua HS, Nilawar DV: Nonsurgical therapy of chalazia. *Am J Ophthalmol* 1982;**94:**424–425. Letter.

English FP, Cohn D, Groeneveld ER: Demodectic mites and chalazion. *Am J Ophthalmol* 1985;**100:**482–483. Letter.

Gills JP, Hustead RF, Sanders DR: *Ophthalmic Anesthesia.* Thorofare, NJ, Slack, 1993.

Katzen LB: Anesthesia, analgesia, and amnesia, in Putterman AM (ed): *Cosmetic Oculoplastic Surgery,* ed 2. Philadelphia, Saunders, 1993, pp 82–93.

King RA, Ellis PP: Treatment of chalazia with corticosteroid injections. *Ophthal Surg* 1986;**17:**351–353.

Last RJ: The eyeball, in Wolff E (ed): *Anatomy of the Eye and Orbit,* ed 6. Philadelphia, Saunders, 1973, pp 30–181.

Lewis G: Parenteral medications, in Perry AG, Potter PA (eds): *Clinical Nursing Skills and Techniques,* ed 3. St. Louis, Mosby, 1994, pp 540–584.

Mohan K, Dhir SP, Munjal VP, Jain IS: The use of intralesional steroids in the treatment of chalazion. *Ann Ophthalmol* 1986; **18:**158–160.

Nesi FA, Waltz KL: *Smith's Practical Techniques in Ophthalmic Plastic Surgery.* St. Louis, Mosby, 1994.

Palva J, Pohjanpelto PEJ: Intralesional corticosteroid injection for the treatment of chalazia. *Acta Ophthalmol* 1983; **61:**933–937.

Pizzarello LD, Jakobiec FA, Hofeldt AJ, et al: Intralesional corticosteroid therapy of chalazia. *Am J Ophthalmol* 1978; **85:**818–821.

Shore JW, McCord CD, Popham JK: Surgery of the eyelids, in Tasman W, Jaeger ED (eds): *Duane's Clinical Ophthalmology.* Philadelphia, Lippincott, 1992, vol 6, pp 1–52.

Talley DK, Bartlett JD: Topical and regional anesthesia, in Bartlett JD, Jaanus SD (eds): *Clinical Ocular Pharmacology,* ed 3. Boston, Butterworth-Heinemann, 1995, pp 463–477.

Thomas EL, Laborder RP: Retinal and choroidal vascular occlusion following intralesional corticosteroid injection of a chalazion. *Ophthalmology* 1986;**93:**405–407.

Townsend DJ: Blepharoplasty, in Borodic GE, Townsend DJ (eds): *Atlas of Eyelid Surgery.* Philadelphia, Saunders, 1994, pp 109–119.

Watson AP, Austin DJ: Treatment of chalazions with injection of a steroid suspension. *Br J Ophthalmol* 1984;**68:**833–835.

Wilson RP: Local anesthesia in ophthalmology, in Tasman W, Jaeger ED (eds): *Duane's Clinical Ophthalmology.* Philadelphia, Lippincott, 1992, vol 6, pp 1–20.

XIV

Ophthalmic Laser Procedures

98   Argon Laser Treatment of Trichiasis

■ **Description/Indications.** Trichiasis, the misdirection of cilia so that they come in contact with the globe, can prove to be a challenging patient management problem. Multiple treatment modalities have been described for this condition, ranging from temporary measures such as epilation (see p. 100) to more permanent surgical excision, electrolysis, high-frequency radio wave electrosurgery, and cryotherapy. Argon laser thermoablation of ciliary follicles for the treatment of trichiasis has been demonstrated to be a safe, effective, and relatively simple alternative for the treatment of this condition.

The blue-green setting of the argon laser emits light with a wavelength of 488 nm. This wavelength is absorbed by the melanin of the treated eyelash and cutaneous tissue, and the subsequent conversion of laser light into heat produces the therapeutic thermoablative effect. The power, spot size, and duration of the argon pulse are all adjusted by the operator to produce the desired effect.

The argon laser is mounted on a slit lamp and activated by a foot pedal control or a pushbutton mounted in the top of the joystick (Fig. 1). The argon laser unit incorporates two red helium-neon (HeNe) aiming beams with a wavelength of 633 nm that are focused (superimposed) using the joystick. This point directly corresponds to the location of the delivery of the argon pulse.

Use of the argon laser allows for precise and accurately controlled ablation of the aberrant lash. Since the follicles of the cilia penetrate to a depth of approximately 1.5 to 2.5 mm below the surface of the lid margin, the laser treatment is delivered to that estimated depth (Fig. 2). Patient discomfort associated with this technique is minimal, likely the result of the extremely short duration of the laser application, the very fast destruction of the tissue, and the minuteness of the area affected by each laser treatment. Although some authors have reported the use of infiltrative anesthesia with this technique (see p. 417), especially if a large number of lashes are to be treated at one sitting, most proceed with the use of topical ophthalmic anesthetic drops only.

■ **Instrumentation.** Slit lamp mounted argon laser, topical ophthalmic anesthetic solution, sterile cotton-tipped applicators, topical ophthalmic antibiotic/steroid combination ointment, sterile rose bengal strips.

■ **Technique.** Perform a thorough ophthalmic examination and assess appropriate systemic findings. Review the risks and benefits of the procedure with the patient, and ask him or her to sign an informed consent. Advise the patient that a slight burning smell will be noted during the treatment.

Proper alignment and focus of the instrumentation is very important. Carefully focus the oculars of the slit lamp biomicroscope. Initially set the laser unit on 50-μm spot size, 0.1 second duration, and 1.0 to 1.2 W power (Fig. 3).

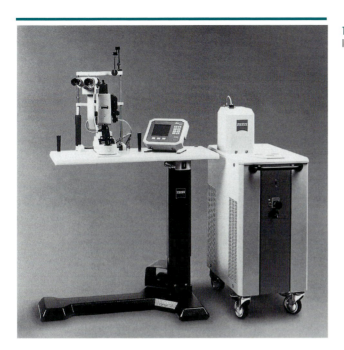

1. A slit lamp-mounted ophthalmic argon laser. (Courtesy of Humphrey Instruments, a division of Carl Zeiss.)

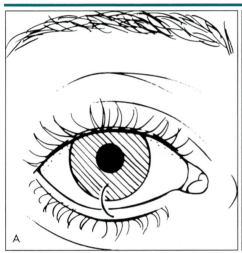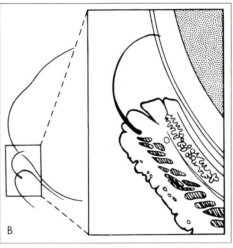

2. A. Frontal view of trichiasis, the result of a misdirected lash on the lower lid. B. Side view of trichiasis. Note that the follicle of the cilium penetrates to a depth of approximately 1.5 to 2.5 mm below the surface of the lid margin.

A

B

3. The initial laser settings for argon laser treatment of trichiasis.

ARGON LASER TREATMENT OF TRICHIASIS

Spot size	50 μm
Duration	0.1 second
Power	1.0 to 1.2 W
Wavelength	Argon blue-green
Contact lens	None

Instill two drops of topical ophthalmic anesthetic solution in each eye. Position the patient comfortably at the slit lamp of the laser unit, ensuring that the forehead is securely against the forehead rest. If necessary, secure the strap around the back of the patient's head or have an assistant hold the patient's head in place. Set the slit lamp magnification at 10X to 16X, and use diffuse illumination of moderate intensity to visualize the lashes that require treatment. Adjust the illumination of the HeNe aiming beams so that they are clearly visible yet not too bright.

To treat the lower lid, ask the patient to look up. Use your forefinger or a sterile cotton-tipped applicator to gently evert the lower lid so that the anticipated path of the laser follows the subcutaneous portion of each cilium (Fig. 4). Use the joystick to focus the aiming beams at the base of the initial lash to be treated. Activate the laser by depressing the foot pedal or the joystick button. Use several applications to initially ablate the shaft of the lash at its base and to create a small crater in the lid margin skin (Fig. 5). The desired thermal effect of the laser produces a darkened charring of the skin within the crater, which absorbs the energy of subsequent burns.

Once the lid margin skin has been disrupted, increase the spot size up to 200 microns to enlarge the crater to the depth of the follicle. The goal of each laser application is to produce a visible thermal effect on the skin surrounding the follicle and to visibly deepen the crater effect (Fig. 6). Because the relative power of individual lasers does vary, adjustments in the spot size, pulse duration, or power may be needed. Increasing the slit lamp magnification to 25X to 40X may permit identification of a small cilia stub to aid in maintaining proper beam orientation.

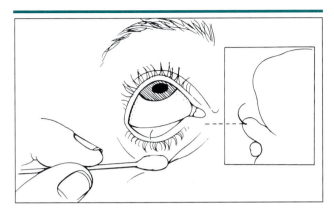

4. To treat the lower lid, the patient is asked to look up, and the forefinger or a sterile cotton-tipped applicator is used to gently evert the lower lid so the anticipated path of the laser beam (dashed line) follows the subcutaneous portion of each cilum. (Inset shows cross-sectional view.)

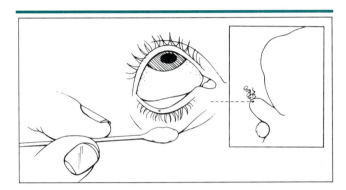

5. The HeNe aiming beams are focused at the base of the lash to be treated, the laser is activated, and several applications are used to initially ablate the shaft of the lash at its base. A small crater will be created at the lid margin. The desired thermal effect produces a darkened charring of the skin within the crater, which absorbs the energy of subsequent burns. (Inset shows cross-sectional view.)

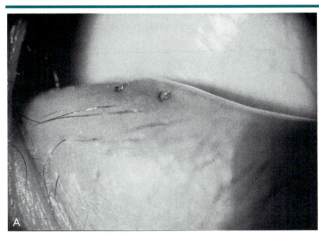

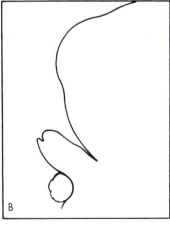

6. Once the lid margin skin has been disrupted, the spot size is increased up to 200 µm to enlarge the crater to the depth of follicle. (A) Note the small spots of thermal charring immediately following the application of argon laser burns to two lashes on the lower lid. (B) The cross-sectional view shows the small resultant crater in the lid margin.

If patient tearing occurs during the course of treatment, use a sterile cotton-tipped applicator to dry the lid margin before resuming the laser applications. To treat the upper lid, ask the patient to look down, retract the upper lid with a cotton-tipped applicator, and proceed in the same fashion (Fig. 7).

Repeat the procedure for each lash to be treated. Record the total number of shots in the patient record and assess systemic findings as indicated. Dismiss the patient with an ophthalmic antibiotic/steroid combination ointment applied to the lid margin two to four times a day and schedule a follow-up appointment in 1 week. To check for lash regrowth, schedule a follow-up examination in 3 to 6 months, sooner if symptoms arise.

For patients with very lightly pigmented lashes and skin, adequate melanin may not be present to effectively absorb the blue-green argon laser light to cause initial vaporization of the lash and the accompanying skin reaction. In this event, rose bengal vital dye may be used to enhance the laser light absorption and effect the desired tissue charring. Remove a rose bengal strip from its sterile package and moisten it slightly with sterile ophthalmic saline (see p. 48). Use the moistened rose bengal strip to "paint" the lid margin at the base of the lashes to be treated, being careful not to "flood" the globe (Fig. 8). Proceed with the laser treatment as described. Similarly, the use of autologous blood placed at the base of the lash from the injection site of infiltrative anesthesia has also been described for this purpose.

■ **Interpretation.** Approximately 12 to 20 laser applications are needed for each lash to create a crater sufficiently deep to destroy the lash follicles, approximately 2 to 3 mm. Some clinicians advocate the use of a depth gauge to ensure adequate laser treatment. Argon laser treatment of trichiasis seems to be most suitable when only a few fine cilia are involved; however, treatment may be repeated for thicker lashes, or a large number of lashes could be treated at several visits when other techniques such as surgical correction of entropion may not be indicated. Should the misdirected cilia regrow, retreatment with the argon laser may be pursued.

The thermal effects to the lid skin heal very quickly without scarring or distortion to the lid. Most patients experience minimal pain with this technique, described as a pinprick or momentary burning sensation. If the patient experiences substantial discomfort during this technique, local infiltrative anesthesia using 1 or 2% lidocaine with epinephrine 1:100,000 may be used (see p. 417). Because injection of the anesthetic produces localized lid distortion so that the exact location of the trichiatic lashes may no longer be determined, it is useful to trim the lashes targeted for laser treatment with an iris scissors before the injection to facilitate their identification.

An alternative approach that has been described for this technique is to set the argon laser in continuous mode at a power of 2.5 W.

■ **Complications/Contraindications.** Patients who are unable to cooperate for positioning at the slit lamp for the necessary duration of time are not candidates for this technique. Treatment failure will manifest as cilia regrowth in several months. This may be the result of an insufficiently deep crater to destroy the lash follicle or an unexpected oblique path of the lash follicle, as in the case of traumatic trichiasis.

Vaporization of even small areas of the tarsal plate can lead to alterations in lid contour such as mild dimpling of the lid margin. As a result, laser applications to the tarsus should be avoided, and conditions such as distichiasis, in which numerous lashes originate from the tarsus, should not be treated with this technique. Focal hypopigmentation of the lid margin has been reported in patients with pigmented skin, but was not found to be cosmetically objectionable.

Although instructing the patient on the appropriate position of gaze during this technique is adequate to protect the globe from exposure to the argon laser, some clinicians use a white plastic lens to protect the globe from beam scatter. Proper safety procedures as recommended by the manufacturer for use of the argon laser should be followed, including setting the laser on standby mode until actual delivery of the shots. Assistants and observers should use appropriate protective eyewear while the argon laser is in use.

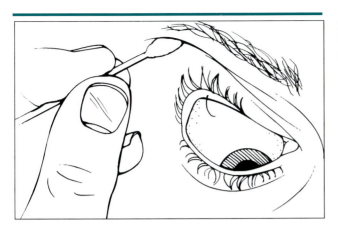

7. To treat the upper lid, the patient is asked to look down, the upper lid is retracted using a cotton-tipped applicator, and the technique is performed in the same fashion.

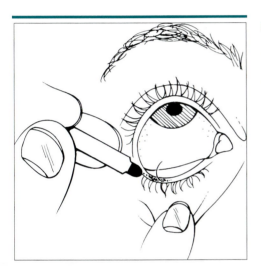

8. For patients with lightly pigmented lashes and skin, rose bengal vital dye may be used to enhance absorption of the blue-green argon laser light. A sterile rose bengal strip is moistened slightly with sterile ophthalmic saline, and the lid margin is carefully "painted" at the base of the lashes to be treated before proceeding with the laser applications.

99

Laser Trabeculoplasty

■ **Description/Indications.** Laser trabeculoplasty (LTP) is a procedure used to reduce intraocular pressure (IOP) in individuals with open-angle glaucoma. Introduced by Wise and Witter in 1979, the argon laser light is absorbed as heat by pigmented tissues of the trabecular meshwork (TM). The original theory suggested that a series of argon laser spots, applied in a nonpenetrating manner, would reopen the spaces in the TM as the adjacent burn sites contract toward their center. The IOP would thus decrease as aqueous outflow was enhanced. Other lasers besides the argon (wavelength, 488 nm), will also enhance aqueous outflow. The diode laser (wavelength, 810 nm), for example, works in a similar fashion to the argon. The major difference between them is that the diode beam, being longer in wavelength, is invisible, making the procedure slightly more difficult. The advantage to the diode laser is that IOP spikes do not appear to occur. However, the argon laser is still the laser most commonly employed and is the one discussed in this chapter.

It is somewhat controversial as to how argon laser trabeculoplasty actually enhances aqueous outflow by decreasing the resistance within the trabecular meshwork. Some proponents still feel, as Wise and Witter originally did, that the burns in the TM caused by the argon laser lead to a tightening of the scleral ring and opening of the spaces in the trabecular meshwork. Another proposed mechanism is that the laser influences biological activity in the TM. Over time, endothelial cells within the TM slowly age with a reduction in their biological activity, which leads to an elevation in the IOP. The laser may stimulate and reawaken these cells, enhancing biological activity and temporarily leading to a better-functioning TM with increased aqueous outflow. Whatever the mechanism, LTP is not a permanent procedure. Its effect diminishes over time, with studies demonstrating that 5 years after LTP, 50% of those treated will return to their pretreatment IOP level.

LTP is indicated for the treatment of open-angle glaucoma, with the Glaucoma Laser Trial indicating its usefulness as an therapeutic modality. At present, LTP is usually performed after several medications have been used and either the glaucoma is progressing or the IOP is felt to be too high for the patient's eye to safely tolerate, requiring additional intervention. LTP works best in older individuals, in primary open-angle glaucoma, and in selected secondary open-angle glaucomas such as pseudoexfoliative or pigmentary glaucoma. This procedure is ineffective in angle recession, uveitic, or neovascular glaucoma. LTP reduces IOP approximately 20 to 30%, similar to the reduction seen by many types of medications. When used, it complements the existing open-angle glaucoma medical regimen and, rarely, will replace a medication.

Because LTP does reduce in efficacy over time, retreatment is only indicated for select cases that showed a good initial response. Even in these cases, however, the second application does not reduce IOP as well as the initial treatment and the effect diminishes at a quicker pace.

There are different philosophies as to the extent and amount of laser treatment that needs to be applied. Some practitioners believe that the entire 360 degrees of the TM should be treated to achieve a longer-lasting effect, with the applications often split between two sessions. Others treat only 180 degrees of the TM, reserving the other half for treatment if the initial procedure is not successful. The trend has been to apply less energy with its resultant fewer complications. The spots can be placed anywhere over the TM to be effective, but the more posteriorly the spots are applied, the greater the inflammation, discomfort, and synechia formation. For this reason, most practitioners recommend placing the burns anteriorly at the juncture of the pigmented and nonpigmented trabecular meshwork. The energy applied is determined by the combination of the power, duration, and diameter of the applications. The power often needs to be adjusted after a test application, watching the site for the creation of a small bubble or tissue blanching.

Different goniolenses are used that are specifically designed for laser procedures. These lenses are similar to the standard Goldmann-type goniolens except that the surfaces have antireflection coatings, which enhance image quality. The Ritch trabeculoplasty lens has four mirrors, two of which have magnifying lenses to increase the lens focus (Fig. 1).

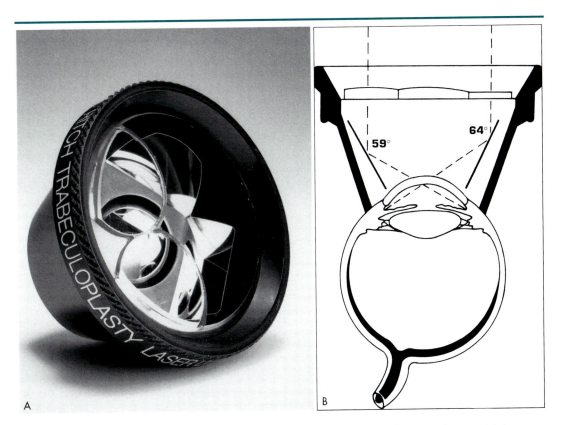

A

B

1. The Ritch trabeculoplasty laser lens (A) has four mirrors: two are angled at 59 degrees and two at 64 degrees (B). The mirrors angled at 64 degrees are best used to treat the superior half of the angle, and the mirrors angled at 59 degrees are best used for the inferior half. A plano-convex button is located over one 59-degree and one 64-degree mirror that provides 1.4X magnification and increases the laser energy by 2X while reducing the spot size from 50 to 35 μm. (Photograph courtesy of Universal Instruments.)

The argon laser is mounted on a slit lamp and activated by a foot pedal control or a push-button mounted in the top of the joystick (see p. 438). The argon laser unit incorporates two red helium-neon (HeNe) aiming beams with a wavelength of 633 nm that are focused (superimposed) using the joystick. This point directly corresponds to the location of the delivery of the argon pulse. There are different lasers available for use. It is important that the manufacturer's guidelines for installation and maintenance are followed to ensure patient safety.

■ **Instrumentation.** Slit lamp mounted argon laser, appropriate laser goniolens, gonioscopic solution, topical 0.5% or 1% apraclonidine ophthalmic solution, topical 2% pilocarpine ophthalmic solution (optional), topical ophthalmic anesthetic solution.

■ **Technique.** Educate the patient thoroughly on the risks and benefits of the procedure. The procedure should be explained so that the patient will understand what to expect. Have the patient review and sign an informed consent form.

One hour prior to treatment, instill one drop of apraclonidine 0.5 or 1.0% ophthalmic solution into the eye to be treated. If necessary, instill one drop of pilocarpine 2% ophthalmic solution to better visualize the trabecular meshwork. Initially adjust the settings on the argon laser so that the spot size is 50 μm, burn duration 0.1 second, and power set at 600 mW with the counter zeroed (Fig. 2).

Prepare the goniolens by placing a gonio solution onto the lens, similar to that used for gonioscopy (see p. 74). Take special care to avoid air bubbles in the solution. Instill one drop of a topical anesthetic in each eye immediately before the procedure. Seat the patient at the slit lamp delivery mechanism of the laser, aligning the lateral canthus with the mark on the slit lamp and ensuring that the patient is comfortable. Use an elbow rest to aid in holding the lens steady and minimize arm fatigue (Fig. 3). Place the goniolens onto the eye and instruct the patient to fixate carefully. Analyze the angle, using 16X to 25X to detect any iris structures, such as iris processes extending into the angle, which if struck by the laser may lead to excessive inflammation. Adjust the small or bullet mirror to maintain a clear view of the angle structures. Precisely focus the aiming beam, kept intentionally dim to minimize light reflections, in the inferior angle at the junction of the posterior pigmented and anterior nonpigmented trabecular meshwork (Fig. 4).

Treat the inferior 180 degrees of the angle at the first session because it is the widest and has the greatest amount of pigmentation and clearest landmarks. A consistent routine is required to ensure the practitioner does not lose track of which areas have previously been treated. A suggested routine is to rotate the bullet mirror to the 9-o'clock position so that the angle at 3 o'clock is treated initially (Fig. 5). The lens is then rotated clockwise to view the last area treated along with the area to be treated next. In lightly pigmented eyes the treatment sites are not obvious, so that proper lens positioning is important. In patients with little angle pigmentation, place the beam midway between the scleral spur and Schwalbe's line, because a tissue reaction may not be observed that could aid in beam localization. If a sharp focus to the aiming beam is not achieved, tilt the lens slightly or have the patient redirect his or her gaze. The beam needs to strike perpendicular to the TM, because an oblique beam loses energy and is less effective. Manipulate the slit lamp joystick to achieve the best placement and focus of the beam.

2. The initial settings for argon laser trabeculoplasty.

ARGON LASER TRABECULOPLASTY

Spot size	50 μm
Duration	0.1 second
Power	600 mW
Wavelength	Argon blue-green
Contact Lens	Ritch lens

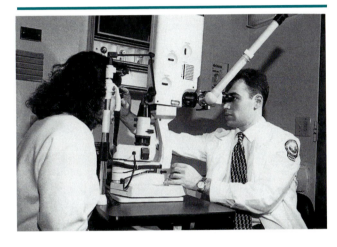

3. The patient is positioned properly and comfortably at the slit lamp delivery system of the laser (a Nd: YAG unit is shown). Either a foot pedal or a button on the joystick of the slit lamp is used to initiate the laser burn.

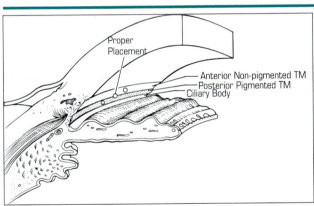

Proper Placement

Anterior Non-pigmented TM
Posterior Pigmented TM
Ciliary Body

4. When performing argon laser trabeculoplasty, the spots are placed at the junction of the pigmented and nonpigmented trabecular meshwork to minimize complications such as inflammation or anterior synechia.

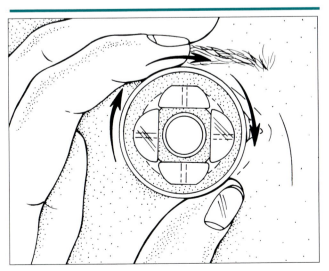

5. A suggested routine for laser trabeculoplasty is to rotate the bullet mirror to the 9-o'clock position so that the angle at 3-o'clock is treated initially. The lens is then rotated clockwise to view the area treated last along with the area to be treated next.

Once ready, depress the foot pedal and view the TM, which should either blanch or exhibit small bubbles at the site immediately after an application (Fig. 6). If no visible signs of treatment are seen, the power setting may be too low, especially for eyes with light TM pigmentation. Consider increasing the power setting in 100-mW steps, never exceeding 1000 mW. If large blisters are produced, the power setting is too high and must be reduced. Rotate the bullet mirror from 9-o'clock towards 12-o'clock, and then finally to the 3-o'clock position, rotating the lens slightly in a clockwise direction every few applications (Fig. 7).

Apply 8 to 9 burns for each clock hour of the angle, so that they are 2 to 3 spot diameters apart, leading to about 40 to 50 burns distributed over 180 degrees, all placed at one session (Fig. 8). Finish the treatment when the bullet lens is at the 3-o'clock position. Separate the burns as evenly as possible and try to keep the aim precise and focused.

In cases of narrow angles where the view of the TM is obscured, have the patient look in the direction of the lens, which should effectively move the iris out of the way, allowing a view of the meshwork. If the TM is still not visible, consider performing argon laser iridoplasty (see p. 450) to open the angle and provide greater access to the structures.

Once the procedure is completed, instill an additional drop of 0.5 or 1.0% apraclonidine ophthalmic solution in the treated eye, rechecking the IOP every hour for 4 hours. Instruct the patient to continue the glaucoma medications, and dismiss the patient if the IOP has not spiked after 4 hours time. In addition, place the patient on a topical ophthalmic steroid drop such as prednisolone acetate 1% four times per day for 5 days.

■ Interpretation.

The patient is examined at 1 day, 1 week, and 1 month after the procedure. The follow-up frequency is then adjusted based upon the characteristics of the case. The examination should include a slit lamp evaluation looking for anterior uveitis, as well as IOP measurement and gonioscopy, looking for anterior synechiae formation. The IOP-lowering effect tends to be maximal around 6 weeks after the procedure. If the IOP reduction is inadequate, the untreated half of the eye may have LTP performed. Also, if LTP reduced the IOP in the range of 15 to 20% but the IOP needs to be lower, a second procedure to treat the remaining 180 degrees of the angle may be considered. The IOP needs to be monitored over time, watching for drift due to loss of efficacy.

The efficacy of IOP control after LTP decreases with time by approximately 10% annually, so that 5 years postoperatively, about 50% of individuals are no longer controlled. Retreatment appears to be somewhat effective in eyes that showed an excellent response to the initial session. Still, the IOP reduction with retreatment is not as effective the second time and the risk for a postoperative IOP spike is enhanced.

■ Contraindications/Complications.

LTP is contraindicated in cases of congenital glaucoma, angle-recession glaucoma, narrow-angle glaucoma, neovascular glaucoma, and uveitic glaucoma. The trabecular meshwork must be visible for LTP to be performed; thus individuals with narrow angles may not be candidates for the procedure. Extensive iris processes or large areas of peripheral anterior synechiae may also make visualization of the trabecular meshwork difficult. Patients with poor fixation or nystagmus may not be candidates for LTP. Corneal edema or significant anterior chamber inflammation may reduce the efficacy of the laser and may be a contraindication for LTP.

Complications of LTP include an acute IOP rise, which occurs in 10 to 30% of cases from 1 to 7 hours after therapy. Apraclonidine 0.5 or 1.0% solution administered 1 hour prior to and immediately after LTP significantly reduces the incidence of acute IOP rise following the procedure. In addition, treating with fewer burns reduces the incidence of postprocedure IOP elevation. If an IOP rise does occur, treatment with appropriate topical and/or oral antiglaucoma therapy should control the increase. Individuals with advanced glaucomatous damage or high IOP measurements pre-LTP are most susceptible to optic nerve head damage from IOP spikes and must be monitored carefully during the postprocedure period. Dividing the treatment into two 180-degree sessions will reduce complications with comparable results to treating 360 degrees of the angle at one session. Late IOP rise that occurs weeks to months after LTP has also been demonstrated. Although unusual, this complication must be watched for and treated with medications.

Mild anterior uveitis is common after LTP and can be controlled with appropriate topical therapy such as prednisolone acetate 1%, used four times daily for 1 week after the procedure. Peripheral anterior synechiae have been noted in up to 33% of patients after undergoing LTP and may be related to the placement of the laser spots. These tent-like adhesions to the spot site do not effect the IOP reduction. Hyphema has been reported in 2 to 5% of eyes undergoing LTP. The hyphema is usually microscopic and clears quickly. Other potential complications include pain, syncope, cystoid macula edema in aphakes, corneal epithelial or endothelial burns, and mild corneal epithelial abrasions. Syncope may be due to anxiety or the vasovagal effect of the goniolens pressing on the eye. If a patient becomes pale, faint, or perspires while undergoing LTP, the procedure should be halted and the episode addressed appropriately.

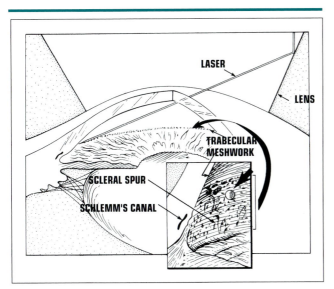

6. Following delivery of the argon laser spot during trabeculoplasty, a small focal blanching or bubble should form (small unlabeled arrow in the inset). If no visible signs of treatment appear, the power may be set too low; if large blisters appear, the power is set too high. (Adapted with permission from Lewis TL, Fingeret M (eds): *Primary Care of the Glaucomas.*)

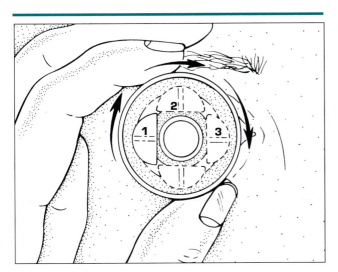

7. To treat the inferior 180 degrees of the angle, the bullet mirror is rotated from 9-o'clock towards 12-o'clock, and then finally to the 3-o'clock position, rotating the lens slightly in a clockwise direction every few applications.

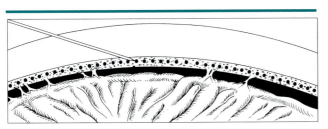

8. Typically, one-half of the extent of the angle is treated at the first session of argon laser trabeculoplasty. Approximately 8 to 9 burns are placed per clock hour, so that 45 to 50 burns are evenly spaced over 180 degrees of the angle.

100

Laser Iridoplasty

■ **Description/Indications.** Laser iridoplasty or gonioplasty is a procedure in which the argon laser is used to create stromal burns in the peripheral portion of the iris. The goal of the procedure is to alter the iris topographic configuration and widen a narrow-angle approach. This is achieved by using long-duration, large burns of low-energy power that cause the tissue at the application sites to contract, pulling the iris away from the angle (Fig. 1).

The argon laser is mounted on a slit lamp and activated by a foot pedal control or a pushbutton mounted in the top of the joystick (see p. 438). The argon laser unit incorporates two red helium-neon (HeNe) aiming beams with a wavelength of 633 nm that are focused (superimposed) using the joystick. This point directly corresponds to the location of the delivery of the argon pulse.

Laser iridoplasty is indicated in cases of narrow-angle glaucoma with subacute or intermittent acute angle-closure attacks to reduce the formation of anterior synechiae. Laser iridoplasty may also be used in an acute angle-closure glaucoma attack that does not respond to medications or laser peripheral iridotomy (see p. 454). In cases of open-angle glaucoma scheduled for argon laser trabeculoplasty (ALT) in which an accompanying narrow angle obscures the view of the trabecular meshwork, laser iridoplasty may widen the angle approach allowing ALT to be successfully performed (see p. 450). Finally, in cases of an acute angle-closure

glaucoma attack with accompanying central corneal edema, the peripheral iris may be the only portion visible that will allow the placement of laser burns. The argon laser may be applied to this region with the subsequent opening of a previously closed angle and the breaking of an acute attack. Once the corneal edema resolves, laser iridotomy is then performed.

There are different lasers available for use. It is important that the manufacturer's guidelines for installation and maintenance are followed to ensure patient safety.

■ **Instrumentation.** Slit lamp mounted argon laser, appropriate laser goniolens, gonioscopic solution, topical 0.5 or 1% apraclonidine ophthalmic solution, topical 2% pilocarpine ophthalmic solution, topical ophthalmic anesthetic solution.

■ **Technique.** Perform a thorough ophthalmic examination and assess appropriate systemic findings. Review the risks and benefits of the procedure with the patient, and ask him or him to sign an informed consent.

Instill one drop of pilocarpine 2% and one drop of apraclonidine 0.5 or 1.0% into the eye to be treated to create miosis, stretch the iris, and prevent IOP spikes. Set the instrument at a spot size of 500 μm, duration of 0.5 seconds, and a power setting of 200 mW (Fig. 2). As with other laser procedures, the lighter the iris color, the greater

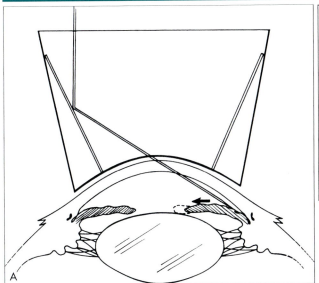

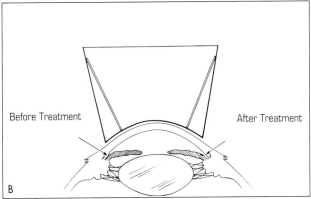

1. A. Laser iridoplasty is used to alter the iris topographic configuration in the presence of a narrow angle. B. The iris tissue contracts at the laser application sites, pulling the iris away from the angle.

2. The initial laser settings for argon laser iridoplasty.

ARGON LASER IRIDOPLASTY

Spot size	500 µm
Duration	0.5 second
Power	200 mW
Wavelength	Argon blue-green
Contact lens	None or Goldmann

the laser power required for the desired response. Instill one drop of topical anesthetic and perform gonioscopy to assess the angle width (see p. 74). Once miosis is complete, seat the patient comfortably at the slit lamp delivery device. A goniolens is not required for the procedure, although many clinicians prefer to use one to keep the eyelids separated and facilitate fixation (Fig. 3). If a goniolens is used, either the central lens or the peripheral bullet mirror can be used.

Aim and focus the beam onto the peripheral portions of the iris surface (Figs. 1A, 4A). Depress the foot switch so that a test burn is performed. Examine the site, looking for sustained contraction of the iris stroma. If an intense burn with pigment liberation occurs, reduce the power or spot duration. If iris reaction is minimal, increase the power or duration. The proper power setting should produce a visible contraction of the iris tissue without charring. The power necessary to produce an adequate burn varies with iris pigmentation and corneal clarity.

Space applications evenly over the entire periphery of the iris, placing 6 applications per quadrant so that 20 to 25 spot burns are placed around the iris. The width of two spots should separate each application with the burn placed in the peripheral region of the iris (Fig. 4). Once the procedure is completed, perform gonioscopy to reinspect the angle looking to see if it has increased in width.

Instill one drop of 0.5 or 1.0% apraclonidine into the eye immediately after the procedure. Also instill a topical steroid drop such as prednisolone acetate with the patient instructed to use it for 1 week, four times per day, at which time the eye is reevaluated. The IOP is measured one hour after the procedure, monitoring for pressure spikes.

■ **Interpretation.** The spot burns should be placed evenly over the circumference of the peripheral iris. Gonioscopy is performed after the procedure to evaluate the success of the procedure. A successful procedure should widen the angle. Patients must be followed at least yearly because the duration of the angle-widening effect is variable. Retreatment may be indicated but is judged on a case-by-case basis.

■ **Complications/Contraindications.** The spots should be spaced so that two burn widths separate each application. Confluence of the spots may occur if they are placed close together, which may lead to iris ischemia and atrophy. Other complications may include syncope, anterior uveitis, IOP elevation, corneal epithelial or endothelial burns, and mild corneal epithelial abrasions. Endothelial burns usually clear without therapy within several days. Syncope may be due to anxiety or the vasovagal effect of the goniolens pressing on the eye. If a patient becomes pale, faint, or perspires while undergoing LTP, the procedure should be halted and the episode addressed appropriately. Patients with poor fixation or nystagmus may not be candidates for the procedure.

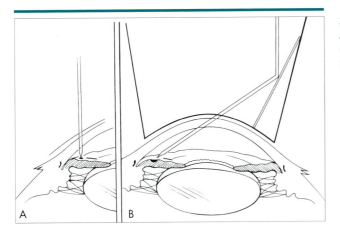

3. Laser iridoplasty may be performed with or without a goniolens. A. Without the goniolens in place, the laser is focused on the iris directly. B. With the goniolens in place, the laser will reflect off the mirror onto the iris.

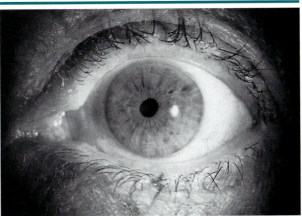

4. A. The laser applications are placed over the entire periphery of the iris, approximately 6 in each quadrant. B. A photograph of a patient following laser iridoplasty. (*See also* Color Plate 100-4.)

101 Laser Iridotomy

■ **Description/Indications.** An iridectomy is a procedure in which an opening is made in the iris to create a new route for aqueous to flow from the posterior to anterior chamber. For many years the procedure was only done surgically with all expense and potential complications associated with an intraocular procedure. In 1956, Meyer-Schwikerath demonstrated that xenon arc photocoagulation could produce a laser iridotomy. Because of numerous complications such as corneal opacities or cataract formation associated with the xenon arc, this modality never gained widespread acceptance. In the 1970s, the continuous-wave argon laser was modified to be delivered through a slit lamp-mounted delivery system that allowed precise focusing in the anterior segment of the eye. As a result, laser iridotomies gained in popularity when the argon laser was demonstrated to successfully create iridotomies with few complications.

In performing a laser iridotomy, several different lasers such as the neodymium:yttrium-aluminum-garnet (Nd:YAG) or argon may be used. In an argon laser iridotomy, a small hole is created in the iris as the iris pigment absorbs the light energy with the subsequent heating and thermal disruption of tissue. The affect of argon laser, which causes photocoagulation, is dependent on iris color and does not work well in eyes with sparse iris pigmentation or in those with thick stromal tissue. The argon laser is mounted on a slit lamp and activated by a foot pedal control or a pushbutton mounted in the top of the joystick (Fig. 1). The argon laser unit incorporates two red helium-neon (HeNe) aiming beams with a wavelength of 633 nm that are focused (superimposed) using the joystick. This point directly corresponds to the location of the delivery of the argon pulse. The laser settings may be modified to either modify the iris contour or achieve iris penetration. Larger spot sizes and lower power settings with a longer duration will modify iris contour and not penetrate the tissue.

The Nd:YAG laser is an alternative modality that works by a different mechanism, namely photodisruption. The neodymium:yttrium-aluminum-garnet (Nd:YAG) laser is a solid-state laser that emits light at an infrared wavelength of 1064 nm. Internal Q-switching produces a short, high-powered, focused laser pulse that is capable of producing the optical breakdown of ocular tissues. The Nd:YAG laser is mounted on a slit lamp biomicroscope and is activated by a foot pedal control or a pushbutton mounted in the top of the joystick (Fig. 2). Although the spot size is fixed, the amount of energy (mJ) as well as the number of pulses per burst delivered (single or multiple) can be adjusted by the operator. Because the wavelength of the Nd:YAG laser is invisible, visible light beams produced by a low-output helium-neon laser are used for aiming. The two red visible-light (633 nm) helium-neon (HeNe) aiming beams are focused (superimposed) using the slit lamp joystick. This point usually corresponds to the focal point of Nd:YAG laser. Compared to the argon laser, the Nd:YAG laser usually requires less energy, produces less postoperative inflammation, and is quicker in achieving iris penetration. The Nd:YAG laser is equally effective on any iris color, produces iridotomies that are less likely to occlude over time, and has replaced the argon as the laser of choice for iridotomies. Because the Nd:YAG laser light does not coagulate tissues, small hemorrhages are common and occur up to 35% of the time.

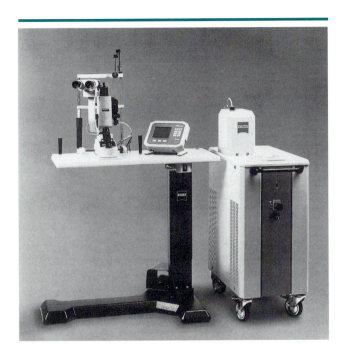

1. A slit lamp mounted ophthalmic argon laser. (Courtesy of Humphrey Instruments, a division of Carl Zeiss.)

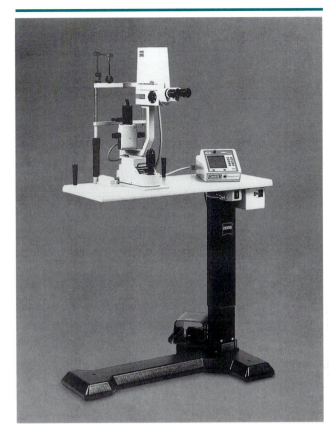

2. A slit lamp mounted Nd:YAG laser. (Courtesy of Humphrey Instruments, a division of Carl Zeiss.)

Laser peripheral iridotomy (LPI) is indicated for angle-closure glaucoma (acute, intermittent, or chronic) caused by primary or secondary pupillary block. In addition, LPI is indicated in the fellow eye when an angle-closure attack is documented. A more controversial indication for LPI is in the individual with narrow angles documented by gonioscopy, with or without elevated IOP. If signs of a past angle-closure attack are present (iris atrophy, misshapen pupil, glaucomflecken) or history of previous attacks (headache, halos) is reported, then an LPI is indicated. Without those signs or symptoms, the decision for prophylactic LPI is more difficult and based upon the clinician's experience and clinical judgment.

In performing a laser iridotomy, a laser contact lens is used to focus the energy onto the iris. In particular, the Abraham (66D button) and Wise (103D button) lenses amplify the energy delivered to the iris while reducing the energy sent to the cornea and retina (Fig. 3). Both lenses have antireflective coatings that reduce laser scatter. Use of the laser lens also aids in keeping the patient's eyelids open during the procedure and enhances patient fixation.

The iridotomy is placed in the peripheral portion of the superior iris in an area where it can be visualized with the slit lamp yet still be covered by the upper eyelid (Fig. 2). The iridotomy is usually placed superior nasally to reduce the risk of macula burn, and is positioned when possible within an iris crypt, which represents a thinned area of iris. For argon laser iridotomy, the site of an iris freckle is used because the extra pigmentation will enhance energy absorption. The site chosen is usually between the 11 and 1-o'clock positions and just inside the limbal border on the iris side, about two thirds to three quarters of the distance between the pupil border and limbus. The 12-o'clock position is avoided, because air bubbles tend to gravitate towards this area, obscuring the underlying iris. The risk of creating lens capsule damage is greater with the Nd:YAG laser, so peripheral placement is important. Areas of corneal arcus should be avoided, which can reduce the efficacy of the laser beam. Some clinicians place two iridotomies, one supratemporal and the other supranasal, for added protection in case one spontaneously occludes.

It is important to follow the manufacturer's guidelines for installation and maintenance of the laser to ensure patient safety.

■ **Instrumentation.** Slit lamp mounted argon or Nd:YAG laser, appropriate laser contact, gonioscopic solution, topical 2% pilocarpine ophthalmic solution, topical 0.5 or 1.0% apraclonidine ophthalmic solution, topical ophthalmic anesthetic solution.

■ **Technique.** Perform a thorough ophthalmic examination and assess appropriate systemic findings. Review the risks and benefits of the procedure with the patient, and ask him or him to sign an informed consent.

One hour before the procedure instill one drop of pilocarpine 2% and one drop of apraclonidine 0.5 or 1.0% into the eye to be treated. Pilocarpine creates miosis, which thins the iris and makes penetration easier; apraclonidine reduces the incidence of intraocular pressure (IOP) spikes occurring after the procedure. Educate the patient as to the procedure and what he or she may expect. Explain that dazzling lights or noises are normal and not cause for alarm. Check the focus and alignment of the laser according to the manufacturer's instructions.

Instill one drop of topical ophthalmic anesthetic solution into each eye immediately before the procedure. Seat the patient at the slit lamp delivery mechanism of the laser with the patient's lateral canthus aligned with the mark on the slit lamp, ensuring that the patient is comfortable. An elbow rest may aid in holding the lens steady and minimizing arm fatigue (Fig. 3). Prepare the laser contact lens by placing a cushioning solution onto the lens, similar to that used for gonioscopy (see p. 74). Place the laser lens onto the eye and instruct the patient to carefully fixate straight ahead.

Argon Laser: Check the settings of the instrument. Initial settings include a 50-μm spot size, 0.1-second duration, and an initial power of 600 mW. The duration of the spot may vary depending on the iris color. For a darker iris, shorter burns (0.02 seconds) in duration are used to prevent char formation (Fig. 4). Longer-duration burns (0.2 seconds), while uncomfortable, aid in penetration in lightly colored irides. Examine the iris, usually in the superior nasal quadrant, to find the optimal laser spot location, looking for iris crypts and pigment spots. Depress the foot pedal to initiate application of the laser. The proper tissue reaction is a pitting or small bubble formation. Charring, in which a black material appears, indicates the laser burn duration is too long and should be reduced.

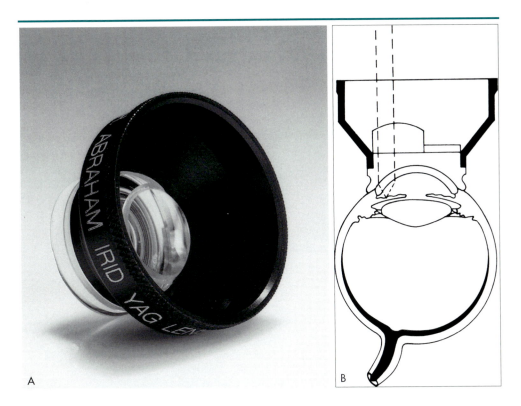

3. A. The Abraham iridotomy Nd:YAG laser contact lens. This Goldmann-style lens contains a 66D plano-convex lens "button." (Courtesy of Universal Instruments.) B. When the button is used for laser iridotomy, the power density is increased by 2.5X and the spot size is decreased by 40%. This aids in achieving iris penetration and reducing complications from the laser energy.

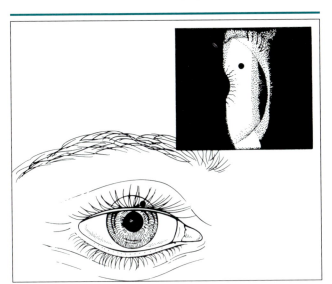

4. The laser iridotomy is typically placed in the superior nasal portion of the peripheral iris, in an area where it is normally covered by the upper eyelid yet can still be visualized with the slit lamp biomicroscope (inset).

There are different techniques used to achieve iris penetration. One approach is to treat the area continuously until iris penetration occurs, making sure the beam is directed away from the macula. Using the aiming beam, focus the light through the button of the laser lens onto the anterior iris stroma, superimposing the burns on top of each other (Fig. 5). After every few applications, inspect the treatment area to see if the lens capsule is visible through the iridotomy site. If so, the iridotomy is patent and the procedure is complete. One sign that penetration has occurred is the sudden appearance of a plume of pigment flowing from the iridotomy site along with deepening of the anterior chamber.

Another approach in performing an argon laser iridotomy is to place stretch burns in a circle around the area of iris to be treated. The stretch burns contract and thin the iris but do not penetrate it (Fig. 6). Used to aid in iris penetration, the contracting spots are created using a 200-μm spot size, 0.2-second duration, and between 200 and 400 mW of power. Six to eight burns are placed in a circle approximately 2 mm in diameter. The central area is then treated within the ring of burns, modifying the settings to allow penetration (50-μm spot size, 0.02 to 0.2-second duration, power of 600 mW). After every few applications of the central area, inspect to see if the lens capsule is visible through the iridotomy site (Fig. 7). If so, the iridotomy is patent and the procedure is complete. The edges of the treated area need to be smoothed, which will aid in further viewing the lens capsule. Reduce the power and duration of the laser, placing burns at the very edge of the opening to reduce the pigment at the edges. The iridotomy must be large enough so that the collection pigment and/or inflammatory debris does not lead to closure of the opening in the first few days following the procedure.

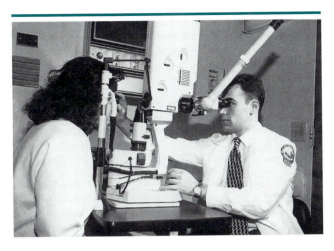

5. The patient is positioned properly and comfortably at the slit lamp delivery device of the laser (a Nd:YAG unit is shown). Either a foot pedal or a button on the joystick of the slit lamp is used to initiate the laser burn.

6. The initial settings for argon laser iridotomy.

ARGON LASER IRIDOTOMY

Spot Size	50 μm
Duration	0.02 to 0.2 second
Power	600 mW
Wavelength	Argon Blue-Green
Contact Lens	Abraham or Wise lens

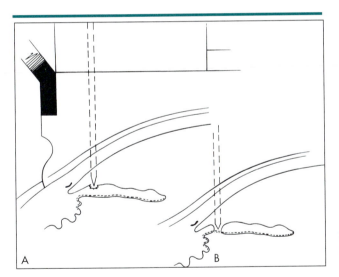

7. One technique used to perform laser iridotomy is to superimpose multiple laser burns in the same location (A) until penetration of the iris occurs (B).

Neodymium:YAG Laser: Examine the iris, looking to place the iridotomy at a site peripherally in the superior nasal portion within an iris crypt if possible. Check the settings for the Nd:YAG laser using the following initial settings: fixed spot size and initial energy between 1 and 12 mJ depending on the laser contact lens used. An initial setting of 3 to 5 mJ is used for the Abraham lens and a 1-mJ initial setting for the Wise lens (Fig. 8). Place either an Abraham or Wise lens onto the eye with the aiming beam precisely focused through the lens button onto the surface of the iris. Use a single burst initially, increasing to 2 to 3 pulses per burst if required. Focus the beam onto the anterior iris stroma, superimposing the applications if necessary. Iris penetration usually occurs with 1 to 12 bursts. If penetration is difficult, increase the energy slowly and carefully, or try a second site. After every application, inspect the treatment area to see if the lens capsule is visible through the iridotomy site (Fig. 9). If so, the iridotomy is patent and the procedure complete. One sign that penetration has occurred is the sudden appearance of a plume of pigment flowing from the iridotomy site along with deepening of the anterior chamber.

Instill one drop of apraclonidine 0.5 or 1.0% solution immediately after the argon or Nd:YAG procedure and measure the IOP hourly for at least 2 hours. If the IOP is unchanged, direct the patient to return in 1 week. Also, place the patient on a topical corticosteroid such as 1% prednisolone acetate four times per day for 1 week. At the 1 week follow-up, measure the IOP, evaluate the patency of the iridotomy, inspect of posterior synechia, and perform gonioscopy. The patient is again seen at 3 and 6 weeks. If the iridotomy is patent at 6 weeks, it is doubtful that it will close in the future.

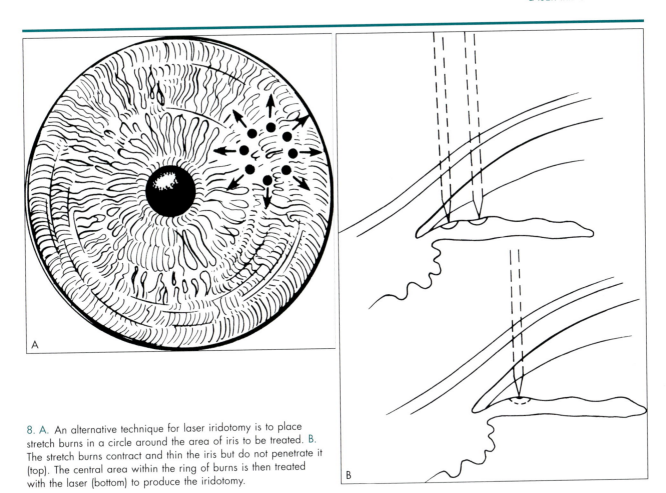

8. A. An alternative technique for laser iridotomy is to place stretch burns in a circle around the area of iris to be treated. B. The stretch burns contract and thin the iris but do not penetrate it (top). The central area within the ring of burns is then treated with the laser (bottom) to produce the iridotomy.

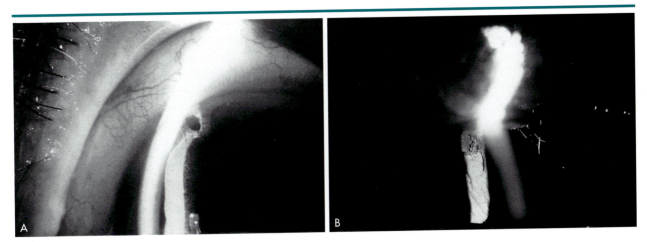

9. A. A patent argon laser iridotomy is visible with the slit lamp biomicroscope. B. This laser iridotomy is not patent. Note the pigment that occludes the opening. (*See also* Color Plates 109–A.)

■ **Interpretation.** The best method to ensure the iridotomy is patent is by visualizing the lens capsule through the newly created opening. Deepening of the peripheral anterior chamber and a release of iris pigment, while signs of patency, do not guarantee penetration. A red reflex seen through the iridotomy using retroillumination also does not guarantee patency. Gonioscopy is indicated after the procedure to analyze the extent to which the angle has changed in configuration and depth.

■ **Complications/Contraindications.** Chronic angle-closure glaucoma due to anterior synechia or neovascularization will not be relieved by an LPI. In cases of acute angle-closure glaucoma with cloudy, edematous corneas that do not clear with hypertonic agents, iridotomy may not be feasible. In this event, the acute attack must be managed medically, or an attempt made to break the attack with iridoplasty (see p. 450) before performing an LPI. Patients with poor fixation or nystagmus may not be candidates for the procedure. Eyes in which iris penetration is difficult with the argon laser will often respond if the Nd:YAG laser is used.

Blurred vision is common immediately after the procedure due to pigment release and/or minor hemorrhage. A low-grade secondary anterior uveitis is common and treated with topical steroids four times per day for 7 days. An elevated IOP may occur that is short lived and rarely seen with the use of apraclonidine. Corneal epithelial or endothelial opacities have been reported if the beam is not properly focused, if the power or energy setting is too high, or if the iris is too close to the cornea. Small epithelial lens opacities have been noted that do not progress to cataract formation. Hyphema formation, usually small, is most common with the Nd:YAG laser. Pressure applied to the eye with the laser contact lens will usually stop any iris bleeding. Retinal or lens damage may occur with poorly placed laser applications. The potential for these complications can be reduced with the use of a laser lens, by ensuring that the laser beam is not directed toward the macula, and reducing the laser energy levels.

Closure of the iridotomy site, especially if the opening is small, may occur within the first few weeks after the procedure and is usually related to anterior chamber inflammation. Minimizing the anterior chamber inflammation and properly sizing the opening will reduce the chance of closure at the site. Monocular diplopia is a potential complication when the iridotomy site is not covered by the upper lid.

Syncope may occur, due either to anxiety or the vasovagal effect of the laser contact lens pressing on the eye. If a patient becomes pale, faint, or perspires while undergoing LTP, the procedure should be halted and the episode addressed appropriately.

ND: YAG LASER IRIDOTOMY

Spot Size	Fixed
Pulse	1—3
Energy	3 to 5 mJ with the Abraham lens
	1 mJ with the Wise lens
Wavelength	Nd-YAG
Contact Lens	Abraham or Wise lens

10. The initial settings for neodymium:YAG laser iridotomy.

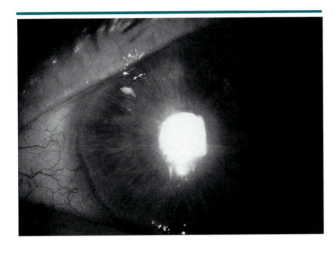

11. A patent Nd:YAG laser iridotomy is noted using retroillumination with the slit lamp biomicroscope. (*See also* Color Plate 101-11.)

102

Nd:YAG Posterior Capsulotomy

■ **Description/Indications.** The neodymium:yttrium-aluminum-garnet (Nd:YAG) laser is a solid-state laser that emits light at an infrared wavelength of 1064 nm. Internal Q-switching produces a short, high-powered, focused laser pulse that is capable of producing optical breakdown of ocular tissue. The resultant ionization, or plasma formation, produces acoustic shock waves slightly "upstream" from the point of the laser focus to produce localized tissue disruption (Fig. 1).

This photodisruptive characteristic of the Nd:YAG laser is used to perform posterior capsulotomies for patients who have developed posterior capsule opacification following extracapsular cataract extraction (ECCE) and secondary intraocular lens (IOL) implantation. Nd:YAG posterior capsulotomy is indicated when, as assessed through appropriate measures, sufficient opacification of the capsule has developed to interfere with the patient's visual acuity, visual function, or both.

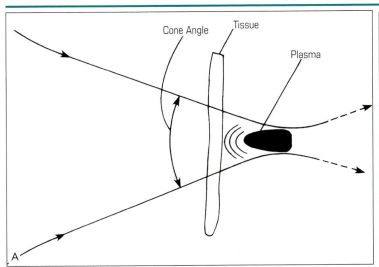
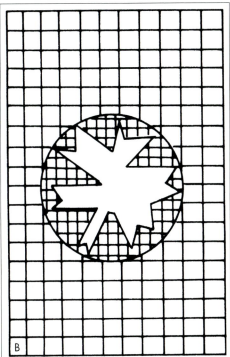

1. The focused Nd:YAG laser pulse results in the formation of plasma that produces an "upstream" shock wave (A). In order to achieve photodisruption (B), the laser is focused slightly behind the tissue to compensate for this shock wave effect. (Modified with permission from Instructions for Use, Visulas YAG II, Carl Zeiss; and Carr LW, Talley DK: Laser-tissue interactions. *Optom Clin* 1995;**4:**18, 28.)

The Nd:YAG laser is mounted on a slit lamp biomicroscope and is activated by a foot pedal control or a push-button mounted in the top of the joystick (Fig. 2). Although the spot size is fixed, the amount of energy (mJ) as well as the number of pulses per burst delivered (single or multiple) can be adjusted by the operator.

Because the wavelength of the Nd:YAG laser is invisible, visible light beams produced by a low-output helium-neon laser are used for aiming. The two red visible-light (633 nm) helium-neon (HeNe) aiming beams are focused (superimposed) using the slit lamp joystick. Because this point usually corresponds to the focal point of the Nd:YAG laser, focusing the aiming beams on the posterior capsule, and then focusing very slightly posterior to the capsule before activating the laser (retrofocusing) will maximize the photodisruptive effect and minimize damage to the IOL. Some manufacturers will set the instrument so that the Nd:YAG pulses are automatically delivered slightly deep to the focused aiming beams to compensate for the upstream shock wave that produces tissue photodisruption.

For a polymethymethacrylate (PMMA) or loop haptic silicone intraocular lens, the pattern of the capsulotomy is most commonly cruciate with the initial shot delivered at the 12-o'clock position, superior to the visual axis (Fig. 3). As a result, if adjustments in the laser settings are needed based upon unintended outcomes from the first shot (such as IOL pitting), the superior location away from the visual axis avoids effects on visual function.

Plate haptic foldable silicone IOLs are becoming more widely used. Anecdotal clinical evidence suggests that the enhanced flexibility of these lenses may make them susceptible to a "watermelon seed" type displacement into the vitreous cavity following posterior capsulotomy. As a result, if a patient with a plate haptic foldable silicone IOL requires a Nd:YAG capsulotomy, it is beneficial to defer it until at least 3 to 4 months postoperatively to allow for some fibrosis and stiffening of the capsular bag. In addition, many clinicians recommend that the pattern of the capsulotomy be delivered to a small central

area in a circular or spiral shape for these types of IOLs to reduce points of capsule tension (Fig. 4). If substantial fibrosis of the anterior capsule rim is present, recent evidence suggests that the Nd:YAG laser may be used to relieve this tensional source as well.

For most lasers, a successful Nd:YAG capsulotomy can be performed using an energy setting of 1 to 2 mJ per pulse. The energy is modified based upon the observed tissue effect; the more densely opacified capsule requires a higher energy setting per pulse. As the posterior capsule opacifies, wrinkles are often observed that indicate lines of tension. Shots placed across these tension lines will produce the largest opening per pulse because the opening will widen as the tension is released.

The elevation in intraocular pressure (IOP) commonly associated with anterior segment laser procedures is effectively controlled by administering apraclonidine HCl drops before and after the procedure. This alpha-adrenergic agonist reduces IOP by decreasing aqueous production.

■ **Instrumentation.** Slit lamp mounted Nd:YAG laser, topical ophthalmic mydriatic/cycloplegic solutions, topical 0.5% or 1% apraclonidine ophthalmic solution, Nd:YAG capsulotomy laser contact lens, artificial tears.

■ **Technique.** Perform a thorough ophthalmic examination and assess appropriate systemic findings. Review the risks and benefits of the procedure with the patient, and ask him or her to sign an informed consent. Check the type and style of the patient's IOL. Instill one or two drops of 0.5 or 1% apraclonidine 1 hour before the procedure. Use the slit lamp to note the location of the undilated pupillary zone and localize a landmark on the capsule. Dilate the patient's pupils with topical ophthalmic mydriatic/cycloplegic solutions.

Carefully focus the oculars of the slit lamp biomicroscope as proper alignment and focus of the instrumentation is very important. Initially set the laser settings on 1.0 to 1.2 mJ and the single pulse setting (Fig. 5).

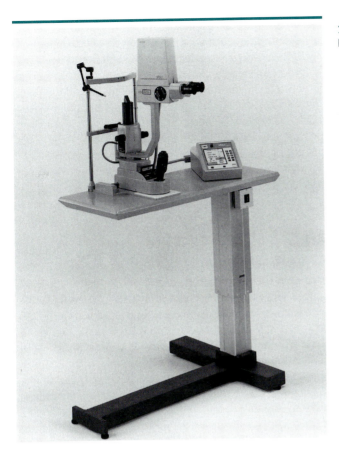

2. A slit lamp-mounted ophthalmic Nd:YAG laser. (Courtesy of Humphrey Instruments, a division of Carl Zeiss.)

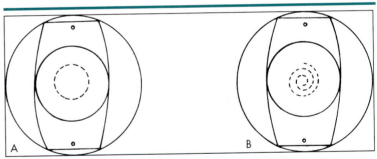

4. Due to its increased flexibility, a circular (A) or spiral (B) pattern is recommended to perform a Nd:YAG posterior capsulotomy for a patient with a plate haptic foldable silicone IOL.

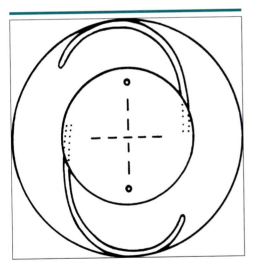

3. A cruciate pattern (dashed lines) is commonly used to perform a Nd:YAG posterior capsulotomy for a patient with a PMMA or loop haptic silicone IOL. The outer circle represents the capsular bag.

5. The initial settings of the Nd:YAG laser for posterior capsulotomy.

Nd: YAG POSTERIOR CAPSULOTOMY

Spot size	Fixed
Pulse	1
Energy	1.0 to 1.2 mJ
Wavelength	Fixed
Contact lens	Usually none

Position the patient comfortably at the instrument, ensuring that the forehead is securely against the forehead rest. If necessary, secure the strap around the back of the patient's head or have an assistant hold the patient's head in place. Advise the patient about the popping noise and flash he or she may notice during the procedure and the need for steady fixation. Set the slit lamp magnification at 10X to 16X, and use diffuse illumination set on moderate intensity (see p. 22). Adjust the illumination of the HeNe aiming beams so that they are clearly visible yet not too bright.

Using the capsule landmarks noted before dilation, use the joystick to focus the aiming beams on the posterior capsule approximately 2 mm above the visual axis; then, if required by the instrument design, focus just slightly behind the capsule to compensate for the upstream shock wave (Fig. 6A). Aim the shot on capsule tension lines in the desired location if possible. Activate the laser by depressing the foot pedal or the joystick button. An aperture in the posterior capsule should appear (Fig. 6B). If not, refocus and adjust the energy setting upward by 0.2 to 0.3 mJ until the desired tissue effect is produced. It is generally not necessary to exceed 2.0 mJ.

Cruciate Pattern: Once a small opening appears after the initial laser shot, lower the slit lamp towards 6-o'clock and focus the aiming beams on the capsule inferior to the edge of the newly created aperture (Fig. 7). Focus just slightly behind the capsule and activate the laser, enlarging the aperture. Continue enlarging the aperture in a vertical direction until it is approximately 4 mm in height and centered with respect to the visual axis. If bridges or substantial flaps of the capsule remain, use appropriately placed laser shots to treat these as well.

Next, focus the aiming beams onto the capsule at the 9-o'clock position adjacent to the capsule aperture, as described (Fig. 8). Focus slightly behind the capsule, activate the laser, and enlarge the capsule opening approximately 2 mm in the 9-o'clock direction. Repeat the process in the 3-o'clock direction so that the aperture is approximately 4 mm wide in the horizontal meridian and centered around the visual axis.

Circular Pattern: Once a small opening appears after the initial laser shot, position the HeNe aiming beams adjacent to the newly created aperture in either a clockwise or counterclockwise direction to effect a circular pattern (Fig. 9). Continue enlarging the aperture opening in a circular direction, maintaining a distance of approximately 2 mm from the visual axis and using the capsule tension lines to your advantage. Use a spiral approach, directed centrally, to treat any substantial remaining flaps or bridges of capsule tissue.

Following the procedure, instill another drop of apraclonidine ophthalmic solution. Record the total number of laser shots and energy in the patient record. Recheck the IOP 1 hour after the procedure, reassess systemic findings as needed, and schedule a follow-up in approximately 1 week. Because a few patients develop anterior uveitis after the procedure, many clinicians recommend topical steroid or nonsteroidal anti-inflammatory ophthalmic drops four times a day for 5 to 7 days. The use of this prophylactic therapy is especially indicated for patients with a prior history of anterior uveitis or for whom an unusually large amount of treatment energy was used during the posterior capsulotomy. Artificial tears may be dispensed to enhance patient comfort following the procedure.

A laser contact lens such as the Peyman or central Abraham lens can be used to increase the cone angle of the laser beam delivered to the capsule, which increases its effectiveness. This relative energy enhancement is useful in the presence of a thicker capsule so that less energy can be used than if the contact lens were not in place. The laser contact lens may also be used to enhance the optical quality of the corneal surface, to control lid and eye movements, such as for a patient who has nystagmus, and to provide some magnification. The technique for inserting the laser contact lens is the same as that used for the three-mirror lens (see p. 74). Use appropriate technique to avoid bubbles in the gonioscopic solution, and increase the illumination of the HeNe aiming beams so that they are clearly visible with the lens in place. Focus on the posterior capsule through the center of the laser lens and proceed with the procedure as described.

■ **Interpretation.** The goal in performing a Nd:YAG posterior capsulotomy is to create an aperture in the opacified capsule that is roughly 4 mm in diameter using the minimal amount of laser energy necessary to do so (Fig. 10). This aperture size is typically sufficient with respect to the patient's natural pupil size to retain good visual function under various lighting conditions, especially because the edges of the capsulotomy tend to retract over time and become more spherical, producing a slightly larger opening. The necessary number of shots to effect a successful capsulotomy aperture will vary depending on the density of the capsule and the treatment pattern used. With the proper refractive correction in place, the patient's visual acuity will improve immediately after the posterior capsulotomy unless other factors intervene, such as the presence of macular abnormalities.

As a result of tissue interaction by the Nd:YAG laser, it is not uncommon for small bubbles to form in the vicinity of the capsule. During the procedure, disruption in the precorneal tear film may compromise focusing of the aiming beams. If this occurs, ask the patient to blink or instill artificial tears if needed. If reflections of the slit lamp illumination off the cornea or IOL interfere with focusing, widen the angle between the slit lamp illumination housing and eyepieces, take the illumination beam slightly out of click (see p. 22), or reposition patient fixation.

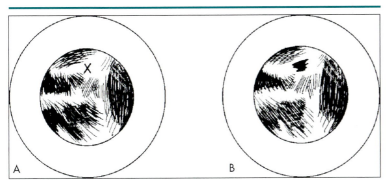

6. Following pupillary dilation, the HeNe aiming beams (X) are focused on the posterior capsule approximately 2 mm above the visual axis at the point of capsule tension lines if possible (A). After focusing slightly behind the capsule, the laser is activated. A small aperture in the posterior capsule should appear (B).

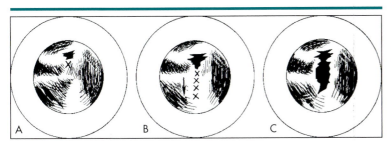

7. To continue the cruciate capsulotomy pattern, the slit lamp is lowered slightly towards 6-o'clock and the HeNe aiming beams are focused (x) on the capsule inferior to the edge of the newly created aperture (A). After focusing slightly behind the capsule, the laser is activated to enlarge the aperture in a vertical direction (arrow) (B). The final vertical component of the cruciate should be approximately 4 mm in height and centered with respect to the visual axis (C).

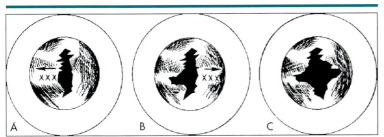

8. To complete the horizontal "arms" of the cruciate posterior capsulotomy, the HeNe aiming beams are focused onto the capsule at the 9-o'clock position adjacent to the capsule aperture (x) (A). After focusing slightly behind the capsule, the laser is activated, and the capsule opening is enlarged approximately 2 mm in the 9-o'clock direction. The process is then repeated approximately 2 mm in the 3-o'clock direction (B). The horizontal component of the cruciate should be approximately 4 mm wide in the horizontal meridian and centered around the visual axis (C).

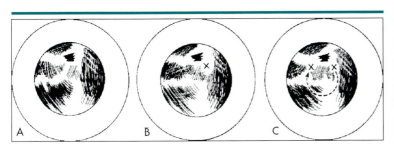

9. To perform a circular capsulotomy pattern for a patient with a plate haptic foldable silicone IOL, the first Nd:YAG laser shot is delivered at the 12-o'clock position approximately 2 mm above the visual axis (A). The HeNe aiming beams (x) are positioned adjacent to the initial aperture opening in either a clockwise or counterclockwise position (B). After focusing slightly behind the capsule, the laser is activated. The treatment is continued in a circular direction, (dashed arrow) maintaining a distance of approximately 2 mm from the visual axis (C).

■ Complications/Contraindications.

If the patient is unable or unwilling to fixate properly, inadvertent damage to adjacent intraocular structures may occur during posterior Nd:YAG capsulotomy. Patients who are unable to cooperate for positioning at the slit lamp for the necessary duration of time are not candidates for this technique.

Posterior Nd:YAG capsulotomy is contraindicated if substantial corneal scarring, irregularity, or edema is present that precludes visualization of the aiming beams or degrades the laser beam optics to prevent reliable and predictable tissue breakdown. The denser the posterior capsule, the more laser energy is needed to effect a successful capsulotomy. As greater levels of energy are transmitted through the vitreous, more complications may ensue.

Elevated IOP is the most common reported complication of YAG posterior capsulotomy, likely the result of debris blocking the trabecular meshwork or from shock wave–induced damage to the meshwork. When it occurs, the IOP elevation usually peaks at 3 to 4 hours postprocedure and returns to baseline after 1 week. Treatment with apraclonidine before and after the procedure effectively prevents this potential IOP elevation in most patients. If administration of apraclonidine is contraindicated for a given patient, a topical beta-blocker or oral carbonic anhydrase inhibitor can be administered before the procedure if no contraindications are present. Postprocedure elevation in the IOP should be treated appropriately. Established glaucoma patients should be monitored closely for potential IOP elevation because they are more susceptible to this complication. These patients will likely benefit from at least an additional follow-up 1 day after the laser procedure.

Pitting of the IOL is not uncommon in the course of Nd:YAG posterior capsulotomy if the laser is focused at or near the surface of the IOL. If infrequent, the pitting is generally not visually significant. Molded PMMA IOLs are more easily damaged than higher molecular weight lathe-cut PMMA lenses. If the laser is inadvertently focused inside the IOL, localized cracks may appear that may cause significant glare for the patient. Silicone lenses tend to pit or exhibit vapor trails more often than PMMA lenses because of their softer consistency. Pits in silicone IOLs tend to appear as dark melted spots, which may be misinterpreted as pigment deposits. If a pit develops in the course of the capsulotomy, reassess the focus and energy level setting.

Known or suspected cystoid macular edema (CME) is a relative contraindication to Nd:YAG posterior capsulotomy until the active process is resolved, if at all possible, due to the possible beneficial affect of an intact posterior capsule in these cases. CME is an uncommon complication of this procedure.

Retinal detachment is an uncommon but reported complication of Nd:YAG capsulotomy, likely the result of vitreous contraction. Patients found to have preexisting peripheral retinal disease prior to the procedure may benefit from prophylactic treatment before proceeding. Efforts to avoid this complication in patients who are at high risk may also include using the least amount of energy and the lowest possible number of shots to form a small capsulotomy aperture.

Other rare but reported complications of posterior Nd:YAG capsulotomy include endophthalmitis caused by *Propionibacterium acnes,* persistent iritis, macular holes, and corneal endothelial cell loss. If a laser contact lens with a button is used and if the laser beam is not sent through the button portion, retinal damage may result.

Proper safety procedures as recommended by the manufacturer for use of the Nd:YAG laser should be followed, including setting the laser on standby mode until actual delivery of the shots.

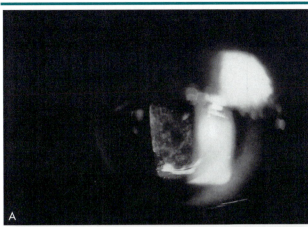

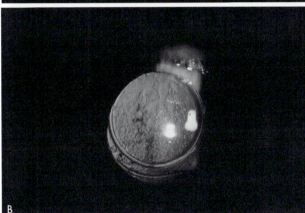

10. A. An opacified posterior capsule as viewed by direct illumination on the slit lamp biomicroscope. B. An opacified posterior capsule is viewed using retroillumination. C. Retroillumination is used to view the capsule aperture following successful Nd:YAG posterior capsulotomy. (C Courtesy of Kevin L. Waltz, MD, OD)

XIV Suggested Readings

Albert DW, Wade EC, Parrish RK, et al: A prospective study of angiographic cystoid macular edema one year after Nd:YAG posterior capsulotomy. *Ann Ophthalmol* 1990;**22:**139–143.

Awan KJ: Argon laser treatment of trichiasis. *Ophthal Surg* 1986;**17:**658–660.

Bartley GB, Lowry JC: Argon laser treatment of trichiasis. *Am J Ophthalmol* 1992;**113:**71–74.

Blacharski PA, Newsome DA: Bilateral macular holes after Nd:YAG laser posterior capsulotomy. *Am J Ophthalmol* 1988; **110:**417–418. Letter.

Brown SVL, Thomas JV, Simmons RJ: Laser trabeculoplasty retreatment. *Am J Ophthalmol* 1985;**99:**8–10.

Campbell DC: Thermoablation treatment for trichiasis using the argon laser. *Aust NZJ Ophthalmol* 1990;**18:**427–430.

Capone AC, Rehkopf PG, Warnicki JW, Stuart JC: Temporal changes in posterior capsulotomy dimensions following neodymium:YAG laser discission. *J Cataract Refract Surg* 1990;**16:**451–456.

Classé JG (ed): *Optometry Clinics,* vol 4, no. 4. *Ophthalmic Lasers.* Norwalk, CT, Appleton & Lange, 1995.

Constable IJ, Ming AS: *Laser: Its Clinical Uses in Eye Diseases.* Edinburgh, Churchill Livingstone, 1990.

Duke-Elder S, Wybar KC: Anatomy of the eye, in Duke-Elder S (ed): *System of Ophthalmology,* vol. 2. St. Louis, Mosby, 1961, p 526.

Ghabrial R, Francis IC, Kappagoda MB: Autologous blood facilitation of lid laser treatment. *Aust NZJ Ophthalmol* 1994;**22:**218. Letter.

Glaucoma Laser Trial Research Group: The glaucoma laser trial, 1. Acute effects of argon laser trabeculoplasty versus topical medication. *Ophthalmology* 1990;**97:**1403–1413.

Gossman MD, Yung R, Berlin AJ, Brightwell JR: Prospective evaluation of the argon laser in the treatment of trichiasis. *Ophthalm Surg* 1992;**23:**183–187.

Gossman MD, Yung R, Berlin AJ, et al: Argon laser treatment of trichiasis. *Am J Ophthalmol* 1993;**114:**379. Letter.

Higginbotham EJ, Shahbazi MF: Laser therapy in glaucoma: An overview and update. *Int Ophthalmol Clin* 1990;**30:** 187–197.

Ladas ID, Karamaounas N, Vergados J, et al: Use of argon laser photocoagulation in the treatment of recurrent trichiasis: Long-term results. *Ophthalmologica* 1993;**207:**90–93.

Laser Therapy for the Anterior Segment. Northeastern State University College of Optometry and the Laser Center, Continuing Education Foundation, Tulsa, 1995.

Mamalis N, Craig MT, Price FW: Spectrum of Nd:YAG laser-induced intraocular lens damage in explanted lenses. *J Cataract Refract Surg* 1990;**16:**495–500.

Moster MR, Schwartz LW, Spaeth GL, et al: Laser iridectomy: A controlled study comparing argon and neodymium:YAG. *Ophthalmology* 1986;**93:**20–24.

Murrill CA, Stanfield DL, VanBrocklin MD: Intermediate to late complications, in: *Primary Care of the Cataract Patient.* Norwalk, CT, Appleton & Lange, 1995, chapter 16.

Newland TJ, Auffarth GU, Wesendahl TA, Apple DJ: Neodymium:YAG laser damage on silicone intraocular lenses. *J Cataract Refract Surg* 1994;**20:**527–533.

Richter CU, Steinert RF: Neodymium:yttrium-aluminum-garnet laser posterior capsulotomy, in Steinert RF (ed): *Cataract Surgery: Technique, Complications, & Management.* Philadelphia, Saunders, 1995, chapter 32.

Ritch R, Palmberry P: Argon laser iridectomy in densely pigmented irides. *Am J Ophthalmol* 1982;**93:**800–801.

Ritch R, Shields MB, Krupin T: *The Glaucomas.* St. Louis, Mosby, 1996, pp 1549–1590.

Rivera AH, Brown RH, Anderson DR: Laser iridotomy vs surgical iridectomy: Have the indications changed? *Arch Ophthalmol* 1985;**103:**1350–1354.

Robin AL, Pollack IP: A comparison of neodymium:YAG and argon laser iridotomies. *Ophthalmology* 1984;**91:**1011–1016.

Robin AL, Pollack IP, Hause B, Enger CL: Effect of ALO-215 on intraocular pressure following argon laser trabeculoplasty. *Am J Ophthalmol* 1987;**105:**646–650.

Romanowski A: Prophylactic use of apraclonidine for intraocular pressure increase after Nd:YAG capsulotomies. *Am J Ophthalmol* 1992;**114:**377–379. Letter.

Sharif KW, Arafat AFA, Wykes WC: The treatment of recurrent trichiasis with argon laser photocoagulation. *Eye* 1991; **5:** 591–595.

Van Buskirk EM: Pathophysiology of laser trabeculoplasty. *Surv Ophthalmol* 1989;**33:**264–272.

Weingeist TA, Sneed SR: *Laser Surgery in Ophthalmology: Practical Applications.* Norwalk, CT, Appleton & Lange, 1992.

Wilensky JT, Jampol LM: Laser therapy for open-angle glaucoma. *Ophthalmology* 1981;**88:**213–217.

Wise JB, Witter AL: Argon laser therapy for open-angle glaucoma: A pilot study. *Arch Ophthalmol* 1979;**97:**319–322.

York K, Ritch R, Szmyd LJ: Argon laser peripheral iridoplasty: Indications, techniques and results. *Invest Ophthalmol Vis Sci* 1984;25(suppl):94.

XV

Infection Control Procedures

103 Disinfection, Sterilization, and Universal Precautions

■ **Description/Indications.** Multiple techniques exist to help prevent the transmission of infectious disease to patients, staff members, and providers in the ophthalmic practice setting. The prevention of exposure to and transmission of disease requires that practitioners and staff members practice certain techniques of proper basic hygiene, as well as appropriate disinfection and sterilization of instrumentation. Potential exposure of eye care personnel to various viruses, including human immunodeficiency (HIV), hepatitis B (HBV), herpes, and adenovirus, as well as organisms such as tuberculosis, pseudomonas, staphylococcus, or streptococcus, all require that cautious measures be taken.

Two distinct areas of concern have been identified in ophthalmic practice. One is the potential transmission of ocular surface infectious agents, which requires that hygienic techniques be practiced such as handwashing and disinfection of tonometers, trial contact lenses, and other instruments. The second is the potential transmission of blood-borne pathogens such as HIV and HBV, requiring the use of personal protective equipment (PPE) such as gloves, masks, gowns, and protective eyewear when indicated; proper handling of needles and waste disposal; proper instrument and equipment cleaning techniques; along with other appropriate precautions, such as hepatitis B vaccinations for at-risk office personnel. Because it is impossible to identify every patient who carries a transmissible disease, all health care personnel should practice the broad guidelines of universal precautions, that is, all blood and body fluids must be treated as if they were infected with pathogens. The purpose of this section is to review basic principles of disinfection, sterilization, and universal precautions, along with their implementation.

Medical and surgical instruments are classified into three categories: critical, semicritical, or noncritical, depending on their risk of transmitting infection and the need to sterilize them between uses. "Critical" includes instruments used for penetration of soft tissue or bone and should be sterilized after each use. "Semicritical" includes instruments that contact tissue such as the eyelids, conjunctiva, and cornea. "Noncritical" includes equipment such as chin and forehead rests that contact intact skin.

■ **Instrumentation.** Liquid hand soap, antimicrobial hand scrub kit, disposable towels, sterile latex examination gloves, nonsterile latex examination gloves, protective eyewear, gowns, masks, isopropyl alcohol swabs, contact lens hydrogen peroxide cleaning system, household bleach, sterile saline solution, puncture resistant sharps container, hazardous waste disposal bags or containers, plastic soft contact lens enzyme vials, sterile cotton-tipped applicators, autoclave.

■ Technique.

Handwashing/Hand Inspection: Wash hands with non-abrasive disinfectant soap, rinse well with running water, and thoroughly dry with a clean cloth or disposable paper towel. Use an antimicrobial soap kit for presurgical hand scrubbing. Perform handwashing before and after each patient encounter, after removal of PPE, after barehanded touching of any object likely to be contaminated by blood or ocular discharge, and after working on or around an environmental surface that may be contaminated. Washing the hands for at least 60 seconds is recommended in precautionary situations. Visually inspect your hands and perform a brief isopropyl alcohol hand lavage at the beginning of each day of patient care, as stinging will assist in identifying any open skin areas or epithelial skin compromise needing additional protective care. Keep all existing cuts covered with clean bandages, even with the use of gloves. Keep fingernails clean and at a reasonable length.

Using Latex Gloves: Wash hands before and after disposable latex glove use. Wear disposable gloves if any open wound or weeping lesion exists on your hands even following proper bandaging. Wear disposable latex gloves if the possibility exists of contact with a patient's blood, ocular discharge, or any weeping skin lesion. Gloves are not a substitute for handwashing. Use nonsterile examination gloves or sterile surgical gloves as circumstances dictate (Fig. 1).

After completion of the patient care procedure and disposal of materials, carefully remove gloves to prevent contamination. With both hands gloved, peel one glove from top to bottom and hold it in the gloved hand (Fig. 2A), being cautious not to touch the exterior of the glove with your skin. With the exposed hand, peel the second glove from the inside (Fig. 2B), tucking the first glove inside the second (Fig. 2C). Dispose of the glove ball in the appropriate receptacle. Wash your hands as described previously after proper glove removal and disposal.

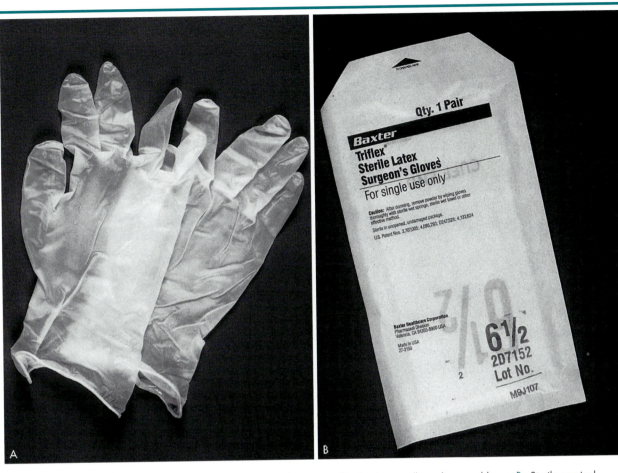

1. A. Nonsterile examination gloves are boxed in quantity and are typically sized as small, medium, and large. B. Sterile surgical gloves are individually packaged and are available in specific sizes.

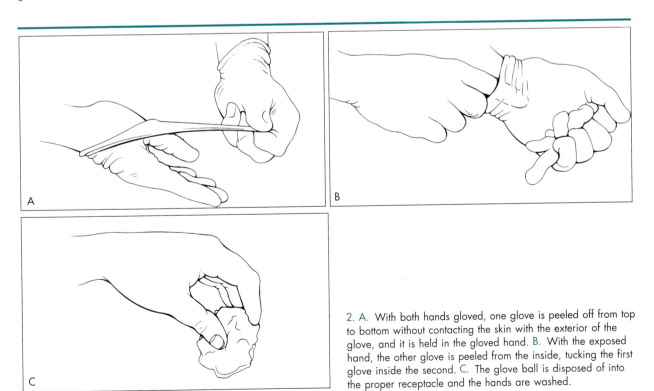

2. A. With both hands gloved, one glove is peeled off from top to bottom without contacting the skin with the exterior of the glove, and it is held in the gloved hand. B. With the exposed hand, the other glove is peeled from the inside, tucking the first glove inside the second. C. The glove ball is disposed of into the proper receptacle and the hands are washed.

Examining the Patient: When examining or assisting with a patient, avoid contact with the patient's eyelids, facial skin, mucous membranes, tears, and other areas of potential discharge by using gloves and/or "no-touch" techniques such as using a cotton-tipped applicator (Fig. 3).

Using Gowns, Masks, and Protective Eyewear: Use gown, mask, and goggles or eyeglasses with solid side shields as barrier precaution whenever the possibility of splattering or splashes of blood or other bodily fluids contaminated with blood or other infectious materials may occur. Also use PPE during minor office surgical procedures and diagnostic testing such as fluorescein angiogra-phy. Use of a disposable surgical mask by the patient and/or examiner for mutual protection should be strongly considered when tuberculosis or any significant upper respiratory infection exists or is suspected (Fig. 4).

Disinfecting Trial Contact Lenses: Disinfect every trial contact lens before reuse. Clean rigid contact lenses with a disinfecting system containing hydrogen peroxide or chlorhexidine. Clean soft contact lenses with a hydrogen peroxide system or use thermal disinfection. Use the standard contact lens cleaning technique recommended by the manufacturer. It is recommended that staff members wear latex gloves when cleaning trial contact lenses.

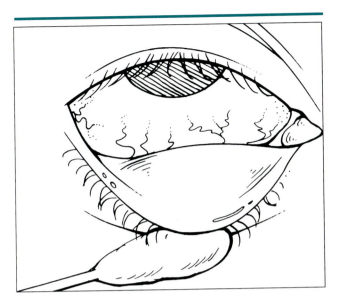

3. The "no-touch" technique for examining the eye. The lower lid is retracted with a cotton-tipped applicator so that the examiner's fingers do not touch the eye.

4. Use of a disposable surgical mask by the patient and/or examiner for mutual protection should be strongly considered when tuberculosis or any significant upper respiratory infection exists or is suspected.

Disinfecting Goldmann Tonometry Tip: Vigorously rub the tonometer tip and its edge with a 70% isopropyl alcohol swab and allow it to air dry for at least 2 minutes before reuse, or dry it with a clean tissue. To avoid damage, do not soak the tip in alcohol. Alternatively, wipe the tip clean with a facial tissue and remove it from holder. Soak the applanating surface and the adjacent 2 to 3 mm of the tonometer tip in a 1:10 dilution of household bleach (1 part) and water (10 parts), or in commercially available 3% hydrogen peroxide or other appropriate disinfectant solution. Pour the needed volume of disinfecting solution into a small plastic vial, such as a soft contact lens enzyme vial, and soak the instrument for 10 minutes (Fig. 5). Remove it from the bath and rinse with distilled water or sterile saline and air dry, or dry with a clean tissue. Alternating the use of two tonometer tips will simplify this process. Do not leave a tonometer tip overnight in solution. Fill a clean vial with fresh solution for each tip soaking, remembering to prepare a new bleach solution daily and to keep the top on the preserved hydrogen peroxide solution overnight. Replace the plastic vials on a frequent basis even with routine cleaning between soaks.

Disinfecting Critical Ophthalmic Instruments: Place the instruments into a container of disinfectant/detergent or water as soon as possible after use to prevent drying of patient material and to make cleaning easier and more efficient. Wear heavy-duty, reusable utility gloves when cleaning these instruments to lessen the risk of hand injuries. Scrub the instruments with soap and water or a detergent solution using a small brush, and rinse well. Once completed, place on an appropriate tray to be autoclaved (steam under pressure) or dry heated. Follow the manufacturer's recommendations for machine use. Unless used immediately after sterilization, wrap the instruments in gauze and place them in sealable sterile packages, following directions from the autoclave manufacturer.

Disinfecting Semicritical and Noncritical Ophthalmic Instruments: Wipe clean all instruments that come into contact with the patient. Immerse most ophthalmic instruments for 5 to 10 minutes in 3% hydrogen peroxide, 1:10 dilution solution of common household bleach with water, 70% ethanol or isopropyl alcohol, or other appropriate disinfection solutions. Thoroughly rinse with distilled water or sterile saline and allow to air dry before reuse.

To disinfect fundus contact lenses, irrigate and mechanically remove any residual debris or solutions from the contact surface of the instrument with tapwater or sterile saline. Do not immerse the entire lens. Vigorously wipe the concave surface and side casing with an isopropyl alcohol swab and allow to air dry. Alternatively, invert the lens and fill the concave surface with 1:10 dilution of household bleach (1 part) and water (10 parts) and allow the surface of the lens to soak for 10 minutes. Irrigate with tapwater or sterile saline and dry with a clean tissue. Use an alcohol wipe on any instrument surfaces that come into contact with the patient's skin, such as instrument forehead and chin rests.

Handling Sharp Instruments: After the use of a needle on a patient, do not remove it from the disposable syringe; do not bend, break, recap, or manipulate the needle by hand. Place used disposable syringes, needles, scalpels, and other sharp items into an infectious waste sharps container that is labeled and/or color-coded red or red-orange. This container should be leakproof, puncture resistant, and closeable. Place nondisposable sharps into a puncture resistant container or tray for proper sterilization. Keep these containers at the procedure site to prevent any unnecessary, unprotected transport of instruments.

HBV Vaccination: Recommend and provide the hepatitis B vaccine for any staff member who has a possibility of occupational exposure to blood or other potentially infectious materials. HBV vaccine is administered by three injections over a 6-month period for at-risk personnel.

Training and Information: Instruct all at-risk personnel regarding universal precautions prior to their initial assignments and on at least an annual or as-needed basis. Provide each individual with information regarding the OSHA standards and an explanation of their contents. Give a general explanation of blood-borne pathogens and their mode of transmission. Also provide an explanation of your practice's exposure control plan. Explain the appropriate methods of recognizing tasks that may involve exposure, and the use and limitations of methods to prevent exposure. Give information on the selection and use of personal protective equipment (PPE). Give information and provide ongoing hepatitis vaccine and periodic titer testing. Instruct all personnel regarding the procedures to follow if an exposure incident occurs and for postexposure evaluation. Keep office records for 3 years of all training sessions including dates and names of attending personnel.

■ **Contraindications/Complications.** Failure to follow the aforementioned precaution procedures can place the patient, staff, or providers at risk for exposure and/or infection. Residual hydrogen peroxide or alcohol left on tonometer tips and other instruments that contact the eye can burn or irritate ocular tissue. Hypersensitivity to latex and powdered-latex gloves has been reported. Alternative measures, such as using nonpowdered gloves or nonlatex materials, should be considered. Individual state laws may preempt the Centers for Disease Control and Prevention (CDC) recommendations for universal precautions, and therefore must be followed.

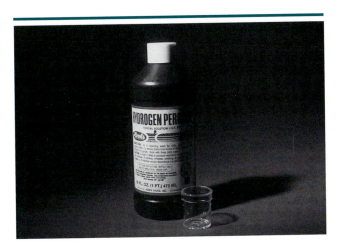

5. Commercially available 3% hydrogen peroxide solution may be poured into a soft contact lens enzyme vial to disinfect certain ophthalmic instruments.

XV Suggested Readings

American Optometric Association, Primary Care and Ocular Disease Committee: Infection Control Guidelines for the optometric practice. *J Am Optom Assoc* 1993;**64:**853–861.

Centers for Disease Control: Recommended infection-control practices for dentistry, 1993. MMWR 1993;42.

Centers for Disease Control: Update, Universal precautions for prevention of transmission of human immunodeficiency virus, hepatitis B virus, and other bloodborne pathogens in health-care settings. MMWR 1988;**37:**377–388.

Department of Labor, Occupational Safety and Health Administration: Occupational exposure to bloodborne pathogens; final rule. 29 CFR part 1910.1030. Fed Reg 1991;**58:**64-175–64182.

Lingel NJ, Coffey B: Effects of disinfecting solutions recommended by the Centers for Disease Control on Goldmann tonometer biprisms. *J Am Optom Assoc* 1992;**63:**43–48.

Index